Essentials of CICS/VS Command Level Programming using COBOL

Essentials of CICS/VS Command Level Programming using COBOL

Robert W. Lowe

Metropolitan Community Colleges

wcb
Wm. C. Brown Publishers
Dubuque, Iowa

Copyright © 1989 by Wm. C. Brown Publishers. All rights reserved

Library of Congress Catalog Card Number: 87–072883

ISBN 0–697–07321–1

Printed in the United States of America by Wm. C. Brown Publishers
2460 Kerper Boulevard, Dubuque, IA 52001

10 9 8 7 6 5 4 3 2

Dedication

This book is dedicated to my wife Jane and my children, Jennifer, Kelly, and Ryan.

Contents

4

CICS/VS Transaction Design

5

BMS Introduction

6

BMS Mapping Operations

7

Menu Transaction Design

8

The Update Transactions

9

Additional CICS/VS Topics

10

File Browsing and Page Building

11

On-Line Help

12

Debugging with EDF

13

Problem Determination

Preface

CICS/VS is a software system used on IBM mainframe computers to provide the capability to use on-line terminals to display and update company information. Reduced costs for hardware has caused a dramatic increase in the number of installations using IBM mainframes, thus resulting in a growing demand for qualified programmers and analysts. Due to increasing costs of human resources, however, companies are demanding more qualifications from their applicants for program development positions. One such qualification is an understanding of CICS/VS program design. A knowledge of the essential CICS commands and programming techniques as presented in this book will provide a competitive edge to any prospective employee.

Nearly every college and university in the nation now has a curriculum in data processing or computer science. Privately owned technical schools specializing in data processing instruction have entered the training market, thus adding to the competition for students. In metropolitan areas, it is not uncommon to find up to a dozen schools offering computer programming courses. To remain competitive in such a market, educators must continuously monitor the job market and modify their curriculum to meet training demands. One way to ride the crest of success in the educational market is to offer one or more courses in CICS programming and design. Employers are looking for people who have training or experience with CICS. Students are searching for a place to acquire these skills.

In the past few years, there has been a growing interest by instructors to develop courses in CICS applications programming. Until now, however, the market has been lacking in textbooks around which to build the framework for such a course. *The Essentials of CICS/VS Command-Level Programming* is suitable for use in an introductory course in CICS programming. This book is not an exhaustive study of CICS; instead, its content describes the commands and techniques that will be used in 80% of all programs. By concentrating on the fundamentals of CICS, the student is not chained to the more complicated but lesser used facilities of this system. The teacher who uses this textbook can thus more easily handle the material within the framework of the academic term.

IBM manuals and some other texts are organized into chapters based on CICS/VS services. While this is advantageous for reference purposes, it is not always conducive to the learning process. *The Essentials of CICS/VS Command-Level Programming* is organized into 13 chapters. These chapters are presented in a logical and progressive manner. With this heuristic approach, each chapter is a step in the building of CICS skills.

The first two chapters contain an introduction to CICS and the Command-Level Interface. The first chapter explains the environment in which CICS operates on an IBM mainframe computer. An overview of the systems management programs and CICS tables establishes a foundation for the chapters that follow. The second chapter introduces the CICS Command-Level Interface. It shows how CICS commands provide functions similar to standard COBOL verbs used in batch programs.

The chapter then describes the format and rules for using CICS commands. At the end of the chapter is a CICS program-compiling exercise. By assigning this laboratory exercise now, the book captures the students' interest early in the course.

The next two chapters contain essential program design topics. In chapter 3, the student learns one way to deal with exceptional conditions that can occur during a program. Then the basic terminal input-output commands are described. After studying this material, the student will be able to design a simple program to communicate with an IBM 3270 terminal.

Chapter 4 opens new horizons for the student. First, it introduces the CICS commands used to process random access files. By studying these commands early in the course, the student will have many opportunities to work with on-line files. The student then learns the fundamentals of CICS transaction design. It is this chapter that introduces the pseudoconversational programming technique. Sample programs are used to illustrate this design strategy. By showing more than one method of designing pseudoconversational programs, the text will better prepare the student to enter the job market where many standards exist.

Chapters 5 and 6 provide an introduction to the Basic Mapping Support facility. In the first of these chapters, the student will learn how to use BMS map definition statements to describe application screens. Then in the following chapter, the student will learn the programming necessary to use BMS. After studying this material, the student will have a concrete knowledge of the most important BMS concepts and services. These concepts will be applied throughout the remainder of the text.

The next four chapters provide additional learning milestones. In chapter 7, students will learn how to design menu-based transactions. The LINK and XCTL commands will be described, and students will learn how to design modular applications. All of the program modules in the remaining chapters will be based on the menu design described in this chapter.

Chapter 8 will introduce the three essential file-update transactions. The student will learn how to design programs to update, add, and delete records from a random access file.

Chapter 9 contains additional topics useful in many programming situations. First, the student is introduced to the Temporary Storage facility. This CICS facility can help to solve even the most complex problems. Then, the FORMATTIME and ASSIGN commands are described. Finally, the student is introduced to the BMS Terminal Paging facility. It is this BMS service that allows a program to display multiple screens without too much difficulty.

In chapter 10, the student will study additional file and BMS topics. The first topic describes how VSAM files can be accessed using alternate key fields. Then, the student learns how to use the CICS file-browsing commands. These commands allow a program to process files sequentially. Finally, the BMS page-building facility is described. This facility is often used with file browsing. It allows a screen to be displayed using a series of smaller BMS maps.

Many instructors will assign chapter 11 as optional reading material. It introduces the concept of an on-line help program. A sample program will demonstrate one technique for providing application help screens.

The last two chapters present topics essential for testing and debugging a CICS program. Chapter 12 provides a comprehensive study of the use of the CICS Execution Diagnostic Facility (EDF). It is the most extensive study of this debugging tool that I have seen to date. Other texts provide only a cursory review of this very important feature of CICS. Many instructors will want to assign this chapter as reading material earlier in the course so students can use EDF while testing their initial lab assignments. Others will present the material later in the course as supplementary material. Chapter 13 describes the CICS problem-determination aids that will eventually be used by any serious programmer. Most instructors will likely wait until the latter part of the academic term before presenting this chapter. Many students may discover the true merit of this chapter only after they leave the classroom and enter the real world.

An Appendix contains a CICS reference summary. The summary contains a list of all of the CICS commands; even those not described in the book. Other reference material such as EIB fields, COBOL restrictions, exception response and return codes, and transaction abend codes are contained in the Appendix. For many students this Appendix will continue to be useful long after the formal course-work has finished.

This book observes the principle of learning by example. Throughout each chapter, the topics are emphasized by coding examples or illustrations. In most chapters the student will find a comprehensive illustration of the theory and concepts that have just been introduced. In the programming chapters, the examples show the use of the commands by integrating them into a complete and operational program.

The Essentials of CICS/VS Command-Level Programming was written for today's students. These students want the practical. The material contained herein is based on generally accepted techniques for the development of on-line programs using CICS/VS. The sample programs represent solutions to real-life applications and thus can be used by the student as initial models for programs that will be written in the lab or on the job. This text represents a fresh new look at the practical approach to teaching and learning CICS programming.

The Essentials of CICS/VS Command-Level Programming requires a working knowledge of COBOL. All of the programming examples are written using this language. No prior knowledge or experience with CICS is required. The commands described in this text can also be used in Assembler and PL/I programs. The programming techniques illustrated also apply to these other languages. The book should therefore be of benefit to those studying CICS command-level techniques in any supported language.

Acknowledgements

I wish to express my appreciation to the people below:

To the Board of Trustees of the Metropolitan Community Colleges, Chancellor Bill Mann, and Vice Chancellor Ron Greathouse for granting me a two month sabbatical leave during the development of this text.

To Larry Judy and Larry Birch for their help in compiling some of the sample programs under the MVS operating system. To Sheryl Blasco, A. Rae Price, and Jack Baker for reviewing some of the early manuscript. To Mark Lamport for tailoring CICS tables for the sample programs and lab assignments. To Ken Becker, Sande Keilhack, Sandy Martin, John Dillard, Lyle Heckathorn, and Bob Pasbach for their assistance with preparing the instructor's manual.

1 CICS/VS Overview

As you study the information in this introductory chapter, you will

1. Develop an increased awareness of the existence and purpose of operating systems to control the multiprogramming capabilities of the IBM mainframe computers.
2. Understand more thoroughly the limitations of the major operating systems that led to the development of CICS/VS.
3. Learn that CICS/VS is not a part of the mainframe operating system but is a software package that allows for the development of on-line programs.
4. Identify the seven major components of CICS/VS.
5. Appreciate the importance of tables in the tailoring of the CICS/VS system.
6. Distinguish between the functions performed by each of the programs in the systems management component of CICS/VS.
7. Observe how the various management programs interact with each other during a typical CICS transaction.
8. Distinguish between the terms *multiprogramming* and *multitasking*.

CICS/VS (Customer Information Control System/Virtual Storage) is a data base/data communications program that allows user-written application programs to be run from on-line terminals connected to an IBM mainframe computer. CICS/VS coexists on the IBM mainframe computer with other software packages and application programs and executes under the control of operating system software. The environment in which CICS operates is often perplexing to those unfamiliar with the architecture of the operating systems that control IBM mainframe computers. A brief glimpse at the development of IBM mainframe hardware and software will help you to understand the software limitations that led to the development of CICS and will provide a basis for further study of this telecommunications software.

Early Mainframe Developments

Two decades ago, IBM announced their first commercial mainframe computer and offered a promise to their customers. That original mainframe was the IBM System/360. The promise was that future mainframe computers would be upward compatible with the System/360. This machine, unlike its predecessors, was capable of simultaneously executing central processing unit instructions with input-output operations. The hardware designers of this early system were keenly aware of the benefits of separating the I/O and CPU functions. They knew that the central processor was capable of executing thousands of instructions during the time it would take to perform a single input-output operation. The primary benefit of this new design was the capability for multiprogramming.

MULTIPROGRAMMING

Multiprogramming is a term whereby a single processor can support several concurrently executing programs. By having more than one program reside in the computer's main storage the central processing unit can be shared. Only one program can be active at any given time, but when that program requests an operation that can be serviced by the Input/Output circuitry of the machine, another program can be given the CPU resources. This program will eventually request I/O services, which will result in the next resident program gaining control of the processor. Eventually, all programs will get sufficient share of the CPU to complete their required functions. This multiprogramming capability first introduced with the System/360, resulted in an enormous increase in machine productivity.

VIRTUAL STORAGE

To some extent, multiprogramming was still limited by hardware. It was not uncommon for a System/360 to be configured with as little as 64K of memory. When compared to today's technology, where it's difficult to find a microcomputer with less than 256K, one would possibly wonder how these machines were able to function. The answer is, not very well. To solve this storage problem, IBM introduced the System/370, a machine upward-compatible from the System/360, as promised. This computer would offer a significant hardware feature called Dynamic Address Translation. DAT would allow the software to use more address space than available on the real machine; put more simply, it was "virtual storage." Virtual addressing was accomplished using direct access storage devices, usually disk, to hold inactive sections of programs. These sections, called *pages,* would be loaded into real storage when needed by the program. With virtual storage, a machine could run as many as 50 batch programs at a time, assuming of course, enough card readers, printers, and tape drives could be allocated. Users of the System/370 had virtually unlimited storage!

OPERATING SYSTEMS

The sixties also introduced a new software era. It was this decade that marked the genesis of operating systems. An operating system consists of a set of software programs that allows for the implementation of the multiprogramming and Virtual Storage functions of the mainframe equipment. The design of the first operating system was closely tied to the multiprogramming hardware features of the System/360. A memory resident supervisor was at the heart of the system. The supervisor program was used to control all other programs in the multiprogramming environment and provided centralized control of the I/O operations directed to the equipment attached to the system. To support this control program, the CPU was configured with a special supervisor mode of operation and a privileged instruction set was provided that could only be executed while in supervisor mode. All application programs would run in problem program mode and issued calls to the supervisor to request input-output services.

User written programs were loaded into separate main storage areas called *partitions* or *regions,* where they would reside until all work was completed. Generally only one application program would be executed in each storage partition (figure 1.1). The duration of the run was determined by the amount of processing to be handled by the program and by the frequency in which the program was given control of the CPU. This process of giving CPU control to an application program, known as *dispatching,* was handled by the supervisor program.

Program dispatching is a key task of the operating system. The allocation of CPU time to each program in a manner that will best utilize the system resources, is perhaps the focal point of the

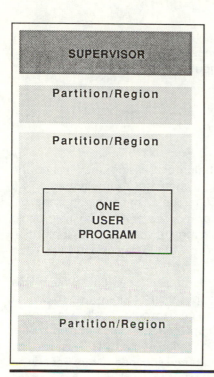

FIGURE 1.1. Generally only one application is executed in each partition

supervisor. Today, there are two predominate methods of program dispatching: time-slice dispatching and demand dispatching. With the time-slice method, each program is given control of the CPU for a given period of time as determined by operating system algorithms. If a program requests services that must be completed to continue operation, it gives up control of the system until its next time slot. Priorities can be assigned so that some programs are guaranteed a greater percentage of the CPU resources. In the demand method, each program is also assigned a relative priority, but once a program is given control of the CPU, it retains exclusive use of the processor until it requires services that must be completed to continue. The dispatcher then selects the highest priority program that is in a ready state. At some later time, after the requested services for the higher priority program are complete, the program is placed back into the dispatch queue in priority order. Each time the dispatcher receives control, it allocates the CPU to the highest priority program.

Time-slice systems tend to work best in on-line applications while demand-based control offers advantages to long-running programs. The first operating system software for the System/360 used the demand-based dispatching technique. In those days, there was no on-line computing; there were no video display terminals. At that time, card readers, printers, tapes, and disk drives were the state of the art. Actually, IBM was still very busy just trying to help its customers computerize their old tabulating machine applications. Over the years prior to the announcement of the System/360, many customers had already designed processing techniques in which data would be batched together for keypunch, sorting, collating, and report processing. Accounting departments freely accepted batch processing since it was a natural extension of their processing methods. It seemed legitimate for the computer system software to reflect a batch architecture. The selection of demand-based dispatching offered the optimum utilization of the System/360, and at that time was truly state-of-the-art.

The design of the early operating systems to support only batch processing imposed some limitations that would eventually affect the way IBM implemented on-line computing. There were three problems with the design of these batch systems. They were

limited number of regions

method of starting a program

language support

First, since IBM system control programs were oriented toward batch processing, they limited the customer to relatively few program partitions. The DOS operating system, for example, had only 5 program areas. The larger OS system limited the user to around 50 regions. For on-line applications, if only one terminal could be allocated to each application program, very few on-line terminals would be serviced. For a single program to handle multiple terminals would require very complex application logic. This logic would be even more complex if different applications were to be supported on each terminal.

The second problem dealt with starting a program. Since the original operating system was designed to support batch processing, the only way to start an application program was to submit job control statements from the card reader. Input data in the form of cards would usually accompany the control statements. This system was designed so that careful planning and scheduling by the computer center would allow for the complete and uninterrupted utilization of the CPU. This was fine for long-running programs, but on-line programs generally take only a few seconds to run. For on-line computing to become a reality some method had to be devised to start an application program directly at the terminal.

A final problem was related to programming language support for on-line terminals. The language translators such as COBOL simply had no input-output instructions to operate CRT terminals. Some way had to be devised for application programs to communicate with on-line terminals.

ON-LINE TERMINALS

In the early seventies, the need for on-line computing became a reality. Advancements in space research had introduced microprocessor technology. A by-product of this technology was the video display terminal. This device, containing some intelligence, was capable of displaying information on a cathode ray tube. The CRT units could be connected to the mainframe to allow input and output operations under control of an application program. There was now an opportunity to develop on-line applications. Prior to the announcement of the System/370, IBM had some major decisions to make. Video display terminals were here and customers wanted on-line applications. When IBM introduced the System/370 they had to make several changes in the software operating system to support the Dynamic Address Translation feature (Virtual Storage). Here was an opportunity to revamp the software to overcome the limitations of the operating system to allow support on-line computing. But these changes would not take place; such a new architecture would require significant conversion efforts by IBM and eventually by its customers. Customer demands for upward compatibility echoed too strongly and prevented any major conversion. This new generation of equipment would inherit the batch characteristics of the original software design.

CICS/VS

Because of the compatibility issue, IBM did not convert their operating systems to accommodate time-sharing. They also did not modify their compilers to support on-line terminals. IBM did, however, develop a program product to handle the on-line systems development needs of their customers.

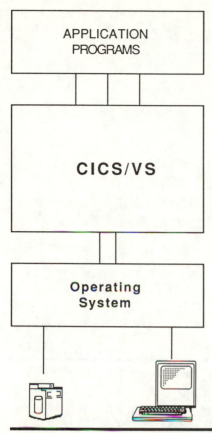

FIGURE 1.2.   CICS/VS is an interface between the applications and the operating system

That product was CICS. The initial release of CICS was implemented on the System/360. It was later enhanced to run on Virtual Storage machines. CICS/VS provides most of the facilities needed in an on-line environment. In doing so, it manages concurrent requests from terminals on a communications network to activate transactions and execute a variety of user-written applications. CICS/VS (figure 1.2) is a database/data communications interface between application programs and the host operating system.

OPERATING ENVIRONMENT

CICS/VS executes as an application task within a VSE partition or an MVS region (figure 1.3). It normally is run in a multiprogramming environment and is usually in one of the highest priority partitions. Batch partitions receive control from the operating system only when CICS/VS has no dispatchable transactions. Thus, as long as there is a transaction ready for processing, CICS/VS maintains system control. Control is released to a job in another partition only when there are no ready transactions. CICS/VS regains control as soon as any previously waiting CICS/VS transaction is ready to continue, or as soon as a new transaction code is entered at a terminal.

Much as the operating system controls concurrent execution of application programs in a multiprogramming environment, CICS/VS controls concurrent execution of application programs within its partition or region. This is called *multitasking*. Whenever one task has to wait for the completion

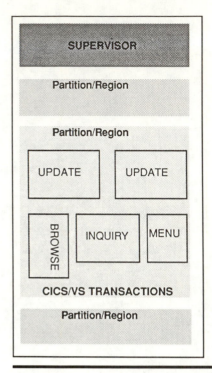

FIGURE 1.3. CICS/VS operates as an application task within a VSE Partition or MVS Region

of an I/O operation, CICS/VS assigns the processing unit to some other task that is ready to use it. This overlapping of I/O operations and processing unit usage between several tasks is called *task switching.*

In CICS/VS, several transactions running concurrently may require the same application program. Rather than having more than one copy of a program in storage at the same time, one copy is used by various transactions. This process is called *multithreading.* An application program, especially one with several I/O operations, may have many concurrently executing transactions associated with it. To control multithreading, CICS/VS uses a task control area for each transaction to determine the point at which each transaction is in a program, or where it should return to resume processing when it receives control.

Since programs may be used by more than one transaction, they must not modify themselves. This requires that code be left in its original condition so that each transaction may be processed in exactly the same manner. For COBOL programs CICS/VS makes a copy of the working-storage section for each transaction so that the programs can be used in the multithreading environment. In this way each task can have its own I/O areas and working variables.

MAJOR COMPONENTS

CICS/VS consists of seven major components (figure 1.4):

1. System Management provides the supervisory and data management functions of CICS/VS. This component comprises the control function of the system and consists of several management programs, which are described in greater detail later in this chapter.

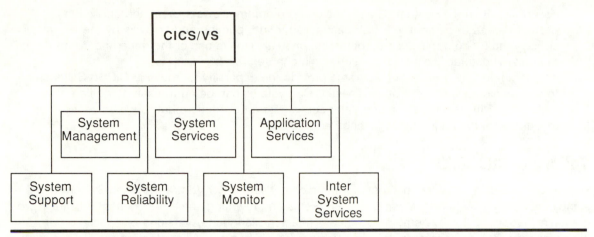

FIGURE 1.4. CICS/VS MAJOR COMPONENTS

2. System Services are ready to use application programs provided by IBM. With new programs added in each release, the number of service programs has increased considerably over the years. One program allows a master operator to open and close data sets dynamically. Another controls the network by activating and deactivating local and remote terminals. Still another allows the systems programmer to modify performance and tuning parameters within the system dynamically. Collecting and reporting system usage statistics is also provided for by systems services programs. Operator sign-on and sign-off programs are included within this group to prevent unauthorized use of the on-line facilities. These and other service programs are used by most installations to provide for the effective utilization of the CICS/VS system.

3. Application Services programs include routines with which to reduce the application-programming effort and thus increase the productivity of the programming staff. A Basic Mapping Support (BMS) function allows programs to be independent of the physical characteristics of the terminals to be used by the application. Most programs will be implemented with BMS, therefore topics describing this facility will appear in many chapters of this book. The Execution Diagnostic Facility, the most recent program to join this component of CICS/VS allows the programmer to test and debug application programs on-line. This program will be described in chapter 12.

4. System Support includes those programs necessary for the operation, tailoring, and recovery of CICS/VS. Program facilities needed to initiate and terminate CICS/VS in a partition or region are included. Macros for the systems programmer are provided to generate, maintain, and tailor all CICS/VS programs and tables. Off-line translator programs allow for the preparation of macro- and command-level programs to run under CICS.

5. System Reliability routines provide for the handling of abnormal conditions. Programs in this group keep the entire CICS system from terminating due to an application program failure. A dynamic transaction back-out program supports the integrity of data sets by ''backing out'' file changes in the event of a program failure. System-level restart of CICS is provided for in case a system failure such as a power outage or operating system problem occurs. Integrity of the on-line system is greatly improved by the programs included in this component.

6. System Monitoring routines are available for testing and debugging all programs. This component consists of an on-line trace and dump program which is available to the applications programmer. The trace program provides for application and system level diagnosis of problems by maintaining a memory resident and disk based trace of all activities

occurring within the system. The on-line dump program allows system and application program areas to be sent to a disk based file for later printing and analysis by the technical support staff. The applications programmer may also make use of the trace and dump routines. These facilities will be described in chapter 13.

7. Intercommunication Facilities programs provide the capability for multiple CICS/VS systems to communicate with each other. These CICS systems can be on the same or different machines. With this facility, an operator can initiate a transaction that requests services or resources that actually reside on another machine.

Tailoring CICS/VS

To provide for efficient operation, most programs comprising CICS/VS are written in System/370 Assembler language. IBM is developing new programs and rewriting some old ones in PLS, their programming language for systems. Load library (machine language) versions of each program are distributed by IBM for ease of installation of the CICS/VS system. All customers receive the distribution files in much the same format. The systems programmer then installs and tailors the system to meet the needs of the installation. There is usually no need to reassemble the control programs, although provision is made to do so. Tailoring is accomplished by defining and assembling CICS *tables* unique to the customer. The most recent releases of CICS/VS provide the capability to maintain most tables with on-line transactions. With each new application, the systems programmer adds the entries to the appropriate tables. As an applications programmer you may need to provide information to the systems programmer so that your new transactions, programs, and files can be added to the system. A description of the essential systems management programs and necessary tables is included in the paragraphs that follow. An understanding of the purpose and operation of each program and table is helpful in discussing your needs and problems with your technical support staff.

Systems Management

The systems management component of CICS/VS is the nucleus of the system. It provides for the control of all transactions, programs, terminals, and files in the partition or region. Several programs are contained within this component, but this text describes only those essential to the operation of the system. Each program performs a unique set of functions and interacts closely with the others during the course of a typical on-line transaction. An example of this interaction is included later in the chapter so that you might gain a better appreciation of the significance of each program.

TERMINAL CONTROL

Terminal control consists of a Terminal Control Program (TCP) and a Terminal Control Table (TCT) (figure 1.5). All input and output operations from the terminal network are controlled by the TCP through the standard operating system access methods (VTAM, BTAM, TCAM). The primary functions of TCP are polling and addressing. Polling checks all remote terminals periodically to determine whether any have input to transmit. Addressing is having the processor check to see if a terminal is ready to receive output. Terminal control also acquires terminal storage I/O areas necessary for proper execution of CICS.

Terminal Control provides the application program with the ability to communicate with the terminal. To display a message on the CRT the program would prepare the message text in working storage, then issue a terminal control SEND command. The application program can cause operator

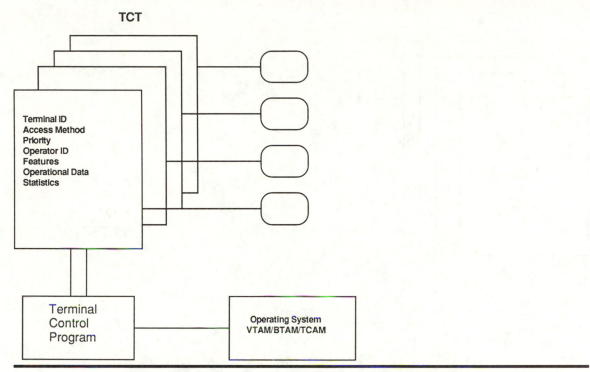

TCT

Terminal ID
Access Method
Priority
Operator ID
Features
Operational Data
Statistics

Terminal
Control
Program

Operating System
VTAM/BTAM/TCAM

FIGURE 1.5. Terminal Control consists of the Terminal Control Program and the Terminal Control Table

input to be moved into working storage by coding a RECEIVE command in the application program. BMS commands, described in chapter 6 also indirectly use terminal control to send and receive formatted display screens.

The Terminal Control Table aids in controlling terminal operations, in that it specifies the types of terminals, special features, and terminal priorities. Operational data such as which task is associated with which terminal is also stored. The Terminal Control Program refers to this table in performing its functions.

TASK CONTROL

Task control consists of a Task Control Program (KCP) and a Program Control Table (PCT) (figure 1.6). The Task Control Program keeps track of the status of all tasks being processed. Transactions are not usually processed through to completion in a single uninterrupted operation. A transaction may be processed up to a file I/O command, for instance, whereupon another waiting task receives control. Therefore, there may be many incomplete tasks which the task control program must control simultaneously. The fastest response can be given to those applications that need it. To do this, priority ratings are allocated to each operator, to each terminal, and to each transaction. The task control program combines these ratings to determine the relative priorities of all tasks under its control.

The task control program is responsible for task initiation. The usual method of initiating a task is through terminal input. The Terminal Control Program determines whether each input message received from a terminal satisfies an outstanding read request placed for that terminal by a currently executing program. If no application program is currently active for the terminal, the Terminal Control Program requests the Task Control Program to perform its task initiation routines. Task initiation refers

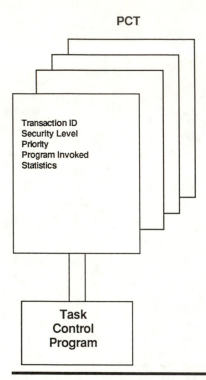

PCT

Transaction ID
Security Level
Priority
Program Invoked
Statistics

Task
Control
Program

FIGURE 1.6.   Task Control consists of the Task Control Program and the Program Control Table

to the identification of an input transaction, the program to be used and the creation of a task to process the transaction. Task control validates transactions by checking the Program Control Table, which lists all valid transaction codes. If the transaction code is valid, the associated program name is used to process the transaction message. If an operator enters an invalid code, task control sends an error message to the terminal and requests that the transaction be resubmitted.

The Task Control Program may be required to purge a stalled task when it would otherwise be held indefinitely in the system. This stall condition can occur when a task is waiting on some action or resource. A terminal operator, for example, can leave the terminal in the middle of a transaction, leaving the task in a wait state. Another task on a different terminal may be suspended because the first task has ownership of a data-base record needed by this task. The Task Control Program is responsible for stall detection and will purge the offending task when possible. A task can be purged in another situation. If a program does not relinquish control to the Task Control Program within a certain time interval, it is treated as a runaway task and will be purged from the system. This situation normally occurs when a program enters a perpetual loop due to errors in logic.

Task termination is a responsibility of the Task Control Program. This involves the release of all resources acquired during the life of the task. Storage areas used for I/O operations are released for use by other programs. Data-base records that have been protected against update operations by other tasks are also released.

The Program Control Table lists all valid transaction codes and the associated programs, so that control may be transferred to the correct program when a task is initiated. Security information is stored in this table and is used by the Task Control Program to prohibit unauthorized use of the transaction. Anticipated storage requirements can also be specified in this table so that task control can preallocate sufficient storage for the transaction during task initiation. The Task Control Program maintains other data, such as usage statistics, in the Program Control Table.

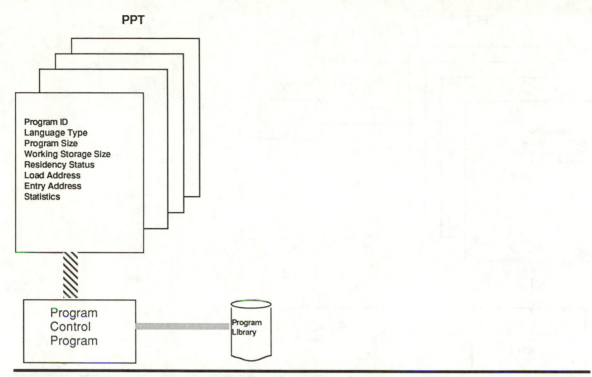

FIGURE 1.7. Program control consists of the Program Control Program and the Program Processing Table

PROGRAM CONTROL

Program control consists of a Program Control Program (PCP), and a Program Processing Table (PPT) (figure 1.7). Program control manages application programs that are stored in the load library (MVS) or core image library (VSE). Some programs are loaded into virtual storage when CICS/VS is initialized and are resident throughout normal operation. Seldom-used programs may be dynamically loaded during program initiation by the Program Control Program and then forced out later, when transaction storage is needed.

During task initiation, task control passes the name of the application program from the PCT to program control to prepare it for processing. The application program is loaded into storage from the program library if necessary; then, for COBOL programs, the Program Control Program acquires storage and makes a copy of the working-storage section to satisfy the multithreading requirements of CICS/VS. At program termination, program control frees the working-storage copy so that storage can be used by other tasks.

The Program Control Program also offers services to the application program. Commands are available that allow a program to pass control and data to other programs. This allows for a system to incorporate a modular design concept and assists in programming menu-driven applications. The program control RETURN command enables a program to return control to a higher-level program or CICS/VS.

The Program Processing Table is used by the Program Control Program. One use is to determine the program's location in Virtual Storage during CICS/VS operation. Programs are relocatable and may be in different main storage locations with each start-up of the system. The table contains the source language, working-storage size, entry point, and other program information. The Program Control Program maintains usage statistics and other data necessary for the proper operation of the system in the PPT.

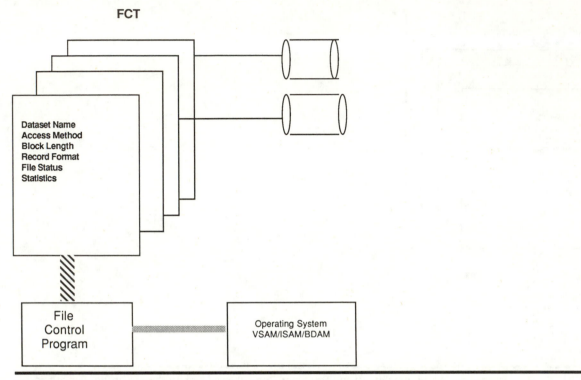

FIGURE 1.8. File Control Consists of the File Control Program and File Control Table

FILE CONTROL

File control consists of the File Control Program (FCP) and the File Control Table (FCT) (figure 1.8). The File Control Program provides file management and file services. It uses the standard access methods available under VSE or MVS (ISAM, BISAM; DAM, BDAM; and VSAM). It supports read-only, update, add, and browse functions.

The File Control Program protects you against the concurrent update of a single data-base record by two or more transactions. This protection is called *exclusive control.* Exclusive control places all tasks, with the exception of the first, into a wait queue, so that only one task at a time updates a record. After a record has been returned to the file, another task may update the record.

When the application program issues a file control command to process a record in the file, the File Control Program performs the necessary processing to accomplish the function. File control may request storage control to acquire an I/O area. It will then communicate with the standard access method to request that the required I/O operation be performed. The File Control Program will request the Task Control Program to place the application program in a wait state until I/O operations are completed as required. When this occurs, another ready task will receive control of the processor, and will maintain control until CICS/VS services are requested. When the I/O operation of the original application is completed, file control will place the program in a ready state and return any data or status information to the program for processing.

The File Control Table contains user-supplied file characteristics for each file, including the access method, record format, length, and block size. The File Control Table also specifies what operations may be performed on each file. A file may be on-line and yet effectively protected against modifications by specifying, read only. CICS/VS does not allow any program to update such a file. The FCT also specifies the status of each file. A file may be closed by the master terminal operator with the use of a CICS/VS service program. When this occurs the entry for the file is set to reflect this condition. No program will be allowed to access the records in the file until it is subsequently reopened by the master terminal operator.

STORAGE CONTROL

Storage control consists of the Storage Control Program (SCP), which communicates with other CICS/VS functions and user-written application programs to satisfy their storage requirements. Transaction storage, acquired by an application program or by a management program on behalf of an application program, is chained together by storage accounting fields maintained by the Storage Control Program. This information is used by storage control to free the storage when it is no longer needed by the transaction.

COMMAND-LEVEL INTERFACE

In a recent CICS/VS release a new high-level programming interface was introduced to simplify writing application programs using COBOL. This new interface, the Command-Level Interface, offered considerable ease-of-use advantages over the earlier macro-level interface. The basic idea behind the Command-Level Interface was to make it possible to write CICS/VS application programs without the need to have a detailed knowledge of CICS/VS architecture, to eliminate the need to be concerned with the addressability of internal control blocks and their formats and contents, and, finally, to eliminate the need to be concerned with storage management.

To accomplish this, an Execute Interface Program was added to the CICS/VS system. It interfaces between the application program and the CICS/VS management programs. The Execute Interface Program (figure 1.9) is used by application programs using the Command-Level Interface. It invokes the required CICS/VS services on behalf of the application program. Data to be transferred to and from the application program may be stored in the COBOL working-storage. An execute interface control block is used to pass information from CICS/VS to the application program.

INTERACTION OF MANAGEMENT PROGRAMS

Throughout the operation of CICS the management programs interact with each other to enable on-line transactions to occur. The following example (depicted in figure 1.10) illustrates how these programs interact during a single CICS transaction. The example is based on a simple inquiry application in which an operator enters an input message consisting of (1) a transaction identification code "VEND" and (2) a vendor number. The application is designed to return an output message to the operator, giving, for example, the current status for the vendor. The example gives a much simplified description of how the system management components of a CICS/VS system interact with each other and with the application program during normal transaction execution. The use of the Command-Level Interface is implied for this example but is not discussed in any detail. Assume now, that an operator has just entered a CICS transaction at an on-line terminal. Here is the sequence of events that would occur within the CICS system to provide the requested services.

1. The Terminal Control Program periodically checks all terminals for input messages. Then on receipt of the input message containing the transaction code ("VEND"), terminal control requests storage control services to create a terminal input-output area (TIOA), then moves the input message to the acquired area. Terminal control then passes control to the Task Control Program to initiate the task.
2. Task control creates a task for the transaction. In doing so, the Task Control Program validates the transaction identification code ("VEND") in the TIOA against the Program

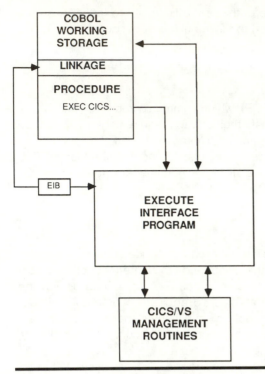

FIGURE 1.9. The Execute Interface Program provides an interface between the application program and the CICS management routines

Control Table. Task control requests storage from the Storage Control Program and creates a task control area and execute interface block. Task control then assigns a priority value to the task and adds the task to the chain of tasks waiting to be executed.

3. Subsequently the Task Control Program dispatches the task. When the VEND task is first dispatched, control is passed to the Program Control Program. Program control locates the required application program and starts its execution. To do this, program control
   A. Inspects the Program Control Table to find the name of the application program associated with the transaction called *VEND.*
   B. Searches the Program Processing Table to obtain the location and entry point of the application program.
   C. Requests storage control services to obtain storage for a copy of the COBOL working-storage section.
   D. Passes control to the application program.

4. The inquiry application program receives the vendor number from the terminal input-output area into a working storage field. The application program next issues a file control command to read the record into working storage. The vendor number is used as the record key for the read operation.

5. The File Control Program initiates the retrieval of the required data. First, the File Control Table is searched for the record length and file type. Then a file input-output area is requested from the Storage Control Program. File control then requests the operating system's data access method to read the required data from the appropriate file into the file input area. File control specifies that this task will wait until the data has been completely read into the file input area. This causes control to be passed to task control.

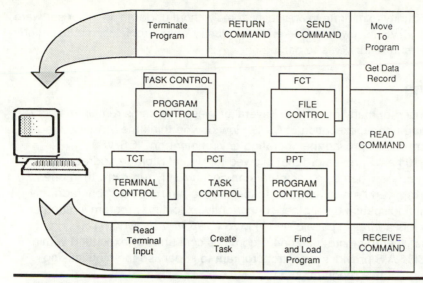

FIGURE 1.10. Example of interaction of Management Programs during a typical CICS/VS transaction

6. Task control causes the inquiry task to wait while the data is being obtained. Task control dispatches other tasks, then dispatches the inquiry task when the requested data is in the file input area; this causes control to be returned to the File Control Program.

7. File control ensures that data has been read into the file input area correctly then returns control to the inquiry application.

8. The inquiry application processes the data to be sent to the operator as an output message in working-storage. It then issues a terminal control SEND command that subsequently causes the output message to be transmitted to a terminal input-output area. The application program finishes execution and returns control to the Program Control Program.

9. Program control notes that execution of the program for this task is complete. Program control returns control to the Task Control Program requesting termination of the inquiry task.

10. Task control releases storage areas associated with this task including the file input area but excluding the terminal input-output area. Task control then dispatches another task.

11. Terminal control subsequently sends the output message from the terminal input-output area to the terminal. It does this when the line to the terminal is free. Terminal control then releases the terminal input-output area.

Our sample transaction is now complete. The operator can view the resulting output on the terminal and then enter another transaction if needed. In each transaction, the various management programs would follow a similar pattern as described above. In doing this CICS/VS meets the needs of the installation to develop and run on-line applications.

Chapter Summary

CICS/VS is a powerful data base/data communications interface between the application program and the IBM mainframe operating systems. Its implementation has allowed IBM to provide on-line support to its customers while maintaining operating systems that are highly efficient and conducive to ongoing batch applications. IBM has taken all measures necessary to protect the investment of its customers by providing new generations of equipment and software compatible with their original mainframe. By designing CICS to operate within the constraints of existing operating system design, customers have had the opportunity to migrate to on-line systems without undergoing major software conversions. By all rights, CICS/VS is now considered the industry standard telecommunications monitor and should retain that status for years to come.

Discussion Questions

1. CICS is a system comprised of many programs. Several of these programs remain memory resident at all times during normal execution of CICS. How do you think the Virtual Storage capabilities of the System/370 improved the operating environment of CICS/VS?
2. What was the System/370 hardware feature that allowed for Virtual Storage addressing?
3. Multiprogramming is a process whereby a computer can concurrently run more than one program. Each program is given its own address space. A program running in one address space is protected from modification by another concurrently executing program in another address space. What is this address space called in MVS (OS)? in VSE (DOS)?
4. Multitasking is a process whereby more than one program is concurrently executing within a single address space. CICS/VS provides a control program to supervise the multitasking function. What is the name of this program?
5. Is there any protection provided by CICS/VS to keep one multitasking program from modifying another program within the CICS/VS address space?
6. Why is CICS/VS normally run in a region that has been assigned a high priority?
7. Multithreading is a process whereby the same application program may be used concurrently. Describe some of the restrictions that have been placed on programs used in the multithreading environment. What provision is made for the use of working-storage in COBOL programs?
8. IBM distributes the same CICS/VS system to all of its customers. Each installation has its own unique operating environment, with a different configuration of terminals, files, transactions, and programs. CICS is implemented in these various environments by configuring tables unique to each installation. Generally, who is responsible for defining and maintaining CICS tables?
9. In the early releases all CICS/VS tables were defined by coding Assembler language macro statements. These statements were then translated by the operating system Assembler and cataloged into a load library. During initialization of CICS/VS these tables were loaded into the region. Generally, the only way to modify a table was to shut down and reload the CICS system. In recent releases of CICS/VS on-line transactions have been provided for dynamic tailoring of tables. Can you describe some of the benefits of this new approach of tailoring CICS?
10. Some transactions may need to run with a higher priority than others. What mechanism is provided by CICS to do this?
11. A program is usually started when an operator keys in a transaction code at a terminal. Which table is used to identify the program that should be started by CICS in response to the keyed transaction code? Which program examines this table?
12. Before an application program can be run, it must be loaded into the CICS region. Which control program is responsible for loading and passing control to the application program?
13. Why is the exclusive control feature of file control necessary in the multitasking environment?
14. Describe some of the benefits of the Command-Level Interface.

2
Command-Level Concepts

As you study the material in this chapter, you will

1. See the analogy between COBOL verbs and CICS commands.
2. Appreciate the ease-of-use features of the Command-Level Interface in comparison to the earlier macro interface.
3. Identify the two components of the Command-Level Interface.
4. Learn how to code the EXECUTE interface commands.
5. Learn that CICS programs are compiled using the standard language translators.
6. Realize that each task using a command-level COBOL program will have its own copy of working-storage.
7. Understand why some COBOL options and statements cannot be used in a CICS program.
8. See how the Execute Interface Program passes useful information to the command-level program.
9. Observe the modifications made to the COBOL source program by the command language translator during the program preparation process.

In this chapter we are going to examine the Command-Level Interface. It is this interface that makes it possible for your application programs to communicate with the CICS management programs. You will first be introduced to the two types of language interfaces provided by CICS. Then, you will learn about the components of the Command-Level Interface that will be used in the remaining chapters. The format and use of commands will be explained so you can begin writing programs in the next chapter. Finally, you will learn about some COBOL restrictions placed on application programs which execute in the CICS environment. At the end of the chapter, you will be given the opportunity to compile and test a simple CICS command-level program.

Language Interfaces

In the first chapter you learned that CICS/VS is an interface between the application program and the operating system. More specifically, it is a data base/data communications interface between the two. It provides the capability for an on-line program to transmit information from a terminal to a computer and to transmit processed information back to the terminal. All of this is accomplished by using the standard languages, such as COBOL, which do not ordinarily support these functions. Is it the magic of CICS and the wizzardry of the systems programmer that makes this possible? Not at all; it is accomplished by a simple and straightforward mechanism called the *language interface*. A definition of *language interface* is a very difficult challenge, so let's use an illustration to describe the term.

```
IDENTIFICATION
ENVIRONMENT
  Select statements for files
DATA
  FD statements for files
PROCEDURE
 OPEN statements for files
 .
 READ statement to get card data record
 .
 READ statement to get master record
 .
 WRITE statements to print report
 CLOSE statement for files
 .
 STOP RUN or GOBACK to terminate program
```

FIGURE 2.1. Batch Program program interface

The CICS/VS language interface is analogous to the functions provided by the various verbs in standard COBOL. Please refer to figure 2.1 as you follow this illustration. Assume that a batch program provides a report containing a printout of the data fields in a record from a vendor master file. This program would contain the four divisions as usual. The Environment and Data divisions would contain the SELECT and FD statements necessary to define the characteristics of the files to be used in the program. The Procedure Division would contain the COBOL OPEN verb to open the files and COBOL READ statements to get the record key, perhaps from a card file, and to read the record randomly from the vendor file. The report would be printed using COBOL WRITE verbs. Prior to terminating the program, the files would be closed with the COBOL CLOSE statement. Finally the program would be terminated with the STOP RUN or GOBACK statement. The COBOL compiler translates all of the I/O verbs in the program to use the standard system operating access methods such as VSAM or ISAM. The STOP RUN or GOBACK statements are translated by the compiler to issue an operating system call to terminate the program. In essence these COBOL statements provide a direct interface to the operating system.

With CICS, these same functions are still provided, but in a different form. Figure 2.2 shows the structure of a CICS COBOL program. This program randomly reads a record from an on-line master file, using a record key provided by the terminal operator. It then displays data fields from the record on a display terminal. In the CICS program, the SELECT and FD statements are not necessary. The equivalents to the SELECT and FD are contained within the CICS/VS File Control Program and File Control Table. The OPEN statements are also omitted from the CICS program since all CICS files are opened and closed by the master terminal operator using one of the System Service programs. When it is necessary for the program to perform an I/O or control function, it will issue a CICS interface instruction to accomplish that task. Each interface instruction will request one or more of the CICS management programs. The management program will, in turn provide the requested service, then, if appropriate, will return control back to the application program. If you can think of the CICS/VS language interface in these terms, then much of your on-line programming will be a simple matter of learning which CICS instructions must be substituted for standard COBOL verbs.

CICS/VS provides two levels of interface instructions: macro and command. This text will concentrate on the Command-Level Interface only. This interface provides several ease-of-use advantages over the macro-level. But, before we begin the study of the Command-Level Interface, let's

```
┌─────────────────────────────────────────────────┐
│  IDENTIFICATION                                   │
│  ENVIRONMENT                                      │
│  DATA                                             │
│                                                   │
│  PROCEDURE                                        │
│  .                                                │
│  .                                                │
│  CICS instruction to get record key    from terminal │
│  .                                                │
│  CICS instruction to get master record            │
│  .                                                │
│  CICS instruction to send output     to terminal  │
│  .                                                │
│  CICS instruction to terminate program            │
│                                                   │
│                                                   │
│                                                   │
│                                                   │
│                                                   │
└─────────────────────────────────────────────────┘
```

FIGURE 2.2.   CICS/VS Program Interface

take a quick look at the problems associated with using the Macro-Level Interface so you won't have any notions of closing this book to pursue a career as a macro-level CICS programmer. More importantly though, this overview will also highlight the noteworthy features of the Command-Level Interface that has subsequently replaced the Macro-Level.

THE MACRO-LEVEL INTERFACE

The early releases of CICS supported only the Macro-Level Interface for the Assembler, COBOL and PL/I languages. The Macro-Level Interface was very rigid and difficult to use. It required the user to code programs in much the same manner as IBM had coded their own management programs. To use macros, it was necessary for programmers to learn much about the CICS/VS internal architecture. The CICS design calls for a variety of storage areas called *control blocks,* which are found at different locations within the on-line partition. To access these control blocks, the COBOL programmer would have to make extensive use of the Linkage Section since that is the only way to access data areas outside of the COBOL object module. With each interface instruction, the programmer had to access the control blocks to deposit or obtain information relating to the operation. Due to the stringent coding requirements with this macro-level interface, extended formal training was often required.

There were also some programming limitations in using the Macro-Level Interface. The working-storage section, for instance, could only be used for program constants. This area was off limits for storing data records and terminal messages for use in input-output interface instructions. There was, of course, a reason for this constraint. IBM had designed this early interface to operate with minimal storage utilization. If you recall from chapter 1, CICS was originally designed to operate on the System/360. With the limited storage on these machines, there was a need for efficient storage utilization. Recall also that CICS supports the multithreading environment, which allows more than one task to use the program actively at the same time. To use working-storage for input-output areas, CICS would have to make a copy of working-storage for each concurrent task using the program. However, to conserve on the limited storage of the early processors, the Macro-Level Interface would not support such a design.

There was also a serious problem, somewhat related to the working-storage limitations described above. This problem dealt with storage violations. A storage violation occurs when one program corrupts the storage of another program. To perform some I/O instructions, programs had to acquire storage from a common pool of so-called dynamic storage. A program's data storage area could therefore be surrounded on either side by storage acquired by other tasks. Because of this, a simple COBOL move statement could easily destroy the storage of another task. Problem diagnosis was often difficult since an error-free program would sometimes fail due to problems in an unrelated program. It was even possible for an application program to corrupt a major CICS control block and crash the entire on-line system. CICS couldn't even protect itself from simple applications errors. The system was vulnerable and subject to reliability problems. But a solution to this problem was eventually at hand.

THE COMMAND-LEVEL INTERFACE

The solution was a new programming interface called the Command-Level Interface. This interface would offer significant ease-of-use advantages and provide some level of protection to the system itself. The Command-Level Interface was designed to overcome all of the limitations and problems of the macro facility. By the time the Command-Level Interface was released by IBM, faster processors with more Virtual Storage were available. Limited storage was no longer a problem. Working-storage constraints were therefore lifted when this new interface was announced. Each task using a program written in the Command-Level Interface would have its own copy of working-storage. A task could use this working-storage copy to provide input-output areas as well as constants to be used by the program. This even allowed for multithreading, or concurrent use of the program by different tasks.

The framework of the Command-Level Interface was also restructured to eliminate the need to access the CICS control blocks directly. Working-storage would be used to hold variables needed by the management programs. Finally, the syntax of the interface instructions was made less rigid. These instructions, called *EXECUTE commands,* even had some likeness to standard COBOL verbs.

Command-Level Components

There are two components that together provide the Command-Level Interface. They are the Command Language Translator and the Execute Interface Program.

THE COMMAND TRANSLATOR

The function of the command translator is to prepare a COBOL program to run under CICS. The COBOL source program that contains EXECUTE commands is input to the translator. The EXECUTE commands appear in the Procedure Division of the COBOL program when it is necessary to request a CICS/VS service. The translator produces an equivalent source program in which the commands have been translated into COBOL language "call" statements. There are some other changes made to the source program. These changes are described in more detail later in the chapter. After the command translator has made the necessary modifications, the program is compiled by the standard COBOL compiler. The compiler produces an executable load module, which is cataloged in the load (or core image) library accessed by CICS.

Like most utility programs, the command translator provides for a number of optional facilities. The translator options are specified along with the compiler options on the COBOL control (CBL) statements that precede the source program. A CICS keyword (CICS or XOPTS) precedes the list of options that may appear in any order and are contained within parentheses. Options are separated by a comma or by one or more blanks. The translator will remove the CICS keyword and its associated options from the CBL card and will pass any remaining options on to the COBOL compiler. For example, a program preceded by

```
CBL CICS (DEBUG,NOSEQ,NOOPT), LIB,SUPMAP,CLIST
         IDENTIFICATION DIVISION.
```

will be passed on to the COBOL compiler as

```
CBL LIB,SUPMAP,CLIST
        IDENTIFICATION DIVISION.
```

A default action will be taken by the translator if any option is not included in the list or if no translator list is provided. If duplicate options are used, the last specification for each option is used. Some of the options are

DEBUG/NODEBUG specifies whether or not the translator is to pass the translator line number to the Execution Diagnostic Facility during program execution. The debug option may be useful to follow the path of the program logic during program testing. It will cause only a small increase to the size of the load module, and will not cause performance problems, even if placed in production versions.

SPACE1/SPACE2/SPACE3 indicates the required type of spacing in the translator listing. SPACE1 is the default and conserves on paper usage.

SOURCE/NOSOURCE SOURCE is the default. NOSOURCE allows the translator to suppress the listing of the COBOL input; this option may be desirable to save paper and print time during latter stages of program debugging.

SEQ/NOSEQ SEQ is the default and will cause the translator to flag source program statements that are out of sequence. Unless your text editor automatically generates line numbers, NOSEQ should be specified.

OPT/NOOPT specifies whether the COBOL compiler will be using the optimizing feature for this compile. This CICS option should match the COBOL option specified for this compile. NOOPT is the default for VSE while OPT is the default for OS/VS.

VBREF/NOVBREF indicates whether the translator is to provide a cross-reference list of all the commands used in the program.

THE EXECUTE INTERFACE PROGRAM

After the program has been prepared for execution by the command translator, it may be started at a terminal. This may be done by an operator keying a transaction code associated with the program (in the PCT). As the program is being executed, the call statements inserted by the translator invoke the Execute Interface Program. These call statements pass arguments that identify the type of request and provide data areas needed to perform the request. The function of the EXEC Interface Program (EIP) is to analyze the arguments to determine the service being requested. It will use the arguments passed by the application program to determine the requested service. The Execute Interface Program will then provide the service or invoke one of the other management programs. In doing so, EIP assigns values to the CICS/VS control blocks and invokes the proper CICS/VS Systems Management programs (figure 2.3).

The Execute Interface Block

Upon return from each management request, EIP determines if the operation was successful. The EXEC Interface Program then returns a response code to the application program along with any data that was requested. Requested data is usually returned to the working-storage copy for the task. The response information is returned to the application program in an Execute Interface Block (figure 2.4). The EIB is defined in the Linkage Section of the COBOL program. A data structure for the EXEC Interface Block is automatically inserted into the Linkage Section by the Command Language Translator and is made addressable during program initialization.

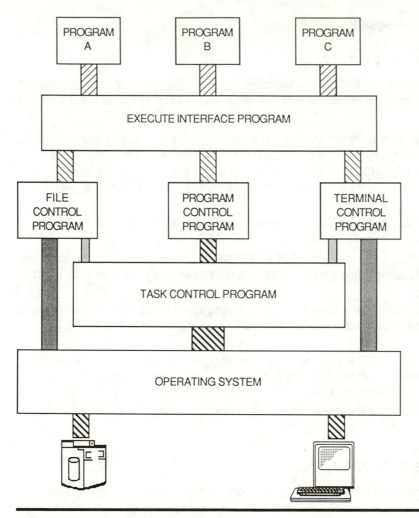

FIGURE 2.3. The Execute Interface Program is an interface between the application program and the CICS/VS management programs

Several data items are defined within the EIB for use by all programs that run within the task. These fields contain information that is useful during the execution of an application program. The most commonly used fields in the EIB are described below.

EIBTRNID contains the CICS transaction identifier that invoked this task. This information can be useful in a program that is invoked by more than one transaction code. In chapter 4, you will see how the EIBTRNID field can be used to select different processing routines in a pseudoconversational program.

EIBTRMID contains the four-character identification of the CICS/VS terminal that has invoked this program. The terminal identification can be displayed on application screens such as the menu. In some cases you may even use this field to limit the access to an application program. For instance, certain terminals may be restricted from using security-sensitive programs, regardless of the operator that is signed on to that terminal.

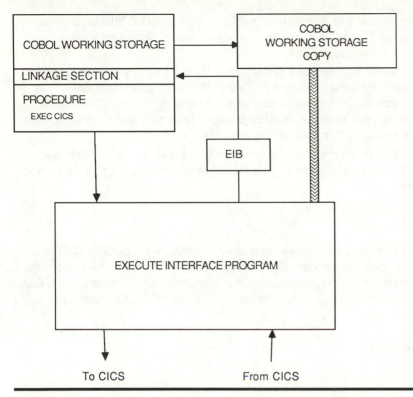

FIGURE 2.4. Task Information is available in the EIB. Data is transferred to and from the working storage copy

EIBAID contains a code indicating which attention key on the terminal was pressed by the operator when the transaction was initiated. The program can use this code to determine actions to be taken. The menu program illustrated in this text, for instance will use the EIBAID value to determine which transaction is being requested by the operator.

EIBCPOSN contains the cursor position on an IBM 3270 video terminal when the transaction was initiated. This field contains a binary (COMP) value that can be used by the program to determine the line or column position of the cursor if needed.

EIBDATE contains the Julian date in COMP-3 format. You may want to use this field to write a date-stamp during file-update operations. A date may also be necessary to the processing logic of your program.

EIBTIME contains the time at which the task was started and this field is in COMP-3 format. With this field, it is possible to time-stamp records written to your files. You may also want to use this field to show the current time on the terminal displays.

EIBCALEN contains the length of the EXEC Interface Communication area that has been passed to this program. If no communication area was passed, the field contains a value of zero. The use of the program communications area is discussed in chapter 7.

EIBDS contains the name of the last data set (file) used by the program.

EIBRSRCE contains the name of the resource used in the last command executed in the program. For file commands, this field contains the same value as field EIBDS. This field can be useful in sending error messages to the operator when some problem with a resource has been encountered.

EIBRCODE contains the response code from the last call returned by the EXEC Interface Program. This hexadecimal response can be analyzed by the application program after each command to determine if the request was successful.

EIBRESP contains a decimal response from the last call returned by the EXEC Interface program. This response code can be analyzed by the application program after each command to determine if the command was successful. The use of this field is similar to the EIBRCODE field but is easier to use since it has a decimal value. Both fields provide for easier design of structured programs in COBOL. Techniques for using this field will be described in chapter 7.

EIBFN contains a hexadecimal value identifying the last command that was executed. This field can be used in conjunction with the response fields in general error-handling routines to determine which command caused the error.

CICS Command Format

As you can now see, the application program can request on-line services by placing CICS commands in the application program. Through the use of the command translator and the Execute Interface Program, these commands produce results similar to the standard COBOL verbs. Let's look at the format and rules for using the various CICS commands. The format of a CICS command is

```
EXECUTE CICS
     function
     option (argument)
     option
     . . .
END-EXEC
```

The EXECUTE CICS (abbreviated EXEC CICS) command *trigger* must appear at the beginning of each CICS command. The command translator will process all statements from this point on, until the END-EXEC delimiter is encountered. The command *function,* which follows the trigger, is required and describes the operation to be performed. The function is analogous to a COBOL verb. It indicates some action to be performed, but in this case by CICS/VS. The command *options* describe the optional facilities of the function being performed. With some commands, one or more options may be required while others are not. Some options have *arguments.* Arguments are values or data areas needed by the function.

CODING EXAMPLES

The examples below illustrate most of the rules and coding conventions for CICS/VS commands.

1. Some commands may contain only a *function* with no options. For instance, the RETURN command, which is used to terminate a program, does not require any options. This command would be coded as follows:

```
EXECUTE CICS
     RETURN
     END-EXEC
```

2. Commands may be coded on one or more lines. The command below would have identical results as the previous example.

```
EXEC CICS RETURN END-EXEC
```

3. *Options* may appear in any order. The order of options contained within a command does not affect the execution of the command in any way. Both commands below would produce the same result even though the options have been coded in different order.

```
EXECUTE CICS READ
    DATASET ('VENFILE')
    RIDFLD (RECORD-KEY)
    INTO (RECORD-AREA)
    LENGTH (RECORD-LENGTH)
    END-EXEC

EXEC CICS READ
    LENGTH (RECORD-LENGTH)
    INTO (RECORD-AREA)
    DATASET ('VENFILE')
    RIDFLD (RECORD-KEY)
    END-EXEC
```

4. Some options will be given a default if not coded by the programmer; in the command below, EQUAL is a default, so both commands would produce the same result.

```
EXECUTE CICS READ
    LENGTH (RECORD-LENGTH)
    INTO (RECORD-AREA)
    DATASET ('VENFILE')
    RIDFLD (RECORD-KEY)
    END-EXEC

EXECUTE CICS READ
    LENGTH (RECORD-LENGTH)
    INTO (RECORD-AREA)
    DATASET ('VENFILE')
    RIDFLD (RECORD-KEY)
    EQUAL
    END-EXEC
```

5. All commands may be coded within IF THEN ELSE constructs, for example,

```
IF (condition)
    EXEC CICS function
        option
        END-EXEC
    MOVE . . . .
    PERFORM . . .
ELSE
    EXEC CICS function
        option
        option
        END-EXEC.
```

COMMAND ARGUMENTS

Some options are followed by an *argument* in parentheses. An argument is a value that may be either a constant or a COBOL name of the correct type for that option. In the following chapters, the argument values in a CICS/VS command are specified as follows:

data-value

data-area

name

label

A *data-value* argument may be replaced by any COBOL name or by a numeric constant that can be converted to the correct type for that argument. The data type varies with different options and will be one of the following:

```
PIC S9999 COMP
PIC S9(8) COMP
PIC X(n) where n is the number of bytes
```

For instance, all output commands require a *data-value* in the LENGTH option. In these commands the LENGTH argument is used to tell CICS/VS the number of characters to be output from the COBOL program. For example, the WRITE commands below could be coded as

```
EXECUTE CICS WRITE
      DATASET ('VENFILE')
      RIDFLD (RECORD-KEY)
      FROM (RECORD-AREA)
      LENGTH (RECORD-LENGTH)
      END-EXEC

EXECUTE CICS WRITE
      DATASET ('VENFILE')
      RIDFLD (RECORD-KEY)
      FROM (RECORD-AREA)
      LENGTH (249)
      END-EXEC
```

where the data-value field *RECORD-LENGTH* is defined in the Data Division as

```
05 RECORD-LENGTH PIC S9999 COMPUTATIONAL VALUE +249.
```

A *data-area* argument may be only replaced by a COBOL data name. This type of argument is used when the command *must* reference a working-storage variable. The data type for this argument type also varies between different options of the various commands. It will be one of the following:

```
PIC S9999 COMP
PIC S9(8) COMP
PIC X(n) where n is the number of bytes
```

Three data-area arguments are used in the command below. These variables are RECORD-LENGTH, VENDOR-RECORD and VENDOR-ID.

```
EXEC CICS READ
      DATASET ('VENFILE')
      RIDFLD (VENDOR-ID)
      INTO (VENDOR-RECORD)
      LENGTH (RECORD-LENGTH)
      EQUAL
      END-EXEC.
```

A *name* argument may be replaced by a COBOL data name or by a literal constant. If a data name is used, it must be defined with a length equal to the maximum length required for the name, and must be padded with trailing blanks if necessary. The size of the COBOL data name will vary between different commands. The DATASET option in the previous example specifies a "name" option and could have been coded as follows:

```
EXEC CICS READ
    DATASET (FILE-NAME)
    RIDFLD (VENDOR-ID)
    INTO (VENDOR-RECORD)
    LENGTH (RECORD-LENGTH)
    EQUAL
    END-EXEC.
```

where FILE-NAME is defined in working-storage as

```
05 FILE-NAME PIC X(8) VALUE 'VENFILE'.
```

A *label* argument specifies the name of a COBOL paragraph or section name. This type of argument is used in a special command known as HANDLE CONDITION. The HANDLE CONDITION command is discussed in detail in the next chapter.

COBOL Restrictions

The standard COBOL compiler used to process batch programs is the same used to prepare CICS/VS application programs for execution. Since CICS operates in a multitasking environment in which several application programs are executing concurrently, certain restrictions apply to a COBOL program that is to be used as an on-line application program. The restrictions can be categorized into four groups:

compiler debugging options
file management functions
compiler special features
execution time subroutines

The following compiler debugging options may not be used: COUNT, FLOW, STATE, SYMDUMP, STXIT, ENDJOB, DYNAM, TEST, AND SYST. These options are available to the batch programmer for execution time debugging and abnormal program recovery handling. The CICS/VS system recovery components provide a mechanism to prevent abnormal termination of the whole system in the event of an application program failure. The use of the debugging options in a COBOL program could override this mechanism, causing CICS/VS to fail.

Environment and Data Division entries and Procedure Division verbs associated with file management cannot be used. All COBOL input-output verbs (i.e., OPEN, CLOSE, READ, WRITE) cause an operating system wait to occur as a part of the I/O operation. When an operating system wait occurs, the region gives up control to the operating system, which may then dispatch a batch program. This action would eliminate the multitasking capability of CICS/VS since the Task Control Program would not receive control to dispatch another task during the I/O delay.

The COBOL verbs ACCEPT, DISPLAY, and EXHIBIT cause input-output operations to occur. They should not be used.

COBOL special features Report Writer, Sort, Trace, and segmentation cannot be used since they will cause input-output operations and program overlay structures to be generated. The I/O operations would impair the multitasking function of CICS while overlay functions are not supported by the Program Control Program.

The verbs INSPECT, SIGN IS SEPARATE, UNSTRING, CURRENT-DATE, DATE, DAY, TIME use execution time subroutines that require the operating system services. These statements should not be used. You should note, however, that many installations do use many of these verbs. It is a common practice, for example, to use the special field CURRENT-DATE.

In addition to the standard COBOL reserved words, CICS command-level programs should not contain names beginning with the letters DFH. This prefix has special meaning to the CICS command translator. You should also not use the names EXEC, CICS, DLI, and END-EXEC. These names are used by the translator for command delimiters.

The COBOL ALTER statement should not be used in a CICS program. The ALTER statement is used to change a GOTO statement so that it branches to a different routine. In effect, the ALTER statement changes the COBOL object module. This could violate an important CICS axiom; that a program should remain reentrant or quasi-reentrant. A reentrant program is one that does not modify itself at all. A quasi-reentrant program is one that may modify itself but always reestablishes itself back to its initial state before issuing another command. Programs should remain at least quasi-reentrant to allow them to be used with multithreading. Recall that *multithreading* means that the same application program may be in use by multiple terminals at the same time. If a task is allowed to modify a program but does not modify it back before returning control to CICS, it could adversely affect another task using the same program. Since the ALTER statement modifies the procedure division, it may make the program lose its quasi-reentrant status. The easiest way to keep this from happening is not to use the ALTER verb.

There is one final statement that should not be used in a CICS program. This statement is discussed last so that you won't forget it. You must never—repeat, never—use a STOP RUN statement. The COBOL STOP statement if used will terminate the whole CICS system! The proper way to end a CICS application program is to use the RETURN command. The basic format of the RETURN COMMAND is simply

```
EXEC CICS RETURN END-EXEC
```

If you use the RETURN command to terminate a program, you may still have to take precautionary measures to keep a STOP RUN from crashing CICS. Some versions of COBOL will automatically insert a STOP RUN at the end of your program. This "free" STOP RUN is inserted only when the compiler determines that you have not provided a COBOL verb to terminate the program. Remember, the RETURN command isn't a COBOL verb. You can prevent the compiler from inserting a STOP RUN at the end of the Procedure Division. This is done by coding a COBOL GOBACK statement somewhere in the program. This GOBACK isn't even executed. Its purpose is simply to prevent the compiler from generating the more devastating STOP RUN. If somehow the GOBACK statement is executed unintentionally, it will not bring down CICS; it will only terminate the COBOL program.

Program Preparation Example

A batch job used to prepare a command-level program for execution by CICS/VS consists of three job steps. Figure 2.5 depicts the processing provided by the job. The listings in figure 2.6 provide an example of the output produced by the command translator and COBOL compiler during the program preparation process.

The first job step invokes the command translator to process the source program containing the CICS commands. The translator will print a listing of the source program and will produce error messages if the source program contains invalid commands. In some instances the command will be deleted from the source code; be sure to check the summary page of the translator listing to verify that your program is still intact.

As explained earlier in this chapter, the command translator will convert the CICS commands into call statements that can be processed by the standard COBOL compiler. To accomplish this a

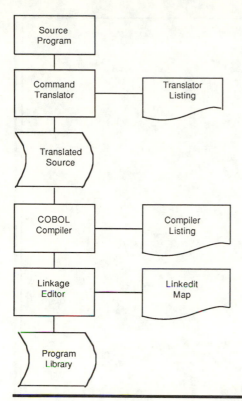

FIGURE 2.5. Preparation of CICS/VS Command Level COBOL Program

disk data set is normally allocated to the job and the translator will write the "new" program to this area. This file is then used as input by the compiler. The compiler produces a listing and an object module that is input to the system Linkage Editor. Output from the Linkage Editor is a load module (OS) or a core image module (VSE).

Several modifications are made to the original program. Please refer to figure 2.6 as you study these paragraphs. The first modification will occur at the very end of the working-storage section. A data structure is inserted into the program. Please refer to page 1 of the listing. Several variable names are included within the data structure. The variables are provided to allow you to specify numeric constants and literals as arguments in your CICS commands. On page 2 of the listing, notice how the two arguments 'MENUMAP' and 'VENDSET' are moved to variable names DFHC0070 and DFHC0071 prior to the call statement generated by the translator. The variables, among others, also appear in the call statement as arguments and are passed on to the Execute Interface Program during program execution.

The next modifications take effect in the Linkage Section. All CICS programs require a Linkage Section, so if you don't specify one, the translator will provide one for you. The translator will also provide a data structure for the Execute Interface Block. Following the EIB, you will find 01-level statements for DFHCOMMAREA, DFHBLLSLOT1, and DFHBLLSLOT2. The first of these areas, DFHCOMMAREA, provides for a program communications area. It will be discussed in chapter 7. The DFHBLLSLOT areas are provided to allow your COBOL object program to access to the EIB and program communications area. You will not have to use these special CICS-provided fields.

The last modifications to your program will appear in the Procedure Division. Notice that a COBOL USING clause has been added to the PROCEDURE DIVISION statement. This clause allows the program to access the Execute Interface Block and Communications area. Be sure not to code your own

```
CICS/VS COMMAND LANGUAGE TRANSLATOR VERSION 1.6                          TIME 15.53 DATE 16 MAR 87    PAGE 1

          CBL LIB,SUPMAP,APOST,NOCLIST CICS(DEBUG SOURCE LINECOUNT (56))

*OPTIONS IN EFFECT*

     CICS
     DEBUG
   NOFE
     SPIE
     EDF
     LINECOUNT(56)
     TABLE(DFHEITAB)
     SOURCE
   NOVBREF
     OPTIONS
     FLAG(W)
     SEQ
     APOST
   NONUM
   NOOPT
     SPACE(1)
     LANGLVL(1)

     LINE        SOURCE LISTING

     00001       IDENTIFICATION DIVISION.
     00002       PROGRAM-ID. EXAMPLE.
     00003       AUTHOR.  BOB LOWE.
     00004       * * * * * * * * * * * * * * * * * * * * * * * * * * * * *
     00005       * THE PURPOSE OF THIS PROGRAM IS TO ILLUSTRATE THE CHANGES
     00006       *     MADE TO A COBOL PROGRAM BY THE CICS/VS COMMAND
     00007       *     TRANSLATOR.
     00008       * THIS PROGRAM CAUSES A FORMATTED MENU SCREEN TO BE
     00009       *     DISPLAYED ON THE TERMINAL.
     00010       * * * * * * * * * * * * * * * * * * * * * * * * * * * * *
     00011       ENVIRONMENT DIVISION.
     00012       DATA DIVISION.
     00013       WORKING-STORAGE SECTION.
     00014       PROCEDURE DIVISION.
     00015       000-MAINLINE.
     00016           EXEC CICS SEND MAP ('MENUMAP') MAPSET ('VENDSET') MAPONLY
     00017           END-EXEC.
     00018           EXEC CICS RETURN END-EXEC.
     00019           GOBACK.

NO MESSAGES PRODUCED BY TRANSLATOR.

TRANSLATION TIME:-  0.03 MINS.
```

FIGURE 2.6.   Program Preparation Example

```
       CBL SUPMAP,CSYNTAX,CLIST,APOST
       CBL LIB,SUPMAP,APOST,NOCLIST
00001       IDENTIFICATION DIVISION.
00002       PROGRAM-ID. EXAMPLE.
00003       AUTHOR.  BOB LOWE.
00004   * * * * * * * * * * * * * * * * * * * * * * * * * * * * * * * *
00005   *   THE PURPOSE OF THIS PROGRAM IS TO ILLUSTRATE THE CHANGES  *
00006   *     MADE TO A COBOL PROGRAM BY THE CICS/VS COMMAND          *
00007   *     TRANSLATOR.                                             *
00008   *   THIS PROGRAM CAUSES A FORMATTED MENU SCREEN TO BE         *
00009   *     DISPLAYED ON THE TERMINAL.                              *
00010   * * * * * * * * * * * * * * * * * * * * * * * * * * * * * * * *
00011       ENVIRONMENT DIVISION.
00012       DATA DIVISION.
00013       WORKING-STORAGE SECTION.
00014       01  DFHLLOVER PIC X(22) VALUE 'LD TABLE DFHEITAB 1-6.'
00015       01  DFHEIDO PICTURE S9(7) COMPUTATIONAL-3 VALUE ZERO.
00016       01  DFHEIBO PICTURE S9(4) COMPUTATIONAL VALUE ZERO.
00017       01  DFHEICB  PICTURE X(8) VALUE IS '        '.
00018
00019       01  DFHEIV16 COMP PIC S9(8).
00020       01  DFHEIV11 COMP PIC S9(4).
00021       01  DFHEIV12 COMP PIC S9(4).
00022       01  DFHEIV13 COMP PIC S9(4).
00023       01  DFHEIV14 COMP PIC S9(4).
00024       01  DFHEIV15 COMP PIC S9(4).
00025       01  DFHB0025 COMP PIC S9(4).
00026       01  DFHEIV5  PIC X(4).
00027       01  DFHEIV6  PIC X(4).
00028       01  DFHEIV17 PIC X(4).
00029       01  DFHEIV18 PIC X(4).
00030       01  DFHEIV19 PIC X(4).
00031       01  DFHEIV1  PIC X(8).
00032       01  DFHEIV2  PIC X(8).
00033       01  DFHEIV3  PIC X(8).
00034       01  DFHEIV20 PIC X(8).
00035       01  DFHC0084 PIC X(8).
00036       01  DFHC0085 PIC X(8).
00037       01  DFHC0320 PIC X(32).
00038       01  DFHEIV7  PIC X(2).
00039       01  DFHEIV8  PIC X(2).
00040       01  DFHC0022 PIC X(2).
00041       01  DFHC0023 PIC X(2).
00042       01  DFHEIV10 PIC S9(7) COMP-3.
00043       01  DFHEIV4  PIC X(6).
00044       01  DFHC0070 PIC X(7).
00045       01  DFHC0071 PIC X(7).
00046       01  DFHDUMMY COMP PIC S9(4).
00047       01  DFHEIV0 PICTURE X(29).
00048       LINKAGE SECTION.
00049       01  DFHEIBLK.
00050       02  EIBTIME  PIC S9(7) COMP-3.
00051       02  EIBDATE  PIC S9(7) COMP-3.
```

FIGURE 2.6. Continued

```
2          EXAMPLE          15.53.29          03/16/87

00052      02  EIBTRNID PIC X(4).
00053      02  EIBTASKN PIC S9(7) COMP-3.
00054      02  EIBTRMID PIC X(4).
00055      02  DFHEIGDI COMP PIC S9(4).
00056      02  EIBCPOSN COMP PIC S9(4).
00057      02  EIBCALEN COMP PIC S9(4).
00058      02  EIBAID   PIC X(1).
00059      02  EIBFN    PIC X(2).
00060      02  EIBRCODE PIC X(6).
00061      02  EIBDS    PIC X(8).
00062      02  EIBREQID PIC X(8).
00063      02  EIBRSRCE PIC X(8).
00064      02  EIBSYNC  PIC X(1).
00065      02  EIBFREE  PIC X(1).
00066      02  EIBRECV  PIC X(1).
00067      02  EIBFIL02 PIC X(1).
00068      02  EIBATT   PIC X(1).
00069      02  EIBEOC   PIC X(1).
00070      02  EIBFMH   PIC X(1).
00071      02  EIBCOMPL PIC X(1).
00072      02  EIBSIG   PIC X(1).
00073      02  EIBCONF  PIC X(1).
00074      02  EIBERR   PIC X(1).
00075      02  EIBERRCD PIC X(4).
00076      02  EIBSYNRB PIC X(1).
00077      02  EIBNODAT PIC X(1).
00078      01  DFHCOMMAREA PICTURE X(1).
00079      01  DFHBLLSLOT1 PICTURE X(1).
00080      01  DFHBLLSLOT2 PICTURE X(1).
00081      PROCEDURE DIVISION USING DFHEIBLK DFHCOMMAREA.
00082          CALL 'DFHEI1'.
00083      000-MAINLINE.
00084      *EXEC CICS SEND MAP ('MENUMAP') MAPSET ('VENDSET') MAPONLY
00085      *END-EXEC.
00086          MOVE '                   00018 ' TO DFHEIV0
00087          MOVE 'MENUMAP' TO DFHC0070
00088          MOVE 'VENDSET' TO DFHC0071
00089          CALL 'DFHEI1' USING DFHEIV0 DFHC0070 DFHEICB DFHDUMMY
00090          DFHC0071.
00091      *EXEC CICS RETURN END-EXEC.
00092          MOVE '           00018 ' TO DFHEIV0
00093          CALL 'DFHEI1' USING DFHEIV0.
00094          GOBACK.
```

FIGURE 2.6. Continued

USING clause since that would upset the normal operation of the program. Finally, all EXECUTE commands are converted into COBOL statements to call the Execute Interface Program, passing various arguments as parameters of the call statement. The MOVE statements preceding the call serve to initialize the parameters in working-storage. The original command remains in the source listing, but is commented out by the translator.

Chapter Summary

In this chapter, you were introduced to the Command-Level Interface of CICS. It is this interface that allows the applications programmer to write on-line programs without requiring a detailed knowledge of CICS. The Command-Level Interface consists of an off-line command translator program and an on-line Execute Interface Program. The coding requirements for the CICS commands that appear in the COBOL program were described. The standard COBOL compiler used to compile batch programs is used to translate CICS command-level programs. The program preparation process, including the COBOL restrictions imposed by CICS were explained. The example translator and compile listing was used to illustrate the translator modifications that are made to the COBOL source program during the program preparation process. You should now be ready to study the various commands presented in the coming chapters.

Discussion Questions

1. A batch program that needs to access a file contains SELECT and FD statements in the Environment and Data Divisions. Why aren't these statements needed in a CICS application program? Where does CICS store the equivalents to these statements?
2. All CICS/VS files are opened and closed by a master terminal operator. Describe how this method provides for central control of CICS file resources. Which COBOL statements are eliminated by this procedure?
3. A STOP RUN statement should never be placed within a COBOL program running under CICS. What would be the effect of executing this statement?
4. Which command is used to terminate a CICS program?
5. COBOL programs using the Command-Level Interface are provided a copy of the original working-storage during program initiation. All constants and I/O areas are set to the original compile-time values. How does this feature affect the multithreading environment provided by CICS?
6. One use of the command translator is to convert CICS commands to COBOL call statements. These call statements pass command arguments to the Execute Interface Program during execution of the COBOL program. How are COBOL literals passed in these call statements?
7. If two CICS commands appear together in a program, is the END-EXEC delimiter necessary?
8. Where are command translator options specified?
9. Which translator option has a COBOL compiler option that should have a corresponding value?
10. The COBOL debugging options, COUNT, FLOW, STATE, and others cannot be used in a CICS application program. What might be the effect of including these options in a compiled program?
11. The Execute Interface Block is used by the program to access CICS values. Why is this control block included in the COBOL Linkage Section instead of working-storage?
12. After a translator run, the original commands appear in the COBOL listing. What method is used to keep these commands from being flagged as errors by the COBOL compiler?
13. Describe the modifications made to the COBOL working-storage section during the translator run.

Review Exercises

1. Code a CBL statement with CICS options to suppress the translator source listing.
2. Write a COBOL statement to move the terminal identification code from the EIB to the field below.

```
05  THE-TERMINAL PIC XXXX.
```

Lab Problems

LAB 1

Prepare the following command-level program for execution under CICS. Use Job Control Language (JCL) statements provided by your instructor. Test the program at a terminal using a transaction code supplied by your instructor.

```
IDENTIFICATION DIVISION.
PROGRAM-ID. MYFIRST.
AUTHOR.  NAME.
ENVIRONMENT DIVISION.
DATA DIVISION.
WORKING-STORAGE SECTION.
01  MESSAGE-AREA PIC X(80) VALUE
    'PROGRAM XXXXXXX WRITTEN BY (your name) IS ON-LINE'.
PROCEDURE DIVISION.
    EXEC CICS SEND FROM (MESSAGE-AREA) ERASE
            LENGTH (80)
            END-EXEC.
    EXEC CICS RETURN END-EXEC.
    GOBACK.
```

3
Programming Introduction

As you study the programming introduction in this chapter, you will

1. Learn how to deal with exceptional conditions that might occur in a CICS/VS command-level program.
2. Understand that the default action for most exceptional conditions is to abend the CICS task.
3. See how the HANDLE CONDITION and IGNORE CONDITION commands can be used to execute exception processing routines within your program.
4. Understand the purpose of various keys on an IBM 3270 keyboard.
5. See how to determine which terminal attention key was used to initiate a transaction.
6. Be able to code a COBOL data structure to process input from a terminal.
7. Learn to use the RECEIVE command to read initial transaction input into the working-storage section of a program.
8. See how the SEND command is used to display messages on the terminal.
9. Learn to use the SEND TEXT and SEND PAGE commands to display multiple message lines on the terminal.

There are two topics in this introductory programming chapter. In the first section, you will learn about CICS exceptional conditions. Every program that you will design will have one or more CICS commands. Most commands can give rise to one or more exceptional conditions. You will learn one way to prevent CICS/VS from abending your programs when these exceptional conditions occur. In the second section, you will learn the commands to perform simple input and output operations on an IBM 3270 terminal. After studying this material, you should be able to write a program to process a transaction message keyed by an operator and send messages back to the operator.

CICS/VS Exceptional Conditions

During execution, CICS command-level programs must deal with errors that can occur at various stages during processing. When these errors occur during the execution of a CICS command, they are referred to as *exceptional conditions*. For each command there are generally one or more conditions which could cause the execution of the command to fail. A command to read a record from a file, for instance, will fail with the NOTOPEN exception if the data set (file) has not been opened by the master terminal operator. It will also fail (with a NOTFND exception) if the requested record is not found in the file.

In most cases when an exceptional condition occurs, the program will not be able to provide the function it was designed to perform. A program initiated to display a master record from a file, for instance, will be unsuccessful when the file is closed. The same program will not be able to display a record if the record is not on file. Both of these circumstances would give rise to a CICS/VS exceptional condition.

In a few situations, exceptional conditions will arise that are acceptable or even expected by the program logic. A program preparing to add a record to a file for example, would generally verify that the record is not already on file. A CICS READ command would be used to do this. The NOTFND exception from the read command in this instance provides the needed verification that the record is not already on file. In this example the exceptional condition NOTFND would actually be a desirable response from the command.

CICS DEFAULT ACTIONS

When the execution of each CICS command is complete, the Execute Interface Program will take some action. The action from a NORMAL command completion is to return control to the application program at the next sequential instruction following the command. When an exceptional condition occurs, however, CICS will perform an exception condition analysis to determine the action to be taken. If the application program does not specify an action to be taken when an exceptional condition occurs, the default action is usually to terminate the task, and display an error message with an ABEND code. For example the message below would be displayed if a program, VEND001 had not specified an action for "file not open" and that condition occurred in the program. A list of Execute Interface Program ABEND codes is shown in figure 3.1.

```
DFH2005I TRANSACTION VEND ABEND AEIS IN PROGRAM VEND001 15:12:42
```

As you can see, this message is not very user friendly. The operator, upon seeing a message like this, will usually call the computer center to get an explanation. A much better way to deal with this situation would be for the program to display a more informative error message such as "VENDOR FILE IS NOT OPEN". But to display such a message you have to prevent CICS from abending the task when an exception occurs. The application program must provide exception condition alternatives in order to prevent CICS from abending a task caused by an exception. There are two alternative actions that can be specified.

First, CICS can be instructed to ignore the exception. When CICS has been instructed to ignore a condition and that condition arises during a command, CICS will return control to the program in a similar manner to normal completion. That is, to the next sequential instruction following the command.

The second alternative is to specify a routine in the program to receive control if an exceptional condition occurs. If a routine has been specified for a given exception, and that exception arises during a command, CICS will transfer control to that routine in the Procedure Division. This exception-processing routine might send an appropriate error message to the operator, then terminate the task. In a few situations, such as our earlier add-record program example, the exception routine would be a normal processing routine for the transaction.

Two commands are provided to activate these exception condition alternatives, namely: IGNORE CONDITION and HANDLE CONDITION. Both of these commands must be placed in the program so they will be executed *prior* to the program issuing a service command that might give rise to an exceptional condition. First let's look at the IGNORE CONDITION command.

AEIA	ERROR	AEI9	MAPFAIL
AEID	EOF	AEYA	INVERRTERM
AEIE	EODS	AEYB	INVMPSZ
AEIG	INBFMH	AEYC	IGREQID
AEIH	ENDINPT	AEYE	INVLDC
AEII	NONVAL	AEYG	JIDERR
AEIJ	NOSTART	AEYH	QIDERR
AEIK	TERMIDERR	AEYJ	DSSTAT
AEIL	DSIDERR	AEYK	SELNERR
AEIM	NOTFND	AEYM	UNEXPIN
AEIN	DUPREC	AEYN	NOPASSBKRD
AEIO	DUPKEY	AEYO	NOPASSBKWR
AEIP	INVREQ	AEYP	SEGIDERR
AEIQ	IOERR	AEYQ	SYSIDERR
AEIR	NOSPACE	AEYR	ISINVREQ
AEIS	NOTOPEN	AEYT	ENVDEFERR
AEIT	ENDFILE	AEYU	IGREQCD
AEIU	ILLOGIC	AEYV	SESSERR
AEIV	LENGERR	AEYY	NOTALLOC
AEIW	QZERO	AEYZ	CBIDERR
AEIZ	ITEMERR	AEY0	INVEXITREQ
AEI0	PGMIDERR	AEY6	LOGIC ERR IN IN DFHEIP
AEI1	TRANSIDERR	AEY8	dynamic storage reg too small
AEI2	ENDDATA	AEY9	invalid EXEC CICS command
AEI3	INVTSREQ		
AEI8	TSIOERR		

FIGURE 3.1. Execute Interface Abend Codes

IGNORE CONDITION COMMAND

The format of the IGNORE CONDITION command is

```
EXEC CICS IGNORE CONDITION
    condition
    END-EXEC
```

This command would be used in a program to specify one or more conditions that are to be ignored by CICS. If any of the conditions occur later during a command CICS will return control back to the application program at the next statement following that command. That is, if a future command gives rise to one of the conditions, the next sequential statement in the COBOL program following the future command will be executed. This has the same effect as if that exception had not occurred.

Up to 16 conditions may appear within the same IGNORE command; additional conditions exceeding the maximum must be specified in further IGNORE commands.

The IGNORE action for a condition remains in effect until a subsequent HANDLE CONDITION command specifying that condition is executed. All IGNORE CONDITION actions are lost when the program is terminated with the RETURN command.

Below is an example of an IGNORE CONDITION command that will cause the condition LENGERR to be ignored in the program. The condition LENGERR will be discussed later in the chapter.

```
EXEC CICS IGNORE CONDITION LENGERR
END-EXEC.
```

HANDLE CONDITION COMMAND

The format of the HANDLE CONDITION COMMAND is

```
EXEC CICS HANDLE CONDITION
    condition [(label)]
    condition [(label)]
    .
    .
    END-EXEC
```

This command is used to specify a routine to receive control when a condition arises. The routine can be a COBOL *paragraph* or *section* name. The COBOL paragraph or section is specified as the *label* argument for each condition.

If a condition is specified *with* a label and that condition occurs later within the program, CICS will transfer control to the associated paragraph or section. CICS generates an equivalent to a GOTO verb to accomplish this transfer. There is no automatic way for an exception condition routine to return to the statement following the command that caused the exception.

The same label may be specified for more than one condition, indicating that the same routine is to be entered if any of the exceptional conditions occurs.

If a condition is specified *without* a label, the default action for that condition will be activated. This option might be specified to reset a condition previously handled, back to its default action. For most conditions this default action is to abend the task and display an abend code on the terminal. Because of this you will rarely specify a condition without a label in a HANDLE CONDITION command.

The label or default action for a condition remains in effect until a subsequent HANDLE CONDITION or IGNORE CONDITION command specifying that condition is executed. All HANDLE CONDITION actions are lost when the program is terminated with the RETURN command.

Up to 16 conditions may appear within the same HANDLE command; additional conditions exceeding the maximum must be specified in further HANDLE commands.

Here is an illustration of the use of the HANDLE CONDITION command:

Assume that a program is going to read a record from a file named VENFILE. But if the file is not open at the time of the read, a routine named 950-NOTOPEN should be entered. Upon entry into the Procedure Division this program issues a HANDLE CONDITION command for the NOTOPEN condition. Later in the program, the READ command is executed. If the NOTOPEN condition occurs as a result of the READ, EIP will cause a branch to the routine named 950-NOTOPEN. Since no other conditions have been handled, if some other exceptional condition occurs, the default action will be taken; otherwise control will be passed to the instruction following the READ command.

```
EXEC CICS HANDLE CONDITION NOTOPEN (950-NOTOPEN) END-EXEC.
EXEC CICS READ
     DATASET ('VENFILE')
     RIDFLD (VENDOR-ID)
     INTO (VENDOR-RECORD)
     LENGTH (RECORD-LENGTH)
     EQUAL
     END-EXEC.
```

statements to process the data record

```
        .
        .
        .
950-NOTOPEN.
    EXEC CICS SEND FROM (NOTOPEN-MESSAGE)
    ERASE LENGTH (80) END-EXEC.
    EXEC CICS RETURN END-EXEC.
```

POSITIONING HANDLE AND IGNORE COMMANDS

There are no set rules for positioning the HANDLE and IGNORE commands within the program. You may place them anywhere as long as the commands are executed sometime prior to issuing a service command that might give rise to the condition. A common practice is to deal with global conditions at the start of the program. Global conditions are those where the action for the condition will not vary throughout the execution of your program. By coding these conditions at the start of the program, you can minimize the number of calls to Execute Interface Program and thus improve the performance of your program. It may also improve the organization and documentation of your program. You shouldn't specify conditions that will never arise during execution. There is no rule against it, but this will cause extra storage requirements for the task and additional processing since EIP must store these condition actions for later use. Here is an example of a HANDLE CONDITION command placed at the start of the Procedure Division:

```
PROCEDURE DIVISION.
    EXEC CICS HANDLE CONDITION
        ERROR (980-ERROR)
        NOTOPEN (950-NOTOPEN)
        NOTFND (960-NOTFND)
    END-EXEC.
```

Some exceptional conditions can occur during the execution of a number of unrelated commands. For example, LENGERR can occur during file control operations, terminal control operations and others. If different actions are desired, HANDLE CONDITION commands specifying these actions are required at appropriate points in the program. This is done by issuing a HANDLE CONDITION or IGNORE CONDITION command prior to issuing the CICS/VS command that might cause the exceptional condition to arise. The coding below illustrates how the program would specify a different label for the condition LENGERR just prior to issuing a second command that might also give rise to the condition.

```
EXEC CICS HANDLE CONDITION
    LENGERR (4000-RECEIVE-LENGERR)
    END-EXEC
EXEC CICS RECEIVE INTO (INPUT-MESSAGE)
    LENGTH (MESSAGE-LENGTH)
    END-EXEC.
        .
        .
EXEC CICS HANDLE CONDITION
    LENGERR (5000-READ-LENGERR)
    END-EXEC
EXEC CICS READ
    DATASET ('VENFILE')
    RIDFLD (VENDOR-ID)
    INTO (VENDOR-RECORD)
    LENGTH (RECORD-LENGTH)
    EQUAL
    END-EXEC.
```

THE ERROR CONDITION

There is a general exceptional condition named *ERROR,* which can be handled in the program. If no HANDLE CONDITION command is active for a condition that arises during a service command but one is active for ERROR, control will be passed to the label specified for ERROR. The error routine might send a general error message to the operator, then terminate the task. A more sophisticated generalized error-handling routine might display the actual exception response code (stored in the EIB) on the terminal. This response code could then be used to help diagnose the problem. One use of a general error routine is to reduce the coding requirements for applications. It can be very costly to handle every exception in every program in an application. Some exceptions will rarely, if ever, occur. Why spend a lot of time and money developing error-handling routines for an exception that is never likely to happen? By coding general error-handling routines you may be able to improve programmer productivity.

EXCEPTIONAL CONDITION LOOPS

Commands should not be included within error routines that might give rise to the same condition that caused the routine to be executed. If this is done, the program could enter an exceptional condition loop. If an exception condition loop occurs, it may require a master terminal operator to cancel your task. You can prevent an exception condition loop by issuing at the start of the routine a HANDLE CONDITION command that will cause a different routine to be executed. You might also specify that the default action is to be taken in the event of an exceptional condition. For example, you might code the following statement in a general error routine. By doing this, if another exception occurs within the error routine, you will not get into an exception condition loop.

```
980-ERROR.
     EXEC CICS HANDLE CONDITION ERROR END-EXEC.
```

When properly used, the IGNORE CONDITION and HANDLE CONDITION commands provide a suitable means to detect application problems, control transaction abends and provide user control of the messages received by the terminal operator. This technique of dealing with exceptional conditions has been used extensively in the past and you will likely see many programs written using this command-level facility. Later, in chapter 7, you will learn other techniques of dealing with exceptional conditions. Let's continue by studying some of the terminal input-output commands.

Terminal Operations

In this section you will learn the programming commands required to communicate directly with an IBM 3270 Video Display Terminal. This type of terminal is widely used in most industry applications. A brief overview of the design of the 3270 terminal will help you to better understand the programming capabilities and requirements for use of this terminal. The remaining chapters of this book concentrate only on this type of terminal. Following the 3270 overview, the chapter contains a description of commands to receive input during a transaction and to send messages using the 3270 terminal.

TERMINAL IDENTIFICATION

The Terminal Control Program is responsible for all communication between the application program and the 3270 terminal. In a batch system, a program is associated with a single partition or region. In CICS/VS, a program is associated with a task running on a single terminal. Each terminal in a CICS/VS network is assigned a unique four-character *identification* code. This user-defined terminal identification is stored in the Terminal Control Table (TCT) during the systems-tailoring process. Terminals are sometimes assigned an identification based upon the location of the device. The chart in figure 3.2 depicts the assignment of terminal identifications for a small network that includes 3270 terminals and printers at five locations. In this example the first letter of the terminal identification indicates the network location of the device; the second letter indicates the type of device, such as terminal or printer, and the last two digits represent the port location assigned to the terminal. This terminal identification is made available to each application program. It is stored in a field named EIBTRMID in the Execute Interface Block. The terminal identification is often displayed along with other information in transaction output messages. It is sometimes used for other purposes, such as to restrict certain functions or access to information. For example, a company with remote locations might limit payroll transactions to the central office terminals only. The terminal identification code can be used to accomplish this function.

	District Office	Longview Campus	Penn Valley Campus	Maple Woods Campus	Pioneer Campus
Terminal ID	DT00	LT00	PT00	MT00	IT00
	DT01	LT01	PT01	MT01	IT01
	DT02	LT02	PT02	MT02	IT02
	DT03	LT03	PT03	MT02	IT03
	..	..	PT04	..	..
	..		..	..	..
	DP30	LP15	..	MP15	IP11
	DP31		PP29		
			PP30		
			PP31		

FIGURE 3.2. Assignment of Terminal Identification by location

IBM 3270 DISPLAY UNIT

The 3270 display station provides image display of data transmitted from the host computer. An attached keyboard enables the operator to enter, modify, or delete data on the display and to cause the revised data to be returned to the computer. Each display station has its own hardware buffer for storing data. As messages are being composed or modified by keyboard operations, the changes are inserted in the buffer and displayed on the screen for operator verification. By using this buffering approach, the host computer is free from interruptions from the terminal during keyboard entry.

3270 KEYBOARDS

There are two types of keyboards commonly used with the 3270 display terminal, namely typewriter keyboard and data entry keyboard. The type of keyboard determines the layout of the keyboard and defines the characters and symbols that can be entered from the station. The typewriter keyboard provides the basic typewriter key layout. Some models provide for both uppercase and lowercase codes. The data entry keyboard closely resembles the layout of the IBM keypunch units used in the past. It is recommended for higher volume data entry operations. Figure 3.3 illustrates the layout of the two keyboards. Both keyboards provide key functions described as follows:

CHARACTER KEYS Alphabetic and alphameric characters can be entered into the display buffer using the character keys. Keyboard entry occurs at the current cursor location.

CURSOR-CONTROL KEYS A group of four keys moves the cursor up, down, left, or right.

FIELD-ORIENTED KEYS A special group of keys supporting 3270 field operations will be discussed later in chapter 5 when the 3270 field capabilities are introduced.

RESET KEY This key is used to ''unlock'' the keyboard. Certain conditions can cause the keyboard to be disabled, thus preventing further input. By pressing this ''panic'' key you can usually recover from most data entry errors.

INSERT KEY This key places the keyboard into insert mode. Pressing any alphameric keys then causes characters to the right of the cursor to be shifted one character to the right to accommodate insertion of the new characters. The new character or characters are inserted at the cursor position. Insert mode is terminated by pressing the RESET key.

DELETE KEY This key deletes the character from the current cursor position. All remaining characters to the right of the cursor shift one character to the left. Unlike the INSERT key, the operator does not have to use the RESET key to terminate DELETE operations.

ERASE EOF is used to erase all characters from the cursor to the end of the screen buffer. Characters preceding the cursor will not be erased.

FIGURE 3.3. (a) 3278 Typewriter Keyboard (b) 3278 Data Entry Keyboard

CLEAR This key clears all of the buffer positions of the terminal and moves the cursor to the upper left corner of the screen. As indicated below, this key also transmits an attention code to the host computer.

PROGRAM ATTENTION KEYS This is a generic term for a group of keys that are used to get the attention of host computer. The program attention keys are ENTER, CLEAR, Program Function Keys PF1 thru PF12 (PF24 on some terminals), and Program Attention Keys PA1, PA2, and PA3. As a result of pressing one of the program attention keys, the terminal generates and transmits an attention identification (AID) character to identify which key caused the interruption. The ENTER key and Program Function Keys also transmit data from the terminal. Upon receiving the input, the Terminal Control Program saves the AID character and the input message for later use by the application program.

STARTING A CICS TASK

One way to start a CICS task is to transmit a transaction message from the terminal. This transaction message must begin with a valid *transaction identification code*. It may contain other information. After using the 3270 keyboard to store the transaction code and any application-dependent information, one of the program attention keys (except CLEAR, PA1, PA2, PA3) is used to transmit the transaction message. The Terminal Control Program stores the transacton message in a terminal input-output area. Task Control Program then starts a task using the transaction identification received from the terminal.

Starting a task involves, among other things, loading and running an application program. The program name that is loaded is associated with the transaction code in the Program Control Table. As an example, assume that you have designed an inquiry program to display information from a vendor master record. Your design requires the operator to start the program by entering a transaction code. Assume that the transaction code for our inquiry program is V001. The operator could start this task and program by simply typing the message below then pressing ENTER or PF1 through PF12.

```
V001
```

USING THE ATTENTION IDENTIFIER

During task initiation, the Execute Interface Program stores the (3270) *attention identifier* code in the EIB. A field in the EIB named EIBAID will contain this code when the program is initiated. You can use the EIBAID value in the Procedure Division to determine which attention key was pressed. It is therefore possible to design the program to perform different functions based upon the key used to start the transaction. You can check this field with a COBOL statement. For example

```
IF EIBAID EQUAL '1'
```

For keys PF1 through PF9, the value in EIBAID corresponds to the numerical value of the PF key. The value for the other keys such as ENTER, CLEAR, and PF10 through PF24 are not as easy to remember. To ease the burden of using attention identifiers, IBM has provided a COBOL copybook which defines a list of names that can be used in the COBOL IF statement. This copy member named DFHAID is shown in figure 3.4. It is copied into working-storage as follows:

```
COPY DFHAID.
```

Once the copy member is included in the working-storage section, the field names can be used to check against the EIBAID field. For instance,

```
IF EIBAID EQUAL DFHPF1
      PERFORM 100-ROUTINE-ONE
ELSE IF EIBAID EQUAL DFHPF2
         PERFORM 200-ROUTINE-TWO
      ELSE PERFORM 800-NORMAL-PROCESSING.
```

PROCESSING INPUT MESSAGES

Sometimes one or more data fields will accompany the transaction code. Let's assume that the operator is allowed to key in a record number when the transaction is started. For our example, let's say that the record number is used by the program to read the record randomly from the master file. This transaction message might appear as follows:

```
V001 100000
```

In this example, the transaction code is accompanied by additional data to be used by the application program. Before the task is started, the transaction message is stored in a terminal input-output area (TIOA) by the Terminal Control Program. When the program first starts, the message is not yet available for processing. It must be transferred to the application program's working-storage before it can be used. The terminal control RECEIVE command (described next) will accomplish this transfer. The

```
01      DFHAID.
 02  DFHNULL   PIC  X  VALUE IS ' '.
 02  DFHENTER  PIC  X  VALUE IS QUOTE.
 02  DFHCLEAR  PIC  X  VALUE IS '_'.
 02  DFHCLRP   PIC  X  VALUE IS 'e'.
 02  DFHPEN    PIC  X  VALUE IS '='.
 02  DFHOPID   PIC  X  VALUE IS 'W'.
 02  DFHMSRE   PIC  X  VALUE IS 'X'.
 02  DFHSTRF   PIC  X  VALUE IS 'H'.
 02  DFHTRIG   PIC  X  VALUE IS '"'.
 02  DFHPA1    PIC  X  VALUE IS '%'.
 02  DFHPA2    PIC  X  VALUE IS '>'.
 02  DFHPA3    PIC  X  VALUE IS ','.
 02  DFHPF1    PIC  X  VALUE IS '1'.
 02  DFHPF2    PIC  X  VALUE IS '2'.
 02  DFHPF3    PIC  X  VALUE IS '3'.
 02  DFHPF4    PIC  X  VALUE IS '4'.
 02  DFHPF5    PIC  X  VALUE IS '5'.
 02  DFHPF6    PIC  X  VALUE IS '6'.
 02  DFHPF7    PIC  X  VALUE IS '7'.
 02  DFHPF8    PIC  X  VALUE IS '8'.
 02  DFHPF9    PIC  X  VALUE IS '9'.
 02  DFHPF10   PIC  X  VALUE IS ':'.
 02  DFHPF11   PIC  X  VALUE IS '#'.
 02  DFHPF12   PIC  X  VALUE IS '@'.
 02  DFHPF13   PIC  X  VALUE IS 'A'.
 02  DFHPF14   PIC  X  VALUE IS 'B'.
 02  DFHPF15   PIC  X  VALUE IS 'C'.
 02  DFHPF16   PIC  X  VALUE IS 'D'.
 02  DFHPF17   PIC  X  VALUE IS 'E'.
 02  DFHPF18   PIC  X  VALUE IS 'F'.
 02  DFHPF19   PIC  X  VALUE IS 'G'.
 02  DFHPF20   PIC  X  VALUE IS 'H'.
 02  DFHPF21   PIC  X  VALUE IS 'I'.
 02  DFHPF22   PIC  X  VALUE IS '¢'.
 02  DFHPF23   PIC  X  VALUE IS '.'.
 02  DFHPF24   PIC  X  VALUE IS '<'.
```

FIGURE 3.4.   DFHAID Copybook

RECEIVE command will transfer the transaction message into a data structure that you provide in working-storage. This data structure is simply a COBOL record layout for the *anticipated* message. The data structure below should be suitable to process our inquiry transaction message.

MESSAGE→V001 100000

```
01      MESSAGE-IN.
        05   TRAN-CODE    PIC XXXX.
        05   FILLER       PIC X.
        05   KEY-INPUT    PIC XXXXX.
```

After the message has been received into the data structure, any data fields are processed using the COBOL names defined in the message area. For instance, you could provide the statement below to determine if the record key supplied by the operator is numeric.

```
IF KEY-INPUT IS NOT NUMERIC
    PERFORM 9000-NONNUMERIC-KEY.
```

THE RECEIVE COMMAND

The terminal control RECEIVE command is used to move an input message from the terminal input-output area (TIOA) to the data structure in working-storage where it can be processed by the program. The format of the RECEIVE command is

```
EXEC CICS RECEIVE
     INTO (data-area)
     LENGTH (data-area)
     END-EXEC
```

INTO (Data-Area)

The INTO data-area argument specifies the name of the receiving data structure in working-storage. The Execute Interface Program will move input from the terminal input-output area to the COBOL field specified as the argument.

LENGTH (Data-Area)

The LENGTH data-area argument is a COBOL field name with a PICTURE S9999 COMPUTATIONAL clause. The value in data area specifies the *maximum* number of characters that CICS should move from the TIOA to the working-storage field. When the command is executed, EIP will limit the number of characters moved into working-storage by the value specified in this field. Any additional data keyed by the operator will be truncated. In the example below, a maximum of 11 characters will be moved to the area named *MESSAGE-IN*.

```
MOVE SPACES TO MESSAGE-IN.
MOVE +11 TO MSG-LEN.
EXEC CICS RECEIVE INTO (MESSAGE-IN)
     LENGTH (MSG-LEN)
     END-EXEC
IF KEY-INPUT IS NOT NUMERIC
     PERFORM 9000-NONNUMERIC-KEY.
```

When the RECEIVE command is executed, the purpose of the LENGTH option is to keep CICS from writing over the COBOL areas immediately following the receiving data structure. CICS doesn't check the COBOL data area to determine field boundaries. It doesn't know if MESSAGE-IN is 11 characters or 11 hundred characters long. CICS simply moves characters from the TIOA to the address you supplied in the INTO option. If for some reason the operator keyed in more characters than the size of your input data structure, you need some way to *truncate* the incoming data. One function of the LENGTH option is to specify the truncation point.

Another function of the LENGTH option is to notify the program of the *actual* number of characters received. After the RECEIVE is complete, the COBOL data area specified in the LENGTH option will contain a new value indicating the actual message length. The actual message length is the number of characters originally transmitted by the terminal. The program can examine the length field to determine the actual number of characters transmitted. For our sample transaction, we needed at least 11 characters to obtain the record key. The following statement could therefore be used to determine if the record key was supplied by the operator:

```
MOVE SPACES TO MESSAGE-IN.
MOVE +11 to MSG-LEN.
EXEC CICS RECEIVE INTO (MESSAGE-IN)
     LENGTH (MSG-LEN)
     END-EXEC
IF MSG-LEN LESS THAN +11
     PERFORM 9005-MSG-TOO-SHORT.
IF KEY-INPUT IS NOT NUMERIC
     PERFORM 9000-NONNUMERIC-KEY.
```

If the transaction message is shorter than the working-storage data structure specified in the INTO option, there is another fact to consider. CICS does not clear the remaining area to spaces or to any other value for that matter. It only changes the *leftmost* positions of the data area. For instance, if only four characters are transmitted by the terminal, only the leftmost four characters of the INTO area will be changed. For this reason, it is a good idea to initialize the transaction input area to a known value prior to issuing the RECEIVE command. This is especially true if you plan to use the fields in the area for logical or arithmetic operations. It is also a good idea if you plan to display the input message contents back on the terminal. Residual "garbage" in the input area can cause unpredictable results when sent to a terminal. In the example above, the program moved SPACES to the message area prior to issuing the RECEIVE command. Another approach is to use a value clause when defining each field in the input area.

RECEIVE EXCEPTIONAL CONDITIONS

When receiving data from an IBM 3270 terminal, there is only one exceptional condition that will generally arise. That condition is LENGERR. It occurs when the transmitted data *exceeds* the size specified in the LENGTH option of the RECEIVE command. You learned earlier that CICS truncates the incoming data. In effect, the LENGERR condition will arise whenever truncation has occurred.

Recall the discussion about exceptional conditions earlier in the chapter. You might remember that the default action for most exceptional conditions is to abend the task. This is the default for LENGERR. If you have not dealt with it in some way, and the operator keys in more characters than your LENGTH argument value, the transaction will be abended. Because of this default action, you will usually want to deal with this condition in some way. Here are two alternatives: First, you could write an error-processing routine to send an error message to the operator. A second and sometimes better alternative is just to *ignore* the error condition.

IGNORING SUPERFLUOUS INPUT

In practice, the normal truncation effect caused by the LENGTH option of the RECEIVE command will be sufficient to most programs. The IGNORE CONDITION command can be used to allow the program to continue execution at the next COBOL statement following the RECEIVE, regardless of excessive input. If necessary, the routine following the RECEIVE will then validate the input message prior to using it. There are a few situations that make this technique advantageous. A common occurrence for instance, is the need to enter a transaction code after an error message has been displayed by an application program or by CICS. For example, assume the CICS message below appears on the terminal.

DFH1001 INVALID TRANSACTION IDENTIFICATION PLEASE RESUBMIT...

If the operator keys over the first part of the message but does not erase the remainder of the screen, the message below would be transmitted by the terminal.

V001 100000ALID TRANSACTION IDENTIFICATION PLEASE RESUBMIT...

The input message keyed by the operator is *logically* valid, but a LENGERR will occur since our program would have specified a truncation point of 11 characters. If the program does not somehow ignore LENGERR, the operator would be required to clear the screen before typing the transaction or use ERASE EOF after typing the message. Why require these extra keystrokes when you can easily bypass the problem? The following coding would be sufficient to receive the sample message above, truncate all but the first 11 characters, then continue processing the input:

```
MOVE SPACES TO MESSAGE-IN.
MOVE +11 TO MSG-LEN.
EXEC CICS IGNORE CONDITION LENGERR END-EXEC.
EXEC CICS RECEIVE INTO (MESSAGE-IN)
    LENGTH (MSG-LEN)
    END-EXEC.
IF MSG-LEN LESS THAN +11
    PERFORM 9005-MSG-TOO-SHORT.
IF KEY-INPUT IS NOT NUMERIC
    PERFORM 9000-NONNUMERIC-KEY.
```

WRITING TERMINAL MESSAGES

Most programs will display some type of output on the terminal. This output is usually a display of the information associated with the transaction. An inquiry program, for instance, will display information from a file or data-base record. In the event of some validation error or exceptional condition, the program might instead display an error message indicating the problem. Either way, the program has sent a message back to the terminal. When using IBM 3270 terminals, it is important for a task always to send some output message back to the terminal.

The importance of sending a message back to the terminal is related to the design of the 3270 display terminal. With this terminal the keyboard becomes "locked" each time the terminal transmits data to the mainframe. If the task terminates without sending some message back to the terminal, the keyboard remains locked and the operator must press the RESET key before additional input can occur. It is very confusing to an operator when a transaction is originated and a reply is not received. Operators generally assume that the system is "down" when the keyboard remains locked for some time. If you follow this principle of sending some message back to the terminal, you will have happier operators and fewer phone calls!

DEFINING MESSAGE AREAS

There are two commands that can be used to transmit a message to the terminal. These are the terminal control SEND command and the BMS SEND TEXT command. Both commands require an output data structure for the message to be sent to the terminal. The layout of an output message area will vary depending on the content of the message to be sent. For error messages, message text indicating the reason for the message is usually displayed. The program might also display the time, terminal identification, or other information useful to the operator. Here is an example of a typical output message and the data structure to support the message:

```
V001 100000 RECORD KEY IS NOT NUMERIC-TRY AGAIN...HH:MM:SS

01  MESSAGE-LINE
    05    SEND-TRANSID      PIC XXXX.
    05    FILLER            PIC X.
    05    SEND-KEY          PIC X(06).
    05    THE-MESSAGE.      PIC X(54).
    05    FILLER            PIC X.
    05    THE-TIME          PIC ZZ9,99,99.
    05    FILLER            PIC XXXXX.
```

The following Procedure Division statements would be used to prepare the message area for transmission to the terminal with the SEND command.

```
9000-NONNUMERIC-KEY.
      MOVE SPACES TO MESSAGE-LINE.
      MOVE EIBTRNID TO SEND-TRANSID.
      MOVE KEY-INPUT TO SEND-KEY.
      MOVE 'RECORD KEY IS NOT NUMERIC-TRY AGAIN'
         TO THE-MESSAGE.
      MOVE EIBTIME TO THE-TIME.
      TRANSFORM THE-TIME FROM ',' TO ':'.
      EXEC CICS SEND FROM (MESSAGE-LINE)
         LENGTH (80) ERASE
         END-EXEC.
```

THE SEND COMMAND

The SEND command is used to send a message from working-storage to a terminal. The basic format of the SEND command is

```
EXEC CICS SEND
      FROM (data-area)
      LENGTH (data-value)
      [ERASE]
      [CTLCHAR (data-value)]
      END-EXEC
```

FROM (Data-Area)

This option specifies the name of the COBOL data area in working-storage containing the message. Each field should be set to a known value through the value clause or by using MOVE statements in the program. If not initialized, residual "garbage" in this working-storage area may be interpreted by the 3270 as special 3270 hardware control orders and might affect the final output message sent to the terminal.

LENGTH (Data-Value)

This option specifies the number of characters from the message data area to be transmitted to the terminal. The argument can be a numeric constant or a COBOL field containing the length value. If a COBOL field name is used, it must be defined as PIC S9999 USAGE COMPUTATIONAL.

ERASE

This option specifies that the screen is to be erased before sending the message. All data, including the input message, will be cleared from the screen. If you are sending a message indicating an error with the input transaction, you may wish to omit this option, so the operator can review the input. If ERASE is omitted, the output message will be displayed beginning at the current *cursor* location. If ERASE is used, the cursor is returned to the upper left corner of the screen during an erase option, thus causing the output message to appear on the top line of the screen.

CTLCHAR (Data-Value)

This option specifies that a control character is to be transmitted to the terminal. The control character will cause certain functions to be performed such as sounding the alarm and unlocking the keyboard. If this option is not specified, a default control character is transmitted; the default will cause the keyboard to be restored (FREE) and the alarm will *not* sound. The data-value argument is a one-character literal or a COBOL field that contains a control character to be transmitted to the terminal. The following list contains some of the commonly used control codes.

```
              FUNCTION              CODE
    ALARM       KEYBOARD

    OFF         LOCK              SPACE
    OFF         FREE              B
    ON          LOCK              D
    ON          FREE              F
```

Here is an example of a SEND command to erase the screen, unlock the keyboard, sound the alarm, then send a message to the terminal:

```
EXEC CICS SEND
     FROM (MESSAGE-LINE)
     ERASE
     CTLCHAR ('F')
     LENGTH (80)
     END-EXEC
```

THE SEND TEXT COMMAND

There is another command that provides functions similar to the SEND command. This command is SEND TEXT. The SEND TEXT command has some options that are particularly useful when you need to display *more* than one line of information. The basic format of the SEND TEXT command is

```
EXEC CICS SEND TEXT
     FROM (data-area)
     LENGTH (data-value)
     [ERASE]
     [FREEKB]
     [ALARM]
     [ACCUM]
     END-EXEC
```

The purpose of the ERASE, FROM, and LENGTH options is the same as described above in the SEND command. You will also notice that the CTLCHAR option is not included in this command. Instead, the ALARM and FREEKB options are used to indicate these actions. If not explicitly coded, the default actions are no ALARM and FREEKB. The only other option shown above is ACCUM.

The ACCUM option, when used, indicates that more than one SEND TEXT command is being used to build a display. If only one line is to be displayed, the ACCUM option is not needed.

If more than one line is to be displayed with the SEND TEXT command (with ACCUM), there is something else to consider. This command inserts a special 3270 terminal formatting character just ahead of each output message. To attain proper alignment of multiple display lines, the length of each message should be one character less than the *width* of the terminal. For instance, if you are writing to an 80-column terminal, each message should have a length of 79 characters.

To see how the SEND TEXT command works with multiple lines, let's look at an example. Assume that we would like to display a screen as follows:

```
SYSTEM INQUIRY
TIME:    HH MM SS
TERMINAL:XXXX
```

The programming necessary to accomplish this is shown in figure 3.5. First, we would need to provide data structures in working-storage for the message area and the data to be displayed. Since we are

```
IDENTIFICATION DIVISION.
PROGRAM-ID. TEXT1.
AUTHOR.  BOB LOWE.
ENVIRONMENT DIVISION.
DATA DIVISION.
WORKING-STORAGE SECTION.
01  DISPLAY-TEXT              PIC X(79).
01  MESSAGE-TEXT.
    05  MESSAGE-1.
        10  FILLER            PIC X(14) VALUE
                              'SYSTEM INQUIRY'.
    05  MESSAGE-2.
        10  FILLER            PIC X(09) VALUE 'TIME:'.
        10  THE-TIME          PIC 99B99B99.
    05  MESSAGE-3.
        10  FILLER            PIC X(09) VALUE 'TERMINAL:'.
        10  THE-TERMINAL      PIC XXXX.
    EJECT
LINKAGE SECTION.
PROCEDURE DIVISION.
*PROCEDURE CODE
    MOVE MESSAGE-1 TO DISPLAY-TEXT.
    EXEC CICS SEND TEXT FROM (DISPLAY-TEXT) ERASE
        LENGTH (79) ACCUM
        END-EXEC.
    MOVE EIBTIME TO THE-TIME.
    MOVE MESSAGE-2 TO DISPLAY-TEXT.
    EXEC CICS SEND TEXT FROM (DISPLAY-TEXT)
        LENGTH (79) ACCUM
        END-EXEC.
    MOVE EIBTRMID TO THE-TERMINAL.
    MOVE MESSAGE-3 TO DISPLAY-TEXT.
    EXEC CICS SEND TEXT FROM (DISPLAY-TEXT)
        LENGTH (79) ACCUM
        END-EXEC.
    EXEC CICS SEND PAGE END-EXEC.
    EXEC CICS RETURN END-EXEC.
    GOBACK.
```

FIGURE 3.5. SEND TEXT ACCUM Example

going to be using an 80-column display, a message area (named *DISPLAY-TEXT*) is defined. This area is 79 characters in length. All message lines are displayed from this area. The *message-staging* areas are defined next. The technique used to display the lines is accomplished in two steps. First, the program will move the variables to be displayed into the staging areas. Then each staging area will be moved into the message area. The SEND TEXT command with the ACCUM option is used to display each message line. The accumulated lines are then sent to the terminal with the SEND PAGE command (described next). Finally the program is terminated with the RETURN command.

THE SEND PAGE COMMAND

The SEND PAGE command is used to send *accumulated* lines of text to the terminal. This command is necessary only when you have specified the ACCUM option of the SEND TEXT. If you forget to use the SEND PAGE after an accumulated SEND TEXT command, the message will never get transmitted to the screen. Of course, if the ACCUM option was not used in the SEND TEXT command, this last command is not necessary.

The basic format of the SEND PAGE command is

```
EXEC CICS SEND PAGE END-EXEC
```

Chapter Summary

In this chapter you have learned the commands necessary to write an elementary CICS/VS program. Most commands can cause exceptional conditions to arise in the event of some CICS or application program problem. To prevent abnormal termination of the task you may execute an IGNORE CONDITION or HANDLE CONDITION command prior to executing the command that might give rise to the exceptional condition. The basic commands and procedures necessary to communicate with an IBM 3270 terminal were also presented. After studying this material, you should be able to construct data areas within your program to receive transaction input and to send simple messages to the operator. The exercises and lab assignments that follow will allow you to write programs that communicate with an IBM 3270 terminal.

Discussion Questions

1. When an exceptional condition occurs, CICS goes through an exceptional condition analysis. If the exception has not been dealt with in some way, CICS takes the default action. What is the default action for most commands?
2. If a task is abended due to the condition LENGERR, which abend code will be displayed on the terminal?
3. Why is it necessary to code a HANDLE or IGNORE CONDITION command prior to issuing a command that might give rise to an exception?
4. How many conditions can be ignored in a single IGNORE CONDITION command?
5. Exceptional conditions occur during many CICS service commands. Some service commands can give rise to the same exceptional condition. If the HANDLE CONDITION command is being used to deal with command exceptions, what action should be taken (1) if a different exception routine is to be used for each service command? (2) if the same exception routine is to handle all occurrences of the exception?
6. How might the use of HANDLE CONDITION commands affect the ability to write structured programs?
7. A program can enter into a looping condition if an exception routine contains a command that gives rise to an exception that again causes the routine to be entered. How can this situation be avoided?
8. What would be the effect of coding an IGNORE CONDITION command for the condition ERROR?
9. When data entry operations are done at the IBM 3270 keyboard, the characters are stored in the 3270 buffer and are displayed on the screen. What action causes the characters to be transferred to CICS?
10. How can you determine which IBM 3270 attention key was used to transmit an input message?
11. The Terminal Control Program stores each input from the terminal into a terminal input-output area (TIOA). Which command is used to cause the TIOA data to be copied into working-storage?
12. How can you limit the amount of incoming data from the TIOA?
13. How can you determine the actual length of the data keyed by the operator?
14. If the operator keyed fewer characters than the size of your working-storage input area, what happens to the remaining positions?
15. Why is it important for a program to send a message back to the terminal before terminating?
16. What would be the result of sending a message to the terminal when the message area has unknown values (garbage)?

17. The SEND command can be used to write messages to the operator. Which option is used to ensure that the screen is cleared as part of the SEND?
18. The SEND TEXT command can be used to display one or more display lines on a terminal. Which option should be used when multiple lines are being sent?
19. Which command is used to transmit accumulated messages to the terminal?

Review Exercises

1. Code a command necessary for the program to ignore conditions LENGERR and DUPKEY.
2. Code a command so that CICS will subsequently transfer control to routines as follows:

   length error   `500-LENGTH-PROBLEM`
   not open   `600-NOT-OPEN`
   not found   `700-NOT-ON-FILE`

3. Code a command to reset the condition LENGERR back to the CICS default action.
4. Code statements necessary to ignore condition LENGERR and to handle condition ERROR to activate routine 800-GENERAL-ERROR.
5. Define an input area necessary to accommodate the following message:

   `V001 999999 XXXXXXXXXXXXXXXXXXXXXXXXXXXXXX`

6. Code statements necessary to receive the transaction message in Exercise 5 above into your input area.
7. Code the field definition for the field MESSAGE-LENGTH used in the command below.

```
MOVE +20 TO MESSAGE-LENGTH.
EXEC CICS RECEIVE INTO (MESSAGE-AREA)
    LENGTH (MESSAGE-LENGTH) END-EXEC.
```

8. Code a SEND command to erase the screen, then send the following message to the operator.

```
05  MESSAGE-1  PIC X(35) VALUE
              'THE MASTER FILE IS CLOSED'.
```

Lab Problems

LAB 1

Write a program to receive a transaction message in the format below. The first four characters represent a CICS transaction code. The numeric field represents an employee number. Compile and test this program using a program name and transaction code assigned by your instructor.

```
TRAN 999999999
```

If the operator keys in more characters than required, send the message, "INPUT TOO LONG-TRY AGAIN." Don't erase the screen when you send this message. After sending the message, terminate the program.

If the employee number entered by the operator is not numeric, send the message, "INVALID EMPLOYEE NUMBER-TRY AGAIN." Don't erase the screen when you send this message. After sending the message, terminate the program.

If the input message is correct, send the message below. Clear the screen when this message is sent.

```
"FROM (your name) THE MESSAGE IS CORRECT--KEY WAS 999999999"
```

LAB 2

Write a program to display the fields from the Execute Interface Block as shown below. Use the SEND TEXT and SEND PAGE commands to display this information. Compile and test this program using a program name and transaction code assigned by your instructor. Use the assigned transaction code to start the program. Try the transaction code with a variety of 3270 attention keys (ENTER, PF1, etc.) to test this program. Test the program a few more times with the cursor in different screen positions.

```
EXECUTE INTERFACE BLOCK DISPLAY BY:(your name)
EIBAID   X
EIBTRNID XXXX
EIBTRMID XXXX
EIBTIME  999999
EIBDATE  999999
EIBCALEN 9999
EIBCPOSN 9999
```

4

CICS/VS Transaction Design

By the time you have finished studying the material in this chapter you will

1. Understand how the file control program supports multitasking within the CICS/VS region.
2. Learn that files can be dynamically opened and closed by a master terminal transaction.
3. Be able to use file control commands to randomly access records in a file.
4. Identify the exceptional conditions that can occur during random file operations.
5. Recognize that the direct transaction initiation method of design is commonly used with CICS applications.
6. Understand how to design noninteractive transactions.
7. Realize that noninteractive transaction design can become difficult for operators to use.
8. Learn how to design interactive transactions to improve the usability of a program.
9. Identify one problem that can result from designing programs using the conversational programming technique.
10. See how the pseudoconversational programming technique can help to utilize CICS dynamic storage more effectively.
11. Learn how to use the pseudoconversational RETURN command.
12. Observe that several methods can be developed to implement the pseudoconversational programming technique.
13. Learn that one or more transaction codes can be assigned to the same application program.

In this chapter you will learn different techniques used in the design of CICS transactions. In the first section, you will be introduced to the primary file control commands. Most transactions involve the use of one or more file control commands. By studying this important topic now, you will have more opportunities to use these commands throughout the text. After the file control topic, the chapter will introduce you to some of the ways to design CICS transactions. First, you will learn how to design simple noninteractive transactions. Then you will see how to develop transactions that interact with the operator to obtain transaction parameters. Finally, you will learn how to design programs using the pseudoconversational programming technique. This technique is the most generally accepted method of writing programs that interact with the operator. It is the "state of the art" in CICS programming.

File Control Introduction

The File Control Program is responsible for providing file access support for all application programs running under CICS/VS. Application programs do not contain native COBOL input-output statements. These statements produce object code that contain *operating system wait* instructions. When an operating system wait occurs, the entire region is suspended by the operating system for the duration of the wait. If programs running under CICS/VS were allowed to execute native I/O statements, CICS/VS would not be able to provide multitasking support. The File Control Program provides all of the services that can be performed with native COBOL input-output statements. This centralized program is, however, designed with multitasking in mind.

Each time an application requests an input-output service, file control performs the appropriate routine to initiate the I/O operation. The standard operating system access methods (ISAM, VSAM, and DAM) are used by the File Control Program. After the access method has begun the I/O function, processor control is returned to the File Control Program. File control then issues a *CICS/VS wait* to suspend the operation of the task. When the CICS wait occurs, the Task Control Program may dispatch other waiting tasks. Later, after the operating system access method completes the I/O operation and another task has issued a CICS command, the task that requested the input-output service is again given control of the CPU.

OPENING AND CLOSING FILES

File management programs are used to open and close CICS/VS files. Files may be opened at the start of the day when CICS is initialized. Unlike batch programs, CICS application programs do not open and close files during each execution. If an application program attempts to access a file that is closed, the File Control Program returns an error indication. For command-level programs, the Execute Interface Program detects this error indication and raises an exceptional condition, NOTOPEN in the application program. The NOTOPEN condition can be handled by the application program; or the default action, which is to abend the task, will be taken by EIP.

Files may also be dynamically opened and closed at certain times of the day. To do this, CICS provides a master terminal transaction that requests these file services. This capability for a master terminal operator to dynamically close a file provides centralized control of the applications using the data set. After a file has been dynamically closed, programs that attempt to access the records will receive the NOTOPEN condition.

FILE CONTROL SERVICES

The File Control Program can provide the following random access services to the application program:

1. random record retrieval
2. random record update
3. random record addition
4. random record deletion (VSAM only)

All of these services are provided in a manner similar to the native COBOL input-output statements. That is, file control takes care of any blocking and deblocking needed. Application programs can access records at the logical record level. Command-level programs can request that a record be read into, or written from, the working-storage section. Both fixed- and variable-length records can be processed by file control.

In keeping with the theme of centralized control, the File Control Program will limit its services for each file to those functions authorized for the application. Some files may be restricted to read-only operations. Other files may have any or all of the services active. The File Control Table, tailored by the Systems Programmer indicates the authorized services for each file when it is opened. A file can be on-line yet protected against update by all programs using the system. If a program issues a command that requests an unsupported service for that file, the File Control Program will return an error indication. For command-level programs, the Execute Interface Program will raise the INVREQ exceptional condition.

CICS provides the capability to modify dynamically the authorized services for a file. This function is provided by a master terminal transaction in a similar fashion to the open-close services. In this way a file can be open for update during certain times of the day and open for read-only operations during other times.

FILE IDENTIFICATION

Each file to be accessed by the File Control Program must be defined in the File Control Table. The File Control Table entry for the data set contains information about the file type (VSAM, ISAM, DAM), blocking factor, and record type. As previously indicated, the FCT also contains information concerning the available services and file status (open or closed). Once a file has been defined to CICS, the application program needing services for the file will issue a file control command in the Procedure Division. Each file control command has a DATASET option indicating the needed file. For example,

```
EXEC CICS READ
          DATASET ('VENFILE')
          .
          .
          .
END-EXEC
```

RECORD IDENTIFICATION

Records in files are identified in a number of ways, depending on the access method used. For Direct Access Method (DAM), records are identified by a block reference, a physical key, and a deblocking argument. For ISAM files, the record identification is the record key. Records in a VSAM file are identified by key, by relative byte address or by relative record number. This book concentrates on the VSAM access method using the record key only. Actually, since the File Control Program uses the Standard Operating System Access Methods and since information concerning the files is stored in the File Control Table, the commands appearing within an application program are generally very similar. In fact, if an ISAM file is converted to VSAM, programs accessing the file by record key can usually be used with no modification. You may not even need to recompile the program.

The RIDFLD option is used in file control commands to access a file using the record key. For example,

```
EXEC CICS READ
          DATASET ('VENFILE')
          RIDFLD (VENDOR-ID)
END-EXEC.
```

File Control Commands

The following commands are provided by the file control program to randomly process records in CICS files:

```
READ
REWRITE
UNLOCK
DELETE
WRITE
```

THE READ COMMAND

The file control READ command is used to randomly read a record from a file. The command identifies the name of the data set to be accessed, the working-storage area into which the record is to be read, and the working-storage area containing the record identification of the record to be read. The basic format of the command is

```
EXEC CICS READ
      DATASET (name)
      RIDFLD (data-area)
      [INTO (data-area)]
      [LENGTH (data-area)]
      [GTEQ | EQUAL]
      [UPDATE]
      END-EXEC
```

The **DATASET** argument contains the name of the file to be accessed. This name must have been defined in the File Control Table. If a COBOL field is used as a name argument, it must be 8 characters in length.

The **RIDFLD** argument contains the name of a field that contains the key of the record to be read.

The **INTO** argument contains the name of the working-storage area where the record is to be read.

The LENGTH argument is an S9999 COMPUTATIONAL field indicating the length of the record to be read. The LENGTH option is not required for fixed length records. If it is used for fixed length records, it must contain the *actual* length defined for the file. For variable length records, the LENGTH argument contains the *maximum* length of the data record.

If the **EQUAL** option is specified or implied (it is the default), file control will attempt to read only the requested record. If that record is not on file the exceptional condition NOTFND will occur.

If the **GTEQ** option is specified and the read is unsuccessful, the first record having a greater key will be read. The exceptional condition NOTFND will only occur if there are no records having a greater key.

The **UPDATE** option is only used when the record is being read for update purposes. This option causes the task to gain exclusive control of the record so that no other task can update the record.

When a record has been read for update, CICS maintains *exclusive control* to prevent another task from updating the record. The method of providing exclusive control depends on the access method for the file. With ISAM files, only the one record is locked. With VSAM files, the entire VSAM control interval containing the record is held. Because of this, it is important that you update the record as soon as possible after issuing the READ UPDATE command. Exclusive control is maintained until the record has been updated or deleted or the program has issued the UNLOCK command. Exclusive control will also be released when the task terminates, even if you haven't updated or unlocked the file.

Let's look at an example of the READ command. The command below would read a record from a VSAM file named VENFILE. The key of the record to be retrieved is 000001 and the record will be moved into the data area in working-storage named VENDOR-RECORD. Exclusive control is *not* being requested.

```
MOVE '000001' TO VENDOR-ID.
MOVE +249 TO VENDOR-RECORD-LENGTH.
EXEC CICS READ
     DATASET ('VENFILE')
     RIDFLD (VENDOR-ID)
     INTO (VENDOR-RECORD)
     LENGTH (VENDOR-RECORD-LENGTH)
     END-EXEC.
```

where VENDOR-RECORD is defined as

```
01   VENDOR-RECORD.
     05    VENDOR-NAME              PIC X(30).
     05    VENDOR-ID               PIC XXXXXX.
     05    VENDOR-ADDR1            PIC X(30).
     05    VENDOR-ADDR2            PIC X(30).
     05    VENDOR-ADDR3            PIC X(30).
     05    VENDOR-ADDR4            PIC X(30).
     05    VENDOR-CONTACT          PIC X(30).
     05    VENDOR-TELE             PIC X(12).
     05    VENDOR-TAXID            PIC X(11).
     05    VENDOR-YTD-SALES        PIC S9(7)V99 COMP-3.
     05    VENDOR-YTD-PAYMENTS     PIC S9(7)V99 COMP-3.
     05    VENDOR-YTD-DISCOUNTS    PIC S9(7)V99 COMP-3.
     05    VENDOR-PAY-HOLD         PIC X.
     05    VENDOR-PRODUCT          PIC XXX.
     05    VENDOR-LAST-CHECK       PIC S9(5) COMP-3.
     05    VENDOR-LAST-CK-DATE     PIC S9(5) COMP-3.
     05    VENDOR-LAST-CK-AMT      PIC S9(7)V99 COMP-3.
     05    VENDOR-DATEA            PIC S9(5) COMP-3.
     05    VENDOR-DATEC            PIC S9(5) COMP-3.
     05    VENDOR-OPE              PIC XXX.
     05    VENDOR-UPDCNT           PIC 9.
```

THE REWRITE COMMAND

The REWRITE command is used to randomly update a record in a file. The format of the command is

```
EXEC CICS REWRITE
        DATASET (name)
        FROM (data-area)
        [LENGTH (data-value)]
        END-EXEC
```

The FROM option contains an argument specifying the area containing the record to be updated.

The LENGTH argument is an S9999 COMPUTATIONAL field or numeric constant indicating the length of the record being updated. This option is not required for fixed-length records. If it is used for fixed-length records, it must contain the actual length defined for the file.

You will notice that there is no RIDFLD option with this command. The record being updated for this file will be the record previously read with the READ UPDATE command.

The file READ command with the UPDATE option must be executed prior to issuing the RE-WRITE command. In response to the READ command, file control will randomly read the specified record, then EIP will move it to the record area in working-storage. The UPDATE option of the READ command specifies that it is the *intent* of the application program to rewrite the record during this same task. For each task, only one READ UPDATE command for the *same* file can be outstanding at one time. The use of the update option will cause CICS to give the task exclusive control of the update rights to the record. This means that no other task will be able to update the record until the task has released exclusive control or has ended.

Here is an example of the REWRITE command. The example will use the vendor master record described in the previous example. First the record will be read with the UPDATE option. Then the fields in the record area are updated. Finally the record is updated with the REWRITE command.

```
MOVE KEY-INPUT TO VENDOR-ID.
MOVE +249 TO VENDOR-RECORD-LENGTH.
EXEC CICS READ UPDATE
     DATASET ('VENFILE')
     RIDFLD (VENDOR-ID)
     INTO (VENDOR-RECORD)
     LENGTH (VENDOR-RECORD-LENGTH)
     END-EXEC.
MOVE NEW-VENDOR-NAME TO VENDOR-NAME.
MOVE NEW-CONTACT-NAME TO VENDOR-CONTACT.
     .
     .
     .
EXEC CICS REWRITE
     DATASET ('VENFILE')
     FROM (VENDOR-RECORD)
     LENGTH (VENDOR-RECORD-LENGTH)
     END-EXEC
```

THE UNLOCK COMMAND

The UNLOCK command is used to release exclusive control of a record. This command is necessary only when the program needs to abandon one update operation in order to perform another update operation. For instance, let's assume that your program has issued a READ UPDATE command for a record. After doing this, if a different record needs to be updated instead or a record needs to be added, an UNLOCK must be issued. If you don't unlock a data set before issuing a second READ UPDATE command, for the same file, the INVREQ condition will occur. It will also occur if a READ UPDATE command has been issued, then a WRITE command is attempted for this file. The format of the UNLOCK command is

```
EXEC CICS UNLOCK DATASET (name) END-EXEC
```

THE DELETE COMMAND

The DELETE Command is used to remove a record from a VSAM file. CICS allows records to be deleted in two ways:

1. following a READ UPDATE command
2. direct delete

A record may be deleted following a READ UPDATE command. The procedure is very similar to the process of updating a record; that is, first the record is read with a READ UPDATE command, then it is deleted. The format of the DELETE command when this procedure is used is

```
EXEC CICS DELETE DATASET (name) END-EXEC
```

When this procedure is used, the record just read in the READ UPDATE command will be deleted. You only have to supply the file name in the DATASET option.

As an alternative, you can directly delete a record from a file. With this method, there is no READ UPDATE; the record is simply deleted. The format of the direct delete command is:

```
EXEC CICS DELETE
     DATASET (name)
     RIDFLD (data-area)
     END-EXEC
```

where the RIDFLD option contains the key of the record to be deleted. If the record is on file, it will be deleted. If the record does not currently exist, CICS will raise the NOTFND exceptional condition. Here's an example: Assume that you have designed a transaction to allow an operator to delete a record. The operator will enter the transaction message below. The coding would be sufficient to delete the record directly.

```
V004 NNNNNN


    05  MSG-LEN     PIC S9999 COMP VALUE +11.
01 MESSAGE-IN.
    05  TRAN-CODE   PIC XXXX.
    05  FILLER      PIC X.
    05  KEY-INPUT   PIC XXXXX.
      . . .
    EXEC CICS RECEIVE INTO (MESSAGE-IN)
    LENGTH (MSG-LENGTH)
    END-EXEC.
    EXEC CICS DELETE DATASET ('VENFILE')
        RIDFLD (KEY-INPUT)
        END-EXEC
```

THE WRITE COMMAND

The WRITE Command is used to add new records to a file. The format of the WRITE command is

```
EXEC CICS WRITE
        DATASET (name)
        RIDFLD (data-area)
        FROM (data-area)
        [LENGTH (data-value)]
        END-EXEC
```

The RIDFLD option contains the full key of the record to be added. The data area may be a field imbedded in the record area, or it may be a field somewhere else in working-storage. In either case, the imbedded key field in the record area must contain the same value as the RIDFLD used in the command.

The FROM option specifies the name of the record area to be written to the file.

The LENGTH option contains the length of the record to be added. If used for fixed length files, the argument must equal the length defined for the file.

Let's look at an example of the WRITE command. Assume that you would like to add a record to our vendor master file. The record key and vendor name will be supplied by the operator in a transaction message. All other fields in the record will be initialized to spaces or zeros. Here's a routine to do this:

```
RECEIVE command to get input
MOVE SPACES TO VENDOR-RECORD.
MOVE ZEROS TO VENDOR-YTD-SALES
              VENDOR-YTD-PAYMENTS
  .
  .
MOVE NAME-INPUT TO VENDOR-NAME.
MOVE KEY-INPUT TO VENDOR-ID.
EXEC CICS WRITE
          DATASET ('VENFILE')
          RIDFLD (VENDOR-ID)
          FROM (VENDOR-RECORD)
          LENGTH (249)
          END-EXEC
```

EXCEPTIONAL CONDITIONS

The exceptional conditions below can occur during file control commands.

DSIDERR occurs if the file name specified in the DATASET option is not in the File Control Table.

DUPREC occurs if an attempt is made to add a record with a record key that already exists on a data set.

ILLOGIC occurs if a READ command for a VSAM file does not fall into one of the other categories. If this exception occurs, the VSAM Return Code and VSAM Error Code are stored in the field EIBRCODE.

INVREQ occurs in a number of situations:

1. If the requested service is invalid for the file. The valid services are specified in the FCT during the tailoring process. They can also be changed by using a CICS master terminal transaction.
2. If a REWRITE or DELETE (without RIDFLD) command is issued but no READ UPDATE command was issued for the file.
3. If there is an outstanding READ UPDATE command for this file and the program issues a direct delete or WRITE command or another READ UPDATE command.

IOERR is similar to the VSAM ILLOGIC condition. It is valid for non-VSAM file types. The field EIBRCODE contains the DAM or ISAM response information.

LENGERR occurs in a number of situations:

1. With variable-length record files, it will occur if the LENGTH option has not been included in the command.
2. For fixed-length files, LENGERR will occur if the value in the LENGTH argument is not the record length specified for the file.
3. During READ operations with variable-length records, LENGERR will occur if the record length exceeds the value stored in the LENGTH argument. In this case the record is truncated, and the length argument is updated with the actual length of the record just read.

NOSPACE occurs if no space is available for adding or updating records.

NOTAUTH occurs if the operator is not authorized to access the file.

NOTFND occurs if the record is not on file.

NOTOPEN occurs if the named data set is closed.

On-Line Transactions

In the last chapter, you learned that an operator can initiate a transaction by transmitting a valid transaction code to CICS/VS. From the terminal operator's viewpoint, entering this transaction code is a means to an end. It is a way to perform a function that is somehow related to his or her job duties. The duties of a clerical worker in the purchasing department, for instance, may require a number of transactions associated with a vendor master file. For example, there may be circumstances when that worker needs to inquire about the status of a particular vendor. An on-line inquiry transaction that provides a display of a single master record would probably be useful to this operator. This same clerical worker may be assigned the duties of updating information about the various vendors for the company. This updating process could include vendor name, address, contact person, and other vendor-related information. On-line transactions provided to perform these functions would likewise be useful to this clerical worker. Another person in the purchasing department may have responsibilities relating to the actual purchasing process. Duties of this person could include the preparation and management of purchase order records. Another set of on-line transactions would prove to be useful to this operator. One transaction, for example, might provide the capability to enter purchase order details. Another transaction might be to print the purchase order document on a CICS printer terminal. Other transactions useful to this worker could include a display of all purchase orders for a vendor, and a display of the status of a particular purchase order. We generally define an on-line application as a set of related transactions available to one or more terminal operators using the system. These applications support an enterprise in conducting its business or performing its mission.

Application Design Methods

There are primarily two methods used when designing on-line applications. These methods deal with the ways in which transactions are initiated. The two methods are

menu transaction selection

direct transaction initiation

One approach is to develop an application menu screen that provides a list of the available transactions within the application. An example of an application menu is depicted in figure 4.1. From the menu, the operator selects the specific transaction and, when necessary, enters any data required to perform the transaction. In this design, one or more menu processing programs are used to interact with the operator and initiate the various transactions. Each transaction processing program is designed to return to the menu after the requested function is completed. In this way the operator can select another transaction without having to start another session.

The other approach used in designing applications is the direct transaction initiation method. This approach requires the operator to enter a transaction code each time a processing function is needed. As a result of entering this transaction code, a transaction processing program will be run to provide the requested function. After each transaction is complete, control will be returned to CICS with the program control RETURN command. The operator will then clear the screen, if necessary, then initiate another transaction by entering a new transaction code.

```
                1         2         3         4         5         6         7         8
       1234567890123456789012345678901234567890123456789012345678901234567890123456789012345678901234567890
 1  ▯VEN0000                                                              ▯DATE▯XX/XX/XX
 2                    ▯VENDOR MASTER MENU                                  ▯TIME▯XX:XX:XX
 3                                                                        ▯TERMINAL▯XXXX
 4
 5              ▯PF1  DISPLAY MASTER RECORD
 6
 7              ▯PF2  UPDATE MASTER RECORD
 8
 9              ▯PF3  ADD MASTER RECORD
10
11              ▯PF4  DELETE MASTER RECORD
12
13              ▯PF5  BROWSE MASTER BY KEY
14
15              ▯PF9  EXIT MASTER MENU
16
17
18  ▯TYPE VENDOR NUMBER▯NNNNNNN▯THEN PRESS APPROPRIATE PF KEY
19
20
21  ▯_____
22
23
24
```

FIGURE 4.1.   Sample Menu Screen

This last design approach was widely used when CICS was first released. This was primarily due to the hardware technologies available at that time. The first on-line terminals had very limited input-output capabilities. Screens were small in size, and provided only limited displays. All input operations were limited to the *top line* of the display only. With just that one line available for operator input, direct transaction initiation was simply the best possible alternative.

Hardware technologies have evolved over the years and have eliminated most of the input-output constraints that faced the early transaction designers. Screen sizes are larger, and input is no longer limited to the first display line. Nevertheless the direct transaction initiation method is still a popular technique for running CICS transactions. In fact most IBM-supplied transactions employ this method of transaction initiation. The popularity of this technique could stem from the fact that it is difficult to break old habits. Or it could simply be due to the ease of program design. It is just much easier to design programs when using this technique.

Ease of program design is the very reason that this technique is used in this chapter. With your limited knowledge of CICS at this point, you should find it easier to understand these techniques. All of the examples and your own programming assignments will use the basic terminal commands that you learned about in chapter 3. Later, in chapter 7, we will study the basic menu program logic.

Direct Transaction Categories

There are two programming methodologies used in the design of direct transactions. These methods deal with the way in which the application program obtains transaction parameters (data) from the operator. For the sake of discussion, let's call these methods (1) noninteractive and (2) interactive. With the noninteractive method, the operator is required to enter all transaction parameters along with the transaction code. With the interactive method, the program establishes and maintains a *conversation* with the operator to obtain any needed transaction parameters. From the programming standpoint, the easiest of these is noninteractive.

NONINTERACTIVE TRANSACTIONS

The noninteractive transaction design technique is by far the easiest to program. In effect this technique shifts the burden from the programmer to the terminal operator. As indicated above, this technique requires the operator to enter all transaction parameters along with the transaction code. This input known as the initial transaction message may be simple or complex, depending on the transaction requirements. Either way the operator is responsible for entering the message in the proper format. Let's look at a couple of examples of noninteractive transactions.

For our first example, assume that we would like to design a program to display a single record from a vendor master file. This simple inquiry program will need, as a minimum, a record key to be supplied in the transaction message. Let's assume that the transaction code will be "V001." The transaction message for such a transaction might appear as follows:

```
-->|V001   NNNNNN
```

To initiate this transaction, the operator would simply type in the transaction code and a record key, then press ENTER. The program for this transaction is shown in figure 4.2. First, in the working-storage section, the program copies the record layout into the program. (This is the same record layout that we used in the file control topics.) The program next defines storage areas for the input transaction message, and an output message area. A couple of length fields are defined for the file and terminal commands. Finally, several staging lines are defined to display the information from the master record. Now, let's move to the Procedure Division. First, the program receives the transaction input message into working-storage to obtain the record key for the master record. The record key is then used to randomly read the master record. Then a series of SEND TEXT commands and the SEND PAGE command is used to display data from the master record. Finally the program issues a RETURN command to return control to CICS. The transaction is now complete. To display another record, the operator will erase the screen, then enter another transaction message.

In our second example we are going to design a transaction to update the company name in a vendor master record. In "real life" an update program would usually update multiple fields in the master record. We'll see how to do that in chapter 8. For now let's just update this one field. With a noninteractive transaction message, we need to design a transaction message for the operator to enter all required data parameters. It might look like this:

```
-->|V002 NNNNNN   XXXXXXXXXXXXXXXXXXXXXXXXXXXXXX
```

To initiate this transaction, the operator would type in the transaction code a record key and a new company name, then press ENTER. The programming logic for this transaction is shown in figure 4.3. For purposes of brevity, those working-storage areas and Procedure Division routines that are identical to those in our last example have been omitted.

In the working-storage section, the program would define storage for the input message and other fields, similarly to the previous example. In the Procedure Division, the program would receive the input message into working-storage to obtain the record key and company name. The record key would be used to randomly read the master record with update intent. The new company name would be moved into the master record. Then the REWRITE command would be used to update the record. A message confirming the update would be transmitted to the terminal with the SEND command. Finally the program would return control to CICS with the program control RETURN command. The transaction is now complete. To update another record, the operator would erase the screen, then enter another transaction message.

```
                IDENTIFICATION DIVISION.
                PROGRAM-ID. VEND001.
                AUTHOR.   BOB LOWE.
                ENVIRONMENT DIVISION.
                DATA DIVISION.
                WORKING-STORAGE SECTION.
                COPY VENDREC.
                01  MESSAGE-IN.
                    05  TRAN-CODE               PIC XXXX.
                    05  FILLER                  PIC X.
                    05  KEY-INPUT               PIC XXXXX.
                01  MISC-AREAS.
                    05  MSG-LEN                 PIC S9999 COMP.
                    05  VENDOR-RECORD-LENGTH    PIC S9999 COMP VALUE +249.
                01  MESSAGE-LINE.
                    05  SEND-TRANSID            PIC XXXX.
                    05  FILLER                  PIC X.
                    05  SEND-KEY                PIC XXXXX.
                    05  FILLER                  PIC X.
                    05  THE-MESSAGE             PIC X(54).
                    05  FILLER                  PIC X.
                    05  THE-TIME                PIC ZZ9,99,99.
                    05  FILLER                  PIC XXXX.
                01  DISPLAY-TEXT                PIC X(79).
                01  LINES-OF-DATA.
                    05  LINE-1.
                        10  FILLER              PIC X(29) VALUE SPACES.
                        10  FILLER              PIC X(22)
                                                VALUE 'VENDOR MASTER INQUIRY '.
                    05  LINE-3.
                        10  FILLER              PIC X(13) VALUE ' RECORD KEY: '.
                        10  KEY-OUT             PIC X(06) VALUE SPACES.
                    05  LINE-4.
                        10  FILLER              PIC X(13) VALUE 'VENDOR NAME: '.
                        10  NAME-OUT            PIC X(30) VALUE SPACES.
                    05  LINE-5.
                        10  FILLER              PIC X(13) VALUE '    ADDRESS: '.
                        10  ADDRESS1-OUT        PIC X(30) VALUE SPACES.
                    05  LINE-6.
                        10  FILLER              PIC X(13) VALUE SPACES.
                        10  ADDRESS2-OUT        PIC X(30) VALUE SPACES.
                    05  LINE-7.
                        10  FILLER              PIC X(13) VALUE SPACES.
                        10  ADDRESS3-OUT        PIC X(30) VALUE SPACES.
                    05  LINE-8.
                        10  FILLER              PIC X(13) VALUE SPACES.
                        10  ADDRESS4-OUT        PIC X(30) VALUE SPACES.
                    05  LINE-10.
                        10  FILLER              PIC X(13) VALUE '    CONTACT: '.
                        10  CONTACT-OUT         PIC X(30) VALUE SPACES.
                        10  FILLER              PIC X     VALUE SPACES.
                        10  TELEPHONE-OUT       PIC X(12) VALUE SPACES.
                    EJECT
                LINKAGE SECTION.
                PROCEDURE DIVISION.
               *PROCEDURE CODE
                000-MAINLINE-ROUTINE.
                    MOVE SPACES TO MESSAGE-LINE, MESSAGE-IN.
                    EXEC CICS IGNORE CONDITION LENGERR END-EXEC.
                    MOVE +11 TO MSG-LEN.
                    EXEC CICS RECEIVE
                        INTO (MESSAGE-IN)
                        LENGTH (MSG-LEN)
                        END-EXEC.
                    IF MSG-LEN LESS THAN +11
                        MOVE 'NEED A RECORD KEY' TO THE-MESSAGE
                        GO TO 990-SEND-ERROR-AND-EXIT.
                    IF KEY-INPUT NOT NUMERIC
                        MOVE 'VENDOR NUMBER NOT NUMERIC' TO THE-MESSAGE
                        MOVE KEY-INPUT TO SEND-KEY
                        GO TO 990-SEND-ERROR-AND-EXIT.
```

FIGURE 4.2.　Non-interactive Inquiry Program

```
        EXEC CICS HANDLE CONDITION
            NOTOPEN  (950-NOTOPEN)
            NOTFND   (960-NOTFND)
            LENGERR  (970-LENGERR)
            ERROR    (980-ERROR)
            END-EXEC.
        EXEC CICS READ
            DATASET ('VENFILE')
            INTO    (VENDOR-RECORD)
            RIDFLD  (KEY-INPUT)
            LENGTH  (VENDOR-RECORD-LENGTH)
            END-EXEC.
        EJECT
        MOVE VENDOR-NAME    TO  NAME-OUT.
        MOVE VENDOR-ID      TO  KEY-OUT.
        MOVE VENDOR-ADDR1   TO  ADDRESS1-OUT.
        MOVE VENDOR-ADDR2   TO  ADDRESS2-OUT.
        MOVE VENDOR-ADDR3   TO  ADDRESS3-OUT.
        MOVE VENDOR-ADDR4   TO  ADDRESS4-OUT.
        MOVE VENDOR-CONTACT TO  CONTACT-OUT.
        MOVE VENDOR-TELE    TO  TELEPHONE-OUT.
        MOVE LINE-1 TO DISPLAY-TEXT.
        EXEC CICS SEND TEXT FROM (DISPLAY-TEXT) ACCUM ERASE
            LENGTH (79)
            END-EXEC.
        MOVE SPACES TO DISPLAY-TEXT.
        EXEC CICS SEND TEXT FROM (DISPLAY-TEXT) ACCUM
            LENGTH (79)
            END-EXEC.
    MOVE LINE-3 TO DISPLAY-TEXT.
        EXEC CICS SEND TEXT FROM (DISPLAY-TEXT) ACCUM
            LENGTH (79)
            END-EXEC.
        MOVE LINE-4 TO DISPLAY-TEXT.
        EXEC CICS SEND TEXT FROM (DISPLAY-TEXT) ACCUM
            LENGTH (79)
            END-EXEC.
        MOVE LINE-5 TO DISPLAY-TEXT.
        EXEC CICS SEND TEXT FROM (DISPLAY-TEXT) ACCUM
            LENGTH (79)
            END-EXEC.
        MOVE LINE-6 TO DISPLAY-TEXT.
        EXEC CICS SEND TEXT FROM (DISPLAY-TEXT) ACCUM
            LENGTH (79)
            END-EXEC.
        MOVE LINE-7 TO DISPLAY-TEXT.
        EXEC CICS SEND TEXT FROM (DISPLAY-TEXT) ACCUM
            LENGTH (79)
            END-EXEC.
        MOVE LINE-8 TO DISPLAY-TEXT.
        EXEC CICS SEND TEXT FROM (DISPLAY-TEXT) ACCUM
            LENGTH (79)
            END-EXEC.
        MOVE SPACES TO DISPLAY-TEXT.
        EXEC CICS SEND TEXT FROM (DISPLAY-TEXT) ACCUM
            LENGTH (79)
            END-EXEC.
        MOVE LINE-10 TO DISPLAY-TEXT.
        EXEC CICS SEND TEXT FROM (DISPLAY-TEXT) ACCUM
            LENGTH (79)
            END-EXEC.
        EXEC CICS SEND PAGE END-EXEC.
        EXEC CICS RETURN END-EXEC.
*  *  *  *  *  *  *  *  *  *  *  *  *  *  *  *  *  *  *  *  *  *  *  *  *  *  *  *
*  *  *  *  *  *  *  *  *  *  *  *  *  *  *  *  *  *  *  *  *  *  *  *  *
*     ERROR PROCESSING ROUTINES
*  *  *  *  *  *  *  *  *  *  *  *  *  *  *  *  *  *  *  *  *  *  *  *  *
 950-NOTOPEN.
        MOVE 'VENDOR FILE NOT OPEN' TO THE-MESSAGE
        GO TO 990-SEND-ERROR-AND-EXIT.
 960-NOTFND.
        MOVE 'RECORD NOT ON FILE' TO THE-MESSAGE
        MOVE KEY-INPUT TO SEND-KEY.
        GO TO 990-SEND-ERROR-AND-EXIT.
```

FIGURE 4.2.   Continued

```
970-LENGERR.
    MOVE 'FILE LENGTH ERROR' TO THE-MESSAGE
    MOVE KEY-INPUT TO SEND-KEY.
    GO TO 990-SEND-ERROR-AND-EXIT.
980-ERROR.
    MOVE 'AN UNDETERMINED ERROR HAS OCCURRED ' TO THE-MESSAGE
    MOVE KEY-INPUT TO SEND-KEY.
    GO TO 990-SEND-ERROR-AND-EXIT.
990-SEND-ERROR-AND-EXIT.
    MOVE EIBTRNID TO SEND-TRANSID.
    MOVE  EIBTIME  TO THE-TIME.
    TRANSFORM THE-TIME FROM ',' TO ':'.
    EXEC CICS SEND
        FROM (MESSAGE-LINE)
        LENGTH (80)
        ERASE
        END-EXEC.
    EXEC CICS  RETURN  END-EXEC.
9999-PARAGRAPH-NOT-USED.
* * * * * * * * * * * * * * * * * * * * * * * * * * * *
* This statement is here to prevent the COBOL compiler from
* generating a STOP RUN.  It will never be executed.
* * * * * * * * * * * * * * * * * * * * * * * * * * * *
    GOBACK.
```

FIGURE 4.2.   Continued

As you can see, the programming logic for the noninteractive method is not too complex. You might also agree that as transactions become more complex, the operator is faced with a much greater burden of remembering the various transaction message formats. With each new parameter that must be entered, there is more chance that a transaction message will be entered in error and will have to be restarted. Transaction restarts result in lower productivity and unhappy users. For this reason, this programming method may be advantageous only for very simple transactions.

INTERACTIVE TRANSACTIONS

The primary problem with the noninteractive design technique is that it places too many demands on the terminal operator. The interactive transaction method is a design technique intended to overcome this problem. The principle behind the technique is to help the operator to enter any needed transaction parameters whenever possible. The result should be more productive operators. There is one trade-off with this technique. Program logic becomes more complex.

The basic design of an interactive transaction requires programming as necessary to *converse* with an operator in order to obtain transaction data. Conversing with an operator involves sending messages to the operator prompting some type of input, then receiving that input for further processing. A simple transaction, such as a master record inquiry, may only require one conversation. More complex transactions could require multiple conversations with the terminal operator. For each conversation with the terminal operator, there is the overhead of programming logic necessary to receive and process the additional transaction data.

Unfortunately, there is more at stake than just a few additional SEND and RECEIVE commands in the application program. If interactive transactions are designed *improperly,* the performance of the entire CICS system can be compromised. In other words, there is a correct way and an incorrect way to design interactive transactions. There is even a name given to each of these methods. The incorrect technique is known as *conversational programming,* and the correct method is called the *pseudoconversational* technique.

```
          IDENTIFICATION DIVISION.
          PROGRAM-ID. VEND002.
          AUTHOR.  BOB LOWE.
          ENVIRONMENT DIVISION.
          DATA DIVISION.
          WORKING-STORAGE SECTION.
          COPY VENDREC.
          01  MESSAGE-IN.
              05   TRAN-CODE          PIC XXXX.
              05   FILLER             PIC X.
              05   KEY-INPUT          PIC XXXXXX.
              05   FILLER             PIC X.
              05   NEW-NAME           PIC X(30).

          01  MESSAGE-LINE. (same as figure 4.2)
          01  MISC-AREAS. (same as figure 4.2)

          LINKAGE SECTION.
          PROCEDURE DIVISION.
         *PROCEDURE CODE
          000-MAINLINE-ROUTINE.
              MOVE SPACES TO MESSAGE-LINE, MESSAGE-IN.
              EXEC CICS IGNORE CONDITION LENGERR END-EXEC.
              MOVE +42 TO MSG-LEN.
              EXEC CICS RECEIVE
                  INTO (MESSAGE-IN)
                  LENGTH (MSG-LEN)
                  END-EXEC.
              IF MSG-LEN LESS THAN +11
                  MOVE 'NEED A RECORD KEY' TO THE-MESSAGE
                  GO TO 990-SEND-ERROR-AND-EXIT.

Check input key for numeric value

Handle conditions (same as figure 4.2)

              EXEC CICS READ UPDATE
                  DATASET ('VENFILE')
                  INTO    (VENDOR-RECORD)
                  RIDFLD  (KEY-INPUT)
                  LENGTH  (VENDOR-RECORD-LENGTH)
                  END-EXEC.
              MOVE NEW-NAME TO  VENDOR-NAME.
              EXEC CICS REWRITE
                  DATASET ('VENFILE')
                  FROM    (VENDOR-RECORD)
                  LENGTH  (VENDOR-RECORD-LENGTH)
                  END-EXEC.
              MOVE 'THE RECORD HAS BEEN UPDATED ' TO THE-MESSAGE
              MOVE KEY-INPUT TO SEND-KEY.
              GO TO 990-SEND-ERROR-AND-EXIT.

error processing routines (same as figure 4.2)

message display routine (same as figure 4.2)

          GOBACK.
```

FIGURE 4.3. Non-interactive Update Program

CONVERSATIONAL PROGRAMMING

First, let's examine the logic of an interactive transaction that uses the conversational approach. I'm going to use a simple inquiry transaction in this example. You might recall from our earlier example that the only transaction parameter needed for an inquiry is the record key for the master record to be displayed. Here's the design for my interactive transaction. First, the operator will initiate the transaction with the code V001 as follows:

V001

```
IDENTIFICATION DIVISION.
PROGRAM-ID. VEND001.
AUTHOR.  BOB LOWE.
ENVIRONMENT DIVISION.
DATA DIVISION.
WORKING-STORAGE SECTION.
COPY VENDREC.
01  MISC-AREAS.
    05  MSG-LEN                    PIC S9999 COMP.
    05  VENDOR-RECORD-LENGTH       PIC S9999 COMP VALUE +249.
    05  PROMPT-MESSAGE             PIC X(50)
        VALUE 'NNNNNN<--TYPE A RECORD KEY AND PRESS ENTER'
    05  KEY-INPUT                  PIC XXXXXX VALUE SPACES.

01  MESSAGE-LINE (same as figure 4.2)
...
01  DISPLAY-TEXT (same as figure figure 4.2)


LINKAGE SECTION.
PROCEDURE DIVISION.
*PROCEDURE CODE
000-MAINLINE-ROUTINE.
    MOVE SPACES TO MESSAGE-LINE.
    EXEC CICS IGNORE CONDITION LENGERR END-EXEC.
    EXEC CICS SEND
        FROM (PROMPT-MESSAGE)
        LENGTH (50)
        END-EXEC.
    MOVE +6 TO MSG-LEN.
    EXEC CICS RECEIVE
        INTO (KEY-INPUT)
        LENGTH (MSG-LEN)
        END-EXEC.
    IF MSG-LEN LESS THAN +6
        MOVE 'NEED A RECORD KEY' TO THE-MESSAGE
        GO TO 990-SEND-ERROR-AND-EXIT.
```

check for numeric record key (same as figure 4.2)

handle conditions (same as figure 4.2)

READ COMMAND...

Move to text area

SEND TEXT SEND PAGE (same as figure 4.2)

error routines (same as figure 4.2)

Send error message routine (same as figure 4.2)

FIGURE 4.4. Conversational Inquiry Program

The program will then send a message to the operator with a *prompt* to type in the record key as follows:

NNNNNN<--TYPE A RECORD KEY AND PRESS ENTER

The program will then display information from the requested master record the same as our first sample inquiry program.

The conversational programming logic for this transaction is shown in figure 4.4. Most of the storage areas and Procedure Division is the same as in our first example. The only difference is in the way the program sends the prompt message and receives the record key. At first glance, this inquiry program seems completely harmless. It simply sends a prompting message to the operator, then receives the input supplied by the operator and displays the master record. Yes, the program works. But this program isn't harmless; it has just violated a very important guideline that is linked to the performance of the CICS system.

As you know, CICS/VS is a multitasking system. As such, it has some inherent limitations that demand certain restrictions on the application programs that operate within its domain. The availability of dynamic storage is perhaps the primary limitation of CICS. Dynamic storage is needed in order to process a transaction running within the system. The number of transactions that can be running at any one time is therefore dependent on the storage that is available. The availability of dynamic storage is dependent on two factors. It first depends on the Virtual Storage allocated to the CICS region. A region with a large amount of allocated storage will have the *potential* to process large numbers of transactions. The second factor in the availability of dynamic storage is how effectively the allocated storage is used.

The problem with our conversational program is related to the effective use of dynamic storage or, rather, the ineffective use of it. Here's the problem with our program: this very short program has the potential of retaining transaction storage for relatively long periods of time. Consider how long it takes for our operator to type in the needed record key, then press enter. Perhaps only a second or two; maybe more. What if it's lunch time and the operator takes a 30-minute break? Well, maybe that's too extreme! But even a second or two of elapsed time is like an eternity to CICS. The system is capable of processing several transactions in that same time—that is, if there is sufficient dynamic storage to do so.

The essence of all this is that conversational programs can retain storage for relatively long periods of time. An *excessive* use of this technique can substantially reduce the amount of dynamic storage available in the system. As a result, the performance of the entire system can suffer. The consequences will be either a slow transaction response rate or a completely unstable on-line system. Because of this, the conversational programming technique has been abandoned by most CICS programmers. It has been replaced by the *pseudoconversational programming technique.*

PSEUDOCONVERSATIONAL PROGRAMMING

Pseudoconversational programming is a technique designed specifically to use CICS/VS dynamic storage more efficiently. The strategy behind this technique is to never leave a program in a task suspended in the system while waiting for terminal input. Does this mean that a pseudoconversational program will not interact with the operator? Not at all. The operator will still see the same prompting messages and will respond with the requested information. From the operator's viewpoint a conversation with the "program" will still take place. What is different with this technique is how we will design the application program or programs to maintain the conversation. In a way we are going to deceive the operator. (The term *pseudo* means "deceptive resemblance.")

Certain programming rules are necessary to adhere to the pseudoconversational programming technique. They are

1. A program will never attempt to receive input from a terminal after it has sent a message to that terminal *in the same task.*
2. A program will never attempt to receive more than one input message from a terminal *in the same task.*

The key words in both of these restrictions are *the same task.* Let's define a *task.* To the CICS system, the basic unit of work is known as a *task.* A task begins when a transaction code is started at a terminal. Each task operates on behalf of the terminal where the transaction code was started. All work completed during the task is done with respect to that terminal only. CICS maintains separate storage areas for each task in the system. Among these storage areas is the Execute Interface Block that you learned about in the preceding chapters. At least one program will be executed during a task. (You will see how more than one program can execute in a single task in chapter 7.) This program is specified in the PCT during the CICS tailoring process. If only one program executes during a task, the task is terminated when the program issues a CICS RETURN command. When a task is ended, all task-related storage areas are released and returned to the storage pool.

There is only one way to interact with an operator during a transaction and not violate the above rules. You must have at least *two* separate tasks. The first task will send output (such as the prompting message) to the terminal. Another task will subsequently receive input (such as the record key) from the terminal. If you can somehow perform this feat of magic, you will have implemented the widely hailed *pseudoconversational* programming technique. You may even become a CICS programming guru. Here's the secret to your success:

PSEUDOCONVERSATIONAL RETURN COMMAND

CICS provides a command specifically designed to support the pseudoconversational programming technique. The command is known as the pseudoconversational RETURN command. The format of this command is

```
EXEC CICS RETURN
      TRANSID (name)
      [COMMAREA (data-area)
      LENGTH (data-value)]
      END-EXEC
```

where TRANSID (name) specifies a transaction code that will be associated with the next operator input.

The primary purpose of the pseudoconversational RETURN command is the same as the standard RETURN. It terminates the program (and usually the task). But when the TRANSID option is used, the transaction code specified in the name argument, becomes *temporarily* assigned to the terminal. More specifically, it is associated only with the *next* input from the terminal. This means that the next time the operator presses ENTER (or any of the AID keys), the transaction code specified in the TRANSID option will be used by CICS to start a task.

The TRANSID option, when used, is like sending a subliminal transaction code to the terminal. But this next transaction code doesn't appear anywhere on the screen. (CICS stores this next transaction code in the Terminal Control Table.)

The COMMAREA and LENGTH options must be used together. These options allow you to pass an area of storage from the current task to the next task that is started on the terminal. These options of the RETURN command can only be used if the TRANSID option is also specified.

COMMAREA (data-area) is a COBOL field or group name containing data that you want to pass to the next task on the terminal.

LENGTH (data-value) is a numeric literal or COBOL field containing the number of characters to be passed. If a COBOL field is used, it must have a PICTURE of S9999, with a COMPUTATIONAL usage.

The COMMAREA and LENGTH options *together* determine what data is passed to the next task. You can effectively pass one field, a group of fields, or even part of a field. Using a COBOL group name does not imply that all of the fields contained within that group will be passed. The group name is simply used as the starting point; the length option tells how many characters are passed to the next task.

PSEUDOCONVERSATIONAL TECHNIQUES

In case you are still confused about how to use the pseudoconversation RETURN command, please read on. I think that some examples describing the various programming techniques will enlighten you more than the command description above. Actually, there are a variety of ways to implement

```
IDENTIFICATION DIVISION.
PROGRAM-ID. VEND001.
AUTHOR.  BOB LOWE.
ENVIRONMENT DIVISION.
DATA DIVISION.
WORKING-STORAGE SECTION.
01  MISC-AREAS.
    05  PROMPT-MESSAGE          PIC X(50)
        VALUE 'NNNNNN<--TYPE A RECORD KEY AND PRESS ENTER'
LINKAGE SECTION.
PROCEDURE DIVISION.
*PROCEDURE CODE
000-MAINLINE-ROUTINE.
    EXEC CICS SEND
        FROM (PROMPT-MESSAGE)
        LENGTH (50)
        END-EXEC.
    EXEC CICS RETURN
        TRANSID ('VOX1')
        END-EXEC.
    GOBACK.
```

FIGURE 4.5.   Pseudo-conversational Inquiry Program (Transid V001)

the pseudoconversational programming technique with this command. Among the most commonly used are

1. Use two programs with two transaction codes
2. Use one program with two transaction codes
3. Use one program with one transaction code

TWO PROGRAMS, TWO TRANSIDS

Let's look at the first method. With this method we use two separate application programs, *each* with its own transaction code. The Program Control Table (PCT) for such a design would appear (logically) as follows:

Transid	Program	Description
V001	VEND001	program to send prompt message
VOX1	VEND0X1	program to receive record key and display master record

Again, I'm going to use the simple inquiry transaction in this example. The interaction with the operator will be the same as our last example. First, the operator will initiate the transaction with the code V001. The operator will then see a message prompting more input. Finally, the operator will then see a display of the requested master record.

1. `-->|V001`

2. `-->|NNNNNNN<--TYPE  A RECORD KEY AND PRESS ENTER`

3. `-->(display of master record)`

Two separate programs will be used in this sample transaction. The first program (VEND001) will be started when the operator enters the transaction code V001. The logic of this program is shown in figure 4.5. The program simply sends the prompt message to the operator, then terminates with a pseudoconversational RETURN. The next transaction will be VOX1. The first task has ended. But because the IBM 3270 terminal is a buffered device, the prompt message remains on the screen awaiting the operator's response.

```
      IDENTIFICATION DIVISION.
      PROGRAM-ID. VENDOX1.
      AUTHOR.  BOB LOWE.
      ENVIRONMENT DIVISION.
      DATA DIVISION.
      WORKING-STORAGE SECTION.
      COPY VENDREC.
      01  MISC-AREAS.
          05  MSG-LEN               PIC S9999 COMP.
          05  VENDOR-RECORD-LENGTH  PIC S9999 COMP VALUE +249.
          05  KEY-INPUT             PIC XXXXXX VALUE SPACES.
      01  MESSAGE-LINE. (same as figure 4.2)

Display area same as figure 4.2)

      LINKAGE SECTION.
      PROCEDURE DIVISION.
     *PROCEDURE CODE
      000-MAINLINE-ROUTINE.
          MOVE SPACES TO MESSAGE-LINE.
          EXEC CICS IGNORE CONDITION LENGERR END-EXEC.
          MOVE +6 TO MSG-LEN.
          EXEC CICS RECEIVE
               INTO (KEY-INPUT)
               LENGTH (MSG-LEN)
               END-EXEC.
          IF MSG-LEN LESS THAN +6
               MOVE 'NEED A RECORD KEY' TO THE-MESSAGE
               GO TO 990-SEND-ERROR-AND-EXIT.

check for numeric key (same as figure 4.2)

handle condition (same as figure 4.2)


READ command (same as figure 4.2)

SEND TEXT, SEND PAGE (same as figure 4.2)

EXEC CICS RETURN END-EXEC.

error processing (same as figure 4.2)

display error message (same as figure 4.2)
```

FIGURE 4.6.   Pseudo-conversational Inquiry Program (Transid V0X1)

Once an operator response occurs, that is, an attention key such as enter is pressed, the next task will be started. The transaction code for that task will be V0X1. Because of our PCT entries, program VEND0X1 will be run. Let's look at the logic (shown in figure 4.6) for that program. Again, much of the logic of this program is the same as shown in the first programming example. The logic of this program simply receives the record key. Then, using that record key, the master record is read and displayed. We now have our first pseudoconversational transaction!

ONE PROGRAM, TWO TRANSIDS

Now let's examine another technique of designing a pseudoconversational transaction. Why not use just one program instead of two? Neither of the programs in the previous example was very large. In fact, they were both extremely short. Why not combine the routines in the two short programs into one longer program. But are we violating the basic principles of pseudoconversational programming? Not at all. Our only rule was that a program would not write to a terminal, then read back from the terminal in the *same task*. This new program design follows our rule. It isolates the receive logic, so that it will not occur in the same task as the send routine. Before we look at this program, we need to see how to specify the PCT entries. The PCT would appear as follows:

```
            IDENTIFICATION DIVISION.
            PROGRAM-ID. VENDOX1.
            AUTHOR.  BOB LOWE.
            ENVIRONMENT DIVISION.
            DATA DIVISION.
            WORKING-STORAGE SECTION.
            COPY VENDREC.
            01  MISC-AREAS.
                05  MSG-LEN              PIC S9999 COMP.
                05  VENDOR-RECORD-LENGTH PIC S9999 COMP VALUE +249.
                05  PROMPT-MESSAGE       PIC X(50)
                    VALUE 'NNNNNNN<--TYPE A RECORD KEY AND PRESS ENTER'.
                05  KEY-INPUT            PIC XXXXXX VALUE SPACES.
            01  MESSAGE-LINE (same as figure 4.2).

display area (same as figure 4.2)

            LINKAGE SECTION.
            PROCEDURE DIVISION.
           *PROCEDURE CODE
            000-MAINLINE-ROUTINE.
                IF EIBTRNID EQUAL 'V001'
                    EXEC CICS SEND ERASE
                        FROM (PROMPT-MESSAGE) LENGTH (50)
                        END-EXEC
                    EXEC CICS RETURN TRANSID ('VOX1')
                        END-EXEC.
                MOVE SPACES TO MESSAGE-LINE.
                EXEC CICS IGNORE CONDITION LENGERR END-EXEC.
                MOVE +6 TO MSG-LEN.
                EXEC CICS RECEIVE
                    INTO (KEY-INPUT)
                    LENGTH (MSG-LEN)
                    END-EXEC.
                IF MSG-LEN LESS THAN +6
                    MOVE 'NEED A RECORD KEY' TO THE-MESSAGE
                    GO TO 990-SEND-ERROR-AND-EXIT.

check for numeric key (same as figure 4.2)

handle condition (same as figure 4.2)

READ command (same as figure 4.2)

Display text (same as figure 4.2)

EXEC CICS RETURN END-EXEC.

error processing routines (same as figure 4.2)

display error message (same as figure 4.2)
```

FIGURE 4.7.   Pseudo-conversational Inquiry Program (Two Transids)

Transid	Program	Description
V001	VEND001	Inquiry Program
VOX1	VEND001	

No, your eyes aren't deceiving you. There are two different transaction codes assigned to the *same* program. Yes, that's perfectly legal too; it's a very common practice.

Let's look at the programming used to implement this technique. I'm going to use the same inquiry transaction and interact with the operator the same as before. The coding for this program is shown in figure 4.7.

This program uses a technique known as the *two-pass* program design. An entry analysis routine at the start of the program is used to determine which pass of the program is to be executed. When the operator first initiates the transaction with the code V001, the entry analysis routine will perform the "first pass" logic. This entry analysis is done by using the field EIBTRNID from the Execute Interface Block. The field EIBTRNID contains the transaction code that started the task.

The "first-pass" routine sends the prompt message, then terminates with the pseudoconversational RETURN command. The TRANSID argument names V0X1 as the next transaction on the terminal. After the operator keys in the required data, then presses an attention key, CICS will start the second task with a transaction code of V0X1. This time, the entry analysis routine will perform the "second-pass" logic. The logic in this second task receives the record key, then displays the requested information. Again, much of this second-pass logic is the same as our original inquiry program.

ONE PROGRAM, ONE TRANSID

There is one additional technique commonly used in the design of pseudoconversational programs. In the previous example you learned how to combine two programs into one, then use two different transaction codes to control the two-pass program logic. Now you will see how to eliminate one of the two transaction codes. Yes, that leaves us with a single transaction code and one program.

In order to use a single transaction code, we must modify the entry analysis routine to check something other than EIBTRNID. We need some other variable to indicate whether the first-pass or second-pass logic should be performed. There is such a variable. It is the field EIBCALEN. This field contains a value indicating the length of the communications area passed to the program. One way to use this field is as follows:

```
IF EIBCALEN EQUAL ZERO
    (first-pass routine)
ELSE
    (second-pass routine).
```

The use of EIBCALEN in the entry analysis routine is based upon an important phenomenon. That is, that there will *never* be a communications area (commarea) passed to a program when the task is started by an operator keying in a transaction code. For an operator to key a transaction code, some previous task must have ended with a simple RETURN command or may have abended. With either of these two actions, there is no commarea associated with the terminal. Therefore when a task is started by keying a transaction code, the value in EIBCALEN will be zero, indicating no commarea is present.

By checking for zero in EIBCALEN, we can now start our first-pass routine. The pseudoconversational RETURN command issued at the end of our first-pass routine is key to using this technique. You might recall that this command provides the capability to pass a communications area to the next task. This is done by using the COMMAREA and LENGTH options of the RETURN TRANSID command. One purpose of these options is to pass some useful information to the next task. This could be a record key entered in the original transaction message, or other information.

In some cases, it may not be important *what* is passed to the next pseudoconversational task. It may only be important that *something* is passed. If you will look again at the entry analysis logic above, you will notice that it is the *presence* of a commarea that is important. This routine doesn't even need to use the contents of the commarea. Later, in chapter 7, you will see how to access the contents of the commarea. For now, let's just use the field EIBCALEN in the entry analysis routine of our pseudoconversational program.

This last sample inquiry program depicted in figure 4.8 makes use of the commarea presence. The entry analysis checks the presence of a commarea. In the first-pass logic, the program sends the prompt message, then issues a pseudoconversational RETURN. The commarea passed in this example is the field EIBAID. Actually, *any* field could have been passed. Remember, it is the presence—not the contents—of the commarea that we are concerned with. After the operator responds to the prompt, the second task will be started. This time, since there is a commarea passed to the program, the entry analysis routine perform will perform the second-pass logic.

```
            IDENTIFICATION DIVISION.
            PROGRAM-ID. VENDOX1.
            AUTHOR.  BOB LOWE.
            ENVIRONMENT DIVISION.
            DATA DIVISION.
            WORKING-STORAGE SECTION.
            COPY VENDREC.
            01  MISC-AREAS.
                05  MSG-LEN                PIC S9999 COMP.
                05  VENDOR-RECORD-LENGTH   PIC S9999 COMP VALUE +249.
                05  PROMPT-MESSAGE         PIC X(50)
                    VALUE 'NNNNNN<--TYPE A RECORD KEY AND PRESS ENTER'.
                05  KEY-INPUT              PIC XXXXXX VALUE SPACES.
            01  MESSAGE-LINE (same as figure 4.2).

display area (same as figure 4.2)

            LINKAGE SECTION.
            PROCEDURE DIVISION.
           *PROCEDURE CODE
            000-MAINLINE-ROUTINE.
                IF EIBCALEN EQUAL ZERO
                    EXEC CICS SEND ERASE
                        FROM (PROMPT-MESSAGE) LENGTH (50)
                        END-EXEC
                    EXEC CICS RETURN TRANSID ('VOO1')
                        COMMAREA (EIBAID) LENGTH (1)
                        END-EXEC.
                MOVE SPACES TO MESSAGE-LINE.
                EXEC CICS IGNORE CONDITION LENGERR END-EXEC.
                MOVE +6 TO MSG-LEN.
                EXEC CICS RECEIVE
                    INTO (KEY-INPUT)
                    LENGTH (MSG-LEN)
                    END-EXEC.
                IF MSG-LEN LESS THAN +6
                    MOVE 'NEED A RECORD KEY' TO THE-MESSAGE
                    GO TO 990-SEND-ERROR-AND-EXIT.

check for numeric key (same as figure 4.2)

handle condition (same as figure 4.2)

READ command (same as figure 4.2)

Display text (same as figure 4.2)

EXEC CICS RETURN END-EXEC.

error processing routines (same as figure 4.2)

display error message (same as figure 4.2)
```

FIGURE 4.8.   Pseudo-conversational Inquiry Program (One Transid)

With the simple technique illustrated above, we are able to design a single inquiry program, using a single transaction code. That program, like the others, implements the pseudoconversational programming technique. The pseudoconversational programming technique is not just limited to the inquiry program. Any program that must interact with the operator can use the techniques just described. Later in the text, you will see how the menu program and others will use this pseudoconversational logic. Once you have mastered these and other techniques, you will be well on your way to a successful career as a CICS programmer.

Chapter Summary

In this chapter you have learned various techniques used in the design of CICS transactions. You have learned how to design both interactive and noninteractive transactions. The basic file control commands were also presented, since most transactions involve the use of these commands. You should now be able to write programs to randomly read and update records in a file. These programs will include the use of the pseudoconversational programming techniques presented in the chapter. This technique and the methods presented in this chapter are commonly used in the design of CICS transactions.

Discussion Questions

1. The File Control Program is designed so that after an I/O operation has begun for one task, it can have the Task Control Program dispatch another task. In this way CICS retains control of the CPU. How does this compare to the way native COBOL I/O verbs operate?
2. Describe some advantages of having a master terminal open and close files instead of placing that function within an application program.
3. Describe the benefits of defining file type and other information in the File Control Table instead of the application program.
4. Describe three actions that will cause exclusive control of a record to be released.
5. Why does the Execute Interface Program raise the exceptional condition INVREQ when a second READ UPDATE command for the same file has been requested without first updating or unlocking the record?
6. Why doesn't the REWRITE command include the RIDFLD option?
7. If the exceptional condition ILLOGIC occurs, where does CICS store the VSAM Return and Error codes?
8. Discuss one problem with the noninteractive transaction design technique.
9. Discuss how the pseudoconversational programming technique can improve the use of dynamic storage resources.
10. An application using the pseudoconversational programming technique sends a screen in one task and receives the operator reply in another task. Which command is used to terminate the first task after the SEND command and "schedule" the next task that will eventually issue the RECEIVE command?
11. A single program can be designed to perform the first-pass logic needed to send a screen as well as the second-pass logic to receive the operator input. In such a program some type of entry analysis must be done to determine which routine should be invoked. Describe some of the ways in which this can be accomplished.
12. What facility makes it possible for information to be passed from one task to the next when using the pseudoconversational programming technique?

Review Exercises

1. Write a command to read a record from a file named PERMAST into the I/O area below. The I/O area extends for a length of 200 bytes. Assume the record key of the record to be read is stored in a field named RECKEYI.

```
      05  PREC-LENGTH PIC S9999 COMP.
01  MASTER-PERSONNEL-RECORD.
      05  PNAME         PIC X(30).
      05  PSSN          PIC 9(9).
      05  PTITLE        PIC XXXXX.
      05  PADDR         PIC X(25).
      05  PCITY         PIC X(15).
      05  PSTATE        PIC XX.
      05  PZIP          PIC X(9).
          .
          .
          .
```

2. Write a command to directly delete a record from the file above. Assume that the record key is stored in a field named RECKEYI.
3. Write a pseudoconversational RETURN command to terminate the current task, "schedule" the transaction code *V$01*, and pass the data stored in the field below.

```
05  RECORD-KEY PIC X(9).
```

Lab Problems

LAB 1

Write a noninteractive program to receive a transaction message as shown below. Use the record key supplied in the transaction message to randomly read the personnel master file. Then display the screen shown below. If an error occurs, send a message back to the operator, then terminate the program. Use the error message layout shown below.

Transaction Input

```
xy01 999999999
```

Error Message Layout

```
xy01 999999999 MESSAGE TO OPERATOR..


              FILE NOT OPEN
              RECORD NOT FOUND
              PLEASE SUPPLY SSN
              UNEXPECTED ERROR


DISPLAY SCREEN
DISPLAY PERSONAL INFORMATION
     SSN:XXX-XX-XXXX
    NAME:XXXXXXXXXXXXXXXXXXXXXXXXXXXXXX
 ADDRESS:XXXXXXXXXXXXXXXXXXXXXXXXXXX
    CITY:XXXXXXXXXXXXXX
   STATE:XX 999999999
   PHONE:9999999
     SEX:X
  ETHNIC:1
     DOB:999999
```

LAB 2

Write a single two-pass pseudoconversational program to display a record from the personnel master file. Use the multiple transaction code technique presented in the chapter to determine first-pass or second-pass logic.

In the first-pass logic, transaction xy01, display a prompt message requesting the operator to enter an employee SSN. Issue a pseudoconversational RETURN command with a transid of xyX1.

Transaction Message

```
    xy01
Prompt Message
    999999999<--ENTER AN EMPLOYEE SSN, PRESS ENTER
```

In the second-pass logic (Transid xyX1), receive the record key. Use that record key to randomly read the record. Then display the screen shown below. If an error occurs, send a message back to the operator, then terminate the program. Use the error message layout shown below.

Error Message Layout

```
    xy01          MESSAGE TO OPERATOR..

                  FILE NOT OPEN
                  RECORD NOT FOUND
                  PLEASE SUPPLY SSN
                  UNEXPECTED ERROR
```

Display Screen

```
DISPLAY PERSONAL INFORMATION

     SSN:XXX-XX-XXXX
    NAME:XXXXXXXXXXXXXXXXXXXXXXXXXXXXX
 ADDRESS:XXXXXXXXXXXXXXXXXXXXXXXXXXXXX
    CITY:XXXXXXXXXXXXX
   STATE:XX 999999999
   PHONE:9999999
     SEX:X
  ETHNIC:1
     DOB:999999
```

LAB 3

Write a pseudoconversational program to delete a record from the personnel master file. Use the commarea presence technique (single transid) presented in the chapter to determine first-pass or second-pass logic.

In the first-pass logic, receive a transaction message as shown below. Use the record key supplied in the transaction message to randomly read the personnel master file. Then display the delete prompt screen. Issue a pseudoconversational RETURN command with a transid of xy05. Pass a commarea to the next task.

Transaction Message

```
    xy05 999999999
```

Display Screen

```
PRESS PF6 TO CONFIRM DELETE
SSN:XXXXXXXXX
NAME:XXXXXXXXXXXXXXXXXXXXXXXXXXXXXX
```

In the second-pass logic, determine if the operator pressed PF6 to confirm the delete operation. If so, delete the record and send a confirmation message to the operator. If any other attention key was pressed, simply send a "RECORD NOT DELETED" message to the operator. In either event, terminate the transaction with a simple RETURN command.

LAB 4

Write a noninteractive program to add a record to the personnel master file. The initial transaction message shown below will contain the employee SSN and employee name. Use the SSN as the record key and store the name in the record. Initialize other fields as follows: Store the date from the EIB in the date-added field in the record. Store your own initials in the last update operator field. All other alphameric fields should contain spaces. All other numeric fields should be initialized to zeros. After adding the record, send a confirmation message to the terminal.

Input Message

```
xy04 999999999 XXXXXXXXXXXXXXXXXXXXXXXXXXXXXX
```

LAB 5

Write a noninteractive program to update a record to the personnel master file. The initial transaction message shown below will contain the employee SSN and employee name. Use the SSN as the record key and use the name to update the record. Initialize other fields as follows: Store the date from the EIB in the last date-updated field in the record. Store your own initials in the last update operator field. All other fields should remain unchanged. After updating the record, send a confirmation message to the terminal.

Input Message

```
xy02 999999999 XXXXXXXXXXXXXXXXXXXXXXXXXXXXXX
```

5

BMS Introduction

As you study the topics in this chapter, you will

1. Learn that the IBM 3270 information display terminal is capable of transferring data at the field level to and from the application program.
2. Understand that each field stored in the IBM 3270 display terminal takes on a set of characteristics.
3. Be able to list the attributes that can be assigned to each field transferred to the IBM 3270 terminal.
4. Recognize the benefits of using BMS to define and process formatted screens for your application.
5. See how the BMS facility of CICS/VS can be used to define complete screens of information for use by the application program.
6. Learn how to use the three BMS screen definition commands to define maps for formatted screens for the IBM 3270 display terminal.
7. Follow the map-generation process needed to define application screens for an application.

In this chapter, you are going to be introduced to Basic Mapping Support. BMS is a CICS application services facility that simplifies programming tasks needed to communicate with IBM terminals. You will first learn that the IBM 3270 terminal has the capability to transfer individual fields to and from the application program. You will see that this capability can require some complex programming without BMS services. After the introductory material, you will learn how to define BMS maps. These maps are used by BMS to process formatted screens. Finally, after learning how to define BMS screens, you will see a BMS map preparation example for two sample screens. The maps for these two screens will be used by various programs in the remaining chapters of the text.

Using Formatted Screens

So far in this book, you used the SEND and SEND TEXT commands to display messages on the IBM 3270 display terminal. These commands, which simply transfer characters to the terminal, are sufficient in many situations, but for most applications, something more than simple message delivery is needed. Let's say, for instance, that you would like your program to produce a display of the application menu screen in figure 5.1. One way to do this would be to develop a group of lines in working-storage. Then, a SEND or SEND TEXT command would be used to transmit the "screen image" to the display terminal. Although this technique will work, it is not really a practical way to construct screen displays.

```
          1         2         3         4         5         6         7         8
1234567890123456789012345678901234567890123456789012345678901234567890123456789 0
UEN0000                                                          DATE 01/31/88
                    VENDOR MASTER MENU                           TIME 06:00:00
                                                                 TERMINAL DT03

          PF1   DISPLAY MASTER RECORD

          PF2   UPDATE MASTER RECORD

          PF3   ADD MASTER RECORD

          PF4   DELETE MASTER RECORD

          PF5   BROWSE MASTER BY KEY

          PF9   EXIT MASTER MENU


      TYPE VENDOR NUMBER  100000  THEN PRESS APPROPRIATE PF KEY
```

FIGURE 5.1.   Sample Menu Screen

One problem with this technique deals with the fact that in many on-line networks, terminals with different screen sizes are connected to the system. Can you imagine what would happen if this screen image, intended for an 80-column by 24-row terminal were to be sent to a terminal with 132 columns by 27 rows? The result would be a garbled view of the information. For a display program to work properly with a variety of screen sizes, you would need to define a screen image for each terminal size to be used in the system. Then, for each task, the program would have to determine the screen width for the terminal that started the transaction. It would then transmit the appropriate image for the terminal using the program. Program maintenance required for screen changes would be more difficult and time-consuming since screen layouts for each terminal size would have to be modified. Likewise, the addition of new terminals, with different screen sizes from those already established, could cause a maintenance nightmare. This would be especially true if a large number of programs had to be modified.

Another limitation of using this native display technique deals with input operations from the terminal. If the application screen is going to invite some type of data entry, it should have a provision for the operator to key in one or more fields. In addition, there should be some way to locate, then process, the keyed input. When a screen is transmitted to the terminal using a series of lines, there is no practical way to locate the information that is subsequently input by the operator. This problem is due to the fact that the entire screen becomes free-form input. All headings, field labels, and input data will be transmitted by the terminal back to the program. Unless the operators strictly adhere to input guidelines, their keystrokes could be lost among the other transmitted characters.

For these and other reasons, the use of the simple CICS data-transfer commands will prove to be ineffective in most of today's interactive applications. The IBM 3270 information display system is designed to support both simple and complex information needs. There are several models of display terminals within the IBM 3270 family. Each model has basic programmable hardware features that can be activated by the application program in response to more complex needs. CICS/VS is designed for full support of the IBM 3270 features as needed to meet these demands in a variety of applications. In the sections that follow, you will be introduced to a few of the features of the IBM 3270 display terminal. You will then see how to use the Basic Mapping Support facility of CICS/VS to display "formatted" screens.

```
                1         2         3         4         5         6         7         8
       1234567890 1234567890 1234567890 1234567890 1234567890 1234567890 1234567890 1234567890
 1 ▮VEN0000                                                          ▮DATE▮XX/XX/XX
 2                ▮VENDOR MASTER MENU                                 ▮TIME▮XX:XX:XX
 3                                                                    ▮TERMINAL▮XXXX
 4
 5           ▮PF1  DISPLAY MASTER RECORD
 6
 7           ▮PF2  UPDATE MASTER RECORD
 8
 9           ▮PF3  ADD MASTER RECORD
10
11           ▮PF4  DELETE MASTER RECORD
12
13           ▮PF5  BROWSE MASTER BY KEY
14
15           ▮PF9  EXIT MASTER MENU
16
17
18 ▮TYPE VENDOR NUMBER▮NNNNNNN▮THEN PRESS APPROPRIATE PF KEY
19
20
21 ▮_____
22
23
24
```

FIGURE 5.2.   Sample Menu Screen Programming View

IBM 3270 Fields

At some time in your data-processing career, you were introduced to the concepts of fields, records, and files (perhaps even data bases). You probably visualize each of these terms with respect to a recording medium such as cards, tape, or disk. Like its input-output ancestors, the IBM 3270 display terminal was designed to support data transfer requirements. It enables you to deal with data by individual elements, or fields, each with its own characteristics, or *attributes*. With disk and tape, field attributes deal primarily with data type, such as character, packed decimal, and binary. With the IBM 3270 terminal, the attributes describe how the field will be displayed on the terminal and what action will be taken if the operator attempts to key into the field during input operations. On the card, disk, and tape mediums, one or more fields constitute a record. With the 3270 devices, the fields combine to produce a complete screen full of information. The result: a display or data entry screen conforming to human requirements for on-line applications.

Please refer again to our menu screen in figure 5.1. The use of menus will be discussed more fully later in the text, but for now let's assume that we would like to design such a screen for display on an IBM 3270 terminal. This screen contains a title indicating the purpose of the display. A screen identification code, in the upper left corner is provided for operator reference. The date, time, and terminal identification are also contained on the display for operator convenience. Following the title area are several lines describing menu functions that can be selected by the operator. Each function is associated with a 3270 PF key. Following the list of available functions is a prompt line with a data entry field to allow the operator to enter a record key. Finally, there is a line used to send messages to the operator.

Now refer to figure 5.2. Here we see the application menu screen from the programming viewpoint. In this figure, a shaded box has been placed just preceding each 3270 field. Each box represents a field delimiter position and will eventually occupy a character location on the screen. This field delimiter position is commonly known as the *attribute byte*. Each data field is physically defined on the 3270 terminals by writing a field attribute code in the first position of the field. Thus, a 3270 field is defined as the attribute character plus all positions following it up to the next attribute character. The attribute byte occupies a character position on the screen, and displays as a space. The placement of attribute characters defines the field lengths. The value in the attribute character determines the field characteristics. Each 3270 field will take on *several* attributes. The attributes will depend on the value of the attribute control code transmitted to the terminal. The following characteristics can be associated with each field:

VISIBILITY

A field is either displayable or nondisplayable. When it is nondisplayable, all characters within the field are not displayed. Nondisplayable data is accepted by the terminal but is not visible on the screen. This nondisplay attribute is useful for entering classified information such as passwords into the terminal. When it is displayable, any nonblank characters contained within the field are displayed. All characters within a displayable field can be displayed at regular brightness or at high intensity. High intensity is often used to highlight an error message or call attention to a field entered in error.

CHARACTER CONTENT

A field is either alphameric or numeric. An operator can enter alphabetic, numeric, or special characters in an alphameric field. The effect of the numeric attribute depends upon which keyboard is attached to the display. On a data entry keyboard the numeric attribute will cause the keyboard to be shifted into numeric mode and will restrict the operator from entering any characters except digits 0–9, a period, and a minus sign. On a standard typewriter keyboard without the numeric lock feature, the numeric attribute has no effect.

PROTECTION

A field is either protected or unprotected. The operator cannot enter or modify data in any location within a protected field. Headings, labels, and titles are commonly specified as *protected*. Some variable content fields appearing on a display screen, such as date and time, would also be specified as *protected.* If a field is defined as *unprotected,* the operator can enter, delete, or modify any of the characters contained within the area. Data entry screens will have one or more unprotected fields on the screen.

MODIFIED DATA TAG

IBM 3270 terminals are designed to allow maximum utilization of data channels and telecommunications circuits. Most CICS commands to read from the terminal result in the 3270 transmitting only fields that have been modified by the operator. When a field is modified by the operator, it takes on a new attribute. This attribute is the *modified data* attribute. The terminal marks or tags each modified data field in the attribute position. In other words a modified data tag is turned on. Only fields with the modified data tag set on are transmitted when an attention key is pressed by the operator.

A program may also send fields to the display with the modified data tag attribute already set on. In this way, the field will be tagged by the terminal as modified. It has the same effect as if the operator had modified the field. On a subsequent read operation, these fields will be returned to the program along with any others actually modified by the operator. They will be transmitted back to the program even if the operator skips over them during data entry. In our sample menu screen, we could set the vendor number data entry field to the modified state. In this way any data in that field will be transmitted to CICS after the operator selects a function on the menu.

EXTENDED HIGHLIGHTING AND COLOR

The newer IBM displays provide for additional highlighting. These terminals feature extended field highlighting such as reverse video, blinking, and underlining. The color terminals have extended color attributes to determine the colors of display fields. On some models, any of seven colors—blue, red, pink, green, turquoise, yellow, and neutral—can be selected. These attributes provide the applications designer with several visual enhancement alternatives.

3270 FIELD-ORIENTED KEYS

When an IBM 3270 terminal display has been written with formatted fields, certain operator keyboard functions are activated to enhance the usability of the terminal. These keyboard functions are as follows:

Tab Key moves the cursor to the first character location of the next unprotected data field. In a display with no unprotected fields, the cursor is repositioned to character location 0.

Backtab Key When the cursor is located in the attribute character or the first character location of an unprotected or in any character location of a protected field, this key moves the cursor to the first character location of the first preceding unprotected data field. When the cursor is located in any character location of an unprotected field other than the first location, this key moves the cursor to the first character location of that field. In a display with no unprotected fields, the cursor is repositioned to character location 0.

New Line moves the cursor to the first unprotected character location of the next line. In a display with no unprotected fields, the cursor is repositioned to character location 0.

Erase EOF If the cursor is located in a character location of an unprotected field, this key clears the character location occupied by the cursor and all remaining character locations in that field to nulls. The modified data tag bit for this field is set on. The cursor does not move when this key is pressed.

Erase Input This key clears all unprotected fields on the screen to nulls and repositions the cursor to the first unprotected character location on the screen. The modified data tag for all unprotected fields is set off.

INSERT Key places the keyboard into insert mode. If the cursor is located in an unprotected data field having a null character in, or to the right of, the cursor location, operation of an alphameric key causes the character to be entered at the cursor location. The character formerly occupying the cursor location and all remaining characters within the field are shifted one character to the right. The modified data tag is set on. The RESET key must be pressed to terminate the insert operation.

DELETE Key If the cursor is located in an unprotected field, the operation of this key deletes the character from the character location occupied by the cursor. All remaining characters in the field, on the same line, shift one character to the left. Vacated characters are filled with nulls and the modified data tag is set on. The RESET key is not necessary to terminate a delete operation.

Formatting 3270 Displays

There are two ways to send formatted screens to the IBM 3270 display terminal. The easiest is to use the Basic Mapping Support facility described in this chapter. The other way, which has been abandoned by most programmers, is to construct *native* 3270 data streams within the program and transmit them using the SEND command. Let's briefly look at what is involved in doing it the hard way. After we do, I think you will agree that BMS is the better way.

To format a screen, complete with the IBM 3270 field definitions, the data stream transmitted to the device must contain a series of *orders*. Orders are special codes written to the terminal to tell the display unit how to format your screen. They also control the creation of fields. There are three basic orders: buffer position order, insert-cursor order, and start-field order.

The buffer position order sets the location of the display terminal buffer for receiving subsequent orders and data. Each terminal has its own buffer for storing attributes and data. The characters that are displayed on the terminal are really just a representation of the buffer contents. The image on a 1,920-character unit is displayed on a 24-row by 80-column screen. There is a fixed relationship between each buffer location and its related character position on the screen. By using the buffer positioning order, a program can build a screen image without sending the entire 1,920 characters to the terminal.

The buffer position order is a three-character hexadecimal value. A hex value of 11 is the first character in the order. The two remaining characters identify the buffer address. There is a unique address for each of the 1,920 buffer positions of a 24-row by 80-column unit. For example the hex address of row 2, column 14 is C15D. So, to condition the terminal to begin receiving subsequent orders or data beginning at this row-column address, the following hexadecimal value would be transferred to the display station: *11C15D*.

The insert-cursor order causes the cursor pointer to be set at the current buffer position. The single character hex code of 13 will set the cursor pointer. This code usually follows a buffer-positioning command that establishes the buffer location. You would transmit the hex order *11D5E413* to the terminal to position the cursor at row-18, column-20.

The field definition order is a two-character sequence. The first byte of the two-byte sequence is a hex code of 1D. The second byte contains the attribute code. When this sequence is encountered, the display station will start a field at the current buffer position. A field definition order usually follows a buffer position order. To start a field definition at row-2, column-14, we would transfer the sequence *11C15D1DF0* to the terminal. The last byte (F0) represents the attribute for a protected, unmodified, normal intensity field.

Start field orders are usually accompanied by the characters to be displayed on the terminal. For example, to display the sample menu screen title shown in figure 5.1, the sequence below would be transmitted to the terminal (hexadecimal codes are underlined).

<u>11C15D1DF0</u>VENDOR MASTER MENU

We would then repeat this order-data sequence for each additional field to build the formatted screen. Figure 5.3 represents a "dump" of a data stream necessary to build our example application menu. The coding necessary to define such a data stream in a COBOL program would be a horrendous task. I'm sure you will agree by now that there has to be an easier way to take advantage of the field definition capabilities of the IBM 3270 terminal. There is; it's called *Basic Mapping Support*.

Basic Mapping Support

Basic Mapping Support (BMS) is an interface between the application program and the terminal. Its primary function is to relieve you from having to deal with the device-dependent data streams needed to communicate with a terminal. The orders previously described are still needed to use fields on the IBM 3270. But BMS takes responsibility for generating the proper orders and merging them along with variables from the program. The result is a data stream that, when sent to a terminal, will produce an application screen with formatted fields. This process is known as *mapping*. By removing the mapping responsibilities from your program, the application development process is much simplified. BMS provides for both input mapping and output mapping. Let's take a much simplified look at both of these mapping processes.

```
                        11D5E413    ...Y.....;.2.NU.
1140401D  F0E5C5D5  F0F0F0F0  11C1C21D    .  .0VEN0000.AB.
F0C4C1E3  C51DF0F0  F161F3F1  61F8F811    0DATE.001/31/88.
C15D1DF0  E5C5D5C4  D6D940D4  C1E2E3C5    A).0VENDOR MASTE
D940D4C5  D5E44011  C2D21DF0  E3C9D4C5    R MENU .BK.0TIME
1DF0F0F6  7AF0F07A  F0F011C3  E21DF0E3    .006:00:00.CS.0T
C5D9D4C9  D5C1D31D  F0C4E3F0  F311C5C8    ERMINAL.0DT03.EH
1DF0D7C6  F14040C4  C9E2D7D3  C1E840D4    .0PF1  DISPLAY M
C1E2E3C5  D940D9C5  C3D6D9C4  11C7E81D    ASTER RECORD.GY.
F0D7C6F2  4040E4D7  C4C1E3C5  40D4C1E2    0PF2  UPDATE MAS
E3C5D940  D9C5C3D6  D9C44011  4AC81DF0    TER RECORD .H.0
D7C6F340  40C1C4C4  40D4C1E2  E3C5D940    PF3  ADD MASTER
D9C5C3D6  D9C44040  4040114C  E81DF0D7    RECORD   .<Y.0P
C6F44040  C4C5D3C5  E3C540D4  C1E2E3C5    F4  DELETE MASTE
D940D9C5  C3D6D9C4  40114FC8  1DF0D7C6    R RECORD .3H.0PF
F54040C2  D9D6E6E2  C540D4C1  E2E3C5D9    5  BROWSE MASTER
40C2E840  D2C5E840  11D1E81D  F0D7C6F9    BY KEY .JY.0PF9
4040C5E7  C9E340D4  C1E2E3C5  D940D4C5    EXIT MASTER ME
D5E44040  40404011  D5501DF0  E3E8D7C5    NU      .N&.0TYPE
40E5C5D5  C4D6D940  D5E4D4C2  C5D91DC1    VENDOR NUMBER.A
D5D5D5D5  D5D51DF0  E3C8C5D5  40D7D9C5    NNNNNN.0THEN PRE
E2E240C1  D7D7D9D6  D7D9C9C1  E3C540D7    SS APPROPRIATE P
C640D2C5  E811D940  1DF0                  F KEY.R .0
```

FIGURE 5.3. Device Dependent Data Stream for Menu

On output, mapping consists of merging variable data from the program with BMS-generated device-dependent orders. The resulting data stream is transmitted to the terminal by BMS and the Terminal Control Program. Please refer to figure 5.4 for this illustration. In preparation for an output mapping operation to the terminal, the application program would initialize the working-storage data fields to be mapped. In the case of our menu application, the date, time, and terminal identification would be moved to mapping fields in working-storage. The program would then issue the BMS SEND MAP command to write the menu screen. The SEND MAP command will cause the BMS on-line mapping program to be executed.

The mapping routines in the BMS on-line mapping program search the Terminal Control Table to get details about the terminal being used. The screen size and other terminal information from the TCT will be used so BMS can generate the proper orders for this type of terminal. BMS then locates information about the screen layout to be mapped to the terminal. The screen layout for the application would have been previously defined using a series of screen definition statements. This information describing the screen layout is called a BMS map. These map definition statements will be discussed fully later in the chapter. Using the TCT, the mapping information, and the data supplied by the program, BMS will construct a device-dependent data stream for this terminal, and then cause this data stream to be transmitted to the terminal. The result of the output mapping operation is a display of the application screen requested in the SEND MAP command.

Now let's look at the input mapping process. Please refer again to the sample menu screen. Assume that an operator has just viewed this menu screen and has entered a vendor record key, then pressed PF1. The objective of input mapping is to cause the *modified fields* transmitted by the terminal to be mapped into the program's working-storage. This process is depicted in figure 5.5. The BMS RECEIVE MAP command would be issued by the program would invoke the on-line BMS mapping program. Upon receiving control, BMS would search the Terminal Control Table to determine the screen size for the terminal running the program. It would then locate the map (MENUMAP) named in the RECEIVE MAP command to determine the screen layout. Using this information, BMS would scan the input data stream, extract the input fields by determining the origin of the data, and move them into the program's working-storage. After completing the input mapping operation, BMS would return control to the application program to process the input in the working-storage fields.

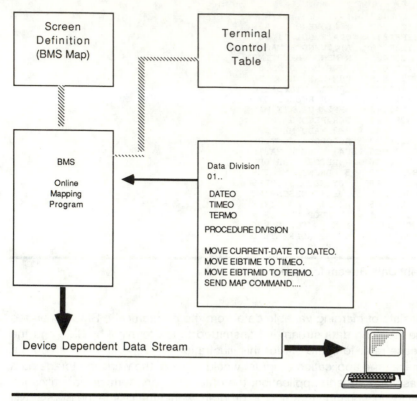

FIGURE 5.4. Output Mapping converts device independent data from the program to a device dependent data stream

BENEFITS OF BMS

There are two principal benefits in using BMS; they are device independence and format independence.

DEVICE INDEPENDENCE

This feature allows the application program to send data to a terminal or to receive data from a terminal without regard for the physical characteristics of the terminal. When sending screens to the IBM 3270 family, device independence deals primarily with the generation of outgoing buffer-positioning orders. For example, on an 80-column by 24-row terminal, the order to position the buffer pointer to row 2, column 14 is 11C15D. But this same order, if sent to a 132-column by 27-row display, would cause the pointer to be set at row 1, column 94. BMS identifies which terminal type is requesting use of the application program by examining the Terminal Control Table. On output, BMS generates the proper device-dependent orders necessary to deliver the application screen to the terminal. On input, BMS scans the device-dependent data stream and properly determines the origin of the incoming fields.

FORMAT INDEPENDENCE

This feature allows the application program to transmit or receive data using a series of fields in the working-storage section. BMS allows constant information such as titles, field labels, and operator messages to be stored in separate areas called maps. The screen constants can be modified and rearranged by changing the maps themselves, not the programs that use them. There is not even a

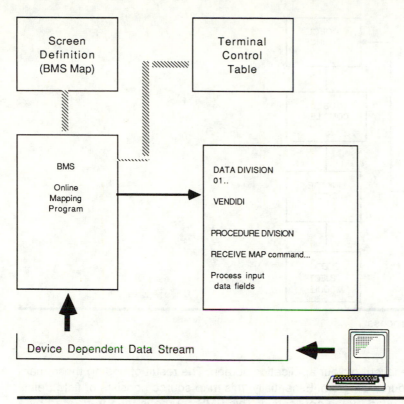

```
┌─────────────────┐         ┌─────────────────┐
│     Screen      │         │    Terminal     │
│   Definition    │         │     Control     │
│   (BMS Map)     │         │      Table      │
│                 │         │                 │
└─────────────────┘         └─────────────────┘

┌─────────────────┐         ┌─────────────────────────────┐
│                 │         │  DATA DIVISION              │
│      BMS        │         │  01..                       │
│                 │   ───▶  │                             │
│     Online      │         │  VENDIDI                    │
│    Mapping      │         │                             │
│    Program      │         │  PROCEDURE DIVISION         │
│                 │         │                             │
│                 │         │  RECEIVE MAP command...     │
│                 │         │                             │
│                 │         │  Process input              │
│                 │         │     data fields             │
└─────────────────┘         └─────────────────────────────┘

┌───────────────────────────────────────┐
│  Device Dependent Data Stream          │   ◀───
└───────────────────────────────────────┘
```

FIGURE 5.5. Input Mapping converts device dependent data from the terminal and sends it to the program

reference to screen constants in the application program. For variable screen data, fields will appear in the application program in a data structure similar to a record layout for a file. During output operations, the on-line BMS routines extract the contents of the fields, and generate the data stream using the screen layout information provided by the map. If the screen layout is later changed, a new data stream is generated as reflected in the updated maps. No *logic* changes are necessary in the program; it is independent of the format of the screen. Similar actions are performed by BMS for input mapping. Screen changes can occur without having to alter the programming logic to process incoming fields. The end result of an input mapping operation is the transfer of modified fields to corresponding fields in working storage.

BMS Map Preparation

As discussed in the preceding overview, the on-line BMS routines use maps to process formatted screens. There are two types of maps, namely the physical map and the symbolic description map. The physical map contains all of the information about the screen layout and the individual fields within the screen. This map resides in the CICS load (program) library until it is needed by the on-line BMS mapping routines. The symbolic description map is a COBOL copybook containing data names for the *variables* to be transferred to and from the program. The data names in the symbolic map are copied into the working-storage of the application program when it is compiled.

The physical and symbolic maps are generated by an off-line (batch) map-preparation process. This map-preparation process is performed in *advance* of compiling and using the application program. You define maps by using a set of map-definition statements. These map-definition statements

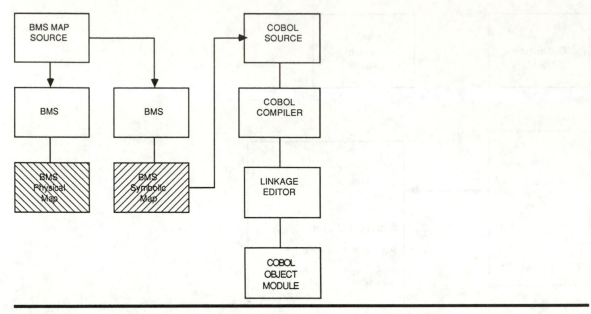

FIGURE 5.6.   Map Preparation Process

contain options that describe the layout of your application screen. The result of coding these map-definition statements is a BMS source program. Essentially, this map source consists of field definitions for each screen that will be used by the application. This BMS source is then translated by a batch process similar to compiling a COBOL program. This batch process is depicted in figure 5.6. The output of the process is the generation of the physical map and the symbolic-description map. As shown in the illustration, the symbolic-description map is then copied into the application program during the COBOL compile process. The physical map is not used until later, when the application program is run and requests a BMS mapping operation using a SEND MAP or RECEIVE MAP command.

STRUCTURE OF BMS SOURCE

The mapset-definition process is accomplished by using three types of BMS statements. Please refer to figure 5.7. The first statement in the map source is a mapset-definition statement (DFHMSD). Many applications require a set of screen definitions. The sample vendor application used in this book, for instance will eventually require a menu screen; a combination display, update and add screen; and a set of browse screens. Since these screens are logically related, it is often useful to group them into an application set. The result is a *mapset.* Conceptually, everything that has been discussed thus far is still the same. There is simply the convenience of multiple map definitions in a single process. After the beginning DFHMSD statement, the map source contains a map-definition statement (DFHMDI) for the first application screen. The map-definition statement is followed by field-definition statements (DFHMDF) for *each* field on that screen. If more than one screen is being defined, there will be another map-definition statement followed by field-definition statements for that map. At the end of the source, there is a final mapset-definition statement (DFHMSD) to indicate the end of the mapset.

```
DFHMSD    TYPE=MAP

DFHMDI
DFHMDF
DFHMDF
DFHMDF

DFHMDI
DFHMDF
DFHMDF

DFHMSD    TYPE=FINAL
```

FIGURE 5.7.   Mapset Coding Structure

```
....5....10....5...20....5....30....5...40....5....50....5....60....5...70..

VENDSET   DFHMSD TYPE=MAP,                                            C
               MODE=INOUT,                                           C
               LANG=COBOL,                                           C
               TIOAPFX=YES
MENUMAP   DFHMDI SIZE=(24,80),LINE=1,COLUMN=1
SCODE     DFHMDF POS=(01,01),LENGTH=07
```

FIGURE 5.8   Example of Mapset Coding Rules

MAPSET CODING RULES

Here are a few of the coding rules that you should follow when defining BMS mapsets. The BMS map-generation statements are written in the form of *assembly language* macros and are processed by the operating system macro assembler. For best results, follow the rules below. Please refer to figure 5.8 as you study these rules.

1.   If a mapset, map or field-definition statement requires a name, the name must begin in column 1. In the example the name VENDSET was provided as the mapset name.
2.   Begin each statement type beginning in column 10.
3.   You should code only a few options per line. It's easier to make changes later in case you make a mistake or want to add another option. A comma should follow each option but the last one. Options can occupy the same line as the statement type. In the example, the TYPE=MAP option follows this rule.
4.   If more than one line is required, a continuation sequence is necessary. For continuations, place any character in column 72 and begin coding the next statement in column 16. The last option should not be followed by a comma. Likewise there is no continuation mark in column 72 of the last line of each statement. This last option rule is the easiest to violate and will cause you the greatest problems.

MAPSET DEFINITION STATEMENT

Information pertaining to an entire mapset is specified in the DFHMSD statement. The operands of the statement define the characteristics of all maps in the map set. The options of the DFHMSD statement are

```
(mapset) DFHMSD  TYPE=MAP | DSECT
                 LANG=COBOL | ASM | PLI | RPG
                 MODE= IN | OUT | INOUT
                 STORAGE=AUTO
                 TIOAPFX= YES | NO
                 CTRL=(FREEKB,ALARM,FRSET)
```

Mapset is a one- to seven-character name of the map set. This name is used in the MAPSET option of the BMS SEND MAP and RECEIVE MAP commands that appear in the Procedure Division of the COBOL program.

TYPE= specifies whether the physical or symbolic map is being generated. The Job Control Language (JCL) options of the batch run can determine the final disposition of this option, so it doesn't really matter what you specify. I usually code TYPE=MAP.

LANG= specifies the source language to be used when generating the symbolic description map (copybook). This option is ignored during the run to create the physical map. The BMS map-generating instructions can create a copybook for COBOL, PL/I, Assembler, and RPGII programs. You should specify LANG=COBOL when you prepare maps for your COBOL programs.

MODE= specifies the type of mapping that will eventually be performed on the maps in the mapset. The valid operands of this option are IN, OUT, and INOUT. If all maps will be used only for input mapping, then IN would be specified. OUT would be specified if all maps will be used for output mapping only. Generally, both input and output mapping will be performed with the maps in a mapset so the operand INOUT is usually specified.

STORAGE=AUTO If this option is specified, the symbolic description map generated for each screen will occupy separate working-storage areas. This will result in greater storage requirements for the program. The option is provided in case the program needs to build multiple maps concurrently and is not normally specified. If this option is not specified, each symbolic map will redefine the storage of the first symbolic map.

TIOAPFX= This option (with YES specified) is required when a map is to be used in a command-level program. TIOAPFX will cause a 12-byte filler to be inserted before the first field in the symbolic description map. If not specified, the fields will be misaligned and will usually result in garbage being displayed on the screen.

CTRL= This option allows you to specify default terminal control functions such as FREEKB, ALARM, and FRSET in the physical map. I prefer to include these same options in the SEND MAP command, where they are more visible for debugging and documentation purposes.

MAP-DEFINITION STATEMENT

The DFHMDI statement is used to define a map within a mapset. The statement provides a name for the map. It also specifies the size of the map and the origin of the map relative to the screen size.

```
(map) DFHMDI
         SIZE=
         LINE=
         COLUMN=
```

Map This is a one- to seven-character name of the map. This name will be used in the MAP option for the BMS SEND MAP and RECEIVE MAP commands. It is also used by BMS to generate the extended map names in the symbolic description map. For instance, if the map name is MENUMAP, the symbolic description map will contain the extended names: MENUMAPI and MENUMAPO.

SIZE= specifies the dimensions of the map in rows and columns. Most of the time the size of a map will correspond to the screen size. For instance, on a terminal with 24 rows and 80 columns, the SIZE option may be coded as: SIZE=(24,80). Later, in chapter 10, you will see how this option can be used to provide some special mapping functions.

LINE= specifies the starting-row position of the map on the screen. Generally you will use the option LINE=1. If a map occupies less than the physical screen size, this option can be used to position the map in a certain area of the screen.

COLUMN= specifies the starting-column position of the map on the screen. Generally you will use the option COLUMN=1. If a map occupies less than the physical screen size, this option can be used to position the map in a certain area of the screen.

FIELD-DEFINITION STATEMENT

The DFHMDF statement is used to define one field in a map. Fields should appear in the map in relative order to their position on the screen; that is, the field in the top left corner of the map should be defined first. Then other fields on that line, from left to right, should be defined. Fields on the next line should be coded next, and so on. Options in the DFHMDF statement are

```
(fld)      DFHMDF POS=
           LENGTH=
           ATTRB=
           PICIN=
           PICOUT=
           INITIAL=
```

(Fld) This option provides a name for the field. The name may be from one to seven characters in length and should begin with a letter. A field must be given a name if it is to contain variable data that will be mapped to or from the application program. Constant fields such as screen titles and labels usually do not need a name. If, however, the value of a screen title or label will vary from one screen to another, it must be given a name.

For each field defined with a name, BMS will provide a group of extended names in the symbolic description map. For example, if a field is defined with the name "DATE" the symbolic map will contain the fields: DATEO, DATEL, DATEF, DATEA, and DATEI. The DATEO and DATEA fields will be used for output mapping. The DATEI, DATEL, and DATEF fields are used for input mapping. These extended names will be discussed fully in the next chapter.

POS= (line,column) indicates the position of the *attribute* for the field.

LENGTH=n This option specifies the length of the *data* portion of the field. The length value does not include the attribute position.

ATTRB= specifies the 3270 attributes for the field. These attributes relate to visibility, protection, and character content as described earlier in the chapter. The valid attributes are described below.

[UNPROT[,NUM] | ASKIP | PROT] Only one of these three groups can be used. Fields with the UNPROT option can be modified by the operator. The NUM operand used with UNPROT can be used to have data entry keyboards shift into numeric mode for an unprotected field.

The ASKIP and PROT attributes are very similar. The difference is noticeable only when the operator is keying into an unprotected field and "runs into" a field with ASKIP or PROT. If an operator is keying in data, and encounters a field with the PROT attribute, the keyboard becomes locked and the operator must press the RESET key to continue typing. On the other hand, if the operator encounters a field with the ASKIP attribute, the cursor will automatically skip to the next unprotected field without locking the keyboard. A screen title or label is generally given the ASKIP attribute. This allows the cursor to automatically skip over the field during input operations. The ASKIP attribute should also be assigned to data fields on inquiry screens since you do not want the operator to begin overkeying these data areas on an inquiry application. One final note: the inadvertent use of NUM with PROT will cause the field to be defined as ASKIP; this happens because of the way 3270 attributes are stored (as individual bits) in the attribute byte.

[BRT | NORM | DRK] Select one of these options to define the visibility of the field. The BRT option might be used for screen headings and labels. This option could also be used on a data field that you want to highlight to draw attention to the operator. The NORM attribute is used to display a field at normal intensity. Most fields will have this attribute. The DRK attribute is normally used to define fields that provide security information to the program. A password field, for instance might be defined with the DRK attribute.

[FSET] specifies that the modified data tag should be set when the field is sent to the terminal. This attribute will cause the 3270 to transmit the field back to the program on the next input even if the operator doesn't key data into the field.

[IC] This parameter is not a field attribute. It specifies that the cursor is to be placed in the first data position of this field when the screen is displayed. If this option is specified for more than one field in a map, the last field for which it is specified takes effect.

INITIAL='character data' This option is used to specify constant data or default data for a field. The INITIAL option is used to define screen titles and headings or labels for the map.

PICIN='COBOL picture' This option can be used for variable fields that will be used in input mapping operations. It provides a way to define an input mapping field with a COBOL picture clause. If this option is not used, a picture clause with PIC X(nn) is used, where nn is the number used in the LENGTH option.

PICOUT='COBOL picture' This option can be used for variable fields that will be used in output mapping operations. It provides a way to define an output mapping field with a COBOL picture clause. If this option is not used, a picture clause with PIC X(nn) is used, where nn is the number used in the LENGTH option.

Mapset-Preparation Example

In this example, we are going to step through the process of defining a mapset for our sample vendor application. This mapset includes two formatted screens. These screens are depicted in figure 5.9. The first screen is our familiar menu screen. The second screen will be used by the inquiry, update, add, and delete transactions described later in the text. Both screens are shown from the pro- grammer viewpoint, with shaded boxes representing field attribute positions. The mapset-definition statements for these screens is shown in figure 5.10. Please refer to these two figures as you follow this example. The coding for this mapset is similar to most of the 3270 mapsets that you will ever use. You may therefore use this example as a master guide for maps that you develop in the future.

The screens depicted in figure 5.9 require the definition of two maps within the mapset. The mapset source begins with the DFHMSD statement as follows:

```
VENDSET  DFHMSD TYPE=MAP,MODE=INOUT,LANG=COBOL,TIOAPFX=YES
```

This coding is fairly static for IBM 3270 terminals. Chances are that you can use these exact state- ments in all of your mapsets. The mapset name is VENDSET. Both input and output mapping will be used with the map(s) in this mapset. The symbolic maps will be generated in the COBOL language.

Following the mapset-definition statement, we will begin coding our first map. Let's begin with the menu screen. The map-definition statement for the menu map is as follows:

```
MENUMAP  DFHMDI SIZE=(24,80),LINE=1,COLUMN=1
```

The map name assigned to this inquiry screen is MENUMAP. This map is 24 rows by 80 columns and begins on the screen in row 1, column 1.

Field-definition statements for each field to appear on the screen will follow the map-definition statement. The first field on the screen is the screen-identification code. This field is defined as fol- lows:

```
SCODE    DFHMDF POS=(01,01),LENGTH=07
```

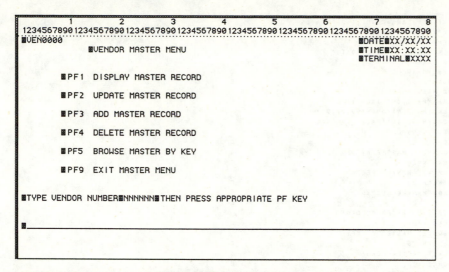

```
          1         2         3         4         5         6         7         8
 1234567890 1234567890 1234567890 1234567890 1234567890 1234567890 1234567890 1234567890
█VEN0000                                                        █DATE█XX/XX/XX
              █VENDOR MASTER MENU                               █TIME█XX:XX:XX
                                                                █TERMINAL█XXXX

         █PF1  DISPLAY MASTER RECORD

         █PF2  UPDATE MASTER RECORD

         █PF3  ADD MASTER RECORD

         █PF4  DELETE MASTER RECORD

         █PF5  BROWSE MASTER BY KEY

         █PF9  EXIT MASTER MENU


█TYPE VENDOR NUMBER█NNNNNNN█THEN PRESS APPROPRIATE PF KEY

█_____
```

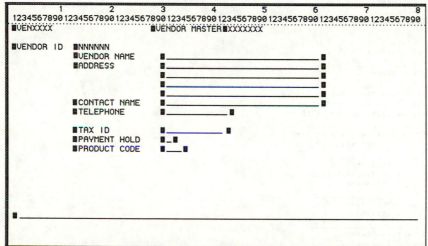

```
          1         2         3         4         5         6         7         8
 1234567890 1234567890 1234567890 1234567890 1234567890 1234567890 1234567890 1234567890
█VENXXXX             █VENDOR MASTER█XXXXXXX

█VENDOR ID  █NNNNNN
            █VENDOR NAME   █_____█
            █ADDRESS       █_____█
                           █_____█
                           █_____█
                           █_____█
            █CONTACT NAME  █_____█
            █TELEPHONE     █_____█

            █TAX ID        █_____█
            █PAYMENT HOLD  █_█
            █PRODUCT CODE  █___█


█_____
```

FIGURE 5.9.   Sample Application Screens Programming View

This field is given a name so the program can ultimately determine the screen code value displayed on the menu screen. The attribute for this field will be in row 1, column 1. You will notice that I have not coded an ATTRB option for this field. If an ATTRB option is not coded, BMS defaults to ATTRB=(ASKIP, NORM). Some installations may have a coding standard requiring you to specify the ATTRB option. This makes it easier for someone else to interpret your maps later during maintenance. Since the field has been implicitly defined as ASKIP, the operator will not be able to change the screen code. It will also display at normal intensity. The field "data" immediately follows in row 1, column 2. Finally, the field is seven characters in length.

The next field on the screen is the field label for the date. It is defined as follows:

```
DFHMDF POS=(01,67),LENGTH=04,INITIAL='DATE'
```

This "constant" field does not require a field name since the program will have no need to change the initial value. The actual constant is defined with the INITIAL option. Again, since no ATTRB option was specified, BMS will supply default attributes to ASKIP, NORM.

```
VENDSET   DFHMSD TYPE=MAP,MODE=INOUT,LANG=COBOL,TIOAPFX=YES
MENUMAP   DFHMDI SIZE=(24,80),LINE=1,COLUMN=1
SCODE     DFHMDF POS=(01,01),LENGTH=07
          DFHMDF POS=(01,67),LENGTH=04,INITIAL='DATE'
DATE      DFHMDF POS=(01,72),LENGTH=08
          DFHMDF POS=(02,14),LENGTH=19,                              C
                 ATTRB=(ASKIP,NORM),                                 C
                 INITIAL='VENDOR MASTER MENU'
          DFHMDF POS=(02,67),LENGTH=04,INITIAL='TIME'
TIME      DFHMDF POS=(02,72),LENGTH=08,PICOUT='99,99,99'
          DFHMDF POS=(03,67),LENGTH=08,INITIAL='TERMINAL'
TERM      DFHMDF POS=(03,76),LENGTH=04
          DFHMDF POS=(05,09),LENGTH=26,                              C
                 INITIAL='PF1  DISPLAY MASTER RECORD'
          DFHMDF POS=(07,09),LENGTH=26,                              C
                 INITIAL='PF2  UPDATE MASTER RECORD'
          DFHMDF POS=(09,09),LENGTH=26,                              C
                 INITIAL='PF3  ADD MASTER RECORD'
          DFHMDF POS=(11,09),LENGTH=26,                              C
                 INITIAL='PF4  DELETE MASTER RECORD'
          DFHMDF POS=(13,09),LENGTH=26,                              C
                 INITIAL='PF5  BROWSE MASTER BY KEY'
          DFHMDF POS=(15,09),LENGTH=26,                              C
                 INITIAL='PF9  EXIT MASTER MENU'
          DFHMDF POS=(18,01),LENGTH=18,                              C
                 INITIAL='TYPE VENDOR NUMBER'
VENDID    DFHMDF POS=(18,20),LENGTH=06,                              C
                 ATTRB=(IC,UNPROT,NUM,NORM,FSET),                    C
                 INITIAL='NNNNNN'
          DFHMDF POS=(18,27),LENGTH=29,                              C
                 INITIAL='THEN PRESS APPROPRIATE PF KEY'
MMESAGE   DFHMDF POS=(21,01),LENGTH=79
DISPMAP   DFHMDI SIZE=(24,80),LINE=1,COLUMN=1
SCODE     DFHMDF POS=(01,01),LENGTH=07
          DFHMDF POS=(01,28),LENGTH=13,INITIAL='VENDOR MASTER'
DTYPE     DFHMDF POS=(01,42),LENGTH=07,INITIAL='INQUIRY'
          DFHMDF POS=(03,01),LENGTH=09,INITIAL='VENDOR ID'
VENDID    DFHMDF POS=(03,13),LENGTH=06
          DFHMDF POS=(04,13),LENGTH=11,INITIAL='VENDOR NAME'
VENNAME   DFHMDF POS=(04,30),LENGTH=30,ATTRB=FSET,                   C
                 INITIAL='_____'
          DFHMDF POS=(04,61),LENGTH=1,ATTRB=PROT
          DFHMDF POS=(05,13),LENGTH=07,INITIAL='ADDRESS'
ADDR1     DFHMDF POS=(05,30),LENGTH=30,ATTRB=FSET,                   C
                 INITIAL='_____'
          DFHMDF POS=(05,61),LENGTH=1,ATTRB=PROT
ADDR2     DFHMDF POS=(06,30),LENGTH=30,ATTRB=FSET,                   C
                 INITIAL='_____'
          DFHMDF POS=(06,61),LENGTH=01,ATTRB=PROT
ADDR3     DFHMDF POS=(07,30),LENGTH=30,ATTRB=FSET,                   C
                 INITIAL='_____'
          DFHMDF POS=(07,61),LENGTH=01,ATTRB=PROT
ADDR4     DFHMDF POS=(08,30),LENGTH=30,ATTRB=FSET,                   C
                 INITIAL='_____'
          DFHMDF POS=(08,61),LENGTH=01,ATTRB=PROT
          DFHMDF POS=(09,13),LENGTH=12,INITIAL='CONTACT NAME'
CONTAC    DFHMDF POS=(09,30),LENGTH=30,ATTRB=FSET,                   C
                 INITIAL='_____'
          DFHMDF POS=(09,61),LENGTH=01,ATTRB=PROT
          DFHMDF POS=(10,13),LENGTH=09,INITIAL='TELEPHONE'
TELE      DFHMDF POS=(10,30),LENGTH=12,ATTRB=FSET,                   C
                 INITIAL='_____'
          DFHMDF POS=(10,43),LENGTH=01
          DFHMDF POS=(12,13),LENGTH=06,INITIAL='TAX ID'
TAXID     DFHMDF POS=(12,30),LENGTH=11,ATTRB=FSET,                   C
                 INITIAL='_____'
          DFHMDF POS=(12,42),LENGTH=01
          DFHMDF POS=(13,13),LENGTH=12,INITIAL='PAYMENT HOLD'
PAHOLD    DFHMDF POS=(13,30),LENGTH=01,ATTRB=FSET,                   C
                 INITIAL='_'
          DFHMDF POS=(13,32),LENGTH=01
          DFHMDF POS=(14,13),LENGTH=12,INITIAL='PRODUCT CODE'
PRODUCT   DFHMDF POS=(14,30),LENGTH=03,ATTRB=FSET,                   C
                 INITIAL='___'
          DFHMDF POS=(14,34),LENGTH=01
DMESAGE   DFHMDF POS=(21,01),LENGTH=79
          DFHMSD TYPE=FINAL
```

FIGURE 5.10. Map definition statements for sample screens (updated)

The screen date field follows the date label. This field is where the actual date will be displayed. Since this field value will be supplied by the application program it requires a field name. It is defined as

```
DATE      DFHMDF POS=(01,72),LENGTH=08
```

The next field to appear on the screen is the title. It is defined much the same as the date label. As you might guess, these field definition statements could easily be copied, then modified with an on-line program editor. In fact I follow this practice as often as I can. It really speeds up the map development process.

The next two fields for the time label and time variable field follow the same pattern as the date entries. The only difference is the PICOUT option for the time field, which provides a COBOL picture clause. For example,

```
TIME      DFHMDF POS=(02,72),LENGTH=08,PICOUT='99,99,99'
```

With this picture clause a program will be able to edit the time field to include commas(,), then change the commas to colons (:) with a COBOL TRANSFORM or EXAMINE verb.

Most of the remaining fields are similar to those just described. There is one field on the screen that is different. It is the data entry field where the operator will type in the record key to be processed by the program. This field is defined as follows:

```
VENDID    DFHMDF POS=(18,20),LENGTH=06,...        C
          ATTRB=(IC,UNPROT,NUM,NORM,FSET),..      C
          INITIAL='NNNNNN'
```

This field requires a name, since it will be mapped to and from the program. The "IC" argument in the ATTRB option indicates that the cursor will be inserted at this field. The FSET option will cause the field to be transmitted with the modified data tag attribute set on. By setting this attribute, this field will later be transmitted back to the program even if the operator doesn't actually key into the field. The UNPROT option allows the operator to change the contents of the field. The UNPROT option is used on all "data entry" type fields. By the way, the options UNPROT and NORM are the default when the *ATTRB* option *is* specified. These two options could have been omitted from the statement.

Finally, a message field is defined to allow the program to display messages that might be useful to the operator. The message field needs a name since the program will supply a variable message. It is protected so the message can not be overtyped by the operator. This completes the field-definition statements for our sample menu screen.

Now let's look at the definitions for the other screen in our mapset. As indicated above, this screen will be used by the inquiry, update, add, and delete programs. The map-definition statement is very similar to the definition for the menu map. The map size and origin is the same. The name of this map is DISPMAP.

```
DISPMAP   DFHMDI SIZE=(24,80),LINE=1,COLUMN=1
```

Like the menu, the first field on this screen is the screen-identification code. This field is defined exactly the same as the screen code on the menu screen. It even has the same name. Because the name has been used previously, BMS will print a warning note during the map-generation process. This warning message is a reminder that your programs may have to take special precautions when using these maps. We'll discuss these precautions in the next chapter.

```
SCODE     DFHMDF POS=(01,01),LENGTH=07
```

The screen title is next. If you look at the screen layout in figure 5.9, you will notice that the title is actually composed of two fields. The coding for these fields is shown below. The first field contains the constant "VENDOR MASTER." The second field is defined with a field name to allow the program to vary the contents of the field. For example, the inquiry program will use the default value, "INQUIRY." The update program would change this value to "UPDATE," the add program would change this value to "ADD," and so on.

```
           DFHMDF POS=(01,28),LENGTH=13,INITIAL='VENDOR MASTER'
DTYPE      DFHMDF POS=(01,42),LENGTH=07,INITIAL='INQUIRY'
```

Next are the definitions for the vendor identification label and display field. There is nothing unusual about these two fields. Both are defined as auto-skip and normal intensity. The definitions are

```
           DFHMDF POS=(03,01),LENGTH=09,INITIAL='VENDOR ID'
VENDID     DFHMDF POS=(03,13),LENGTH=06
```

There are several other label fields on this screen. The field definitions for these other field labels have similar coding to the label for the vendor-identification field. I'm going to skip over these definitions to look at some special fields on this screen. These special fields are the data entry (and display) fields and the skip and stop fields. First let's look at the data entry fields.

As mentioned above, this screen will be used by the update and add programs. The update program will allow the operator to modify a record with data keyed into these fields. The add program likewise will allow the operator to enter new data into these areas. For this reason we are going to define these fields as unprotected. They will also be defined as FSET so the modified data tag will be set on. For example, the name field would be defined as follows:

```
VENNAME   DFHMDF POS=(04,30),LENGTH=30,ATTRB=FSET,         C
          INITIAL='_____'
```

The other data entry fields have similar definitions, so I won't describe them here. The only fields remaining on this screen that we haven't discussed are somewhat related to these data entry fields. You might have noticed in looking at the sample display screen that each of the data entry fields is immediately followed by a shaded box or attribute position. These seemingly useless fields are actually an integral part of the *update* screen design. They are known as *skip* and *stop* fields.

These skip and stop fields are used to establish an "invisible" border behind a data entry field. This border is necessary to prohibit an operator from entering more data into a field than can be transmitted back to the application program. The problem is related to the architecture of the IBM 3270 terminal. Recall that each 3270 field begins at an attribute position and extends up to the next attribute. However, when BMS builds a formatted display, it only stores field attributes at those positions where you have specified that a field is to begin. BMS does not automatically transmit a field terminate attribute to terminate each field. This can result in fields defined on the 3270 terminal which are actually larger than the corresponding symbolic fields defined in the program. If not for the artificial boundaries produced by explicitly defining skip and stop fields, two things would happen: first, the operator could type in more characters than the symbolic map would hold; then BMS would truncate the extraneous characters so they would fit into the symbolic map in the program.

The terms *skip* and *stop* relate to the effect caused when an operator attempts to key past the boundary of a data entry field. A stop field is used to lock up the keyboard if an operator attempts to key beyond a data entry area. Stop fields are generally placed behind a variable-length data entry field where unwanted truncation might normally occur. The operator, upon discovering that the data must be condensed in some way, can unlock the keyboard with the RESET key, then take appropriate action. The following statement would define a stop field behind the data entry field for the name in our example.

```
          DFHMDF POS=(04,61),LENGTH=01,ATTRB=PROT
```

A skip field is used to allow the cursor to skip around an "open" section of the screen to the next unprotected field. Skip fields are usually placed behind fixed-length data entry fields. The effect is that the cursor moves freely from one data entry field to the next without locking the keyboard.

The field below could be defined behind the payment hold data entry field on our sample screen.

```
DFHMDF POS=(13,32),LENGTH=01
```

This concludes the description of the statements for our sample display-update screen. If another screen were to be defined in the mapset, it would follow the last field for this map. Since we don't have another screen to define yet, one more map definition statement would be included in the BMS source.

That statement is the DFHMSD statement. This last statement has only one option, as shown below. Be sure to code this instruction since it is vital to the proper generation of the maps.

```
DFHMSD TYPE=FINAL
```

After the coding for the mapset is complete, the mapset source is submitted to the batch run to produce the physical map and symbolic description map. During the map-generation process, you will most likely have some errors the first time or two. If so, correct them and resubmit the job until your coding errors are eliminated. Be sure to look for your operating system catalog status report to verify that the physical map has been catalogued into the core image or load library and that the symbolic description map has been catalogued into the copy library.

New BMS Developments

Fortunately, many of you will never need to master the intricate details of map preparation that were just described. As mentioned earlier, in many installations, the applications programmer does not have to prepare these maps. In some installations, the map preparation process may be assigned to one group of programmers and another project team would be assigned to design and code the maps that use them. An applications programmer may only see a screen layout, a copy of the map source and the symbolic description map.

There is another reason that you may not need to memorize the details of map preparation. In some installations, this process has been completely eliminated. Instead, on-line utility programs are used to generate BMS maps. Most of these on-line programs allow you to perform a two step "paint-a-screen-and-fill-in-the-blanks" process. In the first step, an application screen is simply "painted" by moving the cursor around the screen, and keying in screen titles and other constants. Variable fields are painted on the screen in a similar manner. Then in the second step the screen generator program requests field attribute information for each field on the application screen.

After the screens are painted, and the attributes are supplied, these automated map generator programs produce their output. The end result needed is still the physical map and the symbolic description map. Some of the more expensive automated programs will directly produce these two maps after the "painting" session. Others will simply produce the BMS source code. This source code will then be processed by the installation as if it had been produced manually.

More and more companies are finding that automated map generator programs can increase productivity and dramatically reduce programming costs. As these products become more predominate, the importance of knowing the intricate details of the map generation statements will likely recede. The concepts behind these statements, however will remain an integral part of your CICS skills. It is likely that even with automated tools, the fundamental concepts and terminology that you have just learned will continue to be important to your future as a CICS programmer.

Chapter Summary

In this chapter, you have learned how to define a formatted screen for use with a CICS application. A formatted screen contains one or more fields that have a set of attributes. These attributes define the visibility, character content, and protection of a field on a terminal. BMS is a facility that simplifies the programming necessary to transmit and receive formatted data using an IBM terminal. BMS makes use of maps that are defined separately from the application program. These maps are generated by coding a series of screen-definition statements. This map source is processed in batch mode to produce the BMS physical map and symbolic maps. In the next chapter, you will learn how to use these maps to read and write formatted screens.

Discussion Questions

1. It is possible to display screens of information by defining several-line images in working-storage and sending these lines to the terminal with the SEND or SEND TEXT commands. What are some limitations of using this technique?
2. Describe some of the problems of using unformatted screens for input operations.
3. The IBM 3270 can store data as unique fields. Each field takes on certain characteristics known as *attributes*. Where are these attributes stored?
4. How does the 3270 define the beginning and end of each field?
5. During normal operations, the 3270 only transmits modified fields to CICS. By what means does the 3270 differentiate between modified and not-modified fields?
6. During output mapping, BMS is responsible for inserting device-dependent orders and control characters for transmission to the 3270 terminal. Where does BMS get information that defines the type of terminal that started the task?
7. Which BMS definition statement is coded at the beginning and the end of the BMS source?
8. When a continuation line is necessary in a BMS definition statement, in which column must you continue coding the specifications?
9. Discuss why the STORAGE=AUTO option should be omitted whenever possible.
10. In the field-definition statement, what are the default attributes when the ATTRB option is *not* used? What if the ATTRB option *is* used?
11. What screen location is specified in the POS option of the DFHMDF statement?
12. Why are title and label fields normally defined with the protected attribute?
13. In coding the mapset-definition statement (DFHMSD), what is the purpose of the LANG= option? What would happen if the wrong option is specified?
14. What is the effect of coding the IC option in the attribute definition for a field?
15. A printer-spacing chart is often used when designing a screen layout. What are some differences between designing a screen layout and a report layout?

Review Exercises

1. Code a field-definition statement for the following title field whose attribute is located at row 2, column 30:

   ```
   PERSONNEL INQUIRY SCREEN
   ```

2. Produce a screen layout that would match the mapset definitions below.

   ```
   PERSET    DFHMSD  TYPE=MAP,MODE=INOUT,LANG=COBOL,TIOAPFX=YES
   INQY      DFHMDI  SIZE=(24,80),LINE=1,COLUMN=1
   SCRNID    DFHMDF  POS=(01,01),LENGTH=07,ATTRB=(ASKIP,NORM,IC)
             DFHMDF  POS=(01,15),INITIAL='MASTER INQUIRY',LENGTH=14
             DFHMDF  POS=(03,01),INITIAL='NAME',LENGTH=04
   MNAME     DFHMDF  POS=(03,10),ATTRB=(UNPROT,NORM),LENGTH=30
             DFHMDF  POS=(05,01),INITIAL='ADDRESS',LENGTH=07
   MADDR1    DFHMDF  POS=(05,10),ATTRB=(UNPROT,NORM),LENGTH=30
   MCITY     DFHMDF  POS=(06,10),ATTRB=(UNPROT,NORM),LENGTH=15
   MSTATE    DFHMDF  POS=(06,26),ATTRB=(UNPROT,NORM),LENGTH=02
   MZIP      DFHMDF  POS=(06,29),ATTRB=(UNPROT,NORM),LENGTH=09
             DFHMSD  TYPE=FINAL
   ```

3. Code a stop field for the data entry field below.

```
EMPNAME    DFHMDF POS=(04,10),LENGTH=30,ATTRB=FSET
```

4. Code a skip field for the data entry field below.

```
EMPTYPE    DFHMDF POS=(10,10),LENGTH=04,ATTRB=FSET
```

Lab Problems

For each lab assigned by your instructor, perform the following steps:

1. Code the BMS screen-definition statements to define the application screen. The symbol "^" represents the position of each attribute character. The symbol "\" represents variable information to be mapped from an application program.
2. Use a job stream (JCL) provided by your instructor to catalog the physical map and the symbolic description map.
3. Use a CICS/VS transaction code provided by your instructor to display the screen. This transaction will display the screen with the initial values and attributes for each field. No variables will be displayed.

LAB 1

PERSONNEL MASTER MENU BMS SCREEN DEFINITION

```
LINE                        <---COLUMN--->
|         1         2         3         4         5         6         7
v 12345678901234567890123456789012345678901234567890123456789012345678901234 5
01^\\\\\\\              ^PERSONNEL MASTER MENU         ^TERMINAL:^\\\\
02                                                     ^DATE:^\\\\\\\\\
03                                                     ^TIME:^\\\\\\\\\
04
05           ^ENTER   DISPLAY PERSONAL INFORMATION
06            ^PF1   DISPLAY COMPANY INFORMATION
07            ^PF2   UPDATE PERSONAL INFORMATION
08            ^PF3   UPDATE COMPANY INFORMATION
09            ^PF4   ADD EMPLOYEE RECORD
10            ^PF5   DELETE EMPLOYEE RECORD
11            ^PF6   BROWSE FILE BY SSN
12            ^CLEAR SCREEN TO EXIT APPLICATION
13
14
15
16
17
18
19
20^TYPE EMPLOYEE SSN THEN PRESS ENTER OR A PF KEY^\\\\\\\\\\\^
21
22^MESSAGE:^\\\\\\\\\\\\\\\\\\\\\\\\\\\\\\\\\\\\\\\\\\\\\\\\\\\\\\\\\\\\
23
24
```

LAB 2

PERSONAL INFORMATION BMS SCREEN DEFINITION

This screen will eventually be used by the personnel inquiry, update, add, and delete lab assignments. Define the screen title as two separate fields to allow these programs to vary the function being performed. Function values will be "INQUIRY," "UPDATE," "ADD," and "DELETE." Set the initial value to "INQUIRY."

```
LINE                        <---COLUMN--->
|            1         2         3         4         5         6
V  1234567890123456789012345678901234567890123456789012345678901234567890123456
01^\\\\\\\            ^PERSONAL INFORMATION^INQUIRY
02
03
04      ^SSN:^\\\\\\\\\
05
06      ^NAME..^\\\\\\\\\\\\\\\\\\\\\\\\\\\\\\\\\\^
07 ^ADDRESS..^\\\\\\\\\\\\\\\\\\\\\\\\\\\\\\\\\\\^
08      ^CITY..^\\\\\\\\\\\^
09     ^STATE..^\\^\\\\\\\\\\^
10
11     ^PHONE..^\\\\\\\^
12       ^SEX..^ ^
13   ^ETHNIC..^\^
14       ^DOB..^\\\\\\^
15
16
17
18
19
20
21^MESSAGE:^\\\\\\\\\\\\\\\\\\\\\\\\\\\\\\\\\\\\\\\\\\
22
23
24
```

LAB 3

COMPANY INFORMATION BMS SCREEN DEFINITION

This screen will eventually be used by the personnel company inquiry and company-update lab assignments. Define the screen title as two separate fields to allow these programs to vary the function being performed. Function values will be "INQUIRY" and "UPDATE." Set the initial value to "INQUIRY."

```
LINE                        <---COLUMN--->
|            1         2         3         4         5         6         7
V  1234567890123456789012345678901234567890123456789012345678901234567890
01^\\\\\\\            ^COMPANY INFORMATION^INQUIRY
02
03^SSN:^\\\\\\\\\
04^NAME:^\\\\\\\\\\\\\\\\\\\\\\\\\\\\\\\\\
05
06
```

```
07  ^EMPLOYEE TYPE..^\\^
08        ^LOCATION..^\\^
09     ^DEPARTMENT..^\\\\^
10
11      ^JOB TITLE..^\\\\\^
12    ^POSITION NO..^\\\\\^
13^EMPLOYMENT DATE..^\\\\\\^
14
15   ^ANNUAL SALARY..^ZZZZ,ZZZ.99^
16
17
18
19
20
21^MESSAGE:^\\\\\\\\\\\\\\\\\\\\\\\\\\\\\\\\\\\\\\\\\\\\\\\\\\\\\\\\\\\\\\\
22
23
24
```

LAB 4

EXTENDED COMPANY INFORMATION BMS SCREEN DEFINITION

This screen will eventually be used by personnel company inquiry and company-update lab assignments. Define the screen title as two separate fields to allow these programs to vary the function being performed. Function values will be "INQUIRY" and "UPDATE." Set the initial value to "INQUIRY."

This assignment is similar to Lab 3. It requires seven additional fields to be defined. These fields are to the right of the data entry display fields. The purpose of these fields is to allow future lab assignments (programs) to display error messages or table look-up data. Define these fields as ASKIP,NORM. Use names such as ETMSG, LOMSG, DEMSG, JTMSG, POMSG, EDMSG, and ASMSG.

```
LINE                      <---COLUMN--->
I         1         2         3         4         5         6         7
V 12345678901234567890123456789012345678901234567890123456789012345678901234567890
01^\\\\\\\              ^COMPANY INFORMATION^INQUIRY
02
03^SSN:^\\\\\\\\\\
04^NAME:^\\\\\\\\\\\\\\\\\\\\\\\\\\\\\\
05
06
07  ^EMPLOYEE TYPE..^\\^              ^\\\\\\\\\\\\\\\\\\\\\\\\\\\\\\\\\\\\\\
08        ^LOCATION..^\\^             ^\\\\\\\\\\\\\\\\\\\\\\\\\\\\\\\\\\\\\\
09     ^DEPARTMENT..^\\\\^            ^\\\\\\\\\\\\\\\\\\\\\\\\\\\\\\\\\\\\\\
10
11      ^JOB TITLE..^\\\\\^           ^\\\\\\\\\\\\\\\\\\\\\\\\\\\\\\\\\\\\\\
12    ^POSITION NO..^\\\\\^           ^\\\\\\\\\\\\\\\\\\\\\\\\\\\\\\\\\\\\\\
13^EMPLOYMENT DATE..^\\\\\\^          ^\\\\\\\\\\\\\\\\\\\\\\\\\\\\\\\\\\\\\\
14
15   ^ANNUAL SALARY..^ZZZZ,ZZZ.99^    ^\\\\\\\\\\\\\\\\\\\\\\\\\\\\\\\\\\\\\\
16
17
18
19
20
21^MESSAGE:^\\\\\\\\\\\\\\\\\\\\\\\\\\\\\\\\\\\\\\\\\\\\\\\\\\\\\\\\\\\\\\\
22
23
24
```

6

BMS Mapping Operations

In this chapter you will

1. Learn how to use the BMS SEND MAP command to display formatted screens.
2. Learn how to use the BMS RECEIVE MAP command to receive formatted data into the program working-storage.
3. Understand how to process terminal input data after a BMS input mapping operation.
4. See how BMS mapping routines perform the needed padding and justification during input mapping operations.
5. Observe how BMS default attributes can be changed when BMS screens are displayed.
6. Understand the CICS/VS table requirements needed to perform BMS mapping operations.
7. Identify the problems associated with defining multiple maps in a BMS mapset.
8. Be able to distinguish between a BMS physical map and symbolic map.

In this chapter, you will learn how to perform BMS mapping operations. There are two types of mapping operations; output mapping and input mapping. Output mapping is the process of converting *device- and format-independent* data to a *device-dependent* data stream for transmission to a terminal. Input mapping is the process of converting a *device-dependent* data stream from a terminal to a *device-independent* format. BMS makes use of maps to perform these mapping functions. These BMS maps are produced from the map-definition statements you learned about in the last chapter.

The topics in this chapter will show you how to use the maps produced during the map-preparation process. First, you will see the layout of the symbolic description map. The symbolic map is the *visible* link between your application programs and BMS. An understanding of the layout and use of the symbolic map is essential to using BMS. After the symbolic map is described, you will learn how to perform output mapping operations. An inquiry program will be used to illustrate the basic output mapping process and some special output mapping functions. You will also see how to use output mapping to display a menu screen. After the output mapping topic, you will learn how to perform input mapping. The menu screen described in the last chapter will be used to demonstrate the input mapping process. But the programming illustrated in this chapter applies to other BMS screens. After studying this material you should be able to perform mapping operations for any application.

BMS Maps

In the last chapter you learned that BMS maps are generated by an off-line map-preparation process. A series of programming statements known as the map source is used to describe the layout of each application screen. Figure 6.1 depicts the map source (developed in the last chapter) for our sample

```
VENDSET   DFHMSD  TYPE=MAP,MODE=INOUT,LANG=COBOL,TIOAPFX=YES
MENUMAP   DFHMDI  SIZE=(24,80),LINE=1,COLUMN=1
SCODE     DFHMDF  POS=(01,01),LENGTH=07
          DFHMDF  POS=(01,67),LENGTH=04,INITIAL='DATE'
DATE      DFHMDF  POS=(01,72),LENGTH=08
          DFHMDF  POS=(02,14),LENGTH=19,                              C
                  ATTRB=(ASKIP,NORM),                                 C
                  INITIAL='VENDOR MASTER MENU'
          DFHMDF  POS=(02,67),LENGTH=04,INITIAL='TIME'
TIME      DFHMDF  POS=(02,72),LENGTH=08,PICOUT='99,99,99'
          DFHMDF  POS=(03,67),LENGTH=08,INITIAL='TERMINAL'
TERM      DFHMDF  POS=(03,76),LENGTH=04
          DFHMDF  POS=(05,09),LENGTH=26,                              C
                  INITIAL='PF1  DISPLAY MASTER RECORD'
          DFHMDF  POS=(07,09),LENGTH=26,                              C
                  INITIAL='PF2  UPDATE MASTER RECORD'
          DFHMDF  POS=(09,09),LENGTH=26,                              C
                  INITIAL='PF3  ADD MASTER RECORD'
          DFHMDF  POS=(11,09),LENGTH=26,                              C
                  INITIAL='PF4  DELETE MASTER RECORD'
          DFHMDF  POS=(13,09),LENGTH=26,                              C
                  INITIAL='PF5  BROWSE MASTER BY KEY'
          DFHMDF  POS=(15,09),LENGTH=26,                              C
                  INITIAL='PF9  EXIT MASTER MENU'
          DFHMDF  POS=(18,01),LENGTH=18,                              C
                  INITIAL='TYPE VENDOR NUMBER'
VENDID    DFHMDF  POS=(18,20),LENGTH=06,                              C
                  ATTRB=(IC,UNPROT,NUM,NORM,FSET),                    C
                  INITIAL='NNNNNN'
          DFHMDF  POS=(18,27),LENGTH=29,                              C
                  INITIAL='THEN PRESS APPROPRIATE PF KEY'
MMESAGE   DFHMDF  POS=(21,01),LENGTH=79
DISPMAP   DFHMDI  SIZE=(24,80),LINE=1,COLUMN=1
SCODE     DFHMDF  POS=(01,01),LENGTH=07
          DFHMDF  POS=(01,28),LENGTH=13,INITIAL='VENDOR MASTER'
DTYPE     DFHMDF  POS=(01,42),LENGTH=07,INITIAL='INQUIRY'
          DFHMDF  POS=(03,01),LENGTH=09,INITIAL='VENDOR ID'
VENDID    DFHMDF  POS=(03,13),LENGTH=06
          DFHMDF  POS=(04,13),LENGTH=11,INITIAL='VENDOR NAME'
VENNAME   DFHMDF  POS=(04,30),LENGTH=30,                              C
                  INITIAL='_____'
          DFHMDF  POS=(04,61),LENGTH=1,ATTRB=PROT
          DFHMDF  POS=(05,13),LENGTH=07,INITIAL='ADDRESS'
ADDR1     DFHMDF  POS=(05,30),LENGTH=30,ATTRB=FSET,                   C
                  INITIAL='_____'
          DFHMDF  POS=(05,61),LENGTH=1,ATTRB=PROT
ADDR2     DFHMDF  POS=(06,30),LENGTH=30,ATTRB=FSET,                   C
                  INITIAL='_____'
          DFHMDF  POS=(06,61),LENGTH=01,ATTRB=PROT
ADDR3     DFHMDF  POS=(07,30),LENGTH=30,ATTRB=FSET,                   C
                  INITIAL='_____'
          DFHMDF  POS=(07,61),LENGTH=01,ATTRB=PROT
ADDR4     DFHMDF  POS=(08,30),LENGTH=30,ATTRB=FSET,                   C
                  INITIAL='_____'
          DFHMDF  POS=(08,61),LENGTH=01,ATTRB=PROT
          DFHMDF  POS=(09,13),LENGTH=12,INITIAL='CONTACT NAME'
CONTAC    DFHMDF  POS=(09,30),LENGTH=30,ATTRB=FSET,                   C
                  INITIAL='_____'
          DFHMDF  POS=(09,61),LENGTH=01,ATTRB=PROT
          DFHMDF  POS=(10,13),LENGTH=09,INITIAL='TELEPHONE'
TELE      DFHMDF  POS=(10,30),LENGTH=12,ATTRB=FSET,                   C
                  INITIAL='_____'
          DFHMDF  POS=(10,43),LENGTH=01
          DFHMDF  POS=(12,13),LENGTH=06,INITIAL='TAX ID'
TAXID     DFHMDF  POS=(12,30),LENGTH=11,ATTRB=FSET,                   C
                  INITIAL='_____'
          DFHMDF  POS=(12,42),LENGTH=01
          DFHMDF  POS=(13,13),LENGTH=12,INITIAL='PAYMENT HOLD'
PAHOLD    DFHMDF  POS=(13,30),LENGTH=01,ATTRB=FSET,                   C
                  INITIAL='_'
          DFHMDF  POS=(13,32),LENGTH=01
          DFHMDF  POS=(14,13),LENGTH=12,INITIAL='PRODUCT CODE'
PRODUCT   DFHMDF  POS=(14,30),LENGTH=03                               C
                  INITIAL='___'
          DFHMDF  POS=(14,34),LENGTH=01,ATTRB=ASKIP
DMESAGE   DFHMDF  POS=(21,01),LENGTH=79
          DFHMSD  TYPE=FINAL
```

FIGURE 6.1. Map definition statements for sample screens (updated) (same as fig. 5.10)

menu and display screens. The map source contains the details about each field on each application screen. This map source is processed by a batch translator to produce the two BMS maps used during mapping operations. These maps are: the physical map and the symbolic description map.

PHYSICAL MAPS

The physical map is a *descriptive table* containing every detail about an application screen. A collection of physical maps can be stored together in a single mapset. Each mapset is cataloged in the CICS program library. The physical maps contained in the mapset, although stored in the program library, are not *executable* members. Instead, they are loaded by BMS during a mapping operation. The various details about the application screens can then be used by BMS to perform mapping operations.

Each physical map contains the attribute position, field length, and attribute values, for each field to appear on an application screen. It also contains the actual values for *constant* fields such as screen titles and field labels. Because these constants are stored in the physical map, they do not even appear within the COBOL application program. From the programming viewpoint, you never really *see* the physical maps. They are "visible" only to the BMS on-line mapping routines. The maps that you do *see* are the symbolic description maps.

SYMBOLIC DESCRIPTION MAPS

The symbolic description maps are cataloged in a system copy library (source statement library in VSE) during the map-generation process. To use these symbolic maps, you copy them into the working-storage section of the program during the COBOL compile process. The symbolic description map is simply a data structure providing COBOL field names used for mapping *variables* to and from the terminal. It is analogous to an input-output area for a file or data-base record.

COPY MEMBER LAYOUT

The contents of the COBOL copy member corresponds to the original map source. It will contain a map area for each map defined in the mapset. Let's use our sample mapset defined in the last chapter to illustrate the layout of the copy member. Figure 6.2 depicts the copybook for our sample display and menu screens. The general layout of this copy member is shown below. You can see that there is an *input* mapping area and an *output* mapping area for each screen definition. You will also notice that the second map area (DISPMAP) is a *redefinition* of the first mapping area. That is, the display map occupies the same storage as the menu map. If the STORAGE=AUTO option is specified in the mapset definition (DFHMSD) statement, each map will occupy separate storage (maps will not be redefined).

```
MENUMAPI
.
input mapping fields for the menu map
.
MENUMAPO REDEFINES MENUMAPI.
.
output mapping fields for the menu map
.
DISPMAPI REDEFINES MENUMAPI.
.
input mapping fields for the display map
.
DISPMAPO REDEFINES DISMAPI.
.
output mapping fields for the display map
.
```

```
01   MENUMAPI.                                      03 ADDR2A     PICTURE X.
     02  FILLER PIC X(12).                          02  ADDR2I PIC X(30).
     02  SCODEL    COMP PIC S9(4).                  02  ADDR3L    COMP PIC S9(4).
     02  SCODEF    PICTURE X.                        02  ADDR3F     PICTURE X.
     02  FILLER REDEFINES SCODEF.                    02  FILLER REDEFINES ADDR3F.
      03 SCODEA     PICTURE X.                          03 ADDR3A     PICTURE X.
     02  SCODEI PIC X(7).                            02  ADDR3I PIC X(30).
     02  DATEL     COMP PIC S9(4).                   02  ADDR4L    COMP PIC S9(4).
     02  DATEF    PICTURE X.                         02  ADDR4F     PICTURE X.
     02  FILLER REDEFINES DATEF.                     02  FILLER REDEFINES ADDR4F.
      03 DATEA     PICTURE X.                           03 ADDR4A     PICTURE X.
     02  DATEI PIC X(8).                             02  ADDR4I PIC X(30).
     02  TIMEL     COMP PIC S9(4).                   02  CONTACL    COMP PIC S9(4).
     02  TIMEF    PICTURE X.                         02  CONTACF    PICTURE X.
     02  FILLER REDEFINES TIMEF.                     02  FILLER REDEFINES CONTACF.
      03 TIMEA     PICTURE X.                           03 CONTACA     PICTURE X.
     02  TIMEI PIC X(8).                             02  CONTACI PIC X(30).
     02  TERML     COMP PIC S9(4).                   02  TELEL     COMP PIC S9(4).
     02  TERMF    PICTURE X.                         02  TELEF    PICTURE X.
     02  FILLER REDEFINES TERMF.                     02  FILLER REDEFINES TELEF.
      03 TERMA     PICTURE X.                           03 TELEA     PICTURE X.
     02  TERMI PIC X(4).                             02  TELEI PIC X(12).
     02  VENDIDL   COMP PIC S9(4).                   02  TAXIDL    COMP PIC S9(4).
     02  VENDIDF    PICTURE X.                        02  TAXIDF    PICTURE X.
     02  FILLER REDEFINES VENDIDF.                    02  FILLER REDEFINES TAXIDF.
      03 VENDIDA     PICTURE X.                          03 TAXIDA     PICTURE X.
     02  VENDIDI PIC X(6).                           02  TAXIDI PIC X(11).
     02  MMESAGEL   COMP PIC S9(4).                  02  PAHOLDL    COMP PIC S9(4).
     02  MMESAGEF    PICTURE X.                       02  PAHOLDF    PICTURE X.
     02  FILLER REDEFINES MMESAGEF.                   02  FILLER REDEFINES PAHOLDF.
      03 MMESAGEA     PICTURE X.                         03 PAHOLDA     PICTURE X.
     02  MMESAGEI PIC X(79).                         02  PAHOLDI PIC X(1).
01   MENUMAPO REDEFINES MENUMAPI.                    02  PRODUCTL    COMP PIC S9(4).
     02  FILLER PIC X(12).                           02  PRODUCTF    PICTURE X.
     02  FILLER PICTURE X(3).                        02  FILLER REDEFINES PRODUCTF.
     02  SCODEO PIC X(7).                               03 PRODUCTA     PICTURE X.
     02  FILLER PICTURE X(3).                        02  PRODUCTI PIC X(3).
     02  DATEO PIC X(8).                             02  DMESAGEL    COMP PIC S9(4).
     02  FILLER PICTURE X(3).                        02  DMESAGEF    PICTURE X.
     02  TIMEO PIC 99,99,99.                         02  FILLER REDEFINES DMESAGEF.
     02  FILLER PICTURE X(3).                           03 DMESAGEA     PICTURE X.
     02  TERMO PIC X(4).                             02  DMESAGEI PIC X(79).
     02  FILLER PICTURE X(3).                   01  DISPMAPO REDEFINES DISPMAPI.
     02  VENDIDO PIC X(6).                           02  FILLER PIC X(12).
     02  FILLER PICTURE X(3).                        02  FILLER PICTURE X(3).
     02  MMESAGEO PIC X(79).                         02  SCODEO PIC X(7).
01   DISPMAPI REDEFINES MENUMAPI.                    02  FILLER PICTURE X(3).
     02  FILLER PIC X(12).                           02  UPTYPEO PIC X(7).
     02  SCODEL    COMP PIC S9(4).                   02  FILLER PICTURE X(3).
     02  SCODEF    PICTURE X.                         02  VENDIDO PIC X(6).
     02  FILLER REDEFINES SCODEF.                    02  FILLER PICTURE X(3).
      03 SCODEA     PICTURE X.                        02  VENNAMEO PIC X(30).
     02  SCODEI PIC X(7).                            02  FILLER PICTURE X(3).
     02  UPTYPEL   COMP PIC S9(4).                   02  ADDR1O PIC X(30).
     02  UPTYPEF    PICTURE X.                        02  FILLER PICTURE X(3).
     02  FILLER REDEFINES UPTYPEF.                    02  ADDR2O PIC X(30).
      03 UPTYPEA     PICTURE X.                       02  FILLER PICTURE X(3).
     02  UPTYPEI PIC X(7).                           02  ADDR3O PIC X(30).
     02  VENDIDL   COMP PIC S9(4).                   02  FILLER PICTURE X(3).
     02  VENDIDF    PICTURE X.                        02  ADDR4O PIC X(30).
     02  FILLER REDEFINES VENDIDF.                    02  FILLER PICTURE X(3).
      03 VENDIDA     PICTURE X.                       02  CONTACO PIC X(30).
     02  VENDIDI PIC X(6).                           02  FILLER PICTURE X(3).
     02  VENNAMEL   COMP PIC S9(4).                  02  TELEO PIC X(12).
     02  VENNAMEF    PICTURE X.                       02  FILLER PICTURE X(3).
     02  FILLER REDEFINES VENNAMEF.                   02  TAXIDO PIC X(11).
      03 VENNAMEA     PICTURE X.                       02  FILLER PICTURE X(3).
     02  VENNAMEI PIC X(30).                         02  PAHOLDO PIC X(1).
     02  ADDR1L    COMP PIC S9(4).                   02  FILLER PICTURE X(3).
     02  ADDR1F    PICTURE X.                         02  PRODUCTO PIC X(3).
     02  FILLER REDEFINES ADDR1F.                     02  FILLER PICTURE X(3).
      03 ADDR1A     PICTURE X.                         02  DMESAGEO PIC X(79).
     02  ADDR1I PIC X(30).
     02  ADDR2L    COMP PIC S9(4).
     02  ADDR2F    PICTURE X.
     02  FILLER REDEFINES ADDR2F.
```

FIGURE 6.2.   Copy book containing Symbolic Maps

For each map there is an input mapping area and an output mapping area. The input mapping area is defined first, then redefined with the output mapping area. These mapping areas will always occupy the same storage (redefined) even if STORAGE=AUTO is not specified. Let's look at each of these mapping areas.

INPUT MAP AREA

Let's examine the input mapping area for our sample menu screen. The first statement in the symbolic map is

```
01   MENUMAPI.
```

This is the extended map name for the screen. The symbolic name is a derivative of original map name "MENUMAP." The extended map name is provided so you can refer to all fields in the data structure at once. For example, prior to an input mapping operation, you could initialize this area to low-values as follows:

```
MOVE LOW-VALUES TO MENUMAPI.
```

Next, we find a 12-byte filler. You should find this filler in all maps that are used with command-level programs. It's not important to know why it is there; it is only important to know that it should be. When testing your programs, if some of the variables look out of place on the screen, check for this filler in the COBOL listing. If it is missing, the map should be regenerated using the TIOAPFX=YES option in the DFHMSD statement.

The input mapping area then contains groups of fields that correspond to each variable field on the screen. The fields in the data structure directly correspond to the *variable* fields on the application screen. Please refer to figure 6.3. This figure depicts our sample menu screen again with a circle around the variable content fields. You will notice that each circled field on the screen corresponds to fields in the data structure. For instance, the input map area contains these definitions:

```
02   SCODEL
02   SCODEF
02   SCODEA
02   SCODEI

02   DATEL
02   DATEF
02   DATEA
02   DATEI
```

These fields are used by the COBOL program for mapping the screen variables. For each screen variable there is a subfield with a different suffix character. The use of each suffixed field in the input map area is as follows:

Suffix-L This is a two-byte computational (binary) field. After an input mapping operation this subfield contains the number of characters transmitted for this data variable. This data-length field is sometimes used by the application program to determine if the field was transmitted. A value of zero indicates that the input field was *not* mapped in from the terminal. It can also signal that the field was modified to nulls (by pressing the erase input or erase input key). A positive value in this field indicates that characters have been received for the field. The value shows the actual number of characters in the incoming field.

This field can also be used for output mapping operations to specify the initial cursor position on the screen. This process will be described later in the chapter under the topic *Symbolic Cursor Positioning*.

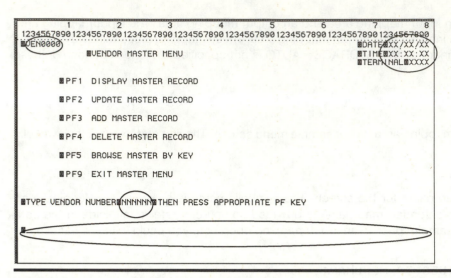

```
         1         2         3         4         5         6         7         8
1234567890123456789012345678901234567890123456789012345678901234567890123456789 00
VEN0000           VENDOR MASTER MENU                          DATE XX/XX/XX
                                                             TIME XX:XX:XX
                                                             TERMINAL XXXX

          PF1  DISPLAY MASTER RECORD

          PF2  UPDATE MASTER RECORD

          PF3  ADD MASTER RECORD

          PF4  DELETE MASTER RECORD

          PF5  BROWSE MASTER BY KEY

          PF9  EXIT MASTER MENU


TYPE VENDOR NUMBER NNNNNN THEN PRESS APPROPRIATE PF KEY
```

FIGURE 6.3. Menu Screen with Variable Fields Circled

Suffix-F This field can be used after an input mapping operation. BMS uses this field to *flag* unusual actions taken by the operator. There is only one "unusual" action flag when using an IBM 3270 terminal. It occurs when an operator sets an unmodified field to a modified state by erasing it with the erase EOF key. This action rarely occurs and you may never use this subfield. It is available in case this special circumstance must be tested by your program. The field will contain low-values under normal conditions. Any other value "flags" the unusual action.

Suffix-A This is a one-byte code that may be used during *output* mapping operations. Its purpose is to allow the program to change the field attribute for a field being mapped to the terminal. This subfield seems to be misplaced here in the input mapping area since it is used only during mapping. There is probably some purpose to its placement here, but I cannot explain IBM's logic in this case. I will discuss the use of this field later in the chapter.

Suffix-I These input fields correspond to the actual variable fields on the application screen. After an input mapping operation, each input subfield will contain the related field data transmitted from the terminal. The underlying purpose of input mapping is this process of moving modified fields from the various screen areas to these fields in the input map area.

Each input field contains a COBOL picture clause corresponding to the size of the data area on the screen. The picture clause is determined by the field-definition statements specified during map generation. It is usually: PICTURE X(nn) where nn is the length of the field as defined in the DFHMDF statement. If the PICIN option was used when defining a field, the input field will use that picture clause instead of the PIC X(nn) clause.

OUTPUT MAP AREA

Now let's look at the output mapping area. The output mapping area will immediately follow the input mapping area. As indicated by the COBOL REDEFINES clause provided by BMS, the output mapping area is a redefinition of the input mapping area. The statements in the output mapping area are as follows:

```
01  MENUMAPO REDEFINES MENUMAPI.
```

MENUMAPO is the extended map name for the screen. It is a derivative of original map name, "MENUMAP." The extended map name is provided so you can refer to all fields in the data structure at once. For instance, to "initialize" the area, you could use the statement

```
MOVE LOW-VALUES TO MENUMAPO.
```

Next, we find the twelve-byte filler caused by the TIOAPFX option in the mapset definition statements. Once again, it's not important to know why it is there; it is only important to know that it should be.

The output mapping area then contains groups of fields that correspond to each variable field on the screen. These output fields are used by the COBOL program for mapping the screen variables. For instance,

```
02   FILLER PIC X(3).
02   SCODEO PIC X(7).

02   FILLER PIC X(3).
02   DATEO PIC X(8).
```

Each "FILLER" field corresponds to the Suffix-L, and Suffix-F (also A) in the input map area. This filler is placed here so the Suffix-O fields will share the same storage area as the Suffix-I fields from the input map area. There is a good reason for this overlapping structure. I will describe this in more detail later in the chapter (p. 127).

Suffix-O These output fields correspond to the actual *variable* fields on the application screen. Prior to issuing an output mapping operation, the program will move field data to be transmitted to the Suffix-O fields.

BMS Mapping

Now that you know the layout of the symbolic description maps, let's discuss the programming requirements needed to perform mapping operations. You will recall that there are two mapping processes. These are *output mapping* and *input mapping*. Since mapping involves the process of transferring information to or from the application program, it stands to reason that a mapping area must be reserved in the program storage. The symbolic description map is the means used to accomplish this transfer. The purpose of the symbolic map is to provide a target area for the mapping process. The first programming step in writing a program that will perform BMS mapping is to copy the symbolic map into working-storage. This is done with the COBOL COPY statement. The COPY statement specifies the copybook name where the symbolic maps are stored. For example,

```
COPY VENDSET [SUPPRESS].
```

It doesn't matter where the COPY statement occurs, as long as it is in working-storage. I prefer to copy it in just *before* the Linkage Section. The field-definition statements in the symbolic description maps sometimes fill several pages on the compile listing. It's best to put them out of the way of the more "important" working-storage fields. Another way to reduce the cluttering effect of these statements would be to include the SUPPRESS option of the COPY statement. This option will totally eliminate the copybook from printing in your listings. Anyway, after you have copied the symbolic description map into the working-storage, you can proceed to the Procedure Division. This is where you will provide the mapping *logic.* We will first look at the output mapping process, then at the input mapping process.

Output Mapping

Output mapping is the process of transferring device-independent data from our application program to the terminal. In other words, output mapping is used to display information on a terminal. For this output mapping example, I am going to use the display map defined in the last chapter. The programming statements will display information from our sample vendor master record shown below. For this example assume that a program has already read a record from the master file into this area.

```
01    VENDOR-RECORD.
      05    VENDOR-NAME             PIC X(30).
      05    VENDOR-ID               PIC XXXXXX.
      05    VENDOR-ADDR1            PIC X(30).
      05    VENDOR-ADDR2            PIC X(30).
      05    VENDOR-ADDR3            PIC X(30).
      05    VENDOR-ADDR4            PIC X(30).
      05    VENDOR-CONTACT          PIC X(30).
      05    VENDOR-TELE             PIC X(12).
      05    VENDOR-TAXID            PIC X(11).
      05    VENDOR-YTD-SALES        PIC S9(7)V99 COMP-3.
      05    VENDOR-YTD-PAYMENTS     PIC S9(7)V99 COMP-3.
      05    VENDOR-YTD-DISCOUNTS    PIC S9(7)V99 COMP-3.
      05    VENDOR-PAY-HOLD         PIC X.
      05    VENDOR-PRODUCT          PIC XXX.
      05    VENDOR-LAST-CHECK       PIC S9(5) COMP-3.
      05    VENDOR-LAST-CK-DATE     PIC S9(5) COMP-3.
      05    VENDOR-LAST-CK-AMT      PIC S9(7)V99 COMP-3.
      05    VENDOR-DATEA            PIC S9(5) COMP-3.
      05    VENDOR-DATEC            PIC S9(5) COMP-3.
      05    VENDOR-OPE              PIC XXX.
      05    VENDOR-UPDCNT           PIC 9.
```

Only three steps are needed to perform an output mapping operation. These steps are

1. Initialize the symbolic description map.
2. Format the symbolic description map.
3. Issue the BMS SEND MAP command.

INITIALIZE THE SYMBOLIC DESCRIPTION MAP

When preparing to build an output screen for the first time, the symbolic description map must be *initialized*. This initialization is necessary since the fields in the cataloged symbolic maps do not contain a *value* clause. They may therefore contain unknown values (garbage) resulting from CICS loading the program over a previously used area. The symbolic description map is initialized by moving low-values to the extended name for the map. The statement below would initialize our sample display map.

```
      MOVE LOW-VALUES TO DISMAPO.
```

In some installations a Linkage Editor statement is used to specify that all areas without a value clause are set to low-values. If this system option is used, the statement above is not necessary. Just remember, it's better to be safe than sorry. This move statement doesn't cost much in CPU time. Once the data structure has been initialized, the program will move the data to be mapped into the output subfields. I call this *formatting* the symbolic map.

FORMAT THE SYMBOLIC DESCRIPTION MAP

After initializing the map area, data values are copied into the symbolic field names. These values may come from working-storage areas, such as our vendor record, from the EIB fields, or from other sources. Sometimes even literals are moved into the symbolic map fields. For our display screen we have mapping fields defined for the screen identification, the screen title, and the display fields from the master record. The COBOL statements below would be used to format the symbolic map.

```
MOVE 'VEN1001' TO SCODEO IN DISMAPO.
MOVE 'INQUIRY' TO DTYPEO.
MOVE VENDOR-NAME TO VENNAMEO IN DISMAPO.
MOVE VENDOR-ID TO VENDIDO IN DISMAPO.
MOVE VENDOR-ADDR1 to ADDR1O IN DISMAPO.
(additional MOVE statements here)
```

After the symbolic description map is formatted, a BMS output mapping operation can be performed. This is done by issuing a SEND MAP command. When the SEND MAP command is issued by the application program, the on-line BMS mapping routines will scan and inspect each field in the symbolic description map. For each field that contains data (not low-values), BMS will use it in the mapping operation. If however, the field contains low-values, BMS will skip over the area and move on to the next field in the map. From the application viewpoint this makes the output mapping process simple and straightforward, and device-independent! To display a data field you only have to copy it to the corresponding field in the symbolic description map prior to issuing the SEND MAP command.

THE SEND MAP COMMAND

The format of the command is

```
EXEC CICS SEND MAP (name)
          [MAPSET (name)]
          [ERASE | ERASEAUP]
          [FREEKB]
          [FRSET]
          [ALARM]
          [CURSOR [(data-value)]]
          [MAPONLY | DATAONLY]
          END-EXEC
```

MAP (name) refers to the name of the map containing the field definitions for this screen. In our sample application the map name is DISPMAP.

MAPSET (name) refers to the "program" name where the *physical map* is stored. This option is required unless the MAPSET name is the same as the MAP name argument. A PPT entry must exist for this name since BMS must load the mapset from the load library. The mapset name VENDSET would be specified here for our sample inquiry application.

ERASE causes the screen to be cleared prior to sending the new screen.

ERASEAUP causes all unprotected fields to be erased before sending the new screen. Protected (and ASKIP) fields will not be erased. This option is normally used with data entry applications.

The CURSOR option is used to specify the initial cursor location on the screen. If used, it will override the initial cursor placement defined in the map. The data-value can be a constant, or a COBOL field defined as S9999 with computational form. The value is relative to position zero; that is, row 1, column 1 on the screen is equivalent to position 0. If the CURSOR option is used without the argument, BMS will use symbolic cursor positioning. This feature is described later in the chapter.

The **MAPONLY** option specifies that BMS is only to use the information from the physical map to display the screen. No variables will be mapped from the program if this option is used. Sometimes screens can be constructed completely from constants stored in the physical map. A "help screen," for instance, might fall into this category.

The **DATAONLY** option specifies that constants from the physical map are *not* to be transmitted to the terminal. When this option is used, only the variables from the symbolic map will be transmitted. This option is generally used with data entry-type screens along with the ERASEAUP option. Chapter 8 will discuss how this option can be used to provide for more efficient data transmission when using the IBM 3270 terminal.

The other options control certain functions of the terminal. They perform similar actions to the CTLCHAR option of the SEND command discussed in chapter 3. These options are

FREEKB will cause the keyboard of the display to be unlocked when the SEND MAP command is issued by the program. If this option is not specified, the keyboard remains locked after operator input, until the operator depresses the RESET key on the keyboard. You will usually want to include this option when a screen is displayed. On some rare occasions, as when a critical error message is being displayed, you might omit FREEKB. This action would require the operator to press the reset key to "acknowledge" the message. If you do omit the FREEKB option, be sure to include a message prompt to tell the operator to press the reset key.

ALARM activates the audible alarm of the display unit. Again, this feature might be used to signal an error condition to the operator. Overuse of this option tends to distract terminal operators. This problem may be compounded when several data entry operators are clustered together in a small work space.

FRSET specifies that the modified data tags (MDTs) of all fields currently in the 3270 buffer are to be reset to a not-modified state before the map data is written. This option is used with data entry-type screens. It can be used with certain programming techniques to reduce the amount of incoming data from a terminal. Since these techniques tend to be more difficult, most installations do not use this option. This text does not expound on these more difficult (less used) techniques.

EXCEPTIONAL CONDITIONS

Exceptional conditions very rarely occur for the SEND MAP command. There is one condition that you might want to handle prior to issuing this command. It is INVMPSZ. INVMPSZ will occur if the specified map is too wide for the terminal. This condition will only occur if your map has been designed for use only on a "wide-screen" terminal such as the IBM 3270 model 5 and the transaction is running on a standard 80-column terminal. A standard-size map can be used on a standard terminal or a wide terminal. You cannot however, use a wide-screen map on a standard-size terminal. If you do, INVMPSZ will occur. This condition may also occur during initial testing if you have made a coding error specifying incorrect map size on the BMS map-definition statement.

CODING EXAMPLE

Basic output mapping is actually a fairly simple process. All you have to do is initialize the symbolic map, format its data to be displayed, then issue the SEND MAP command. Here is the coding necessary to read our vendor master record and display fields on a terminal using the sample display map.

```
EXEC CICS READ
     DATASET ('VENFILE')
     RIDFLD (VENDOR-ID)
     INTO (VENDOR-RECORD)
     LENGTH (VENDOR-RECORD-LENGTH)
     END-EXEC.
```

```
MOVE LOW-VALUES TO DISPMAPO.
MOVE 'VEN1001' TO SCODEO IN DISMAPO.
MOVE VENDOR-NAME TO VENNAMEO IN DISMAPO.
MOVE VENDOR-ID TO VENDIDO IN DISPMAPO.
MOVE VENDOR-ADDR1 TO ADDR10 IN DISPMAPO.
MOVE VENDOR-ADDR2 TO ADDR20 IN DISPMAPO.
MOVE VENDOR-ADDR3 TO ADDR30 IN DISPMAPO.
MOVE VENDOR-ADDR4 TO ADDR40 IN DISPMAPO.
MOVE VENDOR-CONTACT TO CONTACTO IN DISPMAPO.
MOVE VENDOR-TELE TO TELEO IN DISPMAPO.
MOVE VENDOR-TAXID TO TAXIDO IN DISPMAPO.
MOVE VENDOR-PAY-HOLD TO PAHOLDO IN DISPMAPO.
MOVE VENDOR-PRODUCT TO PRODUCTO IN DISPMAPO.
EXEC CICS SEND MAP ('DISPMAP')
     MAPSET ('VENDSET')
     ERASE
     FREEKB
     END-EXEC.
```

OUTPUT MAPPING FEATURES

Let's look at some additional features that can be used when performing BMS output mapping operations. First we will look at how your program can use default data stored in the physical map. We will then see how to override the attribute for a field temporarily. Finally, you will see how to use symbolic cursor positioning. After these topics, we will move on to the input mapping topics.

MAPPING DEFAULT DATA

During output mapping operations, it is possible to transmit *default* data for any variable field in the symbolic map. Default data is stored in the physical map during map generation by using the INITIAL=option in the field-definition statement. Our variable title field on the display map contains default data. This field was defined as follows:

```
DTYPE DFHMDF POS=(01,42),LENGTH=07,INITIAL='INQUIRY'
```

When a variable field is defined this way, BMS may use the default data from the physical map during output mapping. Any data moved into the symbolic map takes precedence over this default data. Recall the output mapping process described earlier. BMS scans the symbolic map during an output mapping operation, searching for data to transmit to the terminal. It skips over any field containing low-values. But prior to moving on to the next field, BMS will first search the physical map for this field to determine if any default data should be sent to the terminal.

For our screen title, if the field DTYPEO contains low-values at the time of an output mapping operation, BMS will use the default value of INQUIRY. The inquiry program would not have to map this literal from the program. The update, add, or delete program can still override the default value. For example, the update program could include the statement below.

```
MOVE 'UPDATE' TO DTYPEO IN DISPMAPO.
```

Other fields with default values appear in our sample display screen. Notice how each data entry field is defined with the underline (_) character. These default values will provide a data entry *template* when used by the add program. That program will simply move low-values to the map area to have BMS display the underline characters. As you can see, this feature adds to the flexibility of BMS. Now, let's examine another useful feature.

3270 ATTRIBUTE BYTES

	UNPROT				ASKIP		PROT	
	NUMERIC	NUMERIC FSET		FSET		FSET		FSET
NORM	&	J	ƀ	A	0	1	-	/
BRT	Q	R	H	I	8	9	Y	z
DRK	*	)	(	(	@	'	%	_

FIGURE 6.4. 3270 attribute graphics

MODIFYING FIELD ATTRIBUTES

Each field mapped to the IBM 3270 terminal will take on a set of attributes. The attributes of visability, protection, and character content are defined for each field during map generation. These *default* attributes are stored in the physical map. The stored attribute code for each field is transmitted along with the field content during the output mapping process. In most cases, the attribute for a given field will not change from one display to another. There are times, however when you may want to override the default attribute for a given field.

Let's use the sample display screen to illustrate a situation where we might want to change a field's attribute. You might recall that many of the fields on our sample display screen are defined with the UNPROT, and FSET attributes. This is fine for update programs, but usually all fields on an inquiry screen are made protected. In this way, the operator will not attempt to key into the inquiry fields.

It is possible to override the attributes for all variable fields that are mapped from the program. This is done by moving a correct attribute value to the symbolic description map. This value is moved to the attribute subfield (Suffix-A) in the symbolic description map. The attribute subfield is defined as PIC X. By moving a correct attribute code to the symbolic map prior to sending the map to the terminal, you are informing BMS that the default attribute is not to be used. During the mapping process, BMS will inspect the attribute subfield (Suffix-A), as it does with the output data fields. If the field contains low-values, BMS will use the default attribute stored in the physical map; anything else will be treated as a new attribute code and will temporarily override the default.

The one-byte code moved to the attribute subfield represents a combination of several attributes. Each bit location of the attribute character is used to determine the attribute settings. The various combinations of attribute bits result in a series of graphic (displayable) characters. Figure 6.4 illustrates the graphics for the most commonly used attributes.

Let's return to our example of protecting the fields on the display screen. Let's set the attribute of each of these to ASKIP,NORM. To cause these attributes to be mapped along with the data field, the application program could include the following statements in the Procedure Division:

```
MOVE '0' TO VENNAMEA IN DISPMAPI.
MOVE '0' TO ADDR1A IN DISPMAPI.
MOVE '0' TO ADDR2A IN DISPMAPI.
MOVE '0' TO ADDR3A IN DISPMAPI.
(other MOVE statements)
```

```
01      DFHBMSCA.
    02    DFHBMPEM   PICTURE X    VALUE   IS   '1'.
    02    DFHBMPNL   PICTURE X    VALUE   IS   '-'.
    02    DFHBMASK   PICTURE X    VALUE   IS   '0'.
    02    DFHBMUNP   PICTURE X    VALUE   IS   ' '.
    02    DFHBMUNN   PICTURE X    VALUE   IS   '&'.
    02    DFHBMPRO   PICTURE X    VALUE   IS   '-'.
    02    DFHBMBRY   PICTURE X    VALUE   IS   'H'.
    02    DFHBMDAR   PICTURE X    VALUE   IS   '<'.
    02    DFHBMFSE   PICTURE X    VALUE   IS   'A'.
    02    DFHBMPRF   PICTURE X    VALUE   IS   '/'.
    02    DFHBMASF   PICTURE X    VALUE   IS   '1'.
    02    DFHBMASB   PICTURE X    VALUE   IS   '8'.
    02    DFHBMEOF   PICTURE X    VALUE   IS   '{'.
    02    DFHBMDET   PICTURE X    VALUE   IS   ' '.
    02    DFHSA      PICTURE X    VALUE   IS   '8'.
    02    DFHCOLOR   PICTURE X    VALUE   IS   '!'.
    02    DFHPS      PICTURE X    VALUE   IS   '"'.
    02    DFHHLT     PICTURE X    VALUE   IS   ' '.
    02    DFH3270    PICTURE X    VALUE   IS   '{'.
    02    DFHVAL     PICTURE X    VALUE   IS   'A'.
    02    DFHALL     PICTURE X    VALUE   IS   ' '.
    02    DFHERROR   PICTURE X    VALUE   IS   '"'.
    02    DFHDFT     PICTURE X    VALUE   IS   ' '.
    02    DFHDFCOL   PICTURE X    VALUE   IS   ' '.
    02    DFHBLUE    PICTURE X    VALUE   IS   '1'.
    02    DFHRED     PICTURE X    VALUE   IS   '2'.
    02    DFHPINK    PICTURE X    VALUE   IS   '3'.
    02    DFHGREEN   PICTURE X    VALUE   IS   '4'.
    02    DFHTURQ    PICTURE X    VALUE   IS   '5'.
    02    DFHYELLO   PICTURE X    VALUE   IS   '6'.
    02    DFHNEUTR   PICTURE X    VALUE   IS   '7'.
    02    DFHBASE    PICTURE X    VALUE   IS   ' '.
    02    DFHDFHI    PICTURE X    VALUE   IS   ' '.
    02    DFHBLINK   PICTURE X    VALUE   IS   '1'.
    02    DFHREVRS   PICTURE X    VALUE   IS   '2'.
    02    DFHUNDLN   PICTURE X    VALUE   IS   '4'.
    02    DFHMFIL    PICTURE X    VALUE   IS   '#'.
    02    DFHMENT    PICTURE X    VALUE   IS   '!'.
    02    DFHMFE     PICTURE X    VALUE   IS   '%'.
    02    DFHUNNOD   PICTURE X    VALUE   IS   '('.
    02    DFHUNIMD   PICTURE X    VALUE   IS   'I'.
    02    DFHUNNUM   PICTURE X    VALUE   IS   'J'.
    02    DFHUNINT   PICTURE X    VALUE   IS   'R'.
    02    DFHUNNON   PICTURE X    VALUE   IS   ')'.
    02    DFHPROTI   PICTURE X    VALUE   IS   'Y'.
    02    DFHPROTN   PICTURE X    VALUE   IS   '%'.
    02    DFHMT      PICTURE X    VALUE   IS   ' '.
    02    DFHMFT     PICTURE X    VALUE   IS   '$'.
    02    DFHMET     PICTURE X    VALUE   IS   '"'.
    02    DFHMFET    PICTURE X    VALUE   IS   '&'.
```

FIGURE 6.5.   DFHBMSCA Copybook

THE DFHBMSCA COPYBOOK

Each of the attribute combinations can be produced by moving a literal (from figure 6.4) as shown in the last example. But the use of literals may present some problems when developing or debugging a program. This is because it is difficult to decipher a graphic back to the attribute combinations. To solve this problem of using literals, IBM has provided a copybook containing symbolic names for many of the attribute characters. The copybook named DFHBMSCA (BMS control characters and attributes) is shown in figure 6.5. Names for most of the standard attribute codes can be found in this copybook. For instance, the name for the ASKIP,NORM (not FSET) attributes is DFHBMASK. If you wanted to use the IBM attributes copybook instead of using a literal to protect the data entry fields, you would first COPY the IBM copybook into the working-storage section, then code statements like the one below:

```
MOVE DFHBMASK TO VENNAMEA IN DISPMAPI.
```

```
01   STANDARD-BMS-ATTRIBUTES.
     02   UNPROT-NORM              PIC X VALUE SPACE.
     02   UNPROT-BRT               PIC X VALUE 'H'.
     02   UNPROT-DRK               PIC X VALUE '<'.
     02   UNPROT-FSET-NORM         PIC X VALUE 'A'.
     02   UNPROT-FSET-BRT          PIC X VALUE 'I'.
     02   UNPROT-FSET-DRK          PIC X VALUE '('.
     02   UNPROT-NUM-NORM          PIC X VALUE '&'.
     02   UNPROT-NUM-BRT           PIC X VALUE 'Q'.
     02   UNPROT-NUM-DRK           PIC X VALUE '*'.
     02   UNPROT-NUM-FSET-NORM     PIC X VALUE 'J'.
     02   UNPROT-NUM-FSET-BRT      PIC X VALUE 'R'.
     02   UNPROT-NUM-FSET-DRK      PIC X VALUE ')'.
     02   PROT-NORM                PIC X VALUE '-'.
     02   PROT-BRT                 PIC X VALUE 'Y'.
     02   PROT-DRK                 PIC X VALUE '%'.
     02   PROT-FSET-NORM           PIC X VALUE '/'.
     02   PROT-FSET-BRT            PIC X VALUE 'Z'.
     02   PROT-FSET-DRK            PIC X VALUE '_'.
     02   ASKIP-NORM               PIC X VALUE '0'.
     02   ASKIP-BRT                PIC X VALUE '8'.
     02   ASKIP-DRK                PIC X VALUE '@'.
     02   ASKIP-FSET-NORM          PIC X VALUE '1'.
     02   ASKIP-FSET-BRT           PIC X VALUE '9'.
     02   ASKIP-FSET-DRK           PIC X VALUE QUOTE.
     02   HILIGHT-DEFAULT          PIC X VALUE LOW-VALUE.
     02   HILIGHT-BLINK            PIC X VALUE '1'.
     02   HILIGHT-REVERSE          PIC X VALUE '2'.
     02   HILIGHT-UNDERSCORE       PIC X VALUE '4'.
     02   COLOR-DEFAULT            PIC X VALUE LOW-VALUE.
     02   COLOR-BLUE               PIC X VALUE '1'.
     02   COLOR-RED                PIC X VALUE '2'.
     02   COLOR-PINK               PIC X VALUE '3'.
     02   COLOR-GREEN              PIC X VALUE '4'.
     02   COLOR-TURKUOISE          PIC X VALUE '5'.
     02   COLOR-YELLOW             PIC X VALUE '6'.
     02   COLOR-WHITE              PIC X VALUE '7'.
```

FIGURE 6.6.   User defined attribute names

There is only one problem with the IBM-supplied copybook: the symbolic names are somewhat obscure. IBM had originally developed this copybook for Assembler language programmers. In that language, symbolic names are limited to eight characters in length. It's difficult to come up with a good mnemonic for two and three combinations of attributes, especially when you reserve three of the eight characters for the CICS prefix DFH. For compatability reasons, IBM decided to use the same symbolic names for COBOL. Many installations, however prefer not to use the IBM copybook. Instead, they develop field names of their own that are not so cryptic. Figure 6.6 illustrates a sample copybook that could be used to replace the standard BMS names. If you decide to use this copybook or develop your own, keep in mind that other installations will probably have their own version with different field names. Someday IBM will probably develop its own standardized version that everyone will use; but it may be a long time.

SYMBOLIC CURSOR POSITIONING

There is one final output mapping feature that I should discuss here, at least briefly. It is symbolic cursor positioning. This feature allows the *program* to specify the cursor position when a screen is displayed. In chapter 5, you learned that the initial position of the cursor can be defined with the BMS field-definition statement. The IC (insert cursor) keyword, when specified in the attribute option, defines the static position of the cursor when the screen is displayed. Symbolic cursor positioning provides an easy way to *override* this static cursor position during output mapping.

To use symbolic cursor positioning, you specify the CURSOR option on the BMS SEND MAP command. For example,

```
EXEC CICS
      SEND MAP ('DISPMAP')
      MAPSET ('VENDSET')
      CURSOR
      END-EXEC.
```

Prior to issuing the command, you must *mark* the field in the symbolic description map that will have the cursor positioned over it. To mark a field, you move the value of minus one (−1) to the length subfield (field name with Suffix-L). For instance, the statement

```
MOVE -1 TO VENNAMEL IN DISPMAPI.
```

would mark the vendor name field for use with the SEND MAP command with the CURSOR option. On output, BMS positions the cursor over the first character of the field. Symbolic cursor positioning can be used with any program, but it is most useful when used with the update and add programs. Later, in chapter 8, you will see how the update program can benefit from this feature. Now, it's time for an example.

OUTPUT MAPPING EXAMPLE

The topics that you have just studied illustrate the most commonly used features of BMS. All of the examples were related to our sample display screen. Now let's look at a complete inquiry program. Figure 6.7 depicts an inquiry program that displays information from our sample vendor master file. If you look back to chapter 4, you will see that most of the logic in this program has not changed. Instead, only the method of displaying the information has been modified. The first change occurs in the working-storage section. Instead of the line images used by the SEND TEXT commands, there is a single COPY statement for the symbolic description map. Then in the Procedure Division the mapping statements have replaced the SEND TEXT ACCUM and SEND PAGE commands. With only a few simple programming changes, we now have a complete inquiry program.

This concludes our discussion of BMS output mapping. These mapping procedures that you have just studied will be used with many other programs. In fact most programs perform output mapping. If you understand these concepts and programming techniques, you have reached another important programming plateau in your climb toward becoming a CICS programmer.

Input Mapping

Input mapping is the process of transferring data received from the terminal into the symbolic description map. Input fields received from a terminal are both device- and format-dependent. First, only modified fields are transmitted from the terminal. Each field transmitted is preceded by a buffer address showing the origin of the field. Finally, fields are variable in length. That is, if the operator typed in a few characters then pressed the erase EOF key, only the keyed data will be transmitted. BMS input mapping provides all of the processing needed to copy the device-dependent data received from the terminal into the symbolic map. In doing so, BMS will analyze the data stream, extract the variable field data, provide padding and justification, then copy the processed fields into the input map area.

Now let's look at the input mapping process. Input mapping implies that the operator has just performed a data entry function, and the program needs to map that input into working-storage. For data entry to happen, some type of data entry screen must have been displayed by a program.

```
IDENTIFICATION DIVISION.
PROGRAM-ID. VEND001.
AUTHOR. BOB LOWE.
ENVIRONMENT DIVISION.
DATA DIVISION.
WORKING-STORAGE SECTION.
01  VENDOR-RECORD.
    05  VENDOR-NAME            PIC X(30).
    05  VENDOR-ID             PIC XXXXX.
    05  VENDOR-ADDR1          PIC X(30).
    05  VENDOR-ADDR2          PIC X(30).
    05  VENDOR-ADDR3          PIC X(30).
    05  VENDOR-ADDR4          PIC X(30).
    05  VENDOR-CONTACT        PIC X(30).
    05  VENDOR-TELE           PIC X(12).
    05  VENDOR-TAXID          PIC X(11).
    05  VENDOR-YTD-SALES      PIC S9(07)V99 COMP-3.
    05  VENDOR-YTD-PAYMENTS   PIC S9(07)V99 COMP-3.
    05  VENDOR-YTD-DISCOUNTS  PIC S9(07)V99 COMP-3.
    05  VENDOR-PAY-HOLD       PIC X.
    05  VENDOR-PRODUCT        PIC XXX.
    05  VENDOR-LAST-CHECK     PIC S9(05)      COMP-3.
    05  VENDOR-LAST-CK-DATE   PIC S9(05)      COMP-3.
    05  VENDOR-LAST-CK-AMT    PIC S9(07)V99 COMP-3.
    05  VENDOR-DATE-ADDED     PIC S9(05)      COMP-3.
    05  VENDOR-DATE-CHANGED   PIC S9(05)      COMP-3.
    05  VENDOR-LAST-OPID      PIC XXX.
    05  VENDOR-UPDCNT         PIC 9.
01  MISC-AREAS.
    05  MSG-LEN               PIC S9999 COMP.
    05  VENDOR-RECORD-LENGTH  PIC S9999 COMP VALUE +249.
    05  PROMPT-MESSAGE        PIC X(50)
        VALUE 'NNNNNN<--TYPE A RECORD KEY AND PRESS ENTER'.
    05  KEY-INPUT             PIC XXXXX VALUE SPACES.
01  MESSAGE-LINE.
    05  SEND-TRANSID          PIC XXXX.
    05  FILLER                PIC X.
    05  SEND-KEY              PIC XXXXX.
    05  FILLER                PIC X.
    05  THE-MESSAGE           PIC X(54).
    05  FILLER                PIC X.
    05  THE-TIME              PIC ZZ9,99,99.
    05  FILLER                PIC XXXX.
* * * * * * * * * * * * * * * * * * * * * * * * * * * * *
*    BMS ATTRIBUTE VALUES INCLUDING HILIGHT AND COLOR
* * * * * * * * * * * * * * * * * * * * * * * * * * * * *
01  STANDARD-BMS-ATTRIBUTES.
    02  UNPROT-NORM           PIC X VALUE SPACE.
    02  UNPROT-BRT            PIC X VALUE 'H'.
    02  UNPROT-DRK            PIC X VALUE '<'.
    02  UNPROT-FSET-NORM      PIC X VALUE 'A'.
    02  UNPROT-FSET-BRT       PIC X VALUE 'I'.
    02  UNPROT-FSET-DRK       PIC X VALUE '('.
    02  UNPROT-NUM-NORM       PIC X VALUE '&'.
    02  UNPROT-NUM-BRT        PIC X VALUE 'Q'.
    02  UNPROT-NUM-DRK        PIC X VALUE '*'.
    02  UNPROT-NUM-FSET-NORM  PIC X VALUE 'J'.
    02  UNPROT-NUM-FSET-BRT   PIC X VALUE 'R'.
    02  UNPROT-NUM-FSET-DRK   PIC X VALUE ')'.
    02  PROT-NORM             PIC X VALUE '-'.
    02  PROT-BRT              PIC X VALUE 'Y'.
    02  PROT-DRK              PIC X VALUE '%'.
    02  PROT-FSET-NORM        PIC X VALUE '/'.
    02  PROT-FSET-BRT         PIC X VALUE 'Z'.
    02  PROT-FSET-DRK         PIC X VALUE '_'.
    02  ASKIP-NORM            PIC X VALUE '0'.
    02  ASKIP-BRT             PIC X VALUE '8'.
    02  ASKIP-DRK             PIC X VALUE '@'.
    02  ASKIP-FSET-NORM       PIC X VALUE '1'.
    02  ASKIP-FSET-BRT        PIC X VALUE '9'.
    02  ASKIP-FSET-DRK        PIC X VALUE QUOTE.
    02  HILIGHT-DEFAULT       PIC X VALUE LOW-VALUE.
    02  HILIGHT-BLINK         PIC X VALUE '1'.
    02  HILIGHT-REVERSE       PIC X VALUE '2'.
    02  HILIGHT-UNDERSCORE    PIC X VALUE '4'.
    02  COLOR-DEFAULT         PIC X VALUE LOW-VALUE.
```

FIGURE 6.7.   Sample Inquiry Program using BMS output mapping

```
            02  COLOR-BLUE              PIC X VALUE '1'.
            02  COLOR-RED               PIC X VALUE '2'.
            02  COLOR-PINK              PIC X VALUE '3'.
            02  COLOR-GREEN             PIC X VALUE '4'.
            02  COLOR-TURKUOISE         PIC X VALUE '5'.
            02  COLOR-YELLOW            PIC X VALUE '6'.
            02  COLOR-WHITE             PIC X VALUE '7'.
       COPY VENDSET.
       LINKAGE SECTION.
       PROCEDURE DIVISION.
      *PROCEDURE CODE
       000-MAINLINE-ROUTINE.
           IF EIBCALEN EQUAL ZERO
               EXEC CICS SEND ERASE
                   FROM (PROMPT-MESSAGE) LENGTH (50)
                   END-EXEC
               EXEC CICS RETURN TRANSID (EIBTRNID)
                   COMMAREA (EIBAID) LENGTH (1)
                   END-EXEC.
           MOVE SPACES TO MESSAGE-LINE.
           EXEC CICS IGNORE CONDITION LENGERR END-EXEC.
           MOVE +6 TO MSG-LEN.
           EXEC CICS RECEIVE
               INTO (KEY-INPUT)
               LENGTH (MSG-LEN)
               END-EXEC.
           IF MSG-LEN LESS THAN +6
               MOVE 'NEED A RECORD KEY' TO THE-MESSAGE
               GO TO 990-SEND-ERROR-AND-EXIT.
           IF KEY-INPUT NOT NUMERIC
               MOVE 'VENDOR NUMBER NOT NUMERIC' TO THE-MESSAGE
               MOVE KEY-INPUT TO SEND-KEY
               GO TO 990-SEND-ERROR-AND-EXIT.
           EXEC CICS HANDLE CONDITION
               NOTOPEN  (950-NOTOPEN)
               NOTFND   (960-NOTFND)
               LENGERR  (970-LENGERR)
               ERROR    (980-ERROR)
               END-EXEC.
           EXEC CICS READ
               DATASET ('VENFILE')
               INTO    (VENDOR-RECORD)
               RIDFLD  (KEY-INPUT)
               LENGTH  (VENDOR-RECORD-LENGTH)
               END-EXEC.
           EJECT


      * ******************************************************
      *     PREPARE AND SEND INQUIRY SCREEN
      * ******************************************************
           MOVE LOW-VALUES          TO             DISPMAPO.
           MOVE 'VEN1001'           TO  SCODEO    IN DISPMAPO.
           MOVE ASKIP-NORM          TO  VENNAMEA  IN DISPMAPI
                                        ADDR1A    IN DISPMAPI
                                        ADDR2A    IN DISPMAPI
                                        ADDR3A    IN DISPMAPI
                                        ADDR4A    IN DISPMAPI
                                        CONTACA   IN DISPMAPI
                                        TELEA     IN DISPMAPI
                                        TAXIDA    IN DISPMAPI
                                        PAHOLDA   IN DISPMAPI.
           MOVE VENDOR-NAME         TO  VENNAMEO  IN DISPMAPO.
           MOVE VENDOR-ID           TO  VENDIDO   IN DISPMAPO.
           MOVE VENDOR-ADDR1        TO  ADDR1O    IN DISPMAPO.
           MOVE VENDOR-ADDR2        TO  ADDR2O    IN DISPMAPO.
           MOVE VENDOR-ADDR3        TO  ADDR3O    IN DISPMAPO.
           MOVE VENDOR-ADDR4        TO  ADDR4O    IN DISPMAPO.
           MOVE VENDOR-CONTACT      TO  CONTACO   IN DISPMAPO.
           MOVE VENDOR-TELE         TO  TELEO     IN DISPMAPO.
           MOVE VENDOR-TAXID        TO  TAXIDO    IN DISPMAPO.
           MOVE VENDOR-PAY-HOLD     TO  PAHOLDO   IN DISPMAPO.
           MOVE VENDOR-PRODUCT      TO  PRODUCTO  IN DISPMAPO.
```

FIGURE 6.7. Continued

```
        EXEC CICS SEND MAP ('DISPMAP')
               MAPSET ('VENDSET')
               ERASE
               FREEKB
               END-EXEC.
        EXEC CICS RETURN END-EXEC.
* * * * * * * * * * * * * * * * * * * * * * * * * * *
* * * * * * * * * * * * * * * * * * * * * * * * * *
*     ERROR PROCESSING ROUTINES
* * * * * * * * * * * * * * * * * * * * * *
    950-NOTOPEN.
        MOVE 'VENDOR FILE NOT OPEN' TO THE-MESSAGE
        GO TO 990-SEND-ERROR-AND-EXIT.
    960-NOTFND.
        MOVE 'RECORD NOT ON FILE' TO THE-MESSAGE
        MOVE KEY-INPUT TO SEND-KEY.
        GO TO 990-SEND-ERROR-AND-EXIT.
    970-LENGERR.
        MOVE 'FILE LENGTH ERROR' TO THE-MESSAGE
        MOVE KEY-INPUT TO SEND-KEY.
        GO TO 990-SEND-ERROR-AND-EXIT.
    980-ERROR.
        MOVE 'AN UNDETERMINED ERROR HAS OCCURRED ' TO THE-MESSAGE
        MOVE KEY-INPUT TO SEND-KEY.
        GO TO 990-SEND-ERROR-AND-EXIT.
    990-SEND-ERROR-AND-EXIT.
        MOVE EIBTRNID TO SEND-TRANSID.
        MOVE EIBTIME  TO THE-TIME.
        TRANSFORM THE-TIME FROM ',' TO ':'.
        EXEC CICS SEND
             FROM (MESSAGE-LINE)
             LENGTH (80)
             ERASE
             END-EXEC.
        EXEC CICS RETURN  END-EXEC.
        GOBACK.
```

FIGURE 6.7. Continued

Maybe an example would help put this into perspective. I'm going to use our sample menu screen to illustrate the input mapping process. Our sample menu is depicted in figure 6.8. Since this menu screen contains an unprotected field (the record key), it qualifies as a data entry screen. To invite input from this menu screen, it must first be displayed. Let's do that now. To display the menu, we must perform a simple output mapping operation. The routine below would do just that.

```
        MOVE LOW-VALUES TO MENUMAPO.
        MOVE EIBTRMID TO TERMO IN MENUMAPO.
        MOVE CURRENT-DATE TO DATEO IN MENUMAPO.
        MOVE EIBTIME TO TIMEO IN MENUMAPO.
        TRANSFORM TIMEO IN MENUMAPO FROM ',' TO ':'.
        MOVE 'VEN0000' TO SCODEO IN MENUMAPO.
        EXEC CICS SEND MAP ('MENUMAP')
             MAPSET ('VENDSET')
             ERASE
             FREEKB
             END-EXEC.
        EXEC CICS RETURN TRANSID ('VEND')
             COMMAREA (EIBAID) LENGTH (1)
             END-EXEC.
```

Now assume that an operator has just viewed this menu screen, has entered a vendor record key, then pressed PF1. To get the record key, the program would need to perform an input mapping

```
         1         2         3         4         5         6         7         8
1234567890123456789012345678901234567890123456789012345678901234567890123456789 0
VEN0000               VENDOR MASTER MENU                          DATE 01/31/88
                                                                 TIME 06:00:00
                                                                 TERMINAL DT03

          PF1  DISPLAY MASTER RECORD

          PF2  UPDATE MASTER RECORD

          PF3  ADD MASTER RECORD

          PF4  DELETE MASTER RECORD

          PF5  BROWSE MASTER BY KEY

          PF9  EXIT MASTER MENU


   TYPE VENDOR NUMBER NNNNNN THEN PRESS APPROPRIATE PF KEY
```

FIGURE 6.8.   Menu Screen

operation. The objective of input mapping is to cause any modified fields transmitted by the terminal to be mapped into the program's working-storage. For our sample menu, input mapping would move the record key into our symbolic map.

RECEIVE MAP COMMAND

At the point in the Procedure Division where you want to perform an input mapping operation you will issue the BMS RECEIVE MAP command. The format of the command is

```
EXEC CICS RECEIVE MAP (name)
          MAPSET (name)
          END-EXEC
```

MAP (name) refers to the name of the map that describes the layout for the screen. In our sample menu application, the name of the map would be MENUMAP.

MAPSET (name) refers to the name of the mapset containing the physical map. For our sample menu application the mapset name would be VENDSET.

The following statement would "map" the menu screen input into the symbolic description map:

```
EXEC CICS RECEIVE MAP ('MENUMAP')
     MAPSET ('VENDSET')
     END-EXEC.
```

PROCESSING BMS INPUT

After successful execution of the BMS RECEIVE MAP command you can process the data in the symbolic description map. Input processing simply involves using the contents of the input fields in working-storage. Like input from other mediums such as tape or disk, you would perform any needed *data validation*. This validation could include such tests as field-verify, reasonableness check, range limit, table search, check digit, and so on. For our sample menu, a verification of the vendor number for valid numeric characters might be coded as follows:

```
IF VENDIDI IN MENUMAPI IS NOT-NUMERIC
     MOVE 'RECORD KEY NOT NUMERIC' TO MMESAGEO
     PERFORM 925-TRANSMIT-MENU-SCREEN.
```

With terminal input, an additional check may be necessary that is not normally found with other input mediums. This is a check for *data presence*. When using the IBM 3270 terminal, there is a possibility that one or more fields may not have been transferred back from the terminal. For instance, if the operator used the erase input or erase EOF key and fails to reenter any data in that field on the terminal, the field will not be mapped in by BMS. There are two ways to detect if a field has not been mapped in by BMS.

1. The input field (symbolic name with Suffix-I) will contain low-values. When no input is received for a field, BMS will move low-values to the input subfield. A COBOL IF statement can easily detect this condition. The statement below could be used for our menu.

```
IF VENDIDI IN MENUMAPI EQUAL TO LOW-VALUES
    MOVE 'NO RECORD KEY ENTERED' TO MMESAGEO
    PERFORM 925-TRANSMIT-MENU-SCREEN.
```

2. The length field (symbolic field name with Suffix-L) will contain a value of zero. If a field is not mapped in by BMS, zeros will be moved to this field. A COBOL IF statement can detect this condition. For example,

```
IF VENDIDL IN MENUMAPI IS NOT POSITIVE
    MOVE 'NO RECORD KEY ENTERED' TO MMESAGEO
    PERFORM 925-TRANSMIT-MENU-SCREEN.
```

If you have specified the PICIN option with a numeric picture, COBOL will not allow you to check the Suffix-I field for low-values. You may have to use the second method described above.

EXCEPTIONAL CONDITIONS

Normally, only two exceptional conditionals will occur during a BMS RECEIVE MAP command. One condition, INVMPSZ, was described earlier in the chapter. The other condition is MAPFAIL. The MAP-FAIL condition will occur under three circumstances:

1. The input screen contains unformatted data. This is usually caused by a logic error in the program where the program "thinks" that a formatted screen is present but in fact unformatted input such as an initial transaction message was transmitted.
2. The terminal transmits only an attention identifier. This will occur if the screen has just been erased with the CLEAR key. It will also happen if the operator uses an attention key such as PA1, PA2, or PA3 that does not transmit data.
3. The input screen was transferred to the program with no *modified* fields. This might have been caused by sending a screen earlier without any FSET fields. In this situation, if the operator retransmits the screen without actually changing one or more of the fields, no data is transferred back to the program, and BMS cannot do a mapping operation. If your output map contained fields with the modified attribute, the operator must have cleared them with the erase input key, and then failed to enter any data. The erase input key will cause all unprotected fields to be set to nulls and the modified data tags set off. BMS cannot do an input mapping operation if no modified fields are sent from the terminal.

When an input mapping operation fails due to an exceptional condition, the input map area in your working storage is not modified by BMS. If you plan to use this area for output mapping, as described in the next paragraph, you may want to initialize the input map area prior to issuing the RECEIVE MAP command. This can be done as shown below. In this way, if the RECEIVE MAP fails, the mapping area is already prepared for you to format it with an error message.

```
MOVE LOW-VALUES TO MENUMAPI.
```

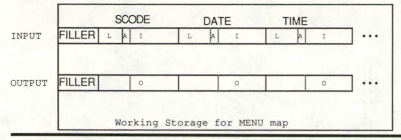

		SCODE		DATE		TIME		
INPUT	FILLER	L	A	I	L	A	I	L	A	I	...

OUTPUT	FILLER	O		O		O	...

Working Storage for MENU map

FIGURE 6.9.   BMS output maps redefine input maps

OUTPUT MAPPING FOLLOWING INPUT MAPPING

In many situations, you will need to retransmit a screen to the terminal *after* performing an input mapping operation. In most cases the data that has just originated from the terminal will be retransmitted to the terminal. The layout of the symbolic description map facilitates this process. As you may recall from an earlier discussion, the output map fields occupy the same storage area as the input fields. This layout is depicted in figure 6.9. Notice that each output field occupies the same working-storage area as the corresponding input field. Unless a field is changed by the program between an input mapping operation and an output mapping process, the same values received will be sent back to the terminal.

If you need to retransmit a screen with data that has just been received from a RECEIVE MAP command, there is one thing that you *should not* do: *don't initialize the output map area.* If your program moves low-values to the output map, your input data will also be erased. So this is one situation in a program where you should not initialize an output map before issuing the SEND MAP command. The coding below illustrates some of the logic of a menu-processing program. This routine receives the input screen, then validates the incoming data. If the data is incorrect, the routine retransmits the menu screen so the operator can make corrections.

```
PROCEDURE DIVISION.
     EXEC CICS RECEIVE MAP ('MENUMAP')
               MAPSET ('VENDSET')
               END-EXEC.
     IF VENDIDI IN MENUMAPI IS NOT-NUMERIC
               MOVE 'RECORD KEY NOT NUMERIC' TO MMESAGEO IN MENUMAPO
               PERFORM 925-TRANSMIT-MENU-SCREEN.
       .
       .
       .
925-RETRANSMIT-MENU-SCREEN.
     MOVE EIBTIME TO TIMEO IN MENUMAPO.
     TRANSFORM TIMEO IN MENUMAPO FROM ',' TO ':'.
     MOVE EIBTRMID TO TERMO IN MENUMAPO.
     MOVE CURRENT-DATE TO DATEO IN MENUMAPO.
     MOVE 'VEN0000' TO SCODEO IN MENUMAPO.
     EXEC CICS SEND MAP ('MENUMAP')
               MAPSET ('VENDSET')
               ERASE
               FREEKB
               ALARM
               END-EXEC.
     EXEC CICS RETURN TRANSID ('VEND')
          COMMAREA (EIBAID) LENGTH (1)
          END-EXEC.
```

```
Contents            UNPROT,NUM          UNPROT
   of                  SPECIFIED           SPECIFIED
 Field

123456              123456              123456
1ºººº               000001              1•••••
ABC•••              ABC•••              ABC•••
ABCººº              000ABC              ABC•••
12ºººº              000012              12••••
12345º              012345              12345•
•••123              •••123              •••123
••123º              0••123              ••123•
```

WHERE º indicates positions cleared with ERASE EOF Key
      • depicts the character space

FIGURE 6.10.   Example of Justify and Padding with NUM option

PADDING AND JUSTIFICATION

There is one final feature of input mapping that needs to be discussed here. That feature is the padding and justification of data as it is moved into the input map area. Suppose you have a six-character BMS field for an input variable, but the operator erases the field, then only keys in two characters. How do you suppose the two characters will be mapped into the six-character working-storage field? Maybe a better question is, How would you *like* the two characters mapped into the six-character field? For numeric-type data, it is usually best if the data is right-justified and contains leading zeros. Alphameric data, on the other hand, is better handled when it is left-justified and contains trailing spaces.

This is exactly how BMS will map the operator data into the various input fields. For our two-character input example, it will be left- or right-justified and padded with spaces or zeros, depending on how the field was defined. The default action for *numeric* fields is to pad short fields with leading zeros as needed to fit the symbolic field. For *nonnumeric* fields the default action is to store the characters left-justified with trailing spaces. The padding and justification depends on whether the NUM option was specified in the *original* definition (the DFHMDF statement) for the field. Please refer to figure 6.10 for an example of field justification and padding during input mapping.

This concludes our discussion of input mapping. You should now be ready to move on to the remaining chapters, where you will be given the opportunity to use this important facility.

Chapter Summary

In this chapter, you have learned how to use BMS to perform output mapping and input mapping operations. Both of these operations use the symbolic map that is generated during the map-preparation process. The symbolic maps are copied into the working-storage with the COBOL COPY statement. These maps then become a target for mapping operations. To perform output mapping you initialize the map area, then move the data to be displayed into the mapping fields. The SEND MAP command is then used to display a formatted screen. During output mapping, your program can use default data stored in the physical map. It can also temporarily override the attributes for any variable field. The program can determine the initial cursor position using symbolic cursor positioning or by specifying the cursor address in the SEND MAP command. Input mapping was also described in the chapter. By using the RECEIVE MAP command, a program can have BMS move device-dependent input into the symbolic map. The program can then perform any needed processing using input fields provided in the symbolic map. Since these fields are properly padded and justified by BMS, processing is similar to that provided with other input mediums. Since most programs perform some type of BMS mapping, an understanding of the topics presented in this chapter is essential to a career as a CICS programmer or analyst.

Discussion Questions

1. Where are the symbolic description maps cataloged during the map-preparation process?
2. How are symbolic maps made available to the COBOL program?
3. How does the use of symbolic description maps provide for format independence?
4. What is the effect of specifying STORAGE=AUTO in the DFHMSD statement? What are the trade-offs in using this option?
5. Why is it necessary for the COBOL program to initialize the symbolic map before an output mapping operation?
6. When new maps are added to an existing mapset, some new field names may duplicate existing names in other maps. How can you prevent the compiler from generating an error when one of these fields is used in a program?
7. Default attributes are stored in the physical map. The program can override the default attribute for any field mapped from the program. How is this accomplished?
8. Why is it common for installations to catalog their own attribute definitions instead of using the IBM-supplied copybook DFHBMSCA?
9. During output mapping, default values for a field can be mapped to the screen. These default values are defined with the INITIAL option during map-preparation and are stored in the physical map. What is necessary to have BMS use a default value for a field?
10. The SEND MAP command has several options that correspond to parameters specified in the CTRL option of the DFHMSD statement. Why would you think that it is preferred to specify these options in the SEND MAP command instead of using the CTRL options?
11. When is the length subfield (Suffix-L) used during output mapping?
12. What would be the result, if a RECEIVE MAP command is issued after the operator cleared the screen?
13. After an input mapping operation, how can the program determine whether a field has been erased?
14. Many times, a RECEIVE MAP command will be followed by a SEND MAP. How does the layout of the symbolic description map facilitate this process?
15. The NUM attribute option is used to cause data entry keyboards to enter into numeric shift mode when the cursor is moved into a field. What is another effect of the NUM option?

Review Exercises

1. Construct a symbolic map for the mapset below the same way BMS would during the map-preparation process.

```
PERSET    DFHMSD  TYPE=MAP,MODE=INOUT,LANG=COBOL,TIOAPFX=YES
INQY      DFHMDI  SIZE=(24,80),LINE=1,COLUMN=1
SCRNID    DFHMDF  POS=(01,01),LENGTH=07,ATTRB=(ASKIP,NORM,IC)
          DFHMDF  POS=(01,15),INITIAL='MASTER INQUIRY',LENGTH=14
          DFHMDF  POS=(03,01),INITIAL='NAME',LENGTH=04
MNAME     DFHMDF  POS=(03,10),ATTRB=(UNPROT,NORM),LENGTH=30
          DFHMDF  POS=(05,01),INITIAL='ADDRESS',LENGTH=07
MADDR1    DFHMDF  POS=(05,10),ATTRB=(UNPROT,NORM),LENGTH=30
MCITY     DFHMDF  POS=(06,10),ATTRB=(UNPROT,NORM),LENGTH=15
MSTATE    DFHMDF  POS=(06,26),ATTRB=(UNPROT,NORM),LENGTH=02
MZIP      DFHMDF  POS=(06,29),ATTRB=(UNPROT,NORM),LENGTH=09
          DFHMSD  TYPE=FINAL
```

2. Write a COBOL statement to initialize the symbolic map in exercise 1 prior to an output mapping operation.

3. Write the statements necessary to display the inquiry screen. Erase the screen, and unlock the keyboard. The screen code should be 'PERS101.' All of the variable fields on the screen should be set to the ASKIP, NORM. Have the cursor display in the *name* field. Fields to be displayed are FNAME, FADDRESS, FCITY, FSTATE, and FZIP.

Lab Problems

LAB 1

PERSONNEL INQUIRY PROGRAM
(PROGRAM XY00001, TRANSID XY01)

Redesign the Lab 1 program from chapter 4 to use BMS output mapping to display information from a master record.

Recall that this program is a noninteractive program with direct transaction input as shown below. If an error occurs, display an error message and terminate the task.

Transaction Message
XY01 999999999

Error Message Layout

```
    XY01              MESSAGE TO OPERATOR..


                      FILE NOT OPEN
                      RECORD NOT FOUND
                      PLEASE SUPPLY SSN
                      UNEXPECTED ERROR
```

☐ Use BMS output mapping to display the personal information screen instead of displaying the fields with the SEND TEXT, and SEND PAGE command. The personal information screen was designed in Lab 2 of chapter 5. The output screen will appear as follows:

```
          1         2         3         4         5         6
 1234567890123456789012345678901234567890123456789012345678901234567890123456
01^PERS101          ^PERSONAL INFORMATION^INQUIRY
02
03
04        ^SSN:^123456789
05
06     ^NAME..^DOE, JOHN A                             ^
07 ^ADDRESS..^123 ANYWHERE STREET                      ^
08    ^CITY..^KANSAS CITY                  ^
09   ^STATE..^MO^641110000^
10
11   ^PHONE..^5551212^
12     ^SEX..^M^
13  ^ETHNIC..^1^
14     ^DOB..^083147^
15
16
17
18
19
20
```

```
21^MESSAGE:^PRESS CLEAR TO START ANOTHER TRANSACTION
22
23
24
```

LAB 2

MENU SCREEN PROCESSING PROGRAM
(PROGRAM XY00000, TRANSID XY00)

Design, code, and test a program to display the personnel master menu screen, then receive input from the screen. Design two-pass logic as follows:

INITIAL ENTRY LOGIC (FIRST PASS) TRANSID-XY00, NO COMMAREA

☐ Initialize the menu map and move date, time, and terminal identification. Use the menu screen cataloged in Lab 1 of chapter 5 of the text. Modify the attribute of the screen code field so that it is FSET,ASKIP,NORM. This will help to prevent a MAPFAIL from occurring when the screen is later received.

☐ Display the menu screen.

☐ Issue a pseudoconversational RETURN naming the menu transaction code. Pass a commarea to be used in the entry analysis logic so the second-pass logic will be invoked in the next task.

```
                 1         2         3         4         5         6         7
        1234567890123456789012345678901234567890123456789012345678901234567890 12345
01^PERS000              ^PERSONNEL MASTER MENU              ^TERMINAL:^XXXX
02                                                          ^DATE:^01/31/88
03                                                          ^TIME:^06 00 00
04
05              ^ENTER   DISPLAY PERSONAL INFORMATION
06               ^PF1    DISPLAY COMPANY INFORMATION
07               ^PF2    UPDATE PERSONAL INFORMATION
08               ^PF3    UPDATE COMPANY INFORMATION
09               ^PF4    ADD EMPLOYEE RECORD
10               ^PF5    DELETE EMPLOYEE RECORD
11               ^PF6    BROWSE FILE BY SSN
12               ^CLEAR SCREEN TO EXIT APPLICATION
13
14
15
16
17
18
19
20^TYPE EMPLOYEE SSN THEN PRESS ENTER OR A PF KEY^\\\\\\\\\\^
21
22^MESSAGE:^\\\\\\\\\\\\\\\\\\\\\\\\\\\\\\\\\\\\\\\\\\\\\\\\\\\\\\\\\\\\\\\\\\\\\
23
24
```

RETURNING LOGIC (SECOND PASS) TRANSID-XY00, COMMAREA PRESENT

☐ If the CLEAR key was used, display a goodbye message and exit the program with a normal RETURN command.

☐ If the CLEAR key was not pressed edit the AID key value in EIBAID. If the operator did not press one of the keys ENTER, PF1, PF2, PF3, PF4, PF5, or PF6, redisplay the menu screen with a message indicating that an invalid function key was pressed. Issue a pseudoconversational RETURN naming the menu transaction code. Pass a commarea to be used in the entry analysis logic so the second-pass logic will again be invoked in the next task.

☐ Receive the menu screen.

☐ Edit the SSN, checking for numeric characters. If the SSN is not numeric, redisplay the menu screen with a message indicating the error. Issue a pseudoconversational RETURN naming the menu transaction code. Pass a commarea to be used in the entry analysis logic so the second-pass logic will again be invoked in the next task.

☐ If the SSN passes the edit, redisplay the menu screen with a message such as "ALL INPUT WAS CORRECT." Issue a pseudoconversational RETURN naming the menu transaction code. Pass a commarea to be used in the entry analysis logic so the second-pass logic will again be invoked in the next task.

Test this program with a number of errors such as nonnumeric SSN, erased SSN, PF8, PA1, and so on. Also test the program with valid PF keys, and valid SSN values entered. The program should continue redisplaying the menu screen until the CLEAR key is pressed. It should then display a good-bye message. After the exit message is displayed, the operator should be able to clear the screen and enter a new transaction code.

7

Menu Transaction Design

In this chapter you will

1. Learn how CICS provides for structured program design in dealing with exceptional conditions.
2. See how to use the NOHANDLE option when coding CICS commands.
3. Be able to use the EIBRCODE and EIBRESP fields following any CICS command.
4. Appreciate how application menus can improve the man-machine communication and increase operator productivity.
5. Develop guidelines for designing application menu screens.
6. Visualize how applications programs run at various logical levels under CICS/VS.
7. Understand the differences between the LINK and XCTL commands.
8. Observe how the communications area is used to pass data from one application program to another.
9. Learn how to design programs that are invoked using a menu program.

In this chapter you will learn additional design techniques that can be used with CICS/VS application programs. In the first topic you will study a new way to deal with exceptional conditions. As an alternative to using the HANDLE and IGNORE commands, a program can check a response code in the Execute Interface Block. This chapter will show how this is done. The chapter will then describe the use of application menus to invoke transaction processing programs. First, you will learn the benefits of using on-line menus and see some of the commonly used techniques for designing menu screens. You will then study the design of a menu processing program.

This chapter will also present some important program control commands and concepts. You will learn how to use the XCTL, LINK, and RETURN commands to allow more than one program to be executed during a single task. These commands provide the capability to design applications in a modular fashion whereby each operator transaction is provided in a separate application program. The menu program described in this chapter is an important part of a modular system. In the remaining chapters you will learn how to design the various transaction programs which are started by the menu program. The design of this sample application is similar to most on-line systems, so the concepts and techniques that follow should provide you with ''real-world'' job skills for developing CICS systems.

CICS/VS Exceptional Conditions

In chapter 3, you learned how to use the CICS HANDLE and IGNORE commands to deal with exceptional conditions. In the past, for designing application programs, this technique was used almost exclusively. But there is one problem with the use of the HANDLE CONDITION command: the HANDLE command makes it somewhat difficult to design a *structured* program. The reason is that the HANDLE CONDITION command introduces an implied GOTO at each point in the program where an exceptional condition can occur. For instance, if a service command is executed that gives rise to an exceptional condition and if that condition has been handled, EIP will cause a direct branch (GOTO) to the exceptional condition–processing routine. There is no automatic return to the point after the service command. If the original service command is within a performed paragraph, there is no guarantee that the exit from the performed paragraph will ever be executed. If it is not, the routine that performed it will not again receive control. Proponents of the structured programming discipline require strict adherence to the principle that each performed processing routine should return control to its calling routine. With the introduction of implied GOTOs for each CICS command, it is difficult to follow this convention.

Some programmers have developed techniques to work around branching logic introduced by the HANDLE CONDITION command. They do this by placing the service command and the exception-handling routines within a performed procedure. The exception routines simply set switches or indicators representing the error, then branch to the exit paragraph. The calling routine can then test these indicators to determine if the function was successful or to identify the specific error, then take the appropriate action. This technique becomes cumbersome if a large number of exceptions are to be detected, since many small HANDLE CONDITION paragraphs must be used to record each exceptional condition indicator value properly.

NOHANDLE OPTION

There is an alternative to setting your own indicators in these clumsy error-handling routines: you can have CICS return control to your program and test a *response code* provided automatically by CICS/VS.

A command option called NOHANDLE, can be used to cause CICS to return control back to your program. When the NOHANDLE option is used, CICS will *always* return control to the program following the command. This option will take precedence over any active IGNORE or HANDLE CONDITION commands. Here is an example of the use of the NOHANDLE option.

```
EXEC CICS READ
     DATASET ('VENFILE')
     RIDFLD (KEY-INPUT)
     INTO (VENDOR-RECORD)
     LENGTH (VENDOR-RECORD-LENGTH)
     NOHANDLE
     END-EXEC
```

After the command has completed, CICS will return control back to the program so you can check the CICS response code. The CICS response code is found in the Execute Interface Block. Depending on the release of CICS/VS you are using, either one or two response code fields are located in the EIB. The early releases (Release 1.6 and below) of CICS provided only one response code field. That field was EIBRCODE.

EXCEPTION	HEX RETURN CODE	DECIMAL VALUE FOR COBOL
PROGRAM CONTROL		
PGMIDERR	01	001
NOTAUTH	D6	214
INVREQ	E0	224
TERMINAL CONTROL		
LENGERR	E1	225
FILE CONTROL		
DSIDERR	01	001
ILLOGIC	02	002
INVREQ	08	008
NOTOPEN	0C	012
DISABLED	0D	013
IOERR	80	128
NOTFND	81	129
DUPREC	82	130
NOSPACE	83	131
NOTAUTH	D6	214
LENGERR	E1	225
TEMPORARY STORAGE		
ITEMERR	01	001
QIDERR	02	002
IOERR	04	004
NOSPACE	08	008
INVREQ	20	032
NOTAUTH	D6	214
LENGERR	E1	225
Basic Mapping Support		
MAPFAIL	04	004
INVMPSZ	08	008

FIGURE 7.1. EIBRCODE values

CHECKING EIBRCODE

The field EIBRCODE is a six-character field containing a *hexadecimal* return code from the last command. The format of the field is PIC X(6). CICS updates this field after each command. If a service command was successful, the field will contain low-values. A simple COBOL statement can test for this value. For example,

```
EXEC CICS READ ....
NOHANDLE
.
.
END-EXEC.
IF EIBRCODE NOT EQUAL LOW-VALUES
    PERFORM 900-FILE-ERROR.
(statements to process record)
```

If a service command is unsuccessful, the EIBRCODE field will contain a *value* indicating which error has occurred. Usually the first byte of the field contains the error return code. Figure 7.1 illustrates the most commonly found exceptions and the resulting return codes that will be stored in the first byte of EIBRCODE. The other positions sometimes contain additional details about the problem. Appendix A contains a summary of the command response values and layout of EIBRCODE.

There is a slight problem in checking the response code field using COBOL. That problem deals with the fact that the response code is in hexadecimal form. For instance, the response for NOTOPEN, is hex 0C; for NOTFND it is hex 81. Unfortunately, COBOL does not provide an easy way to check the value of hexadecimal fields.

```
01     CICS-RETURN-CODE-TEST-AREA.
       05    COMMAND-STATUS-CODE      PIC S9(08) COMP VALUE +0.
       88    NORMAL                              VALUE +0.
       88    DSIDERR                             VALUE +1.
       88    ILLOGIC                             VALUE +2.
       88    MAPFAIL                             VALUE +4.
       88    FC-INVREQ                           VALUE +8.
       88    NOTOPEN                             VALUE +12.
       88    DISABLED                            VALUE +13.
       88    FC-IOERR                            VALUE +128.
       88    NOTFND                              VALUE +129.
       88    LENGERR                             VALUE +225.
       05    FILLER REDEFINES COMMAND-STATUS-CODE.
             10    FILLER            PIC XXX.
             10    CONVERT-TO-DECIMAL        PIC X.
       •
    •
       PERFORM 200-READ-MASTER-RECORD
       THRU      200-READ-MASTER-EXIT.
       IF NOT NORMAL
       PERFORM 900-FILE-ERROR
             PERFORM 999-SEND-ERROR-AND-EXIT.
       •
       •


       200-READ-MASTER-RECORD.
        EXEC CICS READ
             DATASET ('VENFILE')
             INTO (VENDOR-RECORD)
             RIDFLD (KEY-INPUT)
             LENGTH (VENDOR-RECORD-LENGTH)
             NOHANDLE
             END-EXEC.
             MOVE EIBRCODE TO CONVERT-TO-DECIMAL.
       200-READ-MASTER-EXIT.
             EXIT.
       •

       •
       900-FILE-ERROR.
             IF NOTFND
                   MOVE 'RECORD NOT ON FILE' TO THE-MESSAGE
             ELSE
                   IF NOTOPEN
                   MOVE 'VENDOR FILE NOT OPEN' TO THE-MESSAGE
       •
       •
```

FIGURE 7.2.   COBOL Routine to check response codes

Figure 7.2 illustrates one way to get around this problem. This example uses a technique whereby the hexadecimal codes are converted to a corresponding decimal value. The decimal value is then analyzed by the COBOL program to determine the cause of the exception. This is done by using the COBOL REDEFINES clause to provide two different views of a storage area. First, a computational field is defined. This S9(08) computational field provides for a *decimal view* of the area. Four bytes are reserved by this statement. The value clause of zero sets the area to binary zeros. COBOL condition names are then defined using the decimal values corresponding to each hexadecimal response code. These decimal equivalents were taken from figure 7.1. The computational field is then redefined. The redefinition provides a way to move the hexadecimal return code from the EIB to the *last* byte of the COMPUTATIONAL field. Each time a hex value is moved to the last byte of the redefined area, the original COMPUTATIONAL field takes on the decimal equivalent. Then in the Procedure division the condition names are used to test for the CICS exceptional conditions.

EXCEPTION	EIBRESP
ERROR	01
DSIDERR	12
NOTFND	13
DUPREC	14
INVREQ	16
IOERR	17
NOSPACE	18
NOTOPEN	19
ILLOGIC	21
LENGERR	22
ITEMERR	26
PGMIDERR	27
MAPFAIL	36
INVMAPSZ	38
QIDERR	44
NOTAUTH	70

FIGURE 7.3. EIBRESP values

The use of the technique described above provides an easy way to use the EIBRCODE field. If your CICS installation is still using an older release of CICS, this technique should provide a good alternative to using HANDLE CONDITION commands. The sample programs shown in this chapter provide further examples of using this alternative. Now let's look at the latest CICS provisions for checking response codes after a command.

CHECKING EIBRESP

In a recent release of CICS/VS, IBM has provided a much easier way to check the CICS exceptional conditions. They did this by adding another field in the EIB. This field is named EIBRESP. There are two benefits to using this new response field. First, the new field is defined in COBOL as S9(08) COMPUTATIONAL. That is, the new response code is already in decimal form. No conversion routine is required. After each CICS command, this field is updated with a decimal response code. Figure 7.3 illustrates these response codes. The program can easily test the CICS response with an IF statement. For example,

```
EXEC CICS READ ...
NOHANDLE
 ..
END-EXEC.
IF EIBRESP EQUAL +19
    MOVE 'FILE NOT OPEN' TO ERROR-MESSAGE
    PERFORM 990-SEND-ERROR-AND-EXIT.
```

One benefit of using this new field is that the response codes are unique for each exceptional condition. Please refer to figure 7.1 one more time. You will notice that some exceptions such as LENGERR have the same return value for all command types. In other cases, however, the same return code value has different meaning, depending on the type of command that was issued. For example, a return value of hex 01 could indicate PGMIDERR, DSIDERR, or ITEMERR depending on which command has just been executed. The EIBRESP field, on the other hand, contains a *unique* code for each exception.

You might want to define a field in working-storage with condition names as shown below. The use of condition names can make it easier to read and debug a source program. The IF statement below is much easier to read than the previous example.

```
05   WS-RESPONSE            PIC S9(08) COMPUTATIONAL.
     88   NORMAL            VALUE +0.
     88   ERROR             VALUE +1.
     88   DSIDERR           VALUE +12.
     88   NOTFND            VALUE +13.
     88   NOTOPEN           VALUE +19.

EXEC CICS READ ...
    NOHANDLE
    .
    END-EXEC.
MOVE EIBRESP TO WS-RESPONSE.
IF NOTOPEN
    MOVE 'FILE NOT OPEN' TO ERROR-MESSAGE
    PERFORM 990-SEND-ERROR-AND-EXIT.
```

THE RESP OPTION

Along with the EIBRESP field, another new command option has been added to eliminate the need for the COBOL MOVE statement in the example above. This option, when used causes CICS to generate the MOVE statement for you. The RESP option is coded within each command as follows:

```
EXEC CICS function
    option
    option
    RESP (WS-RESPONSE)
    END-EXEC.
```

The RESP option causes the same action as the NOHANDLE option described earlier. The program will always fall through to the statement following the CICS command.

DFHRESP CONDITION TEST

One final way to check the response value was introduced in a recent release of CICS/VS. There is a new command translator keyword that provides an alternative to using COBOL condition names. With this keyword you can directly test a condition after each command. The keyword is "DFHRESP." It is used in a COBOL statement as follows:

```
IF EIBRESP EQUAL TO DFHRESP (NOTOPEN)
    MOVE 'FILE NOT OPEN' TO ERROR-MESSAGE
    PERFORM 990-SEND-ERROR-AND-EXIT.
```

The DFHRESP keyword along with the exception option will cause the command translator to substitute a correct *value* for each condition (such as NOTOPEN, NOTFND, etc.) as shown in the IF statement above.

   If your installation is not yet using the newer releases of CICS, you may have to use the older return code field with your programs. But, with some knowledge of this latest response code, your programs can be designed to convert to the new release easily when it becomes available. If you have the latest release, you can now design programs using the most up-to-date CICS programming techniques. The sample programs in chapter 8 will use the newer response code fields just described.

Program Control

The Program Control Program manages the flow of control between all application programs in CICS. Before a program can be run under CICS, it must first be defined by the systems programmer in the Program Processing Table (PPT). In chapter 4 you learned that one or more transaction codes can be associated with a single application program. This association is defined by the systems programmer by specifying the program name for a transaction code in the Program Control Table (PCT). Once this is accomplished, a terminal operator can thereafter invoke an application (program) by entering the appropriate transaction code. This program then requests terminal and data-base services through the various CICS commands in the procedure division. But CICS does not limit you to using only this one program in a task. There are times when it is useful to have more than one program execute within a single task. Three general situations exist, which may require the use of more than one program during a task. They are (1) use of modular design techniques, (2) language limitations, and (3) CICS interface requirements.

MODULAR DESIGN TECHNIQUES

There are a variety of design techniques used by systems analysts in solving today's problems. Some analysts use a technique whereby the various functions of an application are incorporated into a single program. But other analysts prefer to design systems where the major functions of an application are handled by separate application programs. One reason to do this is to accelerate a project schedule by assigning a different programmer to complete each module of a multifunction application. In some instances, by creating many smaller modules the analyst can simplify and better structure the processing logic of systems. It is also possible that some generalized reusable modules, such as error processing routines, may even be used by programs in different applications.

With modular systems, a menu program is generally used by an operator to select transactions. Figure 7.4 provides an example of the flow of control for a modular system designed to provide inquiry, update, add, delete, and browse services for a vendor master file. You will notice the PCT and PPT entries used to implement this design. Later in the chapter you will see the programs for the sample menu program and inquiry program shown in this design.

LANGUAGE LIMITATIONS

Each programming language provides features that benefit the user in some way. But each language usually has some distinct limitations. COBOL is the most widely used language in both batch and CICS environments. The structure of this language has been clearly defined and standardized across the domain of all computer vendors. Consequently, programmers with training in COBOL can easily adapt their skills to any hardware or software system including CICS. In many regions there is an abundance of COBOL programmers, so employer training costs can be reduced by implementing systems with this language. There are, however, a few limitations to COBOL. To accommodate functions not provided by COBOL, it may be necessary to use the lower-level Assembly language or the high-level PL/I language.

The Assembler language can perform all of the instructions of the host machine. Through the use of hardware registers, machine instructions and a sound understanding of the principles of operation of the IBM/370 processor, any problem can be solved. It can also be used to produce highly efficient code, assuming of course that a skilled programmer is doing the coding. But it has been said that an unskilled programmer may produce less efficient code than a skilled programmer using the COBOL language. The primary disadvantage of this language lies in programmer productivity. Coding in Assembler is a tedius and time-consuming process; many lines of code are often necessary to perform the same operation as one COBOL statement. Nevertheless, to perform special functions, Assembler language programs may be needed in a few situations in the CICS environment.

PL/I is a hybrid language combining the attributes of COBOL, Assembler, and Fortran, and even provides some structured programming capabilities not available in other high-level languages. For some, it is a difficult language to master, and unfortunately (for IBM anyway), most companies have

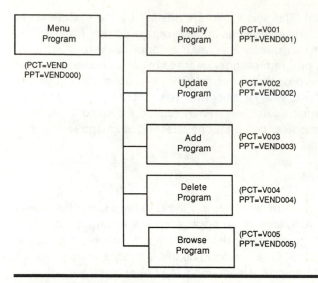

FIGURE 7.4. Modular Design Example

steered away from this language. However, a few companies "bought in" to PL/I and will continue to use it for some time to come. In other situations, some companies have installed purchased "canned" systems and need to interface these programs with newly developed applications.

CICS INTERFACE REQUIREMENTS

Many systems written using the Macro-level interface still exist today. As new application programs are integrated with these systems, they may need to be coded using the newer Command-Level Interface. This may be due to the limited availability of macro-level programmers or may simply be a matter of convenience. As command-level programs are developed, they may need to invoke or be invoked by the macro-level modules.

CICS is flexible enough to accommodate the implementation of a variety of design techniques and to provide capabilities to use programs written in each of the languages described above. A task may be designed to use one or more programs in any language combination as required to meet the demands of the application. It is even possible for programs written using the Command-Level Interface to interact with programs written in the earlier Macro-Level Interface. To accomplish this, CICS provides two program control commands used to pass control from one program to another. These commands are the XCTL and LINK.

PROGRAM LOGICAL LEVELS

Application programs running under CICS/VS are executed at *logical levels.* The first program to receive control within a task is at the highest logical level. This program may pass control to another application program to perform additional processing. When control is passed to another program, CICS will remain at the same logical level or create a lower logical level. The action taken depends on whether the XCTL or LINK command is used to pass control from one program to another. As you study the two commands below, please refer to figure 7.5 to see how each affects the CICS program logical levels.

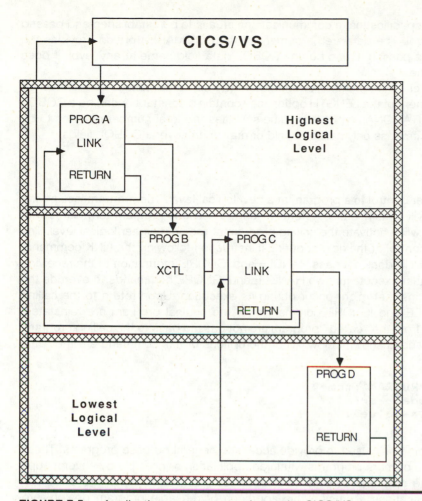

CICS/VS

PROG A

LINK

RETURN

Highest
Logical
Level

PROG B

XCTL

PROG C

LINK

RETURN

PROG D

RETURN

Lowest
Logical
Level

FIGURE 7.5. Application programs running under CICS/VS are executed at various logical levels

THE XCTL COMMAND

The XCTL command is used to pass control from one application program to another and remain at the same logical level. CICS allows only one program to be *active* at the same logical level, so the program issuing the XCTL command is terminated. When the calling program is terminated, CICS will release the working-storage copy and any HANDLE CONDITION information used by the program. HANDLE and IGNORE CONDITION actions are not passed to the new program. The format of the XCTL command is

```
EXEC CICS XCTL PROGRAM (name)
     [COMMAREA (data-area)
     LENGTH (data-value)]
     END-EXEC.
```

The name argument specifies the name of the program to which control will be passed.

The COMMAREA and LENGTH options operate the same as the pseudoconversational RETURN command described in chapter 4. These options perform a similar function with the LINK and XCTL commands. Actually, the only difference is that data is passed to a program in the *same* task.

The COMMAREA option specifies that a communications area is to be established and passed to the program receiving control. The data-area argument of the COMMAREA option provides the start address of the data to be passed. It can be any COBOL data field name at any level; it does not have to be an 01-level name.

The LENGTH option specifies the number of characters (bytes) to be passed to the invoked program. The data-value argument of the LENGTH option may contain a constant or can be a COBOL field of the PIC S9999 COMPUTATIONAL type. This value specifies the total number of bytes to be passed. This number may encompass only part of a field or may span several COBOL fields.

THE LINK COMMAND

The LINK command will transfer control to a program at a new logical level. The program issuing the LINK will be deactivated but will remain in the system. When the "called" program terminates with the RETURN command, CICS will reactivate the calling program at the next-higher logical level. The calling program will be given control at the next sequential instruction following the LINK command. Like the XCTL command, the LINK does not pass HANDLE and IGNORE information to the receiving program. This new program must execute its own HANDLE and IGNORE commands to override the default actions for the conditions that might occur during its execution. Upon return to the calling program, the "stored" HANDLE and IGNORE commands for the original program are reinstated. HANDLE and IGNORE actions from the "called" program are not passed back to the calling program. The format of the LINK command is shown below. All of the options of this command are the same as the XCTL command.

```
EXEC CICS LINK PROGRAM (name)
     [COMMAREA (data-area)
     LENGTH (data-value)]
     END-EXEC.
```

The LINK command is commonly used to provide access to general purpose programs. These programs may be used by one or more programs within an application or possibly by several applications. General error-handling programs or data conversion routines, for example, are commonly invoked by one or more applications. By using this approach of reusable program design, programmer productivity can often be improved.

EXCEPTIONAL CONDITIONS

Two CICS exceptional conditions can occur for the XCTL and LINK commands. The first condition is PGMIDERR. This condition will arise if the program named in the PROGRAM option is invalid. This will usually only occur if the PPT does not contain an entry for the program named in the transfer command. It is also possible for the master terminal operator to disable a program. PGMIDERR will arise if an attempt to transfer control to a disabled program. The second condition that can occur is NOTAUTH. This condition will arise if the operator is not authorized to use the program.

Using the COMMAREA

When the COMMAREA and LENGTH options are used on a XCTL, LINK or pseudoconversational RETURN command, a communications area is created by CICS. The commarea is placed in CICS dynamic storage. It remains there for use by the command-level program receiving control. As mentioned earlier, it is passed to a program in the *same task* when used with the XCTL or LINK command. When created with a pseudoconversational RETURN command, the commarea is passed to a program in the *next task* on that terminal. It doesn't matter how the commarea is created; all programs will access this data in the same manner. Let's pursue the many mysteries of this useful function to get a better understanding of the way in which information can be passed between the programs running under CICS.

ACCESSING THE COMMAREA

The communications area can be accessed by a program that has received control immediately upon entry to the Procedure division. That's assuming of course that an area has been passed. The Execute Interface Program provides addressability to the commarea during program initialization. To use the information in the communications area, you must provide a LINKAGE SECTION statement and a COBOL data structure for the area. The data structure must be an 01-level area with the name DFHCOMMAREA. For example, to access a six-character field either of the two coding methods below would suffice.

```
        LINKAGE SECTION.
        01   DFHCOMMAREA       PIC X(6).
or
        LINKAGE SECTION.
        01   DFHCOMMAREA.
             05   KEY-INPUT  PIC X(6).
```

Figure 7.6 depicts the coding necessary to access data passed in a commarea. In this example you can see how the fields in a "called" program correspond to the layout of the communications area passed from a "calling" program. As you can see, there is no requirement that the data names in the new program be identical to the names in the calling program.

Once the DFHCOMMAREA data structure has been defined in the "called program," there is no further coding required to access the passed communications area. It is a good practice however, to verify that an area has been correctly passed before using any of the data names. One check that can be made is to determine whether the communications area *length* is correct. The field EIBCALEN described in chapter 4 is provided to do this. It will contain a value of zero if no area was passed to the program. Please refer again to the example in figure 7.6. The COBOL IF statement can be used to verify that a correct length COMMAREA has been passed. In this example, PROGB should not refer to the communications area fields if the verification test fails. Use of these fields when no commarea exists (EIBCALEN equal ZERO) may cause program abends or other unpredictable results.

It is possible for a "called" program to pass a communications area that it has received to another program. In figure 7.7, PROGB issues an XCTL to PROGC passing the same six bytes received from PROGA. Notice how the EIBCALEN field was used as the argument for the LENGTH option in PROGB; as an alternative to this, the program could have used a constant of 6. Upon receiving control, PROGC may now access data in the original communications area.

In the case of a LINK operation, it is sometimes necessary to pass some information back to the calling program. In our example, the calling program, PROGA, linked to PROGB. This means that control will eventually be returned to PROGA. Either of the two "called" programs (PROGB and PROGC) may have altered the contents of the communications area fields. When control is eventually returned back to PROGA, it can access the changed fields by simply referring to the original field names passed in the COMMAREA option.

Application Menus

When CICS was first released, almost all application systems were written without using application menus. Instead, most application programs were written to accept simple transaction messages. For instance, to display a vendor master record, an operator might be required to enter the message

```
V001 100000
```

```
┌─────────────────────────────────────────────────────────────┐
│                                                               │
│  CODING REQUIRED IN PROG A                                    │
│                                                               │
│      WORKING-STORAGE                                          │
│      01  PASS-VARIABLE.                                       │
│          05  RECORD-KEY      PIC XXXXXX.                      │
│                                                               │
│                                                               │
│      PROCEDURE DIVISION.                                      │
│      . .                                                      │
│      . .                                                      │
│          EXEC CICS LINK PROGRAM ('PROGB')                     │
│              COMMAREA (PASS-VARIABLE)                         │
│              LENGTH (6)                                       │
│              END-EXEC                                         │
│                                                               │
└─────────────────────────────────────────────────────────────┘


┌─────────────────────────────────────────────────────────────┐
│                                                               │
│                                                               │
│  CODING REQUIRED IN PROG B                                    │
│                                                               │
│      LINKAGE SECTION.                                         │
│      01  DFHCOMMAREA.                                         │
│          05  KEY-INPUT             PIC XXXXXX.                │
│                                                               │
│                                                               │
│      PROCEDURE DIVISION.                                      │
│          Program should not use above field since existence of│
│          commarea has not been verified                       │
│                                                               │
│          IF EIBCALEN EQUAL TO 6                              │
│              PERFORM 1050-GOOD-COMMAREA-PASSED.               │
│              .                                                │
│              .                                                │
│      1050-GOOD-COMMAREA-PASSED.                              │
│          Program can directly use field name: KEY-INPUT      │
│                                                               │
│      1060-XCTL-TO-PROGC.                                     │
│          EXEC CICS XCTL PROGRAM ('PROGC')                    │
│                  COMMAREA (DFHCOMMAREA)                       │
│                  LENGTH (EIBCALEN)                            │
│              END-EXEC                                         │
│                                                               │
└─────────────────────────────────────────────────────────────┘
```

FIGURE 7.6.   Accessing Data Passed in the Commarea

As a result of the transaction code "V001," the inquiry program would be started. This program would then use the RECEIVE command to obtain the record number to be displayed. The record would then be read from the master file and displayed using BMS output mapping. A RETURN command would then terminate the program. To display another record, the operator would have to clear the screen, then reenter another transaction message.

Using this same design technique, these older applications would require other transaction messages to update, add, delete, and browse the master file. For example,

```
V002 100000 to start an update transaction
V003 100000 to start an add transaction
V004 100000 to start a delete transaction
V005 100000 to start a browse by key transaction
```

One problem with this older transaction design technique is that the transaction messages are too difficult to use. You may be surprised or even a bit confused by this last statement. At first glance, these transaction messages don't look too complicated. They may even seem very simple to use. The real problem with this approach does not really surface until you look at the bigger picture. Imagine

```
CODING REQUIRED IN PROG B

    LINKAGE SECTION.
    01   DFHCOMMAREA.
         05   KEY-INPUT              PIC XXXXXX.


    PROCEDURE DIVISION.
         Program should not use above field since existence of
         commarea has not been verified

         IF EIBCALEN EQUAL TO 6
            PERFORM 1050-GOOD-COMMAREA-PASSED.
          .
          .
    1050-GOOD-COMMAREA-PASSED.
         Program can directly use field name: KEY-INPUT

    1060-XCTL-TO-PROGC.
         EXEC CICS XCTL PROGRAM ('PROGC')
                    COMMAREA (DFHCOMMAREA)
                    LENGTH (EIBCALEN)
         END-EXEC
```

```
CODING REQUIRED IN PROG C

    LINKAGE SECTION.
    01   DFHCOMMAREA.
         05   RECORD-KEY             PIC XXXXXX.


    PROCEDURE DIVISION.
    Program should again not use above fields since existence of
    commarea has not been verified

         IF EIBCALEN EQUAL TO 6
            PERFORM 2000-GOOD-COMMAREA-PASSED.
          .
          .
    2000-GOOD-COMMAREA-PASSED.
         Program can directly use field name:
            RECORD-KEY
```

FIGURE 7.7.   Passing Original Commarea to Another Program

that you have just been hired by a very large corporation as a terminal operator. Your job will require you to enter simple transactions such as this, then perform some related task. Assume that this large company has designed all of their transactions using this transaction message approach. Imagine now, that this company has hundreds of these transactions, each requiring a different transaction code, and possibly a different message layout. Each of these transactions individually is fairly simple, but collectively they become a conglomeration of confusion.

As systems grow more complex, and the number of transactions increase, this method of starting transactions is likely to cause many problems. It will affect user-training and productivity. During initial training, operators must rely upon "help" screens and written user guides describing the various transactions and the required input messages. Operator productivity will be low, since many transaction codes will have to be memorized or "looked up." Transaction restarts may occur often, due to miskeying transaction messages. Then, as new functions are added, or as new operators are hired, the learning process starts all over again.

```
                  1         2         3         4         5         6         7         8
         1234567890 1234567890 1234567890 1234567890 1234567890 1234567890 1234567890 1234567890
        ▓VEN0000                                                 ▓DATE▓XX/XX/XX
                     ▓VENDOR MASTER MENU                          ▓TIME▓XX:XX:XX
                                                                 ▓TERMINAL▓XXXX

              ▓PF1  DISPLAY MASTER RECORD

              ▓PF2  UPDATE MASTER RECORD

              ▓PF3  ADD MASTER RECORD

              ▓PF4  DELETE MASTER RECORD

              ▓PF5  BROWSE MASTER BY KEY

              ▓PF9  EXIT MASTER MENU


        ▓TYPE VENDOR NUMBER▓NNNNNNN▓THEN PRESS APPROPRIATE PF KEY


        ▓_____
```

FIGURE 7.8. Sample Menu Screen

In recent years, this older method of starting applications has been replaced by application menus. A systems analyst once told me a story about the discovery of application menus. As the story goes, the idea was conceived by an analyst (naturally, they always take the credit for good ideas) in a dark and dingy cafe, late at night. This analyst was going to have dinner after concluding a long day of physical design for an upcoming application. After staring at the dinner menu for just a few moments the analyst thought, "Why not CRT menus? If a new (untrained) customer in a restaurant can use a menu to select a delicious meal, why can't an operator use a menu to select an on-line transaction?" However they got started, on-line menus have become a huge success.

Application menus can provide several benefits. First, they can simplify the use of the application. With the menu approach, an operator can initiate an application by simply keying in the transaction identification of the menu program. For instance, to enter the vendor master application an operator can simply "key in" the transaction message *VEND*. The menu program started by the transaction code will then display the menu screen containing the list of available functions for the application. This menu screen, introduced in the preceeding two chapters is depicted again in figure 7.8 and might be displayed for our vendor master application. With this menu, the operator is given a list of functions that can be performed by the system. Since the functions are listed right on the menu, the operator wouldn't have to remember the various transaction codes associated with the application programs. Operator training would be minimal and new functions could be added later without impairing operator productivity.

Application menus can also reduce operator keying. With menus, the operator will not have to key in the CICS transaction code each time a function is needed. With proper screen design, the menu screen can provide a data entry template to perform most transactions. Then by redisplaying the menu after each transaction is complete, the operator can immediately perform the next function. Eliminating the need to rekey transaction input can result in an increase in operator productivity.

The design of a menu-oriented application can also provide for the implementation of improved control procedures. The menu program being the standard entry point into the application provides an ideal place to design any special application security provisions. These provisions might include an application sign-on mechanism. This application sign-on could provide for transaction security or other control features for an application.

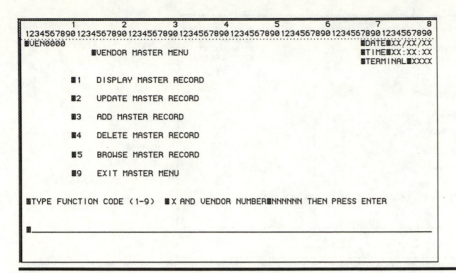

```
          1         2         3         4         5         6         7         8
1234567890123456789012345678901234567890123456789012345678901234567890123456789 0
▪VEN0000                                                   ▪DATE▪XX/XX/XX
            ▪VENDOR MASTER MENU                            ▪TIME▪XX:XX:XX
                                                           ▪TERMINAL▪XXXX

         ▪1    DISPLAY MASTER RECORD

         ▪2    UPDATE MASTER RECORD

         ▪3    ADD MASTER RECORD

         ▪4    DELETE MASTER RECORD

         ▪5    BROWSE MASTER RECORD

         ▪9    EXIT MASTER MENU


▪TYPE FUNCTION CODE (1-9)  ▪X AND VENDOR NUMBER▪NNNNNN THEN PRESS ENTER


▪_____
```

FIGURE 7.9.   Sample Menu Screen Using Function Codes

MENU SCREEN DESIGN

The menu screen depicted in figure 7.8 reflects a commonly used design. In this design the operator will enter a record key then select a transaction by pressing a PF key on the terminal. Since only one PF key can be used on input, only one selection at a time is possible. If you were to survey several installations, you would most likely find many variations to the layout and design of application menus. All of those variations, though, would share the same basic purpose, to provide an ease-of-use method of selecting and invoking transactions. Menu screens should be designed to support the following objectives:

1. Provide a list of available transactions for an application.
2. Provide a means of selecting a transaction.
3. Provide input area(s) for fields needed for the transaction.
4. Provide a way to inform the operator when errors or exceptions occur.

The examples below illustrate the most commonly used screen design techniques for implementing application menus. All of them relate to our sample vendor master application. The only difference between each menu screen is the way in which the transaction is selected. Each of the functions (except EXIT) in this application requires a vendor record key. A data entry field has been provided on all screens for the operator to input this value. Likewise a message line has been provided to inform the operator of any problems in performing a transaction.

The next menu design example is found in figure 7.9. In this design the operator will enter a record key. A function code will also be entered to select a transaction. This design requires more keystrokes than our previous example, since both the record key and function code must be entered. In some cases this design may be better than the PF-key approach. For instance, if more than 12 transactions are to appear on the menu screen, it may be difficult to use PF keys to select them. Some terminals only have keys PF1 through PF12. The function code method would not have this limitation.

The next example is depicted in figure 7.10. In this design, the operator will select a transaction by entering an *X* beside the transaction to be performed. Fields would be defined for the operator to "select" a transaction. After an input mapping operation, the menu program would check each selection field for the *X* character, then—upon determining which selection was made—perform the

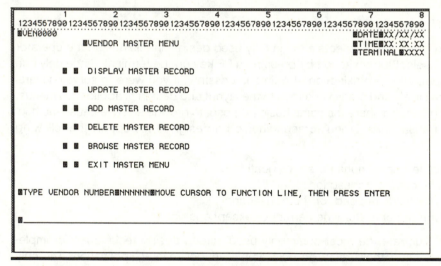

```
              1         2         3         4         5         6         7         8
     1234567890 1234567890 1234567890 1234567890 1234567890 1234567890 1234567890 1234567890
     ▓VEN0000                                                        ▓DATE▓XX/XX/XX
                   ▓VENDOR MASTER MENU                               ▓TIME▓XX:XX:XX
                                                                     ▓TERMINAL▓XXXX

            ▓X▓   DISPLAY MASTER RECORD

            ▓ ▓   UPDATE MASTER RECORD

            ▓ ▓   ADD MASTER RECORD

            ▓ ▓   DELETE MASTER RECORD

            ▓ ▓   BROWSE MASTER RECORD

            ▓ ▓   EXIT MASTER MENU


     ▓TYPE "X" BY FUNCTION DESIRED TYPE VENDOR NUMBER▓NNNNNN▓THEN PRESS ENTER


     ▓_____
```

FIGURE 7.10.   Sample Menu Screen Function Selected with 'X'

```
              1         2         3         4         5         6         7         8
     1234567890 1234567890 1234567890 1234567890 1234567890 1234567890 1234567890 1234567890
     ▓VEN0000                                                        ▓DATE▓XX/XX/XX
                   ▓VENDOR MASTER MENU                               ▓TIME▓XX:XX:XX
                                                                     ▓TERMINAL▓XXXX

            ▓ ▓   DISPLAY MASTER RECORD

            ▓ ▓   UPDATE MASTER RECORD

            ▓ ▓   ADD MASTER RECORD

            ▓ ▓   DELETE MASTER RECORD

            ▓ ▓   BROWSE MASTER RECORD

            ▓ ▓   EXIT MASTER MENU


     ▓TYPE VENDOR NUMBER▓NNNNNN▓MOVE CURSOR TO FUNCTION LINE, THEN PRESS ENTER


     ▓_____
```

FIGURE 7.11.   Sample Menu Screen Function Selected by Cursor Position

transaction. One problem with this design is that the cursor must be moved from the data input area to a selection area. Changes to the record number would require repositioning back to the record key field. Another problem is that some confusion might arise since the operator could make more than one selection. In addition, the extra keystrokes to move the cursor to the desired function could cause a loss of productivity. This design is likely to be inferior to the previously described screens.

Another example is depicted in figure 7.11. In this design, the operator moves the cursor to the function to be selected. The menu program would use cursor position to determine which transaction had been requested. The cursor location is stored in a field in the EIB. Since the cursor can only occupy one position, only one selection is possible. A problem with this design is that changes to the menu screen might cause a loss of format independence afforded by BMS. In addition, like the previous example, repositioning of the cursor from the record key area to the cursor-selection area would cause a loss of productivity.

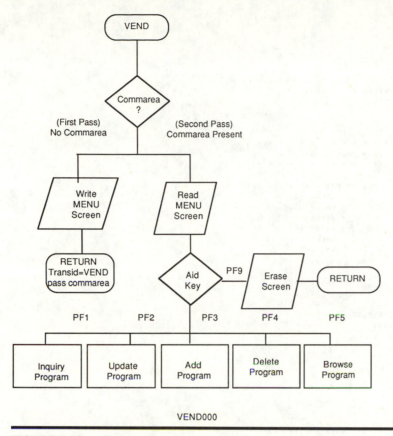

VEND000

FIGURE 7.12. Pseudo-conversational Menu Program Logic

For our sample application we are going to use the menu screen depicted in figure 7.8. Programming requirements to use this menu design will be discussed in the paragraphs that follow. Much of this design would apply to the other menu screen examples just described.

MENU PROGRAM DESIGN

The menu program has three basic functions. These are

1. to send a menu screen to the terminal
2. to receive and validate the menu screen input
3. to transfer control to a transaction processing program

The pseudoconversational programming technique is used to perform these three functions. When using a single program to perform these functions, the two-pass logic is used. Either a second transaction identification code or a commarea presence method as described in chapter 4 can be used. Figure 7.12 depicts the logic of a two-pass menu program using the commarea presence technique. The programming is shown in figure 7.13. The entry analysis routine at the top of the Procedure division checks the commarea length for a value of zero. If no commarea is present, the first-pass routine is performed.

```
        IDENTIFICATION DIVISION.
        PROGRAM-ID. VEND000.
        AUTHOR.  BOB LOWE.
        ENVIRONMENT DIVISION.
        DATA DIVISION.
        WORKING-STORAGE SECTION.
        01  WORK-AREAS.
            05  A-NULL                 PIC X VALUE LOW-VALUES.
            05  PROGRAM-NAME           PIC X(08).
            05  COPY-OF-EIBAID         PIC X.
                88  VALID-AID-KEY-USED  VALUES ARE
                    QUOTE, '1', '2', '3', '4', '5'.
* * * * * * * * * * * * * * * * * * * * * * * * * * * * * * *
*     CICS/VS Release 1.6- Command Exception test area
* * * * * * * * * * * * * * * * * * * * * * * * * * * * * * *
        01  CICS-RETURN-CODE-TEST-AREA.
            05  COMMAND-STATUS-CODE         PIC S9(08) COMP VALUE +0.
                88  NORMAL                      VALUE +0.
                88  DSIDERR                     VALUE +1.
                88  ILLOGIC                     VALUE +2.
                88  MAPFAIL                     VALUE +4.
                88  FC-INVREQ                   VALUE +8.
                88  NOTOPEN                     VALUE +12.
                88  DISABLED                    VALUE +13.
                88  FC-IOERR                    VALUE +128.
                88  NOTFND                      VALUE +129.
                88  NOTAUTH                     VALUE +214.
                88  LENGERR                     VALUE +225.
            05  FILLER REDEFINES COMMAND-STATUS-CODE.
                10  FILLER         PIC XXX.
                10  CONVERT-TO-DECIMAL PIC X.
        COPY  DFHAID SUPPRESS.
        COPY  VENDSET SUPPRESS.
        LINKAGE SECTION.
        PROCEDURE DIVISION.
            MOVE LOW-VALUES TO MENUMAPO.
            IF EIBCALEN EQUAL ZERO
                PERFORM 925-TRANSMIT-MENU-SCREEN.
            IF EIBAID    EQUAL DFHPF9
                EXEC CICS SEND ERASE FROM (A-NULL) LENGTH (1) END-EXEC
                EXEC CICS RETURN  END-EXEC.
            MOVE EIBAID TO COPY-OF-EIBAID.
            IF VALID-AID-KEY-USED
                NEXT SENTENCE
            ELSE
                MOVE 'INVALID PF KEY USED' TO MMESAGEO
                PERFORM 925-TRANSMIT-MENU-SCREEN.
            EXEC CICS RECEIVE MAP ('MENUMAP')
                      MAPSET      ('VENDSET')
                      NOHANDLE
            END-EXEC.
            MOVE EIBRCODE TO CONVERT-TO-DECIMAL.
            IF NORMAL NEXT SENTENCE
              ELSE
              IF MAPFAIL
                 MOVE 'NO INPUT RECEIVED' TO MMESAGEO
                 GO TO 925-TRANSMIT-MENU-SCREEN
              ELSE
                 MOVE 'UNKNOWN BMS ERROR-CALL MIS' TO MMESAGEO
                 GO TO 925-TRANSMIT-MENU-SCREEN.
            IF VENDIDI IN MENUMAPI IS NOT NUMERIC
               MOVE 'RECORD KEY NOT NUMERIC' TO MMESAGEO
               PERFORM 925-TRANSMIT-MENU-SCREEN.
            IF EIBAID EQUAL DFHENTER
               MOVE 'VEND007' TO PROGRAM-NAME
            ELSE
            IF EIBAID EQUAL DFHPF1
               MOVE 'VEND001' TO PROGRAM-NAME
            ELSE IF EIBAID EQUAL DFHPF2
                 MOVE 'VEND002' TO PROGRAM-NAME
                 ELSE IF EIBAID EQUAL DFHPF3
                      MOVE 'VEND003' TO PROGRAM-NAME
                      ELSE IF EIBAID EQUAL DFHPF4
                           MOVE 'VEND004' TO PROGRAM-NAME
                           ELSE IF EIBAID EQUAL DFHPF5
                                MOVE 'VEND005' TO PROGRAM-NAME.
```

FIGURE 7.13.   Sample Pseudo-conversational Menu Program

```
EXEC CICS XCTL PROGRAM (PROGRAM-NAME)
      COMMAREA (VENDIDI IN MENUMAPI) LENGTH (06)
      NOHANDLE
      END-EXEC.
   MOVE 'REQUESTED PROGRAM NOT AVAILABLE' TO MMESAGEO.
925-TRANSMIT-MENU-SCREEN.
   MOVE EIBTRMID   TO TERMO IN MENUMAPO.
   MOVE CURRENT-DATE TO DATEO IN MENUMAPO.
   MOVE EIBTIME TO TIMEO IN MENUMAPO.
   TRANSFORM TIMEO IN MENUMAPO FROM ',' TO ':'.
   MOVE 'VEN0000'  TO SCODEO IN MENUMAPO.
   EXEC CICS SEND MAP ('MENUMAP')
            MAPSET ('VENDSET')
            ERASE
            FREEKB
            END-EXEC.
   EXEC CICS  RETURN  TRANSID (EIBTRNID)
      COMMAREA (EIBAID) LENGTH (1) END-EXEC.
   GOBACK.
```

FIGURE 7.13. Continued

INITIAL ENTRY LOGIC

The first-pass (initial entry) routine (925-TRANSMIT-MENU-SCREEN) first displays the menu screen. This simply involves a BMS output mapping operation. The screen code, date, time, and terminal identification are moved to the mapping area. The screen is then displayed with the SEND MAP command. The first-pass logic is completed by issuing a pseudoconversational RETURN command. A one-byte commarea is passed to the next task.

RETURNING LOGIC

The second-pass logic (returning logic) performs the remaining two menu functions. First, the input is validated, then, if everything is correct, control is transferred to a processing program.

The returning logic begins by checking to see if the operator requested the exit function (PF9 in our sample menu screen). There is no need to perform an input mapping operation if the exit function was requested.

If the exit function was not requested, the AID code is validated. If an invalid attention key is used, the program will not bother to receive the menu input. Instead it will display the menu screen with an error message. The same routine (925-TRANSMIT-MENU-SCREEN) used in the first-pass logic is used to display the menu screen with the error message. A pseudoconversational RETURN again terminates the program. The operator can then press a correct AID key to try again. When this happens, the returning logic will be invoked.

If the AID is correct, the returning logic issues a RECEIVE MAP command to retrieve the record key. The record key field is then validated. In our example, if the record key is not numeric, the menu screen is displayed again, with an error message. The same routine (925-TRANSMIT-MENU-SCREEN) used in the first-pass logic is used to display the menu screen with the error message. A pseudo-conversational RETURN again terminates the program. The operator can then reenter the record key and try again.

If the record key is correct, the returning logic examines the field EIBAID again to determine which function was requested. The logic now identifies the transaction processing program to be used. This is done by moving the appropriate program name to a COBOL variable. This eight-character variable is then used as a *name* argument in the XCTL command that follows the function analysis logic.

The transfer of control function is accommodated by a single XCTL command to pass control to the appropriate processing program. The COBOL variable used as the name argument should contain the program name of the processing program. If the XCTL command fails, the menu screen will be displayed with an error message.

The example depicts one way to design the transfer of control logic. There is another method that could have been used instead. The program could have used statements as shown below. This method might be easier to design in a program with many additional functions.

```
IF EIBAID EQUAL DFHPF1
        EXEC CICS XCTL PROGRAM ('VEND001')
        COMMAREA (VENDIDI IN MENUMAPI) LENGTH (6)
        END-EXEC.
IF EIBAID EQUAL DFHPF2
        EXEC CICS XCTL PROGRAM ('VEND002')
        COMMAREA (VENDIDI IN MENUMAPI) LENGTH (6)
        END-EXEC.
        ...
        ...
```

The logic depicted in this example provides a model that can be used in many menu programs. The logic may vary somewhat for other menu programs due to screen design and other requirements of the program, but the basic functions will remain the same: to provide a way for an operator to select transactions without having to enter CICS transaction codes directly at the terminal. Most of the remaining programming examples in this text will be menu-based, and will interact with the sample program you have just studied. In the next topic you will see how to design a menu-based transaction program. An inquiry program is used in this example. In the chapters that follow, you will then study the update programs, a multiple screen inquiry program, and a file-browse program. All of these programs will be implemented around the menu design just described.

MENU BASED TRANSACTIONS

Throughout this text, you have witnessed the evolution of an inquiry program. The first program, in chapter 4, used the SEND TEXT, and SEND PAGE commands to display information from a record. Then in chapter 5, we designed a BMS map for an inquiry-update screen. In chapter 6, the output mapping example used that BMS screen. All of these examples were implemented using the direct transaction entry design technique. Now let's look at that program one more time. This time, we will develop the logic necessary for the inquiry transaction to interact with the menu program. As with the other examples in this text, this illustration represents the logic of a *typical* application program. Like all programs, there are many variations to this basic design.

The logic of a typical menu-based inquiry program is depicted in figure 7.14. Please refer to this illustration as you study these paragraphs. The programming is shown in figure 7.15. You will notice that much of the logic and the programming shown in these figures is the same as described in the earlier chapters. There is one primary difference. This inquiry program implements the pseudoconversational design technique. It incorporates our familiar two-pass logic. An entry analysis statement at the top of the procedure division will determine which *pass* is being performed.

ENTRY ANALYSIS

Entry to the program will be from either an XCTL from the menu or through a pseudoconversational RETURN with a transaction identification of V001. The entry analysis routine will determine how the program was started. It will determine this by examining the transaction code in the EIB. If the inquiry program has just received control from a pseudoconversational RETURN, the field EIBTRNID will contain the transaction code V001. In this case, the second-pass routine will be performed. If it contains any other value, the entry analysis statement will assume that control has just been passed from the menu program. It will then perform the first-pass routine. This logic is referred to as the initial processing logic.

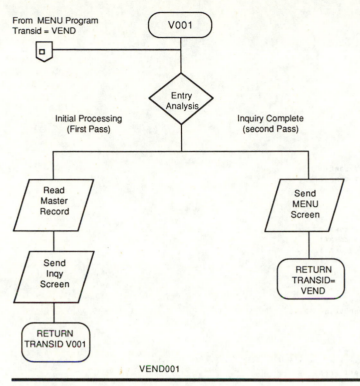

From MENU Program
Transid = VEND

V001

Entry
Analysis

Initial Processing
(First Pass)

Inquiry Complete
(second Pass)

Read
Master
Record

Send
MENU
Screen

Send
Inqy
Screen

RETURN
TRANSID=
VEND

RETURN
TRANSID V001

VEND001

FIGURE 7.14. Inquiry Program Logic

INITIAL PROCESSING LOGIC

The purpose of the first-pass, or initial processing, logic is to display a record. The program will get the record key from the *commarea*. It will use this value for the RIDFLD argument of the READ command. The program will then perform a BMS output mapping operation to display the inquiry screen. Finally, the program does a pseudoconversational RETURN with the transid of V001. It passes a commarea containing the key of the record just displayed. The second-pass logic will use this record key. This second-pass routine is known as the *inquiry complete logic.*

INQUIRY COMPLETE LOGIC

The inquiry complete logic will be started after the operator has viewed the inquiry screen and has pressed an AID key (such as ENTER or CLEAR).

The purpose of the inquiry complete logic is to redisplay the menu screen, and issue a pseudoconversational RETURN to the menu transaction. The operator can then initiate another transaction from the menu screen. In effect, this is the *transition* from the inquiry transaction, back to the menu program. Each of the menu-based transaction programs will "return" to the menu program in this fashion.

ERROR-PROCESSING LOGIC

Now, let's study the error-processing logic for this program. It is essentially the same as our earlier inquiry program examples. The first noticeable difference in the program, is that it checks the CICS return code value instead of using HANDLE CONDITION commands. This process was described earlier in the chapter, and you may want to study it further here. There is another feature illustrated

```
IDENTIFICATION DIVISION.
PROGRAM-ID. VEND001.
AUTHOR.  BOB LOWE.
ENVIRONMENT DIVISION.
DATA DIVISION.
WORKING-STORAGE SECTION.
01   VENDOR-RECORD.
     05   VENDOR-NAME            PIC X(30).
     05   VENDOR-ID              PIC XXXXX.
     05   VENDOR-ADDR1           PIC X(30).
     05   VENDOR-ADDR2           PIC X(30).
     05   VENDOR-ADDR3           PIC X(30).
     05   VENDOR-ADDR4           PIC X(30).
     05   VENDOR-CONTACT         PIC X(30).
     05   VENDOR-TELE            PIC X(12).
     05   VENDOR-TAXID           PIC X(11).
     05   VENDOR-YTD-SALES       PIC S9(07)V99 COMP-3.
     05   VENDOR-YTD-PAYMENTS    PIC S9(07)V99 COMP-3.
     05   VENDOR-YTD-DISCOUNTS   PIC S9(07)V99 COMP-3.
     05   VENDOR-PAY-HOLD        PIC X.
     05   VENDOR-PRODUCT         PIC XXX.
     05   VENDOR-LAST-CHECK      PIC S9(05)    COMP-3.
     05   VENDOR-LAST-CK-DATE    PIC S9(05)    COMP-3.
     05   VENDOR-LAST-CK-AMT     PIC S9(07)V99 COMP-3.
     05   VENDOR-DATE-ADDED      PIC S9(05)    COMP-3.
     05   VENDOR-DATE-CHANGED    PIC S9(05)    COMP-3.
     05   VENDOR-LAST-OPID       PIC XXX.
     05   VENDOR-UPDCNT          PIC 9.
01   MISC-AREAS.
     05   MSG-LEN                PIC S9999 COMP.
     05   VENDOR-RECORD-LENGTH   PIC S9999 COMP VALUE +249.
     05   PASS-EIBRCODE-EIBFN.
          10   PASS-EIBRCODE     PIC XXXXXX.
          10   PASS-EIBFN        PIC XX.
          10   FILLER            PIC X(8).
* * * * * * * * * * * * * * * * * * * * * * * * * * * * *
*    CICS/VS Release 1.6- Command Exception test area
* * * * * * * * * * * * * * * * * * * * * * * * * * * * *
01   CICS-RETURN-CODE-TEST-AREA.
     05   COMMAND-STATUS-CODE          PIC S9(08) COMP VALUE +0.
          88   NORMAL                       VALUE +0.
          88   DSIDERR                      VALUE +1.
          88   ILLOGIC                      VALUE +2.
          88   MAPFAIL                      VALUE +4.
          88   FC-INVREQ                    VALUE +8.
          88   NOTOPEN                      VALUE +12.
          88   DISABLED                     VALUE +13.
          88   FC-IOERR                     VALUE +128.
          88   NOTFND                       VALUE +129.
          88   NOTAUTH                      VALUE +214.
          88   LENGERR                      VALUE +225.
     05   FILLER REDEFINES COMMAND-STATUS-CODE.
          10   FILLER            PIC XXX.
          10   CONVERT-TO-DECIMAL PIC X.
01   ERROR-MESSAGE-LINE.
     05   MESSAGE-NUMBER         PIC X(8).
     05   FILLER                 PIC X.
     05   THE-MESSAGE            PIC X(54).
     05   RC-LABEL               PIC XXXX.
     05   RESPONSE-CODE4-16      PIC X(12).
* * * * * * * * * * * * * * * * * * * * * * * * * * * * *
*    BMS ATTRIBUTE VALUES INCLUDING HILIGHT AND COLOR
* * * * * * * * * * * * * * * * * * * * * * * * * * * * *
01   STANDARD-BMS-ATTRIBUTES.
     02   UNPROT-NORM            PIC X VALUE SPACE.
     02   UNPROT-BRT             PIC X VALUE 'H'.
     02   UNPROT-DRK             PIC X VALUE '<'.
     02   UNPROT-FSET-NORM       PIC X VALUE 'A'.
     02   UNPROT-FSET-BRT        PIC X VALUE 'I'.
     02   UNPROT-FSET-DRK        PIC X VALUE '('.
     02   UNPROT-NUM-NORM        PIC X VALUE '&'.
     02   UNPROT-NUM-BRT         PIC X VALUE 'Q'.
     02   UNPROT-NUM-DRK         PIC X VALUE '*'.
     02   UNPROT-NUM-FSET-NORM   PIC X VALUE 'J'.
     02   UNPROT-NUM-FSET-BRT    PIC X VALUE 'R'.
     02   UNPROT-NUM-FSET-DRK    PIC X VALUE ')'.
     02   PROT-NORM              PIC X VALUE '-'.
     02   PROT-BRT               PIC X VALUE 'Y'.
     02   PROT-DRK               PIC X VALUE '%'.
     02   PROT-FSET-NORM         PIC X VALUE '/'.
```

FIGURE 7.15.   Sample Menu based Inquiry Program

```
          02  PROT-FSET-BRT          PIC X VALUE 'Z'.
          02  PROT-FSET-DRK          PIC X VALUE '_'.
          02  ASKIP-NORM             PIC X VALUE '0'.
          02  ASKIP-BRT              PIC X VALUE '8'.
          02  ASKIP-DRK              PIC X VALUE '@'.
          02  ASKIP-FSET-NORM        PIC X VALUE '1'.
          02  ASKIP-FSET-BRT         PIC X VALUE '9'.
          02  ASKIP-FSET-DRK         PIC X VALUE QUOTE.
          02  HILIGHT-DEFAULT        PIC X VALUE LOW-VALUE.
          02  HILIGHT-BLINK          PIC X VALUE '1'.
          02  HILIGHT-REVERSE        PIC X VALUE '2'.
          02  HILIGHT-UNDERSCORE     PIC X VALUE '4'.
          02  COLOR-DEFAULT          PIC X VALUE LOW-VALUE.
          02  COLOR-BLUE             PIC X VALUE '1'.
          02  COLOR-RED              PIC X VALUE '2'.
          02  COLOR-PINK             PIC X VALUE '3'.
          02  COLOR-GREEN            PIC X VALUE '4'.
          02  COLOR-TURKUOISE        PIC X VALUE '5'.
          02  COLOR-YELLOW           PIC X VALUE '6'.
          02  COLOR-WHITE            PIC X VALUE '7'.
      COPY VENDSET.
      LINKAGE SECTION.
      01  DFHCOMMAREA.
          05  KEY-INPUT              PIC XXXXXX.
      PROCEDURE DIVISION.
      *PROCEDURE CODE
      000-MAINLINE-ROUTINE.
          MOVE LOW-VALUES TO MENUMAPO.
          IF EIBTRNID EQUAL 'V001'
              MOVE KEY-INPUT TO VENDIDO IN MENUMAPO
              PERFORM 925-TRANSMIT-MENU-SCREEN.
          IF EIBCALEN LESS THAN +6
              MOVE 'PROGRAM LOGIC ERROR-NO COMMAREA'  TO MMESAGEO
              GO TO 925-TRANSMIT-MENU-SCREEN.
          IF KEY-INPUT NOT NUMERIC
              MOVE 'VENDOR NUMBER NOT NUMERIC' TO MMESAGEO
              MOVE KEY-INPUT TO VENDIDO IN MENUMAPO
              GO TO 925-TRANSMIT-MENU-SCREEN.
          EXEC CICS READ
              DATASET ('VENFILE')
              INTO    (VENDOR-RECORD)
              RIDFLD  (KEY-INPUT)
              LENGTH  (VENDOR-RECORD-LENGTH)
              NOHANDLE
              END-EXEC.
          IF EIBRCODE NOT EQUAL LOW-VALUES
              PERFORM 940-FILE-ERROR
              MOVE ERROR-MESSAGE-LINE TO MMESAGEO IN MENUMAPO
              GO TO 925-TRANSMIT-MENU-SCREEN.
          EJECT



      * **************************************************
      *    PREPARE AND SEND INQUIRY SCREEN
      * **************************************************
          MOVE LOW-VALUES         TO              DISPMAPO.
          MOVE 'VEN1001'          TO   SCODEO     IN DISPMAPO.
          MOVE ASKIP-NORM         TO   VENNAMEA   IN DISPMAPI
                                       ADDR1A     IN DISPMAPI
                                       ADDR2A     IN DISPMAPI
                                       ADDR3A     IN DISPMAPI
                                       ADDR4A     IN DISPMAPI
                                       CONTACA    IN DISPMAPI
                                       TELEA      IN DISPMAPI
                                       TAXIDA     IN DISPMAPI
                                       PAHOLDA    IN DISPMAPI.
          MOVE VENDOR-NAME        TO   VENNAMEO   IN DISPMAPO.
          MOVE VENDOR-ID          TO   VENDIDO    IN DISPMAPO.
          MOVE VENDOR-ADDR1       TO   ADDR1O     IN DISPMAPO.
          MOVE VENDOR-ADDR2       TO   ADDR2O     IN DISPMAPO.
          MOVE VENDOR-ADDR3       TO   ADDR3O     IN DISPMAPO.
          MOVE VENDOR-ADDR4       TO   ADDR4O     IN DISPMAPO.
          MOVE VENDOR-CONTACT     TO   CONTACO    IN DISPMAPO.
          MOVE VENDOR-TELE        TO   TELEO      IN DISPMAPO.
          MOVE VENDOR-TAXID       TO   TAXIDO     IN DISPMAPO.
          MOVE VENDOR-PAY-HOLD    TO   PAHOLDO    IN DISPMAPO.
          MOVE VENDOR-PRODUCT     TO   PRODUCTO   IN DISPMAPO.
```

FIGURE 7.15.   Continued

```
        EXEC CICS SEND MAP ('DISPMAP')
                MAPSET ('VENDSET')
                ERASE
                FREEKB
                NOHANDLE
                END-EXEC.
    EXEC CICS RETURN TRANSID ('V001')
        COMMAREA (KEY-INPUT) LENGTH (6)
        END-EXEC.
925-TRANSMIT-MENU-SCREEN.
    MOVE EIBTRMID   TO TERMO IN MENUMAPO.
    MOVE CURRENT-DATE TO DATEO IN MENUMAPO.
    MOVE EIBTIME TO TIMEO IN MENUMAPO.
    TRANSFORM TIMEO IN MENUMAPO FROM ',' TO ':'.
    MOVE 'VEN0000'   TO SCODEO IN MENUMAPO.
    EXEC CICS SEND MAP ('MENUMAP')
                MAPSET ('VENDSET')
                ERASE
                FREEKB
                END-EXEC.
    EXEC CICS  RETURN  TRANSID ('VEND')
        COMMAREA (EIBAID) LENGTH (1)
        END-EXEC.




* * * * * * * * * * * * * * * * * * * * * * * * * * *
* * * * * * * * * * * * * * * * * * * * * * * * * *
*    ERROR PROCESSING ROUTINES
* * * * * * * * * * * * * * * * * * * * * * * * *
940-FILE-ERROR.
    MOVE SPACES TO ERROR-MESSAGE-LINE.
    MOVE EIBRCODE TO CONVERT-TO-DECIMAL.
    IF NOTFND
        MOVE 'RECORD NOT ON FILE' TO THE-MESSAGE
        MOVE KEY-INPUT TO VENDIDO IN MENUMAPO
        MOVE 'VEND0950'  TO MESSAGE-NUMBER
    ELSE IF NOTOPEN
            MOVE 'VENDOR FILE NOT OPEN' TO THE-MESSAGE
            MOVE 'VEND0950'  TO MESSAGE-NUMBER
        ELSE PERFORM 980-ERROR.
980-ERROR.
* ********************************************************
* LINK TO VEND010 TO CONVERT HEX RESPONSE CODE TO
* DISPLAY FORM.
* ********************************************************
    MOVE EIBRCODE TO PASS-EIBRCODE.
    MOVE EIBFN    TO PASS-EIBFN.
    EXEC CICS LINK
        PROGRAM ('VEND010')
        COMMAREA (PASS-EIBRCODE-EIBFN)
        LENGTH (16)
        END-EXEC.
    MOVE PASS-EIBRCODE-EIBFN TO RESPONSE-CODE4-16.
    MOVE ' RC=' TO RC-LABEL.
    MOVE 'UNDETERMINED FILE ERROR HAS OCCURRED ' TO THE-MESSAGE
    MOVE 'VEND0980'  TO MESSAGE-NUMBER
999-SUPPRESS-STOP-RUN.
    GOBACK.
```

FIGURE 7.15.   Continued

in this programming example. One of the file error routines makes use of the LINK to "call" an error-handling utility program. This user-written (I wrote it) utility program is depicted in figure 7.16. It's purpose in this example is to convert the CICS hexadecimal return code to display form. (It also allowed me to show an example of the LINK command.) By calling this program, the error-processing routines can now display the "hexadecimal" response value from CICS. This routine or another like it could prove to be a useful problem-determination tool.

We have now converted our inquiry program to *interface* with the menu program. If you compare this program with the examples in the earlier chapters, you will notice that they are very similar. By

Sample Program to convert hex repsonse codes to character form

```
        IDENTIFICATION DIVISION.
        PROGRAM-ID. VEND010.
        AUTHOR.   BOB LOWE.
*  *  *  *  *  *  *  *  *  *  *  *  *  *  *  *  *  *  *  *  *  *  *
*      This is a program to convert the hexadecimal function
*          code and response code to character form so it can
*          be displayed by an application.
*  *  *  *  *  *  *  *  *  *  *  *  *  *  *  *  *  *  *  *  *  *  *
        ENVIRONMENT DIVISION.
        DATA DIVISION.
        WORKING-STORAGE SECTION.
        01   SAVE-PASSED-COMMAREA.
             05   EIBRCODE-PASSED              PIC XXXXXX.
             05   EIBFN-PASSED                 PIC XX.
*  *  *  *  *  *  *  *  *  *  *  *  *  *  *  *  *  *  *  *  *  *  *
*      This group of fields is used in paragraph
*          900-GET-DEBUGGING-INFORMATION
*      The debugging paragraph is entered when some unusual CICS
*          response has been encountered by the program; for
*          instance, ILLOGIC could occurr in a file command.
*          The debugging paragraph converts the hexadecimal
*          function code and response code passed in the
*          commarea to display form.  The display form is
*          passed back to the calling program in the original
*          commarea.
*      See paragraph 900-GET-DEBUGGING-INFORMATION for further
*          comments.
*  *  *  *  *  *  *  *  *  *  *  *  *  *  *  *  *  *  *  *  *  *  *
        01   HEX-TO-DISPLAY-WORK-AREA.
             05   COMP-3-FIELD             COMP-3 PIC S9(13).
             05   SIX-HEX-BYTES REDEFINES COMP-3-FIELD.
                  07   FOUR-HEX-BYTES.
                       09   TWO-HEX-BYTES.
                            11   ONE-HEX-BYTE PIC X.
                            11   FILLER       PIC X.
                       09   FILLER          PIC XX.
                  07   FILLER               PIC XX.
             05   UNPACK-FIELD   PIC S9(13).
             05   SIX-RETURN-CODES REDEFINES UNPACK-FIELD.
                  07   FOUR-RETURN-CODES.
                       09   TWO-RETURN-CODES.
                            11   ONE-RETURN-CODE   PIC XX.
                            11   FILLER            PIC XX.
                       09   FILLER               PIC XXXX.
                  07   FILLER                     PIC XXXX.
*  *  *  *  *  *  *  *  *  *  *  *  *  *  *  *  *  *  *  *  *  *  *
*      CONSTANTS TO TRANSFORM FA,FB,FC,FD,FE,FF to ABCDEF
*  *  *  *  *  *  *  *  *  *  *  *  *  *  *  *  *  *  *  *  *  *  *
             05   FAFBFCFDFEFF.
                  07   HEX-00FAFBFC         PIC S9(8) COMP VALUE +16448508.
                  07   HEX-00FDFEFF         PIC S9(8) COMP VALUE +16645887.
             05   ABCDEF                    PIC X(08)     VALUE ' ABC DEF'.
        LINKAGE SECTION.
        01   DFHCOMMAREA.
             05   PASS-BACK-EIBRCODE        PIC X(12).
             05   PASS-BACK-EIBFN           PIC XXXX.
        PROCEDURE DIVISION.
*  *  *  *  *  *  *  *  *  *  *  *  *  *  *  *  *  *  *  *  *  *  *
*      The debugging paragraph converts the hexadecimal
*          response code passed in the first six bytes
*          of the commarea and the CICS/VS function code
*          passed in the second two bytes of the
*          commarea to character form.  This display form
*          function function code and response code is
*          is returned to the calling program in the original
*          commarea storage.  Of course we need
*          a 16 byte commarea to return the display form of
*          eight hex bytes.
*  *  *  *  *  *  *  *  *  *  *  *  *  *  *  *  *  *  *  *  *  *  *
             MOVE DFHCOMMAREA TO SAVE-PASSED-COMMAREA.
             IF EIBCALEN LESS THAN 16
                 EXEC CICS RETURN END-EXEC.
        900-GET-DEBUGGING-INFORMATION.
```

FIGURE 7.16.   Sample Program to convert hex response codes to character form

```
* * * * * * * * * * * * * * * * * * * * * * * * * * * * *
*       The conversion of a hexadecimal field to display form
*           is accomplished by having the field redefined by
*           COMP-3 variable one byte longer than the hex field.
*           The COMP-3 variable is then moved to a numeric field.
*           This move causes COBOL to generate a S/370 UNPACK
*           instruction.  This unpack instruction causes each
*           hex digit to be placed in the low-order byte of a
*           separate character position and a HEX-F to be placed
*           in the high-order byte of that position.  For example
*           a hexadecimal byte containing 01 would be converted
*           to two bytes containing F0F1.  A byte containing a
*           hex value of E1 would be converted to two bytes of
*           FEF1.  The HEX value of FE does not display as the
*           character "E".  There is a problem with bytes containing
*           FA, FB, FC, FD, FE, and FF.  A COBOL transform
*           statement is used to convert these values to the
*           to the characters A, B, C, D, E, and F.
* * * * * * * * * * * * * * * * * * * * * * * * * * * * *
*       CONVERT EIBRCODE
* * * * * * * * * * * * * * * * * * * * * * * * * * * * *
        MOVE ZEROES TO COMP-3-FIELD.
        MOVE EIBRCODE-PASSED TO SIX-HEX-BYTES.
        MOVE COMP-3-FIELD TO UNPACK-FIELD.
        TRANSFORM SIX-RETURN-CODES FROM FAFBFCFDFEFF
                           TO ABCDEF.
        MOVE SIX-RETURN-CODES TO PASS-BACK-EIBRCODE.
        MOVE ZEROES TO COMP-3-FIELD.

* * * * * * * * * * * * * * * * * * * * * * * * * * * * *
*       CONVERT EIBFN
* * * * * * * * * * * * * * * * * * * * * * * * * * * * *
        MOVE EIBFN-PASSED  TO FOUR-HEX-BYTES.
        MOVE COMP-3-FIELD TO UNPACK-FIELD.
        TRANSFORM SIX-RETURN-CODES FROM FAFBFCFDFEFF
                           TO ABCDEF.
        MOVE FOUR-RETURN-CODES TO PASS-BACK-EIBFN.
        EXEC CICS RETURN END-EXEC.
        GOBACK
```

FIGURE 7.16. Continued

providing a commarea to access the record key, and a little bit of pseudoconversational magic, we have a *real-word* inquiry transaction. As we move into the next chapter to study the update programs you will again see traces of the logic just presented. Most menu-based programs share a common design.

Chapter Summary

This chapter has presented some new programming techniques. First, it described a new method of dealing with exceptional conditions. By using the NOHANDLE command option, and then checking either of two response code fields in the EIB, you can deal with any exceptional condition. This programming technique makes it easier to develop programs in a more structured manner. The chapter also introduced you to some new program control commands that provide for the design of modular systems. The XCTL and LINK commands allow more than one program to be executed during a single task. These commands can pass data from one program to another using the commarea. The basic design of a menu program was also presented in the chapter. The menu program makes it easier for an operator to perform on-line transactions. By using menus, a system can become more user-friendly. Finally, you saw how to design an inquiry-transaction program to interact with the menu program. This same programming will apply to most CICS programs. You should now be ready to proceed to the remaining chapters to study other menu-based transactions.

Discussion Questions

1. The NOHANDLE option can be used to cause CICS to return control to the program after a service command, regardless of whether an exception has occurred. Where is the NOHANDLE option included to cause this action?
2. Why is the EIBRESP field easier to use than EIBRCODE after a command exception?
3. The RESP option can be used to move the value in EIBRESP to a working-storage field. What are some benefits of using this option?
4. Discuss some of the advantages of designing systems consisting of smaller processing modules instead of writing one large general purpose program. Describe any disadvantages.
5. List the languages supported by the CICS Command-Level Interface.
6. Describe the effect of the LINK, XCTL, and RETURN commands with logical levels.
7. The communications area is used to pass variables from one program to another during a task. Why is the DFHCOMMAREA defined in the LINKAGE SECTION of the "called" program?
8. Upon returning control to a "calling" program using the LINK command, where would that program find any returned values?
9. How does a program determine the length of a communications area passed to it?
10. What are the exceptional conditions that can arise from the XCTL and LINK commands? When would they occur?
11. An application menu can make it easier to select a transaction to be run at a terminal. After the menu transaction has been entered, the operator can select from a list of available transactions that are displayed on the menu screen. How does the use of menus improve the productivity of an operator?

Review Exercises

1. Add the command option to the READ command below that would copy the newer CICS response code to the field defined.

```
01   COMMAND-RESPONSE-VALUE PIC S9(8) COMP.
     88  NORMAL              VALUE +0.
     88  DSIDERR             VALUE +12.
     88  NOTFND              VALUE +13.
     88  DUPREC              VALUE +14.

EXEC CICS READ
     DATASET ('PERSFLE')
     RIDFLE (KEY-INPUT)
     LENGTH (PERS-REC-LENGTH)
     INTO (PERSONNEL-MASTER-RECORD)
     (your option)
     END-EXEC.
```

2. Code a statement using the DFHRESP keyword to check for the NOTFND condition. If NOTFND occurs, perform a routine named 9000-NOTFND-ERROR.
3. Write the statement necessary to transfer control to PROGRAMB at the same logical level and pass the data below (these variables have already been initialized).

```
01   PASS-IT.
     05   FUNCTION-CODE PIC S9999 COMPUTATIONAL.
     05   RECORD-KEY PIC X(09).
```

4. Code the LINKAGE SECTION statements for PROGRAMB to access the passed data from the last exercise.

Lab Problems

LAB 1

PERSONNEL MENU PROGRAM
(PROGRAM XY00000, TRANSID XY00)

Design, code, and test a pseudoconversational menu program. This program will send and receive a menu screen and XCTL to a transaction-processing program based upon a selection from the menu screen. Use the menu screen cataloged in Lab 1 of chapter 5 of the text.

The pseudoconversational program logic will include the following functions:

INITIAL ENTRY LOGIC (FIRST-PASS) TRANSID-XY00, NO COMMAREA

☐ Initialize the menu map and move date, time, and terminal identification.

☐ Display the menu screen.

☐ Issue a pseudoconversational RETURN naming the menu-transaction code. Pass a commarea to be used in the entry analysis logic so the second-pass logic will be invoked in the next task.

RETURNING LOGIC (SECOND-PASS) TRANSID-XY00, COMMAREA PRESENT

☐ Receive the menu screen.
☐ Edit the SSN and check the AID key.
☐ XCTL to programs as follows:
>   Program xy00001 if ENTER or PF1 was used
>   Program xy00002 if PF2 was used
>   Program xy00003 if PF3 was used
>   Program xy00004 if PF4 was used
>   Program xy00005 if PF5 was used
>   Program xy00006 if PF6 was used

☐ Pass the SSN to the transaction processing program in the commarea.

Error conditions should be handled by the program. Whenever an error condition is detected, redisplay the menu screen displaying an appropriate message. Error conditions that should be anticipated include MAPFAIL, PGMIDERR, Nonnumeric SSN, invalid AID key.

If the CLEAR key was used, display a good-bye message and exit the program with a normal RETURN command. CLEAR should be the only way to exit the personnel master menu.

LAB 2

PERSONNEL INQUIRY PROGRAM (OPTION 1)
(PROGRAM XY00001, TRANSID XY01)

Design, code, and test a two-pass pseudoconversational inquiry program. The program will perform the following functions:

INITIAL ENTRY LOGIC (FIRST-PASS) TRANSID-XY00

☐ Access the SSN passed from the menu program in the commarea.
☐ Read the personnel master file using the passed SSN.

☐ Display the personal information screen defined in Lab 2 of chapter 5 of the text. Set the attribute of all fields to ASKIP NORMAL. (An example is depicted below.)

☐ Issue a pseudoconversational RETURN command naming the transid of this program (xy01). Pass the SSN in the commarea.

☐ Error conditions should be handled. Whenever an error condition is detected, display the menu screen with an appropriate message. Issue a pseudoconversational RETURN, naming the menu transid (xy00). Pass a suitable commarea so that the second-pass logic of the menu program will be used when that program is next started. Error conditions that should be anticipated include NOTFND, NOTOPEN and any other file errors that you wish to check.

```
                  1         2         3         4         5         6
         1234567890123456789012345678901234567890123456789012345678901234 56
01^PERS101          ^PERSONAL INFORMATION^INQUIRY
02
03
04        ^SSN:^123456789
05
06     ^NAME..^DOE, JOHN A                          ^
07  ^ADDRESS..^123 ANYWHERE STREET                  ^
08     ^CITY..^KANSAS CITY                  ^
09    ^STATE..^MO^641110000^
10
11    ^PHONE..^5551212^
12      ^SEX..^M^
13   ^ETHNIC..^1^
14      ^DOB..^083147^
15
16
17
18
19
20
21^MESSAGE:^PRESS CLEAR TO RETURN TO THE MENU
22
23
24
```

RETURNING LOGIC (SECOND-PASS) TRANSID-XY01

☐ Display the personnel menu screen including the SSN from the commarea.

☐ Issue a pseudoconversational RETURN, naming the menu transid (xy00). Pass a suitable commarea so that the second-pass logic of the menu program will be used when that program is next started.

LAB 3

PERSONNEL INQUIRY PROGRAM (OPTION 2)
(PROGRAM XY00001, TRANSID XY01)

Design, code, and test a two-pass pseudoconversational inquiry program. The program will perform the following functions:

INITIAL ENTRY LOGIC (FIRST-PASS) TRANSID-XY00

☐ Access the SSN passed from the menu program in the commarea.

☐ Read the personnel master file using the passed SSN.

☐ If the value in EIBAID is equal to ENTER, display the personal information screen defined in Lab 2 of chapter 5 of the text. Set the attribute of all fields to ASKIP NORMAL.

```
               1         2         3         4         5         6
      1234567890123456789012345678901234567890123456789012345678901 23
01^PERS101           ^PERSONAL INFORMATION^INQUIRY
02
03
04       ^SSN:^123456789
05
06     ^NAME..^DOE, JOHN A                              ^
07 ^ADDRESS..^123 ANYWHERE STREET                       ^
08    ^CITY..^KANSAS CITY              ^
09   ^STATE..^MO^641110000^
10
11   ^PHONE..^5551212^
12     ^SEX..^M^
13 ^ETHNIC..^1^
14     ^DOB..^083147^
15
16
17
18
19
20
21^MESSAGE:^PRESS CLEAR TO RETURN TO THE MENU
22
23
24
```

☐ If the value in EIBAID is equal to PF1, display the company information screen defined in Lab 3 of chapter 5 of the text. Set the attribute of all fields to ASKIP NORMAL.

```
               1         2         3         4         5         6
      1234567890123456789012345678901234567890123456789012345678901 23
01^PERS201           ^COMPANY INFORMATION^INQUIRY
02
03^SSN:^123456789
04^NAME:^DOE, JOHN A
05
06
07  ^EMPLOYEE TYPE..^01^
08       ^LOCATION..^04^
09     ^DEPARTMENT..^2180^
10
11      ^JOB TITLE..^21805^
12    ^POSITION NO..^00001^
13^EMPLOYMENT DATE..^060686^
14
15  ^ANNUAL SALARY..^  25,000.00^
16
17
18
19
20
21^MESSAGE:^PRESS CLEAR TO RETURN TO THE MENU
22
23
24
```

- Issue a pseudoconversational RETURN command naming the transid of this program (xy01). Pass the SSN in the commarea.
- Error conditions should be handled. Whenever an error condition is detected, display the menu screen with an appropriate message. Issue a pseudoconversational RETURN, naming the menu transid (xy00). Pass a suitable commarea so that the second-pass logic of the menu program will be used when that program is next started.
- Error conditions that should be anticipated include NOTFND, NOTOPEN and any other file errors that you wish to check.

RETURNING LOGIC (SECOND-PASS) TRANSID-XY01

- Display the personnel menu screen including the SSN from the commarea.
- Issue a pseudoconversational RETURN, naming the menu transid (xy00). Pass a suitable commarea so that the second-pass logic of the menu program will be used when that program is next started.

LAB 4

PERSONNEL INQUIRY PROGRAM (OPTION 3)
(PROGRAM XY00001, TRANSID XY01)

Design, code, and test a pseudoconversational inquiry program. The program will perform the following functions:

INITIAL ENTRY LOGIC (FIRST-PASS) TRANSID-XY00

- Access the SSN passed from the menu program in the commarea.
- Read the personnel master file using the passed SSN.
- If the value in EIBAID is equal to ENTER, display the personal information screen defined in Lab 2 of chapter 5 of the text. Set the attribute of all fields to ASKIP NORMAL.

```
              1         2         3         4         5         6
     1234567890123456789012345678901234567890123456789012345678901234567890123456789
01^PERS101           ^PERSONAL INFORMATION^INQUIRY
02
03
04        ^SSN:^123456789
05
06     ^NAME..^DOE, JOHN A                        ^
07 ^ADDRESS..^123 ANYWHERE STREET                  ^
08     ^CITY..^KANSAS CITY           ^
09    ^STATE..^MO^641110000^
10
11    ^PHONE..^5551212^
12      ^SEX..^M^
13   ^ETHNIC..^1^
14      ^DOB..^083147^
15
16
17
18
19
20
21^MESSAGE:^PRESS CLEAR TO RETURN TO THE MENU
22
23
24
```

- [ ] If the value in EIBAID is equal to PF1, display the extended company information screen defined in Lab 4 of chapter 5 of the text. Set the attribute of all fields to ASKIP NORMAL.
- [ ] Use the System Control File (described in Appendix B) to retrieve the description values for the employee type, location, department, and job title codes.

```
            1         2         3         4         5         6
   1234567890123456789012345678901234567890123456789012345678901234556
01^PERS201          ^COMPANY INFORMATION^INQUIRY
02
03^SSN:^123456789
04^NAME:^DOE, JOHN A
05
06
07   ^EMPLOYEE TYPE..^01^          ^ADMINISTRATOR
08        ^LOCATION..^04^          ^PENN VALLEY
09     ^DEPARTMENT..^2180^         ^COMPUTER SERVICES
10
11      ^JOB TITLE..^21805^        ^ANALYST PROGRAMMER
12    ^POSITION NO..^00001^        ^
13^EMPLOYMENT DATE..^060686^       ^
14
15^ANNUAL SALARY..^25,000.00^       ^
16
17
18
19
20
21^MESSAGE:^PRESS CLEAR TO RETURN TO THE MENU
22
23
24
```

- [ ] Issue a pseudoconversational RETURN command naming the transid of this program (xy01). Pass the SSN in the commarea.
- [ ] Error conditions should be handled. Whenever an error condition is detected, display the menu screen with an appropriate message. Issue a pseudoconversational RETURN, naming the menu transid (xy00). Pass a suitable commarea so that the second-pass logic of the menu program will be used when that program is next started. Error conditions that should be anticipated include NOTFND, NOTOPEN and any other file errors that you wish to check.

RETURNING LOGIC (SECOND-PASS) TRANSID-XY01

- [ ] Display the personnel menu screen including the SSN from the commarea.
- [ ] Issue a pseudoconversational RETURN, naming the menu transid (xy00). Pass a suitable commarea so that the second-pass logic of the menu program will be used when that program is next started.

The Update Transactions

By the time you have finished studying the material in this chapter you will

1. See how the on-line update functions can benefit user departments.
2. Develop guidelines for designing update screens.
3. Identify the primary data-editing techniques used with on-line update transactions.
4. See how symbolic cursor positioning can be used with update programs to improve operator productivity.
5. Examine the logic of three typical file-update programs.
6. Recognize that much of the logic in a file-add program is the same as the file-update program.
7. Recognize that pseudoconversational programs can lead to file-update conflict problems.
8. Learn how to protect against multiple update problems when using pseudoconversational programming techniques.
9. Understand how the use of the DATAONLY option of the BMS SEND MAP command can improve system performance and response time.

In this chapter you are going to learn how to design the three primary update transactions. First, the chapter will describe some of the benefits of providing on-line update transactions. Then you will see examples of screens designed for use by the update transactions. The chapter will describe the most commonly used input-editing techniques. Afterwards, the design for each of the update programs will be described. After studying this material, you should be able to design update transactions for a variety of systems. Toward the end of the chapter, two topics related to update programs will be discussed. The first topic will show how the pseudoconversational programming technique can lead to file-update conflicts and present methods to prevent this from happening. Finally, you will see how to use one option of the SEND MAP command to use the IBM 3270 terminal more efficiently.

Update Transaction Benefits

There are three file-update functions shown on the sample vendor master menu. They are (1) update a record; (2) add a record; and (3) delete a record. These update functions can be found in most applications. There are several benefits in developing these update functions for the on-line environment and extending them to the user. The user in this case is the department where the information for the file or data base originates. For instance, the personnel department is the source of much information stored in a payroll-personnel data base. The payroll department updates this same data base with transactions from time and attendance documents. Most operational units have one or more files or data bases that must be updated regularly to support their departmental role. The ability to update departmental information with on-line terminals can have a significant impact on the usefulness of an application. Likewise the efficiency of a user department and even the computer center can be improved by developing on-line update functions. Among the benefits of developing on-line update functions are the elimination of processing delays and improved control of an application.

PROCESSING DELAYS ELIMINATED

Perhaps the most significant benefit of giving users the capability to update their own files is the elimination of processing delays. The transaction flow through a system without on-line update capability often results in delays at several points. First, the department must prepare source documents for the data entry unit. In some cases, the source data is even transcribed from the original source document to a keypunch document that has update transaction codes on the form. Next, the source documents must be delivered to the data entry unit. If both departments are within the same building, this process may take only a matter of minutes. Sometimes, the keypunch department is in another building or even at a remote location. In this case, the transmittal of the source document may be delayed by an hour or even a day.

When the batch of source documents reach the data entry department, there may be some additional delay. The person responsible for data control will usually want to verify the receipt of the batch of changes by recording the receipt in a data entry log. The data control clerk will then give the documents to the keypunch unit supervisor or operator. Unless the transactions have high priority there will usually be some additional delay until an operator becomes available for keypunching the document. If the work has high priority, only a few minutes may elapse, otherwise the documents may remain on the data entry shelf for a long time.

The keypunching process converts the source documents into machine-readable form. These transactions, which may be in the form of cards, tape, or diskette may again have to wait on a shelf for some time until the computer operations unit has a chance to process them. To process the transactions the computer operator will run a batch-update program.

The batch-update program will input each transaction, then perform a validity check or edit on one or more input fields associated with that transaction. The edit will attempt to detect errors in the input fields. These errors may have originated from the source document, or may have been introduced in the transcribing or keypunching process. Upon finding an error, the batch program will list the problem on an exception report. Depending upon the requirements of the application and the severity of the error, the program may completely reject the update transaction or may do a partial update to the file. In either case, the exception report is used to correct problems with the input transactions.

Correcting problems usually involves the return of the source documents and the exception report to the user department. This transmittal process will again cause a delay of minutes, hours, or even a day, depending on the proximity of the department to the computer center. Upon receiving the original batches of documents and exception report, the user department will then have to locate each source document having an error listed on the exception report. After the errors are located and corrected, the process starts all over again. The corrections must be sent to the data entry unit. Transactions must be repunched or corrected. Operations must reschedule the update program to process the transactions. Finally, transaction reports must be sent back to the user department to confirm the update. During this time, hours or even days may have elapsed. In many cases other processing may have been delayed awaiting the update to the master file.

By providing the user with the on-line update functions, some of the processing and most of the delays described in the preceding paragraphs can be eliminated. The transmittal time and interchange of documents is eliminated since the departmental users can key in transactions at their own work station. Data control activities used to control the routing and computer center activities can be eliminated since the documents never leave the user department. Transactions can probably be keyed directly from the document used to collect the information. This eliminates most or all of the work and time required to transcribe data to keypunch forms. The computer operations department is relieved of the responsibilities and time required to schedule the update program and to print transaction and exception listings. Likewise, the user department does not have to wait for the computer center to schedule the update transactions. Updates can occur in a matter of seconds or minutes instead of hours or days.

DEPARTMENTAL CONTROL

A department having on-line update capabilities has better control of its applications. First, as you have just seen, transactions can be processed on demand. Work can be scheduled at the convenience of the user, and the department can better estimate the time it will require to process its transactions. Fewer errors should result from reduced handling of input documents, and errors can be detected and resolved quickly since the user department is most familiar with the application. Other activities that must follow the update functions can begin immediately. The elimination of transaction-update bottlenecks can therefore result in improved work flow for related departments.

Internal security may also be improved through the use of on-line update functions. In some companies, security and privacy are important issues. In the batch-update environment there are many opportunities for vital company information to be viewed by unauthorized people. Unless controlled, unauthorized access to private data can take place at many points in the process. With an on-line update process, many controls can be eliminated since source documents never have to leave the user department.

As you can see, the on-line update functions are an integral part of most applications. The file-update commands and techniques described in this chapter can be used in most update programs. These topics are an essential part of becoming a well-rounded CICS/VS programmer.

Update Screen Design

Now let's look at a screen design technique that is commonly used by the update transactions. A display-update screen for our sample vendor master application is depicted in figure 8.1. You will recall that this screen was used by the inquiry transaction to display information from a vendor master record. The design of this screen also supports the update transactions. Here is a quick review of the screen design features that relate to our update transactions.

Recall that each data entry field was defined with the unprotected, normal, and modified data tag attributes. The unprotected attribute allows the operator to enter or change the value for each field. For the update program, the operator will be able to change the values of these data entry fields. With the add program, the operator can key new values into these fields.

The FSET (modified data tag) attribute is used so that each field will be transmitted back to CICS when an attention key is pressed. Even fields that are not changed by the operator will be mapped into the program's working-storage when the RECEIVE MAP command is used. This design technique is commonly used to simplify the logic of update programs.

The "skip" and "stop" fields are also an important part of the design of the update screen. These user-defined fields, which immediately follow each data entry field, provide a data entry "border." This border prevents an operator from keying in more characters than can be mapped into the program's working-storage. Skip and stop fields are normally defined as one-character fields with either the ASKIP or PROT attribute.

There is another potential use for these skip and stop fields. It is shown in figure 8.2. Most update and add programs will perform some data validation (editing) of the fields entered by the operator. When an input error is detected, it is helpful to display an error message somewhere on

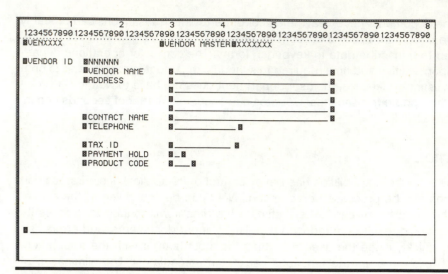

FIGURE 8.1. Update Screen Design

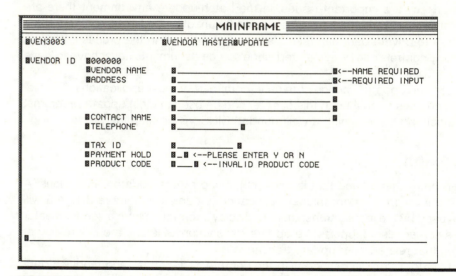

FIGURE 8.2. Update Screen Using Stopper Fields to Display Error Messages

the screen. The skip and stop fields provide an ideal place to display these error messages. Since they are just behind the data entry field, the operator will naturally associate the error message with the error field.

You will have to make some BMS coding changes in order to use these skip-stop fields to display error messages. First, each field will require a BMS name. By defining these fields with a name, the program can then move a variable message to the skip field. You will also have to define the skip-stop fields large enough to hold the error messages. For example, here are the BMS definitions for skip-stop message fields for the screen depicted in figure 8.2:

```
NAMMSG DFHMDF POS=(04,61),LENGTH=17,ATTRB=PROT
     .
AD1MSG DFHMDF POS=(05,61),LENGTH=17,ATTRB=PROT
     .
```

```
PAYMSG DFHMDF POS=(13,32),LENGTH=24,ATTRB=ASKIP

PRDMSG DFHMDF POS=(14,34),LENGTH=24,ATTRB=ASKIP
```

Once the skip-stop message fields are defined this way, the program can use them to display a message. This would be done during the transaction-editing process. For example, the program edit for the payment-hold field might appear as follows:

```
IF PAHOLDI EQUAL 'Y' OR 'N'
     NEXT SENTENCE
ELSE
     MOVE '<--PLEASE ENTER Y OR N' TO PAYMSGO
     MOVE -1 TO PAHOLDL
     MOVE UNPROT-FSET-BRT TO PAHOLDA.
```

Transaction Editing

The update and add programs usually perform some type of data validation as depicted in the example above. This validation process prevents incorrect data from being stored in the file. Invalid data can cause many problems for an application. These problems may range from incorrect reporting to logic errors and program abends. By rejecting invalid data during data entry operations, you can help to maintain the integrity of the application.

Depending on the hardware features available, it may be possible to perform some transaction editing at the terminal. The programmable features of the IBM 3270 terminal can assist in reducing errors at the source of input. For instance, the numeric lock feature can inhibit the input of alphameric characters when keying into a numeric field. Other features providing the capability to define "must-fill" and "must-enter" fields on some newer IBM terminals provide for further transaction editing at the terminal. These programmable features provide for early detection of errors and reduce data transmission and processor usage since the errors can be detected "locally" at the terminal. After local editing is performed, additional validation is then performed by the application program.

At some point, the application program will issue a RECEIVE MAP command to cause BMS to perform an input mapping operation. The input fields will then be moved into the symbolic description map. The data will be right- or left-justified and will have padding characters provided by the BMS. The program may then perform any needed data validation. A CICS/VS application program will perform the same transaction-editing techniques that are commonly used for batch-update programs. Among these techniques are

table search

data set check

reasonableness check

field-verify

limit range

check-digit

sight verification

TABLE SEARCH

This is a commonly used technique that uses the contents of the data field to search a table in the program's working-storage. An exact match between the field and a table entry indicates that the field contents are correct. In some cases, a substitute value or corresponding table description can be displayed on the terminal for sight verification.

DATA SET CHECK

This technique uses the contents of a field from the input transaction to access an on-line dataset. The field may comprise the entire record key of the data set or it may be concatenated with another field or constant to form a complete key. A random read to the data set will determine the validity of the incoming field. A NOTFND condition on the read operation would indicate an error condition. After a successful read using the field, the incoming record may also provide other information that can be used for further validation.

REASONABLENESS CHECK

This check implies that the program will apply various logical tests to ensure that the incoming information is valid for the application. If the criterion for the check is not satisfied, the information is treated as an error. For instance, in an accounting application, certain accounts may be reserved as "nonposting" accounts. An attempt to use one of these accounts in a posting transaction would be treated as an error.

FIELD-VERIFY

A field may be checked to verify that it contains the correct type of data. For instance, a numeric test may be performed on variables prior to use in calculations or output editing. Some applications may require that a field contain some data other than spaces or that a field be completely alphabetic. Fields containing invalid data type or content would be considered in error.

LIMIT RANGE

This technique checks that the value in a field lies between certain limits as defined by the application. A field value outside these limits would be treated as an error.

CHECK-DIGIT

Numeric values such as record identification fields may be checked for validity by means of a check-digit appended to the field. This check-digit, once computed by modulus 10 or modulus 11 procedures, would become an integral part of the field and would be used to check the accuracy of the number each time it is entered.

SIGHT VERIFICATION

This technique involves the display of information related to a field entered by the operator. This information might be a description from a table look-up or from a data set check. Once displayed, the operator can perform a sight verification of the information, then continue with the transaction or change the field contents. One example of this technique is the procedure used in the delete logic of the delete program at the end of the chapter. This logic provides for the display of the record to be deleted in the transaction. After verification that the correct record is being deleted, the operator may cancel or confirm the delete operation.

Error-Correction Techniques

The update program using the editing techniques described above should be able to detect most types of transaction errors. In most applications, you will want to defer the file-update operations until *all* errors have been corrected. Whenever possible, you should check all input fields from the screen and report any errors to the operator for correction. Errors are usually reported by redisplaying the update screen with some form of visual signal.

FIELD HIGHLIGHTING

When an update screen is redisplayed, the operator must be able to identify which fields have errors. Depending on the terminal being used, this can be accomplished a number of ways. On standard terminals, the BRT attribute can be used to "highlight" an error field. Some newer terminals can use extended attributes to highlight errors. These attributes include underlining, reverse video, and blinking. On color terminals, a color attribute could be used to highlight an error. For instance, the color red might be used to signal an error. Whenever possible, you should select a standard way to highlight an error field in all applications at your installation.

ERROR MESSAGES

Field highlighting may be all that is necessary, especially if the operators are familiar with the application. In other situations you may have to provide additional information to help the operator. For instance, you could display a short error message as described earlier. In the case of a field-verify error, a short error message such as "NUMERIC CHARACTERS ONLY" may be sufficient. Errors found by a reasonableness check or table search may require a better explanation than can be accommodated in a short message. In this situation, an error number and abbreviated message could be used. An error number enables the operator to refer to an application-dependent user guide or HELP screen to get a further description of the cause of the error. Some companies have even developed on-line help programs that are field-sensitive. The operator merely moves the cursor to the field in error and invokes a help program that describes the correct field values or edit criteria.

These error messages should be displayed in a conspicuous place on the screen. One technique is to reserve two or three lines at the bottom of the screen for error messages. I prefer to display messages in the skip-stop fields as described earlier. In most cases there is sufficient room here to display a short message. The use of the skip-stop field for displaying error messages can also preclude the need to highlight the actual data entry field to identify an error. In some cases, this may be advantageous. For instance, if a field needs to be corrected because it contains all spaces, the bright attribute may not readily identify the error field since the space character displays the same with normal or bright intensity. The age and quality of the terminal may also impair the effect of the bright attribute. On some terminals, it may be difficult to distinguish between normal and bright intensity.

INITIAL CURSOR POSITION

Each time the update screen is redisplayed due to errors found by the program, the operator will have the opportunity to make corrections. In order to maintain good operator productivity, the cursor should be positioned where input is likely to occur. A good practice is to position the cursor at the *first* error field on the screen. Positioning the cursor at a field also serves as a visual signal that the field contains an error. It will allow the operator to correct the first error field without having to reposition the cursor. To correct other errors, the operator will still have to tab forward using the TAB or NEWLINE keys.

The symbolic cursor positioning technique introduced in chapter 6 can be used to place the cursor on the first error field. You may recall that to use symbolic cursor positioning, the program will use the CURSOR option on the SEND MAP command. Prior to issuing the command, you will also *mark* the field in the symbolic description map where you want the initial cursor position. Recall that to *mark* a field you move the value of minus one (−1) to the length subfield. Let's look at an example to see how this is done. The statements below might appear in the edit routines for our sample vendor master application.

```
IF VENNAMEI IN DISPMAPI EQUAL SPACES
    MOVE -1 TO VENNAMEL IN UPDTMAPI
    MOVE UNPROT-FSET-BRT TO VENNAMEA IN DISPMAPI
    MOVE '<--NAME REQUIRED' TO NAMMSGO IN DISPMAPO.
IF ADDR1I IN DISPMAPI EQUAL SPACES
    MOVE -1 TO ADDR1L IN UPDTMAPI
    MOVE UNPROT-FSET-BRT TO ADDR1A IN DISPMAPI
    MOVE '<--REQUIRED INPUT' TO AD1MSGO IN DISPMAPO.
IF PAHOLDI EQUAL 'Y' OR 'N'
    NEXT SENTENCE
ELSE
    MOVE '<--PLEASE ENTER Y OR N' TO PAYMSGO
    MOVE -1 TO PAHOLDL
    MOVE UNPROT-FSET-BRT TO PAHOLDA.
```

On output, BMS positions the cursor over the first character of the field. If more than one field in the symbolic map is marked for cursor positioning, BMS selects only the first, and ignores the remaining marked fields. This makes it easy to develop logic for cursor positioning over multiple error fields on an update screen. All your program has to do when it encounters an error during data validation is to mark the corresponding "length field." The program doesn't have to "remember" whether it has previously marked another field. And since the order of the fields in the symbolic description map corresponds to the placement on the screen, the cursor will always be inserted at the first error field.

This concludes our discussion of the screen design and transaction-editing techniques used in the update programs. Now let's examine the logic of each of the primary update programs. First, we will look at the update program used to modify existing records in a file. Then we will study the logic of the add program. This program is used to add new records to a file. Finally, we will look at the delete program used to delete a record from a file.

Update Program Logic

The logic of a typical update program is shown in figure 8.3. Please refer to this figure as you study this topic. The update program commonly uses the two-pass pseudoconversational program logic. In this example, the entry analysis routine uses the field EIBTRNID to determine which pass of the program is being performed. If the field contains the transaction code of the update program (V002), the second-pass logic (screen processing) is performed. Otherwise the first-pass (initial processing) logic is performed.

The update program initially receives control from the menu program. The key of the record to be updated is passed in the commarea. Upon receiving control, this *first-pass logic* of the update program will use the record key to randomly read the record from the file. It will then display the record on the terminal using a BMS output mapping operation. Figure 8.4 depicts an update screen using our sample display-update map. Notice how the title has been changed to indicate that an update operation is taking place. The message line has been used to display a prompting message to the operator. After the screen is displayed, the program will issue a pseudoconversational RETURN command. The Transid option will specify the transaction code for the update program (V002 in our example). The record key will be passed in the commarea.

The operator will then make any changes by overtyping the data displayed in the unprotected fields. An attention key such as ENTER will be used to transmit the modified fields. Since all data entry fields have been defined with the FSET attribute, they will be transmitted back to CICS, even if they were not modified by the operator.

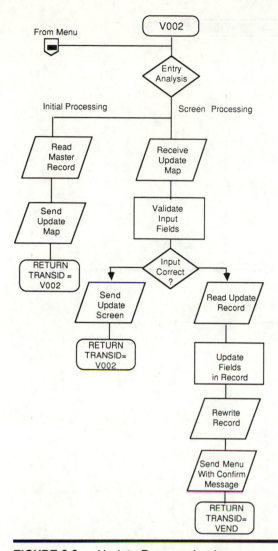

From Menu

V002

Entry
Analysis

Initial Processing ········· Screen Processing

Read
Master
Record

Receive
Update
Map

Send
Update
Map

Validate
Input
Fields

RETURN
TRANSID =
V002

Input
Correct
?

Send
Update
Screen

Read Update
Record

RETURN
TRANSID=
V002

Update
Fields
in Record

Rewrite
Record

Send Menu
With Confirm
Message

RETURN
TRANSID=
VEND

FIGURE 8.3.   Update Program Logic

Because of the pseudoconversational RETURN command previously issued, the update program will again be started. This time the *second-pass logic* will be performed. This logic will use the RECEIVE MAP command to cause the input to be transferred into the symbolic description map. The input fields will then be validated by the program. These data validation routines may be contained in one or more paragraphs or even a COBOL section.

A "error indicator" switch is commonly used to denote whether any errors are found during data validation. The first thing done in the validation routines is to set the indicator or switch to the "no-errors" status. Then validation begins. The data-validation routines will then check each input field as required by the application. The various transaction-editing procedures described earlier will be performed. If an error is found, the program will perform the error-processing routines. A message may be moved to an error message field or the field may be highlighted in some way. In some cases, both of these actions may be performed. The field would also be *marked* for symbolic cursor positioning. Finally, the error indicator would be set to the "errors-found" status.

```
═══════════════════════ Mainframe ═══════════════════════
 VEN3003                VENDOR MASTER UPDATE

 VENDOR ID   900000
             VENDOR NAME      METROPOLITAN COMMUNITY
             ADDRESS              COLLEGES
                              3200 BROADWAY
                              KANSAS CITY, MO. 64111

             CONTACT NAME     RON GREATHOUSE
             TELEPHONE        816-756-0220

             TAX ID           43-1111
             PAYMENT HOLD     N
             PRODUCT CODE     E01




 PLEASE MAKE CHANGES THEN PRESS ENTER
```

FIGURE 8.4. First Pass Logic Displays Record to Be Updated

```
═══════════════════════ Mainframe ═══════════════════════
 VEN3003                VENDOR MASTER UPDATE

 VENDOR ID   900000
             VENDOR NAME      METROPOLITAN COMMUNITY
             ADDRESS              COLLEGES
                              3200 BROADWAY
                              KANSAS CITY, MO. 64111

             CONTACT NAME     BILL MANN
             TELEPHONE        816-756-0220

             TAX ID           43-1111
             PAYMENT HOLD     Ū
             PRODUCT CODE     E01




 PLEASE CORRECT HIGH LIGHTED ERRORS-THEN PRESS ENTER
```

FIGURE 8.5. Update Screen with Errors High Lighted-Cursor on First Error Field

Upon return from the transaction validation routines, the program would check the "error indicator." If any errors were found, the program will redisplay the update screen with the SEND MAP command. The CURSOR option will cause the symbolic cursor-positioning routines of BMS to insert the cursor at the first error field. All error fields will be highlighted in some way. Figure 8.5 depicts a redisplay of our sample update screen. In this figure, the program found an error in the payment-hold field. After issuing the SEND MAP, the program will again issue a pseudoconversational RETURN command. The transid and commarea will be the same as specified in the first-pass logic.

If the update screen is redisplayed, the operator will make corrections then press enter. The program will again be started and will enter the second-pass logic just described. This same process will be repeated until no errors are detected by the validation routines.

When there are no input errors, the update program will rewrite the record with the changes made by the operator. To do this, the program will first issue a READ command with the UPDATE

```
              1         2         3         4         5         6         7         8
     1234567890 1234567890 1234567890 1234567890 1234567890 1234567890 1234567890 1234567890
     VEN0000                                                          DATE 01/31/88
                    VENDOR MASTER MENU                                TIME 06:00:00
                                                                      TERMINAL DT03

              PF1  DISPLAY MASTER RECORD

              PF2  UPDATE MASTER RECORD

              PF3  ADD MASTER RECORD

              PF4  DELETE MASTER RECORD

              PF5  BROWSE MASTER BY KEY

              PF9  EXIT MASTER MENU


     TYPE VENDOR NUMBER 900000 THEN PRESS APPROPRIATE PF KEY


     THE RECORD HAS BEEN UPDATED
```

FIGURE 8.6. After Record Is Updated Menu Screen Is Displayed

option. The record key passed in the commarea will be used to read the record. This read will cause the record contents to be read into the working-storage area of the program. It will also give the task *exclusive control* of the record. Then the program will copy each of the data entry fields from the symbolic description map (input map area) back to the corresponding fields in the record area. The REWRITE command will be used to update the record in the file.

After the record is updated, the program will display the menu screen to begin the transition back to the menu transaction. Figure 8.6 depicts this display. The message area in the menu contains a message that the record was updated. The record key is also displayed on the menu. Finally, the update program issues a pseudoconversational RETURN command, with a transid for the menu program. A commarea is passed so the second-pass logic of the menu program will be used when that program is next started. This completes the update transaction, and provides a transition back to the menu.

The coding for the update program logic that you have just studied is shown in figure 8.7. In addition to the basic logic just described, the program deals with exceptional conditions such as NOTOPEN, and NOTFND. As I promised in the last chapter, this program demonstrates the use of the latest CICS response code field to deal with these exceptions. In general, whenever an exceptional condition is found, the menu is displayed with an appropriate message. You may now wish to study the coding in this sample program before moving on to study the add program. You may find it helpful to read through these last paragraphs as you review the program code.

Add Program Logic

The logic of a typical add program is depicted in figure 8.8. At first glance, it might appear that this logic is the same as that for the update program. Actually, there is a close resemblence to the logic of these two programs. In fact, much of the logic in an add program is the same as the update program. Sometimes installations will even include both of these update transactions in the same application program.

Since these two programs are so alike, I am only going to discuss the different aspects of the add program in this topic. Let's begin with the first-pass routine.

The first-pass (initial entry) routine has two functions. First, it will verify that the record is not already on file. It stands to reason that if the record already exists, it cannot be added. This verification

```
        IDENTIFICATION DIVISION.
        PROGRAM-ID. VEND002.
        AUTHOR.   BOB LOWE.
        * * * * * * * * * * * * * * * * * * * * * * * *
        *    This is a program to update existing records from
        *       the sample vendor master file.  It is called from
        *       the menu program.
        * * * * * * * * * * * * * * * * * * * * * * * *
        ENVIRONMENT DIVISION.
        DATA DIVISION.
        WORKING-STORAGE SECTION.
        01  WS-COMMAREA.
            05  KEY-INPUT              PIC XXXXXX VALUE SPACES.
        01  WORK-AREAS.
            05  VEND-REC-LENGTH        PIC S9999  COMP VALUE +249.
            05  THE-CURSOR-INDICATOR   PIC S9999  COMP VALUE -1.
            05  INPUT-ERROR-INDICATOR   PIC S9999 COMP.
                88  ALL-INPUT-CORRECT    VALUE +0.
        * * * * * * * * * * * * * * * * * * * * * * * *
        *    CICS/VS RELEASE 1.7 RESPONSE FIELD
        * * * * * * * * * * * * * * * * * * * * * * * *
        01  COMMAND-RETURN-VALUE.
            05  COMMAND-STATUS-CODE        PIC S9(08) COMP VALUE +0.
                88  NORMAL                       VALUE +0.
                88  DSIDERR                      VALUE +12.
                88  NOTFND                       VALUE +13.
                88  DUPREC                       VALUE +14.
                88  INVREQ                       VALUE +16.
                88  IOERR                        VALUE +17.
                88  NOSPACE                      VALUE +18.
                88  NOTOPEN                      VALUE +19.
                88  ILLOGIC                      VALUE +21.
                88  LENGERR                      VALUE +22.
                88  ITEMERR                      VALUE +26.
                88  PGMIDERR                     VALUE +27.
                88  MAPFAIL                      VALUE +36.
                88  INVMPSZ                      VALUE +38.
                88  QIDERR                       VALUE +44.
                88  NOTAUTH                      VALUE +70.
                88  DISABLED                     VALUE +84.
        * * * * * * * * * * * * * * * * * * * * * * * *
        *    TWO MESSAGE LINES
        * * * * * * * * * * * * * * * * * * * * * * * *
        01  OUTPUT-MESSAGE.
            05  MESSAGE-NUMBER        PIC X(8).
            05  FILLER                PIC X        VALUE SPACE.
            05  THE-MESSAGE.
                07  FILLER               PIC X(56).
                07  MESSAGE-PARM         PIC X(06).
        * * * * * * * * * * * * * * * * * * * * * * * *
        *    RECORD LAYOUT FOR MASTER RECORD
        * * * * * * * * * * * * * * * * * * * * * * * *
        01  VENDOR-RECORD.
            05  VENDOR-NAME           PIC X(30).
            05  VENDOR-ID             PIC XXXXXX.
            05  VENDOR-ADDR1          PIC X(30).
            05  VENDOR-ADDR2          PIC X(30).
            05  VENDOR-ADDR3          PIC X(30).
            05  VENDOR-ADDR4          PIC X(30).
            05  VENDOR-CONTACT        PIC X(30).
            05  VENDOR-TELE           PIC X(12).
            05  VENDOR-TAXID          PIC X(11).
            05  VENDOR-YTD-SALES      PIC S9(07)V99 COMP-3.
            05  VENDOR-YTD-PAYMENTS   PIC S9(07)V99 COMP-3.
            05  VENDOR-YTD-DISCOUNTS  PIC S9(07)V99 COMP-3.
            05  VENDOR-PAY-HOLD       PIC X.
            05  VENDOR-PRODUCT        PIC XXX.
            05  VENDOR-LAST-CHECK     PIC S9(05)    COMP-3.
            05  VENDOR-LAST-CK-DATE   PIC S9(05)    COMP-3.
            05  VENDOR-LAST-CK-AMT    PIC S9(07)V99 COMP-3.
            05  VENDOR-DATE-ADDED     PIC S9(05)    COMP-3.
            05  VENDOR-DATE-CHANGED   PIC S9(05)    COMP-3.
            05  VENDOR-LAST-OPID      PIC XXX.
            05  VENDOR-UPDCNT         PIC 9.
```

FIGURE 8.7.   Sample Update Program

```
* * * * * * * * * * * * * * * * * * * * * * * * * * * *
*    BMS ATTRIBUTE VALUES INCLUDING HILIGHT AND COLOR
* * * * * * * * * * * * * * * * * * * * * * * * * * * *
 01  STANDARD-BMS-ATTRIBUTES.
     02  UNPROT-NORM            PIC X VALUE SPACE.
     02  UNPROT-BRT             PIC X VALUE 'H'.
     02  UNPROT-DRK             PIC X VALUE '<'.
     02  UNPROT-FSET-NORM       PIC X VALUE 'A'.
     02  UNPROT-FSET-BRT        PIC X VALUE 'I'.
     02  UNPROT-FSET-DRK        PIC X VALUE '('.
     02  UNPROT-NUM-NORM        PIC X VALUE '&'.
     02  UNPROT-NUM-BRT         PIC X VALUE 'Q'.
     02  UNPROT-NUM-DRK         PIC X VALUE '*'.
     02  UNPROT-NUM-FSET-NORM   PIC X VALUE 'J'.
     02  UNPROT-NUM-FSET-BRT    PIC X VALUE 'R'.
     02  UNPROT-NUM-FSET-DRK    PIC X VALUE ')'.
     02  PROT-NORM              PIC X VALUE '-'.
     02  PROT-BRT               PIC X VALUE 'Y'.
     02  PROT-DRK               PIC X VALUE '%'.
     02  PROT-FSET-NORM         PIC X VALUE '/'.
     02  PROT-FSET-BRT          PIC X VALUE 'Z'.
     02  PROT-FSET-DRK          PIC X VALUE '_'.
     02  ASKIP-NORM             PIC X VALUE '0'.
     02  ASKIP-BRT              PIC X VALUE '8'.
     02  ASKIP-DRK              PIC X VALUE '@'.
     02  ASKIP-FSET-NORM        PIC X VALUE '1'.
     02  ASKIP-FSET-BRT         PIC X VALUE '9'.
     02  ASKIP-FSET-DRK         PIC X VALUE QUOTE.
     02  HILIGHT-DEFAULT        PIC X VALUE LOW-VALUE.
     02  HILIGHT-BLINK          PIC X VALUE '1'.
     02  HILIGHT-REVERSE        PIC X VALUE '2'.
     02  HILIGHT-UNDERSCORE     PIC X VALUE '4'.
     02  COLOR-DEFAULT          PIC X VALUE LOW-VALUE.
     02  COLOR-BLUE             PIC X VALUE '1'.
     02  COLOR-RED              PIC X VALUE '2'.
     02  COLOR-PINK             PIC X VALUE '3'.
     02  COLOR-GREEN            PIC X VALUE '4'.
     02  COLOR-TURKUOISE        PIC X VALUE '5'.
     02  COLOR-YELLOW           PIC X VALUE '6'.
     02  COLOR-WHITE            PIC X VALUE '7'.
* * * * * * * * * * * * * * * * * * * * * * * * * *
*    ATTENTION IDENTIFIER CONSTANTS
* * * * * * * * * * * * * * * * * * * * * * * * * *
 COPY    DFHAID SUPPRESS.
 COPY    VENDSET SUPPRESS.
 LINKAGE SECTION.
 01  DFHCOMMAREA            PIC X(06).
 PROCEDURE DIVISION.
*PROCEDURE DIVISION.
 000-ENTRY-ANALYSIS-LOGIC.
     MOVE DFHCOMMAREA TO WS-COMMAREA
     IF EIBTRNID EQUAL 'V002'
         PERFORM 200-SCREEN-PROCESSING-LOGIC
         MOVE LOW-VALUES TO MENUMAPO
         MOVE 'THE RECORD HAS BEEN UPDATED' TO MMESAGEO
         GO TO       850-SEND-MENU-MAP-EXIT
     ELSE
         PERFORM 100-INITIAL-PROCESSING-LOGIC.
 100-INITIAL-PROCESSING-LOGIC.
     IF  KEY-INPUT IS NOT NUMERIC
         PERFORM 905-INVALID-KEY
         GO TO       850-SEND-MENU-MAP-EXIT.
     EXEC CICS READ
             DATASET ('VENFILE')
             RIDFLD  (KEY-INPUT)
             INTO    (VENDOR-RECORD)
             LENGTH  (VEND-REC-LENGTH)
             RESP    (COMMAND-STATUS-CODE)
             NOHANDLE
             END-EXEC.
     IF NORMAL NEXT SENTENCE
     ELSE
         IF NOTFND PERFORM 934-NOTFND-ERROR
         GO TO       850-SEND-MENU-MAP-EXIT
         ELSE
             PERFORM 920-UNEXPECTED-FILE-ERROR
             GO TO       850-SEND-MENU-MAP-EXIT.
```

FIGURE 8.7.   Continued

```
* * * * * * * * * * * * * * * * * * * * * * * * * * *
*     The display/update fields are copied to the BMS
*        symbolic description map.
* * * * * * * * * * * * * * * * * * * * * * * * * * *
        MOVE LOW-VALUES           TO            DISPMAPO.
        MOVE VENDOR-NAME          TO VENNAMEO  IN DISPMAPO.
        MOVE VENDOR-ID            TO VENDIDO   IN DISPMAPO.
        MOVE VENDOR-ADDR1         TO ADDR1O    IN DISPMAPO.
        MOVE VENDOR-ADDR2         TO ADDR2O    IN DISPMAPO.
        MOVE VENDOR-ADDR3         TO ADDR3O    IN DISPMAPO.
        MOVE VENDOR-ADDR4         TO ADDR4O    IN DISPMAPO.
        MOVE VENDOR-CONTACT       TO CONTACO   IN DISPMAPO.
        MOVE VENDOR-TELE          TO TELEO     IN DISPMAPO.
        MOVE VENDOR-TAXID         TO TAXIDO    IN DISPMAPO.
        MOVE VENDOR-PAY-HOLD      TO PAHOLDO   IN DISPMAPO.
        MOVE VENDOR-PRODUCT       TO PRODUCTO  IN DISPMAPO.
        MOVE 'UPDATE'             TO DTYPEO    IN DISPMAPO.
        MOVE 'VEN3003'            TO SCODEO    IN DISPMAPO.
        MOVE 'TYPE INPUT THEN PRESS ENTER' TO DMESAGEO.
        MOVE THE-CURSOR-INDICATOR TO VENNAMEL  IN DISPMAPI.
        EXEC CICS SEND MAP ('DISPMAP')
                  MAPSET ('VENDSET')
                  ERASE
                  FREEKB
                  CURSOR
                  END-EXEC.
        EXEC CICS RETURN
                  TRANSID ('V002')
                  COMMAREA (WS-COMMAREA)
                  LENGTH (06)
                  END-EXEC.
    200-SCREEN-PROCESSING-LOGIC.
* * * * * * * * * * * * * * * * * * * * * * * * * * *
* * * * * * * * * * * * * * * * * * * * * * * * * * *
        EXEC CICS RECEIVE MAP ('DISPMAP')
                  MAPSET ('VENDSET')
                  RESP    (COMMAND-STATUS-CODE)
                  NOHANDLE
                  END-EXEC.
        IF NORMAL NEXT SENTENCE
        ELSE IF MAPFAIL
                PERFORM 288-NO-INPUT-DATA
                GO TO         850-SEND-MENU-MAP-EXIT
             ELSE
                PERFORM 910-UNEXPECTED-BMS-ERROR
                GO TO         850-SEND-MENU-MAP-EXIT.
        PERFORM 250-VALIDATE-INPUT.
        IF NOT ALL-INPUT-CORRECT
           PERFORM 210-SEND-UPDATE-RETURN-TRANSID.
        PERFORM 310-UPDATE-VENDOR-FILE.
    210-SEND-UPDATE-RETURN-TRANSID.
* * * * * * * * * * * * * * * * * * * * * * * * * * *
* * * * * * * * * * * * * * * * * * * * * * * * * * *
        MOVE 'UPDATE'             TO DTYPEO    IN DISPMAPO.
        MOVE 'PLEASE CORRECT HIGH LIGHTED ERRORS-THEN PRESS ENTER'
             TO DMESAGEO.
        EXEC CICS SEND MAP ('DISPMAP')
                  MAPSET ('VENDSET')
                  ERASE
                  FREEKB
                  CURSOR
                  END-EXEC.
        EXEC CICS RETURN
                  TRANSID ('V002')
                  COMMAREA (WS-COMMAREA)
                  LENGTH (06)
                  END-EXEC.
    250-VALIDATE-INPUT.
* * * * * * * * * * * * * * * * * * * * * * * * * * *
* * * * * * * * * * * * * * * * * * * * * * * * * * *
*     VALIDATE FIELDS FROM UPDATE SCREEN
* * * * * * * * * * * * * * * * * * * * * * * * * * *
* * * * * * * * * * * * * * * * * * * * * * * * * * *
* * * * * * * * * * * * * * * * * * * * * * * * * * *
        MOVE +0  TO INPUT-ERROR-INDICATOR.
        TRANSFORM VENNAMEI IN DISPMAPI
                      FROM '_' TO ' '.
        TRANSFORM ADDR1I  IN DISPMAPI
                      FROM '_' TO ' '.
```

FIGURE 8.7.   Continued

```
        TRANSFORM ADDR2I    IN DISPMAPI
                            FROM '_' TO ' '.
        TRANSFORM ADDR3I    IN DISPMAPI
                            FROM '_' TO ' '.
        TRANSFORM ADDR4I    IN DISPMAPI
                            FROM '_' TO ' '.
        TRANSFORM CONTACI   IN DISPMAPI
                            FROM '_' TO ' '.
        TRANSFORM TELEI     IN DISPMAPI
                            FROM '_' TO ' '.
        TRANSFORM TAXIDI    IN DISPMAPI
                            FROM '_' TO ' '.
* * * * * * * * * * * * * * * * * * * * * * * * * *
* * * * * * * * * * * * * * * * * * * * * * * * * *
        IF VENNAMEL IN DISPMAPI
                   IS NOT POSITIVE OR VENNAMEI IN DISPMAPI
                                           EQUAL TO SPACES
            MOVE ALL '_' TO VENNAMEI IN DISPMAPI
            MOVE THE-CURSOR-INDICATOR TO VENNAMEL IN DISPMAPI
                    INPUT-ERROR-INDICATOR
            MOVE UNPROT-FSET-BRT TO VENNAMEA IN DISPMAPI.
        IF VENNAMEI IN DISPMAPI IS ALPHABETIC
        OR    VENNAMEI IN DISPMAPI IS EQUAL ALL '_'
            NEXT SENTENCE
        ELSE
            MOVE THE-CURSOR-INDICATOR TO VENNAMEL IN DISPMAPI
                    INPUT-ERROR-INDICATOR
            MOVE UNPROT-FSET-BRT TO VENNAMEA IN DISPMAPI.
        IF ADDR1L   IN DISPMAPI
                   IS NOT POSITIVE OR ADDR1I    IN DISPMAPI
                                           EQUAL TO SPACES
            MOVE ALL '_' TO ADDR1I    IN DISPMAPI
            MOVE THE-CURSOR-INDICATOR TO ADDR1L   IN DISPMAPI
                    INPUT-ERROR-INDICATOR
            MOVE UNPROT-FSET-BRT TO ADDR1A    IN DISPMAPI.
        IF PAHOLDI IN DISPMAPI EQUAL ' '
            MOVE '_' TO PAHOLDI IN DISPMAPI.
        IF PAHOLDI IN DISPMAPI EQUAL 'Y' OR 'N'
            NEXT SENTENCE
        ELSE
            MOVE THE-CURSOR-INDICATOR TO PAHOLDL IN DISPMAPI
                    INPUT-ERROR-INDICATOR
            MOVE UNPROT-FSET-BRT TO PAHOLDA   IN DISPMAPI.
* * * * * * * * * * * * * * * * * * * * * * * * * *
*  NO OTHER FIELDS ARE VALIDATED IN THIS PROGRAM   *
* * * * * * * * * * * * * * * * * * * * * * * * * *
 288-NO-INPUT-DATA.
* * * * * * * * * * * * * * * * * * * * * * * * * *
* * * * * * * * * * * * * * * * * * * * * * * * * *
* * * * * * * * * * * * * * * * * * * * * * * * * *
* * * * * * * * * * * * * * * * * * * * * * * * * *
        MOVE LOW-VALUES TO MENUMAPO.
        MOVE 'VEND3288' TO MESSAGE-NUMBER.
        MOVE 'UPDATE SCREEN ERASED-TRANSACTION CANCELLED'
            TO THE-MESSAGE.
        MOVE OUTPUT-MESSAGE TO MMESAGEO.
 310-UPDATE-VENDOR-FILE.
* * * * * * * * * * * * * * * * * * * * * * * * * *
* * * * * * * * * * * * * * * * * * * * * * * * * *
        EXEC CICS READ UPDATE
                DATASET ('VENFILE')
                RIDFLD  (KEY-INPUT)
                INTO    (VENDOR-RECORD)
                LENGTH  (VEND-REC-LENGTH)
                RESP    (COMMAND-STATUS-CODE)
                NOHANDLE
                END-EXEC.
        IF NORMAL
            NEXT SENTENCE
        ELSE
            PERFORM 920-UNEXPECTED-FILE-ERROR
            GO TO      850-SEND-MENU-MAP-EXIT.
        PERFORM 340-MOVE-FIELDS-FROM-MAP.
        MOVE EIBDATE TO VENDOR-DATE-CHANGED.
        EXEC CICS REWRITE
                DATASET ('VENFILE')
                FROM (VENDOR-RECORD)
                LENGTH (VEND-REC-LENGTH)
                RESP    (COMMAND-STATUS-CODE)
                NOHANDLE
                END-EXEC.
```

FIGURE 8.7. Continued

```
          IF NORMAL
              NEXT SENTENCE
          ELSE
              PERFORM 920-UNEXPECTED-FILE-ERROR
              GO TO        850-SEND-MENU-MAP-EXIT.
   340-MOVE-FIELDS-FROM-MAP.
* * * * * * * * * * * * * * * * * * * * * * * * *
* * * * * * * * * * * * * * * * * * * * * * * * *
* * * * * * * * * * * * * * * * * * * * * * * * *
       MOVE VENNAMEI IN DISPMAPI TO VENDOR-NAME.
       MOVE ADDR1I   IN DISPMAPI TO VENDOR-ADDR1.
       MOVE ADDR2I   IN DISPMAPI TO VENDOR-ADDR2.
       MOVE ADDR3I   IN DISPMAPI TO VENDOR-ADDR3.
       MOVE ADDR4I   IN DISPMAPI TO VENDOR-ADDR4.
       MOVE CONTACI  IN DISPMAPI TO VENDOR-CONTACT.
       MOVE TELEI    IN DISPMAPI TO VENDOR-TELE.
       MOVE TAXIDI   IN DISPMAPI TO VENDOR-TAXID.
       MOVE PAHOLDI  IN DISPMAPI TO VENDOR-PAY-HOLD.
       MOVE PRODUCTI IN DISPMAPI TO VENDOR-PRODUCT.
   850-SEND-MENU-MAP-EXIT.
* * * * * * * * * * * * * * * * * * * * * * * * *
*     SEND MENU MAP TO OPERATOR
* * * * * * * * * * * * * * * * * * * * * * * * * *
* * * * * * * * * * * * * * * * * * * * * * * * * *
       MOVE 'VEN0003' TO SCODEO IN MENUMAPO.
       MOVE KEY-INPUT  TO VENDIDO IN MENUMAPO.
       MOVE CURRENT-DATE TO  DATEO IN MENUMAPO.
       MOVE EIBTIME TO TIMEO.
       TRANSFORM TIMEO FROM ',' TO ':'.
       MOVE EIBTRMID TO TERMO.
       EXEC CICS SEND MAP ('MENUMAP')
               MAPSET ('VENDSET')
               ERASE
               FREEKB
               NOHANDLE
               END-EXEC.
       EXEC CICS RETURN
               TRANSID ('VEND')
               COMMAREA (KEY-INPUT) LENGTH (06)
               END-EXEC.
* * * * * * * * * * * * * * * * * * * * * * * * *
* * * * * * * * * * * * * * * * * * * * * * * * *
   905-INVALID-KEY.
       MOVE LOW-VALUES TO MENUMAPO.
       MOVE KEY-INPUT TO  VENDIDO IN MENUMAPO.
       MOVE 'RECORD KEY NOT NUMERIC' TO THE-MESSAGE.
       MOVE 'VEND3905'            TO MESSAGE-NUMBER.
       MOVE OUTPUT-MESSAGE TO MMESAGEO.
   910-UNEXPECTED-BMS-ERROR.
       MOVE LOW-VALUES TO MENUMAPO
       MOVE 'BMS ERROR-CALL MIS' TO THE-MESSAGE
       MOVE 'VEND3910'            TO MESSAGE-NUMBER
       MOVE OUTPUT-MESSAGE TO MMESAGEO.
   920-UNEXPECTED-FILE-ERROR.
       IF   ILLOGIC PERFORM 940-VSAM-ERROR
       ELSE IF NOTOPEN PERFORM 944-NOTOPEN-ERROR
           ELSE
               MOVE LOW-VALUES TO MENUMAPO
               MOVE 'VENDOR FILE ERROR-CALL MIS'  TO THE-MESSAGE
               MOVE 'VEND3920'            TO MESSAGE-NUMBER
               MOVE OUTPUT-MESSAGE TO MMESAGEO.
   934-NOTFND-ERROR.
       MOVE LOW-VALUES TO MENUMAPO.
       MOVE 'RECORD NOT ON FILE PRESS PF3 TO ADD' TO THE-MESSAGE.
       MOVE 'VEND3934'            TO MESSAGE-NUMBER.
       MOVE OUTPUT-MESSAGE TO MMESAGEO.
   940-VSAM-ERROR.
       MOVE LOW-VALUES TO MENUMAPO.
       MOVE 'FILE LOGIC ERROR-CALL MIS'  TO THE-MESSAGE.
       MOVE 'VEND3940'            TO MESSAGE-NUMBER.
       MOVE OUTPUT-MESSAGE TO MMESAGEO.
   944-NOTOPEN-ERROR.
       MOVE LOW-VALUES TO MENUMAPO.
       MOVE 'VENDOR FILE CLOSED'  TO THE-MESSAGE.
       MOVE 'VEND3944'            TO MESSAGE-NUMBER.
       MOVE OUTPUT-MESSAGE TO MMESAGEO.
* * * * * * * * * * * * * * * * * * * * * * * * *
   1000-PARAGRAPH-NOT-USED.
       GOBACK.
```

FIGURE 8.7.   Continued

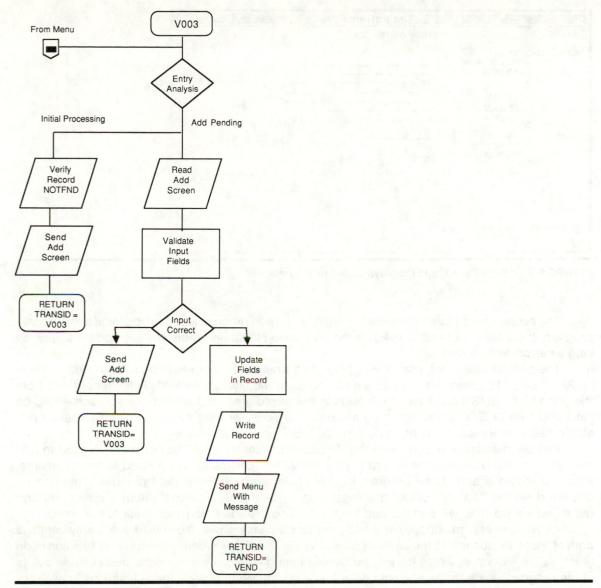

FIGURE 8.8. Add Program Logic

would be done by issuing a READ command using the record key (passed from the menu) in the commarea. In this program a NOTFND condition is considered a good response. Likewise a NORMAL response code is an indication of an error. If the record is already on file, the add program will display the menu screen with an error message and provide a transition back to the menu using a pseudoconversational RETURN.

The second purpose of the first-pass routine is to display an initial data entry screen. A data entry screen for our example is shown in figure 8.9. The screen in our example contains an underscore character for each data entry field. Recall that our sample map has these underscores stored in as *default* values. Of course, any value (such as dashes or dots) could have been mapped from the program. After the initial data entry screen is displayed, the routine will issue a pseudoconversational return. The transid will be V003 (transid of the add program), and the record key will be passed in the commarea.

```
═══════════════════════════ Mainframe ═══════════════════════════
 VEN4004                    VENDOR MASTER ADD

 VENDOR ID    300000
              VENDOR NAME      _____
              ADDRESS          _____

                               _____
                               _____
              CONTACT NAME     _____
              TELEPHONE        _____

              TAX ID           _____
              PAYMENT HOLD     _
              PRODUCT CODE     ___




 TYPE INPUT THEN PRESS ENTER
```

FIGURE 8.9.   First Pass Logic Displays Data Entry Template

The second-pass (screen processing) logic for the add program is almost identical to the update program. It contains routines to validate the transaction input and redisplay the update screen as long as errors were found.

The program *will* differ somewhat at the point where the record is to be added. First, there is no READ UPDATE command. Instead the add program will initialize the fields in the record area from the fields in the BMS input area. Other fields in the record area not found on the add screen will be initialized with COBOL constants such as spaces or zeros, or from other sources. Date and time-stamp fields, for instance, might come from the EIB.

Another difference is found with the file output command. A WRITE command is used to add the record to the data set. The record key for the WRITE command was passed in the commarea. After the record is added, the program logic is again similar to the update program. The menu is displayed with an "add-complete" message, then a pseudoconversational return is issued, naming the menu transid. This will end the add transaction and provide a transition back to the menu.

As you can see, the update and add programs *are* very similar. You could very easily combine both of these functions into the same application program. If this is done, some sort of function code (such as the AID value) would have to be passed through the commarea and tested at those points of the program where the logic would differ. If you do choose to provide these functions in two separate programs, it will be an easy matter to write one of them and "clone" or copy that program to develop the other one. Before we move on to the delete program you should take some time to review figure 8.10. This figure illustrates the coding for the add program. Don't be surprised if you see a lot of coding identical to our earlier update program.

Delete Program Logic

The logic for the DELETE program is depicted in figure 8.11. This logic isn't much like the update or add program. Instead, it's a lot like the inquiry program described in the last chapter. Like that inquiry program, the delete program uses the two-pass programming logic. The entry analysis routine checks the field EIBTRNID to determine which routine should be performed.

The purpose of the first-pass (initial processing) logic is to display the target record on the screen. In this way the operator can confirm that this is indeed the record that should be deleted. If you don't display the record before deleting it, there is a chance that the wrong record could be

```
        IDENTIFICATION DIVISION.
        PROGRAM-ID. VEND003.
        AUTHOR.  BOB LOWE.
        * * * * * * * * * * * * * * * * * * * * * * * * *
        *     This is a program to add new records to the sample
        *         vendor master file.  It is called from the menu
        *         program.
        * * * * * * * * * * * * * * * * * * * * * * * * *
        ENVIRONMENT DIVISION.
        DATA DIVISION.
        WORKING-STORAGE SECTION.
        01  WS-COMMAREA.
            05  KEY-INPUT                PIC XXXXXX VALUE SPACES.
        01  WORK-AREAS.
            05  VEND-REC-LENGTH          PIC S9999  COMP VALUE +249.
            05  THE-CURSOR-INDICATOR     PIC S9999  COMP VALUE -1.
            05  INPUT-ERROR-INDICATOR    PIC S9999 COMP.
                88  ALL-INPUT-CORRECT    VALUE +0.
        * * * * * * * * * * * * * * * * * * * * * * * * *
        *     CICS/VS RELEASE 1.7 RESPONSE FIELD
        * * * * * * * * * * * * * * * * * * * * * * * * *
        01  COMMAND-RETURN-VALUE.
            05  COMMAND-STATUS-CODE          PIC S9(08) COMP VALUE +0.
                88  NORMAL                   VALUE +0.
                88  DSIDERR                  VALUE +12.
                88  NOTFND                   VALUE +13.
                88  DUPREC                   VALUE +14.
                88  INVREQ                   VALUE +16.
                88  IOERR                    VALUE +17.
                88  NOSPACE                  VALUE +18.
                88  NOTOPEN                  VALUE +19.
                88  ILLOGIC                  VALUE +21.
                88  LENGERR                  VALUE +22.
                88  ITEMERR                  VALUE +26.
                88  PGMIDERR                 VALUE +27.
                88  MAPFAIL                  VALUE +36.
                88  INVMPSZ                  VALUE +38.
                88  QIDERR                   VALUE +44.
                88  NOTAUTH                  VALUE +70.
                88  DISABLED                 VALUE +84.
        * * * * * * * * * * * * * * * * * * * * * * * * *
        *     TWO MESSAGE LINES
        * * * * * * * * * * * * * * * * * * * * * * * * *
        01  OUTPUT-MESSAGE.
            05  MESSAGE-NUMBER       PIC X(8).
            05  FILLER               PIC X        VALUE SPACE.
            05  THE-MESSAGE.
                07  FILLER               PIC X(56).
                07  MESSAGE-PARM         PIC X(06).
        * * * * * * * * * * * * * * * * * * * * * * * * *
        *     RECORD LAYOUT FOR MASTER RECORD
        * * * * * * * * * * * * * * * * * * * * * * * * *
        01  VENDOR-RECORD.
            05  VENDOR-NAME          PIC X(30).
            05  VENDOR-ID            PIC XXXXXX.
            05  VENDOR-ADDR1         PIC X(30).
            05  VENDOR-ADDR2         PIC X(30).
            05  VENDOR-ADDR3         PIC X(30).
            05  VENDOR-ADDR4         PIC X(30).
            05  VENDOR-CONTACT       PIC X(30).
            05  VENDOR-TELE          PIC X(12).
            05  VENDOR-TAXID         PIC X(11).
            05  VENDOR-YTD-SALES     PIC S9(07)V99 COMP-3.
            05  VENDOR-YTD-PAYMENTS  PIC S9(07)V99 COMP-3.
            05  VENDOR-YTD-DISCOUNTS PIC S9(07)V99 COMP-3.
            05  VENDOR-PAY-HOLD      PIC X.
            05  VENDOR-PRODUCT       PIC XXX.
            05  VENDOR-LAST-CHECK    PIC S9(05)    COMP-3.
            05  VENDOR-LAST-CK-DATE  PIC S9(05)    COMP-3.
            05  VENDOR-LAST-CK-AMT   PIC S9(07)V99 COMP-3.
            05  VENDOR-DATE-ADDED    PIC S9(05)    COMP-3.
            05  VENDOR-DATE-CHANGED  PIC S9(05)    COMP-3.
            05  VENDOR-LAST-OPID     PIC XXX.
            05  VENDOR-UPDCNT        PIC 9.
```

FIGURE 8.10.   Sample Add Program

```
* * * * * * * * * * * * * * * * * * * * * * * * * * * *
*   BMS ATTRIBUTE VALUES INCLUDING HILIGHT AND COLOR
* * * * * * * * * * * * * * * * * * * * * * * * * * * *
 01  STANDARD-BMS-ATTRIBUTES.
      02  UNPROT-NORM              PIC X VALUE SPACE.
      02  UNPROT-BRT               PIC X VALUE 'H'.
      02  UNPROT-DRK               PIC X VALUE '<'.
      02  UNPROT-FSET-NORM         PIC X VALUE 'A'.
      02  UNPROT-FSET-BRT          PIC X VALUE 'I'.
      02  UNPROT-FSET-DRK          PIC X VALUE '('.
      02  UNPROT-NUM-NORM          PIC X VALUE '&'.
      02  UNPROT-NUM-BRT           PIC X VALUE 'Q'.
      02  UNPROT-NUM-DRK           PIC X VALUE '*'.
      02  UNPROT-NUM-FSET-NORM     PIC X VALUE 'J'.
      02  UNPROT-NUM-FSET-BRT      PIC X VALUE 'R'.
      02  UNPROT-NUM-FSET-DRK      PIC X VALUE ')'.
      02  PROT-NORM                PIC X VALUE '-'.
      02  PROT-BRT                 PIC X VALUE 'Y'.
      02  PROT-DRK                 PIC X VALUE '%'.
      02  PROT-FSET-NORM           PIC X VALUE '/'.
      02  PROT-FSET-BRT            PIC X VALUE 'Z'.
      02  PROT-FSET-DRK            PIC X VALUE '_'.
      02  ASKIP-NORM               PIC X VALUE '0'.
      02  ASKIP-BRT                PIC X VALUE '8'.
      02  ASKIP-DRK                PIC X VALUE '@'.
      02  ASKIP-FSET-NORM          PIC X VALUE '1'.
      02  ASKIP-FSET-BRT           PIC X VALUE '9'.
      02  ASKIP-FSET-DRK           PIC X VALUE QUOTE.
      02  HILIGHT-DEFAULT          PIC X VALUE LOW-VALUE.
      02  HILIGHT-BLINK            PIC X VALUE '1'.
      02  HILIGHT-REVERSE          PIC X VALUE '2'.
      02  HILIGHT-UNDERSCORE       PIC X VALUE '4'.
      02  COLOR-DEFAULT            PIC X VALUE LOW-VALUE.
      02  COLOR-BLUE               PIC X VALUE '1'.
      02  COLOR-RED                PIC X VALUE '2'.
      02  COLOR-PINK               PIC X VALUE '3'.
      02  COLOR-GREEN              PIC X VALUE '4'.
      02  COLOR-TURKUOISE          PIC X VALUE '5'.
      02  COLOR-YELLOW             PIC X VALUE '6'.
      02  COLOR-WHITE              PIC X VALUE '7'.
* * * * * * * * * * * * * * * * * * * * * * * * * * * *
*   ATTENTION IDENTIFIER CONSTANTS
* * * * * * * * * * * * * * * * * * * * * * * * * * * *
 COPY    DFHAID SUPPRESS.
 COPY    VENDSET SUPPRESS.
 LINKAGE SECTION.
 01  DFHCOMMAREA              PIC X(06).
 PROCEDURE DIVISION.
*PROCEDURE DIVISION.
 000-ENTRY-ANALYSIS-LOGIC.
     MOVE DFHCOMMAREA TO WS-COMMAREA
     IF EIBTRNID EQUAL 'V003'
         PERFORM 200-SCREEN-PROCESSING-LOGIC
         MOVE LOW-VALUES TO MENUMAPO
         MOVE 'THE RECORD HAS BEEN ADDED' TO MMESAGEO
         GO TO       850-SEND-MENU-MAP-EXIT
     ELSE
         PERFORM 100-INITIAL-PROCESSING-LOGIC.
 100-INITIAL-PROCESSING-LOGIC.
     IF  KEY-INPUT IS NOT NUMERIC
         PERFORM 905-INVALID-KEY
         GO TO       850-SEND-MENU-MAP-EXIT.
     EXEC CICS READ
             DATASET ('VENFILE')
             RIDFLD  (KEY-INPUT)
             INTO    (VENDOR-RECORD)
             LENGTH  (VEND-REC-LENGTH)
             RESP    (COMMAND-STATUS-CODE)
             NOHANDLE
             END-EXEC.
     IF NOTFND NEXT SENTENCE
     ELSE
         IF NORMAL PERFORM 934-ONFILE-ERROR
         GO TO       850-SEND-MENU-MAP-EXIT
         ELSE
             PERFORM 920-UNEXPECTED-FILE-ERROR
             GO TO       850-SEND-MENU-MAP-EXIT.
```

FIGURE 8.10.   Continued

```
* * * * * * * * * * * * * * * * * * * * * * * * *
*    The display/update fields are copied to the BMS
*       symbolic description map.
* * * * * * * * * * * * * * * * * * * * * * * * *
      MOVE LOW-VALUES            TO            DISPMAPO.
      MOVE KEY-INPUT             TO VENDIDO    IN DISPMAPO.
      MOVE 'ADD'                 TO DTYPEO     IN DISPMAPO.
      MOVE 'VEN4004'             TO SCODEO     IN DISPMAPO.
      MOVE 'TYPE INPUT THEN PRESS ENTER' TO DMESAGEO.
      MOVE THE-CURSOR-INDICATOR TO VENNAMEI  IN DISPMAPI.
      EXEC CICS SEND MAP ('DISPMAP')
                MAPSET ('VENDSET')
                ERASE
                FREEKB
                CURSOR
                END-EXEC.
      EXEC CICS RETURN
                TRANSID ('V003')
                COMMAREA (WS-COMMAREA)
                LENGTH (06)
      END-EXEC.
  200-SCREEN-PROCESSING-LOGIC.
* * * * * * * * * * * * * * * * * * * * * * * * *
* * * * * * * * * * * * * * * * * * * * * * * * *
      EXEC CICS RECEIVE MAP ('DISPMAP')
                   MAPSET ('VENDSET')
                   RESP    (COMMAND-STATUS-CODE)
                   NOHANDLE
      END-EXEC.
      IF NORMAL NEXT SENTENCE
      ELSE IF MAPFAIL
            PERFORM 288-NO-INPUT-DATA
            GO TO      850-SEND-MENU-MAP-EXIT
         ELSE
            PERFORM 910-UNEXPECTED-BMS-ERROR
            GO TO      850-SEND-MENU-MAP-EXIT.
      PERFORM 250-VALIDATE-INPUT.
      IF NOT ALL-INPUT-CORRECT
         PERFORM 210-SEND-UPDATE-RETURN-TRANSID.
      PERFORM 320-ADD-TO-VENDOR-FILE.
  210-SEND-UPDATE-RETURN-TRANSID.
* * * * * * * * * * * * * * * * * * * * * * * * *
* * * * * * * * * * * * * * * * * * * * * * * * *
      MOVE 'ADD'                 TO DTYPEO    IN DISPMAPO.
      MOVE 'PLEASE CORRECT HIGH LIGHTED ERRORS-THEN PRESS ENTER'
          TO DMESAGEO.
      EXEC CICS SEND MAP ('DISPMAP')
                MAPSET ('VENDSET')
                ERASE
                FREEKB
                CURSOR
                END-EXEC.
      EXEC CICS RETURN
                TRANSID ('V003')
                COMMAREA (WS-COMMAREA)
                LENGTH (06)
      END-EXEC.
  250-VALIDATE-INPUT.
* * * * * * * * * * * * * * * * * * * * * * * * *
* * * * * * * * * * * * * * * * * * * * * * * * *
*    VALIDATE FIELDS FROM UPDATE SCREEN
* * * * * * * * * * * * * * * * * * * * * * * * *
* * * * * * * * * * * * * * * * * * * * * * * * *
* * * * * * * * * * * * * * * * * * * * * * * * *
      MOVE +0  TO INPUT-ERROR-INDICATOR.
      TRANSFORM VENNAMEI IN DISPMAPI
                      FROM '_' TO ' '.
      TRANSFORM ADDR1I   IN DISPMAPI
                      FROM '_' TO ' '.
      TRANSFORM ADDR2I   IN DISPMAPI
                      FROM '_' TO ' '.
      TRANSFORM ADDR3I   IN DISPMAPI
                      FROM '_' TO ' '.
      TRANSFORM ADDR4I   IN DISPMAPI
                      FROM '_' TO ' '.
      TRANSFORM CONTACI  IN DISPMAPI
                      FROM '_' TO ' '.
      TRANSFORM TELEI    IN DISPMAPI
                      FROM '_' TO ' '.
      TRANSFORM TAXIDI   IN DISPMAPI
                      FROM '_' TO ' '.
```

FIGURE 8.10. Continued

```
* * * * * * * * * * * * * * * * * * * * * * * * * *
* * * * * * * * * * * * * * * * * * * * * * * * * *
    IF VENNAMEL IN DISPMAPI
                IS NOT POSITIVE OR VENNAMEI IN DISPMAPI
                                    EQUAL TO SPACES
        MOVE ALL '_' TO VENNAMEI IN DISPMAPI
        MOVE THE-CURSOR-INDICATOR TO VENNAMEL IN DISPMAPI
                INPUT-ERROR-INDICATOR
        MOVE UNPROT-FSET-BRT TO VENNAMEA IN DISPMAPI.
    IF VENNAMEI IN DISPMAPI IS ALPHABETIC
    OR     VENNAMEI IN DISPMAPI IS EQUAL ALL '_'
        NEXT SENTENCE
    ELSE
        MOVE THE-CURSOR-INDICATOR TO VENNAMEL IN DISPMAPI
                    INPUT-ERROR-INDICATOR
        MOVE UNPROT-FSET-BRT TO VENNAMEA IN DISPMAPI.
    IF ADDR1L  IN DISPMAPI
                IS NOT POSITIVE OR ADDR1I   IN DISPMAPI
                                    EQUAL TO SPACES
        MOVE ALL '_' TO ADDR1I    IN DISPMAPI
        MOVE THE-CURSOR-INDICATOR TO ADDR1L    IN DISPMAPI
                    INPUT-ERROR-INDICATOR
        MOVE UNPROT-FSET-BRT TO ADDR1A    IN DISPMAPI.
    IF PAHOLDI IN DISPMAPI EQUAL ' '
        MOVE '_' TO PAHOLDI IN DISPMAPI.
    IF PAHOLDI IN DISPMAPI EQUAL 'Y' OR 'N'
        NEXT SENTENCE
    ELSE
        MOVE THE-CURSOR-INDICATOR TO PAHOLDL IN DISPMAPI
                    INPUT-ERROR-INDICATOR
        MOVE UNPROT-FSET-BRT TO PAHOLDA   IN DISPMAPI.
*..     MOVE '<--PLEASE ENTER Y OR N' TO VSTOPPO IN DISPMAPO.
* * * * * * * * * * * * * * * * * * * * * * * * * *
*  NO OTHER FIELDS ARE VALIDATED IN THIS PROGRAM        *
* * * * * * * * * * * * * * * * * * * * * * * * * *
 288-NO-INPUT-DATA.
* * * * * * * * * * * * * * * * * * * * * * * * * *
* * * * * * * * * * * * * * * * * * * * * * * * * *
* * * * * * * * * * * * * * * * * * * * * * * * * *
* * * * * * * * * * * * * * * * * * * * * * * * * *
    MOVE LOW-VALUES TO MENUMAPO.
    MOVE 'VEND4288'  TO MESSAGE-NUMBER.
    MOVE 'UPDATE SCREEN ERASED-TRANSACTION CANCELLED'
            TO THE-MESSAGE.
    MOVE OUTPUT-MESSAGE TO MMESAGEO.
 320-ADD-TO-VENDOR-FILE.
* * * * * * * * * * * * * * * * * * * * * * * * * *
* * * * * * * * * * * * * * * * * * * * * * * * * *
    MOVE SPACES TO VENDOR-RECORD.
    MOVE EIBDATE TO VENDOR-DATE-ADDED.
    MOVE ZEROES TO
        VENDOR-YTD-SALES
        VENDOR-YTD-PAYMENTS
        VENDOR-YTD-DISCOUNTS
        VENDOR-LAST-CHECK
        VENDOR-LAST-CK-DATE
        VENDOR-LAST-CK-AMT
        VENDOR-DATE-CHANGED
        VENDOR-UPDCNT.
    PERFORM 340-MOVE-FIELDS-FROM-MAP.
    MOVE EIBDATE TO VENDOR-DATE-CHANGED.
    EXEC CICS WRITE
            DATASET ('VENFILE')
            RIDFLD (KEY-INPUT)
            FROM (VENDOR-RECORD)
            LENGTH (VEND-REC-LENGTH)
            RESP   (COMMAND-STATUS-CODE)
            NOHANDLE
            END-EXEC.
    IF NORMAL
        NEXT SENTENCE
    ELSE
        PERFORM 920-UNEXPECTED-FILE-ERROR
        GO TO      850-SEND-MENU-MAP-EXIT.
 340-MOVE-FIELDS-FROM-MAP.
```

FIGURE 8.10.   Continued

```
* * * * * * * * * * * * * * * * * * * * * * * * * *
* * * * * * * * * * * * * * * * * * * * * * * * * *
* * * * * * * * * * * * * * * * * * * * * * * * *
      MOVE VENNAMEI IN DISPMAPI TO VENDOR-NAME.
      MOVE KEY-INPUT            TO VENDOR-ID.
      MOVE ADDR1I   IN DISPMAPI TO VENDOR-ADDR1.
      MOVE ADDR2I   IN DISPMAPI TO VENDOR-ADDR2.
      MOVE ADDR3I   IN DISPMAPI TO VENDOR-ADDR3.
      MOVE ADDR4I   IN DISPMAPI TO VENDOR-ADDR4.
      MOVE CONTACI  IN DISPMAPI TO VENDOR-CONTACT.
      MOVE TELEI    IN DISPMAPI TO VENDOR-TELE.
      MOVE TAXIDI   IN DISPMAPI TO VENDOR-TAXID.
      MOVE PAHOLDI  IN DISPMAPI TO VENDOR-PAY-HOLD.
      MOVE PRODUCTI IN DISPMAPI TO VENDOR-PRODUCT.
 850-SEND-MENU-MAP-EXIT.
* * * * * * * * * * * * * * * * * * * * * * * * * *
*     SEND MENU MAP TO OPERATOR
* * * * * * * * * * * * * * * * * * * * * * * * * * * *
* * * * * * * * * * * * * * * * * * * * * * * * * * * *
      MOVE 'VEN0003' TO SCODEO IN MENUMAPO.
      MOVE KEY-INPUT  TO VENDIDO IN MENUMAPO
      MOVE CURRENT-DATE TO  DATEO IN MENUMAPO.
      MOVE EIBTIME TO TIMEO.
      TRANSFORM TIMEO FROM ',' TO ':'.
      MOVE EIBTRMID TO TERMO.
      EXEC CICS SEND MAP ('MENUMAP')
              MAPSET ('VENDSET')
              ERASE
              FREEKB
              NOHANDLE
      END-EXEC.
      EXEC CICS  RETURN
              TRANSID ('VEND')
              COMMAREA (KEY-INPUT) LENGTH (06)
      END-EXEC.
* * * * * * * * * * * * * * * * * * * * * * * * * *
* * * * * * * * * * * * * * * * * * * * * * * * *
 905-INVALID-KEY.
      MOVE LOW-VALUES TO MENUMAPO.
      MOVE KEY-INPUT TO  VENDIDO IN MENUMAPO.
      MOVE 'RECORD KEY NOT NUMERIC' TO THE-MESSAGE.
      MOVE 'VEND4905'         TO MESSAGE-NUMBER.
      MOVE OUTPUT-MESSAGE TO MMESAGEO.
 910-UNEXPECTED-BMS-ERROR.
      MOVE LOW-VALUES TO MENUMAPO
      MOVE 'BMS ERROR-CALL MIS'  TO THE-MESSAGE
      MOVE 'VEND4910'          TO MESSAGE-NUMBER
      MOVE OUTPUT-MESSAGE TO MMESAGEO.
 920-UNEXPECTED-FILE-ERROR.
      IF    ILLOGIC PERFORM 940-VSAM-ERROR
      ELSE IF NOTOPEN PERFORM 944-NOTOPEN-ERROR
           ELSE
              MOVE LOW-VALUES TO MENUMAPO
              MOVE 'VENDOR FILE ERROR-CALL MIS' TO THE-MESSAGE
              MOVE 'VEND4920'           TO MESSAGE-NUMBER
              MOVE OUTPUT-MESSAGE TO MMESAGEO.
 934-ONFILE-ERROR.
      MOVE LOW-VALUES TO MENUMAPO.
      MOVE 'THIS RECORD IS ALREADY ON FILE' TO THE-MESSAGE.
      MOVE 'VEND4934'          TO MESSAGE-NUMBER.
      MOVE OUTPUT-MESSAGE TO MMESAGEO.
 940-VSAM-ERROR.
      MOVE LOW-VALUES TO MENUMAPO.
      MOVE 'FILE LOGIC ERROR-CALL MIS'  TO THE-MESSAGE.
      MOVE 'VEND4940'          TO MESSAGE-NUMBER.
      MOVE OUTPUT-MESSAGE TO MMESAGEO.
 944-NOTOPEN-ERROR.
      MOVE LOW-VALUES TO MENUMAPO.
      MOVE 'VENDOR FILE CLOSED' TO THE-MESSAGE.
      MOVE 'VEND4944'          TO MESSAGE-NUMBER.
      MOVE OUTPUT-MESSAGE TO MMESAGEO.
* * * * * * * * * * * * * * * * * * * * * * * * *
 1000-PARAGRAPH-NOT-USED.
      GOBACK.
```

FIGURE 8.10. Continued

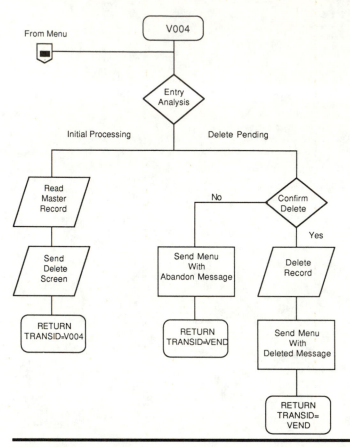

FIGURE 8.11. Delete Program Logic

deleted. It could be a time-consuming task for the operator to add the record back to the file, especially if some of the fields in the record are updated by non-CICS sources.

The initial processing logic begins by reading the record from the data set using the record key passed from the menu program in the commarea. The routine continues by building a BMS screen using the fields from the record. The sample update-inquiry screen depicted in figure 8.12 is again used to display this information. The screen contains a message telling the operator what action needs to be taken to confirm the delete operation. In this example, PF6 will confirm the delete; any other key will cancel it. Of course, any PF or PA key could have been specified to confirm the delete.

After the first-pass routine has sent the delete confirmation screen, it issues a pseudoconversational RETURN command with a transid for the delete program (V004). The record key is passed to the next task in the commarea.

After the operator has viewed the delete screen, some attention key such as PF6 or CLEAR will be pressed. That action will cause the next task to be started. This time the entry analysis will select the second-pass logic. In the logic diagram, this pass is called the delete-pending routine. The purpose of the delete-pending logic is to actually delete the record or to cancel the delete operation. This can be determined by simply checking which AID key was pressed. An input mapping operation is not required. Upon entry to the delete-pending logic, the field EIBAID is tested for PF6. If it was pressed, the routine will issue the DELETE command to remove the record from the file. The record

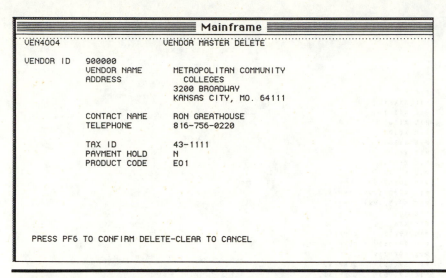

```
╔═══════════════════════ Mainframe ═══════════════════════╗
║ VEN4004                VENDOR MASTER DELETE              ║
║                                                          ║
║  VENDOR ID    900000                                     ║
║               VENDOR NAME      METROPOLITAN COMMUNITY    ║
║               ADDRESS              COLLEGES              ║
║                                3200 BROADWAY             ║
║                                KANSAS CITY, MO. 64111    ║
║                                                          ║
║               CONTACT NAME     RON GREATHOUSE            ║
║               TELEPHONE        816-756-0220              ║
║                                                          ║
║               TAX ID           43-1111                   ║
║               PAYMENT HOLD     N                         ║
║               PRODUCT CODE     E01                       ║
║                                                          ║
║                                                          ║
║                                                          ║
║                                                          ║
║   PRESS PF6 TO CONFIRM DELETE-CLEAR TO CANCEL            ║
╚══════════════════════════════════════════════════════════╝
```

FIGURE 8.12. First Pass Logic Displays Record to Be Deleted

key from the commarea will be used in the delete command. The routine then sends the menu screen with a message confirming that the record was deleted. The pseudoconversational return command with a transid for the menu completes the transition back to the menu program.

If the operator signaled that the delete operation was to be abandoned, the delete-pending logic sends a "delete abandoned" message to the operator, then provides a transition back to the menu the same way as in our earlier example.

A sample delete program is shown in figure 8.13. Before moving on to the last two topics you may want to review this program.

Protecting against Multiple Updates

The pseudoconversational programming technique has been widely accepted as the standard method of writing CICS/VS programs. By designing transactions to release task storage during the time the operator is viewing or changing the screen image, you can maintain the efficiency of CICS. This pseudoconversational design, can however, cause a data integrity problem when updating files or data bases. The problem occurs due to the fact that a pseudoconversational program must read the record image during one task execution and update it during a subsequent task execution. CICS/VS does not provide *exclusive control* of the target record between the separate task executions. In fact, CICS was specifically designed not to maintain exclusive control of a record beyond a single task execution. The exclusive control mechanism is then somewhat limited in protecting records updated by pseudoconversational tasks. Here is an illustration showing how the integrity of a record can be damaged during a pseudoconversational update.

Assume that an operator invokes an update program on terminal ONE (see figure 8.14). During the initial processing logic, the update program reads the target record into working-storage. The program then builds the screen using BMS, and finally does a pseudoconversational return. At this point in the transaction all task storage is released (except the commarea) and exclusive control (if requested) on all files is released. Remember, exclusive control is released at task termination.

At this point the operator on terminal ONE is busy changing the contents of one or more fields on the screen. These fields and the other FSET fields will eventually be read from the screen and used to update the record. This process will occur only after the operator presses ENTER or another AID key.

```
IDENTIFICATION DIVISION.
PROGRAM-ID. VEND004.
AUTHOR.  BOB LOWE.
ENVIRONMENT DIVISION.
DATA DIVISION.
WORKING-STORAGE SECTION.
01   VENDOR-RECORD.
     05   VENDOR-NAME            PIC X(30).
     05   VENDOR-ID              PIC XXXXX.
     05   VENDOR-ADDR1           PIC X(30).
     05   VENDOR-ADDR2           PIC X(30).
     05   VENDOR-ADDR3           PIC X(30).
     05   VENDOR-ADDR4           PIC X(30).
     05   VENDOR-CONTACT         PIC X(30).
     05   VENDOR-TELE            PIC X(12).
     05   VENDOR-TAXID           PIC X(11).
     05   VENDOR-YTD-SALES       PIC S9(07)V99 COMP-3.
     05   VENDOR-YTD-PAYMENTS    PIC S9(07)V99 COMP-3.
     05   VENDOR-YTD-DISCOUNTS   PIC S9(07)V99 COMP-3.
     05   VENDOR-PAY-HOLD        PIC X.
     05   VENDOR-PRODUCT         PIC XXX.
     05   VENDOR-LAST-CHECK      PIC S9(05)     COMP-3.
     05   VENDOR-LAST-CK-DATE    PIC S9(05)     COMP-3.
     05   VENDOR-LAST-CK-AMT     PIC S9(07)V99 COMP-3.
     05   VENDOR-DATE-ADDED      PIC S9(05)     COMP-3.
     05   VENDOR-DATE-CHANGED    PIC S9(05)     COMP-3.
     05   VENDOR-LAST-OPID       PIC XXX.
     05   VENDOR-UPDCNT          PIC 9.
01   MISC-AREAS.
     05   MSG-LEN                PIC S9999 COMP.
     05   VENDOR-RECORD-LENGTH   PIC S9999 COMP VALUE +249.
     05   ASKIP-NORM             PIC X VALUE '0'.
* * * * * * * * * * * * * * * * * * * * * * * * * * * * *
*    CICS/VS RELEASE 1.7 RESPONSE FIELD
* * * * * * * * * * * * * * * * * * * * * * * * * * * * *
01   COMMAND-RETURN-VALUE.
     05   COMMAND-STATUS-CODE         PIC S9(08) COMP VALUE +0.
          88   NORMAL                      VALUE +0.
          88   DSIDERR                     VALUE +12.
          88   NOTFND                      VALUE +13.
          88   DUPREC                      VALUE +14.
          88   INVREQ                      VALUE +16.
          88   IOERR                       VALUE +17.
          88   NOSPACE                     VALUE +18.
          88   NOTOPEN                     VALUE +19.
          88   ILLOGIC                     VALUE +21.
          88   LENGERR                     VALUE +22.
          88   ITEMERR                     VALUE +26.
          88   PGMIDERR                    VALUE +27.
          88   MAPFAIL                     VALUE +36.
          88   INVMPSZ                     VALUE +38.
          88   QIDERR                      VALUE +44.
          88   NOTAUTH                     VALUE +70.
          88   DISABLED                    VALUE +84.
01   ERROR-MESSAGE-LINE.
     05   MESSAGE-NUMBER         PIC X(8).
     05   FILLER                 PIC X.
     05   THE-MESSAGE            PIC X(54).
     05   RC-LABEL               PIC XXXX.
     05   STATUS-DISPLAY         PIC 9999.
COPY VENDSET SUPPRESS.
COPY DFHAID SUPPRESS.
LINKAGE SECTION.
01   DFHCOMMAREA.
     05   KEY-INPUT              PIC XXXXX.
PROCEDURE DIVISION.
*PROCEDURE CODE
000-MAINLINE-ROUTINE.
     MOVE LOW-VALUES TO MENUMAPO.
     IF EIBTRNID EQUAL 'V004'
        PERFORM 400-DELETE-PENDING
        PERFORM 925-TRANSMIT-MENU-SCREEN.
     IF KEY-INPUT NOT NUMERIC
        MOVE 'VENDOR NUMBER NOT NUMERIC' TO MMESAGEO
        MOVE KEY-INPUT TO VENDIDO IN MENUMAPO
        GO TO 925-TRANSMIT-MENU-SCREEN.
```

FIGURE 8.13.   Sample Delete Program

```
       EXEC CICS READ
           DATASET ('VENFILE')
           INTO    (VENDOR-RECORD)
           RIDFLD  (KEY-INPUT)
           LENGTH  (VENDOR-RECORD-LENGTH)
           NOHANDLE
           RESP    (COMMAND-STATUS-CODE)
           END-EXEC.
       IF NORMAL NEXT SENTENCE
       ELSE
           PERFORM 940-FILE-ERROR
           MOVE ERROR-MESSAGE-LINE TO MMESAGEO IN MENUMAPO
           GO TO 925-TRANSMIT-MENU-SCREEN.
* *****************************************************
*      PREPARE AND SEND INQUIRY SCREEN
       MOVE LOW-VALUES          TO            DISPMAPO.
       MOVE 'DELETE'            TO    DTYPEO  IN DISPMAPO.
       MOVE 'VEN4004'           TO    SCODEO  IN DISPMAPO.
       MOVE ASKIP-NORM          TO    VENNAMEA IN DISPMAPI
                                      ADDR1A  IN DISPMAPI
                                      ADDR2A  IN DISPMAPI
                                      ADDR3A  IN DISPMAPI
                                      ADDR4A  IN DISPMAPI
                                      CONTACA IN DISPMAPI
                                      TELEA   IN DISPMAPI
                                      TAXIDA  IN DISPMAPI
                                      PAHOLDA IN DISPMAPI
                                      PRODUCTA IN DISPMAPI.
       MOVE VENDOR-NAME         TO    VENNAMEO IN DISPMAPO.
       MOVE VENDOR-ID           TO    VENDIDO IN DISPMAPO.
       MOVE VENDOR-ADDR1        TO    ADDR1O  IN DISPMAPO.
       MOVE VENDOR-ADDR2        TO    ADDR2O  IN DISPMAPO.
       MOVE VENDOR-ADDR3        TO    ADDR3O  IN DISPMAPO.
       MOVE VENDOR-ADDR4        TO    ADDR4O  IN DISPMAPO.
       MOVE VENDOR-CONTACT      TO    CONTACO IN DISPMAPO.
       MOVE VENDOR-TELE         TO    TELEO   IN DISPMAPO.
       MOVE VENDOR-TAXID        TO    TAXIDO  IN DISPMAPO.
       MOVE VENDOR-PAY-HOLD     TO    PAHOLDO IN DISPMAPO.
       MOVE VENDOR-PRODUCT      TO    PRODUCTO IN DISPMAPO.
       MOVE 'PRESS PF6 TO CONFIRM DELETE' TO DMESAGEO.
       EXEC CICS SEND MAP ('DISPMAP')
                   MAPSET ('VENDSET')
                   ERASE
                   FREEKB
                   NOHANDLE
                   END-EXEC.
       EXEC CICS RETURN TRANSID ('V004')
                   COMMAREA (DFHCOMMAREA) LENGTH (6)
                   END-EXEC.
   400-DELETE-PENDING.
       MOVE 'DELETE CANCELLED' TO MMESAGEO.
       IF EIBAID NOT EQUAL DFHPF6
           GO TO 410-DELETE-PENDING-EXIT.
       EXEC CICS DELETE
           DATASET ('VENFILE')
           RIDFLD (KEY-INPUT)
           NOHANDLE
           RESP    (COMMAND-STATUS-CODE)
           END-EXEC.
       IF NORMAL
           MOVE 'RECORD WAS DELETED' TO MMESAGEO
       ELSE
           IF NOTFND
               MOVE 'RECORD ALREADY DELETED' TO MMESAGEO
           ELSE
               PERFORM 940-FILE-ERROR
               MOVE ERROR-MESSAGE-LINE TO MMESAGEO.
   410-DELETE-PENDING-EXIT.
       EXIT.
   925-TRANSMIT-MENU-SCREEN.
       MOVE EIBTRMID   TO TERMO IN MENUMAPO.
       MOVE CURRENT-DATE TO DATEO IN MENUMAPO.
       MOVE EIBTIME TO TIMEO IN MENUMAPO.
       TRANSFORM TIMEO IN MENUMAPO FROM ',' TO ':'.
       MOVE 'VEN0004'  TO SCODEO IN MENUMAPO.
       EXEC CICS SEND MAP ('MENUMAP')
                   MAPSET ('VENDSET')
                   ERASE
                   FREEKB
                   END-EXEC.
       EXEC CICS RETURN TRANSID ('VEND')
           COMMAREA (EIBAID) LENGTH (1)
           END-EXEC.
```

FIGURE 8.13. Continued

```
* * * * * * * * * * * * * * * * * * * * * * * * * * * * * * * *
* * * * * * * * * * * * * * * * * * * * * * * * * * * *
*     ERROR  PROCESSING  ROUTINES
* * * * * * * * * * * * * * * * * * * * * * * * * * * *
 940-FILE-ERROR.
     MOVE SPACES TO ERROR-MESSAGE-LINE.
     IF NOTFND
        MOVE 'CANNOT DELETE-RECORD NOT FOUND' TO THE-MESSAGE
        MOVE KEY-INPUT TO VENDIDO IN MENUMAPO
        MOVE 'VEND0950'  TO MESSAGE-NUMBER
     ELSE IF NOTOPEN
             MOVE 'VENDOR FILE NOT OPEN' TO THE-MESSAGE
             MOVE 'VEND0950'  TO MESSAGE-NUMBER
          ELSE PERFORM 980-ERROR.
 980-ERROR.
 * ****************************************************
 * THIS ROUTINE PREPARES TO DISPLAY THE CICS RESPONSE CODE
 * ****************************************************
     MOVE COMMAND-STATUS-CODE TO STATUS-DISPLAY.
     MOVE ' RC=' TO RC-LABEL.
     MOVE 'UNDETERMINED FILE ERROR HAS OCCURRED ' TO THE-MESSAGE
     MOVE 'VEND0980'  TO MESSAGE-NUMBER.
 999-PARAGRAPH-NOT-USED.
     GOBACK.
```

FIGURE 8.13.   Continued

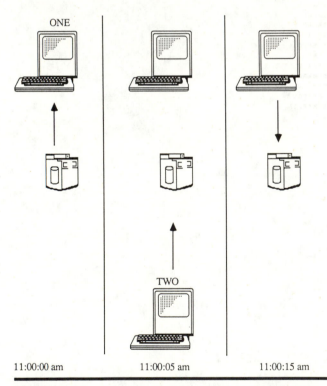

11:00:00 am   11:00:05 am   11:00:15 am

FIGURE 8.14.   Pseudo-conversational update problems

Assume now that before the first operator presses ENTER, a second operator invokes another update program on terminal TWO and *directly* updates any of the same fields being processed by the first terminal. The program running on this terminal will issue a READ UPDATE command to gain exclusive control of the record. Since the task on terminal ONE has ended, exclusive control would be granted. The program on terminal TWO will then change the record contents and issue a REWRITE command. That operator will receive a confirmation message that the file has been updated. But a file integrity problem will soon occur.

When the first operator finally presses an AID key, the original fields will be transferred to CICS and a new task will be started. The program will issue a RECEIVE MAP command to read the fields into the program's working-storage. After passing the field-edit tests, the program will issue a READ UPDATE command. From this point on until the REWRITE is issued, the record is protected against other updates. After moving the fields to the record area, the REWRITE command will update the record and release the record from exclusive control. But one or more of these fields have been written over those just updated on terminal two. We now have a data integrity problem.

PREVENTIVE MEASURES

Now that you understand how a file integrity problem can occur, you can begin to develop strategies to deal with the problem. I have listed below the actions that some installations are taking.

The easiest and most straightforward action is to ignore the problem and not do anything about it. In fact this is just what some people do. This action can even be justified in some cases. One justification is that *procedural* controls can be developed to prevent more than one terminal from updating the file at any one time. In a file maintenance application such as our vendor master update, it may be possible that only one department—or person for that matter—will be responsible for performing the function. In this situation it is not likely that the file integrity problem will ever occur. For other applications such as order entry processing, where the file is highly volatile, this control may not be feasible.

Another adaptation to this principle of manual control is to design programs so that a given function will not violate the "territory" of another function. Again, this assumes that no two operators will be performing the same function on the same record at the same time. In many cases this may be entirely possible.

Another way that some installations deal with the problem is to write their update programs using the *conversational* programming technique. Indeed most of the early CICS programs were written this way. With the conversational programming technique, the update activity occurs within a single task. When the program first gets control, it does a READ UPDATE command to get the record contents and to place exclusive control on the record. The program then displays the record on the screen and in the same task issues a RECEIVE MAP command. This causes the task to be suspended while the operator is keying in changes. While the task is suspended, exclusive control of the record is maintained. After the operator presses enter (or another AID), the task resumes execution. Fields are moved from the input map to the file area, then a REWRITE command is issued to update the record. There is no file integrity problem with this approach.

There are two other problems, however, with the conversational programming technique described above. First, as you learned in chapter 4, all of the storage for the task was tied up during the time the operator was keying in changes. This could have a serious impact on the efficiency of the system if a large number of these transactions enter the system at the same time. Another problem, perhaps even more serious, is that CICS will prevent other users from updating records in this same file during the wait. With the VSAM access method, all of the records in the VSAM control interval are isolated from other update operations when a single record is held under CICS exclusive control. In a highly active system with large VSAM control intervals, a serious bottleneck could occur by using conversational programming techniques. If possible, you should stay away from this programming approach, especially with update programs.

With proper design, you can still prevent file integrity problems while using the pseudoconversational programming technique. In the paragraphs that follow, I will describe two of the design techniques most commonly used today to prevent file-update problems. Both techniques require that all update programs follow the procedures exactly. If they don't, you're right back where you started.

THE UPDATE-INDICATOR APPROACH

The first technique makes use of an "update-in-progress" indicator stored in the record. This update indicator could be as small as a single byte with a "Y" or "N" value (or anything else you prefer). Each update program would be sensitive to this indicator. A pseudoconversational program during its initial processing logic would issue a READ UPDATE command. It would then test the update indicator to see if another transaction had reserved the record. If the test is positive, the program would send a message to the operator indicating that someone else is performing an update to the record. If the update-in-progress test is negative, the program would move the update-in-progress value to the field, then rewrite the record. This would place a "logical" hold on the record, assuming of course that all other update programs honor this indicator. The program would then continue as usual by displaying the screen and doing a pseudoconversational RETURN. In the screen-processing logic of the program, it would again do a READ UPDATE command then move the fields from the screen to the record area. Just before the REWRITE however, the program would turn off the update-in-progress indicator. After the rewrite occurs, other tasks would then be able to access the record for update purposes.

The only problem with this design occurs if the CICS system should terminate before the "owning" transaction has a chance to clear the update-in-progress indicator. If this should happen, all future transactions would be prevented from updating the record. You could design a secret override mechanism to "unlock" the record. The disadvantage here is that someone, probably operations, would have to take corrective action every time this happens. This process could become annoying to both your users and operations.

THE UPDATE-COUNTER APPROACH

There is another technique that I prefer to use. This design provides a field in the record that will serve to prevent a program from updating a record only after determining that a file integrity problem may exist. This design presumes that the integrity problem will seldom happen but prevents it when it would otherwise occur. It makes use of a one-byte counter field stored in the record. The counter field would be initialized to zero when the record is first added to the file. Each update program would be sensitive to this field.

For pseudoconversational transactions, the program would read the record during the initial processing logic and display the screen as usual. It would then issue a pseudoconversational RETURN, passing a commarea. It would, however, save the contents of the file-update counter in the commarea. Later, after all edit tests have passed, the screen-processing logic of the update program would do a READ UPDATE command to gain exclusive control of the record. Before changing its contents, the program would compare the update counter in the record with the original counter in the commarea. If the values are equal, the program would increment the counter in the record, move the other fields from the input map to the record area, then rewrite the record. If the contents of the file-update counter differ from that stored in the commarea, the program would send a message to the operator requesting that the transaction be reinitiated. When this does happen, it may annoy the operator to have to start over, but at least the file is left intact. Remember, this situation is not likely to happen very often so don't get overly concerned about transaction restarts.

There is one final point that you should consider about the use of either the update indicator or update counter. In this discussion, I only used a single indicator counter for the entire record. Depending on the application you may want to use an indicator or counter for different sections or segments of a record. It may be well worth the space and effort to define one or more groups of related areas that are protected against multiple updates. If your application calls for it, use it. If you don't like either of these two techniques, develop one of your own.

Reducing Data Transmission

Efficiency should be the central theme to every program that you write. IBM has provided several features within CICS/VS and with their equipment to allow you to maintain the maximum efficiency of the on-line system. One of these features can be found in the BMS SEND MAP command. It is the DATAONLY option.

The DATAONLY option, as its name implies, allows you to transmit only the data portion of a BMS map to a terminal. This option provides the capability to suppress the mapping of the headings, field labels, and other constants that appear on the screen. Depending on your screen design, the number of characters used for these constants may be quite significant. Each time they are sent to the terminal, these characters must go through a computer's channel or, worse yet, through a tele-communications network. This can have a negative impact on response time. Response time is an important measurement of the success of an on-line system.

There is generally only one time that it is feasible to use the DATAONLY option. These headings and constants must have been previously stored on the screen. Recall that the IBM 3270 terminal is a buffered device. It is capable of storing characters such as headings across one or more task boundaries. We have used this knowledge to allow us to write pseudoconversational programs. With the 3270 terminal, it is also possible to send new data to a terminal while leaving existing fields intact in the screen buffer. This is exactly the purpose of the DATAONLY option. Once the headings have been sent to the terminal in the initial processing logic of the UPDATE and ADD programs, it is no longer necessary to send them again in the second-pass logic. Depending on the number of data errors that require retransmission of the update screen, the DATAONLY option could have a signifi-cant impact on response time. The use of this option is also fairly simple. There are a few rules that you must follow. They are

1. Don't use the ERASE option with the DATAONLY option. The headings will be conspicuously absent from your display.
2. Do move an attribute value to each field in the symbolic map. When the DATAONLY option is used, the default attributes in the physical map are not used in the mapping process. The default attributes, like the default constants, are not mapped. The DATAONLY option really specifies that the BMS mapping routines will get *all* of the mapping data from the symbolic map. BMS will only look at the physical map to determine where the mapped fields are to be placed on the screen.
3. Do move the correct attribute to each field in the symbolic map. If you don't move the correct attribute to the symbolic map, an attribute for a data field will also carry over from a previous display. This could cause problems. For example, a field that was previously highlighted due to an error will still be highlighted if you don't send out a new normal intensity attribute. Except for highlighting, attributes should match those specified in the map-generation process. For instance, if a field is defined as numeric, be sure to use one of the numeric attribute characters. You should also specify FSET if necessary, or the field may not be returned on the next input.

Using the DATAONLY option of the BMS SEND MAP command is fairly simple as long as you un-derstand these rules and the basic concept behind the option. If your network consists of many *remote* terminals, it may be well worth your time to use this technique.

Chapter Summary

In this chapter, you have learned how about the update transactions. Screen design is an important part of this picture. These screens become the data entry template for the update transactions. Skip and stop fields on these screens prohibit the operator from keying too much data for the application. These fields can also double as error message fields.

The chapter also described the most commonly used transaction-editing techniques. By using these editing techniques, you can better assure that only "clean" data enters your application.

The logic of the update, add, and delete programs was also described and sample programs were provided for your review. You should be able to use these sample programs as models for designing your own update transaction-processing programs.

Finally, the chapter described two topics related to the update transactions. In the first topic, you learned that it is possible for one or more pseudoconversational update programs to update the same record. Techniques were described to prevent this from happening. The last topic dealt with one way to reduce the amount of data transmitted to the terminal. By using the DATAONLY option of the SEND MAP command, you might be able to improve the performance of the on-line system.

Discussion Questions

1. Describe some ways in which the Management Information Services (computer center) department can benefit from developing on-line update programs for an application.
2. Internal security for some applications can be improved when on-line update programs are used. This is because fewer people are involved with the update process. How can the on-line update process increase the potential for a single operator to make unauthorized changes to a data base or file?
3. What is the purpose of skip and stop fields on an update screen?
4. What happens if several error fields have been marked with the symbolic cursor value (-1) and the map is displayed with the CURSOR option?
5. Describe some of the techniques for displaying an error message for a field on the update screen.
6. What would happen if attributes for data entry fields are not made FSET? What would be displayed if a screen had to be retransmitted due to errors?
7. Why is it a good practice to display the target record for a delete operation before actually deleting it?
8. How does the DATAONLY option of the SEND MAP command affect default attributes and fields defined with the 'INITIAL' option?
9. Exclusive control is released on a record at task termination. How can this affect the ability of a pseudoconversational program to protect against multiple updates?
10. Describe a problem with using an "update-in-progress" indicator to protect against multiple updates to a file.
11. Discuss how the update-counter approach can be used to protect against multiple updates?

Review Exercises

For the following exercises, assume that the fields listed below appear in a BMS symbolic map that has been copied into the Working-Storage of your program. Assume further that your program has just issued a RECEIVE MAP command in the Procedure division. In each exercise below, perform the validation as directed. If any error is detected, set the field attributes to BRT, FSET, and UNPROT. The field should also be marked for symbolic cursor positioning.

```
UPDPMAP
  DEPTL
  DEPTF
  DEPTA
  DEPTI PIC XXXX.
```

1. Perform a field verify check of the DEPTI field. The field is invalid if it is not numeric.
2. Perform a limit range check. The value of the DEPTI field should be within the range 2000 through 3999 or 5000 through 7999. Any other values should be treated as an error.
3. Perform a data set check using the value in the DEPTI field. Use the System Control File described in Appendix B to validate the field. The record layout of the System Control File pertaining to this exercise is shown below. To validate the DEPTI field, combine the application value 'PE', the table name 'DEPT' and the contents of the DEPTI field to form a complete record key to access the System Control File. Use the record key in a READ comand to randomly access the SCF. A NOTFND condition would indicate an incorrect value in the DEPTI field.

```
01  SYSTEM-CONTROL-RECORD.
*----RECORD-KEY--------------------
    05  PERSCF-RECORD-KEY.
        07  PERSCF-APPL-ID          PIC XX      VALUE 'PE'.
        07  PERSCF-TABLE-NAME       PIC XXXX.
        07  PERSCF-TABLE-VALUE      PIC X(14).
*----RECORD-DATA-------------------
    05  PERSCF-ACTIVE-INACTIVE      PIC X.
    88  PERSCF-ACTIVE-RECORD        VALUE 'A'.
    88  PERSCF-INACTIVE-RECORD      VALUE 'I'.
    05  PERSCF-VARIABLE-DATA        PIC X(2014).
01  PERSCF-DEPT-TABLE REDEFINES SYSTEM-CONTROL-RECORD.
    05  FILLER                      PIC X(21).
    05  PERSCF-DEPT-DESCR           PIC X(30).
```

Lab Problems

LAB 1

UPDATE PERSONAL INFORMATION (OPTION 1)
(PROGRAM XY00002, TRANSID XY02)

Design, code, and test a program to update the personal information section of the personnel master record. Use pseudoconversational two-pass logic.

INITIAL ENTRY LOGIC (FIRST-PASS) TRANSID=XY00

☐ Access the SSN passed from the menu program in the commarea.
☐ Read the personnel master file using the passed SSN.
☐ Display the personal information screen defined in Lab 2 of chapter 5 of the text. An example is depicted below.
☐ Issue a pseudoconversational RETURN command naming the transid of this program (xy02). Pass the SSN in the commarea.
☐ Potential error conditions should be handled. Whenever an error condition is detected, display the menu screen with an appropriate message. Issue a pseudoconversational RETURN, naming the menu transid (xy00). Pass a suitable commarea so that the second-pass logic of the menu program will be used when that program is next started. Error conditions that should be anticipated include NOTFND, NOTOPEN, and any other file errors that you wish to check.

```
                    1         2         3         4         5         6
          1234567890123456789012345678901234567890123456789012345678901 2345
01^PERS201              ^PERSONAL INFORMATION^UPDATE
02
03
04           ^SSN:^123456789
05
06        ^NAME..^DOE, JOHN A                              ^
07   ^ADDRESS..^123 ANYWHERE STREET                        ^
08      ^CITY..^KANSAS CITY                       ^
09     ^STATE..^MO^641110000^
10
11     ^PHONE..^5551212^
12       ^SEX..^M^
13    ^ETHNIC..^1^
14       ^DOB..^083147^
15
16
17
18
19
20
21^MESSAGE:^PRESS CLEAR TO RETURN TO THE MENU
22
23
24
```

UPDATE PENDING LOGIC (SECOND-PASS) TRANSID=XY02

☐ If the CLEAR key was pressed, terminate the update transaction. Send the menu screen with a message indicating that the update was canceled. Use a pseudoconversational RETURN command to cause the next transaction to be the menu program.

☐ Edit the incoming fields from the update screen.
The name field is required. If this field contains spaces or was erased (low-values in input), treat it as an error.

☐ The address field is required. If this field contains spaces or was erased (low-values in input), treat it as an error.

☐ The city field is required. If this field contains spaces or was erased (low-values in input), treat it as an error.

☐ The state abbreviation code is required and must contain alphabetic characters.

☐ The zip-code field is required and must contain numeric characters only.

☐ If the phone number is entered, it must contain numeric characters only.

☐ The sex code is required and must contain a code of either "F" or "M".

☐ The ethnic code is required. It must contain a code of 0–9.

☐ The date-of-birth field is required. It must contain only numeric characters.

☐ Other edit criteria may be assigned by your instructor.

☐ If any of the edits fail, redisplay the update screen with the error fields highlighted. Position the cursor at the first error field. After redisplaying the update screen, issue a pseudoconversational return so the operator can correct the errors.

☐ If all input is correct, update the record with READ UPDATE and REWRITE commands. After updating the record, display the menu screen with a message that the record was updated. Display the SSN on the menu screen.

☐ Issue a pseudoconversational RETURN, naming the menu transid (xy00). Pass a suitable commarea so that the second-pass logic of the menu program will be used when that program is next started.

LAB 2

UPDATE PERSONAL INFORMATION (OPTION 2)

Modify the Lab 1 program to support checking an update counter to determine if other concurrently executing transactions have updated the personal information section of the record. If the counter value prior to your update operation has changed since the transaction was first initiated, send the menu screen indicating that an update conflict was avoided.

If no conflict is detected, increment the update counter and update the record.

LAB 3

UPDATE COMPANY INFORMATION (OPTION 1)
(PROGRAM XY00003, TRANSID XY03)

Design, code, and test a program to update the company information section of the personnel master record. Use pseudoconversational two-pass logic.

INITIAL ENTRY LOGIC (FIRST-PASS) TRANSID-XY00

☐ Access the SSN passed from the menu program in the commarea.
☐ Read the personnel master file using the passed SSN.
☐ Display the company information screen defined in Lab 3 of chapter 5 of the text. An example is depicted below.
☐ Issue a pseudoconversational RETURN command naming the transid of this program (xy03). Pass the SSN in the commarea.
☐ Potential error conditions should be handled. Whenever an error condition is detected, display the menu screen with an appropriate message. Issue a pseudoconversational RETURN, naming the menu transid (xy00). Pass a suitable commarea so that the second-pass logic of the menu program will be used when that program is next started. Error conditions that should be anticipated include NOTFND, NOTOPEN, and any other file errors that you wish to check.

```
                1              2              3              4              5              6
        1234567890 1234567890 1234567890 1234567890 1234567890 1234567890 1234
01^PERS201          ^COMPANY INFORMATION^UPDATE
02
03^SSN:^123456789
04^NAME:^DOE, JOHN A
05
06
07   ^EMPLOYEE TYPE..^01^
08        ^LOCATION..^04^
09     ^DEPARTMENT..^2180^
10
11      ^JOB TITLE..^21805^
12    ^POSITION NO..^00001^
13^EMPLOYMENT DATE..^060686^
14
15   ^ANNUAL SALARY..^  25,000.00^
16
17
18
19
20
21^MESSAGE:^PRESS CLEAR TO RETURN TO THE MENU
22
23
24
```

UPDATE PENDING LOGIC (SECOND-PASS) TRANSID=XY03

☐ If the CLEAR key was pressed, terminate the update transaction. Send the menu screen with a message indicating that the update was canceled. Use a pseudoconversational RETURN command to cause the next transaction to be the menu program.

☐ Edit the incoming fields from the update screen.

Each field except the annual-salary field must contain numeric characters only.

Deedit the annual-salary field to remove any commas and the decimal point. This field should contain a positive value.

Other edit criteria may be assigned by your instructor.

☐ If any of the edits fail, redisplay the update screen with the error fields highlighted. Position the cursor at the first error field. After redisplaying the update screen, issue a pseudoconversational return so the operator can correct the errors.

☐ If all input is correct, update the record with READ UPDATE and REWRITE commands. After updating the record, display the menu screen with a message that the record was updated. Display the SSN on the menu screen.

☐ Issue a pseudoconversational RETURN, naming the menu transid (xy00). Pass a suitable commarea so that the second-pass logic of the menu program will be used when that program is next started.

LAB 4

ADD EMPLOYEE RECORD
(PROGRAM XY00004, TRANSID XY04)

Design, code, and test a program to add a record to the personnel master file. The new record will initially contain data in the personal information section of the record. All other fields will be initialized to zeros (for numeric fields) or spaces (for alphameric fields). Use pseudoconversational two-pass logic.

INITIAL ENTRY LOGIC (FIRST-PASS) TRANSID=XY00

☐ Access the SSN passed from the menu program in the commarea.
☐ Read the personnel master file using the passed SSN.
☐ If the record is already on file, treat this as an error and display the menu screen with an appropriate message.
☐ Display the personal information screen defined in Lab 2 of chapter 5 of the text. An example is depicted below.
☐ Issue a pseudoconversational RETURN command naming the transid of this program (xy04). Pass the SSN in the commarea.
☐ Potential error conditions should be handled. Whenever an error condition is detected, display the menu screen with an appropriate message. Issue a pseudoconversational RETURN, naming the menu transid (xy00). Pass a suitable commarea so that the second-pass logic of the menu program will be used when that program is next started. Error conditions that should be anticipated include *record already on file*, NOTOPEN, and any other file errors that you wish to check.

```
                 1         2         3         4         5         6
        1234567890123456789012345678901234567890123456789012345678901234567890123456
01^PERS401          ^PERSONAL INFORMATION^ADD
02
03
04        ^SSN:^123456789
05
06      ^NAME..^------------------------------^
07   ^ADDRESS..^------------------------------^
08      ^CITY..^--------------------^
09     ^STATE..^--^---------^
10
11     ^PHONE..^-------^
12       ^SEX..^-^
13    ^ETHNIC..^-^
14       ^DOB..^-------^
15
16
17
18
19
20
21^MESSAGE:^PRESS CLEAR TO RETURN TO THE MENU
22
23
24
```

ADD PENDING LOGIC (SECOND-PASS) TRANSID=XY04

☐ If the CLEAR key was pressed, terminate the add transaction. Send the menu screen with a message indicating that the add was canceled. Use a pseudoconversational RETURN command to cause the next transaction to be the menu program.

☐ Edit the incoming fields from the update screen.

The name field is required. If this field contains spaces or was erased (low-values in input), treat it as an error.

The address field is required. If this field contains spaces or was erased (low-values in input), treat it as an error.

The city field is required. If this field contains spaces or was erased (low-values in input), treat it as an error.

The state abbreviation code is required and must contain alphabetic characters.

The zip-code field is required and must contain numeric characters only.

If the phone number is entered, it must contain numeric characters only.

The sex code is required and must contain a code of either "F" or "M".

The ethnic code is required. It must contain a code of 0–9.

The date-of-birth field is required. It must contain only numeric characters.

Other edit criteria may be assigned by your instructor.

☐ If any of the edits fail, redisplay the add screen with the error fields highlighted. Position the cursor at the first error field. After redisplaying the add screen, issue a pseudoconversational return so the operator can correct the errors.

☐ If all input is correct, add the record to the file with the WRITE command. After adding the record, display the menu screen with a message that the record was added. Display the SSN on the menu screen.

☐ Issue a pseudoconversational RETURN, naming the menu transid (xy00). Pass a suitable commarea so that the second-pass logic of the menu program will be used when that program is next started.

LAB 5

DELETE PERSONNEL RECORD
(PROGRAM XY00005, TRANSID XY05)

Design, code, and test a program to delete a record from the personnel master file. Use pseudo-conversational two-pass logic.

INITIAL ENTRY LOGIC (FIRST-PASS) TRANSID=XY00

☐ Access the SSN passed from the menu program in the commarea.
☐ Read the personnel master file using the passed SSN.
☐ Display the personal information screen defined in Lab 2 of chapter 5 of the text. An example is depicted below.
☐ Issue a pseudoconversational RETURN command naming the transid of this program (xy05). Pass the SSN in the commarea.
☐ Potential error conditions should be handled. Whenever an error condition is detected, display the menu screen with an appropriate message. Issue a pseudoconversational RETURN, naming the menu transid (xy00). Pass a suitable commarea so that the second-pass logic of the menu program will be used when that program is next started. Error conditions that should be anticipated include NOTFND, NOTOPEN, and any other file errors that you wish to check.

```
              1         2         3         4         5         6
     1234567890123456789012345678901234567890123456789012345678901234 56
01^PERS201           ^PERSONAL INFORMATION^DELETE
02
03
04        ^SSN:^123456789
05
06     ^NAME..^DOE, JOHN A                          ^
07 ^ADDRESS..^123 ANYWHERE STREET                    ^
08    ^CITY..^KANSAS CITY              ^
09   ^STATE..^MO^641110000^
10
11   ^PHONE..^5551212^
12     ^SEX..^M^
13  ^ETHNIC..^1^
14     ^DOB..^083147^
15
16
17
18
19
20
21^MESSAGE:^PRESS PF3 TO CONFIRM DELETE
22
23
24
```

DELETE PENDING LOGIC (SECOND-PASS) TRANSID=XY02

☐ If any key but the PF3 key was pressed, terminate the delete transaction. Send the menu screen with a message indicating that the delete was canceled.

☐ If the PF3 key was pressed, delete the record from the file. Send the menu screen with a message indicating that the record was deleted.

☐ Issue a pseudoconversational RETURN, naming the menu transid (xy00). Pass a suitable commarea so that the second-pass logic of the menu program will be used when that program is next started.

LAB 6

UPDATE COMPANY INFORMATION (OPTION 2)
(PROGRAM XY00003, TRANSID XY03)

Design, code, and test a program to update the company information section of the personnel master record. Use pseudoconversational two-pass logic.

INITIAL ENTRY LOGIC (FIRST-PASS) TRANSID=XY00

☐ Access the SSN passed from the menu program in the commarea.
☐ Read the personnel master file using the passed SSN.
☐ Display the extended company information screen defined in Lab 4 of chapter 5 of the text. An example is depicted below.
☐ Issue a pseudoconversational RETURN command naming the transid of this program (xy03). Pass the SSN in the commarea.
☐ Potential error conditions should be handled. Whenever an error condition is detected, display the menu screen with an appropriate message. Issue a pseudoconversational RETURN, naming the menu transid (xy00). Pass a suitable commarea so that the second-pass logic of the menu program will be used when that program is next started. Error conditions that should be anticipated include NOTFND, NOTOPEN, and any other file errors that you wish to check.

```
                 1         2         3         4         5         6
        1234567890123456789012345678901234567890123456789012345678901234556
01^PERS201            ^COMPANY INFORMATION^UPDATE
02
03^SSN:^123456789
04^NAME:^DOE, JOHN A
05
06
07  ^EMPLOYEE TYPE..^01^              ^
08      ^LOCATION..^04^               ^
09    ^DEPARTMENT..^2180^             ^
10
11     ^JOB TITLE..^21805^            ^
12   ^POSITION NO..^00001^            ^
13^EMPLOYMENT DATE..^060686^          ^
14
15  ^ANNUAL SALARY..^  25,000.00^      ^
16
17
18
19
20
21^MESSAGE:^PRESS CLEAR TO RETURN TO THE MENU
22
23
24
```

UPDATE PENDING LOGIC (SECOND-PASS) TRANSID=XY03

☐ If the CLEAR key was pressed, terminate the update transaction. Send the menu screen with a message indicating that the update was canceled. Use a pseudoconversational RETURN command to cause the next transaction to be the menu program.

☐ Edit the incoming fields from the update screen.

The employee type, location, department, and job title fields should be validated by using the system control file. If the records corresponding to the codes are not found in the SCF, display an error message in the stop field on the update screen. If the code is found, display the value from the SCF record. An example is depicted below.

Other input fields should be validated the same indicated in Lab 3.

☐ If any of the edits fail, redisplay the update screen with the error fields highlighted and display an error message in the stop field. Position the cursor at the first error field. After redisplaying the update screen, issue a pseudoconversational RETURN so the operator can correct the errors.

```
                 1         2         3         4         5         6
        1234567890123456789012345678901234567890123456789012345678901234 56
01^PERS201           ^COMPANY INFORMATION^UPDATE
02
03^SSN:^123456789
04^NAME:^DOE, JOHN A
05
06
07    ^EMPLOYEE TYPE..^01^          ^ADMINISTRATOR
08         ^LOCATION..^04^          ^<--INVALID CODE ENTERED
09       ^DEPARTMENT..^2180^        ^COMPUTER SERVICES
10
11        ^JOB TITLE..^21805^       ^ANALYST PROGRAMMER
12     ^POSITION NO..^XXXXX^        ^<--MUST BE NUMERIC
13^EMPLOYMENT DATE..^0606AA^        ^<--MUST BE NUMERIC
14
15   ^ANNUAL SALARY..^  25,000.00^  ^
16
17
18
19
20
21^MESSAGE:^PRESS CLEAR TO RETURN TO THE MENU
22
23
24
```

☐ If all input is correct, update the record with READ UPDATE and REWRITE commands. After updating the record, display the menu screen with a message that the record was updated. Display the SSN on the menu screen.

☐ Issue a pseudoconversational RETURN, naming the menu transid (xy00). Pass a suitable commarea so that the second-pass logic of the menu program will be used when that program is next started.

9

Additional CICS/VS Topics

As you study the material in this chapter, you will

1. Discover that CICS/VS provides a Temporary Storage facility that can be used by any application program.
2. Learn how to create a Temporary Storage queue containing one or more records.
3. See how to access Temporary Storage records sequentially and randomly.
4. Understand how Temporary Storage can be used to pass data to programs running on different terminals.
5. Learn to use the ASKTIME and FORMATTIME commands to retrieve various system date and time parameters for use by the program.
6. See how to use the ASSIGN command to obtain special CICS information for use by the program.
7. Learn how a program can display multiple screens of information.
8. Understand how to use BMS Terminal Paging to reduce the programming necessary to display multiple screens.
9. Be able to use the Terminal Paging commands to view multiple screens in any sequence.

This chapter contains topics that are useful as you learn more about CICS. With the first topic, you will be introduced to the Temporary Storage facility provided by CICS. This facility allows a program to store data that might be needed later in a different program or task. By learning to use Temporary Storage, you will be able to design programs to solve more complex problems.

Next, the chapter describes a few miscellaneous commands. The FORMATTIME and ASKTIME commands are presented. These commands enable your program to obtain date and time parameters in a variety of formats. The ASSIGN command is then introduced. This command provides the capability to request certain CICS values that are not provided in the EIB.

Finally, the chapter presents techniques whereby a program can display multiple screens. With some applications, it will often be necessary to provide more than one screen. The topic introduces you to a special BMS facility known as Terminal Paging. This facility enables a program to display multiple screens without much more difficulty than displaying a single screen. The topic also describes the operator commands that can be used to view the various screens in any order.

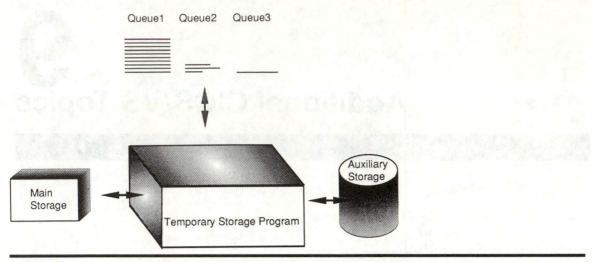

Queue1 Queue2 Queue3

Main Storage

Temporary Storage Program

Auxiliary Storage

FIGURE 9.1. Temporary Storage Queues Are Maintained by the Temporary Storage Program

Temporary Storage

CICS provides a Temporary Storage facility that can be used in a variety of ways to support on-line applications. Temporary Storage can be likened to a scratch pad or chalk board. You can store information in the facility, then at a later time retrieve and process the data. Data stored in the Temporary Storage facility can be maintained in the system across task boundaries or for that matter for any period of time. Stored information can even be kept intact between each daily start-up of CICS.

The Temporary Storage facility is controlled by the CICS/VS Temporary Storage management program. Please refer to figure 9.1. This program manages groups of related records called *queues*. Each queue of records can be maintained in either main storage or on an auxiliary data set. Main storage queues are held in CICS dynamic storage. Auxiliary storage queues are maintained in a single VSAM data set defined during the CICS tailoring process.

A queue can have one or more records. The only limitation to the number of records that can be stored in a queue is the amount of CICS dynamic storage available in the system or the size of the Temporary Storage data set. In the last few releases of CICS, there is no limit to the record length. In earlier releases, the record length was limited for queues maintained in auxiliary storage.

Each record stored in a queue can be variable in length. The length of each record is determined when it is written to the queue. New records can be added to a queue at any time. As new records are added with the WRITEQ TS command, they are added to the *end* of the queue. New records cannot be inserted between existing records.

Existing records can also be updated randomly. The WRITEQ TS command with the REWRITE option is used to do this. When updating records, the ITEM option is used to specify which record is to be updated. Both the content and length of a record can be changed during an update operation.

Records in a queue can be read sequentially. For sequential access, a next-record pointer is maintained by the Temporary Storage program. By issuing the READQ TS command with the NEXT option, the next record will be presented to the program. Records can also be accessed randomly. Each record in a queue has an item number that can be specified in the READQ TS command. When a program retrieves a record by item number the next record pointer is also updated. In this way, a program can start a sequential access at any point in the queue.

A single record cannot be deleted from a queue. Only an entire queue can be deleted. To do this the DELETEQ TS command is provided.

Once a queue has been created by a program, it can be accessed by any other program in the system until it is deleted. This program may be running on any terminal. A program can create a queue during one task and access it later in the same task or a different task. Temporary Storage is often used to pass information from one task to another in this way. It can be used like a permanent multirecord commarea. It can also be used to store *global* information such as application parameters or tables that might be used by all programs within an application.

CREATING A QUEUE

A Temporary Storage queue can be dynamically created by an application program. There is no table name required (as in file control) to limit access to a queue. Each queue is identified by a symbolic queue name. Each queue name is from one to eight characters in length. A queue is created and new records are added using the WRITEQ TS command. The format of the command is

```
EXEC CICS WRITEQ TS
     QUEUE (name)
     FROM (data-area)
     LENGTH (data-value)
     [ITEM (data-area)]
     [MAIN | AUXILIARY]
     END-EXEC
```

The queue name is identified in the QUEUE option. If a constant is used, it must be enclosed within apostrophes. If a COBOL name is used, it must be an eight-character field and must contain the name of the queue to be created or extended. When the WRITEQ TS command is executed, if the queue does not exist, one will be created and the record will be added. If the queue does exist, the record will be added to the end of the queue.

The use of the FROM option is similar to other output commands. The argument is the name of the data area containing the record to be written.

The LENGTH argument can be a constant or can name a COBOL field with a usage of COMPUTATIONAL and a PICTURE of S9999. The value stored in the length argument represents the length of the record to be written. It must be a positive value or the exceptional condition INVREQ will occur.

The ITEM option is not required when adding records to a queue. If used, the argument must contain a COBOL variable with a usage of COMPUTATIONAL and a picture of S9999. After the WRITEQ TS command has been executed, this field will contain the item number of the record that has just been written to the queue. For the first record written to the queue, it will contain a value of one. As new records are written, the appropriate item number is returned to the program.

If the MAIN option is used the queue will be created and maintained in CICS dynamic storage. Access to the queue is faster since it does not require an input-output operation. Main storage queues, however, reduce the amount of dynamic storage available to other tasks. Unless the access time is critical, main storage queues should be avoided. Also, queues maintained in MAIN are lost when CICS is shut down.

AUXILIARY specifies that the queue will be created and maintained in the system auxiliary Temporary Storage data set. With this option it is possible for the queue to be passed to a subsequent restart of the entire CICS system.

CICS/VS will force all WRITE requests with the same queue name to use the same storage facility specified in the first WRITEQ TS request.

Here is an example of the WRITEQ TS command. The following statements would write a record to an auxiliary Temporary Storage queue named MYQUEUE. After the command is complete, the item number of the record is returned in the variable WHICH-ITEM.

```
    05    TS-REC-LENGTH PICTURE S9999 COMPUTATIONAL.
    05    WHICH-ITEM PICTURE S9999 COMPUTATIONAL.
01 TS-QUEUE-RECORD    PICTURE X(100).
    .
    .
    .
    MOVE +100 TO TS-REC-LENGTH.
    EXEC CICS WRITEQ TS
        QUEUE ('MYQUEUE')
        FROM (TS-QUEUE-RECORD)
        LENGTH (TS-REC-LENGTH)
        ITEM (WHICH-ITEM)
        AUXILIARY
        END-EXEC
```

READING TEMPORARY DATA

Individual records in temporary storage can be accessed by a program using the READQ TS command. They can be accessed both sequentially and randomly. For sequential access, each record is retrieved based on a next-record pointer maintained by the Temporary Storage Program. There is only one next-record pointer for the entire queue. The record read will be based on the last record read by a program in any task.

During sequential access, an exceptional condition ITEMERR, is returned to the program when a sequential retrieval operation requests a record beyond the end of the queue. A program may reset the next-record pointer by performing a random access to another record.

With random retrieval, any record in the queue can be requested by the application program. The program can switch between sequential and random retrieval at any time.

The format of the READQ TS command is

```
    EXEC CICS READQ TS
        QUEUE (name)
        INTO (data-area)
        LENGTH (data-area)
        [NUMITEMS (data-area)]
        [ITEM (data-area) | NEXT]
        END-EXEC
```

The queue name is identified in the QUEUE option. The same rules as specified for WRITEQ TS apply to this command. If the queue name specified does not exist the exceptional condition QIDERR will occur.

The INTO option specifies the receiving area for the record to be read. It should be large enough to hold the maximum anticipated record.

The LENGTH option specifies a COBOL field with a usage of COMPUTATIONAL and a picture of S9999. This field must be initialized to a value corresponding to the maximum anticipated record length. If a longer record is read, it will be truncated, and LENGERR will occur. The field specified in the argument will be set to length of retrieved record.

The NUMITEMS option can be used to obtain the number of records currently stored in the queue. The data-area argument is a COBOL field with a usage of COMPUTATIONAL and a picture of S9999.

The ITEM option is used to request *random* retrieval. The argument must name a COBOL field with a usage of COMPUTATIONAL and a picture of S9999. Prior to executing the READQ TS command, the field should be initialized to a value specifying the record number to be read from the queue. If that item does not exist, the exceptional condition ITEMERR will occur.

The NEXT option is the default and specifies that *sequential* retrieval is desired. The Temporary Storage Program returns the next record in the queue as determined by a queue-dependent item number counter maintained by Temporary Storage. This counter is updated when any task requests a record. There is only one counter per queue, so if multiple tasks are concurrently using the queue, this counter represents the last record read by the system. This counter is updated by both random and sequential requests to the queue.

The following instructions would read the first record from a Temporary Storage queue named MYQUEUE. The maximum record length expected is 100 bytes.

```
    05    TS-REC-LENGTH PICTURE S9999 COMPUTATIONAL.
    05    WHICH-ITEM PICTURE S9999 COMPUTATIONAL.
 01 TS-QUEUE-RECORD     PICTURE X(100).
    .
    .
    .
    MOVE +100 TO TS-REC-LENGTH.
    MOVE +1 TO WHICH-ITEM.

    EXEC CICS READQ TS
        QUEUE ('MYQUEUE')
        INTO (TS-QUEUE-RECORD)
        LENGTH (TS-REC-LENGTH)
        ITEM (WHICH-ITEM)
        END-EXEC
```

UPDATING RECORDS

Individual records in Temporary Storage queues can be updated by any application program. As mentioned earlier, records can be added to the queue. But existing records can also be updated, including modification of the record length. Existing records in a queue are updated using the WRITEQ TS command with the REWRITE option. The format of this command is

```
    EXEC CICS WRITEQ TS
        QUEUE (name)
        FROM (data-area)
        LENGTH (data-value)
        ITEM (data-area)
        REWRITE
        END-EXEC
```

All options as earlier described have the same effect with the following exceptions:

The QUEUE option must contain a value corresponding to the Temporary Storage queue to be updated. If the queue does not exist the exceptional condition QIDERR will arise.

The ITEM option must contain a value corresponding to the record number to be updated. If that record does not exist, the exceptional condition ITEMERR will arise.

DELETING QUEUES

Temporary Storage queues can be deleted by any application program. Once a queue is created with the WRITEQ TS command, the queue will remain in the system until deleted. Individual records in a queue cannot be deleted. A queue is deleted with the DELETEQ TS command. The format is

```
EXEC CICS DELETEQ TS QUEUE (name) END-EXEC
```

The QUEUE option must contain a value corresponding to the Temporary Storage queue to be deleted. If the queue does not exist, the exceptional condition QIDERR will arise. This is the only exceptional condition for this command.

EXCEPTIONAL CONDITIONS

NOSPACE This exceptional condition is one of the few CICS conditions that will not cause the task to be abended. It occurs when there is not sufficient space to add or update a queue.

A program may issue a HANDLE CONDITION or IGNORE CONDITION command prior to updating a queue. If it does and the NOSPACE condition occurs, control will be returned to the application program. Either the HANDLE CONDITION label will be started or the response codes in the EIB will be set to reflect the condition. If the condition has not been dealt with, the program will be *suspended* until Temporary Storage space becomes available.

IOERR might arise when creating or updating Temporary Storage records on auxiliary storage. It will occur if some input-output error occurs on the data set.

NOTAUTH occurs if the Temporary Storage queue name has been defined with resource-level security and the operator security code for the terminal does not have a matching resource-level security.

TEMPORARY STORAGE USE

There are a number of ways to use the Temporary Storage facility. As you learn more about CICS, and the design of on-line programs, you will inevitably find many uses for it.

Let's look at an example where a Temporary Storage queue could be used to ease the burden of program maintenance. Many times, programs have to be modified due to changes in a table required by an application. Tables are commonly used in programs to provide table look-up values. In our sample vendor application, for example, there might be a table used to provide descriptions for the various product codes. You might recall that the vendor record contains a product code field.

Many of our sample programs could have used a product code table in their processing routines. The inquiry program, for instance, might have displayed the product description along with the product code on the inquiry screen. The update and add programs could have used a product table to validate the product code entered by the operator.

One technique that is commonly used is to "hard code" table descriptions in each application program. Figure 9.2 illustrates how our sample product table might be defined in a program. This procedure involves the use of one series of COBOL fields to provide the table values. The area is then redefined, and a COBOL *occurs* clause is used to provide a *table* structure.

One problem with this technique deals with program maintenance. Any time the table values are changed, all programs which use them must be recompiled. This process can be facilitated by storing the tables in a source library to be copied during the compile process. This reduces the maintenance burden somewhat, but the programs still have to be recompiled to use the changes. In a large application with many programs, this recompiling process can consume a lot of time.

```
01   PRODUCT-TABLE-AREA.
     05   PRODUCT-TABLE-CONSTANTS.
          10   FILLER PIC X(33) VALUE 'A03AUTOMOTIVE PARTS'.
          10   FILLER PIC X(33) VALUE 'C01MAINFRAME COMPUTER EQUIPMENT'.
          10   FILLER PIC X(33) VALUE 'C10MICROCOMPUTER EQUIPMENT'.
          10   FILLER PIC X(33) VALUE 'C19COMPUTER PRINTERS'.
          10   FILLER PIC X(33) VALUE 'C25COMPUTER TAPE DRIVES'.
          10   FILLER PIC X(33) VALUE 'C80COMPUTER SOFTWARE'.
          10   FILLER PIC X(33) VALUE 'D01VIDEO RECORDING EQUIPMENT'.
          10   FILLER PIC X(33) VALUE 'D18VIDEO PROJECTION EQUIPMENT'.
          10   FILLER PIC X(33) VALUE 'D22VIDEO CAMERAS'.
          10   FILLER PIC X(33) VALUE 'O01OFFICE FURNITURE'.
          10   FILLER PIC X(33) VALUE 'P10PAPER SUPPLIES'.
          10   FILLER PIC X(33) VALUE 'R01BIOLOGY LAB EQUIPMENT'.
          10   FILLER PIC X(33) VALUE 'S22PAINTING SUPPLIES&EQUIPMENT'.
          10   FILLER PIC X(2871) VALUE SPACES.
     05   PRODUCT-TABLE REDEFINES PRODUCT-TABLE-CONSTANTS
                    OCCURS 100 INDEXED BY PRODUCT-INDEX.
          10   PRODUCT-CODE        PIC X(03).
          10   PRODUCT-DESCRIPTION PIC X(30).
```

FIGURE 9.2.   Coding to define Product Table

There is a better design technique that is commonly used. This technique involves storing the table look-up values outside of the program. These values can then be dynamically read into a COBOL data structure defined with the occurs clause. The structure would be large enough to accommodate table additions. By using this technique, program maintenance can be greatly reduced and programmer productivity can be improved.

There are a variety of design techniques used to store tables so they are external to the programs which use them. Tables are sometimes stored in a file. Each record in the file could represent an entire table, or it could contain only a single table look-up value. The system control file described in Appendix B uses the latter approach.

There is another simple technique that you might want to use for your CICS programs. This technique involves a variation of the "hard coding" method described earlier. By using Temporary Storage, it is possible to limit the table definitions to only a single program. When a table is changed, only that one program would need to be recompiled.

By using Temporary Storage, the table values can be passed to other CICS programs. This can be accomplished by storing the table values in a Temporary Storage queue. Figure 9.3 depicts a program designed to use Temporary Storage to share a table. This program contains table definitions in the usual way. When executed, it writes the table values to a queue named 'VNTABLE.'

This program could be executed automatically at the start of the day or could be "called" by another program using the LINK command. When executed, it would *load the table* out to the Temporary Storage queue for use by other programs.

Figure 9.4 depicts the programming logic for a program needing access to the product table. This program contains an "empty" table area in working-storage. The table is loaded dynamically by reading the first item from the Temporary Storage queue VNTABLE. If the queue does not exist, the update program will LINK to the table load program to build the queue. After the queue is created, the load program will return control to the calling program. This program would then access the queue to load the product table.

In this example, a single table was shared using a Temporary Storage queue. Multiple tables could also be shared using additional records (items) in the same queue. The ability to randomly access records in a queue would easily support these multiple tables. I hope this example will inspire you to come up with your own ideas for using this scratch-pad facility.

```
        IDENTIFICATION DIVISION.
        PROGRAM-ID. VEND008.
        AUTHOR.  BOB LOWE.
      * * * * * * * * * * * * * * * * * * * * * * * *
      *    This is a program to create a vendor product code
      *       table record.  The table record is saved in a
      *       Temporary Storage Queue named "VNTABLE".  Other
      *       programs, such as the update, and add program can
      *       read this table into their working storage.
      *       Program maintenance due to product table changes
      *       will be reduced since only this program will have
      *       to be re-compiled.  Aftwards, the other programs
      *       will be able to access the new table values.
      * * * * * * * * * * * * * * * * * * * * * * * *
        ENVIRONMENT DIVISION.
        DATA DIVISION.
        WORKING-STORAGE SECTION.
        01   PRODUCT-TABLE-AREA.
            05   PRODUCT-TABLE-CONSTANTS.
                10   FILLER PIC X(33) VALUE 'A03AUTOMOTIVE PARTS'.
                10   FILLER PIC X(33) VALUE 'C01MAINFRAME COMPUTER EQUIPMENT'.
                10   FILLER PIC X(33) VALUE 'C10MICROCOMPUTER EQUIPMENT'.
                10   FILLER PIC X(33) VALUE 'C19COMPUTER PRINTERS'.
                10   FILLER PIC X(33) VALUE 'C25COMPUTER TAPE DRIVES'.
                10   FILLER PIC X(33) VALUE 'C80COMPUTER SOFTWARE'.
                10   FILLER PIC X(33) VALUE 'D01VIDEO RECORDING EQUIPMENT'.
                10   FILLER PIC X(33) VALUE 'D18VIDEO PROJECTION EQUIPMENT'.
                10   FILLER PIC X(33) VALUE 'D22VIDEO CAMERAS'.
                10   FILLER PIC X(33) VALUE 'O01OFFICE FURNITURE'.
                10   FILLER PIC X(33) VALUE 'P10PAPER SUPPLIES'.
                10   FILLER PIC X(33) VALUE 'R01BIOLOGY LAB EQUIPMENT'.
                10   FILLER PIC X(33) VALUE 'S22PAINTING SUPPLIES&EQUIPMENT'.
        01   THE-MESSAGE PIC X(80).
        PROCEDURE DIVISION.
            EXEC CICS DELETEQ TS QUEUE ('VNTABLE')
                NOHANDLE
                END-EXEC.
      * NOTE THE LENGTH FIELD MUST BE UPDATED EACH TIME AN ELEMT IS ADDED
      *  TO THE TABLE ABOVE.
            EXEC CICS WRITEQ TS QUEUE ('VNTABLE')
                FROM (PRODUCT-TABLE-AREA)
                LENGTH (429)
                END-EXEC.
            IF EIBTRNID EQUAL 'V008'
                MOVE 'THE PRODUCT TABLE HAS BEEN WRITTEN TO TS'
                    TO THE-MESSAGE
                EXEC CICS SEND
                    FROM (THE-MESSAGE)
                    LENGTH (80)
                    ERASE
                    END-EXEC.
            EXEC CICS RETURN END-EXEC.
```

FIGURE 9.3.   Program to Write Product Table to Temporary Storage

System Date and Time

The EIB provides many of the system parameters needed by a CICS/VS application program. Among these are the EIBDATE and EIBTIME fields, which provide the system date and time at the start of the task. But in most cases these fields must be processed further by the program, to be usable. For instance, the EIBDATE field is provided in the Julian format. To display this date in calendar form, the program must provide a Julian-to-calendar conversion routine. The time value in EIBTIME is also stored in COMP-3 format, and usually must be edited by the COBOL program for display purposes. In a

```
IDENTIFICATION DIVISION.
PROGRAM-ID. VEND002.
AUTHOR. BOB LOWE.
ENVIRONMENT DIVISION.
DATA DIVISION.
WORKING-STORAGE SECTION.
01  WORK-AREA.
    05  MAX-PRODUCT-TABLE-SIZE  PIC S9999 COMP VALUE +3300.
01  PRODUCT-TABLE-AREA.
    05  PRODUCT-TABLE OCCURS 100 INDEXED BY PRODUCT-INDEX.
      10  PRODUCT-CODE        PIC X(03).
      10  PRODUCT-DESCRIPTION PIC X(30).



PROCEDURE DIVISION.


* LOAD THE PRODUCT TABLE FROM TEMPORARY STORAGE QUEUE VNTABLE.
*    IF QIDERR OCCURS, LINK TO VEND008 TO BUILD IT, THEN TRY
*    AGAIN.  IF EITHER THE LINK OR THE SECOND READQ FAILS
*    WE WILL LET CICS ABEND THE TASK DUE TO THE EXCEPTIONAL
*    CONDITION.
    MOVE SPACES TO PRODUCT-TABLE-AREA.
    EXEC CICS READQ TS QUEUE ('VNTABLE')
        INTO (PRODUCT-TABLE-AREA)
        ITEM (1)
        LENGTH (MAX-PRODUCT-TABLE-SIZE)
        RESP (COMMAND-STATUS-CODE)
        END-EXEC.
    IF QIDERR
        EXEC CICS LINK PROGRAM
            ('VEND008')
            END-EXEC
        EXEC CICS READQ TS QUEUE ('VNTABLE')
            INTO (PRODUCT-TABLE-AREA)
            ITEM (1)
            LENGTH (MAX-PRODUCT-TABLE-SIZE)
            END-EXEC.
```

FIGURE 9.4.   Product Table Is Loaded into Empty Table Area

recent CICS release, IBM has provided a new command to make it easier to get date and time parameters in other formats. This command is the FORMATTIME Command. The format of the command is

```
EXEC CICS FORMATTIME
        [ABSTIME (data-value)]
        [DATE (data-area)]
        [DATESEP (data-value)]
        [DAYCOUNT (data-area)]
        [DAYOFWEEK (data-area)]
        [DAYOFMONTH (data-area)]
        [MONTHOFYEAR (data-area)]
        [YEAR (data-area)]
        [YYDDD (data-area)]
        [TIME (data-area) [TIMESEP (data-value)]]
        END-EXEC
```

where

ABSTIME (data-value) specifies a value that is to be converted to one of the other formats. The data value may be a constant or may specify a COBOL field name defined as S9(15) COMPUTATIONAL-3. The data value contains a number representing the number of milliseconds that have elasped since 0000 hours on 1 January 1900. This value is *input* to the command. The other options name output fields from the command. To get this input value for the current time, another command ASKTIME may be used. The ASKTIME command will be described later in this section.

DATE (data-area) specifies a field name defined as PIC $\times$(08) to receive the date in the standard form specified for your system. For example MMDDYY. If the DATESEP option (described next) is not present, the system date is provided as six characters without a separator between the month and the day or the day and the year.

DATESEP [(data-value)] specifies that a date separator is to be inserted between the month, day, and year values in the DATE option. If no argument (data-value) is supplied, a slash (/) will be used to separate the day, month, and year. A data value may be supplied as a one-character literal or COBOL field to provide a different date separator.

DAYCOUNT (data-area) specifies a field where CICS will store a value indicating the number of days that have elapsed since 1 January 1900 (day 0). This value may be useful in computing the number of days between two dates. The format of this field is PIC S9(8) COMP.

DAYOFWEEK (data-area) specifies a PIC S9(8) COMP field to get the relative day of the week. Sunday = 0, Saturday = 6.

DAYOFMONTH (data-area) specifies a field where CICS returns the day of the month in PIC S9(8) COMP form.

MONTHOFYEAR (data-area) specifies a field where CICS stores the month of the year in S9(8) COMP form.

YEAR (data-area) specifies a field where the corresponding year value is stored. This field, like the four previous ones, is in PIC S9(8) COMP form.

YYDDD (data-area) specifies a field where the corresponding Julian value is stored. This field is a type PIC $\times$(06).

TIME (data-area) TIMESEP (data-value) The data area for the time argument is a PIC $\times$(8) type. If the TIMESEP option is omitted, six bytes are returned in the field. The TIMESEP option indicates that a separator between the hour, minute, and second values is needed. If the data value is omitted the colon (:) is used as a default. If some other separator is desired, use a one-character literal or COBOL field to specify the separator character.

As indicated earlier, input to the FORMATTIME command is the ABSTIME argument. This value may have been stored in a data base record as a time-stamp. You may have also stored this value somewhere in an earlier task. In most cases, though, you will want to use the current system date and time as input to the FORMATTIME command. Another command is provided to retrieve this information. It is the ASKTIME command. The format of the ASKTIME command is

```
EXEC CICS ASKTIME [ABSTIME (data-area)] END-EXEC
```

where

ABSTIME (data area) specifies a COBOL field PIC S9(15) COMPUTATIONAL, where CICS will store the current date in time in milliseconds that have elapsed since hour 0000, 1 January 1900. This field is suitable for input to the FORMATTIME command.

If the ABSTIME option is not used, CICS will only update the fields EIBDATE and EIBTIME. These fields normally contain the date and time when the task first started. If you need these fields updated for more precise time measurement, the ASKTIME command will do nicely.

ASKTIME AND FORMATTIME EXAMPLE

The following commands provide an example of how to retrieve the current date and time in various formats:

```
WORKING-STORAGE SECTION.
01   DATES-PROGRAM-PARAMETERS.
     05   CALENDAR-DATE        PIC X(08).
     05   DAY-COUNT            PIC S9(08) COMP.
     05   DAY-OF-WEEK          PIC S9(08) COMP.
     05   DAY-OF-MONTH         PIC S9(08) COMP.
     05   MONTH-OF-YEAR        PIC S9(08) COMP.
     05   THE-YEAR             PIC S9(08) COMP.
     05   ABSOLUTE-DATE        PIC S9(15) COMP-3.
PROCEDURE DIVISION.

     EXEC CICS ASKTIME ABSTIME (ABSOLUTE-DATE) END-EXEC
     EXEC CICS FORMATTIME
         ABSTIME (ABSOLUTE-DATE)
         DATE (CALENDAR-DATE)
         DATESEP
         DAYCOUNT (DAY-COUNT)
         DAYOFWEEK (DAY-OF-WEEK)
         DAYOFMONTH (DAY-OF-MONTH)
         MONTHOFYEAR (MONTH-OF-YEAR)
         YEAR (THE-YEAR)
         END-EXEC.
```

The Assign Command

The Execute Interface Block contains several variables that are useful during a task. There are many other CICS variables that are not stored in the EIB but can be made available to the program. These variables can prove to be useful in some programming situations. Let's look at a couple of these variables and the command that is used to obtain them. The command is ASSIGN. The format of the command is

```
EXEC CICS ASSIGN
     OPTION (data-area)
     OPTION (data-area) . . .
     END-EXEC
```

where OPTION specifies a keyword naming the CICS area to be obtained. The data-area argument specifies the name of a COBOL working-storage variable where CICS will store the requested value. The size and format of the data area will vary depending on the option used in the command.

We are only going to examine a few of these data areas. This will give you an idea of how to use the command. A complete list of the CICS areas available is provided in Appendix A. When you have time, you might browse through this material to get a better feel for the data areas that are available.

One variable that is sometimes used is the operator identification code. It is possible (although not required) to assign a unique identification code to each terminal operator. This is done during the CICS tailoring process using a sign-on table. The code is copied from the sign-on table to the TCT when the operator "signs on" to CICS. This code can then be used by any application program running on that terminal. To access the operator code, you would use the command

```
EXEC CICS ASSIGN OPID (OPERATOR-CODE) END-EXEC.
```

where the data area OPERATOR-CODE is defined as PIC XXX. After issuing the command, the code would be stored in this field.

One use for the code might be to produce an *audit trail* for programs that update security-sensitive files. The program could include the operator code in an audit record whenever a file has been modified.

Another variable that is sometimes used contains the operator security codes. These codes are also stored in the TCT when an operator signs on to CICS.

The keyword to obtain the operator security codes is OPSECURITY. A data area of PIC XXX is needed to store the transaction security codes. The following statement would retrieve the security codes.

```
05   OPERATOR-KEY     PIC XXX.

EXEC CICS ASSIGN OPSECURITY (OPERATOR-KEY) END-EXEC.
```

There are 24 different standard transaction security codes provided by CICS. These 24 codes are stored in the three-character locations in binary form. Each storage location contains eight bits corresponding to 8 of the 24 codes. All 24 codes can therefore be stored in 3 locations as follows:

```
00000000 00000000 00010010

22222111 11111110 00000000
43210987 65432109 87654321
```

Each bit position can be numbered from 1 to 24 beginning with the *rightmost* position. A bit value of 1 in a position indicates that the operator has been assigned that operator security code. A value of 0 indicates that the operator is not assigned that code. In the illustration above, the operator is assigned security codes of 2 and 5.

In COBOL, it is difficult to work with individual bits within a character position. Since the operator security codes are stored in a bit pattern, it may be necessary to convert the bit pattern to a form more palatable to the COBOL language. One approach is to convert each bit into a single-character position in display form. Each "zero bit" could be stored as a character 0 and each "one bit" converted to character 1. Then, by storing these characters into an array, you could easily determine the security codes for the operator.

In a recent release of CICS, additional operator security keys were provided. Up to 64 security codes are now available to the application program. The ASSIGN command is still used to retrieve the 64 codes. The keyword option for the extended codes is OPERKEYS. It will also require an eight-byte working-storage field to store the 64 codes.

One other area that can be accessed with the ASSIGN command is OPCLASS. The operator class codes are similar to the transaction security codes. At present there are 24 class codes that are stored in a similar fashion to the basic operator security codes. These operator class codes can be used independently or in conjunction with the operator security codes to add another level of security.

When used in the MENU program or another program, all of these operator codes can provide some useful design strategies for application security. Consider using them when you develop your security-sensitive applications.

Displaying Multiple Screens

In most applications, one or more inquiry programs will be used to provide a display of information from a master or transaction file. The sample inquiry program described in the earlier chapters displayed information from the vendor master file. This inquiry program used the BMS SEND MAP command to display a single-screen image. For our sample application, we presumed that this single screen contained all of the information needed by an operator. But what if additional information was needed?

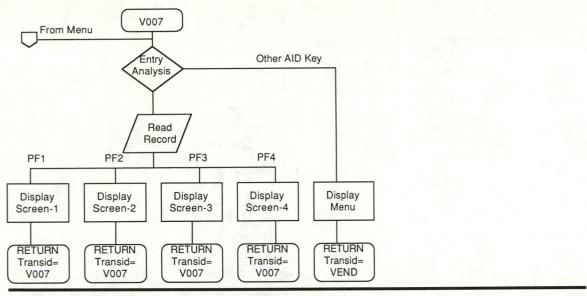

FIGURE 9.5. Presentation Logic to Display Multiple Screens

One alternative is to display more fields on the same screen. To an extent, this may be practical. Sometimes, however, there may be too many fields to "pack" onto a single display screen. A screen can become so cluttered with information that is actually becomes difficult to read. For larger data records it may be physically impossible to display all of the needed information on a single screen. In these cases, another alternative is needed.

That second alternative is to design multiple inquiry screens. For some applications, such as our sample vendor master file, only one additional screen would be necessary to display all of the fields from the record. In other applications, such as a payroll-personnel system, several screens might be required to display a complete record. Each screen could contain a logical section of the record. A good design technique is to display a group of related fields on the same screen.

This will involve defining an additional BMS MAP for each display screen. It will also require additional programming to display the multiple screens. But, how do we design the program(s) to present the multiple screens? One way would be to write a single inquiry program for each display screen. Each screen could then be individually selected from a menu by the operator. This design would be easy to program but could also be counterproductive for the operator. Switching back and forth between the menu screen and each inquiry screen would require multiple keystrokes. There could be a loss of continuity, and time would be wasted while switching to and from the menu.

PROGRAM-CONTROLLED DISPLAYS

Another design strategy is to provide a single menu selection for a transaction program that can display the multiple screens. An example of the logic of such a program is depicted in figure 9.5. This transaction-processing program contains logic to display four individual screens, but only one at a time during a single task. If a program is allowed to display more than one screen during a single task, each new screen will *overlay* the previous screen. The operator would only get a very quick glance at each display. However, the pseudoconversational programming technique allows more than one screen to be displayed before returning to the menu.

The program dipicted in the figure requires an entry analysis routine to determine which screen to display. The logic is fairly simple; the attention identifier value is used to identify which screen is

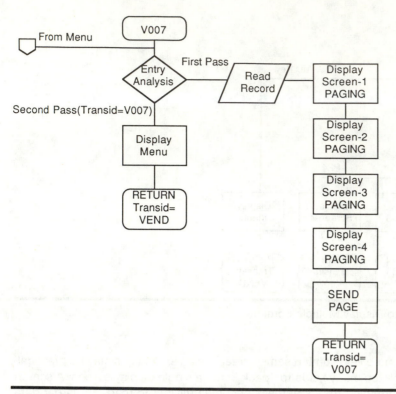

FIGURE 9.6.   Logic to Display Mutliple Screens Using Terminal Paging

to be displayed. The program will only have to check the field EIBAID, and perform a different display routine for each assigned PF key. It will return to the menu only when an unassigned AID key is pressed by the operator. To display a screen, the program will randomly read the target record, then perform a BMS output mapping operation. After the screen is displayed, the program will issue a pseudoconversational RETURN command to allow the operator to view the screen.

BMS-CONTROLLED DISPLAYS

There is another method of designing programs to display multiple screens. This method involves the use of a BMS service known as Terminal Paging. With Terminal Paging, all of the presentation logic can be removed from the transaction-processing program. Screen presentation is controlled completely by a separate BMS Terminal Paging Program. Figure 9.6 depicts the logic of a program providing four separate display screens. Compare this logic with that illustrated in the previous figure. You will notice that the screen-presentation logic has been completely omitted. The remaining entry analysis logic is similar to the single-screen inquiry program described in chapter 7.

Right now you might be thinking that this last example contradicted my earlier statement that only one screen should be displayed in a single task. Well, that rule is still valid, but when using BMS Terminal Paging, you can have multiple mapping operations in the same task. These screens are not transmitted directly to the terminal. Instead, BMS stores the screen images in Temporary Storage. This process is depicted in figure 9.7. In this figure, you can see that four screen images have been stored by BMS. Other control information, such as the total number of screens, will also be stored here by BMS.

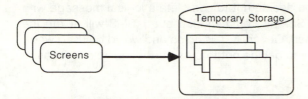

FIGURE 9.7. With BMS Terminal Paging Screens Are Stored in Temporary Storage

You will use two familiar commands in your program in order to use the BMS Terminal Paging facility. These commands are SEND MAP and SEND PAGE. The format of the SEND MAP command with Terminal Paging is the same as described in chapter 6. The new command option to request Terminal Paging is *PAGING*. The PAGING option tells BMS to begin storing screen images as a part of a logical message in Temporary Storage. These screen images will be retrieved later by BMS in response to a series of page retrieval commands entered at the terminal.

Once a logical message has been started, all SEND MAP commands should use the PAGING option until the logical message has been completed. A logical message is completed by using the SEND PAGE command. The format of this command is

```
EXEC SEND PAGE
    [OPERPURGE]
    [RETAIN | [[RELEASE] TRANSID (name)]
    END-EXEC
```

The OPERPURGE option is normally not used. When it is used, the operator will have to enter a message termination command at the terminal to purge the logical message. You might use this option to store one or more screens that will be of later use to the operator. For our sample vendor application, a list of valid product codes could be stored for later use. When the screens are no longer needed, they can be purged by the operator. If OPERPURGE is not specified, the logical message will be purged automatically by BMS after the operator has finished viewing them.

The RETAIN option is rarely used. This option specifies that the program issuing the command should be suspended immediately in order for BMS to begin displaying the screens. These screens will be displayed by entering Terminal Paging commands (described later) at the terminal. While the various screens are being displayed, the task enters a *conversational* status. Later, after the pages have been displayed, the program resumes at the statement following the SEND PAGE command. You should not use this option, since it *does* place the program into conversational mode.

The RELEASE option is rarely used with menu-driven transactions. This option performs the same function as the standard RETURN command. If used, you would not be able to provide transition back to the menu transaction.

The TRANSID option can be used only when the RELEASE option has been specified. Together, these options cause a pseudoconversational RETURN to be performed. The only problem with these BMS command options, is that a commarea cannot be passed. After displaying multiple screens, if you need to pass a commarea, you will still have to use the RETURN TRANSID command. Therefore, the simple form of the SEND PAGE command will normally be used; that is

```
EXEC CICS SEND PAGE END-EXEC.
```

Before moving on to the page retrieval topic, let's look at one more command that you might need when using BMS terminal paging. The command is

```
EXEC CICS PURGE MESSAGE END-EXEC.
```

This command would be used in the event that you decide not to complete a logical message with the SEND PAGE command. When the PURGE MESSAGE command is issued, BMS will delete the portions of the logical message previously constructed. Generally, this command would be used when some fatal error has occurred in the program, and you decide not to present the multiple screens to the operator.

BMS TERMINAL PAGING PROGRAM

As discussed earlier, the SEND MAP command with the PAGING option and the SEND PAGE command are used to store a logical message in CICS Temporary Storage. This logical message can consist of any number of screen images to be viewed by the operator. After the task that stored the logical message is terminated (or has used the RETAIN option), a BMS Terminal Paging Program can be used to display the screens. Depending on the status of the terminal, the Terminal Paging Program may be started automatically by BMS. When it is, the first screen of the logical message is displayed. Thereafter, other screens can be displayed by entering a series of Terminal Paging commands at the terminal. In some cases, the Terminal Paging Program will not be started automatically by BMS. This depends on the mode of the terminal defined during CICS tailoring. If the terminal mode is not set to have the Terminal Paging Program started automatically, the operator will have to request it explicitly. This can be done by keying the CICS supplied transaction code for the program. The transaction code is *CSPG*. The Terminal Paging Program can also be started by keying a Terminal Paging command at the terminal.

TERMINAL PAGING COMMANDS

Once the Terminal Paging Program has been started (automatically or manually), the operator can then enter a series of Terminal Paging commands. These paging commands provide for complete control of the logical messages pertaining to the terminal. Each paging command consists of an installation-defined command-identification code followed by a command operation code. Many installations have used the command-identification code examples from the IBM systems programming manuals. I will therefore use these "defacto" standard codes in my examples.

The paging commands fall into four categories. These commands and their "defacto" standard identification codes are

message retrieval commands (P/..)

message termination commands (T/..)

message copy commands (C/..)

message chaining commands (X/..)

The message retrieval commands (P/..) are used to request the display of a single page. The various operation codes allow the operator to view pages in any sequence. These operation codes are shown below. For example, to display the last page of a message, the operator could enter P/L; to display page 3 of a message the operator would enter P/3; to back up two screens from the current screen, P/−2 could be entered. A page from a previously stored message can also be displayed if the OPERPURGE option was used on the SEND PAGE command. This is done by specifying the message identification for the message.

Command	Function	Examples
P/N	Display next page.	P/N
P/P	Display previous page.	P/P
P/L	Display last page.	P/L
P/n	Display page no. *n*.	P/1
		p/4
		P/2
P/+n	Display *n* pages forward.	P/+3
		P/+2
P/−n	Display *n* pages backward.	P/−1
		P/−3
P/Q	Query (display) the identification codes of all logical messages destined for this terminal. The identification consists of a six-character hexadecimal message number assigned when the message was stored.	P/Q
P/n[,hhhhhh]	Display a specific logical message. If a value is not supplied, the oldest message is returned.	P/1,020406
		P/L,020406
		P/L

The message termination commands are used to erase a logical message. Usually, messages will be purged automatically by BMS. This occurs when the operator stops entering Terminal Paging commands during a session. If a message has been stored with the OPERPURGE option, a message-termination command will be necessary. The basic termination commands are shown below.

Command	Function	Examples
T/A	Purge all messages destined for this terminal.	T/A
T/B	Purge the current logical message only.	T/B

The message-copy command allows the operator to copy the screen being displayed to another terminal. This terminal could be another display terminal or a printer terminal. The format of this command is C/term; where *term* is the terminal identification of the terminal to receive the current display screen.

The message-chaining command is a special page retrieval command that is not normally used with menu-driven transactions. I will therefore not spend much time describing this command. Basically, the message-chaining command allows an operator to enter another CICS transaction code while viewing a logical message. This transaction could display a screen directly with a SEND MAP command. It could also use the SEND MAP command with the PAGING option to create another logical message. In the latter case, the logical message would be *chained* to the current logical message; hence the term *message chaining*. If message chaining has been used, a variation of message retrieval and message-termination commands would be needed to view the messages at different logical levels. These variations were not described above.

This concludes my description of message chaining. If this brief discussion has whetted your appetite for more learning, I suggest that you acquire the appropriate IBM manual for further study. Since this powerful facility is rather advanced, I recommend that you wait until you achieve the *expert rating* as a CICS programmer.

SCREEN DESIGN REQUIREMENTS

Generally, the Terminal Paging facility is only used for inquiry-type programs. There is no specific restriction placed by CICS, but the service is just better suited to display only screens. To use all of the Terminal Paging commands described above, you will probably have to modify the design of your inquiry screens. Most inquiry screens have all fields set to the protected or auto-skip attribute. But

```
├───────────────────────── Mainframe ─────────────────────────┤
 P/N                    VENDOR MASTER INQUIRY

   VENDOR ID    444444
                VENDOR NAME    METROPOLITAN COMMUNITY COLLEGE
                ADDRESS        3200 BROADWAY
                               KANSAS CITY, MO. 64111


                CONTACT NAME   RON GREATHOUSE
                TELEPHONE      816-756-0220

                TAX ID         00000000000
                PAYMENT HOLD   Y
                PRODUCT CODE   E01
```

```
├───────────────────────── Mainframe ─────────────────────────┤
 P/1                    VENDOR MASTER SALES

   VENDOR ID    444444
                VENDOR NAME    METROPOLITAN COMMUNITY COLLEGE

                YTD SALES              .00
                YTD PAYMENTS          0.00
                YTD DISCOUNTS         0.00

                LAST CHECK                    RECORD STATUS

                NUMBER         22             DATE ADDED      87 216
                DATE       88 001             DATE CHANGED    87 229
                AMOUNT     500.00             LAST OPID       ZBL
```

FIGURE 9.8.   Screen Design to Provide Data Entry of Paging Commands

if paging commands are to be entered by the operator, you will need to define an *unprotected* field on the screen. This field needs to be large enough for the operator to enter the longest paging command that you plan to support. For instance, if you want to support the message-copy command (C/ term), you will need to provide an unprotected field at least six-characters long.

The paging command field must also be the *first* unprotected field on the screen. It can be anywhere, even on the last line, as long as it is the first unprotected field. If the paging command field follows another unprotected field, and that field is modified by the operator, or FSET by the program, the paging command will be ignored by CICS.

It is also possible to initialize the unprotected field with a valid Terminal Paging command. Then, if the field attribute is set to FSET, the paging command will be returned to CICS even if the operator doesn't modify it. If this technique is used, the operator only has to press the ENTER key to transmit the paging command. Of course, the operator can still type over a new value before pressing enter.

An example of this screen design technique is depicted in figure 9.8. In this example, two screens for our vendor master application have been defined. The first screen is our standard display screen that we have used throughout the text. The second screen provides for a display of additional information from the vendor master record. Notice how the screen-identification code field has been used to provide a data entry area for the Terminal Paging commands. The sample program described later has also initialized these fields with paging commands. The first screen contains the value "P/N"; the second contains the value "P/1." To switch back and forth between these two screens, the operator only has to press the ENTER key.

SINGLE-KEYSTROKE RETRIEVAL

Before moving on to the sample program, let's look at one more paging facility provided by CICS. This facility, is known as Single-Keystroke Retrieval (SKR). The SKR service allows you to equate the various PA or PF keys to the different paging commands. For example, you could associate the "P/N" command with the PF1 key; the "P/P" to PF2; "P/L" to PF12; and so on.

These key definitions are user-defined; that is, each installation can determine which PA or PF keys are to be associated with the different paging commands. This means that these key definitions can vary from one installation to another. Some installations will not use them at all. A PF or PA key that has been assigned to a paging command can still be used for other purposes. The key definitions are only active during a Terminal Paging session.

The SKR facility provides a way to use multiple inquiry screens without defining a data entry field as discussed earlier. This might be of some benefit if you want to reuse an existing inquiry screen that does not have a provision for a data entry field. You will be limited to the paging commands defined for your installation. In most cases however, this facility will prove to be most useful.

SAMPLE PROGRAM

Now let's look at a sample program to illustrate the process of displaying multiple screens. In this example, you will see a program that will display the two screens depicted in figure 9.8. This program is a slight variation to the single-screen inquiry program described in chapter 7. The first screen is our regular inquiry screen from the earlier chapters. The second screen contains a display of additional fields from the vendor master record. The BMS map for this screen is depicted in figure 9.9. There is nothing unusual about this screen definition, so I won't go into any more detail about the specific fields. Before moving on, you may want to take a moment to compare the screen layout to the map shown in the figure.

The coding for the program is depicted in figure 9.10. As indicated earlier, this program has the same basic design as the single-screen inquiry program. The two-pass pseudoconversational logic is used. In the first-pass logic, the master record is read using the key supplied in the commarea. Then two separate BMS mapping operations are performed. The SEND MAP commands include the PAGING option to have BMS store the logical message in Temporary Storage. The SEND PAGE command is used to complete the logical message. Finally, the first-pass logic issues a pseudoconversational RETURN command, naming the transaction code for the program as the next task. The record key is passed in the commarea.

It is at this point that the operator will be able to view the screens, one at a time. If the terminal is set for automatic Terminal Paging, the first screen will be displayed. If not, the transaction CSPG, or a paging command (such as P/1) will start the Terminal Paging Program. Since the program has initialized the screen-identification code field with paging commands and has set the attribute to FSET, the operator will be able to use the enter key to switch between the two displays. If SKR has been defined, the assigned PF keys could be used to view the screens. At some point the operator will no longer want to view the screens. To terminate the page retrieval session the operator will press some AID key (not assigned to SKR), such as CLEAR. When this is done, the Terminal Paging Program will purge the logical message. It will then have CICS start the pseudoconversational transaction named in the earlier RETURN command.

```
STATMAP   DFHMDI  SIZE=(24,80),LINE=1,COLUMN=1
SCODE     DFHMDF  POS=(01,01),LENGTH=07
          DFHMDF  POS=(01,28),LENGTH=19,INITIAL='VENDOR MASTER SALES'
          DFHMDF  POS=(03,01),LENGTH=09,INITIAL='VENDOR ID'
VENDID    DFHMDF  POS=(03,13),LENGTH=06
          DFHMDF  POS=(04,13),LENGTH=11,INITIAL='VENDOR NAME'
VENNAME   DFHMDF  POS=(04,30),LENGTH=30
          DFHMDF  POS=(06,13),LENGTH=09,INITIAL='YTD SALES'
YTDSAL    DFHMDF  POS=(06,30),LENGTH=12,                                C
                  PICOUT='Z,ZZZ,ZZZ.99'
          DFHMDF  POS=(07,13),LENGTH=12,INITIAL='YTD PAYMENTS'
YTDPAY    DFHMDF  POS=(07,30),LENGTH=12,                                C
                  PICOUT='Z,ZZZ,ZZ9.99'
          DFHMDF  POS=(08,13),LENGTH=13,INITIAL='YTD DISCOUNTS'
YTDDIS    DFHMDF  POS=(08,30),LENGTH=12,                                C
                  PICOUT='Z,ZZZ,ZZ9.99'
          DFHMDF  POS=(10,13),LENGTH=10,INITIAL='LAST CHECK'
          DFHMDF  POS=(10,51),LENGTH=13,INITIAL='RECORD STATUS'
          DFHMDF  POS=(12,13),LENGTH=06,INITIAL='NUMBER'
CKNUM     DFHMDF  POS=(12,24),LENGTH=07,                                C
                  PICOUT='ZZZZZZZ'
          DFHMDF  POS=(12,51),LENGTH=10,INITIAL='DATE ADDED'
DATADD    DFHMDF  POS=(12,67),LENGTH=06,                                C
                  PICOUT='99B999'
          DFHMDF  POS=(13,13),LENGTH=04,INITIAL='DATE'
CKDATE    DFHMDF  POS=(13,25),LENGTH=06,                                C
                  PICOUT='99B999'
          DFHMDF  POS=(13,51),LENGTH=12,INITIAL='DATE CHANGED'
DATCHG    DFHMDF  POS=(13,67),LENGTH=06,                                C
                  PICOUT='99B999'
          DFHMDF  POS=(14,13),LENGTH=06,INITIAL='AMOUNT'
CKAMT     DFHMDF  POS=(14,21),LENGTH=10,                                C
                  PICOUT='ZZZZZZ9.99'                                   C
          DFHMDF  POS=(14,51),LENGTH=09,INITIAL='LAST OPID'
LASTOP    DFHMDF  POS=(14,67),LENGTH=03
SMESAGE   DFHMDF  POS=(21,01),LENGTH=79
```

FIGURE 9.9. BMS Map Definition for Second Inquiry Screen

The program will again be started. This time, the entry analysis routine selects the second-pass logic. The purpose of this logic is to provide transition back to the menu. To do this, it displays the menu screen, and issues a pseudoconversational RETURN naming the menu transid. The multiple-screen inquiry transaction is now complete.

The programming techniques you have just studied will be useful in many applications. By incorporating your own multiscreen presentation logic or using the Terminal Paging facility, you will be able to write programs that display as much information as needed for any application.

Chapter Summary

In this chapter you have learned some commands and techniques that can be used to solve more complex problems. First, you learned how to use the Temporary Storage facility. This CICS feature allows any program to store data to be used at a later time. The data are stored in queues that consist of one or more records of related information. These records can then be read and updated by any other program in the system. Records can be read sequentially or randomly.

The chapter also introduced you to a few miscellaneous commands. The FORMATTIME and ASKTIME command can be used to retrieve date and time parameters. The ASSIGN command can be used to retrieve system information useful to some programs. The operator identification, security codes, and operator class codes can be retrieved with this command. Other data areas provided by the ASSIGN command have been listed in Appendix A.

```
IDENTIFICATION DIVISION.
PROGRAM-ID. VEND007.
AUTHOR.   BOB LOWE.
ENVIRONMENT DIVISION.
DATA DIVISION.
WORKING-STORAGE SECTION.
01  VENDOR-RECORD.
    05  VENDOR-NAME              PIC X(30).
    05  VENDOR-ID               PIC XXXXXX.
    05  VENDOR-ADDR1            PIC X(30).
    05  VENDOR-ADDR2            PIC X(30).
    05  VENDOR-ADDR3            PIC X(30).
    05  VENDOR-ADDR4            PIC X(30).
    05  VENDOR-CONTACT         PIC X(30).
    05  VENDOR-TELE            PIC X(12).
    05  VENDOR-TAXID           PIC X(11).
    05  VENDOR-YTD-SALES       PIC S9(07)V99 COMP-3.
    05  VENDOR-YTD-PAYMENTS    PIC S9(07)V99 COMP-3.
    05  VENDOR-YTD-DISCOUNTS   PIC S9(07)V99 COMP-3.
    05  VENDOR-PAY-HOLD        PIC X.
    05  VENDOR-PRODUCT         PIC XXX.
    05  VENDOR-LAST-CHECK      PIC S9(05)    COMP-3.
    05  VENDOR-LAST-CK-DATE    PIC S9(05)    COMP-3.
    05  VENDOR-LAST-CK-AMT     PIC S9(07)V99 COMP-3.
    05  VENDOR-DATE-ADDED      PIC S9(05)    COMP-3.
    05  VENDOR-DATE-CHANGED    PIC S9(05)    COMP-3.
    05  VENDOR-LAST-OPID       PIC XXX.
    05  VENDOR-UPDCNT          PIC 9.
01  MISC-AREAS.
    05  MSG-LEN                 PIC S9999 COMP.
    05  VENDOR-RECORD-LENGTH    PIC S9999 COMP VALUE +249.
    05  PASS-EIBRCODE-EIBFN.
        10  PASS-EIBRCODE       PIC XXXXXX.
        10  PASS-EIBFN          PIC XX.
        10  FILLER              PIC X(8).
01  ERROR-MESSAGE-LINE.
    05  MESSAGE-NUMBER          PIC X(8).
    05  FILLER                  PIC X.
    05  THE-MESSAGE             PIC X(54).
    05  RC-LABEL                PIC XXXX.
    05  RESPONSE-CODE4-16       PIC X(12).
* * * * * * * * * * * * * * * * * * * * * * * * * * * * * * *
*    CICS/VS Release 1.6- Command Exception test area
* * * * * * * * * * * * * * * * * * * * * * * * * * * * * * *
01  CICS-RETURN-CODE-TEST-AREA.
    05  COMMAND-STATUS-CODE             PIC S9(08) COMP VALUE +0.
        88  NORMAL                          VALUE +0.
        88  DSIDERR                         VALUE +1.
        88  ILLOGIC                         VALUE +2.
        88  MAPFAIL                         VALUE +4.
        88  FC-INVREQ                       VALUE +8.
        88  NOTOPEN                         VALUE +12.
        88  DISABLED                        VALUE +13.
        88  FC-IOERR                        VALUE +128.
        88  NOTFND                          VALUE +129.
        88  NOTAUTH                         VALUE +214.
        88  LENGERR                         VALUE +225.
    05  FILLER REDEFINES COMMAND-STATUS-CODE.
        10  FILLER              PIC XXX.
        10  CONVERT-TO-DECIMAL  PIC X.
* * * * * * * * * * * * * * * * * * * * * * * * * * * * *
*    BMS ATTRIBUTE VALUES INCLUDING HILIGHT AND COLOR
* * * * * * * * * * * * * * * * * * * * * * * * * * * * *
01  STANDARD-BMS-ATTRIBUTES.
    02  UNPROT-NORM             PIC X VALUE SPACE.
    02  UNPROT-BRT              PIC X VALUE 'H'.
    02  UNPROT-DRK              PIC X VALUE '<'.
    02  UNPROT-FSET-NORM        PIC X VALUE 'A'.
    02  UNPROT-FSET-BRT         PIC X VALUE 'I'.
    02  UNPROT-FSET-DRK         PIC X VALUE '('.
    02  UNPROT-NUM-NORM         PIC X VALUE '&'.
    02  UNPROT-NUM-BRT          PIC X VALUE 'Q'.
    02  UNPROT-NUM-DRK          PIC X VALUE '*'.
    02  UNPROT-NUM-FSET-NORM    PIC X VALUE 'J'.
    02  UNPROT-NUM-FSET-BRT     PIC X VALUE 'R'.
    02  UNPROT-NUM-FSET-DRK     PIC X VALUE ')'.
    02  PROT-NORM               PIC X VALUE '-'.
    02  PROT-BRT                PIC X VALUE 'Y'.
    02  PROT-DRK                PIC X VALUE '%'.
```

FIGURE 9.10.   Sample Program to Display Inquiry Screens

```
        02  PROT-FSET-NORM          PIC X VALUE '/'.
        02  PROT-FSET-BRT           PIC X VALUE 'Z'.
        02  PROT-FSET-DRK           PIC X VALUE '_'.
        02  ASKIP-NORM              PIC X VALUE '0'.
        02  ASKIP-BRT               PIC X VALUE '8'.
        02  ASKIP-DRK               PIC X VALUE '@'.
        02  ASKIP-FSET-NORM         PIC X VALUE '1'.
        02  ASKIP-FSET-BRT          PIC X VALUE '9'.
        02  ASKIP-FSET-DRK          PIC X VALUE QUOTE.
        02  HILIGHT-DEFAULT         PIC X VALUE LOW-VALUE.
        02  HILIGHT-BLINK           PIC X VALUE '1'.
        02  HILIGHT-REVERSE         PIC X VALUE '2'.
        02  HILIGHT-UNDERSCORE      PIC X VALUE '4'.
        02  COLOR-DEFAULT           PIC X VALUE LOW-VALUE.
        02  COLOR-BLUE              PIC X VALUE '1'.
        02  COLOR-RED               PIC X VALUE '2'.
        02  COLOR-PINK              PIC X VALUE '3'.
        02  COLOR-GREEN             PIC X VALUE '4'.
        02  COLOR-TURKUOISE         PIC X VALUE '5'.
        02  COLOR-YELLOW            PIC X VALUE '6'.
        02  COLOR-WHITE             PIC X VALUE '7'.
    COPY VENDSET.
    LINKAGE SECTION.
    01  DFHCOMMAREA.
        05  KEY-INPUT               PIC XXXXXX.
    PROCEDURE DIVISION.
    *PROCEDURE CODE
    000-MAINLINE-ROUTINE.
        IF EIBTRNID EQUAL 'V007'
            MOVE LOW-VALUES TO MENUMAPO
            MOVE KEY-INPUT TO VENDIDO IN MENUMAPO
            PERFORM 925-TRANSMIT-MENU-SCREEN.
        IF KEY-INPUT NOT NUMERIC
            MOVE 'VENDOR NUMBER NOT NUMERIC' TO MMESAGEO
            MOVE KEY-INPUT TO VENDIDO IN MENUMAPO
            GO TO 925-TRANSMIT-MENU-SCREEN.
        EXEC CICS READ
            DATASET ('VENFILE')
            INTO    (VENDOR-RECORD)
            RIDFLD  (KEY-INPUT)
            LENGTH  (VENDOR-RECORD-LENGTH)
            NOHANDLE
            END-EXEC.
        IF EIBRCODE NOT EQUAL LOW-VALUES
            PERFORM 940-FILE-ERROR
            MOVE ERROR-MESSAGE-LINE TO MMESAGEO IN MENUMAPO
            GO TO 925-TRANSMIT-MENU-SCREEN.
    * ******************************************************
    *     PREPARE AND SEND INQUIRY SCREEN
    * ******************************************************
        MOVE LOW-VALUES             TO          DISPMAPO.
        MOVE 'P/N  '                TO  SCODEO   IN DISPMAPO.
        MOVE UNPROT-FSET-NORM       TO  SCODEA   IN DISPMAPI.
        MOVE PROT-NORM              TO  VENNAMEA IN DISPMAPI
                                        ADDR1A   IN DISPMAPI
                                        ADDR2A   IN DISPMAPI
                                        ADDR3A   IN DISPMAPI
                                        ADDR4A   IN DISPMAPI
                                        CONTACA  IN DISPMAPI
                                        TELEA    IN DISPMAPI
                                        TAXIDA   IN DISPMAPI
                                        PAHOLDA  IN DISPMAPI.
        MOVE VENDOR-NAME            TO  VENNAMEO IN DISPMAPO.
        MOVE VENDOR-ID              TO  VENDIDO  IN DISPMAPO.
        MOVE VENDOR-ADDR1           TO  ADDR1O   IN DISPMAPO.
        MOVE VENDOR-ADDR2           TO  ADDR2O   IN DISPMAPO.
        MOVE VENDOR-ADDR3           TO  ADDR3O   IN DISPMAPO.
        MOVE VENDOR-ADDR4           TO  ADDR4O   IN DISPMAPO.
        MOVE VENDOR-CONTACT         TO  CONTACO  IN DISPMAPO.
        MOVE VENDOR-TELE            TO  TELEO    IN DISPMAPO.
        MOVE VENDOR-TAXID           TO  TAXIDO   IN DISPMAPO.
        MOVE VENDOR-PAY-HOLD        TO  PAHOLDO  IN DISPMAPO.
        MOVE VENDOR-PRODUCT         TO  PRODUCTO IN DISPMAPO.
        EXEC CICS SEND MAP ('DISPMAP')
                MAPSET ('VENDSET')
                PAGING
                ERASE
                FREEKB
                END-EXEC.
```

FIGURE 9.10. Continued

```
          MOVE LOW-VALUES              TO          STATMAPO.
          MOVE 'P/1    '               TO  SCODEO   IN STATMAPO.
          MOVE UNPROT-FSET-NORM        TO  SCODEA   IN STATMAPI.
          MOVE VENDOR-YTD-SALES        TO  YTDSALO  IN STATMAPO.
          MOVE VENDOR-YTD-PAYMENTS     TO  YTDPAYO  IN STATMAPO.
          MOVE VENDOR-YTD-DISCOUNTS TO     YTDDISO  IN STATMAPO.
          EXEC CICS SEND MAP ('STATMAP')
                 MAPSET ('VENDSET')
                 PAGING
                 ERASE
                 FREEKB
                 END-EXEC.
          EXEC CICS SEND PAGE END-EXEC.
          EXEC CICS RETURN TRANSID ('V007')
                 COMMAREA (KEY-INPUT)  LENGTH (6)
                 END-EXEC.
925-TRANSMIT-MENU-SCREEN.
      MOVE EIBTRMID   TO TERMO IN MENUMAPO.
      MOVE CURRENT-DATE TO DATEO IN MENUMAPO.
      MOVE EIBTIME TO TIMEO IN MENUMAPO.
      TRANSFORM TIMEO IN MENUMAPO FROM ',' TO ':'.
      MOVE 'VEN0000' TO SCODEO IN MENUMAPO.
      EXEC CICS SEND MAP ('MENUMAP')
                 MAPSET ('VENDSET')
                 ERASE
                 FREEKB
                 END-EXEC.
      EXEC CICS  RETURN  TRANSID ('VEND')
             COMMAREA (EIBAID) LENGTH (1)
             END-EXEC.
* * * * * * * * * * * * * * * * * * * * * * * * * * * * * * *
* * * * * * * * * * * * * * * * * * * * * * * * * * * *
*     ERROR PROCESSING ROUTINES
* * * * * * * * * * * * * * * * * * * * * * * * * * * *
940-FILE-ERROR.
      MOVE SPACES TO ERROR-MESSAGE-LINE.
      MOVE EIBRCODE TO CONVERT-TO-DECIMAL.
      IF NOTFND
         MOVE 'RECORD NOT ON FILE' TO THE-MESSAGE
         MOVE KEY-INPUT TO VENDIDO IN MENUMAPO
         MOVE 'VEND0950' TO MESSAGE-NUMBER
      ELSE IF NOTOPEN
              MOVE 'VENDOR FILE NOT OPEN' TO THE-MESSAGE
              MOVE 'VEND0950' TO MESSAGE-NUMBER
           ELSE PERFORM 980-ERROR.
  980-ERROR.


* *****************************************************
* LINK TO VEND010 TO CONVERT HEX RESPONSE CODE TO
* DISPLAY FORM.
* *****************************************************
      MOVE EIBRCODE TO PASS-EIBRCODE.
      MOVE EIBFN    TO PASS-EIBFN.
      EXEC CICS LINK
            PROGRAM ('VEND010')
            COMMAREA (PASS-EIBRCODE-EIBFN)
            LENGTH (16)
            END-EXEC.
      MOVE PASS-EIBRCODE-EIBFN TO RESPONSE-CODE4-16.
      MOVE ' RC=' TO RC-LABEL.
      MOVE 'UNDETERMINED FILF ERROR HAS OCCURRED ' TO THE-MESSAGE
      MOVE 'VEND0980'  TO MESSAGE-NUMBER
      GOBACK.
```

FIGURE 9.10. Continued

Finally, the chapter described methods whereby a program can display multiple screens. You can write your own procedures to display multiple screens. BMS also provides a more flexible method to do this. With BMS, the operator can request a screen in any sequence and even copy a screen to another terminal.

Discussion Questions

1. Which program manages the Temporary Storage Facility?
2. Where are Temporary Storage records stored?
3. What are the two ways in which a program can read records in a Temporary Storage queue?
4. What is a Temporary Storage ITEM?
5. Can you delete individual records in a Temporary Storage queue?
6. When new records are written to a queue, where are they positioned?
7. Which CICS command is used to update a record in a queue?
8. What value must be supplied to enable the FORMATTIME command to provide the date and time?
9. Which command is used to obtain the system date and time for use by the FORMATTIME command?
10. How could a program use the DAYCOUNT value provided by the FORMATTIME command?
11. How can a program obtain the operator identification of the operator signed on to a terminal?
12. Which BMS SEND MAP command option is used to request the Terminal Paging facility?
13. Where does the BMS Terminal Paging facility store the screens to be displayed by an operator?
14. If multiple screens are to be displayed using Terminal Paging, when does the program issue the SEND PAGE command?
15. Which Terminal Paging command is used by an operator to display the last screen?
16. When would a program issue the PURGE MESSAGE command?
17. How does the screen design affect the ability to enter a Terminal Paging command?
18. What is Single Keystroke Retrieval?

Review Exercises

1. Write a command to delete a Temporary Storage queue named "ABCQUEUE."
2. Code the statements necessary to write the record below to a Temporary Storage queue. The queue name should be composed of the terminal identification concatenated (plus) the transaction code where the program is executing.

   ```
   01   SAVE-VENDOR-RECORD PIC X(249).
   ```

3. Code the statements necessary to read the first record from a Temporary Storage queue. The queue name should be composed as OPEIDxxx, where xxx is the identification of the operator signed on at the terminal. Read the record into the area below.

   ```
   01   OPERATOR-SIGNON-RECORD.
        05   OPE-TERMINAL PIC XXXX.
        05   OPE-TIME      PIC S9(7) COMPUTATIONAL.
   ```

4. Write a routine to retrieve the 24 operator security codes and convert each bit to character format with a value of zero or one. Use an array to store the character values.

Problems

LAB 1

PERSONNEL INQUIRY PROGRAM—BMS PAGING
(PROGRAM XY00001, TRANSID XY01)

Design, code, and test a two-pass pseudoconversational inquiry program. This program will display the personal information screen, and company information screen. The program will perform the following functions:

INITIAL ENTRY LOGIC (FIRST-PASS) TRANSID–XY00

☐ Access the SSN passed from the menu program in the commarea.

☐ Read the personnel master file using the passed SSN.

☐ Use BMS Terminal Paging to store the following screens in Temporary Storage.

the personal information screen defined in Lab 2 of chapter 5 of the text

the company information screen defined in Lab 3 of chapter 5 of the text

☐ Set the attribute of all fields to ASKIP NORMAL with the exception of the screen-identification code.

☐ Set the screen-identification code field of each screen to the FSET attribute and initialize these fields with the Terminal Paging commands as shown in the sample screens.

☐ Transmit the logical message.

☐ Issue a pseudoconversational RETURN command naming the transid of this program (xy01). Pass the SSN in the commarea.

☐ Error conditions should be handled. Whenever an error condition is detected, display the menu screen with an appropriate message. Issue a pseudoconversational RETURN, naming the menu transid (xy00). Pass a suitable commarea so that the second-pass logic of the menu program will be used when that program is next started. Error conditions that should be anticipated include NOTFND, NOTOPEN, and any other file errors that you wish to check.

```
                    1         2         3         4         5         6
      1234567890123456789012345678901234567890123456789012345678901234 5678
01^P/N                ^PERSONAL INFORMATION^INQUIRY
02
03
04          ^SSN:^123456789
05
06      ^NAME..^DOE, JOHN A                            ^
07   ^ADDRESS..^123 ANYWHERE STREET                    ^
08      ^CITY..^KANSAS CITY                  ^
09     ^STATE..^MO^641110000^
10
11     ^PHONE..^5551212^
12       ^SEX..^M^
13   ^ETHNIC..^1^
14       ^DOB..^083147^
15
16
17
18
19
20
21^MESSAGE:^PRESS CLEAR TO RETURN TO THE MENU
22
23
24
```

```
                    1         2         3         4         5         6
          1234567890123456789012345678901234567890123456789012345678901 2
01^P/P              ^COMPANY INFORMATION^INQUIRY
02
03^SSN:^123456789
04^NAME:^DOE, JOHN A
05
06
07   ^EMPLOYEE TYPE..^01^
08       ^LOCATION..^04^
09     ^DEPARTMENT..^2180^
10
11      ^JOB TITLE..^21805^
12    ^POSITION NO..^00001^
13^EMPLOYMENT DATE..^060686^
14
15   ^ANNUAL SALARY..^  25,000.00^
16
17
18
19
20
21^MESSAGE:^PRESS CLEAR TO RETURN TO THE MENU
22
23
24
```

RETURNING LOGIC (SECOND-PASS) TRANSID=XY01

☐ Display the personnel menu screen including the SSN from the commarea.
☐ Issue a pseudoconversational RETURN, naming the menu Transid (xy00). Pass a suitable commarea so that the second-pass logic of the menu program will be used when that program is next started.

10

File Browsing and Page Building

After studying the advanced topics in this chapter you will

1. Learn that VSAM files can be accessed using one or more alternate key fields.
2. Follow the steps necessary to use a VSAM alternate key field.
3. Discover that the same commands used to access a file by primary key are used to access a VSAM file by alternate key.
4. Learn that CICS provides the capability to access files sequentially.
5. See how file browsing can start at any point in a file using the STARTBR command.
6. Understand the difference between a full-key browse and a generic mode browse.
7. Observe how the RESETBR command can be used to change the browse position and status of a browse operation.
8. Learn how to perform skip sequential operations to process different sections of a file.
9. Understand why file browsing operations should be limited to as few records as possible.
10. Learn that BMS is capable of building a single display screen using multiple maps.
11. See how BMS page building can be used with browse programs to display information from multiple records.
12. Observe how to design page overflow routines for programs that use page building.

This chapter contains an introduction to the more advanced file handling and BMS mapping functions provided by CICS.

In the first topic you will learn how to access VSAM files using an alternate key field. There are several ways to benefit from accessing a file using different record keys. Files are commonly accessed by an alternate key using the CICS browse commands.

In the second topic, you will learn how to use the CICS browse commands to access a file sequentially. Any part of a file can be processed sequentially by a CICS program. This processing can be performed to display multiple records or to perform calculations on groups of records. An understanding of the browsing process is an integral part of becoming an experienced CICS programmer.

In the final topic you will learn how to use multiple BMS maps to build a display screen. This process, known as *page building*, is also used many times with file-browsing programs. The ability to browse a file and display multiple records provides some good program design strategies.

VSAM Alternate Keys

In this chapter, you will learn how to use the file-browsing commands to access records in a file sequentially. These browsing operations are commonly performed on files that have been defined with alternate keys. Let's briefly examine the VSAM alternate index facility. It is this facility that allows access to a file using an alternate key. Then we will move ahead to learn how to access records in a file sequentially.

With many applications it is necessary to access a file with more than one key. When using VSAM key-sequenced data sets (KSDS files), it is possible to construct alternate indexes to permit access to the file using secondary keys. Programs may then access the original records in a sequence that differs from the primary key. Any number of alternate indexes may be defined for a single KSDS file. One index, for example, could be defined to give access by a name field. By using the name index, the program would be able to retrieve records in name sequence. Another index could be defined using a department code field. Access to records would then be in department value sequence. This unique feature of VSAM can provide many benefits and design strategies if used properly. Let's look at the mechanics of using VSAM alternate indexes.

First, a primary data set, known as the *base cluster,* must be defined. This file will contain the actual data records. Each record in the primary data set contains a unique record key which is used as the record identification. Random access to records in the primary data set is performed using the record key. For our vendor file, the record key is the vendor number. Please refer to figure 10.1 as you study this material.

After the base cluster is defined, an alternate index can be defined. An alternate index definition is made by a process similar to defining the base cluster. A single data area (one or more fields) from the original record layout is used as the alternate key field. For the current release of VSAM, this key field must occupy contiguous positions in the record. This limitation may change in the future. For our sample vendor master file, we could use the VENDOR-NAME field as an alternate key field.

Unlike the base data set, an alternate key field can be *nonunique;* that is, there may be more than one record in the file with the *same value.* For instance, in our sample vendor master file, an identical vendor name could appear one or more times as shown in the figure. When the alternate index file is loaded, there will be a single index record for each alternate index value from the primary data set. This index record contains a slot for each primary record key containing this alternate index value. In figure 10.1, you can see how the alternate index record for "UNIVERSITY OF MISSOURI" contains 4 slots. Each of these slots contains the primary record key from the base cluster having that vendor name. When accessing a record through the alternate index, VSAM first retrieves the index record. VSAM will then retrieve the data records using the primary keys stored in the slots of that index record. This process is performed automatically by VSAM when the program requests access to records using an alternate index. Even with all this overhead, it is still a fairly efficient process.

It is also possible to define an alternate index using a *unique* value field. A payroll master file, for example, may have a unique position number field as well as a social security number field. One of these fields would be assigned to the base data set; the other could be used as an alternate key. In this case, the index record will contain a single search key and one slot containing the original record key field. Most of the time you won't be so fortunate as to have two unique key eligible fields in the same record. It is still possible, however, to define a unique alternate index.

This can be done by simply defining the primary key field immediately behind the alternate index field. Our vendor master file has this design as shown below. In this example, it would be possible to define a unique alternate index over the name field. It would be done by telling VSAM to create the index beginning at the name field for 36 bytes.

```
01   VENDOR-RECORD.
     05   VENDOR-NAME PIC X(30).
     05   VENDOR-ID   PIC X(6).
```

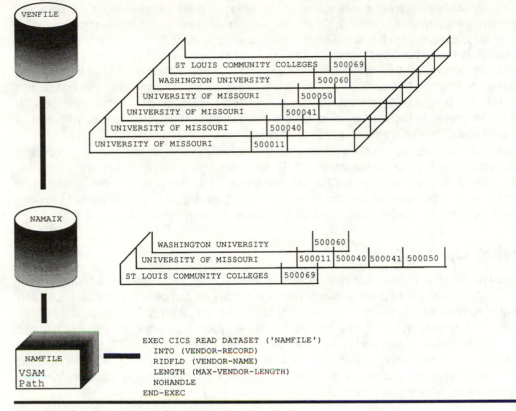

FIGURE 10.1. Access to File Using Alternate Index

If for some reason you need to define multiple unique alternate indexes, you could define a second field the size of the primary key and copy the primary key to this field each time a record is added to the base file. For large files, this could consume a significant amount of disk storage. You might really have a difficult time justifying the cost of using this technique. At least, it's something to consider.

After the alternate index is defined, a VSAM utility is run to build the index. This utility will read the base cluster. Do some sorting and load the index data set. If you define the index as upgradable, VSAM will automatically update the index file as you update the primary data set. The build-index run will only be needed again when the primary data set is reloaded.

The final step is to define a VSAM PATH. This process is again accomplished by using a VSAM utility. It is similar to defining the base cluster and alternate index. In most cases, these functions are performed by the Systems Support staff. The VSAM PATH definition contains information that relates the alternate index to the cluster. Your programs access the alternate index and base file using the data set name provided for the PATH. This is also shown in figure 10.1.

It isn't really important that you understand all of the mechanics just described. You don't have to know how to perform these steps to use an alternate index. You don't even have to know where all of this information is stored. With CICS, you only have to know two things: The data set name and the record layout.

If you know the record layout for the primary data set, you know the layout for every index. It's the same. To access a record, you must provide a different name in the DATASET option of the file commands. It's not important that this data set name is the PATH name. To you, it's just a data set name. To access a record using an alternate index, you use the same file commands as you do when accessing a primary data set. Of course, the RIDFLD argument must contain a value appropriate for the alternate key field. Everything else is the same—with one exception!

That exception is the exceptional condition DUPKEY. It can occur when accessing a file using an alternate index defined with the NONUNIQUE attribute. The DUPKEY condition indicates that there is more than one record having this same key value. When using the READ command, the first record only is presented to the program for processing. To process additional records you must perform file browsing. This is discussed in the next section. Before moving on to the browse topic, we need to discuss one more consideration when using VSAM alternate keys.

That consideration deals with update operations. There is only one guideline. Always update, add, and delete records using the primary data set. To say it another way, never update a data set by using an alternate index data set name. Chances are that your systems people have defined all "index" data set names with read-only access. If they haven't, they probably should have. Updating through an alternate path can lead to integrity exposures and recovery problems with CICS.

File-Browsing Operations

In chapter 4 you learned the various commands to randomly access a file. These random access commands are used in a variety of programs including the inquiry and update programs. CICS also provides a set of commands that provide for *sequential* access of files. With CICS, sequential access is called *file browsing.* Browsing can be performed for all file types supported by the File Control Program. These include ISAM, BDAM, and VSAM. For VSAM, all file types—KSDS, ESDS, and RRDS—can be browsed. You will notice that sequential files were not listed. Except for the VSAM ESDS file type, sequential files are not processed by the File Control Program. Browsing is therefore defined as sequential processing of random access files.

BROWSE KEYS

Browsing can occur by record key or record location. The browse type is specified when browsing is started with the STARTBR command. For DAM and VSAM ESDS files, each browse request (READ-NEXT command) obtains the next record as it is physically stored in the data set. For VSAM RRDS files, records are presented in order by relative record number.

Generally, browsing works best when accessing a file by record key. This is in fact the most commonly used browse method. For this reason, it is the only method described in detail in this text. The record key browse is valid for ISAM and VSAM KSDS files. For each browse request, the program is presented with the next record in ascending key sequence. For VSAM, backwards browsing is possible. In this case, records are presented to the program in descending key sequence. You can even browse a VSAM KSDS file using an alternate record key. In this case, records are presented to the program in order by the alternate key.

BROWSE INITIATION

A browse is initiated by using the start-browse (STARTBR) command. The primary purpose of browse initiation is to acquire system resources and establish a browse position within the file. System resources include the file input-output areas and, for VSAM, a placeholder called a *VSAM string* is acquired. This VSAM string is released when the browse is ended or when the task is terminated. If a VSAM string is not available, the task is suspended until one is released by another task.

The browse position is determined by the record key and other options in the start-browse command. Browsing can start anywhere in the file. To start a browse at the first record in the file, a record key of low-values would be specified. For VSAM files, a record key of high-values will start a backward browse at the last record. There is another way to start a browse at the beginning of the file. You can do this by specifying options of GENERIC and KEYLENGTH (0) in the STARTBR command.

The use of the GENERIC and KEYLENGTH options also determines the *mode* of the browse operation. There are two browse modes: *full-key* and *generic key.* There are also two browse types: EQUAL and GTEQ. The browse mode and browse type will determine how some browsing operations are performed and will prohibit certain functions.

With the full-key EQUAL browse, a complete record key is supplied in the start-browse command. CICS will use this key value in attempting to establish a browse position within the file. When using this mode and type, the exact record must exist in the file. If it does not, the NOTFND exception will be raised, and the start-browse command will fail.

The full-key GTEQ browse also requires a complete record key. With this browse type, CICS will first attempt to find a record matching the supplied record key. If that record is not in the file, CICS will establish positioning at the record with the next greater key. The NOTFND condition will *not* arise unless the supplied key is greater than the highest record in the file.

A generic key browse is specified by using the GENERIC and KEYLENGTH options in the start-browse command. With this browse mode, only a partial key is required to establish a browse position within the file. More specifically, only the *leftmost* characters of the record key are used. The actual number of characters to be used to establish positioning is determined by the value specified in the KEYLENGTH option of the start-browse command. This value can range from one (1) to one less than the full-key length. For instance, if the full-key length is six (6), the generic key length can range from one to five.

A generic EQUAL browse can be requested in the start-browse command. If an EQUAL type browse is requested, CICS will attempt to establish positioning using the leftmost characters of the record key. The KEYLENGTH argument will determine the number of leftmost characters to be used. If a record with the same starting characters cannot be found, the NOTFND exception will be raised, and the start-browse command will fail.

If a generic GTEQ browse is requested, the generic key will be used to locate a record. If a record having the same generic value is not found, CICS will attempt to locate a record with a greater key value than the requested record. If no such record exists, the NOTFND condition will be raised, and the browse command will fail.

For some applications, a partial key browse will have no practical use. This is generally true whenever the leftmost characters of the key have no special meaning. Our sample vendor master key, for instance, has no special significance. There would probably not be a reason to perform a generic browse on this key.

For other applications, the leftmost positions of a record key will have some special meaning and would benefit from a generic mode browse. For instance, a record key in a course master file for a college might be constructed as L-CCCCC-SS, where the key is composed of the *L*ocation, *C*ourse number, and *S*ection number. A program needing to start a browse operation at the beginning of a particular location could do so by moving the location value to the record key field. A keylength of one (1) would be specified to indicate that only the first position of the key should be used to establish browse positioning.

A generic mode browse is often used when browsing a file by an alternate key. Let's say, for example, that an alternate key has been defined for a name field. With this design, an operator could request a browse with a single character or a few starting characters. For example, find the first name in the file beginning with the letter *S;* or find the first name beginning with the characters *SMITH.*

BROWSE RETRIEVAL

After a browse operation is started, the program can retrieve one or more records from the file sequentially. This is accomplished with the READNEXT command. A record does not actually become available until the READNEXT command is used. Each time the command is used, a new record towards the end of the file is presented to the program.

With VSAM files, the program can also use the READPREV command to perform backwards retrieval. Each time this command is used, the next record towards the beginning of the file is presented to the program. A program can also switch between the READNEXT and READPREV commands. If this is done, the switching will cause CICS to return the same record just processed. The next READNEXT or READPREV command will read the next record towards the end or beginning of the file.

BROWSE TERMINATION

Browsing can continue until the last (or first) record in the file has been read. The next sequential request will raise the ENDFILE condition. When ENDFILE occurs, the browsing operation is terminated. To perform further browsing, the program must issue another start-browse command.

Except for the ENDFILE condition, there is no physical limit to the number of records that can be processed during a browsing operation. It is therefore possible for a program to browse through an entire file. Generally, though, it is not feasible to do that. Can you imagine what would happen to response time if two or three transactions were to browse completely through a 200 thousand-record master file?

Usually, there will be some logical point where a browse can end. A browse starting at a particular group of records might be ended after the last record in that group has been processed. A browse to display a series of records could be ended after a screen has been filled. The program could even set a counter to limit processing to some maximum number of records. Any of these techniques or others can be used to produce a logical end of file during browse operations.

The ENDBR command is used to terminate a browse operation at a logical point in the file. It is important to limit a browse operation to the fewest number of records possible. This is because of the resources held during the browse. The most critical of these resources is perhaps the VSAM strings. There are generally only a few strings allocated to each file. A lengthy browse through a file will tie up a string for excessive periods. Other tasks needing access to this file may be suspended for lack of VSAM strings.

RESETTING A BROWSE

Sometimes a program will need to change certain parameters of a browse operation after one or more records have been retrieved. The RESETBR command is used to do this. There are two reasons for a program to reset a browse operation.

One purpose of the reset command is to change the browse mode and/or the browse type. As mentioned earlier, some functions are not available or will have a different effect depending on the current mode or type of browse. A READPREV command, for instance, cannot be used in a generic mode browse. A program might need to reset to a full-key browse prior to issuing the READPREV command.

Another reason to use the reset command is to change to a new record position within the file. Some programs may be designed to process multiple logical sections of a file. Such a program could start a browse at the first logical section and retrieve those records. It could then issue a reset-browse command to reposition to the next (or previous) logical section for further processing. Then, after all sections have been processed, it would issue the ENDBR command.

SKIP SEQUENTIAL PROCESSING

When using VSAM files, there is another alternative to the reset-browse command. This alternative is known as skip sequential processing. With this facility, the program can simply change the record key value, then issue the READNEXT command to reposition to a higher record key. The new record is also retrieved during the process. Skip sequential processing eliminates the need to use the reset-browse command. There are some limitations to this feature.

First, only VSAM is supported. If you are processing an ISAM file, you must still use the RE-SETBR command to perform the repositioning.

Next, the record key must be greater than the record just retrieved by the program. The logical section must be somewhere ahead of the current position. If it isn't, you will still have to use the RESETBR command.

The browse mode also affects how CICS interprets your skip sequential request. If you are performing a generic browse, CICS will perform a skip sequential operation only if the READNEXT command specifies the KEYLENGTH option. The keylength argument *value* may differ from the original STARTBR or last RESETBR command.

Finally, the browse type can affect skip sequential processing. If you are performing an EQUAL browse and attempt to skip to a record that is not in the file, the NOTFND condition will occur. For this reason, you may need to specify a GTEQ browse type if you plan to perform skip sequential processing.

MULTIPLE BROWSING

There is one final browsing feature to discuss before moving on to the command formats. This feature is multiple browsing. Most of the other browsing options have similar counterparts in the COBOL batch world. This is one area where CICS provides a unique function. With multiple browsing you have the capability to establish multiple concurrent browse positions within a single file. The only limit to the number of concurrent positions is the CICS resources required to perform the function. For VSAM files, that resource is probably going to be the number of strings allocated for the file. Each position will require a placeholder. For example if only four (4) strings are allocated, that is the maximum number of concurrent positions that can be established. Needless to say, these operations should be kept to a very minimum. Don't use multiple browsing if skip sequential processing or a reset-browse command will do the job.

Actually, there won't be many occasions where you will need to use multiple browsing. The only example that I can conjure up is a program that needs to merge records from multiple logical sections of a file to produce a display. There may be other reasons for you to use this facility. Just be careful not to abuse it.

STARTBR COMMAND

Now that you have seen the browsing procedures and services provided CICS, let's look at the various commands and options needed to use this powerful facility. We will begin with the STARTBR command. The purpose of this command is to establish the starting position, mode, and type for the browse operation. If multiple browsing is needed, the command also provides a browse request identifier for this browse.

The format of the STARTBR command is

```
EXEC CICS STARTBR
      DATASET (name)
      RIDFLD (data-area)
      [KEYLENGTH (data-value) [GENERIC]]
      [GTEQ | EQUAL]
      [REQID (data-value)]
      [RBA | RRN]
      END-EXEC
```

The DATASET option is the same as specified for the random access commands. It contains the name of the file. Either a literal or a COBOL data name may be specified. If a COBOL name is specified, the field must be eight characters in length.

The RIDFLD option specifies the data area that contains the record identification. For VSAM KSDS files, this area contains the record key. This same data area must also be specified in each browsing command related to this start-browse command. The RIDFLD data area must be large enough to hold the full record key even if a generic browse is being started. This is because the READNEXT and READPREV commands update the field with the key of the retrieved record.

To begin a full-key browse at the start of the file, move low-values to the RIDFLD argument. Move high-values to this argument to start a backwards browse at the end of the file.

The GENERIC option is used to indicate that a "partial key" browse is being started. When this option is used, only the leftmost characters of the record key are used to satisfy the search for a record. The number of leftmost characters to be used is specified in the KEYLENGTH option.

A generic mode browse can be started at the beginning of the file by specifying KEYLENGTH (0) with the GENERIC option.

The KEYLENGTH option is used to specify the number of characters in the record key to be used to find a record. The data-value argument is a numeric literal or a COBOL data area defined as S9999 COMPUTATIONAL. The KEYLENGTH and GENERIC options are usually used together. If GENERIC is specified, the KEYLENGTH argument contains a value indicating the number of *leftmost* characters in the RIDFLD data area that are to be used to search for a record. For instance, if a length of two is specified, only the first two characters of the record key will be used to find a record.

The EQUAL option indicates that CICS is to search only for a record matching the record key specified in the RIDFLD option. If a generic browse is being requested, a record must exist that contains the same starting characters in the RIDFLD. In this case the KEYLENGTH argument determines the number of starting characters to examine. If a full-key browse (no GENERIC option) is being requested, the actual record must exist in the file. If the generic or full-key record is not in the file, CICS will raise the NOTFND exception, and the start-browse command will be unsuccessful.

The GTEQ option indicates that CICS is to search for a record matching the record key specified in the RIDFLD option. If that search is unsuccessful, the first record having a greater key will satisfy the search. Like the EQUAL option, this option is valid for both full-key and generic key operations. This option will usually result in a successful start-browse operation. The browse will be unsuccessful only if the record key is greater than the last record in the file. In this case the NOTFND exception will be raised, and the browse will not be started.

The REQID option is used when multiple browsing for the same file is being performed. The data-value argument can be a numeric literal or a COBOL data name defined as S9999 COMPUTATIONAL. For each multiple browse to the same file, a unique request identifier must be specified. The request identifier is simply a value, such as zero, one, two, and so on. For instance, if two concurrent browse operations are to be started, the first STARTBR command could specify a REQID of zero. The second STARTBR command would specify a value of one. If not specified, CICS assigns a default REQID value of zero.

With multiple browsing, each of the related browsing commands would also need to specify the REQID option. This request identifier in effect provides a relationship between the browsing commands and the start-browse command.

The RBA option is used with VSAM files to indicate that the record key field is a relative byte address. This option is valid when browsing KSDS and ESDS files. The RRN option is used with VSAM relative record data sets only. If either of these two options is not specified, CICS will access the file by record key.

Here is an example of a start-browse command for our sample vendor master file. In this example, the record key is stored in the field "ENTRY-KEY." A full key browse is being requested. If the requested record does not exist, the browse is to be started at the next greater key in the file.

```
05  ENTRY-KEY PIC XXXXXX.

EXEC CICS STARTBR
     DATASET ('VENFILE')
     RIDFLD (ENTRY-KEY)
     GTEQ
     NOHANDLE
     RESP (COMMAND-STATUS-CODE)
     END-EXEC
```

Here is an example of a generic start-browse command using the vendor name path shown earlier in the chapter. In this example, part of a name is moved to the vendor name field. If the requested record does not exist, the browse is to be started at the next greater alternative key in the file.

```
MOVE 'UNIVER' TO VENDOR-NAME.
EXEC CICS STARTBR
     DATASET ('VENNAME')
     RIDFLD (VENDOR-NAME)
     GENERIC KEYLENGTH (6)
     GTEQ
     NOHANDLE
     RESP (COMMAND-STATUS-CODE)
     END-EXEC
```

THE ENDBR COMMAND

This command is used to end a browse operation. If an ENDBR command is not issued, CICS will perform the equivalent of this command at task termination. One use of this command deals with update operations during browsing. Sometimes, after a browse operation has been started, a program will need to update a record from the same data set. If an update is needed, you should issue an ENDBR command prior to issuing a READ UPDATE command.

The format of the ENDBR command is

```
EXEC CICS ENDBR
     DATASET (name)
     [REQID (data-value)]
     END-EXEC
```

The DATASET option specifies the file for which browsing is to be terminated.

The REQID option is used only if the program is using multiple browsing. It would also be used if a browsing operation was started with a REQID option specifying a nonzero argument value. If used, the REQID value must be the same as specified in an earlier STARTBR command.

To end a simple browse operation for our sample vendor master file, you would code,

```
EXEC CICS ENDBR
     DATASET ('VENFILE')
     END-EXEC
```

THE RESETBR COMMAND

This command is used to perform any or all of the actions described below.

Reset the browse position to another record in the file. This position can be a lower or a higher record key than the record just processed.

Reset the record identification to a different type. For VSAM files, browsing can occur by record key, relative byte address, or relative record number.

Reset the browse to generic or full-key mode. There are some situations when it is convenient to change from generic mode to full-key mode. Backwards browsing, for instance, cannot occur when in generic mode. Skip sequential processing is also mode-dependent. You may need to change to or from full-key mode prior to performing a skip sequential operation.

Reset the browse type to EQUAL or GTEQ. Some operations such as skip sequential processing can benefit from activating the GTEQ option. You could start a browse with the EQUAL option, then use the RESETBR command to change to the GTEQ option.

The format of the RESETBR command is

```
EXEC CICS RESETBR
     DATASET (name)
     RIDFLD (data-area)
     [KEYLENGTH (data-value) [GENERIC]]
     [GTEQ | EQUAL]
     [REQID (data-value)]
     [RBA | RRN]
     END-EXEC
```

The various options of the RESETBR command are the same as described with the STARTBR command. There is only one important rule: you need to use the same data area in the RIDFLD option as specified in the original start-browse command.

THE READNEXT COMMAND

This command is used to read the next sequential record in the file. The first READNEXT command issued after a browse is started will read the record that was located by the STARTBR command. Each subsequent READNEXT command will retrieve the record with the next greater record key.

The format of the command is

```
EXEC CICS READNEXT
     DATASET (name)
     RIDFLD (data-area)
     [INTO (data-area)]
     [LENGTH (data-area)]
     [KEYLENGTH (data-value)]
     [REQID (data-value)]
     END-EXEC
```

The RIDFLD option contains the name of the data area where the record key is stored. This must be the same data-area address used in the original STARTBR command.

For VSAM files, the READNEXT command can also be used to request skip sequential processing. To perform skip sequential processing, you simply replace the contents of the RIDFLD argument with another record key. This record key must be greater than the record just retrieved with the previous READNEXT command. When CICS discovers that you have modified the record key, it will reposition to that record, and present the new record to the program. There are a couple of rules associated with skip sequential processing. These are

If you specify the EQUAL option in the STARTBR command, the NOTFND condition can arise during skip sequential processing. This occurs if the new record key is not in the file. For this reason, you may want to specify the GTEQ option if you plan to perform skip sequential processing.

If a generic mode browse is in progress, you must perform a generic mode skip sequential operation. This is done by using the KEYLENGTH option in the READNEXT command. The value of the KEYLENGTH argument may be different than specified in the previous STARTBR or RESETBR command.

If a generic mode browse is in progress, and you need to perform a full-key skip sequential operation, you must change to full-key browse mode. This can be done by using a RESETBR command. The READNEXT following this reset command will retrieve the requested record (or one with a greater key). Thereafter, you may request skip sequential operations by changing the record key and issuing the READNEXT command again. Be sure not to code the KEYLENGTH option on these full-key READNEXT commands.

The INTO option contains the name of the data area for the data record. For variable-length files, this area must be large enough to accommodate the largest record to be processed.

The LENGTH option contains a data area specifying the length of the record. For fixed-length files, the argument must contain the actual record length defined for the file. For variable-length files, the argument contains the maximum length of the record area. This S9999 COMPUTATIONAL field will be updated with the actual length of the record just read.

Usually more than one record will be retrieved during the execution of a program. With variable-length files, you will need to restore the length argument back to the maximum value. If you don't, the first time a longer record is read, the exception LENGERR will occur. A COBOL MOVE statement just prior to the READNEXT command will ensure that the length argument is restored.

The KEYLENGTH option is only used if you are performing a generic browse and need to perform skip sequential processing. If this option is not specified, CICS will return the next sequential record in the usual manner. One common mistake is to assume that you must use the KEYLENGTH option here if you started the browse in generic mode. If you do this, and do not change the RIDFLD value, the same record will be retrieved over and over. Therefore, only use this option when you want to perform a generic skip sequential operation.

The REQID option is only needed when multiple browsing has been started. The data value should correspond to the original REQID value specified in the related STARTBR command.

Here is an example of a READNEXT command for our sample vendor file:

```
MOVE +249 TO VENDOR-RECORD-LENGTH.
EXEC CICS READNEXT
     NOHANDLE
     DATASET ('VENFILE')
     RIDFLD (ENTRY-KEY)
     INTO (VENDOR-RECORD)
     LENGTH (VENDOR-RECORD-LENGTH)
     END-EXEC.
```

THE READPREV COMMAND

This command is used to read records in reverse sequential order; that is, records are read sequentially towards the beginning of the file. The READPREV command is valid only for VSAM files. The format and options of the READPREV command are much the same as the READNEXT command.

The format of the command is

```
EXEC CICS READPREV
     DATASET (name)
     RIDFLD (data-area)
     [INTO (data-area)]
     [LENGTH (data-area)]
     [REQID (data-value)]
     END-EXEC
```

There are a few special rules that you must consider if you plan to use this command. These are as follows:

If the READPREV command is issued after a READNEXT command, the same record will be returned. Thereafter, the next record toward the beginning of the file will be read.

You may not use this command in a generic mode browse operation. If you do, the INVREQ condition will arise. If you must do a generic browse and still want to read records in reverse, there is a way to get around this problem. First, you would issue the STARTBR with the GENERIC option. Then a READNEXT would be issued to retrieve the first record. Finally, by using the updated value in the RIDFLD, you would issue a RESETBR command *without* the GENERIC option. This would alter the browsing operation to a nongeneric mode. The READPREV command would now be acceptable.

If a READPREV command immediately follows a STARTBR command, the record must be in the file. If it is not, the NOTFND condition will arise. If you plan to issue a READPREV immediately after starting a browse operation, you should therefore specify the EQUAL option on the STARTBR command. This will avoid getting the NOTFND on the first READPREV command when the record does not exist.

Do not attempt to use skip sequential processing with the READPREV command. That is, do not modify the contents of the RIDFLD argument between successive READPREV commands.

BROWSE EXCEPTIONAL CONDITIONS

DSIDERR occurs if the data set name has not been defined in the FCT.

DUPKEY occurs if a record is retrieved using an alternate key, if the key is not unique. This condition will arise on all but the last record having the same key value.

ENDFILE occurs if the end of file has been reached. The previous READNEXT command would have read the last record. If backwards browsing is used, the front of the file has been reached. The last READPREV command would have just processed the first record in the file.

ILLOGIC occurs if some VSAM error has occurred that is not covered by the other exceptional conditions.

INVREQ occurs in a number of situations. These are

The browsing function is not available for this file. This is reflected in the FCT. Browsing can be enabled using a master terminal transaction.

A READNEXT, READPREV, ENDBR, or RESETBR command has been issued for which no previous STARTBR command has been issued.

The KEYLENGTH and GENERIC option has been specified on the STARTBR or RESETBR command, and the argument value of the KEYLENGTH option is less than zero, or greater than or equal to the length of the full key.

A STARTBR command is issued for a REQID argument value already in use by another browse operation.

The key type RBA, RRN, or record key in a READNEXT or READPREV command differs from the STARTBR or last RESETBR command.

LENGERR occurs if the record length exceeds the maximum length specified in the LENGTH argument.

NOTFND can occur on a READPREV command that immediately follows a STARTBR command if the record is not in the file. It can also occur during skip sequential processing if the new record key is not in the file and EQUAL was specified in the STARTBR or last RESETBR command.

NOTAUTH occurs if the operator's resource security does not match that of the file.

NOTOPEN occurs if the file is not open.

BMS Page Building

All of the examples so far in the text have used a single SEND MAP command to produce a screen image. The menu, inquiry, and update programs described in the previous chapters used this simple mapping approach. In the last chapter you learned how to use more than one SEND MAP command to produce multiple screens. A sample program using the BMS Terminal Paging facility was used to display two inquiry screens. Each screen was produced by a separate SEND MAP command.

There is one additional service provided by BMS. This service is known as *page building*. Page building is a process whereby multiple SEND MAP commands are used to construct a *single* screen image. To use page building, you must define maps that are smaller than the screen size. These maps also contain special options that tell BMS where they are to be *positioned* on the screen. After the maps are defined, the application program will use the SEND MAP command with a special page-building option.

Page building is often used in conjunction with file browsing. Many file-browsing programs are designed to display multiple records on the same screen. Page building can help to simplify the logic of these programs. The screen depicted in figure 10.2 was produced by a file-browsing program using the page-building feature. The heading area of this screen contains a screen identification code and a screen title. Following the title area is a display of information from up to 20 records. Then at the bottom of the screen, there is a message area.

The browse screen was produced using three separate maps. These maps that contain special page-building options are depicted in figure 10.3. The headings for the screen are provided by a type of map called a *header* map. The size of this map is 2 by 80. The detail lines are provided by a single *detail* map. The size of this map is 1 by 80. The program will repeatedly send this map to display the detail data. The message at the bottom is displayed in a special map known as a *trailer* map. This trailer map, which is 2 by 80, is displayed at the bottom of the screen.

The logic of the browse program that pertains to the page-building process is shown in figure 10.4. The exception logic, such as NOTOPEN, NOTFND, and ENDFILE, have been omitted from the diagram. The program will begin by initiating a browse operation using the STARTBR command. If the browse is successful, the program will begin the page-building process. First, it will reserve space on the screen for the trailer map. It will then issue a SEND MAP command to display the headings. The program will then enter a processing cycle to read and display information for each data record. After each record has been read with the READNEXT command, the program will move the data fields to be displayed to fields in the detail map. The program will then issue a SEND MAP command

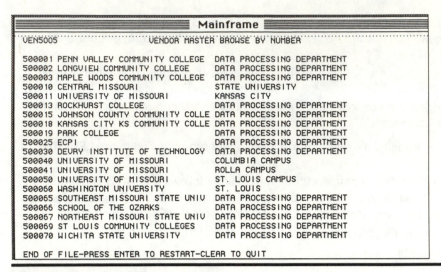

```
═══════════════ Mainframe ═══════════════
VEN5005                VENDOR MASTER BROWSE BY NUMBER

500001 PENN VALLEY COMMUNITY COLLEGE   DATA PROCESSING DEPARTMENT
500002 LONGVIEW COMMUNITY COLLEGE      DATA PROCESSING DEPARTMENT
500003 MAPLE WOODS COMMUNITY COLLEGE   DATA PROCESSING DEPARTMENT
500010 CENTRAL MISSOURI               STATE UNIVERSITY
500011 UNIVERSITY OF MISSOURI         KANSAS CITY
500013 ROCKHURST COLLEGE              DATA PROCESSING DEPARTMENT
500015 JOHNSON COUNTY COMMUNITY COLLE  DATA PROCESSING DEPARTMENT
500018 KANSAS CITY KS COMMUNITY COLLE  DATA PROCESSING DEPARTMENT
500019 PARK COLLEGE                   DATA PROCESSING DEPARTMENT
500025 ECPI                           DATA PROCESSING DEPARTMENT
500030 DEVRY INSTITUTE OF TECHNOLOGY  DATA PROCESSING DEPARTMENT
500040 UNIVERSITY OF MISSOURI         COLUMBIA CAMPUS
500041 UNIVERSITY OF MISSOURI         ROLLA CAMPUS
500050 UNIVERSITY OF MISSOURI         ST. LOUIS CAMPUS
500060 WASHINGTON UNIVERSITY          ST. LOUIS
500065 SOUTHEAST MISSOURI STATE UNIV   DATA PROCESSING DEPARTMENT
500066 SCHOOL OF THE OZARKS           DATA PROCESSING DEPARTMENT
500067 NORTHEAST MISSOURI STATE UNIV   DATA PROCESSING DEPARTMENT
500069 ST LOUIS COMMUNITY COLLEGES    DATA PROCESSING DEPARTMENT
500070 WICHITA STATE UNIVERSITY       DATA PROCESSING DEPARTMENT

END OF FILE-PRESS ENTER TO RESTART-CLEAR TO QUIT
```

FIGURE 10.2.　Sample Browse Screen

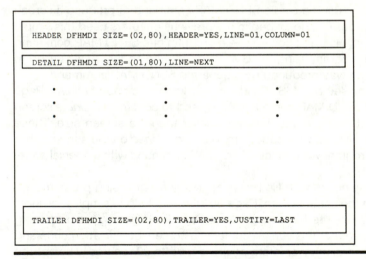

```
HEADER DFHMDI SIZE=(02,80),HEADER=YES,LINE=01,COLUMN=01

DETAIL DFHMDI SIZE=(01,80),LINE=NEXT

TRAILER DFHMDI SIZE=(02,80),TRAILER=YES,JUSTIFY=LAST
```

FIGURE 10.3.　BMS Maps for Sample Browse Screen

to display a single line. This process will be repeated until the BMS page-building routines raise an exceptional condition that the screen is full. The program will then issue a SEND MAP command to display the message at the bottom. The message will be written using the trailer map.

The logic of this browse program is somewhat analagous to a batch program designed to produce a report. By using the BMS page-building feature, the program simply writes "lines" to the terminal in the same way they would be written to a batch printer. The screen output is also device-independent. That is, the same logic would work for terminals with a different number of available lines and columns.

Now let's examine the programming requirements needed to use this powerful feature of BMS. First, we will look at the map definition statements. Then we will study the CICS commands used to perform page building. Finally, we will examine the programming needed when the page overflow (screen full) condition occurs during page building.

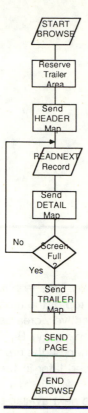

FIGURE 10.4. Program Logic for Browse Screen

BMS MAP DEFINITION

As indicated earlier, you will define maps smaller than the screen size in order to use the page-building feature. You might recall from chapter 5 that maps are defined with the map definition (DFHMDI) statement. At that time, I skipped over the options normally used with the page-building feature. Let's look at the map definition statement again with the new options. The complete format of the DFHMDI statement is

```
(mapname) DFHMDI SIZE=(lines,columns)
         LINE={nn | SAME | NEXT}
         COLUMN={nn | SAME | NEXT}
         JUSTIFY=[{LEFT | RIGHT}][{FIRST | LAST}]
         HEADER=YES
         TRAILER=YES
```

There are a variety of new options shown above. By using different combinations of these options you can design almost any screen imaginable. In fact, you may never use some of these special options, but they are available in case you need to.

The SIZE option is fairly straightforward. It simply defines the size of the map in terms of lines (rows) and columns. Of course, to use page building, a map must be smaller than the actual screen (page) size. To be smaller, a map must contain fewer lines and/or fewer columns than the screen size. For instance, a map could be defined as SIZE=(12,40) or as SIZE=(12,80).

All field definitions for maps are defined with respect to the map size. A map defined as 03 by 80 may therefore only have fields that fall within this range. For instance, you could not define a field on line 04 for a 03-by-80 map. Keep this in mind as you code your field definitions.

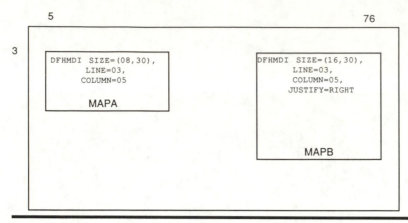

FIGURE 10.5.   Map Positioning Using Left and Right Justification

The LINE option is used to specify the line where the top of the map will display. Line=nn is used to explicitly specify the line number. For instance, if LINE=03 is specified, the top of the map will display on line 03. During page building, as each map is sent, the line number effectively creates a *top margin* for the screen. If another map is sent with a line number lower than the top margin, BMS will treat this as page overflow. It will either raise the overflow condition or place the map on the next screen at the specified line and column number. The overflow condition is discussed later in the chapter.

If LINE=NEXT is used—or taken by default—the map will be displayed on the next available line on the screen. If a map with LINE=NEXT is the first one used for a screen, the map will display on line 1. If previous maps *have been* accumulated for the screen, the map will display on the next completely empty line.

If LINE=SAME is specified, BMS will attempt to display the map on the same line as the previous map. If, however, the map is too wide to fit on the same line, it will be displayed on the next completely empty line.

The COLUMNS option is a little more complex than the line option. This is due to the fact that column specifications work in conjunction with the JUSTIFY=LEFT, or JUSTIFY=RIGHT specifications.

The COLUMN=nn option specifies the number of columns that the map is to be positioned from the *edge* of the screen. If JUSTIFY=LEFT has also been specified, the nn value indicates the number of columns from the left edge of the screen. For instance, if COLUMN=05 has been specified, and the map is left-justified, the left side of the map will begin in column 5 of the screen. On the other hand, if the map is right-justified, the right side of the map will be in column 76 (of an 80 column terminal). This process is depicted in figure 10.5.

Left or right reference pointers are also established when BMS sends a map with the COLUMN=nn specification. If the map is left-justified, the left reference pointer is set to nn. If the map is right-justified, the column containing the right edge of the map becomes the right reference point. BMS maintains these pointers until another map is sent with the COLUMN=nn specification.

If a map is used with the COLUMN=SAME specification, BMS positions the map based on the reference pointers. If the map is left-justified, the left edge of the map is positioned in the left reference column. This will be the position established by the last left-justified map using the nn specification. If there was no previous left-justified map with the nn specification, the left reference is column 1. If the map is right-justified, BMS will align the right side of the map with the right reference. The right reference point either will be the right side of the screen or will have been established as described in the last paragraph.

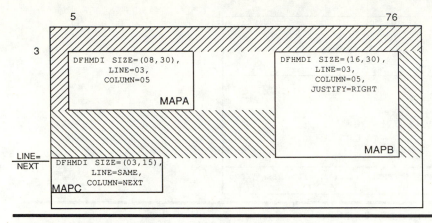

FIGURE 10.6.   Top, Bottom, Left Margins, and NEXT Line
After MAPA and MAPB Accumulated

When COLUMN=SAME is used, BMS will make all attempts to position the map according to this specification. In fact, if LINE=SAME and COLUMN=SAME are both specified, the column specification will be given the higher priority.

The COLUMN=NEXT option is used to position the map in the next available column on the current line. The next available column is determined by the previously sent map with similar justification. For example, in figure 10.5, after MAPA is sent, the next available column is 35. When another left-justified map is sent, BMS will attempt to position it in column 35. If the map will *not fit* on the current line, BMS will position the map beginning in column 1 of the next completely empty line as if LINE=NEXT had been specified. This process is depicted in figure 10.6.

If LINE=NEXT and COLUMN=NEXT are both specified, the map will be positioned on the left or right side of the screen, depending on the justification of the map. The map will also be positioned on the next completely empty line.

The JUSTIFY=FIRST option is normally used with header maps only. Only the first header map on a page can use the JUSTIFY=FIRST specification. If additional header maps are used, they must not specify this option, or else another page will be started.

The JUSTIFY=LAST option is normally used with trailer maps. This option is used to position a trailer map at the very bottom of the screen. If a detail map is defined with the JUSTIFY=LAST option, the map will be justified at the bottom of the screen if there are no trailer maps. It will be placed just above the trailer area if trailer maps are to be used.

The HEADER=YES option is used to define a header map. Header maps are displayed at the top of the screen, and usually contain information such as the page number and screen and column titles. More than one header map can be defined in the mapset. If multiple header maps are used, only the first may contain the JUSTIFY=FIRST option. Refer to figure 10.7 for an example of header and trailer maps.

The TRAILER=YES option is used to define a trailer map. Trailer maps are usually displayed at the very bottom of the screen. To do this, the JUSTIFY=LAST would also be used for the map. If multiple trailer maps specify JUSTIFY=LAST, BMS must be able to position them horizontally at the bottom of the screen. A trailer map without the JUSTIFY=LAST option can also be positioned just below the last detail map by specifying the LINE=NEXT option.

There are many different combinations of options that can be selected when defining maps to be used with page building. There is a good rule to follow until you become familiar with the page-building process. That rule is, Keep your maps simple. Don't get fancy with multiple header and trailer maps if it is not necessary. If your maps become too complicated, it may be more difficult to maintain the programs which use them. Now let's look at the CICS commands necessary to use page building.

```
DFHMDI SIZE=(08,30),        DFHMDI SIZE=(08,50),
      LINE=01,COLUMN=01          LINE=SAME,COLUMN=NEXT,
      HEADER=YES,                 HEADER=YES
      JUSTIFY=FIRST

HEADER1                     HEADER2




DFHMDI SIZE=(02,40),TRAILER=YES,    DFHMDI SIZE=(02,40),TRAILER=YES,
      JUSTIFY=LAST                        JUSTIFY=LAST
```

FIGURE 10.7.   Multiple Header and Trailer Maps

CICS COMMANDS NEEDED

There are three commands that are provided to control the page-building process. Two of these commands are required. The third command is optional but is used in most page-building programs.

The first command is SEND MAP. As you saw in the introduction, this command is used for each map to be displayed. A new option, ACCUM is used to request page building. When the ACCUM is used, BMS will consider that the map is part of an accumulated page- (screen-) building process. BMS will then begin to construct the logical message (screen image) in dynamic storage. Each subsequent SEND MAP command with the ACCUM option will cause BMS to construct the screen image further. Here is an example of the SEND MAP command used to accumulate the first header map depicted in figure 10.7.

```
EXEC CICS SEND MAP ACCUM
     MAP ('HEADER1')
     MAPSET ('VENDSET')
     ERASE
     FREEKB
     END-EXEC
```

The second command is SEND PAGE. When the program is ready to transmit the screen image, it will use the SEND PAGE command. The format and options of this command were described in chapter 9.

The third command that is often used in page-building programs is optional. Actually, there are two commands in this category. The commands are HANDLE CONDITION and IGNORE CONDITION. The condition used with these commands is OVERFLOW. When the HANDLE or IGNORE command is used with the OVERFLOW option, two actions are taken by BMS.

The first action is to reserve lines at the bottom of the screen for any trailer maps needed by the program. The area reserved will then be unavailable for displaying detail maps. If a trailer area is not reserved, the entire screen can be used for accumulating detail maps. In effect, the HANDLE or IGNORE command, with the OVERFLOW option, draws an invisible line between the trailer area and the rest of the screen. The number of trailer lines reserved is determined by the size of the trailer maps defined for the application. BMS will not be able to determine the trailer size until a subsequent SEND MAP command has been issued by the program. When this occurs, BMS will examine the mapset to determine the trailer size. Each mapset contains a value corresponding to the *largest* trailer map in the mapset. If there are no trailer maps in the mapset, the trailer size value is set to zero. If the trailer size is zero, no lines will be reserved on the screen.

There is a second action taken when the HANDLE or IGNORE command (with OVERFLOW) is used. This action deals with the page overflow condition itself. Page overflow occurs when a SEND MAP command is issued, and the map will not fit in the detail area of the screen. The presence of a trailer area will affect the size of the detail area, as described above. BMS has two ways to deal with page overflow.

The *default* BMS action is taken when the program has *not* issued a HANDLE or IGNORE command for overflow. The default action is to start a new screen and place the target map on that screen. BMS will not even inform the program that this action has occurred; that is, the exceptional condition overflow will not be raised. The program can continue to send additional maps. If another screen becomes full, BMS will take the same action. Another new screen will be started, and the map will be positioned on that screen.

This default action is acceptable only in a few situations. The program would somehow have to be aware that new pages (screens) were being started. To display these multiple screens, the program would also have to specify the Terminal Paging option (PAGING) in the various SEND MAP commands. Programs designed to display a single screen would have to develop other logic to *prevent* page overflow. A line counter, for example, might be used in a program to limit the number of mapping commands issued.

A better approach is to activate the page overflow condition. To do this, you must issue a HANDLE CONDITION (label) or IGNORE CONDITION command for the overflow condition. Once you issue the HANDLE or IGNORE command, BMS assumes that you want to provide your own page overflow logic.

Later, during a mapping operation when overflow occurs, BMS will raise the overflow condition. If you have specified the HANDLE CONDITION command, CICS will branch to the overflow routine in your program. If the IGNORE CONDITION command was used, you can check one of the response codes in the EIB, and perform the overflow routine if necessary.

OVERFLOW PROCESSING

The processing performed when page overflow occurs usually depends on the program design. Page-building programs generally fall into one of two categories. These are

multiple-page display programs
single-page display programs

The *standard* overflow logic for a program that displays multiple pages (screens) is depicted in figure 10.8. Multiple-page display programs usually display header and trailer maps on each screen. The logic depicted in the figure follows this procedure. This program, like the one in the Introduction, is a browse program designed to display detail information from each record. It begins with a start-browse to establish positioning within the file.

After the browse is started, the program will issue the HANDLE CONDITION command with the OVERFLOW option. This will activate the BMS page overflow routine, and prepare BMS to reserve space for a trailer map.

Next, the header map for the first screen is sent. Because page building is being used, each SEND MAP command will contain the ACCUM option. Since multiple pages are anticipated, the PAGING option is also used so the screens will be stored in Temporary Storage. BMS will also reserve trailer lines using the size of the largest trailer map in the mapset.

After the header map is sent, the program enters a processing cycle to read and display information for each data record. A detail map will be used to display each record. After each SEND MAP command, the program will return to the beginning of the processing cycle.

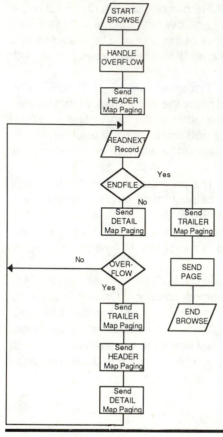

FIGURE 10.8. Multiple Page Overflow Logic

This process will continue until the OVERFLOW condition is raised. Recall that this condition is raised when a map will no longer fit in the detail area. When overflow is raised, the map that caused the overflow condition is *not accumulated* on that page. The program will have to save the map contents or move the fields to the detail map again, in order to display that record on the next screen.

Because of the HANDLE CONDITION command, the overflow routine will be entered. The overflow routine begins by displaying the trailer map. After the trailer map is sent, it sends the header map for the next screen. This will start a new page. Finally, the detail map is sent again. If the program fails to send the detail, and branches back to the READNEXT command, the record that caused the overflow condition will not be displayed.

To display the detail map, the program might have to copy the fields from the record back to the fields in the detail map. A few COBOL MOVE statements will accomplish this process. There is one situation when this process may not be necessary. If the STORAGE=AUTO option had been specified for the mapset, each of the maps would occupy separate storage. In this case the symbolic description area for the detail map will still contain the original fields. If STORAGE=AUTO is not specified, the data would have been modified when mapping fields to the header or trailer areas.

There is only one piece of logic missing in this example. That is a check to determine when to stop the browse operation.

This program will continue to build screens until the ENDFILE condition is raised or a maximum display counter is reached. Without such a counter, the program could potentially browse through the entire file. A program variable or the COBOL ON statement could be used to provide the counter.

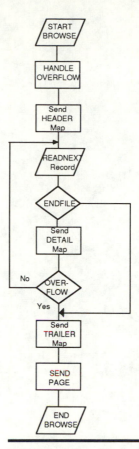

FIGURE 10.9. Single Page Overflow Logic

Another way would be to use a screen counter that could be checked in the overflow routine. For instance, it could stop after three screens have been displayed. The program logic depicted in this figure is fairly complete and standard for multiple-screen displays.

Now let's quickly look at the overflow logic for a program designed to display only a single page. Essentially, this logic was depicted in the Introduction. It is shown again in figure 10.9.

Much of the program logic is the same as depicted in the multiple-screen display program. The program differs only in the overflow routine. In this program, the overflow routine only has to send the trailer map, then issue the SEND PAGE command. As you can see, the overflow logic for the single-page display program is not very complex.

A SAMPLE PROGRAM

Let's top off the chapter by examining a sample program. The logic for this program is depicted in figure 10.10. This sample program is much like the single-page display program in the last example. It is designed to work with the menu program described in chapter 7. The menu program will pass a record key to this program in the commarea in the same way as it did for the other sample programs used in the text. When the browse program has finished displaying records, it will provide a transition back to the menu in the *standard* way.

This browse program is designed to display multiple screens. However, it does not use the Terminal Paging feature. Instead, it uses a design technique that I like to call *pseudobrowsing*. This

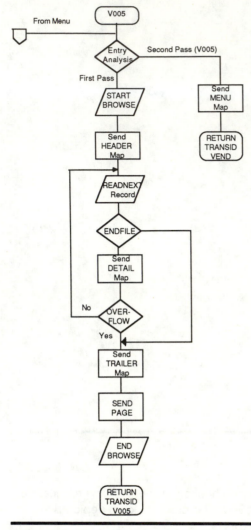

FIGURE 10.10. Logic for Sample Browse Program

technique involves browsing the file and displaying detail information one screen at a time. Each screen is produced during a single *pass* of a pseudoconversational browse program. The first screen is displayed in the first-pass logic of the program. Each additional screen is displayed in the second-pass logic.

The initial record key used to start the browse will be supplied by the menu program. After starting the browse, the program will produce the first screen using BMS pagebuilding. First, the header map will be accumulated. Next, the detail map will be used to display records from the file, one line at a time. This will be accomplished by browsing through the file, and accumulating as many detail maps as needed to fill the screen. When the overflow condition occurs, the trailer map will be accumulated. The SEND PAGE command will be used to transmit the browse screen to the terminal.

The program will then save the record key of the record that caused the overflow condition. It will then issue a pseudoconversational RETURN, naming the transid of the browse program. It will pass the saved record key to the next task using the COMMAREA and LENGTH options of the RETURN command.

```
================================= Mainframe =================================
  VEN5005              VENDOR MASTER BROWSE BY NUMBER

   500001 PENN VALLEY COMMUNITY COLLEGE  DATA PROCESSING DEPARTMENT
   500002 LONGVIEW COMMUNITY COLLEGE     DATA PROCESSING DEPARTMENT
   500003 MAPLE WOODS COMMUNITY COLLEGE  DATA PROCESSING DEPARTMENT
   500010 CENTRAL MISSOURI               STATE UNIVERSITY
   500011 UNIVERSITY OF MISSOURI         KANSAS CITY
   500013 ROCKHURST COLLEGE              DATA PROCESSING DEPARTMENT
   500015 JOHNSON COUNTY COMMUNITY COLLE DATA PROCESSING DEPARTMENT
   500018 KANSAS CITY KS COMMUNITY COLLE DATA PROCESSING DEPARTMENT
   500019 PARK COLLEGE                   DATA PROCESSING DEPARTMENT
   500025 ECPI                           DATA PROCESSING DEPARTMENT
   500030 DEVRY INSTITUTE OF TECHNOLOGY  DATA PROCESSING DEPARTMENT
   500040 UNIVERSITY OF MISSOURI         COLUMBIA CAMPUS
   500041 UNIVERSITY OF MISSOURI         ROLLA CAMPUS
   500050 UNIVERSITY OF MISSOURI         ST. LOUIS CAMPUS
   500060 WASHINGTON UNIVERSITY          ST. LOUIS
   500065 SOUTHEAST MISSOURI STATE UNIV  DATA PROCESSING DEPARTMENT
   500066 SCHOOL OF THE OZARKS           DATA PROCESSING DEPARTMENT
   500067 NORTHEAST MISSOURI STATE UNIV  DATA PROCESSING DEPARTMENT
   500069 ST LOUIS COMMUNITY COLLEGES    DATA PROCESSING DEPARTMENT
   500070 WICHITA STATE UNIVERSITY       DATA PROCESSING DEPARTMENT

  PRESS ENTER FOR MORE RECORDS-CLEAR TO QUIT
```

```
HEADMAP    DFHMDI SIZE=(2,80),LINE=01,COLUMN=01,HEADER=YES,JUSTIFY=FIRST
SCODE      DFHMDF POS=(01,01),LENGTH=07                                    X
           DFHMDF POS=(01,26),LENGTH=32,                                   X
                  INITIAL='VENDOR MASTER BROWSE BY NUMBER'
DETLMAP    DFHMDI SIZE=(1,80),LINE=NEXT,COLUMN=01
DETAIL     DFHMDF POS=(1,1),LENGTH=79
FOOTMAP    DFHMDI SIZE=(02,56),TRAILER=YES,JUSTIFY=LAST
FOOTMSG    DFHMDF POS=(2,01),LENGTH=52,                                    X
                  INITIAL='PRESS ENTER FOR MORE RECORDS-CLEAR TO QUIT'
```

FIGURE 10.11.   Sample Browse Screen and BMS Map Definitions

At this point the operator will be able to view the browse screen. This screen is depicted in figure 10.11. The message in the trailer area informs the operator of the next action required. After the operator has finished viewing the screen, the CLEAR key can be pressed to terminate the browse. Any other key will cause the browse to continue.

When the operator has pressed an attention key, the browse program will again be started. The entry analysis routine will determine the action to be taken. If the CLEAR key was pressed, the program will send the menu screen and provide transition back to the menu program with a pseudo-conversational RETURN.

If another AID key was used, the program will get the next record key from the commarea. The browse will again be started using this key to reestablish position in the file. A second screen will be displayed in the same manner as the first. This process will be repeated, until the end-of-file condition has been encountered or the operator requests browse termination.

When you examine the program listing in figure 10.12, you will notice that the program has another feature. When end of file is encountered and the operator does not request termination, the original browse key is used to start the process over again. If you don't like this particular feature, you don't have to use it. It was strictly my design choice.

The pseudobrowsing technique shown in this last example has some good performance benefits. It effectively allows the operator to browse as many records as needed, without using too many CICS resources. In any one execution of the program, only a few records are read. This provides good utilization of the VSAM strings needed during browsing. By displaying only one screen at a time, the Terminal Paging facility is not required. It does not have to use Temporary Storage. And finally, the program is fairly short and, hopefully, easy to understand. Before moving on to the chapter summary, you might want to take a few minutes to study this program.

```
IDENTIFICATION DIVISION.
PROGRAM-ID. VEND005.
AUTHOR. BOB LOWE.
ENVIRONMENT DIVISION.
DATA DIVISION.
WORKING-STORAGE SECTION.
01  WS-COMMAREA.
    05  ENTRY-KEY               PIC XXXXXX VALUE ZERO.
    05  FIRST-KEY               PIC XXXXXX VALUE ZERO.
01  DETAIL-LINE.
    05  D-KEY           PIC XXXXXX      VALUE SPACES.
    05  FILLER          PIC X           VALUE SPACES.
    05  D-NAME          PIC X(30)       VALUE SPACES.
    05  FILLER          PIC X           VALUE SPACES.
    05  D-ADDRESS       PIC X(30)       VALUE SPACES.
    05  FILLER          PIC X(11)       VALUE SPACES.
01  VENDOR-RECORD.
    05  VENDOR-NAME             PIC X(30).
    05  VENDOR-ID               PIC XXXXXX.
    05  VENDOR-ADDR1            PIC X(30).
    05  VENDOR-ADDR2            PIC X(30).
    05  VENDOR-ADDR3            PIC X(30).
    05  VENDOR-ADDR4            PIC X(30).
    05  VENDOR-CONTACT          PIC X(30).
    05  VENDOR-TELE             PIC X(12).
    05  VENDOR-TAXID            PIC X(11).
    05  VENDOR-YTD-SALES        PIC S9(07)V99 COMP-3.
    05  VENDOR-YTD-PAYMENTS     PIC S9(07)V99 COMP-3.
    05  VENDOR-YTD-DISCOUNTS    PIC S9(07)V99 COMP-3.
    05  VENDOR-PAY-HOLD         PIC X.
    05  VENDOR-PRODUCT          PIC XXX.
    05  VENDOR-LAST-CHECK       PIC S9(05)    COMP-3.
    05  VENDOR-LAST-CK-DATE     PIC S9(05)    COMP-3.
    05  VENDOR-LAST-CK-AMT      PIC S9(07)V99 COMP-3.
    05  VENDOR-DATE-ADDED       PIC S9(05)    COMP-3.
    05  VENDOR-DATE-CHANGED     PIC S9(05)    COMP-3.
    05  VENDOR-LAST-OPID        PIC XXX.
    05  VENDOR-UPDCNT           PIC 9.
01  WORK-AREAS.
    05  VEND-REC-LENGTH         PIC S9999  COMP VALUE +249.
    05  OVERFLOW-TRAP-VALUE     PIC S9999  COMP VALUE +1.
    05  MENU-SEND-INDICATOR     PIC S9999  COMP VALUE +0.
        88  MENU-TO-BE-SENT                VALUE +1.
    05  COPY-OF-EIBRCODE.
        10  EIBRCODE-BYTE-1     PIC X.
        10  EIBRCODE-BYTE-2     PIC X.
        10  EIBRCODE-BYTE-3     PIC X.
01  CICS-RETURN-CODE-TEST-AREA.
    05  COMMAND-STATUS-CODE         PIC S9(08) COMP VALUE +0.
        88  NORMAL                      VALUE +0.
        88  DSIDERR                     VALUE +1.
        88  BMS-OVERFLOW                VALUE +1.
        88  ILLOGIC                     VALUE +2.
        88  FC-INVREQ                   VALUE +8.
        88  NOTOPEN                     VALUE +12.
        88  DISABLED                    VALUE +13.
        88  ENDFILE                     VALUE +15.
        88  FC-IOERR                    VALUE +128.
        88  NOTFND                      VALUE +129.
        88  NOTAUTH                     VALUE +214.
        88  LENGERR                     VALUE +225.
    05  FILLER REDEFINES COMMAND-STATUS-CODE.
        10  FILLER              PIC XXX.
        10  CONVERT-TO-DECIMAL  PIC X.
01  OUTPUT-MESSAGE.
    05  MESSAGE-NUMBER          PIC X(8).
    05  FILLER                  PIC X       VALUE SPACE.
    05  THE-MESSAGE             PIC X(62).
COPY  DFHAID.
COPY VENDSET SUPPRESS.
LINKAGE SECTION.
01  DFHCOMMAREA             PIC X(12).
PROCEDURE DIVISION.
*PROCEDURE DIVISION.
0000-MAINLINE-PROCEDURE-CODE.
```

FIGURE 10.12. Sample Browse Program

```
* * * * * * * * * * * * * * * * * * * * * * * * *
*     ENTRY ANALYSIS
* * * * * * * * * * * * * * * * * * * * * * * * *
* * * * * * * * * * * * * * * * * * * * * * * * *
      IF EIBCALEN NOT EQUAL ZERO
          MOVE DFHCOMMAREA TO WS-COMMAREA.
      IF EIBTRNID EQUAL 'V005'
          IF EIBAID EQUAL TO DFHCLEAR
             MOVE LOW-VALUES TO MENUMAPO
             MOVE 'CLEAR KEY PRESSED BROWSE STOPPED'
                                              TO THE-MESSAGE
             MOVE 'VEND5205'       TO MESSAGE-NUMBER
             MOVE OUTPUT-MESSAGE TO MMESAGEO
             PERFORM 925-TRANSMIT-MENU-SCREEN
          ELSE NEXT SENTENCE
      ELSE
          MOVE ENTRY-KEY TO FIRST-KEY.
      PERFORM 100-INITIAL-ENTRY
      THRU   109-INITIAL-ENTRY-EXIT.
      IF MENU-TO-BE-SENT
          EXEC CICS PURGE MESSAGE END-EXEC
          PERFORM 925-TRANSMIT-MENU-SCREEN
      ELSE
          EXEC CICS RETURN TRANSID ('V005')
                    COMMAREA (WS-COMMAREA) LENGTH (12)
                    END-EXEC.

* * * * * * * * * * * * * * * * * * * * * * * * *
*     ENTRY FROM MENU
* * * * * * * * * * * * * * * * * * * * * * * * *
  100-INITIAL-ENTRY.
      EXEC CICS STARTBR
                DATASET ('VENFILE')
                RIDFLD (ENTRY-KEY)
                GTEQ
                NOHANDLE
      END-EXEC.
      MOVE EIBRCODE TO CONVERT-TO-DECIMAL.
      IF NORMAL NEXT SENTENCE
      ELSE MOVE +1 TO MENU-SEND-INDICATOR
           IF NOTFND
              PERFORM 935-NOTFND-ERROR
                 GO TO 109-INITIAL-ENTRY-EXIT
           ELSE PERFORM 920-UNEXPECTED-FILE-ERROR
                GO TO 109-INITIAL-ENTRY-EXIT.
* * * * * * * * * * * * * * * * * * * * * * * * *
*     If a handle condition for OVERFLOW is not active
*     the overflow condition will not be raised.  We will
*     issue a NOHANDLE option in the SEND MAP command and
*     test the response code for OVERFLOW.
* * * * * * * * * * * * * * * * * * * * * * * * *
      EXEC CICS IGNORE CONDITION OVERFLOW
                END-EXEC.
* * * * * * * * * * * * * * * * * * * * * * * * *
*     Initialize all of the map areas.  The maps were defined
*       with the STORAGE=AUTO option so each map occupies
*       its own working-storage space.
* * * * * * * * * * * * * * * * * * * * * * * * *
      MOVE LOW-VALUES TO  HEADMAPO, DETLMAPO, FOOTMAPO.
      MOVE SPACES TO DETAIL-LINE.
      EXEC CICS SEND MAP ('HEADMAP')
                MAPSET ('VENDSET')
                ERASE
                FREEKB
                ACCUM
                NOHANDLE
      END-EXEC.
      MOVE EIBRCODE TO CONVERT-TO-DECIMAL.
      IF NOT NORMAL PERFORM 910-UNEXPECTED-BMS-ERROR
                    MOVE +1 TO MENU-SEND-INDICATOR
                    GO TO 109-INITIAL-ENTRY-EXIT.
      PERFORM 120-DISPLAY-RECORDS
      THRU    150-DISPLAY-RECORDS-EXIT
      UNTIL   BMS-OVERFLOW OR ENDFILE OR NOT NORMAL
      EXEC CICS  SEND MAP ('FOOTMAP')
                 MAPSET ('VENDSET')
                 FREEKB
                 ACCUM
      END-EXEC.
```

FIGURE 10.12.   Continued

```
            MOVE EIBRCODE TO CONVERT-TO-DECIMAL.
            IF NOT NORMAL PERFORM 910-UNEXPECTED-BMS-ERROR
                        MOVE +1 TO MENU-SEND-INDICATOR
                        GO TO 109-INITIAL-ENTRY-EXIT.
            EXEC CICS SEND PAGE END-EXEC.
   109-INITIAL-ENTRY-EXIT.
            EXIT.
   120-DISPLAY-RECORDS.
            ON 24  MOVE OVERFLOW-TRAP-VALUE TO COMMAND-STATUS-CODE
                   GO TO 150-DISPLAY-RECORDS-EXIT.
            MOVE +249 TO   VEND-REC-LENGTH.
            EXEC CICS READNEXT
                    INTO     (VENDOR-RECORD)
                    DATASET  ('VENFILE')
                    LENGTH   (VEND-REC-LENGTH)
                    RIDFLD   (ENTRY-KEY)
                    NOHANDLE
            END-EXEC.
            MOVE EIBRCODE TO CONVERT-TO-DECIMAL.
            IF NORMAL NEXT SENTENCE
            ELSE IF ENDFILE
                    MOVE
                    'END OF FILE-PRESS ENTER TO RESTART-CLEAR TO QUIT'
                    TO FOOTMSGO
                    MOVE FIRST-KEY TO ENTRY-KEY
                    GO TO 150-DISPLAY-RECORDS-EXIT
                ELSE PERFORM 920-UNEXPECTED-FILE-ERROR
                    MOVE +1 TO MENU-SEND-INDICATOR
                    GO TO 150-DISPLAY-RECORDS-EXIT.
            MOVE VENDOR-ID    TO D-KEY.
            MOVE VENDOR-NAME   TO D-NAME.
            MOVE VENDOR-ADDR1  TO D-ADDRESS.
            MOVE DETAIL-LINE   TO DETAILO.
            EXEC CICS SEND MAP ('DETLMAP')
                    MAPSET    ('VENDSET')
                    FREEKB
                    ACCUM
            END-EXEC.
            MOVE EIBRCODE TO CONVERT-TO-DECIMAL.
            IF NOT NORMAL PERFORM 910-UNEXPECTED-BMS-ERROR
                        MOVE +1 TO MENU-SEND-INDICATOR
                        GO TO 150-DISPLAY-RECORDS-EXIT.
            MOVE EIBRCODE TO COPY-OF-EIBRCODE.
            MOVE EIBRCODE-BYTE-3 TO CONVERT-TO-DECIMAL
   150-DISPLAY-RECORDS-EXIT.
            EXIT.
   925-TRANSMIT-MENU-SCREEN.
            MOVE EIBTRMID   TO TERMO IN MENUMAPO.
            MOVE CURRENT-DATE TO DATEO IN MENUMAPO.
            MOVE ENTRY-KEY   TO VENDIDO IN MENUMAPO
            MOVE EIBTIME TO TIMEO IN MENUMAPO.
            TRANSFORM TIMEO IN MENUMAPO FROM ',' TO ':'.
            MOVE 'VEN0005' TO SCODEO IN MENUMAPO.
            EXEC CICS SEND MAP ('MENUMAP')
                    MAPSET ('VENDSET')
                    ERASE
                    FREEKB
                    END-EXEC.
            EXEC CICS RETURN  TRANSID ('VEND')
                COMMAREA (EIBAID) LENGTH (1)
                END-EXEC.
* * * * * * * * * * * * * * * * * * * * * * * * *
* * * * * * * * * * * * * * * * * * * * * * * * *
* * * * * * * * * * * * * * * * * * * * * * * * *
*    ERROR PROCESSING ROUTINES
* * * * * * * * * * * * * * * * * * * * * * * * *
*    These error processing routines are performed by other
*       routines within the program.  Generally, the purpose of
*       these routines is to move an error message for display
*       on the MENU screen.  These routines then perform the
*       routine to display the menu screen and issue a pseudo-
*       conversational return to the menu program.  Although
*       PERFORMS are used, the program eventually terminates
*       with the return command.
* * * * * * * * * * * * * * * * * * * * * * * * *
   910-UNEXPECTED-BMS-ERROR.
            MOVE LOW-VALUES TO MENUMAPO
            MOVE 'BMS ERROR-CALL MIS'  TO THE-MESSAGE
            MOVE 'VEND5910'                TO MESSAGE-NUMBER
            MOVE OUTPUT-MESSAGE TO MMESAGEO.
```

FIGURE 10.12.   Continued

```
920-UNEXPECTED-FILE-ERROR.
    IF   ILLOGIC PERFORM 940-VSAM-ERROR
    ELSE IF NOTOPEN PERFORM 944-NOTOPEN-ERROR
        ELSE
            MOVE LOW-VALUES TO MENUMAPO.
            MOVE 'VENDOR FILE ERROR-CALL MIS'  TO THE-MESSAGE
            MOVE 'VEND5920'             TO MESSAGE-NUMBER
            MOVE OUTPUT-MESSAGE TO MMESAGEO.
935-NOTFND-ERROR.
    MOVE LOW-VALUES TO MENUMAPO.
    MOVE 'RECORD KEY GREATER THAN END OF FILE D' TO THE-MESSAGE.
    MOVE 'VEND5935'             TO MESSAGE-NUMBER.
    MOVE OUTPUT-MESSAGE TO MMESAGEO.
940-VSAM-ERROR.
    MOVE LOW-VALUES TO MENUMAPO.
    MOVE 'FILE LOGIC ERROR-CALL MIS'  TO THE-MESSAGE.
    MOVE 'VEND5940'             TO MESSAGE-NUMBER.
    MOVE OUTPUT-MESSAGE TO MMESAGEO.
944-NOTOPEN-ERROR.
    MOVE LOW-VALUES TO MENUMAPO.
    MOVE 'VENDOR FILE CLOSED'  TO THE-MESSAGE.
    MOVE 'VEND5944'             TO MESSAGE-NUMBER.
    MOVE OUTPUT-MESSAGE TO MMESAGEO.
1000-PARAGRAPH-NOT-USED.
    GOBACK.
```

FIGURE 10.12. Continued

Chapter Summary

In this chapter, you were introduced to additional services provided by file control and BMS. In the first topic, you learned that VSAM files can be accessed by one or more alternate key fields. CICS programs can access files with alternate key fields using the normal file control commands. Alternate indexes are often used by CICS browsing programs.

The second topic described the commands and procedures necessary to access a file sequentially. With CICS, this is known as *browsing*. Several browsing commands are provided by CICS to allow programs to solve a variety of problems. A browse operation can be started anywhere in a file. Browsing can be started using a full key or a partial key. A RESETBR command can be used to change many of the options specified when the browse was initiated. A program accessing a VSAM file can process multiple logical sections of the file. This can be done with skip sequential processing. It is even possible to process multiple sections of a file concurrently. Files can be processed in ascending key sequence with the READNEXT command or in reverse order with the READPREV command.

The final topic described a BMS service that is often used with file-browsing programs. This service, which allows a screen to be constructed from multiple maps, is called *page building*. To use page building, the program can define maps with special screen-positioning options. Maps can be positioned in fixed locations on a screen or can be displayed relative to other maps. The SEND MAP command with the ACCUM option is used to request page building. Instead of sending the screens directly to the terminal, the ACCUM option causes BMS to accumulate the maps in storage. The SEND PAGE command is then used to transmit the screen image. The program can also use the HANDLE or IGNORE CONDITION to activate screen overflow processing logic. In this way, the program's page overflow routines can be performed when a screen becomes full. These overflow routines allow trailer maps to be displayed at the bottom of the screen. When used with the Terminal Paging feature described in chapter 9, page building can be used to display multiple screens.

Discussion Questions

1. Describe one technique where a field that normally contains nonunique values can be defined as a unique alternate index.
2. Which commands are used by a CICS program to access a file using an alternate index?
3. What process is needed to update alternate indexes when updating records in the base data set?
4. How would a generic browse be of benefit when accessing a file by an alternate index using a name field?
5. What happens when a full key GTEQ browse is started and the requested record is not on file?
6. What is the purpose of skip sequential processing? How is it accomplished?
7. What would cause the NOTFND condition to arise during a skip sequential operation?
8. What VSAM resource is maintained during a browse operation?
9. What is the limit to the number of records that can be processed during a browse operation?
10. What is the purpose of reinitializing the LENGTH argument when browsing files with variable-length records?
11. Which browse options can be reset with the RESETBR command?
12. During page building, if LINE=SAME has been specified for a map, where does BMS position the map if it will not fit on the same line as the previous map?
13. Which map specification is used to establish a left- or right-column reference?
14. If a map with the COLUMN=SAME and JUSTIFY=LEFT specifications is displayed, where does BMS position the map?
15. How does BMS determine the number of lines to be reserved for a trailer area?
16. What process is needed to signal to BMS that a trailer area is to be reserved?
17. Which byte of the field EIBRCODE contains the return code indicating that the OVERFLOW condition has occurred?

Review Exercises

1. Code the statements necessary to begin a browse operation at the first record of the department table in the system control file described in Appendix B.
2. Code the BMS map definition statements to define a trailer map. The map should be defined as 3 lines by 80 columns and will display at the bottom of the screen.
3. Code the BMS map definitions to allow a program to display a screen as shown below. Only a single map should be necessary to display this screen. Assume that no trailer maps will be defined in the mapset. The screen will be produced by a file-browsing program. For each record, the program will display the SSN on line 1 of the map. The remaining four lines will contain the name (2), address (3), city, state, zip (4), and telephone number (5). Line 6 will contain no fields. Code field definitions for this map. The program will move the city, state, and zip fields from the record to an area defined as shown below. That field will be moved to the field defined on line 4.

```
        05  LINE4.
            10  CITY PIC X(20).
            10  FILLER PIC X.
            10  STATE PIC XX.
            10  FILLER PIC X.
            10  ZIP-CODE PIC 9(9).
```

```
             1         2         3         4         5         6         7         8
    1234567890123456789012345678901234567890123456789012345678901234567890123456789 0
01^123456789                          ^123456789
02^XXXXXXXXXXXXXXXXXXXXXXXXXXX        ^XXXXXXXXXXXXXXXXXXXXXXXXXXX
03^XXXXXXXXXXXXXXXXXXXXXXXXXXX        ^XXXXXXXXXXXXXXXXXXXXXXXXXXX
04^XXXXXXXXXXXXXXXXXXXXXXXXXXXXXX     ^XXXXXXXXXXXXXXXXXXXXXXXXXXXXXX
05^XXXXXXXXXXXXXXXXXXXXXXXXXXX        ^XXXXXXXXXXXXXXXXXXXXXXXXXXX
06
07^123456789                          ^123456789
08^XXXXXXXXXXXXXXXXXXXXXXXXXXX        ^XXXXXXXXXXXXXXXXXXXXXXXXXXX
09^XXXXXXXXXXXXXXXXXXXXXXXXXXX        ^XXXXXXXXXXXXXXXXXXXXXXXXXXX
10^XXXXXXXXXXXXXXXXXXXXXXXXXXXXXX     ^XXXXXXXXXXXXXXXXXXXXXXXXXXXXXX
11^XXXXXXXXXXXXXXXXXXXXXXXXXXX        ^XXXXXXXXXXXXXXXXXXXXXXXXXXX
12
13^123456789                          ^123456789
14^XXXXXXXXXXXXXXXXXXXXXXXXXXX        ^XXXXXXXXXXXXXXXXXXXXXXXXXXX
15^XXXXXXXXXXXXXXXXXXXXXXXXXXX        ^XXXXXXXXXXXXXXXXXXXXXXXXXXX
16^XXXXXXXXXXXXXXXXXXXXXXXXXXXXXX     ^XXXXXXXXXXXXXXXXXXXXXXXXXXXXXX
17^XXXXXXXXXXXXXXXXXXXXXXXXXXX        ^XXXXXXXXXXXXXXXXXXXXXXXXXXX
18
19^123456789                          ^123456789
20^XXXXXXXXXXXXXXXXXXXXXXXXXXX        ^XXXXXXXXXXXXXXXXXXXXXXXXXXX
21^XXXXXXXXXXXXXXXXXXXXXXXXXXX        ^XXXXXXXXXXXXXXXXXXXXXXXXXXX
22^XXXXXXXXXXXXXXXXXXXXXXXXXXXXXX     ^XXXXXXXXXXXXXXXXXXXXXXXXXXXXXX
23^XXXXXXXXXXXXXXXXXXXXXXXXXXXXXX     ^XXXXXXXXXXXXXXXXXXXXXXXXXXXXXX
24
```

Lab Problems

LAB 1

Code the BMS MAP definition statements for the screen below. The program will display the screen using page building while browsing the personnel master file. The first three lines of the screen should be defined using a header map. There are no fields in the third header line. The trailer map should be defined to reserve two lines at the bottom of the screen. The trailer map will always be displayed at the bottom of the screen. The detail lines will be produced with a single map display for each detail record.

```
             1         2         3         4         5         6         7         8
    1234567890123456789012345678901234567890123456789012345678901234567890123456789 0
01^XXXXXXX                     ^PERSONNEL MASTER BROWSE (BY SSN)
02^----SSN----     ^------------NAME-----------^-----------ADDRESS-----------
03
04^999-99-9999     ^XXXXXXXXXXXXXXXXXXXXXXXXXXXXX^XXXXXXXXXXXXXXXXXXXXXXXXXXXXXXXX
05^999-99-9999     ^XXXXXXXXXXXXXXXXXXXXXXXXXXXXX^XXXXXXXXXXXXXXXXXXXXXXXXXXXXXXXX
06^999-99-9999     ^XXXXXXXXXXXXXXXXXXXXXXXXXXXXX^XXXXXXXXXXXXXXXXXXXXXXXXXXXXXXXX
07^999-99-9999     ^XXXXXXXXXXXXXXXXXXXXXXXXXXXXX^XXXXXXXXXXXXXXXXXXXXXXXXXXXXXXXX
            .
            .
            .
23
24^XXXXXXXXXXXXXXXXXXXXXXXXXXXXXXXXXXXXXXXXXXXXXXXXXXXXXXXXXXXXXXXXXXXXXXXXXXXXXXXXXX
```

LAB 2

Write a browse program to produce the display shown in Lab 1. Use two-pass pseudoconversational logic. The first-pass logic should be performed when the program first receives control from the menu program. The purpose of the first-pass logic is to display the screen using BMS page building. The record key of the first record to be displayed will be passed in the commarea.

Display the header map and as many detail lines as will fit on the screen. Use the overflow condition to determine when detail lines will no longer fit. After the overflow condition or ENDFILE occurs, display the trailer map. A message should be displayed in the trailer map.

Issue a pseudoconversational RETURN naming the browse transid and pass the SSN of the record that caused overflow.

The purpose of the second-pass logic is to provide transition back to the menu. Display the menu screen with the SSN that caused overflow. Issue a pseudoconversational RETURN naming the menu transid. Pass a suitable commarea to cause the second-pass logic of the menu to be performed in the next task.

LAB 3

Design a program similar to the Lab 2 assignment with the following differences:

Modify the second-pass logic to allow the operator to reinitiate the browse operation using the SSN passed in the commarea. After the browse is started, perform the same processing as the first-pass logic.

If the ENDFILE condition occurs in either the first-pass or second-pass browse logic, display the trailer map. Then perform the processing needed to cause the program to begin the browse at the first record in the file on the next entry to the program.

After viewing any screen, the operator will request a cancelation of the browse by pressing the CLEAR key. When the second-pass logic detects this request, provide transition back to the menu program as indicated in Lab 2.

LAB 4

Code the BMS MAP definition statements for the screen below. The program will display the screen using page building while browsing the System Control File. Terminal Paging will also be used to allow multiple pages to be displayed.

The first three lines of the screen should be defined using a header map. A page-number field is displayed on the first line. There are no fields in the third header line; it is used to provide a blank line between the header and the first detail line.

The trailer map should be defined to reserve two lines at the bottom of the screen. The trailer map will always be displayed at the bottom of the screen. The trailer map contains a field to allow the operator to enter paging commands. Initialize this field with the P/N command on all screens but the last. On the last screen initialize the field with the value "P/1." In either case the field should be set to "modified" by the program. All other fields (in all maps) should be defined as protected.

The detail lines will be produced with a single map displayed for each detail record. Each detail line will display information from the department table records in the system control file.

```
                    1         2         3         4         5         6
          1234567890123456789012345678901234567890123456789012345678901234567
01^XXXXXXX          ^PERSONNEL DEPARTMENT TABLE--PAGE^NN
02^CODE       ^A/I. DESCRIPTION
03
04^XXXX       ^X  ^XXXXXXXXXXXXXXXXXXXXXXXXXXXXX
05^XXXX       ^X  ^XXXXXXXXXXXXXXXXXXXXXXXXXXXXX
06^XXXX       ^X  ^XXXXXXXXXXXXXXXXXXXXXXXXXXXXX
07^XXXX       ^X  ^XXXXXXXXXXXXXXXXXXXXXXXXXXXXX
           .
           .
           .
24^P/N...^
```

LAB 5

DISPLAY DEPARTMENT RECORDS

Write a browse program to produce the display shown in Lab 4. Use two-pass pseudoconversational logic. The first-pass logic should be performed when the program first receives control from the menu program. You will have to modify the menu program to select this program. Use an unassigned PF key to do this. No data will have to be passed to the department display program. Start the browse operation at the first department table record in the System Control File.

The purpose of the first-pass logic is to display one or more screens using BMS page building and Terminal Paging.

Display the header map and as many detail lines as will fit on the screen. Use the overflow condition to determine when detail lines will no longer fit. When page overflow occurs, display the trailer map. Repeat this process until the end of the department table is reached or ENDFILE occurs. Complete the logical message with the SEND PAGE command.

Issue a pseudoconversational RETURN naming the browse transid.

The purpose of the second-pass logic is to provide transition back to the menu. Display the menu screen. Issue a pseudoconversational RETURN naming the menu transid. Pass a suitable commarea to cause the second-pass logic of the menu to be performed in the next task.

11 On-Line Help

As you study the topics in this chapter you will

1. See how to use the BUFFER option of the RECEIVE command to read the entire buffer contents of the 3270 terminal.
2. Understand the format of data received by the BUFFER option of the RECEIVE command.
3. Observe the use of the BMS SEND CONTROL command to perform control functions on the 3270 terminal.
4. Learn about some useful options of the SEND TEXT command.
5. Examine the design and logic of a general purpose HELP program.
6. See how to design logic in a transaction-processing program to provide linkage to a general help program.

In this chapter, you are going to learn how to provide on-line help screens for your transactions. On-line help screens are displays that contain messages or text that assist the operator in using the transaction. This chapter is going to show you how to design a general purpose help program. This help program will be called by a transaction-processing program whenever help is requested by an operator.

In the first part of the chapter, you are going to learn some of the commands that can be used by a general purpose help program. Then you will see one design technique that can be used to implement a general purpose on-line help program. After studying these topics, you should be able to design your own on-line help programs. You may even be able to develop some other programming strategies using the commands described in the chapter.

The Receive Buffer Option

In chapter 3, you learned how to use the RECEIVE command to "read" transaction input into working-storage. In the early chapters, this transaction input included the initial transaction message as well as other input requested by interactive programs. Then you learned how to use BMS to receive operator input from formatted screens. After learning BMS, we somewhat abandoned the RECEIVE command. Now it's time to consider another use for it.

The RECEIVE command has a rarely used option that can provide a useful function. This option is BUFFER. The BUFFER option causes CICS to read the entire buffer contents from the terminal. The format of the command is

```
EXEC CICS RECEIVE BUFFER
     INTO (data-area)
     LENGTH (data-area)
     END-EXEC
```

After the terminal buffer is read, the Execute Interface Program copies it into the working-storage named as the INTO argument. Of course, your working-storage area must be large enough to hold the buffer contents. The size of the input area will depend on the terminal model and the number of fields currently on the screen. For instance, if an 80-column-by-24-row screen is read, you will need a working-storage area of at least 1,920 characters to store the entire buffer. If the screen contains field attributes, you will need even more storage. Let's see why.

When the IBM 3270 buffer is read, each buffer position is transmitted, beginning at the first location on the screen. All characters, including nulls, are transmitted as they appear in the buffer. When a field attribute position is encountered, there will be *two* characters transmitted. The first of these two characters is the hexadecimal value for the "start-field" order. You may recall from chapter 5 that the start-field control code is *hex 1D*. The second character of the sequence is the actual attribute for the field. After the two-character sequence, each buffer position for that field is transmitted until the next attribute position is encountered. This process continues until the end of the buffer is reached. The current cursor position is also transmitted during a buffer-read operation. CICS stores this address in the field EIBCPOSN.

By now, you might be wondering how this RECEIVE BUFFER command could be used. One use is to allow a program to save the entire contents of a screen in order to display something else. A help program, for instance, might save an application screen prior to displaying one or more help screens. After the help screen or screens have been viewed by the operator, the help program could *restore* the original application screen from the saved area.

The SEND command is used to transmit a buffer image back to a terminal. Since a buffer image contains start-field orders and attributes, all fields will be reinstated with their original status. There is one exception. Terminals with *extended* attributes such as color and blinking do not transmit these attributes on the buffer read. Only the standard attributes are read, so any extended features will be lost when the screen is refreshed. Let's look at a short example of the process just described. Later in the chapter you will see a more complete illustration in the sample on-line help program. In the example below, a program at some point would issue the RECEIVE command with the BUFFER option. This would cause the screen buffer, including field definitions, to be read into the area "SCREEN-BUFFER." The actual buffer length would be stored in the field "BUFFER-LENGTH." This area could then be saved somewhere; perhaps in Temporary Storage. Later in the program (even in another task), the saved areas are used to *refresh* the screen using the SEND command.

```
05    BUFFER-LENGTH PIC S9999 COMP VALUE +4090.
05    SCREEN-BUFFER PIC X(4090).

      EXEC CICS RECEIVE BUFFER
           INTO (SCREEN-BUFFER)
           LENGTH (BUFFER-LENGTH)
           END-EXEC.
      .
      .
      .
      EXEC CICS SEND
           FROM (SCREEN-BUFFER)
           LENGTH (BUFFER-LENGTH)
           ERASE
           END-EXEC.
```

The BMS Send Control Command

In the preceding example, the SEND command was used to redisplay a saved screen image. There was one minor flaw in that example. When the screen was refreshed, the cursor would have been displayed in the corner of the screen. The SEND command, unfortunately, does not have an option to position the cursor. There is another command that does have this option. It is the BMS SEND CONTROL command. The format of this special BMS command is

```
EXEC CICS SEND CONTROL
      [FREEKB]
      [FRSET]
      [ALARM]
      [ERASE | ERASEAUP]
      [CURSOR[(data-value)]]
      END-EXEC
```

This command is used to send control codes to a terminal. You might recall that these options also appeared on the BMS SEND MAP command. With the SEND CONTROL command, however, no mapping is performed; only the control functions are transmitted to the terminal.

Let's see how this command could be used in our previous example to reposition the cursor to its original location. First the RECEIVE BUFFER command would be issued. The program would then move the cursor position (binary address) from the EIB to a save area. Later, the screen is redisplayed with the SEND command. Finally the SEND CONTROL command would reposition the cursor to its original location. Now we have completely refreshed the terminal back to its original state before the buffer-read command.

```
05    CURSOR-LOCATION PIC S9999 COMPUTATIONAL.
05    BUFFER-LENGTH   PIC S9999 COMP VALUE +4090.
05    SCREEN-BUFFER   PIC X(4090).


      EXEC CICS RECEIVE BUFFER
            INTO (SCREEN-BUFFER)
            LENGTH (BUFFER-LENGTH)
            END-EXEC.
      MOVE EIBCPOSN TO CURSOR-LOCATION.
            .
            .
      EXEC CICS SEND
            FROM (SCREEN-BUFFER)
            LENGTH (BUFFER-LENGTH)
            ERASE
            END-EXEC
      EXEC CICS SEND CONTROL
            CURSOR (CURSOR-LOCATION)
            END-EXEC
```

The commands just described were presented within the context of a help program. Later in the chapter you will see how a pseudoconversational help program is able to save an application screen, display a help screen, then reinstate an application to its starting point. But these commands are not just limited to the help program. Hopefully, as you gain more experience with CICS, you will be able to develop other program design strategies based upon these commands.

BMS Text Processing

In this topic we are going to examine the advanced options of the BMS SEND TEXT command. This command is used in the sample help program later in the chapter. After looking at the new options, we will study the text-processing capabilities of this useful command.

NEW SEND TEXT OPTIONS

The format of the SEND TEXT command is shown below. The advanced options appear at the bottom.

```
EXEC CICS SEND TEXT
     FROM (data-area)
     LENGTH (data-value)
     [CURSOR]
     [ERASE]
     [FREEKB]
     [ALARM]
     [ACCUM]
     [TERMINAL | PAGING]
     [JUSFIRST | JUSLAST |
      JUSTIFY (data-value)]
     [HEADER (data-area)]
     [TRAILER (data-area)]
     END-EXEC
```

The PAGING option specifies that the output screen is to be placed in Temporary Storage. One or more screens can be stored when using Terminal Paging. The screens will then be displayed in response to BMS Terminal Paging commands or PF key equivalents as described in chapter 9.

JUSFIRST specifies that the text is to be placed at the top of the screen. If a page has already been partially formatted with prior SEND TEXT commands, this option causes a new page to be started. If the HEADER option is also specified, the header data precedes the text.

JUSLAST positions the text at the bottom of the screen. If the TRAILER option is also specified, the trailer text will follow the data text. If additional text is formatted with another SEND TEXT command, it will start on a new screen.

The JUSTIFY option is used to specify the line of the page at which the text is to be positioned. The *data-value* argument is a numeric constant or COBOL field with a picture of S9999 and usage of COMPUTATIONAL (binary). The value must be in the range of 1 through 240. If a COBOL data name is used, this option can be used to dynamically specify JUSFIRST or JUSLAST. A value of -1 or -2 (respectively) will signify these options.

The HEADER and TRAILER options provide the capability to place header and trailer text on the screen. This text will accompany the data specified in the FROM option. Header text will be placed at the top of the screen and trailer text will be positioned at the bottom.

If several SEND TEXT ACCUM commands are used to format one or more screens, the HEADER and TRAILER options should be specified on each of these commands. These options will be ignored unless a page boundary occurs.

Header text will be placed at the top of each screen. Trailer text will be placed at the bottom of each screen, except the last one. To place the trailer text on the last screen, you must issue the SEND PAGE command with the TRAILER option. The format of this command is

```
EXEC CICS SEND PAGE TRAILER (data area) END-EXEC
```

The *data-area* specified in the HEADER and TRAILER options has a special format. This format is depicted in figure 11.1. Essentially, the header and trailer areas consist of a fixed-length (4-byte) prefix, followed by a variable-length text area. The length of the *text area* is specified as the first field

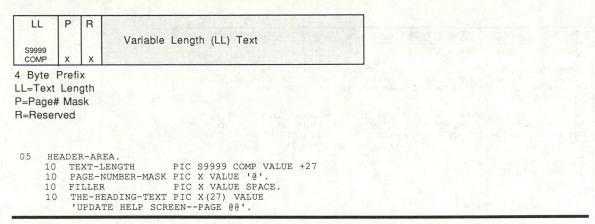

```
4 Byte Prefix
LL=Text Length
P=Page# Mask
R=Reserved


05   HEADER-AREA.
     10   TEXT-LENGTH        PIC S9999 COMP VALUE +27
     10   PAGE-NUMBER-MASK PIC X VALUE '@'.
     10   FILLER            PIC X VALUE SPACE.
     10   THE-HEADING-TEXT PIC X(27) VALUE
          'UPDATE HELP SCREEN--PAGE @@'.
```

FIGURE 11.1. Format of Header and Trailer Areas for SEND TEXT Command

in the prefix. This length field is an S9999 COMPUTATIONAL value. The third byte of the prefix is used to specify automatic page numbering during text building. The fourth byte is reserved for BMS.

One purpose of the header and trailer text is to provide automatic page numbering. These page numbers are computed by BMS during the page-building process. Page numbers begin at one and are incremented when each new page is started. These variable page numbers can be displayed anywhere within the header or trailer text. To do this a page number *mask* is stored in the third position of the header or trailer prefix. In the example, the "@" character is used as the mask. Actually, any nonblank character can be specified here, but generally a special character is used. When the header or trailer data is displayed, BMS will scan the variable-text area, looking for a page number "field" containing these mask characters. A single "field" with up to five (5) mask characters can be specified. BMS will replace the mask character field in the text with the automatic page number.

The "full function" BMS options just described, give you the capability to control the format of text-oriented screens. Now let's look at a standard feature of the SEND TEXT command that can also help to control the layout of your text screens.

You might recall from the early chapters that the SEND TEXT command was used to display multiple lines of text. In those early examples, this command was used to display text on a line-by-line basis. At that time I told you that each text line was preceded by a control character. I also said that this command works best when the display text is one-character shorter than the terminal width. For example, on an 80-column terminal, we displayed each line with 79 characters. The result was a nicely formatted screen. I must now admit that I misled you. Actually, we don't have to use that procedure, but the application at the time required this technique.

The truth is that the SEND TEXT command is not intended to be used on a line-by-line basis. In fact, the real power of this command is its capability to handle large blocks of text. A block of text can encompass a paragraph, a single screen, or even multiple screens. Furthermore, when these large blocks of data are transmitted, the real purpose of the command begins to surface.

TEXT PROCESSING

The primary purpose of the SEND TEXT command is to perform text processing. When blocks of text are transmitted with the SEND TEXT command, BMS splits the text into lines whose length is less than or equal to the terminal width. It also ensures that *words* are not split across a line boundary. If a word will not fit at the end of a line, BMS will insert enough spaces to force the word to the next line. If the text exceeds the screen boundary, BMS continues the text on another screen. If multiple

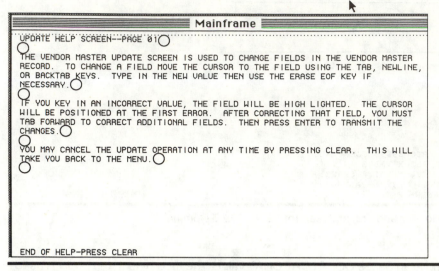

FIGURE 11.2. Sample Help Screen-Line-Feeds Circled

screens are built, each previous screen will be overwritten. You can use the PAGING option to prevent this from happening. If this option is included, the operator can use the Terminal Paging commands (or PF keys) to view each screen.

As indicated in the previous paragraph, BMS formats the text into lines that will fit on the size of the terminal running the program. This terminal width, taken from the TCT, is always used to determine where a line ending will occur. But BMS provides you with the capability to ''force'' a new line. You can do this by inserting the new-line character into your data stream. The new-line character is a value of hexadecimal 15 (X'15'). When this character is encountered, BMS will start formatting the next character on a new line. You can get the appearance of a paragraph by placing two (2) new-line characters together in the text. This process is depicted in figure 11.2. Notice how a ''paragraph break'' occurs at each point corresponding to the placement of double new-line characters (depicted by circles) in the text data.

Now we have another problem. Again IBM has used a hexadecimal character that is somewhat difficult for COBOL to deal with. But they have provided a solution. Recall the BMS attributes copybook? This copybook (DFHBMSCA) also contains a field with the new-line value. The field is DFHBMPNL. Just in case you are really trying to evade using that copybook, there's another way to get the hex value. Look at the field definition below. Actually, this coding would produce two bytes, each containing a hex 15. My hexadecimal-to-decimal calculator helped to solve this problem. A similar technique could be used to define four (4) hex-15 characters. I prefer this method to using the IBM copybook.

```
05   TWO-HEX-15S.
     10   FILLER PIC S9999 COMP VALUE +5397.
```

DEFINING TEXT

Before moving on to the help program topic, I want to discuss a couple of design techniques for producing the text blocks to be used with the SEND TEXT command. The easiest way is to simply define a series of constants in working-storage. An example of this is depicted in figure 11.3. This coding was used to ''define'' the help screen shown in the last figure. Notice how several COBOL ''filler'' areas were used to construct a single continuous stream of characters. Paragraphs were formed

```
01  DISPLAY-TEXT-4-SCREEN-VEN3.
    05  TWO-HEX15S-1  PIC S9999 COMP VALUE +5397.
    05  FILLER PIC X(40) VALUE
            'THE VENDOR MASTER UPDATE SCREEN IS USED '.
    05  FILLER PIC X(40) VALUE
            'TO CHANGE FIELDS IN THE VENDOR MASTER RE'.
    05  FILLER PIC X(40) VALUE
            'CORD.  TO CHANGE A FIELD MOVE THE CURSOR'.
    05  FILLER PIC X(40) VALUE
            ' TO THE FIELD USING THE TAB, NEWLINE, OR'.
    05  FILLER PIC X(40) VALUE
            ' BACKTAB KEYS.  TYPE IN THE NEW VALUE TH'.
    05  FILLER PIC X(40) VALUE
            'EN USE THE ERASE EOF KEY IF NECESSARY.  '.
    05  TWO-HEX15S-2  PIC S9999 COMP VALUE +5397.
    05  FILLER PIC X(40) VALUE
            'IF YOU KEY IN AN INCORRECT VALUE, THE FI'.
    05  FILLER PIC X(40) VALUE
            'ELD WILL BE HIGH LIGHTED.  THE CURSOR WI'.
    05  FILLER PIC X(40) VALUE
            'LL BE POSITIONED AT THE FIRST ERROR.  AF'.
    05  FILLER PIC X(40) VALUE
            'TER CORRECTING THAT FIELD, YOU MUST TAB '.
    05  FILLER PIC X(40) VALUE
            'FORWARD TO CORRECT ADDITIONAL FIELDS.  T'.
    05  FILLER PIC X(40) VALUE
            'HEN PRESS ENTER TO TRANSMIT THE CHANGES.'.
    05  TWO-HEX15S-3  PIC S9999 COMP VALUE +5397.
    05  FILLER PIC X(40) VALUE
            'YOU MAY CANCEL THE UPDATE OPERATION AT A'.
    05  FILLER PIC X(40) VALUE
            'NY TIME BY PRESSING CLEAR.  THIS WILL TA'.
    05  FILLER PIC X(40) VALUE
            'KE YOU BACK TO THE MENU.               '.
    05  TWO-HEX15S-3  PIC S9999 COMP VALUE +5397.
    05  FILLER PIC X(40) VALUE
                                                    '.

01  HEADERS-TRAILERS.
    05  HEADER-AREA.
        10  TEXT-LENGTH PIC S9999 COMP VALUE +27.
        10  PAGE-NUMBER-MASK PIC X     VALUE '@'.
        10  FILLER          PIC X     VALUE ' '.
        10  THE-HEADING-TEXT PIC X(27) VALUE
                        'UPDATE HELP SCREEN--PAGE @@'.
    05  TRAILER-AREA.
        10  TEXT-LENGTH PIC S9999 COMP VALUE +25.
        10  FILLER          PIC X     VALUE ' '.
        10  FILLER          PIC X     VALUE ' '.
        10  THE-HEADING-TEXT PIC X(27) VALUE
                        'END OF HELP-PRESS CLEAR'.
    EXEC CICS SEND TEXT
        FROM (DISPLAY-TEXT-4-SCREEN-VEN3)
        LENGTH (640)
        HEADER (HEADER-AREA)
        ERASE
        FREEKB
        END-EXEC.
    EXEC CICS SEND PAGE
        TRAILER (TRAILER-AREA)
        END-EXEC.
```

FIGURE 11.3. Programming to produce Sample Help Screen

by placing two new-line characters at the appropriate places in the text. The header and trailer blocks were defined in separate storage. The figure also depicts the Procedure Division statements necessary to display the help screen.

Another technique is to store the text somewhere outside of the working-storage. A help file, for instance, could be used to store help text used by an application or an entire system. These text records could then be read into a working area for use with the SEND TEXT command. Multiple-text screens could even be processed with the file-browsing commands.

You could even develop programs to create and update these text records. For example, a program to create a help screen might perform the following steps:

1. Format a screen (using BMS mapping) to allow the operator to enter a help record key and any header or trailer text.
2. Receive that information.
3. Format a "blank" screen to allow free-form text to be entered. Some special character such as " | " could be used to denote a new-line character.
4. Use the RECEIVE command with the BUFFER option to read that text. Examine the text, replacing each new-line symbol with a hex 15.
5. Store the header, trailer, and text information in a random access file for later use.

I don't have an example of that program. I can only offer these suggestions for you to consider if you want to design such a program. I'm sure that someone will take the challenge and even improve on this basic design just offered. For now, let's move on to the help program topic.

On-Line Help

An important measure of the success of an on-line system is its usability. Good screen design techniques will go a long way to help operators use an application. A few screen messages can also help to improve the usability of a system. In most cases, these measures alone will provide all the assistance necessary to use an application. However, there are always a few transactions where additional help may be needed.

One way to provide additional help is to develop on-line help screens. These help screens may be as simple as a few lines of text explaining how to use a transaction. Some companies have even gone as far as developing field-sensitive help screens. With this design an operator can move the cursor to a field on a transaction screen, then press a help key (usually a PF key). The system will then respond by displaying a help screen for that data entry field.

There are different design techniques for providing help screens for an application. A simple way is to develop one or more transaction-specific help programs and provide access to them with a menu selection. The menu program would then XCTL to each help program in the same way it does for other transaction-processing programs.

Another technique is to design one or more help routines within each transaction-processing program. These transaction-related help routines could then be performed by the entry analysis logic. This technique would also be fairly simple to implement.

Still another technique that is sometimes used is to develop a single generic help program. With this design, the help program would be "called" by one or more transaction-processing programs when the operator requested help. The help program would then display the appropriate help screen(s) for the operator. Afterwards, it would provide a transition back to the original transaction-processing program.

This is the technique that we are going to describe in this chapter. In the paragraphs that follow you will see one method of designing a generic help program. First, you will see how to provide the "linkage" from a transaction-processing program to the help program. This linkage involves some coding in a transaction-processing program to "call" the help program. After discussing the program logic needed to invoke the help program, we will examine the design of the sample help program.

HELP REQUEST LOGIC

As mentioned above, some logic will be necessary for a transaction-processing program to provide a linkage to the help program. I'm going to use the sample update program to illustrate this help

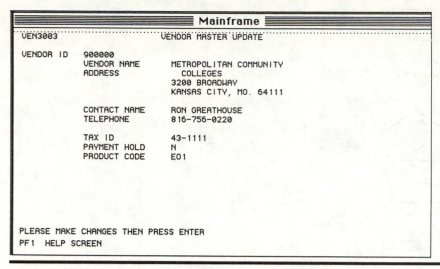

```
╔════════════════════ Mainframe ════════════════════╗
  VEN3003                  VENDOR MASTER UPDATE

  VENDOR ID   900000
              VENDOR NAME     METROPOLITAN COMMUNITY
              ADDRESS            COLLEGES
                              3200 BROADWAY
                              KANSAS CITY, MO. 64111

              CONTACT NAME    RON GREATHOUSE
              TELEPHONE       816-756-0220

              TAX ID          43-1111
              PAYMENT HOLD    N
              PRODUCT CODE    E01




  PLEASE MAKE CHANGES THEN PRESS ENTER
  PF1  HELP SCREEN
```

FIGURE 11.4.   Update Screen with HELP menu prompt

request logic. Let's review the processing logic of that update program. You will recall that the two-pass pseudoconversational logic was used by the update program. In the first pass, the program displayed the update screen. It then issued a RETURN command with the transid option and passed a commarea containing the record key. At this point the operator would be able to change the un-protected fields. A sample update screen is illustrated in figure 11.4.

Assume now that we have provided a help screen for the update transaction. Notice that a menu prompt has been placed at the bottom of the update screen. Of course, it would require a BMS coding change to display this prompt. A simple display field would be sufficient here. Let's say that the operator makes a few data entry changes but then decides to press the "help key." This attention key would cause CICS to start the update program again. This time, the second-pass logic of the update program would be executed. Recall that the second-pass logic will validate the input and update the record. But since our operator has requested help, we don't want the normal second-pass logic to be performed. Instead, we need the update program to provide linkage to the help program. To do that we need to modify the second-pass logic.

Please refer to figure 11.5. This diagram illustrates the logic necessary to pass control to our sample help program. You will notice that the first-pass logic has not changed in this program. There is a minor difference in the second-pass logic. It occurs at the very start of this routine, prior to the RECEIVE MAP command. This updated program simply determines if the operator has pressed the help key (PF1). If so, the program issues an XCTL to the generic help program, passing a commarea. The coding for this design might appear as follows:

```
200-SCREEN-PROCESSING-LOGIC.
       * * * * * * * * * * * * * * * * * * * * * * * * * * * * * *
       * * * * * * * * * * * * * * * * * * * * * * * * * * * * * *
       IF EIBAID EQUAL DFHPF1
           EXEC CICS XCTL PROGRAM ('VEND009')
                 COMMAREA (DFHCOMMAREA)
                 LENGTH (EIBCALEN)
                 END-EXEC.
           EXEC CICS RECEIVE MAP ('DISPMAP')
                 MAPSET ('VENDSET')
                 RESP      (COMMAND-STATUS-CODE)
                 NOHANDLE
                 END-EXEC.
```

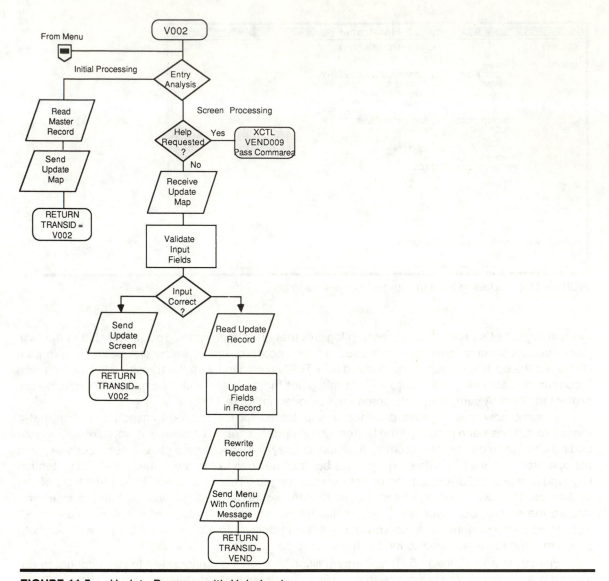

FIGURE 11.5. Update Program with Help Logic

For our sample update program the commarea passed to the help program is the original commarea sent to the second-pass logic. The help program will save the commarea while the help screen(s) are being displayed. When help is complete, the help program will redisplay the update screen. It will then issue a pseudoconversational return naming the update transid (V002) and passing back the original commarea. The effect of this is that the operator will be able to resume the update transaction exactly where it was interrupted when help was requested.

HELP PROGRAM LOGIC

The sample help program is designed to be a generic program to be "called" by one or more application programs when help is requested by the operator. The logic of the help program is depicted in figure 11.6. The coding for this program is shown in figure 11.7. This help program is implemented using the two-pass pseudoconversational technique.

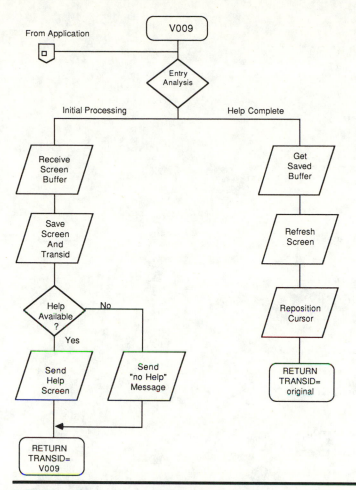

FIGURE 11.6. Sample Help Program Logic

The entry analysis logic will determine which pass of the program is being executed. The transaction code (from EIBTRNID) is used to do this. If the transaction code is not its own (V009), the first-pass logic will be performed.

The purpose of the first-pass or initial entry logic is twofold. First, it must save status information about the "calling" transaction. This information will be used later to reinstate the calling transaction back to its original status at the time help was requested. To accomplish this, three things must be saved. They are

1. the screen image including cursor position
2. the transaction code
3. the commarea

The screen image is read using the RECEIVE BUFFER command described earlier in the chapter. The cursor address is taken from the field EIBCPOSN. The transaction code is taken from the field EIBTRNID. The commarea can be accessed by using the field DFHCOMMAREA.

All of this information will be used in the second-pass logic to reinstate the original transaction. The help program therefore needs some way to get this information to the second-pass logic. Passing the commarea is a simple matter. It is passed using the pseudoconversational RETURN command, naming DFHCOMMAREA as the beginning address and EIBCALEN as the length argument.

```
       IDENTIFICATION DIVISION.
       PROGRAM-ID. VEND009.
       AUTHOR.   BOB LOWE.
     * * * * * * * * * * * * * * * * * * * * * * * * * * * * * *
     *    * * * * Method Of Operation * * * * * *
     *  Entry Analysis selects:
     *     Initial Processing
     *        Read Screen Buffer
     *        Save Screen Buffer in TS
     *        Send Help Screen with SEND TEXT
     *        Return naming next transid of help program
     *     Help Complete processing
     *        Read Screen image from TS
     *        Refresh Screen image
     *        Return to CICS with original Transid and Commarea
     * * * * * * * * * * * * * * * * * * * * * * * * * * * * * * *
       ENVIRONMENT DIVISION.                                    STP00040
       DATA DIVISION.                                           STP00050
       WORKING-STORAGE SECTION.
       01  DISPLAY-TEXT-4-SCREEN VEN3.
           05  TWO-HEX15S-1  PIC S9999 COMP VALUE +5397.
           05  FILLER PIC X(40) VALUE
                   'THE VENDOR MASTER UPDATE SCREEN IS USED '.
           05  FILLER PIC X(40) VALUE
                   'TO CHANGE FIELDS IN THE VENDOR MASTER RE'.
           05  FILLER PIC X(40) VALUE
                   'CORD.  TO CHANGE A FIELD MOVE THE CURSOR'.
           05  FILLER PIC X(40) VALUE
                   ' TO THE FIELD USING THE TAB, NEWLINE, OR'.
           05  FILLER PIC X(40) VALUE
                   ' BACKTAB KEYS.  TYPE IN THE NEW VALUE TH'.
           05  FILLER PIC X(40) VALUE
                   'EN USE THE ERASE EOF KEY IF NECESSARY.  '.
           05  TWO-HEX15S-2  PIC S9999 COMP VALUE +5397.
           05  FILLER PIC X(40) VALUE
                   'IF YOU KEY IN AN INCORRECT VALUE, THE FI'.
           05  FILLER PIC X(40) VALUE
                   'ELD WILL BE HIGH LIGHTED.  THE CURSOR WI'.
           05  FILLER PIC X(40) VALUE
                   'LL BE POSITIONED AT THE FIRST ERROR.  AF'.
           05  FILLER PIC X(40) VALUE
                   'TER CORRECTING THAT FIELD, YOU MUST TAB '.
           05  FILLER PIC X(40) VALUE
                   'FORWARD TO CORRECT ADDITIONAL FIELDS.  T'.
           05  FILLER PIC X(40) VALUE
                   'HEN PRESS ENTER TO TRANSMIT THE CHANGES.'.
           05  TWO-HEX15S-3  PIC S9999 COMP VALUE +5397.
           05  FILLER PIC X(40) VALUE
                   'YOU MAY CANCEL THE UPDATE OPERATION AT A'.
           05  FILLER PIC X(40) VALUE
                   'NY TIME BY PRESSING CLEAR.  THIS WILL TA'.
           05  FILLER PIC X(40) VALUE
                   'KE YOU BACK TO THE MENU.               '.
           05  TWO-HEX15S-3  PIC S9999 COMP VALUE +5397.
           05  FILLER PIC X(40) VALUE
                   '                                       '.
       01  HEADERS-TRAILERS.
           05  HEADER-AREA.
               10  TEXT-LENGTH PIC S9999 COMP VALUE +27.
               10  PAGE-NUMBER-MASK PIC X       VALUE '@'.
               10  FILLER          PIC X        VALUE ' '.
               10  THE-HEADING-TEXT PIC X(27) VALUE
                             'UPDATE HELP SCREEN--PAGE @@'.
           05  TRAILER-AREA.
               10  TEXT-LENGTH PIC S9999 COMP VALUE +25.
               10  FILLER          PIC X        VALUE ' '.
               10  FILLER          PIC X        VALUE ' '.
               10  THE-HEADING-TEXT PIC X(27) VALUE
                             'END OF HELP-PRESS CLEAR'.
       01  HELP-CONTROL-AREA.
           05  THE-CURSOR-ADDRESS     PIC S9999 COMP.
           05  THE-CALLING-TRANSID    PIC XXXX.
           05  INPUT-BUFFER.
               10  SCREEN-ID-STRT-FLD-ATT PIC XX.
               10  SCREEN-ID              PIC XXXX.
               10  REMAINDER-OF-BUFFER    PIC X(4084) VALUE SPACES.
```

FIGURE 11.7.   Sample On-Line Help program

```
* * * * * * * * * * * * * * * * * * * * * * * * * *
*     The Temporary-Storage queue used to save the screen
*         information is named "HELPterm" where term is
*         the terminal identification of the terminal running
*         the task.  The queue identification is 'built' in
*         a field below.
* * * * * * * * * * * * * * * * * * * * * * * * * *
 01   MISC-AREAS.
      05   HELPNAME.
           10  FILLER             PIC XXXX VALUE 'HELP'.
           10  HELP-TERMINAL      PIC XXXX.
      05   TS-QUEUE-LENGTH        PIC S9999 COMP VALUE +4096.
      05   BUFFER-MAXIMUM         PIC S9999 COMP VALUE +4090.
      05   NOHELP-MESSAGE         PIC X(50) VALUE
           'NO HELP SCREEN AVAILABLE-PLEASE CLEAR TO RESUME '
 LINKAGE SECTION.
 01  DFHCOMMAREA                  PIC X.
 PROCEDURE DIVISION.                                      STP00840
* * * * * * * * * * * * * * * * * * * * * * * * * *
*     ENTRY-ANALYSIS-- If the Transaction code that started
*         the program is V009 (Transid of the HELP Program)
*         the help complete logic is performed.  If the transid
*         is not V009 the initial processing logic is performed.
*         The initial processing logic concludes by doing a
*         RETURN with a transid of V#05.
* * * * * * * * * * * * * * * * * * * * * * * * * *
* * * * * * * * * * * * * * * * * * * * * * * * * *
* * * * * * * * * * * * * * * * * * * * * * * * * *
      IF   EIBTRNID NOT EQUAL 'V009'
           PERFORM 100-INITIAL-PROCESSING
              THRU 100-INITIAL-PROCESSING-EXIT
* * * * * * * * * * * * * * * * * * * * * * * * * *
*     After the help screen is displayed, the program does a
*         pseudo-conversational return, passing on the original
*         commarea.  After the operator has viewed the help screen
*         an AID key such as clear will be pressed.  This program
*         will then be started by CICS.
* * * * * * * * * * * * * * * * * * * * * * * * * *
           EXEC CICS RETURN
                TRANSID ('V009')
                COMMAREA (DFHCOMMAREA)
                LENGTH (EIBCALEN)
           END-EXEC
      ELSE
* * * * * * * * * * * * * * * * * * * * * * * * * *
*     If the transid is V009 then the help complete logic is
*         performed.  The help complete logic will re-display
*         the original application screen then issue a pseudo
*         conversational RETURN to the transid specified in the
*         original commarea.  The commarea originally received
*         by the help program will be passed back to the next
*         transaction.  This process should serve to put the
*         terminal back to the same logical status as when the
*         operator requested the help function.
* * * * * * * * * * * * * * * * * * * * * * * * * *
           PERFORM 200-HELP-COMPLETE
           EXEC CICS RETURN
                TRANSID (THE-CALLING-TRANSID)
                COMMAREA (DFHCOMMAREA)
                LENGTH (EIBCALEN)
           END-EXEC.
      EJECT
 100-INITIAL-PROCESSING.
* * * * * * * * * * * * * * * * * * * * * * * * * *
*     This routine is entered when the help program has been
*         entered from an application program.  The purpose of
*         this routine is to save the application screen contents
*         in temporary storage, then display the help screen.
*     The terminal identification is moved to working storage
*     The Temporary Storage queue name will be "HELPterm"
*         where term is the terminal identification of the
*         terminal running this transaction.
* * * * * * * * * * * * * * * * * * * * * * * * * *
      MOVE EIBTRMID   TO HELP-TERMINAL.
      MOVE EIBTRNID   TO THE-CALLING-TRANSID.
```

FIGURE 11.7.   Continued

```
* * * * * * * * * * * * * * * * * * * * * * * * *
*    The terminal screen is read using the buffer option. This
*        option caused all buffer positions from the screen to
*        be transmitted to the program.  For each 3270 field
*        attribute, the terminal transmits a one byte field
*        start character (Hex 1D) followed by the attribute
*        code.  Extended attribute information is not
*        transmitted, so these attributes will be lost when
*        the screen is ultimately re-displayed.
* * * * * * * * * * * * * * * * * * * * * * * * *
     EXEC CICS RECEIVE
          INTO (INPUT-BUFFER)
          LENGTH (BUFFER-MAXIMUM)
          BUFFER
          NOHANDLE
     END-EXEC.
* * * * * * * * * * * * * * * * * * * * * * * * *
*    The Temp storage record will contain the screen buffer
*        plus the cursor address (two bytes).  The record
*        length is computed as the actual screen buffer length
*        received plus 2.
* * * * * * * * * * * * * * * * * * * * * * * * *
     ADD +6, BUFFER-MAXIMUM GIVING TS-QUEUE-LENGTH.
     MOVE EIBCPOSN TO THE-CURSOR-ADDRESS.
* * * * * * * * * * * * * * * * * * * * * * * * *
*    A Temporary Storage DELETEQ command insures that the
*        screen image is saved in item 1.
*    The screen buffer and cursor address are saved
* * * * * * * * * * * * * * * * * * * * * * * * *
     EXEC CICS DELETEQ TS
          QUEUE (HELPNAME)
          NOHANDLE
     END-EXEC.
     EXEC CICS WRITEQ TS
          QUEUE (HELPNAME)
          FROM (HELP-CONTROL-AREA)
          LENGTH (TS-QUEUE-LENGTH)
          NOHANDLE
     END-EXEC.

* * * * * * * * * * * * * * * * * * * * * * * * *
*    The first FOUR (4) characters of the screen identification
*        code are used to DETERMINE WHICH HELP SCREEN IS
*        TO BE DISPLAYED.  IF THERE IS NO HELP SCREEN FOR THE
*        REQUESTING TRANSACTION, A MESSAGE WILL BE DISPLAYED.
* * * * * * * * * * * * * * * * * * * * * * * * *
     IF SCREEN-ID EQUAL 'VEN3'
          PERFORM 150-HELP-ROUTINE-FOR-VEN3
          GO TO 100-INITIAL-PROCESSING-EXIT.
     EXEC CICS SEND
          FROM (NOHELP-MESSAGE)
          LENGTH (50)
          ERASE
          END-EXEC.
100-INITIAL-PROCESSING-EXIT.
     EXIT.
150-HELP-ROUTINE-FOR-VEN3.
     EXEC CICS SEND TEXT
          FROM (DISPLAY-TEXT-4-SCREEN-VEN3)
          LENGTH (640)
          HEADER (HEADER-AREA)
          ERASE
          FREEKB
          END-EXEC.
     EXEC CICS SEND PAGE
          TRAILER (TRAILER-AREA)
          END-EXEC.
200-HELP-COMPLETE.
* * * * * * * * * * * * * * * * * * * * * * * * *
*    This routine is entered when the help program has been
*        entered after the help screen has been viewed.  The
*        purpose of this routine is to 'restore' the terminal
*        logically back to the same status as before help
*        was requested.  This involves re-displaying the
*        application screen and issuing a pseudo-conversational
*        return to the original transid, passing the original
*        commarea.
```

FIGURE 11.7. Continued

```
*  *  *  *  *  *  *  *  *  *  *  *  *  *  *  *  *  *  *  *
*    The Temporary Storage queue name is "HELPterm" where
*       TERM is the terminal id from the EIB.
*    The information is read from Temp Storage back to the
*       Working-Storage of this program.
*    The Temporary Storage Queue is then deleted
*  *  *  *  *  *  *  *  *  *  *  *  *  *  *  *  *  *  *  *
     MOVE EIBTRMID    TO HELP-TERMINAL.
     EXEC CICS READQ TS
          QUEUE (HELPNAME)
          INTO (HELP-CONTROL-AREA)
          LENGTH (TS-QUEUE-LENGTH)
          ITEM (1)
          NOHANDLE
     END-EXEC.
     EXEC CICS DELETEQ TS
          QUEUE (HELPNAME)
          NOHANDLE
     END-EXEC.
*  *  *  *  *  *  *  *  *  *  *  *  *  *  *  *  *  *  *  *
*    The SEND command will re-display the application screen
*       but there is no CURSOR option for the send command.
*    The SEND CONTROL command positions the cursor to the
*       original position.  After the screen is displayed
*       the calling paragraph at the top of the program will
*       issue the pseudo-conversational return back to the
*       original transid passing back the original commarea.
*  *  *  *  *  *  *  *  *  *  *  *  *  *  *  *  *  *  *  *
     SUBTRACT +6  FROM TS-QUEUE-LENGTH GIVING BUFFER-MAXIMUM.
     EXEC CICS SEND
          FROM (INPUT-BUFFER)
          LENGTH (BUFFER-MAXIMUM)
          ERASE
     END-EXEC.
     EXEC CICS SEND CONTROL
          CURSOR (THE-CURSOR-ADDRESS)
          ALARM
     END-EXEC.
900-PARAGRAPH-NOT-EXECUTED.
     GOBACK.
```

FIGURE 11.7. Continued

The screen buffer, cursor address, and transaction code will be saved in Temporary Storage. The Temporary Storage WRITEQ command saves this information. The program uses a queue name of "HELPterm," where "term" is the terminal identification code taken from the field EIBTRMID.

After saving the screen image and transaction code, the first-pass logic will perform the second function. It will display a help screen for the requesting transaction code. In our sample program, the SEND TEXT command is used to display the help screen. The text is defined in working-storage as a series of constants.

By now, you have probably been wondering how the help program determines which help screen to display. If this is truly a generic help program, it must be prepared to display help for more than one transaction. One technique would be to use the calling transaction code to determine which help screen to display. This would be a perfectly valid method. In this case, the help program logic would be "transaction sensitive."

Let's examine another design technique, whereby the help program logic is "screen sensitive." This is the technique used by our sample help program. To be screen-sensitive, the help program must be able to locate some value that identifies the screen for which help is being requested. We have such a value on our sample update screen and the other screens used in this text. It is the screen identification code. You will recall that this screen identification code has been consistently placed in the upper left corner of the screen. This is an ideal position, since the help program can easily locate this data.

The help program will extract the screen identification code from the "buffer contents" read earlier with the RECEIVE BUFFER command. Specifically, the screen code should be stored in positions 3 through 8 of the input area. Positions 1 and 2 would contain the codes for the start-field order and attribute for the screen code field. To get the first four (4) characters of the screen code, the sample help program defines fields in the input buffer as follows:

```
05   INPUT-BUFFER.
     10   SCREEN-ID-STRT-FLD-ATT PIC XX.
     10   SCREEN-ID PIC XXXX.
```

By using the field "SCREEN-ID," the help program can determine which help screen to display. If a help screen has not been "defined" for the calling transaction, the help program will display the message, "HELP NOT AVAILABLE." After the HELP screen or error message is displayed on the terminal, the help program issues a pseudoconversational RETURN command naming its own transaction code in the transid option. The original commarea passed from the calling transaction is passed to the next task.

The second-pass (help complete) logic is started when the operator clears the help screen (or no-help message). The purpose of the second-pass logic is to provide transition back to the calling transaction. The program must now "reset" the terminal to the same status as before the operator requested help. This involves refreshing the transaction screen and performing a pseudoconversational RETURN with the original transaction code and commarea.

The help complete routine first retrieves the saved screen buffer and transaction code from Temporary Storage. The queue name is "HELPterm" where "term" is the terminal identification where the program is running. Once all of the information is in the working-storage of the help program, the Temporary Storage queue is deleted.

To refresh the original screen, the program issues the terminal control SEND command with the FROM option specifying the working-storage area that contains the original buffer image. Since this buffer image contains start-field orders, attributes, and display characters, the transaction screen is formatted as it was when the operator requested help, except for one thing, the cursor is in the upper left corner of the screen. The BMS SEND CONTROL command is used to reposition the cursor.

The final action of the help complete routine is to issue a pseudoconversational RETURN using the transid of the original transaction code. The original commarea is also passed to this transaction. The transition back to the calling transaction is now complete. The terminal is in the same "status" as before help was requested.

Chapter Summary

This chapter described some commands and techniques that can be used to develop on-line help programs. The commands are, however, not limited to just the help program. First, the BUFFER option of the RECEIVE command was described. With this command, a program can read the entire contents of a terminal. A program might do this in order to display another screen. The screen image can be restored later with the SEND command.

The BMS SEND CONTROL command was also described. With this command, a program can send control codes to the terminal. These control codes can be used to perform such functions as clearing the screen, positioning the cursor, and other functions similar to the SEND MAP command.

The chapter also described the advanced options and functions of the SEND TEXT command. This powerful command can be used to send large blocks of text to a terminal. BMS will split the text into lines, taking special care not to split a word between two lines.

Finally, a sample help program was described. This program was very basic but should provide you with the essential logic and commands necessary to design your own on-line help programs.

Discussion Questions

1. The BUFFER option of the RECEIVE command can be used to read the entire 3270 screen buffer into working-storage. Where is the address of the cursor stored when this command is executed?
2. When the RECEIVE BUFFER command is used, what is transmitted when a field attribute is encountered?
3. How do the options on the SEND CONTROL command compare with those on the SEND MAP command?
4. What features of the SEND TEXT command make it convenient to use on terminals of varying widths?
5. How can you force a new line when formatting a screen with the SEND TEXT command?
6. What are some of the advantages of providing on-line help screens?

Review Exercises

1. Write a SEND CONTROL command to clear the screen, unlock the keyboard, and sound the alarm.
2. Show the Data Division statements to define a header block with the message below.

    `'INQUIRY HELP SCREEN-PAGE NUMBER#####'`

Lab Problems

LAB 1

TRANSACTION CODE XY07 (PROGRAM XY00007)
ON-LINE HELP PROGRAM

Design, code, and test a pseudoconversational help program.

1. Develop the first-pass logic to perform the following functions:

    Read the current screen contents. Save the calling transaction code, the buffer image and the cursor address in a Temporary Storage queue. The queue name should be a concatenation of the literal "HELP" and the terminal identification.

    Send a help screen consisting of a few lines of text to include one or two paragraphs. Define a header block for this text. Define the text and header in working-storage.

    Issue a pseudoconversational RETURN, naming the transaction code for the help program. Pass the original commarea to the next task.
2. Develop the second-pass logic to perform the following functions:

    Read the Temporary Storage record containing the cursor address, screen image, and transaction code.

    Redisplay the transaction screen, including positioning the cursor position at its original location.

    Issue a pseudoconversational RETURN to the original calling transaction code. Pass the commarea back to that task.

LAB 2

Write the same program as indicated above, with the following exception:

Use the calling transaction code to randomly read a help record from the System Control File. The record layout of the help record is described in Appendix B.

12

Debugging with EDF

As you follow the illustrations and examples in this chapter you will

1. Recognize the importance of adequate testing for CICS/VS programs.
2. Learn how to invoke the Execution Diagnostic Facility to checkout command-level programs.
3. Determine when EDF normally intercepts the execution of a CICS/VS task to display the status of the program.
4. Observe the use of EDF menus and Program Function Keys to request special actions during the debugging session.
5. See how to suppress displays during an EDF session to speed up the testing process.
6. Identify the conditions that can stop the user transaction during a suppress-display operation.
7. Learn how to modify the commands and working-storage dynamically during the execution of a task.
8. Examine the process of locating the failing statement in a COBOL program after a Program Check Interruption occurs in a task.
9. Follow the steps to locate any field in the working-storage section for viewing or modification with the EDF storage display function.
10. Develop a better awareness of the layout of the COBOL object module and find out how to locate the module with EDF.
11. See how a knowledge of the COBOL object module can increase the usefulness of EDF in special debugging applications.

Adequate testing is vital to the successful operation of any programming system. Information is the lifeblood of a company and the central element of good decisions. Program errors with on-line systems can cause havoc with a company. Many times departments and sometimes entire corporations come to rely on the computer system being on-line. When the computer is ''down,'' the operation of an entire company can become crippled. The repair of a corrupted company data base caused by a program error can cause delays even more serious than a power or equipment failure. Managers have recognized the need for timely and correct information in the hands of people making decisions. But incorrect information caused by an error in a program can cause wrong decisions to be made, generally at some cost to the company. Program testing is an important part of the program development cycle.

CICS/VS provides application services programs to assist you in testing application programs written using the Command-Level Interface. The Execution Diagnostic Facility (EDF) enables you to carry out comprehensive on-line tests of application programs. In many cases, temporary modifications to the program can be carried out without recompiling the source program. This provides the capability to uncover more than one error during a single test session. By reducing the number of compilations, the application development process can be shortened. The ease of use features of EDF invites more thorough testing, which in turn results in systems with fewer errors, a goal that we all strive to accomplish.

Starting EDF

The Execution Diagnostic Facility is an on-line testing tool. With it, the test results can be viewed at the terminal. EDF can run either on the same terminal as the transaction requiring checkout or on a different terminal. To run EDF on the same terminal requiring checkout, clear the screen, then type the transaction identification code CEDF at the terminal.

EDF should respond with the message, "THIS TERMINAL: EDF MODE ON." Once EDF has displayed the confirming message, you may initiate the transaction to be tested.

For different terminal checkout, go to another terminal, clear the screen, and enter the transaction message.

```
CEDF TTTT
```

where TTTT is the terminal identification of the terminal requiring checkout. EDF will respond with a message that EDF mode is on for that terminal. If a transaction is already running on the target terminal, EDF will then associate itself with that task, otherwise it will be activated with the next task initiated on that terminal.

Format of EDF Displays

During the execution of a transaction in debug mode, EDF intercepts the Command-Level Programs at various points. At each interception EDF provides a screen display allowing you to checkout the program status and, in many cases, to modify data areas or the command in progress. An example of a typical EDF screen is given in figure 12.1. Although the content of each screen will vary, certain areas of each screen have a common layout as follows.

The *top line* of the screen contains the transaction identification code, program, and task number associated with the EDF session. The number at the right of this line indicates the current display number. It is possible to recall any of the last 10 screen displays in the session by overtyping this number. The current display is numbered 00, and each previous display −01, −02, and so on. To view the earliest display you would move the cursor to the top line and press the tab key then type −10 in the display field. If the number entered exceeds the number of remembered displays EDF will display the actual display number of the recalled screen. As an alternative to keying the screen number on the top line, you can use PF10 and PF11 (previous and next displays) in the EDF menu to view the various displays.

The five lines at the bottom of the screen provide a *menu* or list of functions that can be performed by EDF. These functions are invoked by pressing the ENTER or PF keys on the terminal. These menu functions can change from one display to another and certain PF keys may become undefined at times. If the terminal you are using does not have PF keys, you can still invoke the menu functions by positioning the cursor next to the required menu item and pressing the ENTER key. If the ENTER key is pressed while the cursor is outside the menu area, the function specified for the ENTER key is performed.

```
╔══════════════════════ Mainframe ══════════════════════╗
║ TRANSACTION: VEND  PROGRAM: VEND001   TASK NUMBER: 0000023   DISPLAY:  00 ║
║ STATUS:  ABOUT TO EXECUTE COMMAND                        ║
║ EXEC CICS SEND MAP                                       ║
║   MAP ('MENUMAP')                                        ║
║   FROM ('.............VEND000...11/05/86...07:22:20...ZBL...DT04.......'...) ║
║   MAPSET ('VENDSET')                                     ║
║   TERMINAL                                               ║
║   FREEKB                                                 ║
║   ERASE                                                  ║
║                                                          ║
║                                                          ║
║                                                          ║
║                                                          ║
║   OFFSET:X'000F1E'   LINE:00206        EIBFN=X'1804'     ║
║                                                          ║
║                                                          ║
║ ENTER:  CONTINUE                                         ║
║ PF1 : UNDEFINED        PF2 : SWITCH HEX/CHAR   PF3 : UNDEFINED    ║
║ PF4 : SUPPRESS DISPLAYS PF5 : WORKING STORAGE  PF6 : USER DISPLAY ║
║ PF7 : SCROLL BACK      PF8 : SCROLL FORWARD    PF9 : STOP CONDITIONS ║
║ PF10: PREVIOUS DISPLAY PF11: UNDEFINED         PF12: ABEND USER TASK ║
╚══════════════════════════════════════════════════════════╝
```

FIGURE 12.1.   EDF Screen Display Format

The line above the menu section is used by EDF to display *messages.* These messages usually indicate that some type of error has occurred or may prompt you to complete some action. The *status line,* located below the top line, identifies the screen display or describes the activity that is about to take place or that has just been completed.

The *data area* between the status and message lines will vary depending on the type of EDF screen being displayed.

Primary EDF Displays

There are eight basic EDF displays. They are

program initiation
command interception
the user display
display on condition
task termination
transaction abend
storage display
Temporary Storage browse

THE PROGRAM INITIATION SCREEN

At the start of each command-level program, prior to giving control to the Procedure Division state-ments, EDF displays the Program Initiation Screen (figure 12.2). If a communications area was passed to the program, EDF will display it on the first line of the data area. The data area also contains a display of the Execute Interface Block. The EIB fields will not all fit on one screen, so the PF7 and PF8 keys in the menu are assigned to scroll forward and backward to view the entire EIB. You can modify most of the EIB fields for this task. This is not ordinarily done, but it does offer some flexibility during testing. To modify a field, you just move the cursor to the field on the EDF display, type over a new value, and press ENTER.

```
╔══════════════════════ Mainframe ══════════════════════╗
 TRANSACTION: VEND   PROGRAM: VEND001   TASK NUMBER: 0000023   DISPLAY:  00
 STATUS:  PROGRAM INITIATION

     EIBTIME      = +0072220
     EIBDATE      = +0086309
     EIBTRNID     = 'VEND'
     EIBTASKN     = +0000023
     EIBTRMID     = 'DT04'

     EIBCPOSN     = +00004
     EIBCALEN     = +00000
     EIBAID       = X'7D'                              AT X'00B4546A'
     EIBFN        = X'0000'                            AT X'00B4546B'
     EIBRCODE     = X'000000000000'                    AT X'00B4546D'
     EIBDS        = '........'
   + EIBREQID     = '........'



 ENTER:  CONTINUE
 PF1 : UNDEFINED            PF2 : SWITCH HEX/CHAR     PF3 : END EDF SESSION
 PF4 : SUPPRESS DISPLAYS    PF5 : WORKING STORAGE     PF6 : USER DISPLAY
 PF7 : SCROLL BACK          PF8 : SCROLL FORWARD      PF9 : STOP CONDITIONS
 PF10: PREVIOUS DISPLAY     PF11: UNDEFINED           PF12: UNDEFINED
```

FIGURE 12.2. Program Initiation Screen

```
╔══════════════════════ Mainframe ══════════════════════╗
 TRANSACTION: VEND   PROGRAM: VEND001   TASK NUMBER: 0000023   DISPLAY:  00
 STATUS:  ABOUT TO EXECUTE COMMAND
 EXEC CICS READQ TS
   QUEUE ('OPEZBL  ')
   INTO ('...  ..                       ..........')
   LENGTH (+00052)
   ITEM (+00001)
   NOHANDLE




   OFFSET:X'001022'    LINE:00229         EIBFN=X'0A04'


 ENTER:  CONTINUE
 PF1 : UNDEFINED            PF2 : SWITCH HEX/CHAR     PF3 : UNDEFINED
 PF4 : SUPPRESS DISPLAYS    PF5 : WORKING STORAGE     PF6 : USER DISPLAY
 PF7 : SCROLL BACK          PF8 : SCROLL FORWARD      PF9 : STOP CONDITIONS
 PF10: PREVIOUS DISPLAY     PF11: UNDEFINED           PF12: ABEND USER TASK
```

FIGURE 12.3. Command Interception Screen (Before Execution)

THE COMMAND INTERCEPTION SCREEN

Once the Procedure Division is given control, EDF intercepts the program at each "call" to the Execute Interface Program, that is, each time an EXEC CICS command is executed. At each interception, *prior* to executing the command, EDF displays the command including the keywords, options, and argument values. Please refer to figure 12.3. To assist in locating the instruction in the source program, the hexadecimal offset within the program is also displayed. If the DEBUG option was specified in the translator run, the line number of the command in the translator listing (not the compiler listing) is displayed beside the offset.

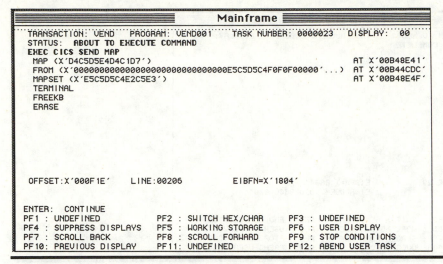

```
═══════════════════════════════ Mainframe ═══════════════════════════════
  TRANSACTION: VEND   PROGRAM: VEND001   TASK NUMBER: 0000023   DISPLAY: 00
  STATUS:  ABOUT TO EXECUTE COMMAND
  EXEC CICS SEND MAP
    MAP (X'D4C5D5E4D4C1D7')                               AT X'00B48E41'
    FROM (X'00000000000000000000000000000000E5C5D5C4F0F0F00000'...)  AT X'00B44CDC'
    MAPSET (X'E5C5D5C4E2C5E3')                            AT X'00B48E4F'
    TERMINAL
    FREEKB
    ERASE




    OFFSET:X'000F1E'    LINE:00206          EIBFN=X'1804'


  ENTER:  CONTINUE
  PF1 : UNDEFINED         PF2 : SWITCH HEX/CHAR    PF3 : UNDEFINED
  PF4 : SUPPRESS DISPLAYS PF5 : WORKING STORAGE    PF6 : USER DISPLAY
  PF7 : SCROLL BACK       PF8 : SCROLL FORWARD     PF9 : STOP CONDITIONS
  PF10: PREVIOUS DISPLAY  PF11: UNDEFINED          PF12: ABEND USER TASK
```

FIGURE 12.4.   Hexadecimal Display Mode (PF2)

At this point of the interception you are allowed to interact with the applicaton in several ways. Here are a few of the things that can be done:

You can cancel the execution of the command by overtyping the command with the keyword NOOP or NOP.

Any argument value can be changed by overtyping the value that is displayed on the screen. Noncharacter information can be overtyped in hexadecimal, but you must first switch to hex display mode by using a menu function.

You can switch the display mode to and from hex format with the PF2 key. In character mode EDF displays only the first 65 characters of an argument on the command interception screen. The hex mode (shown in figure 12.4) displays the first 23 bytes of an argument and also provides the actual storage address of the argument.

You can display or modify any working-storage variable using the working-storage display menu function key PF5. You may have to use the working-storage display menu function to display and modify large arguments such as BMS or file I/O areas. Modification is done by locating the field and typing over the working-storage display screen. The use of the working-storage display function is described in more detail later in this chapter.

EDF also displays the command interception screen after the requested action is performed but before the HANDLE CONDITION action is performed (see figure 12.5). The return code from the EIB is displayed in hexadecimal and the condition response is interpreted and displayed in the message area. At this point of the interception you are allowed to

Change any argument or working-storage value as indicated in the previous paragraphs.

Modify the response from the command execution. Response from a few commands such as RETURN and XCTL cannot be modified. The response from most commands, however, can be modified. EDF allows any valid response for the command just executed to be overtyped. This allows you to test error routines for exceptional conditions that might otherwise be difficult to obtain. An exceptional condition response can also be changed to NORMAL causing the next sequential instruction after the command to be executed as if the condition had not occurred.

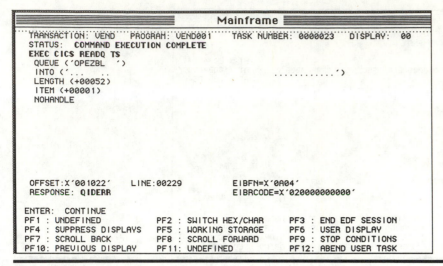

```
================================ Mainframe ================================
TRANSACTION: VEND   PROGRAM: VEND001   TASK NUMBER: 0000023   DISPLAY: 00
STATUS:  COMMAND EXECUTION COMPLETE
EXEC CICS READQ TS
  QUEUE ('OPEZBL  ')
  INTO ('...  ..                              ...........')
  LENGTH (+00052)
  ITEM (+00001)
  NOHANDLE




  OFFSET:X'001022'   LINE:00229        EIBFN=X'0A04'
  RESPONSE: QIDERR                     EIBRCODE=X'020000000000'

ENTER:  CONTINUE
PF1 : UNDEFINED          PF2 : SWITCH HEX/CHAR      PF3 : END EDF SESSION
PF4 : SUPPRESS DISPLAYS  PF5 : WORKING STORAGE      PF6 : USER DISPLAY
PF7 : SCROLL BACK        PF8 : SCROLL FORWARD       PF9 : STOP CONDITIONS
PF10: PREVIOUS DISPLAY   PF11: UNDEFINED            PF12: ABEND USER TASK
```

FIGURE 12.5. Command Interception Screen (After Execution)

```
          1         2         3         4         5         6         7         8
1234567890123456789012345678901234567890123456789012345678901234567890123456789012345678901234567890
VEN0000                                                        DATE 01/31/88
              VENDOR MASTER MENU                               TIME 06:00:00
                                                               TERMINAL DT03

       PF1  DISPLAY MASTER RECORD

       PF2  UPDATE MASTER RECORD

       PF3  ADD MASTER RECORD

       PF4  DELETE MASTER RECORD

       PF5  BROWSE MASTER BY KEY

       PF9  EXIT MASTER MENU


TYPE VENDOR NUMBER 100000 THEN PRESS APPROPRIATE PF KEY
```

FIGURE 12.6. User Display Screen

In addition to being able to modify the commands, arguments, and responses during the execution of a program, these command interception screens effectively allow you to trace the execution path of a program. By following the commands and referencing your translator listings you can often locate logic errors in your program. While the program statements cannot be corrected with EDF, the capability to detect these errors can be invaluable in the debugging process.

THE USER DISPLAY

During an EDF session, it is sometimes helpful to be able to view the user display. The user display is the screen that would normally be displayed on the terminal at a particular point if EDF were not active. After a command such as SEND MAP, EDF will show the user display on the terminal. The display in figure 12.6 was produced as a result of the execution of the command in figure 12.4. This display will remain on the screen until you acknowledge the display by pressing the ENTER key. You can also view the user display at other EDF command interception screens by pressing the PF6 menu key.

THE DISPLAY ON CONDITION SCREEN

The interceptions just described can consume a great deal of testing time. EDF's normal action is to stop the program execution at each interception, to await your acknowledgement. Although this is quite useful during initial testing, it can be distracting during the final testing stages. Say, for instance, you want to test the logic of a program after a pseudoconversational return. Chances are that you wouldn't even want to examine the displays in the first pass through the program. You would step through each display, and finally respond "YES" to the EDF prompt on the task termination screen. Finally in the second pass of the program, you would begin to examine the EDF displays closely.

To speed up the testing process, EDF provides the SUPPRESS-DISPLAYS menu option. This menu option will cause EDF to suppress the display of each command interception screen until a stop condition occurs. The suppress-display mode can be activated on most EDF command interception screens by using the PF4 menu function. When this function is invoked, EDF bypasses the display of the command interception screens until a predefined stop condition occurs. Testing of partially-working programs can be done at a more rapid pace this way.

When debug mode is first activated, the default stop conditions are

any CICS exceptional condition

at transaction abend

at normal task termination

at abnormal task termination

You can, however, change the conditions for which EDF will stop suppressing displays. This is done with the DISPLAY ON CONDITION screen. This menu option (PF9) will cause EDF to display the screen depicted in figure 12.7. This screen displays the current conditions which will later deactivate the suppress-displays mode. You may then activate any of the options on this screen by overtyping the appropriate field. These new stop conditions will remain active throughout the current EDF session, even across task boundaries (if you respond "YES" on the task termination screen). The next time you reactivate the suppress-displays mode with the PF4 key, EDF will stop the displays until one of the stop conditions has arisen.

Let's examine some of the options. One alternative is to enter a CICS command. Let's say, for instance, that you overtype RECEIVE and then invoke suppress-displays. EDF will suppress all displays until the command interception point corresponding to the "ABOUT TO EXECUTE" for the RECEIVE command. That's assuming, of course, one of the other stop conditions doesn't occur first. You then have the opportunity to perform any other EDF function as described in the preceding paragraphs.

EDF can also be conditioned to stop suppressing displays when a command on a specific line number or offset in the program is about to be executed. To use this option, DEBUG must be specified in the command translator, and the translator listings must be on hand during testing. The line number must be specified exactly as it appears on the translator listing and must be the line on which the command starts. The offset method is more difficult to use since the value specified must correspond to the address of the machine language "call" instruction generated by the compiler. This information can only be found in the full Procedure Division map of the compiler listing.

Another useful option is to specify a CICS exceptional condition. Suppose that you are testing a transaction, and for some unknown reason are getting a LENGERR exceptional condition. By telling

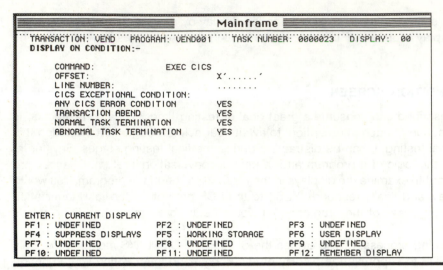

FIGURE 12.7. Display on Condition Screen

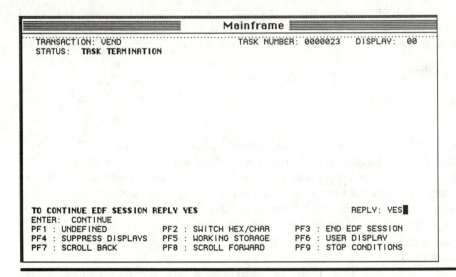

FIGURE 12.8. Task Termination Screen

EDF to stop on that condition you can then suppress displays until a command gives rise to LEN-GERR. EDF will respond by bypassing the display of the interception screens up to the point of the error. It is important to note that EDF still remembers the display screens, it just doesn't display them. When suppress-displays is stopped, you can use the top line or menu function to recall these earlier screens.

THE TASK TERMINATION SCREEN

When a program at the highest logical level issues a RETURN command, CICS will terminate the task. At task termination EDF will display the task termination screen (see figure 12.8). On this screen you are prompted with a message allowing you to continue with the EDF session. If you reply YES,

```
══════════════════════════════════ Mainframe ══════════════════════════════════
  TRANSACTION: VEND   PROGRAM: VEND001   TASK NUMBER: 0000765   DISPLAY:  00
  STATUS:  AN ABEND HAS OCCURRED
       COMMAREA   = '..      200000ZBL11/05/86'
       EIBTIME    = +0075627
       EIBDATE    = +0086309
       EIBTRNID   = 'VEND'
       EIBTASKN   = +0000765
       EIBTRMID   = 'DT04'

       EIBCPOSN   = +01248
       EIBCALEN   = +00023
       EIBAID     = X'7D'                              AT X'00B44452'
       EIBFN      = X'0A04'   READQ                    AT X'00B44453'
       EIBRCODE   = X'000000000000'   NORMAL           AT X'00B44455'
       EIBDS      = '........'
  +    EIBREQID   = '........'
   OFFSET:X'001996'                INTERRUPT: DATA EXCEPTION
   ABEND :    ASRA                  PSW: X'03BD2000 00C691D4 00060007'

   ENTER:   CONTINUE
  PF1  : UNDEFINED           PF2  : SWITCH HEX/CHAR    PF3  : END EDF SESSION
  PF4  : SUPPRESS DISPLAYS   PF5  : WORKING STORAGE    PF6  : USER DISPLAY
  PF7  : SCROLL BACK         PF8  : SCROLL FORWARD     PF9  : STOP CONDITIONS
  PF10: PREVIOUS DISPLAY     PF11: UNDEFINED           PF12: REGISTERS AT ABEND
```

FIGURE 12.9.   Transaction ABEND Screen (Program Interrupt)

EDF will remain active on the checkout terminal. When EDF is allowed to remain active, all previous displays up to the maximum will still be available for review. This option is particularly useful in debugging pseudoconversational programs since EDF will remain active across task boundaries.

THE TRANSACTION ABEND SCREEN

A task may not run to normal completion. There are a variety of reasons that will cause CICS to abnormally end (ABEND) a program. For example, a BMS mapping command specifying an invalid mapname, will cause an abend. Likewise CICS will abend a program in a never-ending loop. Sometimes the execution of a program will be interrupted by a program check detected by the system. A number of program check interruptions can cause a program failure. For instance a data exception, or "OC7," will occur if the program attempts to use a decimal field that does not contain a valid data format. When a program check occurs, CICS recovers from the failure and abends the offending task.

When a task is abended, EDF displays the transaction abend screen to assist in the debugging process. The screen shows the abend code along with the fields from the EIB. If the abend was caused during the execution of a command, you can use the PREVIOUS DISPLAY menu option to display the offending command along with its options and arguments. This information is usually sufficient to determine the problem. In the event of a program check interruption, EDF displays the offset of the failing instruction and the reason for the failure. A transaction ABEND screen caused by a program interrupt, is depicted in figure 12.9. The program status word (PSW) is also provided but is only needed in special situations.

When a program check interruption occurs, you will want to find the source statement corresponding to the failure. EDF does not directly display the source statement number, but it does provide all the information needed to get there. As stated earlier, the offset of the failing machine instruction is provided on the EDF abend screen. This offset can be used to determine the COBOL source statement that has failed. Use the procedure below to locate a failing instruction. Figure 12.10 contains extracts of the compiler listing for our failing program.

1. Write down the offset of the failing instruction. It is shown on the left side of the transaction abend screen. In figure 12.9, the offset is hex 001996.
2. Locate the Procedure Division map in the compile listing. For our example see figure 12.10. This PMAP (CLIST in VSE) is necessary to locate the COBOL source statement containing

```
00619                    MOVE TS-TIME-IN TO FINAL-TIME-IN
00620                    TRANSFORM FINAL-TIME-IN FROM ',' TO ':'
00621                    MOVE TS-TIME-LAST TO FINAL-TIME-LAST
00622                    TRANSFORM FINAL-TIME-LAST FROM ',' TO ':'
00623                    MOVE TS-READS    TO FINAL-READ-COUNT
00624                    MOVE TS-UPDATES TO FINAL-WRITE-COUNT
00625                    MOVE TS-ADDS     TO FINAL-ADD-COUNT
00626                    MOVE TS-DELETES TO FINAL-DELETE-COUNT
00627                    MOVE 'VEND900' TO FINAL-MESSAGE-NUMBER
00628                    MOVE FINAL-LINE-1 TO MMESAGEO
00629                    MOVE FINAL-LINE-2 TO MMESAG2O.


594   VERB  1   001858   595   VERB  1   001862   596   VERB  1   001872
597   VERB  1   001878   605   VERB  1   00187E   606   VERB  1   00188E
607   VERB  1   001894   612   VERB  1   0018D2   613   VERB  1   0018F4
614   VERB  1   001902   615   VERB  1   00190C   617   VERB  1   00191C
619   VERB  1   00192C   619   VERB  2   001932   620   VERB  1   001944
621   VERB  1   001958   622   VERB  1   00196A   623   VERB  1   00197E
624   VERB  1   001996   625   VERB  1   0019AE   626   VERB  1   0019C6
627   VERB  1   0019DE   628   VERB  1   0019E4   629   VERB  1   0019F4
630   VERB  1   001A04   632   VERB  1   001A12   633   VERB  1   001A22
639   VERB  1   001A40   640   VERB  1   001A50   641   VERB  1   001A56
642   VERB  1   001A5C   645   VERB  1   001A92   646   VERB  1   001AA2
648   VERB  1   001ABE
```

FIGURE 12.10.   Procedure Division Statements and PMAP (CLIST with VSE)

the machine instruction that failed. The condensed PMAP in this example contains the offset of the first machine instruction for each statement in the Procedure Division. Depending on the compiler option, the actual verb or verb number will be listed. Beside the statement and verb number is the offset of the first machine instruction. For example, verb 1 on statement number 619 begins at offset 00192C in the program. Verb 2 on statement number 619 begins at offset 1932.

3.   Locate the COBOL statement and verb number that correspond to the offset of the failing instruction. Look for an offset that exactly matches, or is less than, the offset shown on the transaction ABEND screen. In our example, the offset of the failing instruction corresponds to the COBOL statement on line number 624, verb 1. The statement is

`MOVE TS-UPDATES TO FINAL-WRITE-COUNT`

4.   Using the description of the interrupt provided on the transaction ABEND screen, analyze the source statement on the compiler listing. In our example, the reason for the interruption was a "DATA EXCEPTION," or OC7. This error is caused when the machine attempts to use a COMP-3 field in a calculation or editing operation and the field contains an invalid data format. Other errors such as "DIVIDE BY ZERO" will give similar clues to the problem.

Many times you may be able to determine the cause of the problem without further use of EDF. This can be done by identifying the fields involved in the operation and analyzing prior use of such fields. For instance, a COMP-3 field may have been used but may not have been previously initialized. Sometimes a more thorough analysis is needed. You may have to use EDF to display the contents of the fields involved in the operation to determine the cause of the failure. EDF provides the capability to view these fields. Working-storage fields can be viewed by using the storage display function (PF5).

```
┌──────────────────────────────────────────────────────────────────────┐
│  ═══════════════════════════  Mainframe  ══════════════════════════    │
│  TRANSACTION: VEND   PROGRAM: VEND001    TASK NUMBER: 0000765  DISPLAY:  00  │
│    ADDRESS:  00B44A4C                    WORKING STORAGE                │
│  00B44A40   000000                           00024040        ...........│
│  00B44A50   000004    4040F2F0 F0F0F0F0 E9C2D3F1 F161F0F5    200000ZBL11/05│
│  00B44A60   000014    61F8F600 E5C5D5C4 D6D940D4 C1E2E3C5    /86.VENDOR MASTE│
│  00B44A70   000024    D9404040 40404040 40404040 C4E3F0F4    R      DT04  │
│  00B44A80   000034    1105186C 0072220C 0073817C 00002C40    ...%......aə...│
│  00B44A90   000044    40400000 0C00000C 40404040 40404040    ......    │
│  00B44AA0   000054    40404040 40DFF1F1 61F0F561 F8F6F0F7    .11/05/8607│
│  00B44AB0   000064    7AF5F67A F2F7F0F7 6BF5F66B F2F74040    :56:2707,56,27│
│  00B44AC0   000074    40404040 40400034 D6D7C5E9 C2D34040    ..OPEZBL  │
│  00B44AD0   000084    40404040 40404040 40404040 40404040             │
│  00B44AE0   000094    40404040 40404040 40404040 40404040             │
│  00B44AF0   0000A4    4780F62E 40404040 40404040 40404040    ..6.       │
│  00B44B00   0000B4    40404040 40404040 40404040 5CC5D4D7             *EMP│
│  00B44B10   0000C4    D3404040 40404040 4040D9D4 C1E3C9D6    L      RMATIO│
│  00B44B20   0000D4    D55C4040 E2C5E2E2 C9D6D540 E2E3C1E3    N*  SESSION STAT│
│  00B44B30   0000E4    C9E2E3C9 C3E27AE2 C9C7D540 D6D57E40    ISTICS:SIGN ON=│
│                                                                        │
│   ENTER:   CURRENT DISPLAY                                             │
│   PF1 :  UNDEFINED          PF2 : BROWSE TEMP STORAGE PF3 :  UNDEFINED │
│   PF4 :  EIB DISPLAY        PF5 : WORKING STORAGE     PF6 :  USER DISPLAY│
│   PF7 :  SCROLL BACK HALF   PF8 : SCROLL FORWARD HALF PF9 :  UNDEFINED │
│   PF10:  SCROLL BACK FULL   PF11: SCROLL FORWARD FULL PF12: REMEMBER DISPLAY│
└──────────────────────────────────────────────────────────────────────┘
```

FIGURE 12.11.   Display Working Storage (Initial)

THE STORAGE DISPLAY SCREEN

EDF can be used to display the program's working-storage generally anytime after the program initialization screen. Fortunately EDF includes this function at task abend time. When the storage display function key (PF5) is selected, the address of the beginning of working-storage is displayed along with the first hex 100 (sometimes fewer) bytes of the area. Please refer to figure 12.11. In this example working-storage starts at address B44A4C. You can scroll forward and backward in the working-storage area with PF keys 7, 8, 10, and 11. Each new screen contains the storage address of the displayed area, the current offset into working-storage and an offset column for the display.

Many times you will want to locate a specific field in working-storage. In our earlier discussions you learned that the address of an argument can be found by turning on the hex mode during a command interception screen. If a field that you want to locate was an argument of an earlier command, and you happened to write down the address, it's a simple matter. If you know the address of a field, you can simply overtype the address value on any storage display screen. EDF will respond with a display beginning at that address. Generally, you're not going to be fortunate enough to know the address of a field when you need it. There is, however, a simple procedure that you can follow to locate any working-storage field. Let's resume our transaction abend problem analysis from the previous section. It will provide an opportunity to see how to locate a working-storage field.

Recall that the transaction had abended with a "DATA EXCEPTION" in statement number 624. The statement was "MOVE TS-UPDATES TO FINAL-WRITE-COUNT." After an analysis of the statement, you might conclude, as I have, that something is wrong with the contents of field TS-UPDATES. We'll use the procedure below to locate this suspect field.

1. First, locate the field in the compiler listing, Data Division map. The Data Division map contains a line for each COBOL data name defined. Figure 12.12 contains an extract of the Data Division fields and map for our sample problem. In the data map, each line entry contains the source field name, a reference to a bass locator (BL) number and a hexadecimal displacement within the BL.

    At compile time, a base locator is assigned to each 4096 (hex 1000) bytes of working-storage. During execution of the program, the base locator plus the displacement value is used by the processor to locate the field. The field named TS-UPDATES has been assigned to base locator 1, and has a displacement of 043 within the BL.

```
00055                    01   TS-RECORD.
00056                         05   TS-APPLICATION        PIC X(24).
00057                         05   TS-TERMID             PIC XXXX.
00058                         05   TS-DATE               PIC S9(7)  COMP-3.
00059                         05   TS-TIME-IN            PIC S9(7)  COMP-3.
00060                         05   TS-TIME-LAST          PIC S9(7)  COMP-3.
00061                         05   TS-READS              PIC S9(5)  COMP-3 VALUE +0.
00062                         05   TS-UPDATES            PIC S9(5)  COMP-3 VALUE +0.
00063                         05   TS-ADDS               PIC S9(5)  COMP-3 VALUE +0.
00064                         05   TS-DELETES            PIC S9(5)  COMP-3 VALUE +0.
```

```
DNM=2-132  02  ENTRY-OPERATOR   BL=1  00C   DNM=2-132  DS 3C     DISP
DNM=2-156  02  ENTRY-DATE       BL=1  00F   DNM=2-156  DS 8C     DISP
DNM=2-176  01  TS-RECORD        BL=1  018   DNM=2-176  DS 0CL52  GROUP
DNM=2-198  02  TS-APPLICATION   BL=1  018   DNM=2-198  DS 24C    DISP
DNM=2-222  02  TS-TERMID        BL=1  030   DNM=2-222  DS 4C     DISP
DNM=2-241  02  TS-DATE          BL=1  034   DNM=2-241  DS 4P     COMP-3
DNM=2-258  02  TS-TIME-IN       BL=1  038   DNM=2-258  DS 4P     COMP-3
DNM=2-278  02  TS-TIME-LAST     BL=1  03C   DNM=2-278  DS 4P     COMP-3
DNM=2-300  02  TS-READS         BL=1  040   DNM=2-300  DS 3P     COMP-3
DNM=2-318  02  TS-UPDATES       BL=1  043   DNM=2-318  DS 3P     COMP-3
DNM=2-338  02  TS-ADDS          BL=1  046   DNM=2-338  DS 3P     COMP-3
DNM=2-355  02  TS-DELETES       BL=1  049   DNM=2-355  DS 3P     COMP-3
DNM=2-375  01  WORK-AREAS       BL=1  050   DNM=2-375  DS 0CL52  GROUP
DNM=2-398  02  MSG-LEN          BL=1  050   DNM=2-398  DS 1H     COMP
DNM=2-415  02  ABSOLUTE-DATE    BL=1  052   DNM=2-415  DS 2F     COMP
DNM=2-438  02  CALENDAR-DATE    BL=1  05A   DNM=2-438  DS 8C     DISP
```

FIGURE 12.12.   Data Division Entries and Map

2.   Next, locate the beginning of working-storage. This is a simple matter; just press PF5. For our example, refer again to figure 12.11. This screen is produced by pressing the storage display menu function. From the display, you can see that working-storage starts at B44A4C. This also happens to be the value stored in the first COBOL base locator cell.

3.   If the field that you want to locate is referenced by the first BL, you can simply add the offset given in the Data Division map to the working-storage address and then overtype this new address to find the field. In our example, by adding 043 to the working-storage address of B44A4C, we come up with B44A8F. Figure 12.13 was produced by overtyping the computed address of B44A8F. You can verify that you have found the right location by comparing the working-storage offset value in the upper left corner of the screen with the offset used in the computation. In our example the offset is 000043. In examining the contents of TS-UPDATES, we can see that spaces have somehow made their way into the COMP-3 field. This of course, was the cause of the data exception.

4.   To find the address of a field referenced by other than BL1, you must compute the sum of the three values: the start of working-storage, the base locator offset, and the field displacement. The base locator and field displacement are taken directly from the Data Division map. The base locator offset is a multiple of 4096 or hex 1000 bytes as indicated below.

BL=2   001000
BL=3   002000
BL=4   003000
etc.

```
╔══════════════════════════════ Mainframe ══════════════════════════════╗
  TRANSACTION: VEND    PROGRAM: VEND001    TASK NUMBER: 0000765   DISPLAY:  00
   ADDRESS: 00B44A8F                   WORKING STORAGE+X'000043'
  00B44A80   000000                          40                ..............
  00B44A90   000001   40400000 0C00000C 40404040 40404040       ......
  00B44AA0   000011   40404040 40DFF1F1 61F0F561 F8F6F0F7       .11/05/8607
  00B44AB0   000021   7AF5F67A F2F7F0F7 6BF5F66B F2F74040      :56:2707,56,27
  00B44AC0   000031   40404040 40400034 D6D7C5E9 C2D34040         ..OPEZBL
  00B44AD0   000041   40404040 40404040 40404040 40404040
  00B44AE0   000051   40404040 40404040 40404040 40404040
  00B44AF0   000061   4780F62E 40404040 40404040 40404040      ..6.
  00B44B00   000071   40404040 40404040 40404040 5CC5D4D7            *EMP
  00B44B10   000081   D3404040 40404040 4040D9D4 C1E3C9D6      L      RMATIO
  00B44B20   000091   D55C4040 E2C5E2E2 C9D6D540 E2E3C1E3      N* SESSION STAT
  00B44B30   0000A1   C9E2E3C9 C3E27AE2 C9C7D540 D6D57E40      ISTICS:SIGN ON=
  00B44B40   0000B1   F0F77AF2 F27AF2F0 40D3C1E2 E340E3D9      07:22:20 LAST TR
  00B44B50   0000C1   C1D5E2C1 C3E3C9D6 D540F0F7 7AF3F87A      ANSACTION 07:38:
  00B44B60   0000D1   F1F74040 D9C5C1C4 7E404040 40404040      17  READ=
  00B44B70   0000E1   F240E4D7 C4C1E3C5 7E40F6AA 40404040      2 UPDATE= 6.

  ENTER:  CURRENT DISPLAY
  PF1 :  UNDEFINED            PF2 :  BROWSE TEMP STORAGE PF3 :  UNDEFINED
  PF4 :  EIB DISPLAY          PF5 :  WORKING STORAGE     PF6 :  USER DISPLAY
  PF7 :  SCROLL BACK HALF     PF8 :  SCROLL FORWARD HALF PF9 :  UNDEFINED
╚════════════════════════════════════════════════════════════════════════╝
```

FIGURE 12.13. Storage Display for Field TS-UPDATES

Let's use a new example to illustrate this calculation. Assume that a field is listed in the Data Division map with BL=6 and a field displacement of 3E4. Assume also that working-storage is at address 0045CE4C. The address of the field is computed as follows:

```
        WORKING-STORAGE              0045CE4C
        BL-6 OFFSET                      5000
        FIELD DISPLACEMENT                3E4
        ADDRESS                      00462230
```

After using EDF to locate this field, you could verify that your computations are correct by checking the EDF offset in the upper right corner. For this last example, the working-storage offset should be equal to 00053E4.

TEMPORARY STORAGE BROWSE DISPLAY

A recent feature of EDF provides the capability to browse through temporary storage queues. Temporary Storage is often used in designing CICS transactions, so the ability to look at Temporary Storage records can be quite useful in the debugging process. To browse a Temporary Storage queue, you must first invoke the storage display function using PF5. This action causes working-storage to be displayed as usual but redefines the PF2 key to activate the browse-Temp Storage function. When this browse function is first invoked, the Temporary Storage browse program will initially attempt to locate a queue with a name of

```
        CEDFTTTT
```

where TTTT is the terminal identification of the EDF checkout program. If that queue doesn't exist, a message will appear, indicating that queue is empty. This can be corrected.

The top line of the Temporary Storage display screen provides a data entry field allowing you to enter a new queue identification. Please refer to figure 12.14. This screen was produced by entering the queue name of "OPEZBL" on the top line of the display. A command prompt line is provided on

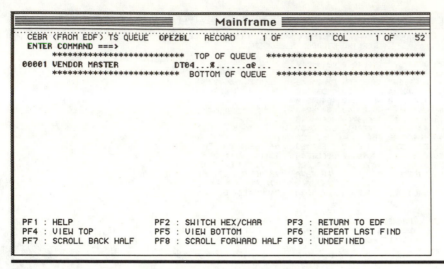

```
┌═══════════════════════════════════════════════════════════════════┐
│                            Mainframe ═══                             │
│═══════════════════════════════════════════════════════════════════ │
│ CEBR (FROM EDF) TS QUEUE  OPEZBL   RECORD    1 OF   1   COL   1 OF  52 │
│ ENTER COMMAND ===>                                                    │
│      ************************* TOP OF QUEUE ************************* │
│ 00001 VENDOR MASTER            DT04...%......ae...   .......          │
│      ************************ BOTTOM OF QUEUE ************************ │
│                                                                      │
│                                                                      │
│                                                                      │
│                                                                      │
│                                                                      │
│                                                                      │
│                                                                      │
│                                                                      │
│                                                                      │
│ PF1 : HELP              PF2 : SWITCH HEX/CHAR     PF3 : RETURN TO EDF │
│ PF4 : VIEW TOP          PF5 : VIEW BOTTOM         PF6 : REPEAT LAST FIND │
│ PF7 : SCROLL BACK HALF  PF8 : SCROLL FORWARD HALF PF9 : UNDEFINED     │
└═══════════════════════════════════════════════════════════════════┘
```

FIGURE 12.14. Temporary Storage Browse Display

the second line of the Temporary Storage browse screen to allow you to enter browsing commands for the queue. Some of the commands that can be entered are as follows:

1. QUEUE XXXXXXXX names a queue that you want to become the current queue. This has the same effect as overtyping the name on the top line. The command line, however, provides the capability to enter a queue name in hexadecimal mode, for example: X'FFFFC1C2'.
2. PURGE erases the contents of the active queue. This has the same effect as executing a CICS DELETEQ command.
3. LINE NNNN causes the specified queue item to be displayed in the data area.
4. COLUMN NNNN causes the specified column to be displayed as the first column in the data area.
5. FIND /character string/ causes a search of the queue. If the string is found, the line containing the string will be displayed first in the data area. The character "/" is a delimiting character. It does not have to be "/" but must not be a character that appears in the search string. For example, to search for the string "/ABC," you could enter FIND $/ABC$ on the command line, where "$" is the delimiting character.

    Finally, a list of menu options allows you to perform other browsing operations, switch between character and hex mode, and return to the EDF storage display screen.

Displaying COBOL Areas

EDF allows you to view any storage area within the CICS region. This can be done by overtyping the required address on the storage display screens. If a storage area is not within the address range of the working-storage copy, EDF protects the corresponding data area against input. Thus, you cannot modify these other areas, but you can view them. The usefulness of this function will increase as you learn more about CICS/VS. It is not the purpose of this book to discuss the internal architecture of CICS. Fortunately, you don't have to know about the internals of CICS to write programs in the Command-Level Interface. However, a knowledge of the layout of the COBOL object module and an understanding of the methods used by CICS to initialize and run your program will make it easier to debug the more difficult programs with EDF. The following section presents an overview of the internal structure of the COBOL object module and describes techniques that can be helpful in the debugging process.

```
┌─────────────────────────────┐
│  INIT1                       │
├─────────────────────────────┤
│  WORKING-STORAGE             │
├─────────────────────────────┤
│  TASK GLOBAL TABLE           │
├─────────────────────────────┤
│  LITERALS                    │
├─────────────────────────────┤
│  PROCEDURE DIVISION          │
│                              │
└─────────────────────────────┘
```

FIGURE 12.15.   The COBOL Object Module

COBOL OBJECT MODULE

The object module produced by the COBOL compiler is shown in figure 12.15. Other areas do exist within the actual object module, but those areas not relevant to this discussion have been omitted from the diagram.

The *Initialization 1* routine (INIT1) begins at relative location zero and is constant in length for every compilation. The size and layout will vary somewhat between MVS and VSE compilers. The routine is entered when the program is first executed for the purpose of initializing the object module prior to passing control to the Procedure Division code. In addition to the initialization code INIT1 area contains some address pointers to the various areas of the object module. These pointers include the Task Global Table (described later) and the start of the Procedure Division. The date and time the program was compiled are also contained within the INIT1 area. These fields may be useful during the debugging process in verifying that the program you are testing corresponds to your compiler listing. Later, we'll see how to locate the INIT1 routine with EDF.

Working-storage contains reserved storage for the working-storage section of the Data Division. The data items for which value clauses were specified have been initialized. In CICS/VS this working-storage area is used as the "master copy" for all tasks using this program. You might recall from chapter 2 that the Execute Interface Program makes a copy of this area for each task using the program.

Task Global Table (TGT) is used by the Procedure Division to record and save information needed during the execution of the program. It can be considered as a special class of working-storage since it contains save areas and intermediate work areas used by the program. Like working-storage, there is a copy of the TGT for every task using this program. The size of the TGT is variable and depends on various factors. A map of the TGT structure is included in every COBOL compiler listing. Some of the data areas in the TGT are described below.

A *save area* used by subprograms to save the registers of the COBOL program. During each call to the Execute Interface Program, EIP uses this area to save the registers of the calling program. These registers are restored from this area just prior to returning control to your program.

Tally is a fullword available for source program reference to the special register TALLY.

Base locator (BL) cells are fullwords containing addresses of data areas in working-storage. A base locator is assigned to each block of 4096 (hex 1000) bytes of working-storage.

Base Locators for Linkage (BLL) are fullwords containing the addresses of areas passed to the program. There is one BLL for each 01-level entry used in the Linkage Section of the program. In CICS/VS command-level programs these cells are used to access the Execute Interface Block and DFHCOMMAREA.

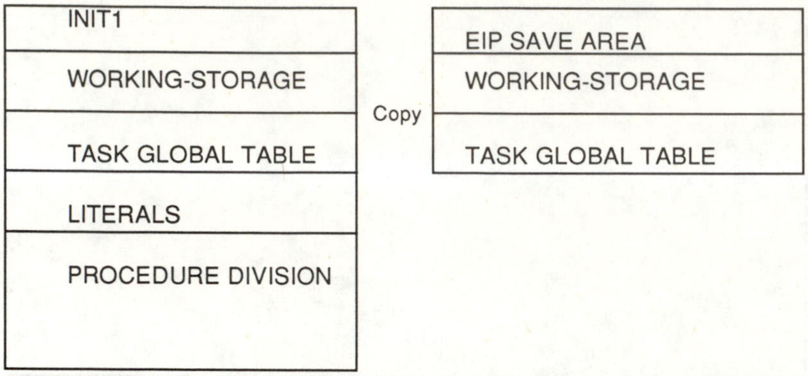

FIGURE 12.16. The COBOL AREA Is Created During Program Initiation

The original working-storage and TGT is used as a "master copy" for all tasks using this program. Each task will be provided a copy of these areas so that COBOL programs can be multithreaded.

Literals are read-only variables that are produced by the compiler in response to Procedure Division statements specifying numeric or character constants. For example, the statement MOVE 'TEST' TO FILE-NAME. would cause the literal 'TEST' to be stored in the literals area. Extensive use of literals instead of working-storage constants can reduce the storage requirements of your program since only one copy of this area will be produced for all tasks using the program.

Procedure Division instructions follow the literals in the object module. The offset of the instructions produced by each statement appear in the compiler listing if a procedure map is requested at compile time.

FINDING INIT1

Any of the areas described above can be viewed by EDF. After locating the area, the listings produced by the compiler can be used to locate specific fields. The following paragraphs describe the procedure to locate the INIT1 routine:

During program initialization for each CICS command-level COBOL program, the program control program acquires a storage area large enough to hold a copy of the original working-storage and TGT. The working-storage and TGT are then copied into this area for use by the program. The original areas are only used as a base for creating new COBOL areas. This process is depicted in figure 12.16. At the top of this COBOL area, just before working-storage, is a register save area for use by the Execute Interface Program. One of the fields in the register area points to the COBOL INIT1 routine. You can find this field with EDF as follows:

1. First press the storage display menu function to get to the working-storage copy (figure 12.17). Make note of the address then subtract hex 10 from it. This negative offset value has been valid from the earliest release of CICS supporting the command-level feature but may change in a future release.
2. Next, overtype the new computed address and press enter (figure 12.18). The contents of the fullword first displayed on this screen will point to INIT1.
3. Make a note of the address of INIT1, then overtype this new address; this should provide a display of the area (figure 12.19). You should see the date and time the program was compiled as indicated on your compile listing. This information is sometimes useful in verifying that the program you are testing is the one that corresponds to the compiler listing you are using. If they don't match up, then you don't have the correct listing or you haven't told CICS to use the latest compiled program.

```
═══════════════════════ Mainframe ═══════════════════════
 TRANSACTION: VEND   PROGRAM: VEND001    TASK NUMBER: 0000765   DISPLAY:  00
   ADDRESS: 00B44A4C                WORKING STORAGE
 00B44A40   000000                              00024040    .............
 00B44A50   000004   4040F2F0 F0F0F0F0 E9C2D3F1 F161F0F5    200000ZBL11/05
 00B44A60   000014   61F8F600 E5C5D5C4 D6D940D4 C1E2E3C5    /86.VENDOR MASTE
 00B44A70   000024   D9404040 40404040 40404040 C4E3F0F4    R           DT04
 00B44A80   000034   1105186C 0072220C 0073817C 00002C40    ...%....aℓ...
 00B44A90   000044   40400000 0C00000C 40404040 40404040    ......
 00B44AA0   000054   40404040 40DFF1F1 61F0F561 F8F6F0F7      .11/05/8607
 00B44AB0   000064   7AF5F67A F2F7F0F7 6BF5F66B F2F74040    :56:2707,56,27
 00B44AC0   000074   40404040 40400034 D6D7C5E9 C2D34040    ..OPEZBL
 00B44AD0   000084   40404040 40404040 40404040 40404040
 00B44AE0   000094   40404040 40404040 40404040 40404040
 00B44AF0   0000A4   4780F62E 40404040 40404040 40404040    ..6.
 00B44B00   0000B4   40404040 40404040 40404040 5CC5D4D7            *EMP
 00B44B10   0000C4   D3404040 40404040 4040D9D4 C1E3C9D6    L      RMATIO
 00B44B20   0000D4   D55C4040 E2C5E2E2 C9D6D540 E2E3C1E3    N* SESSION STAT
 00B44B30   0000E4   C9E2E3C9 C3E27AE2 C9C7D540 D6D57E40    ISTICS:SIGN ON=

 ENTER:  CURRENT DISPLAY
 PF1 : UNDEFINED            PF2 : BROWSE TEMP STORAGE PF3 : UNDEFINED
 PF4 : EIB DISPLAY          PF5 : WORKING STORAGE     PF6 : USER DISPLAY
 PF7 : SCROLL BACK HALF     PF8 : SCROLL FORWARD HALF PF9 : UNDEFINED
 PF10: SCROLL BACK FULL     PF11: SCROLL FORWARD FULL PF12: REMEMBER DISPLAY
```

FIGURE 12.17. Locating INIT1 (Step 1-Working Storage Display)

```
═══════════════════════ Mainframe ═══════════════════════
 TRANSACTION: VEND   PROGRAM: VEND001    TASK NUMBER: 0000765   DISPLAY:  00
   ADDRESS: 00B44A3C
 00B44A30   000000                              00C67838    ............F..
 00B44A40   000004   00C680A0 00C67CD0 00B20778 00024040    .F...Fℓ.......
 00B44A50   000014   4040F2F0 F0F0F0F0 E9C2D3F1 F161F0F5    200000ZBL11/05
 00B44A60   000024   61F8F600 E5C5D5C4 D6D940D4 C1E2E3C5    /86.VENDOR MASTE
 00B44A70   000034   D9404040 40404040 40404040 C4E3F0F4    R           DT04
 00B44A80   000044   1105186C 0072220C 0073817C 00002C40    ...%....aℓ...
 00B44A90   000054   40400000 0C00000C 40404040 40404040    ......
 00B44AA0   000064   40404040 40DFF1F1 61F0F561 F8F6F0F7      .11/05/8607
 00B44AB0   000074   7AF5F67A F2F7F0F7 6BF5F66B F2F74040    :56:2707,56,27
 00B44AC0   000084   40404040 40400034 D6D7C5E9 C2D34040    ..OPEZBL
 00B44AD0   000094   40404040 40404040 40404040 40404040
 00B44AE0   0000A4   40404040 40404040 40404040 40404040
 00B44AF0   0000B4   4780F62E 40404040 40404040 40404040    ..6.
 00B44B00   0000C4   40404040 40404040 40404040 5CC5D4D7            *EMP
 00B44B10   0000D4   D3404040 40404040 4040D9D4 C1E3C9D6    L      RMATIO
 00B44B20   0000E4   D55C4040 E2C5E2E2 C9D6D540 E2E3C1E3    N* SESSION STAT

 ENTER:  CURRENT DISPLAY
 PF1 : UNDEFINED            PF2 : BROWSE TEMP STORAGE PF3 : UNDEFINED
 PF4 : EIB DISPLAY          PF5 : WORKING STORAGE     PF6 : USER DISPLAY
 PF7 : SCROLL BACK HALF     PF8 : SCROLL FORWARD HALF PF9 : UNDEFINED
 PF10: SCROLL BACK FULL     PF11: SCROLL FORWARD FULL PF12: REMEMBER DISPLAY
```

FIGURE 12.18. Locating COBOL INIT1 (Step 2-Offset Hex-10 from Working Storage)

Recall that INIT1 is also located at offset zero in your COBOL compiler listing. With this address and the various maps provided by the compiler, you can virtually locate any storage area in the program. For instance, the procedure map can provide offsets of actual machine instructions corresponding to your procedure statements. Although not very useful to most programmers, this information could be helpful to advanced users.

Chapter Summary

In this chapter you have learned to use the Execution Diagnostic Facility to checkout command-level programs. The EDF utility is an integrated part of the Command-Level Interface and provides a tool for program debugging. Its use is limited only by your knowledge of CICS. As you become more familiar with CICS, it's features will become more important and most impressive.

```
▓▓▓▓▓▓▓▓▓▓▓▓▓▓▓▓▓▓▓▓▓▓▓▓▓    Mainframe    ▓▓▓▓▓▓▓▓▓▓▓▓▓▓▓▓▓▓▓▓▓▓▓
 TRANSACTION: VEND   PROGRAM: VEND001   TASK NUMBER: 0000765  DISPLAY:  00
   ADDRESS: 00C67838
 00C67830  000000                        05F00700 900EF00A  .........0....0.
 00C67840  000008  47F0F082 00CA723C 00B44384 00C67908  .00b.......d.F..
 00C67850  000018  00B44A10 00C67880 00B204D0 00B44000  ..c..F.........
 00C67860  000028  00C67838 00AED074 00C685D0 00B23F2C  .F.......Fe.....
 00C67870  000038  80B442D8 00B44140 00B44394 50AED2DA  ...Q.....m&.K..
 00C67880  000048  00C67938 50C693B6 00C69520 00AE64E0  .F..&FI..Fn.....
 00C67890  000058  00C67838 40C6939E 00C67938 00C67EEF  .F.. FI..F...F=.
 00C678A0  000068  00C67EF0 00C6935C 00C67838 00C67838  .F=0.FI*.F...F..
 00C678B0  000078  00C680A0 00C67CD0 00B20778 58C0F0C6  .F...Fe.......0F
 00C678C0  000088  58E0C000 58D0F0CA 9500E000 4770F0A2  ......0.n... .0s
 00C678D0  000098  9610D048 92FFE000 47F0F0AC 98CEF03A  o...k....00.q.0.
 00C678E0  0000A8  90ECD00C 185D989F F0BA9110 D0480719  .....)q.0.j.....
 00C678F0  0000B8  07FF0700 00C6935C 00C67838 00C67838  .....FI*.F...F..
 00C67900  0000C8  00C680A0 00B44DE4 00C685D0 00C69342  .F....(U.Fe..FI.
 00C67910  0000D8  C3D6C2C6 F3F0F0F0 E5C5D5C4 F0F0F140  COBF3000VEND001
 00C67920  0000E8  00C67FFC F1F161F0 F461F8F6 F1F24BF3  .F".11/04/8612.3

 ENTER:   CURRENT DISPLAY
 PF1 : UNDEFINED            PF2 : BROWSE TEMP STORAGE PF3 : UNDEFINED
 PF4 : EIB DISPLAY          PF5 : WORKING STORAGE     PF6 : USER DISPLAY
 PF7 : SCROLL BACK HALF     PF8 : SCROLL FORWARD HALF PF9 : UNDEFINED
 PF10: SCROLL BACK FULL     PF11: SCROLL FORWARD FULL PF12: REMEMBER DISPLAY
```

FIGURE 12.19.   COBOL INIT1 (VSE)

Discussion Questions

1. EDF can be invoked on the same terminal as a transaction to be debugged or can be started on a different terminal. Can you describe any circumstances that might need different terminal checkout?

2. When the program initiation screen is displayed, many of the fields in the EIB can be displayed and modified. Among these fields are EIBAID and EIBTRMID. How could this be useful when debugging a program?

3. If a communications area has been passed a program, it is displayed on the program initiation screen. Modification of the commarea and the field EIBCALEN is also possible. When would this modification be useful during debugging?

4. How are EDF menu functions selected on terminals without PF keys?

5. During program checkout a command interception screen is displayed before each command is executed. What can be done if you decide that the command should not be executed but that the program should continue?

6. At the command interception screen prior to executing a command, the argument values can be changed. What should be done if an argument needs to be changed but the characters that should be modified are beyond the area displayed on the screen?

7. The command interception screen is also displayed after a command has been executed but before control is returned to the program. The command response is displayed on this screen and can be changed if necessary. Any valid response for the command can be overtyped on this screen. How could this be useful in testing very unusual command exceptions?

8. On each command interception screen EDF displays the translator line number for the command. How could this be useful in tracing the logic flow of a program? Where does EDF get this line number value?

9. Explain how EDF could be used to repair a corrupted record in a file?

10. How could you cause EDF to skip over all command interception screens until a READQ command has been encountered?

11. An EDF session is normally ended at task termination. How can you instruct EDF to continue a session across a task boundary? How would this be useful in checking out a pseudoconversational program?

12. Describe how to locate a failing COBOL statement after a transaction abend screen has been displayed by EDF.

13. Why is it important to have a COBOL Data Division map when using EDF to locate a working-storage field?

14. Describe the purpose of base locators in addressing COBOL working-storage. How many bytes (in decimal) can be addressed by one COBOL base locator?

15. How can EDF be used to delete a Temporary Storage queue?

16. The INIT1 routine of a COBOL object module contains the date and time the COBOL program was compiled. This information should correspond to the date and time printed on the compiler listing. What should you do if there is a conflict with these two sources?

17. When each command-level COBOL program is initialized, the Execute Interface Program makes a copy of the original COBOL working-storage and Task Global Table (TGT). When changes are made during an EDF session, the copy of working-storage is modified, not the original version. How would you make changes to the permanent working-storage?

Review Exercises

1. Assume that a field ZIP-CODE appears in the Data Division map as shown below. If, by using the PF5 key during an EDF session, you determine that Working-Storage begins at location 53FE4C, what is the address of the target field?

   ```
   ZIP-CODE BL=2 DISPLACEMENT=0CC
   ```

2. Assume that PF5 has been used to locate working-storage and that the address displayed is 45CE4C. What address would you overtype as the first step in locating the COBOL INIT1 routine?

3. Assume that a task termination screen has been displayed and that the offset of the interrupt shown on the display is 1B1A. Assume further that the COBOL Procedure Division Map shows the information below. On which statement did the interrupt occur?

   ```
   Line Verb Offset
   1039 1    001ADE
   1040 1    001AEE
   1042 1    001B0A
   1043 1    001B14
   1044 1    001B24
   1045 1    001B2A
   ```

Lab Problems

Demonstrate the use of EDF by completing the following tasks at a terminal. Use any of your programs for this lab. Make sure that you have a current program listing, containing the Data Division and Procedure Division maps.

1. Start an EDF session for same terminal checkout.
2. Trace program execution by tracking EDF screens and using the translator listing.
3. Use the SUPPRESS DISPLAYS menu function to speed up the testing process.
4. Modify an argument before or after a command is executed.

5. Modify a command execution response (i.e., NORMAL to some error or some error to NORMAL).
6. Select a working-storage field from the Data Division map. Compute its address using the base locator and displacement shown. Display that field. Modify the field.
7. Locate an argument using the address displayed in hexadecimal mode.
8. Force a task abend from EDF.
9. Locate the EIP save-area pointer that contains the address to INIT1. Type this address on a storage display screen to find the COBOL INIT1. On VSE systems INIT1 starts with X'05F0'; on MVS INTI1 begins with X'90EC'. Use the SCROLL FORWARD PF key to find the date and time compiled. Compare this with your compiler listing. It should match.

13

Problem Determination

As you follow the topics and illustrations in this chapter you will

1. Identify three CICS/VS service aids that can be used to analyze problems in application programs.
2. Understand why EDF may not always be available for problem diagnosis.
3. Learn to use the CICS/VS transaction dump to perform problem diagnosis.
4. See how to use the CICS/VS trace table in doing problem determination.
5. Examine the process of using the transaction dump to locate the failing statement in a COBOL program after a program check interruption occurs in a task.
6. Identify one or more ways to locate the working-storage of a COBOL program in a transaction dump.
7. Follow the steps to locate a specific working-storage field in a transaction dump.
8. Find out how to locate the Execute Interface Block in a transaction dump.
9. See how to use the CICS/VS DUMP and ENTER commands to assist in problem determination.

In the last chapter, you learned to use the Execution Diagnostic Facility in the program testing and debugging process. In this chapter you will learn how to use the standard CICS/VS service aids for the diagnosis of failures in application programs. You may be asking yourself why CICS provides two facilities to do essentially the same thing; locate problems and debug programs. There are three reasons:

First, the service aids were designed prior to the introduction of the Command-Level debugging facility. As with most other features of CICS, IBM continues to support the service aids.

The second reason for the service aids is that EDF may not always be available for problem analysis, and you need something else to fall back on. Oftentimes for security reasons, EDF is not generated in the *production* environment. EDF provides the capability to do many things such as modify working-storage areas prior to file updates. For this and other reasons, some auditors often make recommendations to have the production CICS tailored without EDF support. Generally, in this situation, a separate version of CICS is used in another region for program development and testing and only the test version contains EDF support.

The final reason for the service aids is that unexpected problems often occur in the production environment. The use of EDF presumes that a problem is anticipated since you have to activate it on a terminal. Problems may occur after a program is put into production. Sometimes programs are not adequately tested and errors surface sometime later. At other times records in files or data bases become corrupt by some means. Incorrect contents in data records can cause abends or logic problems. The service aids allow for problem analysis in these situations.

CICS/VS Service Aids

The primary service aids are the transaction dump, internal trace, and auxiliary trace. These service aids are produced by the System Monitoring component of CICS/VS. Afterwards, when the problem has been discovered, a hard-copy printout can be produced by batch utility programs. The following paragraphs will briefly describe these service aids. The remainder of the chapter presents a more detailed description of the listings. These topics include procedures for using these listings. These procedures should be useful as you perform your own problem analysis.

THE TRANSACTION DUMP

A transaction dump is taken by CICS any time a transaction terminates abnormally. A dump can also be requested by the application program with the DUMP command. The transaction dump contains those storage areas related to the transaction and are generally useful in locating the source of a problem. The dump may also contain a formatted printout of an internal trace table that is maintained by CICS.

TRACE TABLE

The trace table is a main storage table that contains a record of actions taken by the CICS management programs. User trace entries can also be made by an application program with the ENTER command. The internal trace table has a *limited* number of slots. As CICS makes trace entries in the internal trace table, it wraps around whenever it becomes full. That is, when the end of the table is reached, CICS begins making new trace entries at the beginning of the table, overwriting old entries. To avoid losing information, an auxiliary trace function may be activated.

AUXILIARY TRACE

The auxiliary trace function makes use of a disk file to record trace entries. Essentially, the same trace entries that are made in the internal trace table are recorded in the auxiliary trace data set. Sometimes, for efficiency reasons, the auxiliary trace function is not activated unless a problem has been anticipated. In these situations, you may have to rely on the internal trace table produced with the transaction dump or activate the auxiliary trace function and try to recreate the problem.

The Transaction Dump

As indicated earlier, the transaction dump is printed by an off-line utility program. This Dump Utility Program reads the dump data set and prints all dumps contained therein. It is possible that other programs have failed or that the program you are analyzing has produced more than one dump. For each dump produced by the system monitoring programs, the Dump Utility Program will print the information in the format shown in figure 13.5.

DUMP LAYOUT

A heading line appears at the top of each page of the transaction dump. This line contains the transaction identification of the task and the date and time the task started. An abend code or dump code is also printed in the heading line. If the dump was caused by an abend, the CICS abend code is printed. If the DUMP command was used to request the dump, the dump code specified in the program is printed. The DUMP command will be described later in this chapter.

The second line of the first page of the transaction dump contains a "short symptom string." This line is intended to be used as a search string for on-line software support programs available on some systems. It contains the abend code, CICS/VS component name and release level, and the name of the program that caused the abend. The program name is useful when more than one program is executed during a task, since it helps you to locate the offending program more quickly.

If the transaction dump was produced due to a program check interruption, the first page will contain the program status word at the time of the failure. Unlike the EDF transaction abend screen, the Dump Utility Program does not print the offset of the instruction or give the reason for the failure. You must interpret the PSW to do this. This procedure will be described later on in this chapter.

The next two lines contain the contents of general registers 14 through 11 at the time the dump was produced. In most cases these registers can be used to locate the program's working-storage and object module load address. Procedures to do this will be covered later in the chapter.

After the registers, the Dump Utility Program prints two task control areas. These task-related control blocks are not usually used in debugging command-level programs but may be necessary in some special instances. The first of these blocks, however, usually contains the Execute Interface Block. By using the layout of the EIB from the linkage section, you can locate individual fields in this area. The literal "DFHEIB" immediately precedes the EIB. It serves as a visual marker to help locate the area.

The transaction dump continues with a printout of any commareas acquired for the task. These areas are labeled *program communication area*.

Following the commareas is another CICS/VS control block, the common system area. The CSA is not generally needed for debugging command-level programs.

The internal trace table follows the CSA. The layout of the trace table will be described later.

After the trace table, there are the various storage areas that have been acquired for the task. Preceding each storage area is a header line that identifies the type of storage and the address range of the storage area. Each line of the dumped area contains up to 32 characters in both hexadecimal and character format. Unprintable characters are translated to the character ".". The left column of each line contains the storage offset of the first character of the line while the right column contains the actual storage address of that character. One or more lines may be suppressed if consecutive lines contain the same contents as an earlier line. If this happens, a "SAME AS ABOVE" message appears, indicating that lines were suppressed.

After the printout of the transaction storage areas, the dump program prints the Terminal Control Table entry for the terminal, and any Terminal Storage areas associated with the task. The Terminal Control Table entry contains the terminal identification as the first four characters. Other information is not normally needed for debugging purposes with command-level programs.

Finally, the program areas are dumped. The program areas usually consist of the COBOL object module(s). A BMS physical map may also appear in the dump listing if a mapping operation has been performed by the task.

PROBLEM DIAGNOSIS

Problem diagnosis using the transaction dump is analogous to procedures that were described in the last chapter. The major difference is that you will be performing the procedures while examining a dump instead of using EDF displays. You might recall from the last chapter that three procedures for problem diagnosis were described. In problem diagnosis using a dump these same tasks are usually necessary. These tasks, listed below, will be described in the paragraphs that follow.

Locating Working-Storage

Locating a Failing Instruction

Locating a Working Storage Field

Locating Working Storage

Generally, most of the program check interrupt problems that occur in a Command-level program are caused by invalid data found in working-storage fields. Because of this, it is important for you to know how to locate the working-storage (copy) in the transaction dump. Once you have found the start of working-storage, you can locate any field. The process of locating a *specific* field is described later. For now, let's see how to find the address of working-storage. Here are two commonly used methods.

1. Usually, one of the registers printed at the top of the dump points to the start of working-storage. Most releases of VSE and MVS COBOL use register 6 to point to working-storage. This is the case in our sample dump. From the printout in figure 13.5, you can see that register 6 contains the address: B8723C. Please take a moment to find this address in the printout.

2. Here is a second procedure that can be used to locate working-storage. It is a little more difficult than the technique just described. First, locate the dumped area with the label *TASK CONTROL AREA (SYSTEM AREA)*. It should be the second storage area in the dump listing. Locate the offset 0040 (hex) in the system TCA. The full-word at that offset contains the address of the COBOL area. The COBOL area contains: a register save area used by the Execute Interface Program, the COBOL working-storage copy, and the COBOL TGT. In our sample dump, the address of the COBOL area (stored at offset hex-40 in the TCA) is B871F0. Please locate the COBOL area at that address. You should find it on page 9 of the dump.

   To find the working-storage copy advance to offset 4C (hex) of the COBOL area. The COBOL working-storage begins at that address. As you can see, we have found working-storage at the same address as we did in our earlier procedure.

Locating a Failing Instruction

As with EDF, when a program check interruption occurs, you will want to find the source statement corresponding to the failure. With EDF you are given the offset of the failing machine instruction which can be used to determine the COBOL source statement that has failed. The offset is not provided in the transaction dump, but information is provided to allow you to *compute* the offset. To compute the offset, use the procedure below.

1. Locate the PSW at the top of the dump. The PSW contains two subareas needed to compute the offset. First, it contains the address of the machine instruction that follows the failing instruction. On the sample dump, this address is: C09302. The PSW also contains the *length* of the failing instruction. The length in the sample dump is 0006.

2. Subtract the instruction length from the next instruction address. The resulting address is the address of the failing instruction. For example:

```
PSW Address                    C09302
Instruction Length             -0006
Failing Address                C092FC
```

3. Next, locate load point of the COBOL object module that contains the failing instruction. Generally, one of the registers at the top of the dump listing contains the address of the load point. From my experience, Register A (decimal 10) is usually used in both MVS and VSE. In our sample dump, register A contains the address C08038. Your COBOL compiler version may use a different register to point to the load module. It is also possible that the pointer register will change with a future release of your COBOL compiler. In either case it may require a little research to identify which register is used.

From Procedure Division Listing

```
00761      *  ********************************************************
00762      *      MODIFY ATTRIBUTES OF SPECIAL FIELDS
00763      *  ********************************************************
00764          IF   VENDOR-PAY-HOLD EQUAL TO 'Y'
00765               MOVE ASKIP-BRT        TO    PAHOLDA   IN DISPMAPI
00766               MOVE COLOR-RED        TO    PAHOLDC   IN DISPMAPO
00767               MOVE HILIGHT-REVERSE TO    PAHOLDH   IN DISPMAPO.
00768      *  *  *  *  *  *  *  *  *  *  *  *  *  *  *  *  *  *  *  *  *  *  *
00769      * THIS LINK TO VEND006 WILL CONVERT THE JULIAN CHECK DATE
00770      *      TO CALENDAR FORM MM/DD/YY RETURN DATE IN CALENDAR DATE
00771      *  *  *  *  *  *  *  *  *  *  *  *  *  *  *  *  *  *  *  *  *  *  *
00772          MOVE VENDOR-LAST-CK-DATE  TO    JULIAN-DATE.
00773          MOVE +2 TO DATES-FUNCTION.
```

From Procedure Division Map

736	VERB	1	00117C	736	VERB	2	001182	737	VERB	1	0011A0
741	VERB	1	0011BE	742	VERB	1	0011CC	743	VERB	1	0011D2
744	VERB	1	0011D8	745	VERB	1	0011DE	746	VERB	1	0011E4
747	VERB	1	0011EA	748	VERB	1	0011F0	749	VERB	1	0011F6
750	VERB	1	0011FC	751	VERB	1	001202	752	VERB	1	001208
753	VERB	1	00121A	754	VERB	1	00122C	755	VERB	1	00123E
756	VERB	1	001244	757	VERB	1	00126C	758	VERB	1	00127E
759	VERB	1	001290	760	VERB	1	0012A2	764	VERB	1	0012A8
765	VERB	1	0012B2	766	VERB	1	0012B8	767	VERB	1	0012BE
772	VERB	1	0012C4	773	VERB	1	0012CA	778	VERB	1	0012D0
779	VERB	1	0012E0	780	VERB	1	0012EA	781	VERB	1	0012F0
783	VERB	1	00131E	784	VERB	1	00132C	785	VERB	1	001332
786	VERB	1	001338	793	VERB	1	001356	794	VERB	1	001366
795	VERB	1	00136C	796	VERB	1	001372	827	VERB	1	0013AE
828	VERB	1	0013BE	830	VERB	1	0013DC	831	VERB	1	0013F8

FIGURE 13.1.   Procedure Division Statements and PMAP (CLIST with VSE)

Let's look at one more technique of locating the load point of the object module. Some optimizing versions of the COBOL compiler do not use a register to point to the load module. Therefore, you may have to use this more difficult process to locate the area.

First, locate the address of the working-storage copy. This process was described in the previous section. In the sample dump, recall that we found working-storage at address B8723C. Next, back up 16 bytes (hexadecimal 10) from this address. You might remember from the EDF chapter that the full-word at minus hex-10 from working-storage contains the address of the load module. If you look at the dump now on page 9, you will see that the full-word at hex-10 bytes back from working-storage contains the address C08038. This is the same value that we found in register A.

4. Subtract the load address from the computed address of the failing instruction. The result is the offset of the failing instruction. This is the same offset displayed on the EDF abend screen. Write down this offset.

```
failing address                C092FC
load point                    -C08038
failing offset                  012C4
```

The next two steps are the same as described in the EDF chapter (12).

5. Locate the Procedure Division map in the compile listing. An extract of a Procedure Division map is shown in figure 13.1. This PMAP (CLIST in VSE) is necessary to locate the COBOL source statement containing the machine instruction that failed. The condensed PMAP in this

```
0001 Operation Exception
0002 Priviledged Operation Exception
0003 Execute Exception
0004 Protection Exception
0005 Addressing Exception
0006 Specification Exception
0007 Data Exception
0008 Fixed Point Overflow
0009 Fixed Point Divide
000A Decimal Overflow Exception
000B Decimal Divide Exception
000C Exponent Overflow Exception
000D Exponent Underflow Exception
000E Significance Exception
000F Floating Point Divide
```

FIGURE 13.2.   System/370 Program Interrupt Codes

example contains the offset of the first machine instruction for each statement in the Procedure Division. Depending on the compiler option, the actual verb or the verb number will be listed.

6. Locate the COBOL statement and verb number which corresponds to the offset of the failing instruction. Look for the offset (12C4) computed above. In our example, this statement is on line number 772, verb 1.

7. Next, determine the reason for the interrupt. An interrupt code is stored in the PSW to allow you to do this. Figure 13.2 lists the program check interruption codes and descriptions that can occur on an IBM mainframe computer. Using figure 13.2 and the interrupt code from the PSW, determine the reason for the interrupt. Now analyze the source statement on the compiler listing. In our example, the reason for the interruption was a "DATA EXCEPTION," or OC7. This error is caused when the machine attempts to use a COMP-3 field in a calculation or editing operation and the field contains an invalid data format.

Many times you may be able to determine the cause of the problem without further use of dump. This can be done by identifying the fields involved in the operation and analyzing prior use of such fields. For instance, a COMP-3 field may have been used but may not have been previously initialized. Sometimes a more thorough analysis is needed. You may have to locate and examine the contents of the fields involved in the operation to determine the cause of the failure. Most often these fields reside in working-storage.

LOCATING A WORKING-STORAGE FIELD

The following paragraphs describe a procedure that you can follow to locate any working-storage field. Let's resume our transaction abend problem analysis from the previous section.

Recall that the transaction had abended with a "DATA EXCEPTION" in statement number 772. The statement was "MOVE VENDOR-LAST-CK-DATE TO JULIAN-DATE." After an analysis of the statement, you might conclude, as I have, that something is wrong with the contents of field "VENDOR-LAST-CK-DATE." We'll use the procedure below to locate this suspect field.

1. First, locate the field in the compiler listing, Data Division map. The Data Division map contains a line for each COBOL data name defined. Figure 13.3 is an extract from a compiler listing. This figure depicts a Data Division map showing definitions for our suspect field. Each line entry contains the source program name, a reference to a base locator (BL) number and

Data Division Listing

```
00053                 05  VENDOR-LAST-CHECK      PIC S9(05)     COMP-3.
00054                 05  VENDOR-LAST-CK-DATE    PIC S9(05)     COMP-3.
00055                 05  VENDOR-LAST-CK-AMT     PIC S9(07)V99  COMP-3.
00056                 05  VENDOR-DATE-ADDED      PIC S9(05)     COMP-3.
00057                 05  VENDOR-DATE-CHANGED    PIC S9(05)     COMP-3.
00058                 05  VENDOR-LAST-OPID       PIC XXX.
```

Data Division Map

```
DNM=3-156  02  VENDOR-LAST-CHECK     BL=1  0F9   DNM=3-156  DS 3P  COMP-3
DNM=3-183  02  VENDOR-LAST-CK-DATE   BL=1  0FC   DNM=3-183  DS 3P  COMP-3
DNM=3-212  02  VENDOR-LAST-CK-AMT    BL=1  0FF   DNM=3-212  DS 5P  COMP-3
DNM=3-240  02  VENDOR-DATE-ADDED     BL=1  104   DNM=3-240  DS 3P  COMP-3
DNM=3-267  02  VENDOR-DATE-CHANGED   BL=1  107   DNM=3-267  DS 3P  COMP-3
DNM=3-296  02  VENDOR-LAST-OPID      BL=1  10A   DNM=3-296  DS 3C  DISP
```

FIGURE 13.3.　Data Division Entries and Map

a hexadecimal displacement within the BL. At compile time, a base locator is assigned to each 4096 (hex 1000) bytes of working-storage. During execution of the program, the base locator plus the displacement value is used by the processor to locate the field. The field named VENDOR-LAST-CK-DATE has been assigned to base locator 1 and has a displacement of OFC within the BL.

2. Next, locate the beginning of working-storage. This process was described earlier. In the sample dump, the start of working-storage is at address B8723C.

3. If the field that you want to locate is referenced by the first BL, you can simply add the offset given in the Data Division map to the working-storage address to compute the actual address of the field. In our example, by adding OFC to the working-storage address of B8723C, we come up with B87338.

4. Using the addresses supplied in front of each dumped area, locate the storage area that contains this address. Then, using the address on the right column, locate the line and finally the storage location containing the field. In examining the contents of VENDOR-LAST-CK-DATE, we can see that high-values have somehow made their way into this COMP-3 field.

5. To find the address of a field referenced by other than BL1, you must compute the sum of the three values: the start of working-storage, the base locator offset, and the field displacement. The base locator and field displacement are taken directly from the Data Division map. The base locator offset is a multiple of 4096 or hex 1000 bytes as indicated below. This process was described in more detail in chapter 12.

```
BL=2        001000
BL=3        002000
BL=4        003000
etc.
```

LOCATING THE EIB

Sometimes you will need to locate the Execute Interface Block to determine the reason for a transaction abend. When an abend is caused by a CICS exceptional condition, a transaction dump may be produced. In some cases, you won't even need to examine the dump to determine the problem. For example, if the dump code is AIES, you can quickly determine that a "file-not-open" condition existed in a transaction. Chances are that by the time you even see the dump, the problem has been corrected. In other situations, further analysis may be required. For instance, one exceptional condition that will cause an abend and produce a dump is "ILLOGIC" or abend code "AEIU." This condition occurs when some program error occurs with a VSAM file. In this situation the EIB contains the VSAM return code. You might need this to determine the VSAM problem. The EIB is usually easy to locate. As mentioned earlier, the constant "DFHEIB" is placed just ahead of the EIB fields in the dump. Just look for this marker. It can be found in one of two storage areas:

1. Most often the EIB is found towards the end of the control block identified as "TASK CONTROL AREA (USER AREA)." This is the first control block in the dump.
2. If abend occurs in the very first execution of the task for the day, the EIB will not be in the TASK CONTROL AREA. It will be in one of the areas labeled "TRANSACTION STORAGE-USER." The EIB is one of the first storage areas acquired for the task and will therefore be towards the end of the dump as one of the last storage areas.

Once you have located the "DFHEIB" marker, use the COBOL layout in the LINKAGE SECTION to locate the specific EIB field.

THE DUMP COMMAND

A transaction dump can be requested by an application program by using the DUMP command. The DUMP command can be an effective tool for trapping special problem situations for later analysis. The format of the DUMP command is

```
EXEC CICS DUMP
          DUMPCODE (name)
          FROM (data-area)
          LENGTH (data-value)
          TASK
          END-EXEC
```

where

DUMPCODE (name) specifies a four-character code that will be printed in dump listing on the heading line.

FROM (data-area) is the name of a COBOL area to be dumped.

LENGTH (data-value) specifies the total number of bytes to be dumped. This can be a numeric constant or an S9999 COMPUTATIONAL field that contains a value indicating the number of bytes to be dumped.

In response to this command, CICS will dump all of the areas shown in the sample dump at the end of the chapter, with the exception of the PSW information. The FROM data area will be identified in the dump as "SEGMENT STORAGE" and will contain the number of bytes specified in the LENGTH option.

Here is an example of a command that might be used in a program to dump the EIB so it will be easier to locate in the listing.

```
EXEC CICS DUMP
          DUMPCODE ('A256')
          FROM (DFHEIB)
          LENGTH (256)
          TASK
          END-EXEC
```

This capability to produce a transaction dump presents some useful design strategies for problem determination. There may be problem situations that a program can logically detect but that still might require further problem diagnosis. For example, file operations can result in two exceptional conditions, IOERR and, for VSAM, ILLOGIC. When either of these conditions occurs, the Execute Interface Program provides the response code from the operating system access methods (VSAM, ISAM, BDAM) to the program in the field EIBRCODE. If the program has a HANDLE CONDITION active for these conditions, EIP will return control to the program without producing a dump. The program probably cannot recover from the error but may end the transaction with an error message to the terminal operator. It could also produce a dump to document the problem and capture the response code. The dump could then be printed and analyzed at a later time.

PROBLEM CONTROL

In an on-line system, many problems often go unreported. Oftentimes an operator, upon seeing an error message, will clear the screen and try the transaction again. Sometimes the problem just "goes away" and the operator is able to continue with another similar transaction, but perhaps with another record. In other cases the operator may abandon the transaction and work on something else. What happens if the operator never reports the error message? Chances are there is a program or file problem that must be corrected. In many installations, it is a common practice for operations to print the dump data set at certain intervals and deliver the listing to someone responsible for identifying system problems. In a production CICS environment, the presence of a dump is a good indication that a problem exists. The DUMP command provides an opportunity to document problems that might otherwise go unnoticed. By implementing problem control design strategies with the dump facility, the stability on an on-line system can often be improved. This practice should result in fewer problems and better productivity of the systems support staff.

The Internal Trace Table

The CICS/VS trace table is a debugging and problem determination aid for application programmers and system programmers. When activated by the master terminal operator, the Trace Control Program records information in the trace table at three points:

at entry to each management program

at exit from each management program

at user-specified monitor points

You might recall from chapter 1 that there is a great deal of interaction between the management programs during the execution of a single task. The trace function records this interaction for use in system and application debugging. Let's take, for example, a single command from an application program and look at the trace entries that would be made. Assume that you have a program that has just issued a READ command against a master file. That command would be translated into a call to EIP. Upon calling Execute Interface Program, an EIP trace entry would be made. EIP would in turn call the File Control Program to perform the read function. Upon entry to FCP, a trace entry would be made. File control would have to call storage control to acquire storage for the read operation. A trace entry for SCP would be made. Storage control would then return control back to file control with an acquired area. Upon exit from SCP, a trace entry would be made. File control would then proceed with a read or "get" function. Knowing that an I/O operation had been started, FCP would issue a task control wait function. Upon entry to task control, a KCP trace entry would be made. Later after the I/O has been completed, file control would be activated and would return control to EIP. At exit from FCP a trace entry would be made. EIP would then return control back to the application program. An EIP trace entry would record this fact. Processing would then continue in the application program. All of the trace entries that are made are intended to allow a complete trace of system activities that occur during the life of a transaction. These detailed trace entries are normally needed by the systems programmer only in resolving system-level problems. As a command-level programmer you can usually perform transaction-level problem resolution by examining only the EIP trace entries. Therefore in this book we will only describe the contents of the EIP trace entries.

TRACE TABLE FORMAT

The internal trace table printout includes a trace table header and individual trace entries. The trace table header contains some information about the actual address of the trace table; you won't need this information in debugging an application program. Individual trace entries follow the header. Trace entries are printed in columns for ease of use. The columns are

TIME OF DAY The time of day accurate to the microsecond is printed. This information might be used in analyzing the performance of a system.

ID The hexadecimal trace identification of the CICS/VS program making the trace entry. Each CICS program has its own unique trace identification code. Your application can also make trace entries with the ENTER command (described later). These trace entries can have hex codes ranging from "00" through "C7."

REG 14 The contents of register 14 at entry to the CICS management or service. For CICS commands, register 14 contains the address of the point in the application program immediately following the call to CICS.

REQD A two-byte code indicating the requested service.

TASK The unique task number assigned to the task. This corresponds with the field EIBTASKN in your transaction.

FIELD A, FIELD B Hexadecimal values. They vary for each trace entry. I will describe the contents of these fields in the next section.

CHARS The character representation of FIELD A and FIELD B.

RESOURCE For some entries, this column represents a CICS/VS resource being used. For example, in a LINK or XCTL command, the program name is printed.

TRACE TYPE These two columns represent an interpreted description of the ID and REQD columns. The first column contains the abbreviation of the CICS/VS management program name that requested the trace. The second column contains a brief description of the request.

INTERVAL The time delay between this trace entry and the previous entry is printed. If the time interval exceeds 12,800 milliseconds, the entry is flagged with an asterisk. This can be useful to the systems programmer in dealing with performance problems.

EIP TRACE ENTRIES

As mentioned earlier, you can usually diagnose problems by examining only the Execute Interface Program trace entries. In this section we will look at the important fields in the EIP entries in more detail.

EIP trace entries can be identified in two ways:

by trace ID

by trace type

The trace ID for EIP is a hexadecimal code of "E1." The corresponding TRACE TYPE code will indicate "EIP." You will probably agree that the TRACE TYPE column is easier to use.

As indicated earlier, a trace entry is made upon entry to the management program and upon return to the calling program. In the case of EIP trace entries, the TRACE TYPE will indicate "EIP COMMAND ENTRY" and the EIP exit entry will specify "EIP COMMAND RESPONSE." The contents of the other trace fields are as follows:

FOR EIP ENTRY

The REG 14 field contains the address of the instruction in the application program following the generated call statement to EIP.

The register 14 value can be used to determine the COBOL statement number of the command in the source program. To determine the statement number follow this procedure:

The TASK field contains the unique task number. Since the trace table contains trace entries for all tasks, this code can be used to isolate trace entries for your task. For example, assume that you are following the trace activity for task number 17846. Other trace entries may appear for task numbers 17844, 17845, and 17847. You would ignore the entries for those tasks and only look at the EIP entries for task 17846.

FIELD A contains the address of COBOL working-storage. This field provides another way of locating the working-storage if you need to find a specific field or data area using the COBOL listings. If you examine the trace entry that occurred at 20:04:11. 118752 on page 8 of the dump, you will see that FIELD A contains the address of working-storage for our dumped program (VEND002).

FOR EIP RESPONSE

FIELD A and the first two bytes of FIELD B contain the hexadecimal response code from the command. This response code corresponds to the response code returned to the application program in the EIB field EIBRCODE. If these bytes contain low-values, the command response was normal. If other than low-values appear in these locations, there was an exceptional condition. Appendix A shows some of the return codes that can appear in FIELD A and FIELD B when an exceptional condition occurs. The last two bytes of FIELD B contain the original function code. This code corresponds to the contents of field EIBFN. See Appendix A for a list of command function codes.

The REG 14 field contains the actual return address to the application program. If the command response was normal or the NOHANDLE option was used (or implied), this address should be the same as the REG 14 contents in the EIP—ENTRY trace entry. But if an exceptional condition occurred and the program had a HANDLE CONDITION active, REG 14 contains the address of the paragraph or section that EIP branched to as a result of the exceptional condition. The COBOL statement number can be determined by computing the offset of this address and referring to the COBOL PMAP. The procedure to compute the offset of a statement was described earlier in the chapter.

THE ENTER COMMAND

A user trace entry can be recorded in the trace table by issuing the ENTER command. The format of the ENTER command is

```
EXEC CICS ENTER
          TRACEID (data-value)
          FROM (data-area)
          RESOURCE (name)
          END-EXEC
```

where

TRACEID (data-value) specifies a value in the range 0 through 199.

FROM (data-area) specifies an eight-byte data area whose contents are to be entered into the FIELD A and FIELD B areas of the trace entry.

RESOURCE (name) specifies an eight-byte name that is to be entered into the resource area of the trace entry.

Exceptional Condition The only exceptional condition for the ENTER command is INVREQ. It will be raised if the TRACEID argument value is greater than 199. The CICS management modules use these larger values.

USING THE ENTER COMMAND

By placing the ENTER command at strategic points in your program, you can make program debugging easier. For instance, you could place it at the start of each paragraph or section to show that the program has entered that routine. An ENTER command could even be placed before and after processing routines within a paragraph. Each of these trace points would appear in the transaction dump for reference. These commands would also show up during an EDF session to assist you in following your program logic.

Auxiliary Trace

There may be times when the printout of the internal trace table will not adequately provide for complete problem determination. First, the internal trace table is limited in size. On a highly active system, the sheer number of trace entries may cause CICS to wrap around to the beginning of the table every few seconds, causing the earlier entries to be erased. This means that you may not have all of the trace entries you need when the dump is produced. Another problem with the trace table printout in the transaction dump is that all trace entries are printed. In some instances this is useful, especially when you are trying to find out if another transaction is somehow causing yours to fail. But in most cases you have to skip over the trace entries that are not related to your task. To alleviate these problems, CICS/VS provides an auxiliary trace function.

Like the internal trace function, the auxiliary trace facility is activated by the master terminal operator. When activated, CICS opens an auxiliary trace data set to enable trace entries to be recorded. Each trace entry in the format described earlier is placed in an output buffer. When the buffer becomes full, it is written to the auxiliary trace file. By doing this, no trace entries are lost as in the case when the internal trace table wraps around. When the data set becomes full, the operator is informed, and the file is closed. The contents of this data set can be printed by using the Trace Utility Program.

TRACE UTILITY PROGRAM

The Trace Utility Program is a batch utility that formats and prints trace records stored in the auxiliary trace data set. The printout (depicted in figure 13.4) looks similar to the internal trace entries in the transaction dump. The trace can then be printed by the operator or browsed in the system queues by an on-line program provided by the operating system.

One nice feature of the Trace Utility Program is the ability to extract and format selected records from the trace data set. The selection options are

all trace entries

entries written for one or more terminals

entries written for one or more transaction codes

entries written for one or more trace codes

entries written to the trace data set within specified time ranges

Through combinations of the selection criteria it is possible to reduce the trace printout to a manageable size. As an example, you could request a printout of only the USER and EIP trace entries on a particular terminal for a given transaction code. This is one reason why the auxiliary trace is often more useful than the internal trace produced in the transaction dump.

SELECTION PARAMETERS:
    DEVICE=DISK,TERMID=DT03,TYPETR=(00-C7,E1),
    TRANID=(VEND,V#02,V#03,V#04,V#05,V#06)

AUXILIARY TRACE ACTIVATED AT - 20:03:44.32

TIME OF DAY	ID	REG 14	REQD TASK	FIELD A	FIELD B	CHARS	RESOURCE	TRACE TYPE	INTERVAL
20:03:55.142112	E1	50C10EB2	0004 17822	00B82EAC	0000208	......		EIP ASSIGN ENTRY	00.000512
20:03:55.142624	E1	50C10EB2	00F4 17822	00000000	0000208	......		EIP ASSIGN RESPONSE	00.000544
20:03:55.143168	E1	50C1105C	0004 17822	00B82EAC	0000A04	......		EIP READQ-TS ENTRY	00.003296
20:03:55.146464	E1	50C1105C	00F4 17822	0000000C	0000A04	......		EIP READQ-TS RESPONSE	00.000544
20:03:55.147008	E1	50C10F58	0004 17822	00B82EAC	0001804	......		EIP SEND-MAP ENTRY	00.018112
20:03:55.165120	E1	50C10F58	00F4 17822	00000000	0001804	......		EIP SEND-MAP RESPONSE	00.000448
20:03:55.165568	E1	50C10FA6	0004 17822	00B82EAC	0000E08	......		EIP RETURN ENTRY	*04.740960
20:03:59.906528	E1	50C11408	0004 17829	00B86A4C	0001802	......		EIP RECEIVE-MAP ENTRY	*04.034912
20:03:59.941440	E1	50C11408	00F4 17829	00000000	0001802	......		EIP RECEIVE-MAP RESPONSE	00.000544
20:03:59.941984	E1	50C11640	0004 17829	00B86A4C	0000E04	......		EIP XCTL ENTRY	*00.032160
20:03:59.974144	E1	50C0900E	0004 17829	00B8723C	0001A04	......		EIP ENTER ENTRY	00.000544
20:03:59.974688	10	50C0900E	00F4 17829	0000ESC5	DSC44040	.VEND	VEND001	USER 016	00.000224
20:03:59.974912	E1	50C0900E	00F4 17829	00000000	0001A04	......		EIP ENTER RESPONSE	00.000704
20:03:59.975616	E1	50C0995C	0004 17829	00B8723C	0000602	......		EIP READ ENTRY	*00.014656
20:03:59.990272	E1	50C0995C	00F4 17829	00000000	0000602	......		EIP READ RESPONSE	00.001664
20:03:59.991936	E1	50C09356	0004 17829	00B8723C	0000E02	......		EIP LINK ENTRY	00.011616
20:04:00.003552	E1	50C0697C	0004 17829	00B86C6C	0000E02	......		EIP RETURN ENTRY	00.003264
20:04:00.006816	E1	50C09356	00F4 17829	0000000D	0000E02	......		EIP LINK RESPONSE	00.000576
20:04:00.007392	E1	50C09712	0004 17829	00000000	0000A04	......		EIP READQ-TS ENTRY	00.003264
20:04:00.010656	E1	50C09712	00F4 17829	0000000D	0000A02	......		EIP READQ-TS RESPONSE	00.000544
20:04:00.011200	E1	50C097C2	0004 17829	00B8723C	0000A02	......		EIP WRITEQ-TS ENTRY	00.003200
20:04:00.014400	E1	50C097C2	00F4 17829	00000000	0000A02	......		EIP WRITEQ-TS RESPONSE	00.000480
20:04:00.014880	E1	50C093E0	0004 17829	00B8723C	0001804	......		EIP SEND-MAP ENTRY	*00.017024
20:04:00.031904	E1	50C093E0	00F4 17829	00B8723C	0000E08	......		EIP SEND-MAP RESPONSE	00.000448
20:04:00.032352	E1	50C0910C	0004 17829	00B86A4C	0001804	......		EIP RETURN ENTRY	*02.298144
20:04:02.330496	E1	50C0900E	0004 17832	00000000	0001A04	......		EIP ENTER ENTRY	00.000512
20:04:02.331008	10	50C0900E	0002 17832	0000ESC5	DSC44040	.VEND	VEND001	USER 016	00.000224
20:04:02.331232	E1	50C0900E	00F4 17832	00000000	0001A04	......		EIP ENTER RESPONSE	00.000832
20:04:02.332064	E1	50C098BC	0004 17832	00B86A4C	0000602	......		EIP SEND-MAP ENTRY	*00.013856
20:04:02.345920	E1	50C09906	0004 17832	00000000	0001804	......		EIP SEND-MAP RESPONSE	00.000416
20:04:02.346336	E1	50C11408	0004 17836	00B86A4C	0000E08	......		EIP RETURN ENTRY	*02.514528
20:04:04.860864	E1	50C11408	00F4 17836	00000000	0001802	......		EIP RECEIVE-MAP ENTRY	00.011232
20:04:04.872096	E1	50C11640	0004 17836	00B86A4C	0000E04	......		EIP RECEIVE-MAP RESPONSE	00.000576
20:04:04.872672	E1	50C0900E	0004 17836	00B86A4C	0001A04	......		EIP XCTL ENTRY	*00.013024
20:04:04.885696	10	50C0900E	0002 17836	0000ESC5	DSC44040	.VEND	VEND001	USER 016	00.000512
20:04:04.886208	E1	50C0900E	00F4 17836	00000000	0001A04	......		EIP ENTER RESPONSE	00.000224
20:04:04.886432	E1	50C0995C	0004 17836	00B8723C	0000602	......		EIP READ ENTRY	00.000480
20:04:04.886912	E1	50C0995C	00F4 17836	00000000	0000602	......		EIP READ RESPONSE	*00.017152
20:04:04.904064	E1	50C09356	0004 17836	00B8723C	0000E02	......		EIP LINK ENTRY	00.001600
20:04:04.905664	E1	50C0697C	0004 17836	00B86C6C	0000E08	......		EIP RETURN ENTRY	00.011072
20:04:04.916736	E1	50C09356	00F4 17836	0000000D	0000E02	......		EIP LINK RESPONSE	00.003488
20:04:04.920224	E1	50C09712	0004 17836	00B8723C	0000A04	......		EIP READQ-TS ENTRY	00.000512
20:04:04.920736	E1	50C09356	00F4 17836	00000000	0000A04	......		EIP READQ-TS RESPONSE	00.003296
20:04:04.924032	E1	50C09712	0004 17836	00000000	0000A04	......		EIP WRITEQ-TS ENTRY	00.000480
20:04:04.924512	E1	50C097C2	00F4 17836	00B8723C	0000A02	......		EIP WRITEQ-TS RESPONSE	00.003680
20:04:04.928192	E1	50C097C2	00F4 17836	00000000	0000A02	......		EIP WRITEQ-TS RESPONSE	00.000480
20:04:04.928736	E1	50C093E0	0004 17836	00B8723C	0001804	......		EIP SEND-MAP ENTRY	00.000544

FIGURE 13.4. Auxiliary Trace Listing

TIME OF DAY	ID	REG 14	REQD	TASK	FIELD A	FIELD B	CHARS	RESOURCE	TRACE TYPE	INTERVAL
20:04:04.953888	E1	50C093E0	00F4	17836	00000000	00001804	....		EIP SEND-MAP RESPONSE	*00.025152
20:04:04.954336	E1	50C0910C	0004	17836	00B8723C	00000E08	....		EIP RETURN ENTRY	00.000448
20:04:07.515168	E1	50C0900E	0004	17840	00B86A4C	00001A04	....		EIP ENTER ENTRY	*02.560832
20:04:07.515680	10	50C0900E	0002	17840	000DE5C5	D5C44040	..VEND	VEND001	USER 016	00.000512
20:04:07.515904	E1	50C0900E	00F4	17840	00000000	00001A04	....		EIP ENTER RESPONSE	00.000224
20:04:07.516736	E1	50C098BC	0004	17840	00B86A4C	00001804	....		EIP SEND-MAP ENTRY	00.000832
20:04:07.543520	E1	50C098BC	00F4	17840	00000000	00001804	....		EIP SEND-MAP RESPONSE	*00.026784
20:04:07.544000	E1	50C09906	0004	17840	00B86A4C	00000E08	....		EIP RETURN ENTRY	00.000480
20:04:11.092256	E1	50C11408	0004	17846	00B86A4C	00001802	....		EIP RECEIVE-MAP ENTRY	*03.548256
20:04:11.104288	E1	50C11408	00F4	17846	00000000	00001802	....		EIP RECEIVE-MAP RESPONSE	00.012032
20:04:11.104960	E1	50C11640	0004	17846	00B8723C	00001A04	....		EIP XCTL ENTRY	00.000672
20:04:11.118752	E1	50C0900E	0004	17846	00B86A4C	00001A04	....		EIP ENTER ENTRY	*00.013792
20:04:11.119296	10	50C0900E	0002	17846	000DE5C5	D5C44040	..VEND	VEND001	USER 016	00.000544
20:04:11.119520	E1	50C0900E	00F4	17846	00000000	00001A04	....		EIP ENTER RESPONSE	00.000224
20:04:11.119936	E1	50C0995C	0004	17846	00B8723C	00000602	....		EIP READ ENTRY	00.000416
20:04:11.141248	E1	50C0995C	00F4	17846	00000000	00000602	....		EIP READ RESPONSE	*00.021312

END OF AUXILIARY TRACE DATA -   TOTAL TIME ACTIVE   00:00:34.54
                                    TRACE RECORDS READ   8,063
                                    TRACE RECORDS SELECTED   63

EOJ TRACCICS   DATE 11/04/86, CLOCK 20/06/01, DURATION 00/00/13

FIGURE 13.4.   Continued

CUSTOMER INFORMATION CONTROL SYSTEM STORAGE DUMP   CODE=ASRA   TASK=VEND   DATE=11/04/86   TIME=20:04:11   PAGE   1

SYMPTOMS= AB/UASRA PIDS/5746XX300 FLDS/F000KC RIDS/VEND002

CICS/VS LEVEL = 0160

PSW   03BD0000   00C09302   0006D007   00000000

REGS 14-4 50B1F0A0   00C0916A   00B87707   00000000   00C092FC   60C09290   00B86384
REGS 5-11 40C09ECC   00B8723C   00B87A73   00000000   00C09E8A   00B87A74   00C08038

TASK CONTROL AREA (USER AREA)   ADDRESS 00B86140 TO 00B869FF   LENGTH 0008C0

```
0000000  00B86000 00AE6224 01ADF970 00AE64E0  00B86570 00B439A0 2000FE00 C03100A0  *-.......9.......................*   00B86140
0000020  50B283FA 00000000 00000000 00B86B38  50B269FC 00B279FC 00B86BF4 00000000  *.c.............,4.............*   00B86160
0000040  00B86AC0 00B25C98 00B28030 00B25C20  00B86BE0 00B86B30 50B1F0A0 00B86AC0  *.....*q....*.....0..........*   00B86180
0000060  40B1EEC8 C1E2D9C1 00B87707 00006000  00B1FB00 60C09290 00CA7230 00B1EC94  *...HASRA...-...8....k....m*   00B861A0
0000080  FE006BE0 E5C5D5C6 C9D3C540 C1E2D9C1  03BD0000 00C09302 00060007 00000000  *..,.VENFILE ASRA.....k...l*   00B861C0
00000A0  50B1F0A0 00C0916A 00B87707 00000000  00C092FC 60C09290 00C08038 40C09ECC  *.0...j....k.....k..d*   00B861E0
00000C0  00B8723C 00B87A74 00C09E8A 00000000  00C08038 06020000 00000000 00000000  *..........................*   00B86200
00000E0  00B86AC0 8C0000A8 24F40000 00000000  00000000 00000000 00000000 00000000  *.......y.4.................*   00B86220
0000100  00000000 00000000 00000000 00000000  00000000 00000000 00000000 00000000  *..........................*   00B86240
0000120  LINES TO 00000140 SAME AS ABOVE
0000160  00000000 00000000 8B000028 00B862A8  00000000 00B23E90 00000000 00000000  *...........y......y......*   00B862A0
0000180  00000000 00000000 00000000 00000000  00000028 00B862A8 00000238 00B862D8  *........Q.........y...Q.*   00B862C0
00001A0  00B86438 00000000 00000000 00000000  00000000 40404040 00ADF970 00000000  *......       ...9.*   00B862E0
00001C0  00000000 00000000 00B25C20 00000000  00000000 00000000 00000000 00B871C0  *.....*..............*   00B86300
00001E0  00000000 00000000 00000000 80B26480  00000000 3FFF0000 00000004 00008000  *..........*........0.*   00B86320
0000200  00B863F0 00000000 00000000 00000000  00000000 00000004 00B871C0 00017000  *..0.................0.*   00B86340
0000220  00000000 00000000 00B86438 00B87854  00000000 00000000 00B871C0 00B37854  *.........H....d.a.*   00B86360
0000240  00000000 00000000 80B871C8 00B86384  00B8723C 00C08108 00CA723C 00B204D0  *.......H...d.a.*   00B86380
0000260  50AED2DA 50C0803A 00CA723C 00C08FA0  00C08108 00B87200 00C08080 00B204D0  *.K.....d.a....Q./*   00B863A0
0000280  00B86000 00C08038 00AED074 00000000  00B23F80 00B862D8 00B86140 00000000  *.-...........d..h.*   00B863C0
00002A0  00000000 00000000 00000000 00B86A08  80B86388 00B86388 00000000 00000000  *.............d..h.*   00B863E0
00002C0  00000000 00000000 00000000 00B86A08  00000000 00B86438 00B86438 00B87C28  *................*   00B86400
00002E0  00000000 00000000 00000000 000004E1  40C4C6C8 C5C9C240 0200411C 0086308F  *......DFHEIB....f.*   00B86440
0000300  E5C5D5C4 0017846C C4E3F0F3 000004E1  00017FD06 C5D5C6C9 C5D5C6C9 00000000  *VEND..d.DT03....VENFI*   00B86460
0000320  D3C54000 00000000 000000E5 C5D5C6C9  D3C54000 00000000 00000000 00000000  *LE ...VENFILE.*   00B86480
0000340  LINES TO 000003A0 SAME AS ABOVE
00003C0  00000000 00000000 00000000 00000000  00000238 00B862D8 00000000 00B3FFD0  *.........Q.O.*   00B86500
00003E0  00000001 00B3EE2C 00000000 00B3EDCC  00000001 00B3EE2C 00000002 00000000  *...................*   00B86520
0000400  00000000 00000000 00000000 00000000  00000000 00000000 00000000 00000000  *...................*   00B86540
0000420  00000000 00000000 D3C9C6D6 E2E3D6D9  42000068 00000000 FFB865D8 40B262D6  *.....LIFOSTOR....Q..O*   00B86560
0000440  00B873BA 90B26448 00B87C28 00B87834  00B86A08 00B8734C 00000000 00B86EC  *...............*   00B86580
0000460  00000000 00AED950 00B25D10 00B25C20  00B86140 00B86D10 00AE60E0 FEB865D8  *...........Q./.-..Q*   00B865A0
0000480  F000D2C3 00AE8980 00000000 00000000  00000000 00000000 480000B0 00B86570  *0.KC.i.........*   00B865C0
00004A0  FFB86688 00000000 C0040000 00000000  00B8665C 50B269FC 00B279FC 00B865F1  *..h..............1*   00B865E0
00004C0  00B873BA 00B86000 480000B0 00B28EB8  00B25D10 00B862D8 00B86140 00000000  *..............9...Q./*   00B86600
00004E0  00AE60E0 FEB86688 F500C6C3 00B26C10  01000000 00000000 10B86BE0 E5C5D5C6  *.-...h5.FC....,.VENF*   00B86620
0000500  C9D3C540 00B25C20 000004DF 00000000  00B86AA8 00000000 00000000 00000000  *ILE.*........y.*   00B86640
```

FIGURE 13.5.   CICS/VS Transaction Dump

TASK CONTROL AREA (USER AREA)   ADDRESS 00B86140 TO 00B869FF   LENGTH 0008C0

```
00000520  00000000 00000000  00000000 00000000  00000000 00000000  00000000 00000000  *................................*  00B86660
00000540  00000000 FEB86610  48000178 00B865D8  01020505 00020505  00000000 00000020  *.........Q......................*  00B86680
00000560  F0F0F140 00ADF970  D4C5D5E4 D4C1D740  E5C5D5C4 E2C5E340  00AED074 000001A4  *001 .....MENUMAP VENDSET ..u....*  00B866A0
00000580  00000000 00B86668  00000000 80B19136  00B1A3CC FEB86800  EA00E3D4 00B1805C  *.........j..t...TM.**  00B866C0
000005A0  00000034 07800000  80B18100 00CA7320  00B40B25 00B86130  80B181CA 00000000  *.........a.......*  00B866E0
000005C0  00000034 00B861C4  80B18274 00B40B25  00B861C4 00B48E04  80B181CA 00000000  */D.b..t.../..*  00B86700
000005E0  00B3EE2C 00B86518  00000000 00000000  00000000 00000000  00000000 00000303  *................*  00B86720
00000600  00000000 00000000  00000000 00000000  00000000 00000000  00000000 80B19136  *...............j*  00B86740
00000620  00000000 00000000  00000000 00000000  00000000 00000000  00000000 00000000  *................*  00B86760
00000640  00B1A3CC 00B40B25  00B1A3CC 00000000  00000019 00B861C4  00000000 00000000  *.t.../..*  00B86780
00000660  00CA7320 00B865C0  00B8610C 00B86130  00000000 00B86518  00000000 00000000  *.*.../D*  00B867A0
00000680  00B25C20 00B3DB24  00B40B19 00000000  00000000 00000000  00000000 00000000  *.*....*  00B867C0
000006A0  00000000 00000000  00000000 00000000  00000505 00000000  00000000 00000000  *................*  00B867E0
000006C0  00500050 00000000  48000178 00B86638  00000000 00000000  00000000 00000000  *................*  00B86800
000006E0  00000000 00000000  00000000 00000000  00000000 00000000  00000000 00000000  *................*  00B86820
00000700  EA00E3D4 00B1805C  00000000 00000000  00000000 FEB86988  00000000 00000000  *.TM.*.........h.*  00B86840
00000720  80B181CA 00000000  80B18274 00B1A3CC  00B8610C 00B3EDD8  00B8610C 00000000  *.a...b..t..Q./.*  00B86860
00000740  80B181CA 00000000  80B18274 00B1A3CC  00000000 00000000  00000000 00000000  *.a...b..t..*  00B86880
00000760  00000000 00000000  00000000 00000000  00000000 00000000  00000000 00000000  *................*  00B868A0
00000780  LINES 00000780  TO 000007A0 SAME AS ABOVE
000007C0  00000000 00B3EDD8  00B8610C 00000000  00000000 0000001B  00B861C4 00000000  *...Q..............j..t...Q./D*  00B868C0
000007E0  00000000 00CA7320  00B86130 00000000  00000000 00B3EDCC  00B86518 00000000  */D*  00B86920
00000800  00000000 00B23E90  00B48E04 00000000  00000000 00B3EDCC  00000000 00000000  *................*  00B86940
00000820  00000000 00000000  00000000 00000000  00000303 00000000  00000000 00000000  *................*  00B86960
00000840  LINES 00000840  TO 00000880 SAME AS ABOVE
00000860  00000000 00000880  00000000 00000000  00000000 8A0409F8  00B86AC0 00000000  *..............8....*  00B869A0
00000880  00000000 00000000  00000000 00000000  00000000 00000000  00000000 00000000  *................*  00B869E0
```

TASK CONTROL AREA (SYSTEM AREA)   ADDRESS 00B86000 TO 00B8613F   LENGTH 000140

```
00000000  8A0409F8 00B86AC0  00B86B70 8017846C  00B1D8CC 00B43980  00000000 00000000  *...8.......d..Q..........*  00B86000
00000020  00AE6968 00000000  00000000 00000000  FFB23F80 00B87854  00000000 00000000  *.y.................*  00B86020
00000040  00B871F0 00B862A8  00000000 00000000  00000000 00000000  00B862D8 00000000  *..0...y.......Q.*  00B86040
00000060  00000000 00000000  80000000 C1E2D9C1  00000000 00000000  00B862D8 00000000  *....ASRA.....Q.*  00B86060
00000080  FEB86988 00000000  FEB86560 00AE7B68  00B86570 00000000  00B862D8 00000000  *.h....-.8......Q.*  00B86080
000000A0  00ADF970 00000000  FEB869F8 E5C5D5C4  00000000 00000000  00000000 00000000  *.9....8.VEND.......*  00B860A0
000000C0  C1E2D9C1 00000005  00B86AC0 E5C5D5C4  00000000 00000000  00C0F808 50180101  *ASRA....VEND.........8..*  00B860C0
000000E0  00000000 00C08008  E5C5D5C4 E2C5E340  00C0F808 50180101  8 00000000  *....VEND SET .8..*  00B860E0
00000100  00000000 00C08038  F0F0F140 00B86518  00C0F808 00000000  00000000 00000000  *...001 ...8...*  00B86100
00000120  0C000100 00B1DBCC  00600000 00B86140  01000300 00B861C4  00B23F80 00000000  *......./D*  00B86120
```

FIGURE 13.5.   Continued

```
LIFO STACK ENTRY OWNED BY DFHKCP

CUSTOMER INFORMATION CONTROL SYSTEM STORAGE DUMP    CODE=ASRA    TASK=VEND           DATE=11/04/86    TIME=20:04:11    PAGE    3

00000000  42000068 00000000 FFB865D8 40B262D6   9B26448  00B87C28 00B87834            *..............Q..O.........*     00B86570
00000020  00B86A08 00B8734C 00000000 00B86CEC   00000000 00AED950 00B25D10 00B25C20   *..........R...)..*               00B86590
00000040  00B862D8 00B86140 00AE60E0 F000D2C3   00AE8980 00000000 00000000            *..Q../.-...QO.KC..i..*           00B865B0
00000060  00000000 00000000 00000000                                                  *...*                             00B865D0

PROGRAM COMMUNICATION AREA          ADDRESS 00B871C8 TO 00B871DE    LENGTH 000017

00000000  00014040 404F1F0 F0F0F0F0 E9C2D3F1   F161F0F4 61F8F6                         *.. 1000002BL11/04/86 *          00B871C8

       REGS  0 THRU 15                ADDRESS 00CA4130 TO 00CA416F    LENGTH 000040

00000000  00B87707 00000000 00C092FC   60C09290 00B86384 40C09ECC 00B8723C 00B87A73   *.....k.-k....d ...*              00CA4130
00000020  00B87A74 00C09E8A 00C08038   00C08038 00B87854 50C0997E 00C0916A            *...........r=..j.*               00CA4150

COMMON SYSTEM AREA                    ADDRESS 00AE60E0 TO 00AE64DF    LENGTH 000400

00000000  00000000 00000000 70CBFCA6   0047BFA0 00000010 00AD85A8 00B5BC98            *..........w.....eY..q*           00AE60E0
00000020  B0AF9BC0 00B4181C 00B38578   70AF95A2 00B41800 00AD85A8 00ADF970            *........e...ns.....eY..9*        00AE6100
00000040  00AD80A0 00AE6968 0011999C   2004111F 00B43A80 07D00100 00000000            *....r./ .........*               00AE6120
00000060  06E3F19 00012C00 0000562C   00003000 00AD8000 00D1FFF 0086308F              *........f..*                     00AE6140
00000080  00AE70C8 E8FFFFFE 00000096   00000007D 00B3CCF0 C513C616                    *HY.....;.o.Y.i.OE.F*             00AE6160
000000A0  00000000 00AE617C 00AE617C   00B43980 00AE6798 00AE6968 C50C0FF00           *........q....q..E..*             00AE6180
000000C0  00140005 00090400 00AE64E0   00000000 00000000 00AE1AB4                     *........E..*                     00AE61A0
000000E0  40AE7E88 00B1A580 00B1F800   0CCBFC7E 00AD8738 00B268A4 00B2DA0C            *=h.v..8....g..u....*             00AE61C0
00000100  00B29BBC 00000000 00CACF74   00000000 00AEEBB4 01AF39B8 00CA75A0            *....g......=.....*               00AE61E0
00000120  00000000 00000000 00AD80A0   00B2D4F8 00B3C820 00B42000 00000000            *.......M8..H....*                00AE6200
00000140  00000000 00CA4030 00AE14B0   00B2C240 00CA3A60 00000000 00000000            *........h..B. - ..*              00AE6220
00000160  00CB3A32 00000000 00CC6B60   0064FC58 02000000 00000000 00CA3B70           *FWQ...*                          00AE6240
00000180  00000000 00000000 00CC6B60   00000000 00AE7CF4 FFAE6090                     *........4--..*                   00AE6260
000001A0  070E58F0 D19C07FF 014ABDCA   00BB800 00000000 E6D6D9D2 C1D9C5C1             *.0J......WORKAREA*               00AE6280
000001C0  00000002 01C01C10C 17846C02   62435C02 01031C00 0C000C00 0C000CC0           *....d....*                       00AE62A0
000001E0  4C005C00 0C000C00 0C000C0C   00001C00 00C0000 0C000CC0 00000C00             *.*                               00AE62C0
00000200  00000000 00000000 00000000   00000000 00000000 00000000                    *.*                               00AE62E0
00000220  LINES TO 000003C0  SAME AS ABOVE                                                                              00AE6300
000003E0  00000000 00000000 00000000   00000000 00000000 00000000 00000000            *.*                               00AE64C0

CSA OPTIONAL FEATURE LIST             ADDRESS 00AE64E0 TO 00AE671F    LENGTH 000240

00000000  00000000 00000000 00CC13D0   00B3326A 00000000 00CC3658 00CC3688            *..............h*                 00AE64E0
00000020  00CB3934 00CB3600 20CB2FE4   00000200 00000000 00000000 00000000            *..U.......*                      00AE6500
00000040  80000000 01F4D5D6 0000000    00CAD556 00000000 00000000 00000000            *.4NO...N...*                     00AE6520
00000060  00AE7B68 00CBEFB0 0000025C   00CBF430 0086308F 0086308F 00AE60E0            *........*..4..f.. -*             00AE6540
00000080  00000000 00000000 00CBC950   00CBF70 00000000 00000000 00000000             *.....I...*                      00AE6560
000000A0  00000000 00AED074 00AEC4F0   00AF21F0 00B25D10 00B2D770 00B29820            *.........DO..0..).P..q.*         00AE6580
000000C0  00B1A450 00B21160 00CC4C40   00CC36C0 00AEEA10 00B32950 00CACDE0            *.u..4--....2....*                00AE65A0
000000E0  00CC0F80 00CBF490 00CC1FD0   00B2F270 00000000 00000000 00AF17A0            *.....2....*                      00AE65C0
00000100  00B0C1A0 00CBEDF0 00CBEAF0   00AF77A0 00AF3510 00000000 00B3054A            *.A..0..e...*                     00AE65E0
00000120  00B0D260 00B10F10 00CC233A   00B3785A 00B31830 00B357BA 00000000            *.K-.......*                      00AE6600
00000140  00B3002A 00B33FEC 00B39630   00B3648A 00B1EC94 00000000 00000000            *........m..*                     00AE6620
```

FIGURE 13.5.   Continued

CUSTOMER INFORMATION CONTROL SYSTEM STORAGE DUMP   CODE=ASRA   TASK=VEND   DATE=11/04/86   TIME=20:04:11   PAGE   4

CSA OPTIONAL FEATURE LIST   ADDRESS 00AE64E0 TO 00AE671F   LENGTH 000240

```
00000160  00000000 00B18024 00B2087A 00CA9520  00000000 00000000 00000000 00000000  *..............n.*  00AE6640
00000180  00CA74B0 00B2087A 00AE0960 00000000  00000000 00AE7B08 00AE6720 00000000  *...........#....*  00AE6660
000001A0  00CA7460 00AE0960 00000000 00000000  00000000 00CA3BC8 00000000 00000000  *.-.......H......*  00AE6680
000001C0  00000000 00000000 00000000 00008000  00000000 00000000 00000000 00000000  *................*  00AE66A0
000001E0  00000000 00000000 00000000 00000000  00000000 9BC6E6C3 67E80000 00000000  *.........FWC.Y..*  00AE66C0
00000200  9BC6E6C3 67E80000 00000000 00CC5A88  67E80000 00000000 00000000 00000000  *.FWC.Y...h......*  00AE66E0
00000220  00000000 00000000 00000000 00000000  00000000 00000000 00000000 00000000  *................*  00AE6700
```

TRACE TABLE

TRACE HDR   00CA7BE0   00CA75C0   00CA94E0   ADDRESS 00CA75C0 TO 00CA94FF   LENGTH 001F40

TIME OF DAY	ID	REG 14	REQD	TASK	FIELD A	FIELD B	CHARS	RESOURCE	TRACE TYPE	INTERVAL
20:04:10.545248	F1	60C701FA	4004	17844	00B5BD20	01ADBA70	....		SCP FREEMAIN	00.000384
20:04:10.545632	C9	50B1A8C6	0004	17844	00B5BD20	85000068	....		SCP RELEASED TERMINAL STORAGE	00.000800
20:04:10.546432	F2	40C6EEF8	0404	17844	00000000	00000000	....		PCP LOAD	00.000544
20:04:10.546976	EA	40B1F062	0005	17844	01000300	00B911C4	.......D	OLLE6000	TMP PPT LOCATE	00.000896
20:04:10.547872	EA	40B19114	4004	17844	01000300	00B21F10	.....	OLLE6000	TMP RETN NORMAL	00.001600
20:04:10.549472	F0	40B20282	4004	17844	80000000	00B43860	.......-		KCP WAIT DCI=SINGLE	00.001760
20:04:10.551232	D0	50AE9F70	0504	17844	00000000	00000000	....		KCP DISPATCH	00.000832
20:04:10.552064	F2	40C6FEF8	0404	17844	00000000	00000000	....		PCP LOAD	00.000480
20:04:10.552544	EA	40B1F062	0003	17844	01000300	00B911C4	.......D	OLLE6002	TMP PPT LOCATE	00.000928
20:04:10.553472	EA	40B19114	0005	17844	01000300	00B21F58	.....	OLLE6002	TMP RETN NORMAL	00.001632
20:04:10.555104	F0	40B20282	4004	17844	80000000	00B43860	.......-		KCP WAIT DCI=SINGLE	00.001248
20:04:10.556352	D0	50AE9F70	0504	17844	00000000	00000000	....		KCP DISPATCH	00.000800
20:04:10.557152	F1	40C701C2	8504	17844	00B509D8	01ADBA70	......Q.		SCP GETMAIN	00.001376
20:04:10.558528	C8	50B1A890	0004	17844	00B5A800	85B509E8	.......Y		SCP ACQUIRED TERMINAL STORAGE	00.005248
20:04:10.563776	F1	40C70020	CC04	17844	00000470	8C000478	.......-		SCP GETMAIN INITIMG	00.000736
20:04:10.564512	C8	50B1A890	0004	17844	80000000	00B93478	....		SCP ACQUIRED USER STORAGE	00.003840
20:04:10.568352	F0	40C706CA	4004	17844	00000000	00000000	....		KCP WAIT DCI=SINGLE	*00.016896
20:04:10.585248	D0	50AE9F70	0904	KCP	00020001	C7A1D187	....G.J.		KCP SYSTEM RESUME	00.000896
20:04:10.586144	D0	50AE9F70	0504	TCP	00000000	00000000	....		KCP DISPATCH	00.001824
20:04:10.587968	F1	40B00532	E504	TCP	00000050	00ADC730	....&.G.		SCP GETMAIN CONDITIONAL INITIMG	00.000672
20:04:10.588640	C8	50B1A890	0004	TCP	00B5BD20	85000068	......G.		SCP ACQUIRED TERMINAL STORAGE	00.000544
20:04:10.589184	F0	50B0AC96	1B04	TCP	D4E6F1F6	D6D3D3C9	MW16OLLI		KCP ATTACH-CONDITIONAL	00.000416
20:04:10.589600	EA	70AE847A	0003	TCP	01040100	00AE6A00	....	OLLI	TMP PCT LOCATE	00.000800
20:04:10.590400	EA	40B19114	0025	TCP	01040100	00B1CB24	....		TMP RETN NORMAL	00.000352
20:04:10.590752	F1	50AEB5E8	EA04	TCP	006005F8	00ADC730	-.8.G.		SCP GETMAIN CONDITIONAL INITIMG	00.003872
20:04:10.594624	C8	50B1A890	0604	TCP	00B8E000	8A0405F8	...8		SCP ACQUIRED TCA STORAGE	00.000768
20:04:10.595392	D0	50AE9364	0604	17845	D4E6F1F6	D6D3D3C9	MW16OLLI		KCP CREATE	00.000416
20:04:10.595808	EA	40AE897C	0003	TCP	0C000100	00B1CB24	....	OLLI	TMP PCT TRANSFER	00.000864
20:04:10.596672	EA	40B19114	0025	TCP	00000000	00000000	....		TMP RETN NORMAL	00.000352
20:04:10.597024	D0	50AE9F70	0504	TCP	00000000	00000000	....		KCP DISPATCH	00.007392
20:04:10.604416	F0	40AF36B8	4004	TCP	44000000	00AE1480	....		KCP WAIT DCI=TCP	00.000800
20:04:10.605216	D0	50AE9F70	0504	TCP	00000000	00000000	....		KCP DISPATCH	00.007008
20:04:10.612224	F0	40AF36B8	4004	TCP	44000000	00AE1480	....		KCP WAIT DCI=TCP	00.001120
20:04:10.613344	D0	50AE9F70	0504	17844	00000000	00B93460	....		KCP DISPATCH	*00.052128
20:04:10.665472	F1	60C7003E	4004	17844	00B93460	01ADBA70	....		SCP FREEMAIN	00.000480
20:04:10.665952	C9	50B1A8C6	0004	17844	00B93460	8C000478	.......-		SCP RELEASED USER STORAGE	

FIGURE 13.5.   Continued

TIME OF DAY	ID	REG 14	REQD	TASK	FIELD A	FIELD B	CHARS	RESOURCE	TRACE TYPE	INTERVAL
20:04:10.666624	F1	40C70020	CC04	17844	00000470	01ADBA70	......		SCP GETMAIN INITIMG	00.000672
20:04:10.667328	C8	50B1A890	0004	17844	00B93460	8C000478	......		SCP ACQUIRED USER STORAGE	00.000704
20:04:10.671104	F0	40C706CA	4004	17844	80000000	00B93478	......		KCP WAIT DCI=SINGLE	00.003376
20:04:10.672128	D0	50AE9F70	0504	TCP	00000000	00000000	......		KCP DISPATCH	00.001024
20:04:10.693120	F0	40AF36B8	4004	TCP	44000000	00AE1480	......		KCP WAIT DCI=TCP	*00.020992
20:04:10.694240	D0	50AE9F70	0504	17844	00000000	00000000	......		KCP DISPATCH	00.001120
20:04:10.725216	FC	50C70132	0103	17844	00010000	00ADBA70	......		ZCP ZARQ APPL REQ WRITE	*00.030976
20:04:10.725728	FC	40AF3D06	0105	17844	0035A800	0035A800	......		ZCP RETN ZARQ APPL REQ WRITE	00.000512
20:04:10.726880	F1	60C7003E	4004	17844	00B93460	01ADBA70	......		SCP FREEMAIN	00.001152
20:04:10.727296	C9	50B1A8C6	0004	17844	00B93460	8C000478	......		SCP RELEASED USER STORAGE	00.000416
20:04:10.728128	F7	40C70586	4803	17844	5BD6D3D3	01D4D1D9	$OLL.MJR		TSP PUT	00.000832
20:04:10.728864	F1	40B29DD8	0B03	17844	B0171F58	86B91470	.....&		SCP GETMAIN CONDITIONAL ANY	00.000736
20:04:10.736320	C8	50B1A890	0004	17844	00B61650	971F0E50	....&		SCP ACQUIRED TSMAIN STORAGE	00.007456
20:04:10.738496	F7	40C700C2	4803	17844	00B61650	971F0E50	....&		TSP RETN NORMAL	00.002176
20:04:10.739072	F7	40B2ABAE	00B5	17844	5BD6D3D3	FFD4D1D9	$OLL.MJR		TSP PUT	00.000576
20:04:10.739776	F1	40B29DD8	0004	17844	B0171F00	86B91470	..H....		SCP GETMAIN CONDITIONAL ANY	00.000704
20:04:10.741568	C8	50B1A890	0004	17844	00B7C800	971F0730	..H....		SCP ACQUIRED TSMAIN STORAGE	00.001792
20:04:10.742816	F7	40B2ABAE	00B5	17844	00B7C800	971F0730	..H....		TSP RETN NORMAL	00.001248
20:04:10.743360	F2	60C6FFE4	1004	17844	00000000	00000000	......	OLLE1000	PCP RETURN	00.000544
20:04:10.744192	F0	40B1FB30	0304	17844	00B93478	00000000	......		KCP DETACH	00.000832
20:04:10.744800	D2	40AE8AD2	0304	17844	00000000	00000000	......		KCP DEQALL	00.000608
20:04:10.745216	D0	50AE9F70	0504	17844	00000000	00000000	......		KCP DISPATCH	00.000416
20:04:10.763168	DC	50AE9364	0704	17844	03380400	D6D3D3C9	....OLLI		KCP TERMINATE	*00.017952
20:04:10.763648	FC	50AE8B26	0B03	17844	04000000	00ADBA70	......		ZCP ZISP ISC FREE DETACH	00.000512
20:04:10.764160	FC	40AF7700	0B05	17844	00ADBA70	00ADBA70	......		ZCP RETN ZISP ISC FREE DETACH	00.000352
20:04:10.764512	F1	40AE8C72	4A04	17844	00B91000	8A0405F8	8		SCP FREEMAIN	00.000448
20:04:10.764960	D0	50AE9F70	0504	17844	00000000	00000000	......		SCP RELEASED TCA STORAGE	00.010944
20:04:10.775904	FC	05AF5610	0503	17845	00010000	00ADC730	..G....		KCP DISPATCH	00.000608
20:04:10.776512	FC	50AF56CC	0C03	17845	00000000	00000000	......		ZCP ZSUP START UP TASK	00.000640
20:04:10.777152	E5	50AF5E64	8804	17845	00000000	00000000	......	OLLI.*.:	XSP SECURITY	00.000416
20:04:10.777568	EA	40B1FD62	0003	17845	01000300	00B8E1C4	......D	OLLE1000	PCP XCTL-CONDITIONAL	00.000576
20:04:10.778144	EA	40B19114	0005	17845	01000300	00B21778	......	OLLE1000	TMP PPT LOCATE	00.000832
20:04:10.778976	EA	40B20282	4004	17845	80000000	00B439A0	......Y		TMP RETN NORMAL	00.001696
20:04:10.780672	F0	40B20282	4004	17845	00000000	00000000	......		KCP WAIT DCI=SINGLE	00.001184
20:04:10.781856	D0	50AE9F70	0504	17845	00000000	00000000	......		KCP DISPATCH	00.000416
20:04:10.782272	FC	40B2ABAE	0004	17845	00010000	01ADC730	..G....		SCP GETMAIN INITIMG	00.001472
20:04:10.783744	C8	50C6F858	CC04	17845	00B8E600	8C0014E8	..G....		SCP ACQUIRED USER STORAGE	00.000448
20:04:10.784192	F2	50B1A890	0004	17845	00000000	8C0014E8	..G...Y	OLLE3000	PCP LOAD	00.000544
20:04:10.784736	EA	40C6FA78	0404	17845	01000300	00B8E1C4	......D	OLLE3000	TMP PPT LOCATE	00.000896
20:04:10.785632	EA	40B1FD62	0005	17845	01000300	00B21778	......		TMP RETN NORMAL	00.001568
20:04:10.787200	F0	40B19114	4004	17845	80000000	00B439A0	......Y		KCP WAIT DCI=SINGLE	00.001152
20:04:10.788352	D0	40B20282	0504	17845	00000000	00000000	......		KCP DISPATCH	00.000704
20:04:10.789056	F7	50AE9F70	9003	17845	01D4D1D3	01D4D1D3	$OLL.MJL		TSP GET	00.002016
20:04:10.791072	F7	40B2ABAE	00B5	17845	00000000	00000000	$OLL.MJL		TSP RETN NORMAL	00.000448
20:04:10.791520	F7	40C70556	2003	17845	5BD6D3D3	01D4D1D3	$OLL.MJL		TSP RELEASE	00.000704
20:04:10.792224	F1	60B2A938	0004	17845	5BD6D3D3	86B8E470	....U...		SCP FREEMAIN	00.000448
20:04:10.792672	C9	50B1A8C6	0004	17845	4001778	971F0E50	....U...		SCP RELEASED TSMAIN STORAGE	00.003264
20:04:10.795936	F7	40B2ABAE	00B5	17845	00B78730	971F0E50	.....&		TSP RETN NORMAL	00.000544
20:04:10.796480	F7	40C70094	8003	17845	5BD6D3D3	FFD4D1D3	$OLL.MJL		TSP GET	00.000704
20:04:10.797312	F1	40B2A2F6	AE04	17845	00B70710	01ADC730	..G....		SCP GETMAIN CONDITIONAL	00.000544
20:04:10.797856	C8	50B1A890	0004	17845	00B8FAF0	8EB7D718	.O....		SCP ACQUIRED TEMPSTRG STORAGE	00.000544

FIGURE 13.5. Continued

TIME OF DAY	ID	REG 14	REQD	TASK	FIELD A	FIELD B	CHARS	RESOURCE	TRACE TYPE	INTERVAL
20:04:10.798752	F7	40B2ABAE	00B5	17845	00B8FAF0	8EB70718	..0...		TSP RETN NORMAL	00.000896
20:04:10.799264	F7	40C700DE	2003	17845	5BD6D3D3	FFD4D1D3	$OLL.MJL		TSP RELEASE	00.000512
20:04:10.799968	F1	60B2A938	0004	17845	40001700	86BE470	.....U.		SCP FREEMAIN	00.000704
20:04:10.800448	C9	50B1A8C6	0004	17845	971F0730	971F0730	......		SCP RELEASED TSMAIN STORAGE	00.000480
20:04:10.800992	F7	40B2ABAE	00B5	17845	00B4A000	971F0730	......		TSP RETN NORMAL	00.000544
20:04:10.801344	F1	40C70020	CC04	17845	00000100	01ADC730	....G.		SCP GETMAIN INITIMG	00.000352
20:04:10.801984	C8	50B1A890	0004	17845	00B90210	8C000108	......		SCP ACQUIRED USER STORAGE	00.000640
20:04:10.804992	F7	40C70094	8003	17845	5BD6D3D3	20D4D1D3	$OLL.MJL		TSP GET	00.003008
20:04:10.805568	F1	40B2A2F6	AE04	17845	00B9012F	01ADC730	...G.		SCP GETMAIN CONDITIONAL	00.000576
20:04:10.806144	C8	50B1A890	0004	17845	00B90320	8EB90138	......		SCP ACQUIRED TEMPSTRG STORAGE	00.000576
20:04:10.806560	F7	40B2ABAE	00B5	17845	00B90320	8EB90138	...G.		TSP RETN NORMAL	00.000416
20:04:10.807136	F1	60C701FA	4004	17845	00B5BD20	01ADC730	...G.		SCP FREEMAIN	00.000576
20:04:10.807520	C8	50B1A8C6	0404	17845	00B5BD20	85000068	......		SCP RELEASED TERMINAL STORAGE	00.000384
20:04:10.808448	F2	40C6FEF8	0404	17845	00000300	00B8E1C4	.....D	OLLE6000	PCP LOAD	00.000928
20:04:10.816192	EA	40B1FD62	0003	17845	00000300	00B21F10	......	OLLE6000	TMP PPT LOCATE	00.007744
20:04:10.817120	EA	40B19114	0005	17845	01000300	00B439A0	......		TMP RETN NORMAL	00.000928
20:04:10.818624	F0	40B20282	4004	17845	80000000	00000000	......		KCP WAIT DCI=SINGLE	00.001504
20:04:10.819680	D0	50AE9F70	0504	17845	00000000	00000000	-		KCP DISPATCH	00.001056
20:04:10.820480	F2	40C6FEF8	0404	17845	00000300	00B8E1C4	.....D	OLLE6002	PCP LOAD	00.000800
20:04:10.820896	EA	40B1FD62	0003	17845	01000300	00B21F58	......	OLLE6002	TMP PPT LOCATE	00.000416
20:04:10.821824	EA	40B19114	0005	17845	01000300	00B439A0	......		TMP RETN NORMAL	00.000928
20:04:10.823264	D0	50AE9F70	0504	17845	80000000	00000000	......		KCP WAIT DCI=SINGLE	00.001440
20:04:10.824320	D0	50AE9F70	0504	17845	00000000	00000000	-		KCP DISPATCH	00.001056
20:04:10.825184	F1	40C701C2	8504	17845	00B509D8	01ADC730	..Q..G.		SCP GETMAIN	00.000864
20:04:10.825664	C8	50B1A890	0004	17845	00B5B1F0	85B509E8	...0..Y		SCP ACQUIRED TERMINAL STORAGE	00.000480
20:04:10.828992	F1	40C70020	CC04	17845	00000470	01ADC730	...G.		SCP GETMAIN INITIMG	00.003328
20:04:10.829760	C8	50B1A890	0004	17845	00B90460	8C000478	-		SCP ACQUIRED USER STORAGE	00.000768
20:04:10.832192	D0	40C706CA	4904	17845	80020001	C7A1D1C7	.G.JG		KCP WAIT DCI=SINGLE	*00.002432
20:04:10.864480	D0	50AE9F70	0904	KCP	00000000	00000000	......		KCP SYSTEM RESUME	*00.032288
20:04:10.869924	D0	50AE9F70	0504	TCP	00000000	00AE1480	......		KCP DISPATCH	*00.005344
20:04:10.873600	F0	40AF36B8	4004	TCP	44000000	00AE1480	......		KCP WAIT DCI=TCP	00.003776
20:04:10.896384	D0	50AE9F70	0904	KCP	00020001	C7A1D1D1	.G.JJ		KCP SYSTEM RESUME	*00.022784
20:04:10.897344	D0	50AE9F70	0504	TCP	00000000	00000000	......		KCP DISPATCH	00.000960
20:04:10.898688	F1	50AFE58A	4004	TCP	00B5BBE0	00ADDFA0	......		SCP FREEMAIN	00.001344
20:04:10.899168	C9	40AF36B8	0004	TCP	00B5BBE0	85B50138	......		SCP RELEASED TERMINAL STORAGE	00.000480
20:04:10.911872	F0	40AF36B8	4004	TCP	44000000	00AE1480	......		KCP WAIT DCI=TCP	00.012704
20:04:10.912640	D0	50AE9F70	0504	TCP	00000000	00000000	-		KCP DISPATCH	00.000768
20:04:10.935256	F0	40AF36B8	4004	TCP	44000000	00AE1480	......		KCP WAIT DCI=TCP	*00.023616
20:04:10.937408	D0	50AE9F70	0504	TCP	00000000	00000000	-		KCP DISPATCH	00.001152
20:04:11.022848	FC	50C70132	0103	17845	00010000	00ADC730	....G.		ZCP ZARQ APPL REQ WRITE	*00.085440
20:04:11.023424	FC	40CF3D06	0105	17845	00000000	00B5B1F0	0		ZCP RETN ZARQ APPL REQ WRITE	00.000576
20:04:11.024384	F1	60C7003E	4004	17845	00B90460	01ADC730	.-..G.		SCP FREEMAIN	00.000960
20:04:11.024896	C9	50B1A8C6	0004	17845	00B90460	8C000478	......		SCP RELEASED USER STORAGE	00.000512
20:04:11.025664	F7	40C70586	4803	17845	5BD6D3D3	01D4D1D3	$OLL.MJL		TSP PUT	00.000768
20:04:11.026432	F1	40B29DD8	0004	17845	B0171F58	86BBE470	....U.		SCP GETMAIN CONDITIONAL ANY	00.000768
20:04:11.032640	C8	50B1A890	0004	17845	00B6DC30	971F0E50	....&		SCP ACQUIRED TSMAIN STORAGE	00.006208
20:04:11.034592	F7	40B2ABAE	00B5	17845	00B6DC30	971F0E50	....&		TSP RETN NORMAL	00.001952
20:04:11.035168	F7	40C700C2	4803	17845	5BD6D3D3	FFD4D1D3	$OLL.MJL		TSP PUT	00.000576
20:04:11.035872	F1	40B29DD8	0004	17845	B0171F00	86BBE470	....U.		SCP GETMAIN CONDITIONAL ANY	00.000704
20:04:11.038080	C8	50B1A890	0004	17845	00B4A000	971F0730	......		SCP ACQUIRED TSMAIN STORAGE	00.002208
20:04:11.039328	F7	40B2ABAE	00B5	17845	00B4A000	971F0730	......		TSP RETN NORMAL	00.001248

FIGURE 13.5. Continued

CUSTOMER INFORMATION CONTROL SYSTEM STORAGE DUMP   CODE=ASRA   TASK=VEND   DATE=11/04/86   TIME=20:04:11   PAGE   7

TIME OF DAY	ID	REG 14	REQD TASK	FIELD A	FIELD B	CHARS	RESOURCE	TRACE TYPE	INTERVAL
20:04:11.039776	F2	60C6FFE4	1004	17845	00000000	00000000	....	OLLE1000	PCP RETURN	00.000448
20:04:11.040640	F0	40B1FB30	8004	17845	00000000	00000000	....		KCP DETACH	00.000864
20:04:11.041088	F0	40AE8AD2	0304	17845	00B90478	00000000	....		KCP DEQALL	00.000448
20:04:11.041600	D0	50AE9F70	0504	17845	00000000	00000000	....		KCP DISPATCH	00.000512
20:04:11.041952	D0	50AE9364	0704	17845	03380400	D6D3C9	...OLLI		KCP TERMINATE	00.000352
20:04:11.042624	FC	50AE8B26	0B03	17845	04000000	01ADC730	....G.		ZCP ZISP ISC FREE DETACH	00.000672
20:04:11.043232	FC	40AF7700	0B05	17845	04000000	0CADC730	....G.		ZCP RETN ZISP ISC FREE DETACH	00.000608
20:04:11.043904	F1	40AE8C72	4A04	KCP	00B8E000	00000000	....		SCP FREEMAIN	00.000672
20:04:11.044256	C9	50B1A8C6	0004	KCP	00B8E000	8A0405F8	8		SCP RELEASED TCA STORAGE	*00.012832
20:04:11.057088	D0	50AE9F70	0504	TCP	00000000	00000000	....		KCP DISPATCH	00.001024
20:04:11.058112	FC	70AF362E	1404	TCP	012A0001	0ADF970	9		ZCP ZRAC RECEIVE ANY	00.000416
20:04:11.058528	FC	50AFA582	1304	TCP	00000001	00ADF970	9		ZCP ZGET GETMAIN	00.000800
20:04:11.059328	EE	70AF974C	2314	TCP	012A01A0	01ADF970	9		VIO RECEIVE OIC DATA	00.000224
20:04:11.059552	EE	70AF974C	0024	TCP	00107DD3	6111D34C	..'L/.L		VIO DATA	00.000512
20:04:11.060064	F1	50AF9ABC	A504	TCP	00B500A0	01ADF970	9		SCP GETMAIN CONDITIONAL	00.000512
20:04:11.060576	C8	50B1A890	0004	TCP	00B5BBE0	85B500B8			SCP ACQUIRED TERMINAL STORAGE	00.004512
20:04:11.065088	FC	40AF7B04	1103	TCP	00200001	00ADF970	9		ZCP ZATT ATTACH	00.000736
20:04:11.065824	F0	50AF5446	1304	TCP	C4E3F0F3	ESC5D5C4	DT03VEND		KCP ATTACH-CONDITIONAL	00.000384
20:04:11.066208	EA	70AE847A	0003	TCP	01040100	00AE6A00		VEND	TMP PCT LOCATE	00.000832
20:04:11.067040	EA	40B19114	0025	TCP	01040100	00B1D8CC	...Q.		TMP RETN NORMAL	00.000352
20:04:11.067392	F1	50AE85E8	EA04	TCP	005209F8	01ADF970	..8.9		SCP GETMAIN CONDITIONAL INITIMG	00.005216
20:04:11.072608	C8	50B1A890	0004	TCP	00B86000	8A0409F8	-...8		SCP ACQUIRED TCA STORAGE	00.000832
20:04:11.073440	D0	50AE9364	0604	17846	C4E3F0F3	ESC5D5C4	DT03VEND		KCP CREATE	00.000448
20:04:11.073888	EA	40AE897C	0003	TCP	0C000100	00B1D8CC	...Q.	VEND	TMP PCT TRANSFER	00.000768
20:04:11.074656	EA	40B19114	0025	TCP	0C000100	00000000	....		TMP RETN NORMAL	00.000384
20:04:11.075040	D0	50AE9F70	0504	TCP	00000100	00000000	....		KCP DISPATCH	00.000352
20:04:11.075392	FC	40AF554E	1125	TCP	00000000	00AE1480			ZCP RETN ZATT ATTACH	00.000384
20:04:11.075776	F0	40AF36B8	4004	TCP	44000000	00ADF970	9		KCP WAIT DCI=TCP	00.005888
20:04:11.081664	D0	50AE9F70	0504	TCP	00000000	00000000	....		KCP DISPATCH	00.000640
20:04:11.082304	FC	0SAF5610	0503	17846	00200001	00ADF970	9		ZCP ZSUP START UP TASK	00.000672
20:04:11.082976	E5	40AF56CC	0C03	17846	00000000	00000000	VEND.*..		XSP SECURITY	00.000640
20:04:11.083616	F2	50AF5E64	8004	17846	00000000	00000000		VEND001	PCP XCTL-CONDITIONAL	00.000416
20:04:11.084032	EA	40B1FD62	0003	17846	01000300	00B861C4	...../D	VEND001	TMP PPT LOCATE	00.000864
20:04:11.084896	EA	40B19114	0005	17846	01000300	00B23F2C			TMP RETN NORMAL	00.001408
20:04:11.086304	F0	40B20282	4004	17846	80000000	00B439A0			KCP WAIT DCI=SINGLE	00.001088
20:04:11.087392	D0	50AE9F70	0504	17846	00000000	00000000			KCP DISPATCH	00.000512
20:04:11.087904	F1	60B207BE	8C04	17846	000007AC	01ADF970	9		SCP GETMAIN	00.000832
20:04:11.088736	C8	50C11408	0004	17846	00B86A00	8C0007B8			SCP ACQUIRED USER STORAGE	00.003520
20:04:11.092256	E1	50CC1408	0004	17846	00B864C0	00001802			EIP RECEIVE-MAP ENTRY	00.000672
20:04:11.092928	FA	50B32A26	0003	17846	00025505	00000020			BMS MAP MAPSET MAP-FROM IN	00.000384
20:04:11.093312	FA	40B3336C	0003	17846	00025505	00000020			BMS MAP MAPSET MAP-FROM IN	00.000384
20:04:11.093696	F2	50B319C0	8404	17846	00000000	00000000		VENDSETM	PCP LOAD-CONDITIONAL	00.000544
20:04:11.094240	EA	40B1FD62	0003	17846	01000300	00B861C4	...../D	VENDSETM	TMP PPT LOCATE	00.000544
20:04:11.095296	F2	50B319F0	0405	17846	01000304	00000000			TMP RETN NOT FOUND	00.000768
20:04:11.095808	EA	40B1FD62	0003	17846	01000000	00000000		VENDSET	PCP LOAD	00.000288
20:04:11.096608	EA	40B19114	0005	17846	01000300	00B23E90			TMP PPT LOCATE	00.000512
20:04:11.098208	F0	40B20282	4004	17846	80000000	00B439A0		VENDSET	TMP RETN NORMAL	00.000800
20:04:11.099360	D0	50AE9F70	0504	17846	00000000	00000000	...../D		KCP WAIT DCI=SINGLE	00.001600
20:04:11.099968	F1	60B31BC2	C504	17846	000000E5	01ADF970	..V..9		KCP DISPATCH	00.001152
20:04:11.100640	C8	50B1A890	0004	17846	00B5BCA0	850000F8	8		SCP GETMAIN INITIMG	00.000608
								SCP ACQUIRED TERMINAL STORAGE	00.000672

FIGURE 13.5. Continued

TIME OF DAY	ID	REG 14	REQD	TASK	FIELD A	FIELD B	CHARS	RESOURCE	TRACE TYPE	INTERVAL
20:04:11.101728	F1	50B31FFE	4004	17846	00B5BBE0	01ADF970	.......9.		SCP FREEMAIN	00.001088
20:04:11.102112	C9	50B1A8C6	0004	17846	00B5BBE0	85B500B8			SCP RELEASED TERMINAL STORAGE	00.000384
20:04:11.102816	FA	40B32676	0005	17846	00000000	00000000			BMS RETN	00.000704
20:04:11.103072	FA	40B3338A	0005	17846	00000000	00000000			BMS RETN	00.000256
20:04:11.103456	F1	50AEDC34	4004	17846	00B5BCA0	01ADF970	.......9.		SCP FREEMAIN	00.000384
20:04:11.103872	C9	50B1A8C6	0004	17846	00B5BCA0	850000F8	8		SCP RELEASED TERMINAL STORAGE	00.000416
20:04:11.104288	E1	50C11408	00F4	17846	00000000	00001802			EIP RECEIVE-MAP RESPONSE	00.000416
20:04:11.104960	E1	50C11640	0004	17846	00B86A4C	00000E04			EIP XCTL ENTRY	00.000672
20:04:11.105376	F2	60B21188	8204	17846	00000000	00000000		VEND002	PCP LOCATE	00.000416
20:04:11.105984	EA	40B1FD62	0004	17846	01000300	00B861C4	..../D	VEND002	TMP PPT LOCATE	00.000608
20:04:11.106848	EA	40B19114	0005	17846	01000300	00B23F80			TMP RETN NORMAL	00.000864
20:04:11.107200	F1	60AEDC34	8C04	17846	00B50017	01ADF970	.......9.		SCP GETMAIN	00.000352
20:04:11.107808	C8	50B1A890	0004	17846	00B871C0	8CB50028			SCP ACQUIRED USER STORAGE	00.000608
20:04:11.108192	F1	50AEDC34	4004	17846	00B7BFD0	01ADF970	.......9.		SCP FREEMAIN	00.000384
20:04:11.108480	C9	50B1A8C6	0004	17846	00B7BFD0	93000030			SCP RELEASED SHARED STORAGE	00.000288
20:04:11.109920	F2	40AEDEF4	0204	17846	00000000	00000000		VEND002	PCP XCTL	00.001440
20:04:11.110400	F1	60B1FFCE	4004	17846	00B86A00	01ADF970	.......9.		SCP FREEMAIN	00.000480
20:04:11.110784	C9	50B1A8C6	0004	17846	00B86A00	8C0007B8			SCP RELEASED USER STORAGE	00.000384
20:04:11.111328	EA	40B1FD62	0003	17846	01000300	00B861C4	..../D	VEND002	TMP PPT LOCATE	00.000544
20:04:11.112256	EA	40B19114	0005	17846	01000300	00B23F80			TMP RETN NORMAL	00.000928
20:04:11.113856	F0	40B20282	4004	17846	80000000	00B439A0			KCP WAIT DCI=SINGLE	00.001600
20:04:11.115072	D0	50AE9F70	0504	17846	00000000	00000000			KCP DISPATCH	00.001216
20:04:11.115616	F1	60B207BE	8C04	17846	00B80A4C	01ADF970	.......9.		SCP GETMAIN	00.000544
20:04:11.116160	C8	50B1A890	0004	17846	00B871F0	8CB80A58			SCP ACQUIRED USER STORAGE	00.000544
20:04:11.118752	E1	50C0900E	0004	17846	00B8723C	00001A04			EIP ENTER ENTRY	00.002592
20:04:11.119296	10	50C0900E	0002	17846	000DE5C5	D5C44040	.VEND	VEND001	USER 016	00.000544
20:04:11.119520	E1	50C0900E	00F4	17846	00000000	00001A04	..0...		EIP ENTER RESPONSE	00.000224
20:04:11.119936	E1	50C0995C	0004	17846	00B8723C	00000602			EIP READ ENTRY	00.000416
20:04:11.120576	F5	40B25E2A	F103	17846	00000000	00000000		VENFILE	FCP CTYPE LOCATE	00.000640
20:04:11.120992	EA	40B28F7C	0005	17846	01000500	00B861C4	..../D	VENFILE	TMP FCT LOCATE	00.000000
20:04:11.121792	EA	40B19114	0005	17846	01000500	00B25C20			TMP RETN NORMAL	00.000800
20:04:11.122016	F5	40B27FA2	00B5	17846	01000500	00B25C20	.......*		FCP RETN NORMAL	00.000224
20:04:11.122304	F1	60AEDC34	CC04	17846	00000090	01ADF970	.......9.		SCP GETMAIN INITIMG	00.000288
20:04:11.122816	C8	50B1A890	0004	17846	00B86A00	8C000098			SCP ACQUIRED USER STORAGE	00.000512
20:04:11.123360	F1	60AEDC34	8C04	17846	00B8000C	01ADF970	.......9.		SCP GETMAIN	00.000544
20:04:11.123776	C8	50B1A890	0004	17846	00B86AA0	8CB80018			SCP ACQUIRED USER STORAGE	00.000416
20:04:11.124224	F5	50B26192	8003	17846	00000000	00000000		VENFILE	FCP GET	00.000448
20:04:11.124800	F1	50B2905E	9D04	17846	00C0C054	01ADF970	.......9.		SCP GETMAIN	00.000576
20:04:11.125248	C8	50B1A890	0004	17846	00000094	9D5C0068	.......*		SCP ACQUIRED DWE STORAGE	00.000448
20:04:11.125504	F1	50B28D42	CF04	17846	00000094	01ADF970	.......9.		SCP GETMAIN INITIMG	00.000256
20:04:11.132608	C8	50B1A890	0004	17846	00B86B30	8F0000A8			SCP ACQUIRED FILE STORAGE	00.007104
20:04:11.133088	F1	40B28D42	CF04	17846	0000011E	01ADF970	.......9.		SCP GETMAIN INITIMG	00.000480
20:04:11.133536	C8	50B1A890	0004	17846	00B86BE0	8F000128			SCP ACQUIRED FILE STORAGE	00.000448
20:04:11.136128	F0	50B283FA	4004	17846	20000000	00B439A0			KCP WAIT DCI=DISP	00.002592
20:04:11.137248	D0	50AE9F70	0504	17846	00000000	00000000			KCP DISPATCH	00.001120
20:04:11.137728	F1	40B28EB6	0004	17846	00B86AC0	01ADF970	.......9.		SCP FREEMAIN	00.000480
20:04:11.138272	C9	50B1A8C6	0004	17846	00B86AC0	9D5C0068	.......*		SCP RELEASED DWE STORAGE	00.000544
20:04:11.138560	F1	40B28EB6	4004	17846	00B86B30	01ADF970	.....9.		SCP FREEMAIN	00.000288
20:04:11.138912	C9	50B1A8C6	0004	17846	00B86B30	8F0000A8			SCP RELEASED FILE STORAGE	00.000352

FIGURE 13.5. Continued

```
CUSTOMER INFORMATION CONTROL SYSTEM STORAGE DUMP   CODE=ASRA   TASK=VEND        DATE=11/04/86   TIME=20:04:11   PAGE   9

TIME OF DAY      ID  REG 14    REQD TASK  REQD TASK   FIELD A   FIELD B   CHARS      TRACE TYPE                INTERVAL

20:04:11.139264  F5  40B27FA2  00B5 17846  8F000DA8  8F000DA8  .......   FCP RETN NORMAL              00.000352
20:04:11.139936  F5  40B262D6  1003 17846  10B86BE0  00000200  .......   FCP RELEASE                 00.000672
20:04:11.140288  F1  50B28EB6  4004 17846  00B86BE0  01ADF970  ......9.  SCP FREEMAIN                00.000352
20:04:11.140608  C9  50B1A8C6  0004 17846  00B86BE0  8F000128  .......   SCP RELEASED FILE STORAGE   00.000320
20:04:11.140928  F5  40B27FA2  00B5 17846  00B86BE0  8F000128  .......   FCP RETN NORMAL             00.000320
20:04:11.141248  E1  50C0995C  00F4 17846  00000000  0000D602  .......   EIP READ RESPONSE           00.000320
20:04:11.144000  F2  80CB3CA4  6004 17846  C1E2D9C1  00000000  ASRA...   PCP ABEND                   00.002752
20:04:11.144512  F1  40B1EEC8  CC04 17846  000000A0  01ADF970  ......9.  SCP GETMAIN INITIMG         00.000512
20:04:11.145088  C8  50B1A890  0004 17846  00B86AC0  8C0000A8  .......   SCP ACQUIRED USER STORAGE   00.000576
20:04:11.145440  F4  50B1F0A0  FE04 17846  00000000  C1E2D9C1  ....ASRA  DCP TRANSACTION             00.000352
20:04:11.151968  F0  40CCA70  4004 17846  80000000  00CA0000  ......-   KCP WAIT DCI=SINGLE         00.006528
20:04:11.153152  D0  50AE9F70  0504 17846  00000000  00000000  .......   KCP DISPATCH                00.001184

TRANSACTION STORAGE -USER           ADDRESS 00B86AC0 TO 00B86B6F   LENGTH 0000B0

00000000  8C0000A8  00B86AA0  00000000  C4C6C8E3  C1C3C240  80600000  C1E2D9C1  *.......y.......DFHTACB .-..ASRA*  00B86AC0
00000020  E5C5D5C4  F0F0F240  00000000  00000000  00000000  00C092FC  00000000  *VEND002........REGS.PSW.........*  00B86AE0
00000040  00000000  D9C5C7E2  50D7E2E6  D9C5C7E2  00B87707  00000000  00C09290  *....REGS.PSW........k..k...*  00B86B00
00000060  00B86384  40C09ECC  00B87223C  00B87A73  00B87A74  00C09E8A  00C08038  *...d............r=..........k..*  00B86B20
00000080  00B86140  00AE60E0  50C0997E  00C0916A  03BD0000  00C09302  00060007  *.../.....r=..j..........l.....*  00B86B40
000000A0  00000000  00000000  8C0000A8  00B86AA0                              *............y..*                00B86B60

TRANSACTION STORAGE -USER           ADDRESS 00B86AA0 TO 00B86ABF   LENGTH 000020

00000000  8CB80018  00B86A00  F1F0F0F0  F0F0F0F0  F1F1F2F0  8CB80018  00B86A00  *........1000001000001120........*  00B86AA0

TRANSACTION STORAGE -USER           ADDRESS 00B86A00 TO 00B86A9F   LENGTH 0000A0

00000000  8C000098  00B871F0  E5C5D5C6  C9D3C540  00000000  08B25C20  00600006  *.......q....OVENFILE ....*....y.*  00B86A00
00000020  80B87242  00000000  00000000  00000000  00000000  00000000  00000000  *...............................*  00B86A20
00000040  00000000  00000000  00000000  00000000  00000000  00000000  00000000  *...............................*  00B86A40
00000060  00000000  00000000  00000000  00000000  00000000  00000000  00000000  *...............................*  00B86A60
00000080  00000000  00000000  00000000  00000000  00000000  FF000000  8C000098  *.......................q....0.*  00B86A80

TRANSACTION STORAGE -USER           ADDRESS 00B871F0 TO 00B87C4F   LENGTH 000A60

00000000  8CB80A58  00B871C0  00000000  00C08138  50C09EE4  00C0A050  00AE64E0  *........a...U...*                00B871F0
00000020  CA9442FC  40C09ECC  00C08138  00C0896F  00C09E8A  00C08038  00C08038  *.m....a..i..a...i..*             00B87210
00000040  00C08B40  00C08750  00B20778  00014040  404F1F0  F0F0F0F0  E92C03F1  *..g....100000ZBL11/04*           00B87230
00000060  61F8F604  D4C9C4E6  C5E2E340  C3D6D4D4  E4DC9C3  C1E3C9D6  5DE24040  */86.MIDWEST COMMUNICATIONS*      00B87250
00000080  4040F1F0  F0F0F0F0  40E2B4C2  40E2B4C2  4CC1E2E2  D6C3C9C1  E3C5E26B  *100000 SYSTEMS ASSOCIATES,*      00B87270
000000A0  4B404040  4040D74B  D64B40C2  D68C40F7  F9F24040  40404040  40C9D5C3  *.. P.O. BOX 792        INC*      00B87290
000000C0  40404040  D3C5C57D  E2404040  4D4C9E3  6B40D4D6  4B40F6F4  F0F6F340  *...LEE'S SUMMIT, MO. 64063*      00B872B0
000000E0  40404040  40404040  40404040  40404040  40404040  40404040  40404040  *                       *         00B872D0
00000100  C2D6C240  D3D6E6C5  40404040  40404040  40404040  4040F8F1  40404040  *BOB LOWE          81*            00B872F0
00000120  F660F5F2  F460F4F8  F7F0F4F3  60F1F2F3  F4F5F6F7  40000000  00000C00  *6-524-487043-1234567 ...*        00B87310
00000140  0000000C  E800365C  1234500C  86305C86  307CE9C2  D3F10000  5020C48C  *.Y.*...f.*f..ZBL1...D.*          00B87330
```

FIGURE 13.5. Continued

```
CUSTOMER INFORMATION CONTROL SYSTEM STORAGE DUMP    CODE=ASRA    TASK=VEND        DATE=11/04/86    TIME=20:04:11    PAGE    10

TRANSACTION STORAGE -USER

                        ADDRESS 00B871F0 TO 00B87C4F    LENGTH 000A60

00000160  9101C4CF 47E0C710 5850C494 41330004 40350000 58DD0008 58100018 D2031000  *.j...G....Dm.....K..*  00B87350
00000180  C4945811 00000C00 000C0000 0C00000C 07FED200 00015060 00000008 0000000C  *Dm...........K...-..*  00B87370
000001A0  9101C579 4710C866 9601C579 91105049 4710C75C 5040C49C 5020C494 0001C780  *.j.E..H.o.E.j...G*. D..Dm..G.*  00B87390
000001C0  D6D7C56C 58414040 40000F8 58210004 5020C400 FAFBFC00 FDEFFF40 C1C2C340  *OPE.......8....D....ABC*  00B873B0
000001E0  C4C566E2 91204010 4780C790 906CCB14 47F0C9DE 951A4014 4780C836 91104014  *DEFSj......G.....I.n....H.j.*  00B873D0
00000200  4710C7B8 95204014 4780C836 00000000 4026D202 401DCAE1 47F0C866 40025074  *....G.....H.......K....OH..E.*  00B873F0
00000220  4025D201 C484404A 91C04020 4770C804 91024049 5840C49C 4710C7F0          *.K....D.j...H...H.j.D..GO*  00B87410
00000240  4B40C4BA 91044000 5840C49C 4710C80A 47F0C804 4B404040 40404040 40404040  *..D.j...D....H.....H....*  00B87430
00000260  40404040 4040C49C E4D5C5E7 D7C5C3E3 C5C440C5 D9D9D6D9 D709D6C7 D9C1D440  *....D.UNEXPECTED ERROR IN PROGRAM*  00B87450
00000280  E5C5D5C4 F0F0F26B 40D3C9D5 C5404B20 C4BA5040 C6D57E40 40404040 D9C37E40  *VEND002, LINE..D.FN=    RC=*  00B87470
000002A0  40404040 40404040 40404040 7EF0F080 40C84CC1 C94D50D8 5CD1D95D          * RESP=00. H.AI(.Q*JR)*  00B87490
000002C0  60E8C661 E96DF0F8 7CF1F97D 00F1F2F3 F4F5F6F7 50494780 007D6D6A          *-Y./.08.19.124.1234567..'.*  00B874B0
000002E0  7EE6F788 7F6C6E6B F1F2F3F4 F5F6F7F8 F97A7B7C C1C2C3C4 C5C6C7C8 C94AB4C  *=Wh..123456789..ABCDEFGHI..*  00B874D0
00000300  58F10010 40040040 00000000 00000000 000000B5 C5D5C4F1 F0F10000          *.1...........VEND101..*  00B874F0
00000320  00F1F0F0 F0F0F0F0 00000000 00000000 0000D4C9 C4E6C5E2 E340C3D6 D4D4E4D5  *.100000........MIDWEST COMMUN*  00B87510
00000340  C9C3C1E3 C9D6D5E2 40404040 40404040 40000040 E2E8E2E3 C5D4E240          *ICATIONS...........SYSTEMS*  00B87530
00000360  C1E2E2D6 C3C9C1E3 C5E26B40 C9D5C34B 40404040 40000000 D74BD64B          *ASSOCIATES, INC.........P.O.*  00B87550
00000380  40C2D6E7 40F7F9F2 40404040 40404040 40404040 40000000 00000000          *.BOX 792............*  00B87570
000003A0  00D3C5C5 7DE240E2 E4D4D4C9 E36B40D4 D64B40F6 F4F0F6F3 40404040          *.LEE'S SUMMIT, MO. 64063....*  00B87590
000003C0  40404040 40404040 000000C2 D6C240D3 D6E6C540 40404040 40404040          *........BOB LOWE......*  00B875B0
000003E0  40404040 40404040 000000C2 D6C240D3 F8F1F660 F5F2F460 F4F8F7F0          *........43-1234567...816-524-4870.*  00B875D0
00000400  40404040 40404040 00000000 00000000 F4F0F6F3 F4F0F6F3 F4F4F8F0          *...............0.*  00B875F0
00000420  0000F0F4 F360F1F2 F3F4F5F6 F7400000 40404040 404040F0 40404BF0          *..0....1234567....0.....0.00...*  00B87610
00000440  F0000000 40404040 40404040 F2000E800 00000040 40404040 F5000000          *0.............0....*  00B87630
00000460  40404F0  4BF0F200 00F8F200 F200E800 00000000 00000040 4040F3F6          *.....0..82.2.Y.....6.*  00B87650
00000480  00000000 F8F640F3 F0F50000 000040F1 4BF00000 00000000 0000E9C2          *....86 305....0.00...ZB*  00B87670
000004A0  F8F640F3 F0F70000 000040F1 4BF0F4F5 4BF0F000 0000E9C2 0000E9C2          *86 307....12345.00...ZB*  00B87690
000004C0  D3000000 00000000 00000000 00000000 00000000 00000000 00000000          *L...................*  00B876B0
000004E0  00000000 00000000 00000000 00000000 00000000 00000000 00000000          *....................*  00B876D0
00000500  C1C23C5 40C4C6C8 C5C9E3C1 C240F160 00000010 C5709280 3C40E3          *ABLE DFHEITAB 1-6....E.k.LD T*  00B876F0
00000520  CA8A8124 40404040 40404040 C240F160 F64B58F0 F00041D0 000047F0          *.a....   ..6....0.....0.*  00B87710
00000540  C5480F4 00000000 00000000 0010906C CB1458D0 C410986C          *.E.4....   ..5.5....D.q*  00B87730
00000560  D200C200 811DD200 E2D6D9E3 40404040 00003F6D4 8134D200 60C98101          *...D..SORT.......6Ma.K.-Ia*  00B87750
00000580  D2006106 61228139 D200613E 802BD200 0003FC76 00000000 0003F6FC          *...K./.a.K./..K....6.*  00B87770
000005A0  90EC00C0 585D0004 E5C5D5C6 C9D3C540 5010C498 58F0C490 9101C57A          *.....N.VENFILE..Dq.0D.j.E:*  00B87790
000005C0  4780C87C 9101C57B 4780CB6E 18D547F0 CCF6D503 1000CB34 4780CB7C 41FF0006  *.H..j.E..N.O.6N....*  00B877D0
000005E0  58D50004 9102D049 4780CBA8 5850D208 12554780 5001C3C0 92205000          *.N.j...y.K..c.k.*  00B877F0
00000600  9101C583 4710CBA8 92015000 D5031000 C344780 CC1C5811 00001B66 585C4A8  *.j.Ec..yk..N.......Dy*  00B87810
00000620  9101C4CF 4780CBD6 D201C4BE 10004850 C4E4B50 00044161 60005820          *.j.D..OK.D...D..-/-..*  00B87830
00000640  C4081255 0602F000 25000080 00F0F0F4 F7F94040 40404040 40404040          *.D....0....00479.....*  00B87850
00000660  40384F0  00000001 00B86394 5CC0997E 5CC09F10 00C0914E 00C08C28          *....0.....r=....j+..*  00B87870
00000680  00C0A050 00000001 00B86384 40C09ECC 00C09F10 5051000 00C09E8A          *...0....m....d.......q.*  00B87890
000006A0  00C08038 00C08B40 2012804B 00C08038 00AED254 00000000          *.0.........K....*  00B878B0
000006C0  C4B09110 50494780 CCF65020 C4005845 C5845060 41440000          *...K.Ed....6.D...-K.Ed.-*  00B878D0
000006E0  47F0CCF6 41500008 581D0018 50510000 98EC000C 07FE90EC          *.0.6........K.E...q.*  00B878F0
00000700  D00C185D 58CD0044 58AD003C 50C05020 C4909101 C57A4780          *.0....E.D.j.E:.*  00B87910
00000720  CCD45810 C498D503 1000CB34 47F0CC84 9601C57A 5810C498          *.M.DqN.......0.do.E:.Dq*  00B87930
00000740  58F0C490 58DD0004 D5031000 CB344780 CC1C5810 C499101          *.0....N....E.D.j.Ed....n..*  00B87950
00000760  C57C4710 CE089601 C57C5040 C49C9180 CE089511 40114780          *E....o.E..D.j.Ed....n....*  00B87970
00000780  40144780 CD489520 40144780 CD84951A C4AA402E 91044015          *...E..o.E..D.j..dK.D..*  00B87970
000007A0  4780CE08 9601C57E 47F0CE08 91044010 4710CDC4 91024024 9201C582  *.o.E=.0.j....k.Eb*  00B87990
```

FIGURE 13.5.   Continued

TRANSACTION STORAGE -USER   ADDRESS 00B871F0 TO 00B87C4F   LENGTH 000A60

```
000007C0  5800C4B0 4B00C4BA 5000C4B0 91404015 4780CD78 9601C57D 47F0CD40 91204015  *.D...D..D.j....o.E'.O.  j..*  00B879B0
000007E0  4710CD40 47F0CE08 951A4014 4770CD98 91804015 00000000 00C08C84           *....O...n....qj.......d*    00B879D0
00000800  00C08AEC 41604000 0038CDBC E5C5D5C4 F0F0F240 00C8038 50006050 9200C4BC   *.-....VEND002...-.k.D.*     00B879F0
00000820  91024010 47000000 9201C580 5800C400 4B00C4BA 5000C4B0 47F0CE08 91024064  *.j....k.E..D...D..D...j.*   00B87A10
00000840  00000000 9201C582 5800C4B0 4B00C4BA 5000C4B0 91404015 4780CE08 9601C57D  *..k.Eb..D...D..D.j....E'*   00B87A30
00000860  47F0CD40 91084064 00000000 CB344780 C5824780 F0F8F5861 00005820 C4B09180  *.O.j......n.Eb.086 3075.00*  00B87A50
00000880  00B8723C 00000000 0000365C CE529501 C5824780 F0F8F7F5 F3F0F7F5 4BF0F0F0  *......*..n.Eb.086 3075.00*  00B87A70
000008A0  F0A84155 00044052 00004122 00045850 C4A847F0 CEAED201 C4BE6000 4850C4BE  *0y.......*Dy.O..K.D-...D.*   00B87A90
000008C0  9501C582 4780CE78 9501C580 4B50C4BA 41660004 47F0CEAE 9101C57D 4BF0F0F0  *n.Eb....n.E....D....j.E'*    00B87AB0
000008E0  4780CEAE 5830C4AC 193547B0 C49C4540 CAF21841 58F10010 45EF0014 45EF0014  *....D....D...2..1....d*      00B87AD0
00000900  05F058F0 F212986C F00041D0 C40C5020 C4B01255 47CCCF3A 4950CF38 4740CED2  *.0.02.q.0..D..D.....K*       00B87AF0
00000920  D2FF2000 60004B50 CF384A20 CF3847F0 CEAE0650 4B50C4BA 4450CF32 47F0CF3A  *K..........-..0..0.*        00B87B10
00000940  5800C4A8 18509101 C4CF4780 CEAED201 4BE6000 4850C4BE 4B50C4BA 18054166  *.Dy..j.D...K.D-..D..D..*     00B87B30
00000960  00447F0 CEAE5800 C4B01820 48320000 4540CAF2 184158F1 0010456F 00C005F0  *.01mq.0..0...K..2..1....0*   00B87B50
00000980  58F0F194 986CF000 47F0CF7A 41500004 D2004004 00000000 00B86438 80B871C8  *.01mq.0..0....K..1..rd*      00B87B70
000009A0  00B87B90 00AE60E0 00000000 CF869501 C5804780 00C093E6 CAF21841 00C09984  *...0.....fn.E...lw.2..rd*    00B87B90
000009C0  45EF000C 05F058F0 F14E986C F0009101 C57E4780 CF7A5020 C4B05030 CAC41D0  *...0.01+q.0.j.E=...D...D*     00B87BB0
000009E0  C40C4150 CC8841E0 CC8841E0 00C09B42 CAF21841 58F4000C 00C09CBE 000058F0  *D.....D...2...4....0*        00B87BD0
00000A00  00C096B2 00C0990C 00C09BCC 00C09B78 00C09D12 00C09D48 00C09C84 00C09808  *.o..r....rd...d..q..*        00B87BF0
00000A20  00C09A94 00C09BCC 00C09B78 00C09E24 00C09D12 00B86453 80B873FC 80B873FC  *.......m...........*         00B87C10
00000A40  00B87254 00B873BA 80B87242 986CF000 9234C4BC 00000000 8CB80A58 00B871C0  *.......q.0.k.D....*          00B87C30
```

TRANSACTION STORAGE -USER   ADDRESS 00B871C0 TO 00B871EF   LENGTH 000030

```
00000000  8CB50028 00B86000 00014040 4040F1F0 F0F0F0F0 E9C2D3F1 F161F0F4 61F8F600  *......-...1000002BL11/04/86.*  00B871C0
00000020  00000000 8CB50028 8CB50028 00B86000 F0F0F0F0                              *.......-.*                     00B871E0
```

TERMINAL CONTROL TBL USER AREA   ADDRESS 00AE12E0 TO 00AE12FF   LENGTH 000020

```
00000000  00000000 00000000 00000000 00000000 00000000 00000000 00000000 00000000  *................*  00AE12E0
```

TERMINAL CONTROL TABLE   ADDRESS 00ADF970 TO 00ADFB2F   LENGTH 0001C0

```
00000000  C4E3F0F3 91F20006 00ADF974 00000000 00B86140 00000000 00AE12E0 20000000  *DT03j2..9..../.....*         00ADF970
00000020  00000000 0CE9C2D3 F8047FFD 00000990 04E17DBC E225E3C2 FCF0F740 00000000  *..ZBL8........SETB007...*    00ADF990
00000040  20000000 20000000 07801850 00000000 01C00000 00000000 00000000 00000100  *..........*                 00ADF9B0
00000060  00000001 00AEOCB0 00B43004 00ADFB0C 01C00000 00000000 00000000 00000000  *....-.....*                 00ADF9D0
00000080  00000000 00840000 00AE0960 00000001 2E001700 00005900 02000000 00800000  *....-...........*           00ADF9F0
000000A0  00000000 00000000 00000000 2A000001 00A00000 00005900 00800000 00000000  *...............d...*        00ADFA10
000000C0  00000000 00000000 00000000 00000000 100307D1 012A012D 00000200 00000000  *.......J.*                  00ADFA30
000000E0  00000000 FFFF5040 00000000 3A008400 012A012D 00000000 00000000 00000000  *...............d.*          00ADFA50
00000100  00000000 00000000 012D0001 00000000 00000000 00000000 701E7007 00000000  *.........*                  00ADFA70
00000120  00000000 01230000 012D0001 00000000 00000000 00000000 00000000 00000000  *.........*                  00ADFA90
00000140  00000000 20E00002 01002010 01000000 00000000 00000000 000000AAC 00000000  *.........*                  00ADFAB0
00000160  000000E0 20E00002 00000000 00000000 01000000 00000000 10000000 00000000  *.........*                  00ADFAD0
00000180  00000014 00000000 00000082 00000000 00000000 00000000 24000000 00000000  *.........*                  00ADFAF0
000001A0  01000018 50000000 000000D4 D4000000 00000000 00000000 00000000 00000000  *...b..MM.*                  00ADFB10
```

FIGURE 13.5. Continued

PROGRAM STORAGE

ADDRESS 00C08008 TO 00C0A4BF   LENGTH 0024B8

```
00000000  C4C6C8E8 C3F1F6F0 58F00014 58F0F0B4 58F0F00C 58FF000C 07FF58F0 001458F0  *DFHYC160.0...00..00.........0*  00C08008
00000020  F0B458F0 F0858FFF 018407FF 00C858FF 05F00700 900EF00A 47F0F082 00CA723C  *0..00..H..d..0....0..00b..*      00C08028
00000040  00B86384 00C08108 00B87200 00C08080 00B204D0 50AED2DA 00C08138 00AED074  *...d.a............m.K..a..U*     00C08048
00000060  00C08FA0 00B23F80 00B862D8 00B86140 00B86394 00C08138 00C08138 50C09E44  *.........Q../....m.K.a...i.*     00C08068
00000080  00C0A050 00AE64E0 CA9442FC 40C09ECC 00C08138 00C0896F 00C08970 00C09E8A  *...........m....a..i...i...*     00C08088
000000A0  00C08038 00C08038 00C08B40 00C08750 00B20778 58C0F0C6 5E0C000 5ED0F0CA  *...........g....g..o.....0.*     00C080A8
000000C0  9500E000 4770F0A2 9610D048 92FFE000 47F0FAC 98CEF03A 90DCD000 185D989F  *n....0so..k...00.q.0....)q.*     00C080C8
000000E0  F0BA9110 D0480719 07FF0700 00C09E8A 00C08038 00C08038 00C08B40 00B87854  *0.j............00.q.0....q..*     00C080E8
00000100  00C09FA0 00C09E70 C3D6C2C6 F3F0F00F E5C5D5C4 F0F0F240 00C08A84 F1F161F0  *...........COF3000VEND002...d11/0*  00C08108
00000120  F461F8F6 F1F84BF4 F84BF2F7 0008581D D5C44040 40404040 40404040 4040F0F9  *4/8618.48.27....VEND          9*  00C08128
00000140  F961F9F9 61F9F904 41550008 50510000 98ECD00C 07FE0000 00000000 00090EC  *9/99/99......q.......9*          00C08148
00000160  D00C585D 000450D5 000858C5 47F0C73C 003C9101 C5774710 C63A9601 C57747F0  *...).....N...E..v..j.E..F.o.E..0*  00C08168
00000180  C6489101 C5784780 C64818D5 47F0C73C 58D50004 9102D049 4780C668 5840D208  *F.j.E...F..N.OG..N.j...F..K.*     00C08188
000001A0  12444780 C6689202 4000D202 4001C3C0 58F0C48C 4540CC02 23BD00C 4540D208  *....F.k..K...0D...K..E.q..*       00C081A8
000001C0  D01405EF 47F0E064 90EC000C 185D58DD 018C58CD 004458AD 003CD23B C528980C  *.....0....K.E...........K.E.*     00C081C8
000001E0  5000C3FC 12444780 C6C89601 C5789110 50494780 C73C4840 C5888940 00030640  *........FHo.E.j......K...*        00C081E8
00000200  4440C72E 4140C4E8 5040C56C 47F0C73C 58DD0008 581D0018 58110004 D2031000  *.....G...DY..E..j.......G...Ehi*  00C08208
00000220  C73498EC D00C07FE 90EC000C 185D58DD 018C58CD 004458AD 003CD23B 528500C  *G.q............G......K.E.*       00C08228
00000240  5020C48C 9101C4CF 47F0C710 5850C494 41330004 40350000 58DD0008 581D0018  *...D.j.D...G........K.E.*         00C08248
00000260  D2031000 C4945811 00C0C000 00C0C000 0C00000C 07FED200 00015060 00000008  *....K...Dm.........K..*           00C08268
00000280  0000000C 9101C579 4710C866 9601C579 91105049 4710C75C 5040C49C 5020C494  *........J.E...H.o.E.j...G*.....D...Dm*  00C08288
000002A0  001C1780 D6D7C56C 58414040 4780C790 58210004 47F0C9DE FAFBFC00 FDFEFF40  *....G..OPE......8......Om..H.*    00C082A8
000002C0  C1C2C340 C4C5C6E2 91204010 4780C836 00000000 4026D202 951A4014 4780C836  *ABC DEFSj....0In....H.*           00C082C8
000002E0  9110A014 4710C7B8 95204014 4780C836 00000000 4026D202 401DCAE1 47F0C866  *j...G-n......K....OH..*           00C082E8
00000300  40025741 4025D201 C4B4404A 91C04024 4770C804 584D0004 47F0C804 5840C49C  *...E..K.D...j....H...D.*          00C08308
00000320  4710C7F0 4B40C4BA 91044000 5840C49C 4710C80A 47F0C804 91C0C024 40404040  *...E.K.D...j..D..H.OH..*          00C08328
00000340  40404040 40404040 E4D5C5E7 D7C5C3E3 C5C440C5 D9D9D6D9 40C9D540 D7D9D6C7  *...GO..D..H.OH..*                 00C08348
00000360  D9C1D440 E5C5D5C4 F0F0F26B 40D3C9D5 C5404B20 C6D57E40 40404040 40404040  *RAM VEND002, LINE .D. FN=*        00C08368
00000380  D9C37E40 40404040 40404040 40404040 D9C5E2D7 7EF0F080 00C84CC1 C94D50D8  *RC=......RESP=00. H.AI(.Q*        00C08388
000003A0  5CD1D95D 60E86C61 E96DF0F8 7CF1F97D 00F1F2F3 F4F5F6F7 50494780 5049F780  **JR)..Y./Z.08.19..124.123456 7....*  00C083A8
000003C0  007D6D6A 7EE6E788 7F6C6E6B F1F2F3F4 F5F6F7F8 F97A7B7C C1C2C3C4 C5C6C7C8  **=WXh...12345 6789..ABCDEFGH*     00C083C8
000003E0  C94A484C 58F10010 45EF0008 05F058F0 F0004100 C40C9101 C4CF7010 4CCF4710  *I..=.HF....0.08.q.0...D.j.D..*    00C083E8
00000400  C97E9501 C5814770 C8C64122 000458DD 00185021 00005811 0005811D 0004D203  *I=n.Ea..HF.............K.K*       00C08408
00000420  1000C738 98ECD00C 07FE1814 41E0C8F8 4540CAF2 184158F4 00C051F 04020080  *...G.q......H8...2...4......*      00C08428
00000440  58F0E7B8 986CF000 41D0C40C 5810C49C D5011060 C3EA47F0 C92C95F1 10604780  *...Ox.q.0...D.N..-C..I.nl.-.*     00C08448
00000460  CAB258F0 C3CCD501 1060C564 478F0000 47FF0008 400CC4B4 9101C4CF 4710C986  *....0C.N...E.........D.j.D..If*   00C08468
00000480  47F0C8C6 5800C3FC 4B00C4BA 18204150 CAE05000 CAE44540 CAF21841 58F10010  *...OHF..C..D........j.D..HF.*     00C08488
000004A0  45EF0008 05F058F0 F7529860 F0004100 C40C4032 00009101 C4CF4710 C8C64122  *....OHfn.Ea..HF..D...D...D.*      00C084A8
000004C0  000447F0 C8C69501 C5814780 05F058F0 C8C65840 C4BA4850 C4BA4155 00044050  *D.K..D...D...IK....I.K*           00C084C8
000004E0  C4B4D203 4000C4BA 4B50C4BA 4050C4B4 125547C0 C9D24950 5810C49C C9CCD2FF  *...D...OHF.0..06.q.0...D.j..*     00C084E8
00000500  40042000 B50CF38 41D0C40C 47F0C9A8 06504450 CF2C5820 CF384740 C4084B20  *....j.........j...K..E.m...2.*    00C08508
00000520  C4BA47F0 C8C605F0 58F0F6D0 986CF000 41DCC40C 5810C49C 951A1014 4780CA12  *.0j...........0...7..0.....0*     00C08528
00000540  91201014 4780CA00 91101014 4780CA12 D2021025 C57494EF 10204540 CAF21841  *00...0.............07...0.*       00C08548
00000560  05F09102 D0494710 F0220700 5010F016 4110F73E 4500F01A 00000000 0A0205F0  *.06.q.0...D.j....bj...*           00C08568
00000580  47F0F01E 05F01801 05105000 10084510 110E0700 4500F01A 58F0F722 05EF05F0  *...bK...0j...FH..Eh.*             00C08588
000005A0  58F0F658 986CF000 41DCC40C 585D0004 5810C49C 91201014 4780CA82 91105049  *FH..E...E.k.E.k.Ea.OG*.E.k.*      00C085A8
000005C0  47E0CA82 D2EF1000 10F09110 5840C588 C5840640 4040C588 5810C49C 12444780  *LD TABLE DFHEITAB 1-6...0....*    00C085C8
000005E0  C6C85840 C56C4144 00085040 C56C9200 C57F2000 C58147F0 C75C5010 C5709280  *D.q.E..4.......SORT....6Ma.K.*    00C085E8
00000600  D3C40DE3 C1C2D3C5 40C4C6C8 C5C9E3C1 C240F160 F64B58F0 0000000C F00041D0  *LD TABLE DFHEITAB 1-6...0....*    00C08608
00000620  000047F0 CA8A8124 40404040 40404040 0003F51C 58F50008 07FF906C CB1458D0  *.0.a......5.5...*                 00C08628
00000640  C410986C C54807F4 00000000 00000000 E2D6D9E3 40404040 0003F6D4 8134D200  *D.q.E..4.......SORT....6Ma.K.*    00C08648
```

PROGRAM STORAGE

ADDRESS 00C08C08 TO 00C0A4BF   LENGTH 0024B8

```
0000660  60C98101 D2006106 811DD200 61228139   D200613E 802BD200 00C08C08 0003FC76 00000000   *-Ia.K./.aK./..K....K.*   00C08668
0000680  0003F6FC 90EC000C 585D0004 50D50008   58C50044 58A5003C 5010C498 58F0C490            *..6.....).....N....E...v..Dq.0D.*   00C08688
00006A0  9101C57A 4780CB7C 9101C57B CCF6D503   1000CB34 4780CB6E                              *.jE.....jE....j...N.0.6N..*   00C086A8
00006C0  41FF0006 58D50004 9102D049 5850D208   12554780 CBAD202 5001C3C0                      *......N...j....y.K....yK...C*   00C086C8
00006E0  92205000 9101C583 4710CBA8 D5031000   CB344780 CC1C811 00001B66                      *k...j.Ec..yk..N........*   00C086E8
0000700  5850C4A8 9101C4CF 4780CBD6 D201C4BE   C4BE4B50 C4BA4160 0004161                       *.Dy].D..OK.D...D...D-...*   00C08708
0000720  60005820 C4081255 47C0CC1C 4950CF38   4740CC16 D2FF2000 60004B50 CF384A20             *...D....K...4....D...K......*   00C08728
0000740  CF384A60 CF3847F0 00000000 00CA723C   00000000 5810C3C8 92081026 07F40650             *.-...0.......CHk.....4.*   00C08748
0000760  4450CF32 4540CC02 5810C408 D23BD00C   D01C05EF 47F0E06A 90EC000C                      *D.K..Eq....D.K...0j....*   00C08768
0000780  185D58CD 018C58CD 004458AD 003C023B   2012804B 00000000 00B20778                      *.)........D.j......-..*   00C08788
00007A0  00000000 C4B09110 50494780 CCF65020   C4005845 060D200 C5845060                       *.....D.j....6..D...-K.Ed.-*   00C087A8
00007C0  41440000 47F0CCF6 41500008 581D0018   58110008 50510000 98ECD00C                      *.....0.6........q....*   00C087C8
00007E0  07FE90EC D00C185D 58DD018C 58DD0044   D23BD528 50050020 C4909101                       *...........K.E...D.j.*   00C087E8
0000800  C57A4780 CCD5810 C498D503 1000CB34   4780CC80 47F0CC84 9601C57A                       *E...M..DqN.......0.do.E.*   00C08828
0000820  5810C498 58F0C490 58DD0004 D5031000   C57C5040 4710CDC4 47F0CD68                       *.Dq.0D.....N.....o.E=.0....*   00C08848
0000840  C4989101 C57C4710 CD84951A 40144780   C584710 000647F0 47F0CD40                        *......E....dn.....dK.D.*   00C08868
0000860  C4989101 CD489520 40144780 CE08 9601C57E 40144780 9601C57E 47F0CD68           *......E....dn...........qj.*   00C08888
0000880  91044015 4780CE08 9601C57E 4B00C4B0   91404015 9601C57D 47F0CD40                       *.k.Eb..D..j....o.E.0.*   00C088A8
00008A0  9201C582 580C4BA 4B00C4BA 4770CD98   91804015 00000000 50006050                        *j.......o........VEND002*   00C088C8
00008C0  47104D40 00C08C84 41604000 0038CDB4   F0F0F240 5000C8038 47F0CE08                       *.k.D.j...k.E...D...D.0.*   00C08908
00008E0  9200C4BC 91024010 47000000 9201C580   4B00C4B0 91404015 4780CE08                        *.j........0..E.j.o.j.*   00C08928
0000900  47F0CF3A 91024064 91084064 9201C582   CB344780 CFF85861 0003C820                        *.0.j..............8./.*   00C08948
0000920  9601C57D 47F0CD40 00C08138 CE3A9501   CE529501 C5824780 CEAC4780                        *.o.E.0....n.Eb..n.E..*   00C08968
0000940  C4B09180 00C08138 C4A47FD8 00044052   0004830 CEAD201 C4BE6004 47F0CEAE                 *D...D.y...j.D...Dy.0..K.D.-*   00C08988
0000960  CE4A5850 C4A84155 4780CE78 4850C4BA   4B50C4BA 4160004 47F0CEAE                         *.D.n.Eb...n.E....D-*   00C089A8
0000980  9101C57D 4780CEAE 5830C4AC CEAE5810   C49C4540 CAF21841 58F10010                        *jE'...D..n.E...D...2.1*   00C089C8
00009A0  45EF0014 05F058F0 F212986C C40C5020   C4B01255 47CCF3A 4950CF38                         *j.E....0...D..........Dy.*   00C089E8
00009C0  4740CED2 D2FF2000 60004B50 CF384A20   CEAD650 CEAD650 4450CF38                           *..KK..j....0......-...0.*   00C08A08
00009E0  47F0CF3A 5800C4A8 18509101 CEAED201   C4BE6000 4850C4BE 4B50C4BA                         *.0..Dy..j.D...K.D...D.*   00C08A28
0000A00  18054166 CEAE5800 C4B01820 45400CAF2   18415F1 00104EF1                                 *.....D...K.D...2.*   00C08A48
0000A20  00C05F0 58F0F194 986CF000 00000000   41500004 2004000 00000000                          *.0.01mq.0..0...K.......2.*   00C08A68
0000A40  00000000 00000000 00000000 00000000   C5804780 CF024540 CAF21841                        *..............fn.E...2*   00C08A88
0000A60  58F10010 45EF000C 05F058F0 F14E986C   C57A4780 CF7A5020 C4B05030                         *.1....0..01+q.0.j.E=...D.*   00C08AA8
0000A80  C4AC41D0 C40C4150 00447D1 CAF21841E   CAF21841 58F4000C 051F0800                          *.D...D....K.D...0.d...2.4....D*   00C08AC8
0000AA0  00C058F0 00000000 00C0990C 00C09BC0   00C09984 00C09D12 00C09CBE                        *..0.....r..lW...rd.....d*   00C08AE8
0000AC0  00C09F10 00C0A2C0 00C01C8 00C093E6    986CF000 00C093E6 00C09B42                          *........o.q.0.k.D.*   00C08B08
0000AE0  00C09808 00C09990 00C0990C 00C0A94E   00C09924 00C09D12 00C09B78                        *-E....t...s..H.j..lW....o*   00C08B28
0000B00  00C09BCC 00C09CBE 00C090C 00C09D12    00C09B42 00C093BC 00C09B42                          *....q..q..r..rd..m....*   00C08B48
0000B20  00C0904C 00C0907A 00C0909E 00C090D4   986CF000 00C09024 00C0902A 00C0909E              *.....a..d......b*   00C08B68
0000B40  00C0916A 00C091F6 00C091BA 00C0918E   00C091AC 00C091D0 00C091EE 00C09092FC           *...+...j6.j...j.j+*   00C08B88
0000B60  00C0936A 00C09386 00C09414 00C0940C   00C09430 00C09482 00C0949E 00C094F0             *...j6.j...j.j.k..*   00C08BA8
0000B80  00C09510 00C09598 00C095D0 00C095AC   00C095C2 00C0961E 00C09610                        *...1f.m..m..m..mb..m0*   00C08BC8
0000BA0  00C09634 00C09680 00C0968E 00C096A4   00C09748 00C09610 00C09802                        *...n.nq..n...nB.nU....o*   00C08BE8
0000BC0  00C09A24 00C09A3E 00C09A44 00C09A64   00C09A78 00C09BBE 00C09BF0                        *.....o*.o...ou..p..p..q..o*   00C08C08
0000BE0  00C09C7E 00C09C22 00C09D04 00C09976   00C09D04 00C09E18 00C09632                        *..=....o.....o.*   00C08C28
0000C00  00C09510 00C09E6 00C09B42 00C09D12    00C09C84 00C09808 00C09A94                         *...r..lW....rd..q..m*   00C08C48
0000C20  00C09BCC 00C09B78 00C09E24 00C09D12   CA9442FC 00020001                                 *.....r....m.......m.*   00C08CA8
```

FIGURE 13.5.   Continued

PROGRAM STORAGE

                    ADDRESS 00C08008 TO 00C0A4BF   LENGTH 0024B8

```
000000C0  0017000D 40206B20 20206B20 20211B20  2040206B 2021204B 20212204B 20204020  *..........................*  00C08CC8
000000E0  20202020 20204020 20206B20 21204B20  20F02120 20220024 00220024 00341CF0  *...................0......0*  00C08CE8
00000D00  2021206B 20206B20 20000050 0003001B  00150013 08E00005 00000000 04E00005  *.,..,.............*           00C08D08
00000D20  22000000 F0F0F2F3 F7404040 E5C5D5C4  F0F0F10E 08E00005 00001000 F0F0F2F7  *........0237     VEND001.....0027*  00C08D28
00000D40  F8404040 E57BF0F2 E5C5D5C4 F1F0F10E  02E00005 00000100 00020400 F4404040  *8   V.02VEND101.........00334*  00C08D48
00000D60  E5C5D5C4 F0F0F66F 6F616F6F 616F6F18  04D00025 0DE20400 0020F0F0 0020F0F0  *VEND06../../.....B..S.....00*  00C08D68
00000D80  F3F4F240 4040C4C9 E2D7D4C1 D7E2C5E3  C2F0F0F7 0E04E000 25000002 00F0F0F3  *342    DISPMAPSETB007.....003*  00C08D88
00000DA0  F8F14040 40E5C5D5 C4F0F0F5 0E04E000  25000002 00F0F0F3 F8F84040 40E5C5D5  *81    VEND005.......00388   VEN*  00C08DA8
00000DC0  C4F0F0F3 180200D0 25000900 00020F0  F0F3F9F6 4040400A 04E80025 04E80025  *D003..........0396     .Y.*  00C08DC8
00000DE0  00008900 F0F0F4F2 F5404040 E3C8C540  E2C9C7D5 D6D540E2 E3C1E3C9 E2E3C9C3  *..i.00425    THE SIGNON STATISTIC*  00C08DE8
00000E00  E240D9C5 C3D6D9C4 40C8C1E2 40C2C5C5  D540D3D6 E2E30A02 E8002500 004500F0  *S RECORD HAS BEEN LOST..Y...0*  00C08E08
00000E20  F0F4F4F0 40404040 C9D9D9D6 40C9D540  E4D7C4C1 E3C9D5C7 40E2C9C7 D5D6D540  *0440    ERROR IN UPDATING SIGNON*  00C08E28
00000E40  D9C5C3D6 D9C41804 D0002500 C2000000  E2040000 20F0F0F4 F6F84040 40D4C5D5  *RECORD.......B..S...00468   MEN*  00C08E48
00000E60  E4D4C1D7 0E08E000 05000010 00F0F0F4  F7F44040 400602F0 00250000 8000F0F0  *UMAP......00474   .0.....00*  00C08E68
00000E80  F4F7F940 404040E5 C5D5C6C9 D3C5C3D9  C9E3C9C3 C1D340C5 D5E3D9E8 C5D9D9D6  *479    VENFILECRITICAL ENTRY ERRO*  00C08E88
00000EA0  D9E5C5D5 C4F1F9F0 F0180400 C2000000  E2040000 20F0F0F5 F2F54040 F5404040  *RVEND1900.....B..S...00525*  00C08EA8
00000EC0  0E080000 05000010 00F0F0F5 F3F14040  40D9C5C3 D6D9C440 D2C5E840 D5D6E340  *......00531    RECORD KEY NOT*  00C08EC8
00000EE0  D5E4D4C5 D9C9C3E5 C5D5C4F1 F9F0F5C2  D4E2C0C5 D9D9D6D9 60C3C1D3 D340D4C9  *NUMERICVEND1905BMS ERROR-CALL MI*  00C08EE8
00000F00  E2E5C5D5 C4F1F9F1 F0E5C5D5 C4D6D940  C6C9D3C5 40C5D9D9 D6D96043 C1D3D340  *SVEND1910VENDOR FILE ERROR-CALL*  00C08F08
00000F20  D4C9E2E5 C5D5C4F1 F9F2F0D9 C5C3D6D9  C440D5D6 E340D6D5 40C6C9D3 C540D7D9  *MISVEND1920RECORD NOT ON FILE PR*  00C08F28
00000F40  C5E2E240 C5D5E3C5 D940E3D6 40C1C4C4  E5C5D5C4 F1F9F3F4 C6C9D3C5 40D3D6C7  *ESS ENTER TO ADDVEND1934FILE LOG*  00C08F48
00000F60  C9C340C5 D9D9D6D9 60C3C1D3 D340D4C9  E2E5C5D5 C4F1F9F4 F0E5C5D5 C4D6D940  *IC ERROR-CALL MISVEND1940VENDOR*  00C08F68
00000F80  C6C9D3C5 40C3D3D6 E2C5C4E5 C5D5C4F1  F9F4F440 40400000 58400018 C1E39240  *FILE CLOSEDVEND1944   ...K..8ATk*  00C08F88
00000FA0  58104000 5010D334 58104004 1B1158F0  C00405EF D21065F8 5010D3D4 .......  *..L....L....0...K..8ATk*     00C08FA8
00000FC0  6609D20A 660A6609 D2016508 656C01F4  92406567 5010D3E0 4110D3D4 ........  *..K....A.K..-A4k ....8.-LM*   00C08FC8
00000FE0  41106000 5010D3D8 41106508 5010D3DC  9680D3E0 C1884110 9680D3E0 4110D3D4  *.........LQ..K..-L.o.L..LM*   00C08FE8
00001000  58F0C004 05F58E00 D3344830 E0184930  C18258F0 C060078F 58E0D338 D2166000  *.0.....Ad.0-...L.K.-*         00C09008
00001020  E0004830 60004930 C18458F0 C064077F  5000348 5800C068 5000D39C ........  *....Ad.0....L.K.-*            00C09028
00001040  5810C01C 07F15800 D3485000 D39C4830  617C4930 C18658F0 C064078F 5800D3AC  *..1..L..L../..Af.0....L.*     00C09048
00001060  5000D34C 5800C06C 5810C02C 07F15800  D34C5000 D3A04830 6000D3AC 60004930  *.L...l...L...l...d..L*        00C09068
00001080  C18658F0 C070078F 4830617C 4930C186  58F0C074 077F5800 D3505000 D3A45000  *Af.0.......Af.0...Lu..L*      00C09088
000010A0  C0785000 D3A45810 C01807F1 5800D350  C2016000 C1842010 65F85010 65F8C1F8  *..Lu.....l..L..LuK.-AdK..8A.*  00C090A8
000010C0  92406609 D20A660A 6609D203 6538C20C  D2016508 C1884110 65F85010 D3D44110  *k..K..B.K..Ah...8.-LM.*       00C090C8
000010E0  65385010 D3D84110 60005010 D3DC4110  65085010 D3E09680 D3E04110 D3D458F0  *....LQ..L...L.o.L..LM.0*      00C090E8
00001100  58F0C004 05EF58E0 5800D354 5800C07C  C060078F 5800D348 5800C084 5000D3AC  *.0.....Ly..L..Ly.L...L.L.*    00C09108
00001120  D3A84830 60004930 C18658F0 D3585000  D3AC5000 C08077F 5810C08C 5000D3AC  *Ly...Af.0....L..L..d..L*      00C09128
00001140  5810C030 07F15800 D3585000 C090077F  58F0C074 077F5800 C080077F 5810C08C  *.1/...Af.0......Ab.0.h...*    00C09148
00001160  07F15830 61C04930 C18A58F0 C090077F  5800D3C0 C2016000 C1842010 5800D3B0  *.1..L..L.../..A.0....L*..m..L*  00C09168
00001180  07F15800 D35C5000 D3B85800 5810C08C  07F15800 D3605830 C180077F 5800D3AC  *..L....L*..L*.....q..L...*    00C09188
000011A0  C02C07F1 5800D360 5810C08C D3C04110  65085010 D3E09680 D3645800 C9C5000  *..1..L-..1..L..L..L..L...*    00C091A8
000011C0  D3B45810 C04807F1 5800D364 5800D3B4  D380D3A0 5800D3A0 5800C0A0 5000D3A0  *.L...L..l..L..L....A..K..*    00C091C8
000011E0  5810C02C 07F15800 D3685000 D3A04100  62B84110 02135830 C1DCC0E0 D2062C2B  *.....1...A...K...*            00C091E8
00001200  C210D21D 62E66018 D0562D9 630B603C  D21D6330 605AD21D 6355607B 18CDE0C  *B.K..W-K..R-K..-K..--*        00C09208
00001220  D21D637A 6096D21D 639F60B4 60D22D0A  63D760DE 63FCD231 D20CD230 18CDE0C  *K..-oK...-K.D-KK..P-K.K.A.*   00C09228
00001240  D23060E9 D20B63E9 D231D20C D230C199  60EED20B 63FCD231 D20CD230 D230C1A6  *K.-ZK..ZK.K.K.Ar..K.K.K.K.*   00C09248
00001260  C199DE0C D23060F3 D20B640F D231D200  642260F8 F872D220 D20CD230 D230C1A6  *Ar..K.-3K...K.K..-88.K.-9K.K.Aw*  00C09268
00001280  DE07D230 D2096461 D231D206 9240D231  D230C2B9 DE06D230 6104D205 6438D231  *.K.K...K.K.K.K..K.K.K.*       00C09288
000012A0  C1AEDE0A D23060F7 D2306107 D2306107  D231D202 6472610A 5820C0A4 60FCD201  *A..K..-K..K.K.A..K./.K..-K.*  00C092A8
000012C0  D206D230 C1B9DE06 D2306454 2286D200  64206282 F8226152 95E860F8 6148C184  *K.K.A..K../.K.K...unY-8*      00C092C8
000012E0  0772D200 64ID627B D200641E 660A6609  D2066560 C2289240 6567D201 6508C1C0  *K..A....fK...b8/.-.K./.Ad*    00C092E8
00001300  D21065F8 C2179240 6609D20A 660A6609  ........ ........ ........ ........  *K..8B.k..K...-B.k..K..A.*    00C09308
```

```
CUSTOMER INFORMATION CONTROL SYSTEM STORAGE DUMP    CODE=ASRA    TASK=VEND         DATE=11/04/86    TIME=20:04:11    PAGE   15

PROGRAM STORAGE                  ADDRESS 00C08008 TO 00C0A4BF     LENGTH 0024B8

0001320  411065F8 5010D3D4 41106560 5010D3D8  41106148 5010D3DC 41106508 5010D3E0  *.8..LM..-..LQ./...L.*  00C09328
0001340  9680D3E0 4110D3D4 58F0C004 05EF4830  61484930 C18258F0 C0A807AF D207614A  *o.L..LM.O...../..Ab.o.y..K./.*  00C09348
0001360  C22FD207 6445614A 5800D3B8 5000D3C   5800C0AC 5810C024 07F15800            *B.K../..../..L...../..K./.*  00C09368
0001380  D36C5000 D3B8D216 65F8C237 9240660F  D2046610 660FD206 65E0C24E D20665E8  *L..L.K..8B.k....K..K.B+K.Y*  00C09388
0001390  C2554110 65E05010 D3D44110 65E05010  62885010 D3DC4110 65F05010            *B....L..LQ......L...0..*  00C093A8
00013C0  D3E04110 65E85010 D3E49680 D3E44110  D3D458F0 C00405EF 5810D3A4 07F15820  *L..Y..LUo.LU..LM.O../..*  00C093C8
00013E0  C0B58E50 D334D500 E01A6291 07725800  D3BC5000 C0B45000 D3BC5810            *..L.N...j...L..L...*  00C093E8
0001400  C03407F1 5800D370 5000D3BC 629C0782  5BE0D334 D500E01A 629C0782 5820C0BC  *...1..L.L...b...*  00C09408
0001420  D5006180 629C0772 58E0D334 D2036602  E008D210 65F8C25C 9240660A D20A660A  *N./..L.K.-.K..8B*k...*  00C09428
0001440  6609D206 6560C26D 92406567 92406567  5010D3D8 4110650D8 4110600   41106000  *..K.-B.k....8.LM..K..*  00C09448
0001460  5010D3DC 4110E018 5010D3E0 9680D3E0  58F0C004 05EF5820 C0C058E0 C0C058E0  *..LQ....L..L.O...L..O.*  00C09468
0001480  D334D500 07825820 C0C4D500 C0C4D500  6180629D 0772D201 6000C186 D21065F8  *.L..b..DN..K.-AfK..8*  00C09488
00014A0  C2749240 6609D20A 660A6609 D2066560  C2859240 6567411 D3D44110  D3D44110  *B.k..K..-Bek...8.LM.*  00C094A8
00014C0  65605010 D3D84110 60005010 D3344110  D3344110 E0185010 D3E04680 D3E04110  *..LQ-..L..L..L.o.L.*  00C094C8
00014E0  D3D458F0 C00405EF 920062B8 62B85820  62B85820 D334D500 D334D500 E01A6291  *LM.O....Y...H.LN..j*  00C094E8
0001500  07825810 C02007F1 D21665F8 C28C9240  660FD204 66106607 D20665E0 C24ED206  *..b...1K..8B.k..K-.B+K.*  00C09508
0001520  65E8C255 411065F8 5010D3D4 4110650   5010D3D8 411062B8 5010D3DC 411065F0  *.YB...8.LM..LQ...0*  00C09528
0001540  5010D3E0 4110650E8 5010D3E4 9680D3E4  4110D3D4 58F0C004 05EF5810 D3344110  *..L..Y..LUo.LU.LM.O..L*  00C09548
0001560  E01B5010 D3D44110 65C05010 D3D89680  D3D84110 65F05010 C00805EF 583061C0  *..LM./..LQo.LU.LM.O../.*  00C09568
0001580  4930C182 58F0C0CC 077F5810 C0D007F1  583061C0 4930C1C2 58F0C0D4 077F5810  *..Ab.O...1./..AB.0.M..*  00C09588
00015A0  C02007F1 5800D3C0 5000D374 5800CDD8  5000D3C0 5810C044 07F15800 D3745006  *..1..L..L..Q.L...1K-.*  00C095A8
00015C0  D3C05810 C02007F1 48306D2D 4930C182  5800C0DC 072F5810 C02007F1 D2056006  *L...1..K.Ab.0...1K-.*  00C095C8
00015E0  62D95820 C00CDDD5 60062000 5810C0E0  07815800 D3C45000 CC45000 CCE45000  *.R...a..LD.L...U..*  00C095E8
0001600  D3C45810 C04007F1 5800D378 5000D3C4  5810C020 07F15800 D3AC5000 D37C5800  *LD...1.LD.-1.L...Ab.0.*  00C09608
0001620  C0B85000 C03007F1 5800D37C 5000D3AC  5000D3AC 4930C182 58F0C0EC 58F0C0FC  *K.-AfK./Af..1.Ab.0.*  00C09628
0001640  077F0201 6000C186 D2016171C C1865810  C02007F1 583061C0 4930C18A 58F0C0F0  *..K.-AfK./.A..0.0*  00C09648
0001660  077F5800 D3B05800 C0F45000 CF45000  D3B05810 C04C07F1 5800D3B0 5000D3B0  *..L..L..4..l.L..l.Ld*  00C09668
0001680  5810C020 07F15800 D3845800 C04807F1  C04807F1 C0805EF 9680D3E8 9680D384  *..L..8..l.LM..Ld..8Btk*  00C09688
00016A0  5000D3B4 5810D39C 07F1D202 6177600C  D2016172 C1C4D210 65F8C2A3 92406609  *L..L..../-.K/.ADK..8Btk*  00C096A8
00016C0  D20A660A 6609D201 6508C186 411065F8  5010D3D4 61061 74 5010D3D8 41106110  *..K..Af..8.LM../..LQ./.*  00C096C8
00016E0  E01B5010 D3D44110 65C05010 D3D89680  4110650 8 5010D3E0 9680D3E8 9680D384  *..LM./..LU.LM.O..LYo.LY*  00C096E8
0001700  4110D3D4 58F0C004 05EF58E0 C00805EF  D3D44110 61C05010 D3D89680 D3D89680  *..LM./..L...LM.*  00C09708
0001720  D3D84110 D3D458F0 583061C0 C00805EF  4930C182 077F5810 C10007F1 C10007F1  *.LM./-K./.ADK.8Btk*  00C09728
0001740  D2296474 C2B49240 64A6D223 64A764A6  5810C028 07F1FA20 6138C1C6 58E0D334  *K..K.m.K.K.K.AG..K.K.K.-*  00C09748
0001760  F8336134 65F8C2DE 9240660A D20A660A  D20A660A 6609D201 6508C1C4 411065F8  *8./..K..8B.k.LYo.LY.*  00C09768
0001780  5010D3D4 41106174 5010D3D8 41106110  5010D3DC 41106508 5010D3E0 411065F0  *..LM./..LQ./..L..0*  00C09788
00017A0  5010D3E4 41106170 5010D3E8 9680D3E8  58F0C004 05EF58E0 C00805EF 5E0D334   *..LU...LYo.LY.LM.O.*  00C097A8
00017C0  E01B5010 D3D44110 61C05010 D3D89680  D3D84110 D3D458F0 C00805EF 583061C0  *..LM./..LU.wK..x.w..l./.AF.l.*  00C097C8
00017E0  4930C182 58F0C104 078FD21E 647CC2EF  9240649B 22264 9C 649B5810 D3B807F1  *..Ab.0.8..K..8B.k..L.L.l*  00C097E8
0001800  D20662C7 C285D205 62F86006 D20262E7  600CD207 62D1600F 58E0D334 F873D220  *K..GBeK..8-.K.X-.K.-J-.L.1*  00C09808
0001820  E000D703 D220D224 940FD224 D209D203  C1C7DE09 D230D224 D20762DC D2325820  *.P.K.m.K.K.K.AG.K.K.K.-*  00C09828
0001840  C010D2FF D2302000 927AD29B DC0762DC  D23058E0 D334D203 62EDE010 D2016000  *.K.K..8c.k..k.K..*  00C09848
0001860  C184D216 65F8C30E 9240660F D2046610  660FD206 65E0C325 D2065810 C2554110  *.AdK..8c.k..K..C.K.YB..*  00C09868
0001880  65F85010 D3D44110 65F05010 D3E04110  62B85010 65F05010 D3E04110 D3E04110  *..8..LM..LQ..L..K.*  00C09888
00018A0  65E85010 D3E49680 D3E44110 D3D458F0  C00405EF 65F05010 C32C9240 6609D20A  *.Y..LUo.LU..LM.O...K..8C.k*  00C098A8
00018C0  66A6609 D2036538 C1F4D201 6508C188  411065F8 5010D3D4 41106538 5010D3D8  *..K..A4K..Ah..8.LM..LQ*  00C098C8
00018E0  4110600 D2036538 58F0C0C4 C00805EF  9680D3E0 4110D3DC C34E9240 58F0C0C4  *..8..L.o.L..LM.O.*  00C098E8
0001900  D3A07F1 D21065F8 C3309240 6609D20A  660A6609 D2066560 C34E9240 65674110  *L..1K.8C.k..K.-C+k*  00C09908
0001920  65F85010 D3D44110 65605010 D3D84110  60185010 617E5010 D3E04110 D3E04110  *.8..LM.-..LQ.--.L..L*  00C09928
0001940  60065010 D3E49680 D3E44110 D3D458F0  58E0D334 4110E01B 5010D3D4 5810D3D4  *..LUo.LU..LM*  00C09948
0001960  411061C0 5010D3D8 9680D3D8            58F0C008 05EF5810 D3AC07F1 58E0D334  *..../..LQo.LM..L..L.*  00C09968
```

FIGURE 13.5. Continued

PROGRAM STORAGE   ADDRESS 00C08008 TO 00C0A4BF   LENGTH 0024B8

```
00001980  D2006180 E01AD707 D220D220 D201D226 E0164820 E0168E20 00204850 C1D21D25  *K.../...P.K.K.K.........+K.P.K.K..*  00C09988
000019A0  5030D22C 40306181 4830D22E 4C30C1D2 485DD226 1B53AE50 D228D704 D228D228  *.K..  /a.K..<.AK.]K...+.P.K.K.*     00C099A8
000019C0  940FD22D 4F30D228 40306181 4830C186 4A306181 4E30D228 D704D228 D228940F  *m.K.O.K.  /a.K.Af./a+.K.P.K.K.m.*   00C099C8
000019E0  D22D4F30 D2284030 61814830 61834E30 D228D704 D228D228 940FD22D 940FD22D  *K../.K. /a..a.N.K.P.K.K.m.K.*       00C099E8
00001A00  4F30D228 40306181 48306183 40306181 58F0C108 07AF5810 C03807F1 48306181  *.K.  /a..a.  /a.0A....1./a*          00C09A08
00001A20  4930C188 58F0C10C 077FD201 5810C110 07F1D201 6181C1D4 D2016185 D2016185  *.K..c./a.Ah.0A.....1../a*           00C09A28
00001A40  C1864830 61834930 C1C458F0 D2016185 C1C45810 C1D45810 C11807F1 48306183  *.Ah.0A..K./aAb..A..lK./aAMK./e*    00C09A48
00001A60  4930C1D6 58F0C118 07DFD201 6185C184 4A306185 4A306185 4E30D228 F3026180  *Af.0A..AD.0A..K./eAd..a../e+.K.3./.* 00C09A68
00001A80  D22D96F0 61805810 D3BC07F1 62B8D213 61D1C355 92406185 92406185 92406185  *K.o0/..k..l.k..KY....K./JC.k./V*    00C09A88
00001AA0  D22261E6 61E5D207 61C8C369 D24C6301 634ED200 634F634E D21665F8 D21665F8  *K./W/VK./HC.K../Hk.+K...+K..8*      00C09AA8
00001AC0  C3719240 660FD204 610660 0F D20665E0 C325D206 65E8C255 411065F8 501 0D3D4  *C.k...K..C.K..YB...8..LM*           00C09AC8
00001AE0  411065E0 5010D3D8 411062B8 58F0C004 411065E0 5010D3E4 411065E0 5010D3E4  *.K...LM.0...L...Y..LU*              00C09AE8
00001B00  9680D3E4 4110D3D4 58F0C004 05EFD210 65F8C388 92406609 D20A660A 66094110  *o.LU.LM.0....K..8Chk..K..*          00C09B08
00001B20  65F85010 D3D49680 D3D44110 D3D458F0 C00405EF 5810D3A8 07F19200 62B8D2E8  *.8..LMo.LM.LM.0..Ly.lk..KY*         00C09B28
00001B40  62B96288 D21561D1 C399240 0 61E7D220 61BB61E7 D2076IC8 C3AFD24C 63016IC8  *.K./JCrk./XK/Y/XK./HC.K../H*        00C09B48
00001B60  924063 4E D200634F 634E5810 D3C407F1 920062B8 D2E862B9 62B8D211 61D1C3B7  *.k.+K...+.LD.lk..KY../K./JC*        00C09B68
00001B80  924061E3 D22461E4 61E3D207 61C8C3C9 D24C6301 61C89240 634F634E 634F634E  *k./TK./U/TK./HCIK../Hk.+K..+*       00C09B88
00001BA0  5800D3C8 5000D388 5800C11C 5000D3C8 5810C058 07F15800 D3885000 D3C85810  *.LH..Lh..A..LH...l..LH..LH.*        00C09BA8
00001BC0  D3C007F1 583061C0 4930C1D8 58F0C120 077F5800 D3CC5000 D38C5800 C1245000  *L.l../.A..AQ.0A...L..LA..KY*        00C09BC8
00001BE0  D3CC5810 C05007F1 5800D38C 5000D3CC 5810C128 07F15830 5810C054 C1DA58F0  *L..l...l..L..A..l./..A..0*          00C09BE8
00001C00  C12C077F 5800D3D0 5000D390 5800C130 5000D3D0 5810C054 D3905000 D3905000  *A...L..L..A..L..L.*                 00C09C08
00001C20  D3D05810 C12807F1 920062B8 D2E862B9 62BD2D70 61D1C3D1 924061EB D21C61EC  *.L..A..lk...KY...K./JCJk./L./*      00C09C28
00001C40  61EBD207 61C8C3EB D24C6301 61C89240 634ED200 634F634E 5800D3C8 5000D394  */.K./HC.K../Hk..+K...+..LH..Lm*     00C09C48
00001C60  5800C134 5000D3C8 5810C058 07F15800 D3945000 D3B407F1 920062B8 92F362F4  *.A...LH...l..Lm..LH..L..lk*         00C09C68
00001C80  D2E862B9 62B8D224 61D1C3F3 924061F6 D21161F7 61F6D207 61C8C418 92F362F4  *KY...K./JC3k./6K./7/6K./HD.k3.4*    00C09C88
00001CA0  24C6301 61C89240 634ED200 634F634E 5810D3B0 07F19200 62B8D2E8 62B962B8  *KY../Hk.+K../.K./HD.K../Hk.+*       00C09CA8
00001CC0  D2181D1 C4209240 61EAD21D 61EB61EA D20761C8 C439D24C 630161C8 92406340E  *K./JD.K../.K./.K./HD.K../Hk.+*      00C09CC8
00001CE0  D200634F 634E5800 D3C85000 D3985800 C1385000 C05807F1 C4419240 61E3D224  *K..+..LH..Lq..A...LH...l./Lq*       00C09CE8
00001D00  5000D3C8 5810D3CC 07F19200 62B8D2E8 62B962B8 D21161D1 C4419240 61E3D224  *.LH..l.lk..KY...K./JD.k./TK.*       00C09D08
00001D20  61E461E3 D20761C8 C453D24C D200634F 634E5810 D200634F D3D007F1 D3D007F1  */U/TK./HD.K../Hk.+K...+..L..l*      00C09D28
00001D40  D2066197 C1DC58E0 D3342D05 6197E01D 47D6619E 6101D217 C010D2FF D2302000  *K./pA...L.K./p..3F//.p...K.K.*      00C09D48
00001D60  41100007 1B220539 4301618F 1B220530 6101D217 07B3DC0B 619ED230 619ED230  *....K..../.g..K.*                   00C09D68
00001D80  D20B6253 619ED206 6197C1DC 58E0D334 47D6619E E01B9240 6199D200 619A6199  *K./pA.../.K./pA...L.K./p..k/rK.//r* 00C09D88
00001DA0  4202D230 06101211 07B3DC0B 619B5820 619B5830 C1C04E30 D228F314 43216187  *3F//.p...K.K......./.g*             00C09DA8
00001DC0  D20B6253 96F06266 D20D61AB 65F85820 61B42000 5810C13C 0771D204 47E9620   *.K../.K.K..../...+./.K.3*           00C09DC8
00001DE0  62425B4 5810C140 1EAB5040 10087I6 D24E6353 62185810 C3C807F1 05F058E0  *.K.oO.K./..8....A...K*              00C09DE8
00001E00  D1B09110 D04900E0 E04847E0 F02E94EF D0485810 C0009200 10001B11 58F0C014  *J.J...q...q......q..0.Jj.*          00C09E08
00001E20  05EF58E0 D1B0980E E00C07FE 58D0D004 98ECD00C 07FE05F0 95002000 07792FF   *.q....q......n....k...o.*           00C09E28
00001E40  471F01A 900EE048 50D05008 5050D004 5820C010 95002000 20009610 9110D048  *K......0j...0...q....*              00C09E48
00001E60  D04850E0 D05405F0 9120D048 47E0FO16 5800B048 982B0050 58E0D054 07E9620   *.....0j...0..00.....A.*             00C09E68
00001E80  D0489110 D04847E0 F02C58F0 C00041F0 F01005EF 41600004 411C0018 4170C180  *.K.oO.K./..8....A...K*              00C09E88
00001EA0  06700550 58401000 1EAB5040 10087I6 D21C4170 D21F0510 58E00D54 58E0D054  *.....gf.K.K..K..K...*               00C09EA8
00001EC0  1E0B5000 80008786 1000D237 D39CC144 5860D21C 58E01D61 906DD060 18B19180  *.....j.......q..K...j.*             00C09EC8
00001EE0  07FE101E 07FE9104 90ECD00C 18CF182D 41D0C0F0 50200008 50D20008 18B19180  *..gf.K.L.A..-K..J...K.*             00C09EE8
00001F00  B00447E0 C0705840 B0005850 50504000 95004002 47800C70 2015002 2015002   *...........j........o....K...j.*    00C09F08
00001F20  C13B8200 50004000 B2005001 40024180 C07A4170 C0EA4160 0044D501 80005000  *.............o....K...*             00C09F28
00001F40  4780C064 8786C052 47F0C06A D2015002 8002D701 00150608 00120684 98ECD00C  *........P...n....K...*              00C09F48
00001F60  07FE02E0 01004E0 00110681 00D00682 000E0683 00120684 0010060C 04606E1   *A.K...K..........N...K...*          00C09F68
00001F80  054060F 00140680 00110681 00160601 00160601 00150608 00D00682 04606E1   *..gf...0.K.......q..*               00C09F88
00001FA0  00160A01 001A0A02 002C0A04 00110A08 00110A08 00120A20 00460AE1 0016E001  *.......a..b..c..d..0....*           00C09FA8
00001FC0  00160A01 001A0A02 002C0A04 00110A08 00110A08 00120A20 00460AE1 0016E001  *...............*                    00C09FC8
```

FIGURE 13.5. Continued

```
CUSTOMER INFORMATION CONTROL SYSTEM STORAGE DUMP      CODE=ASRA    TASK=VEND          DATE=11/04/86    TIME=20:04:11    PAGE   17

PROGRAM STORAGE                          ADDRESS 00C08008 TO 00C0A4BF      LENGTH 0024B8

0001FE0  001B0EE6 00100ED6 00461801 00101804 00241AE0 01101040 91201015 0B87854   *.........O.........j......*   00C09FE8
0002000  F3E0AA00 07F7189B 4B901054 50901044 4BB01050 5BEE0000 47F0F150 9547E000   *3=..7.........01.n..*        00C0A008
0002020  4770F1F8 9518E003 077E947F 101507FE 947F1015 5BEE0000 507DF460 987DF464   *..18n..=..m....-4.4.*        00C0A028
0002040  00011015 478DF224 FF000000 F0F761F2 58EE0000 90ECD00C 987DF460 05B047F0   *......2......-..0*           00C0A048
0002060  B01CC9D3 C2C4D7D9 D4F0F3F0 F0F761F2 F1F34BF3 F31450D0 B08E41F0 4780B07E   *..ILBDPRM03007/25/8113.33....0*  00C0A068
0002080  B08A50FD 000818DF 58A0B0DE 9280A001 58100014 0A215890 1071299 4780B07E    *....k....r.=*                00C0A088
00020A0  D207B0D5 90004120 B0D44150 20074140 0001D501 2000B0D2 4770B066 947FA001   *K.N...M...N....K...m.*       00C0A0A8
00020C0  47F0B07A 95C12001 4770B07A 95D52000 4780B07A 9640A001 8724B054 58D0B08E   *.0.:nA...:nN....o..g.*       00C0A0C8
00020E0  98ECD00C 1BFF07FE 00000000 00000000 00000000 00000000 00000000 00000000   *q.................*          00C0A0E8
0002100  00000000 00000000 00000000 00000000 D5C40000 00000000 00000000 00C0A050   *.................ND.*        00C0A108
0002120  00000000 00000000 00000000 40C9D3C2 C4D7D9D4 F000B0F8 B0FA00FC B0FEB100   *.......PATCH AREA - ILBDPRM0..8....*  00C0A128
0002140  D7C1E3C3 C840C1D9 C5C14060 40C9D3C2 C2F14OC3 D6D7E8D9 C9C7C8E3 40C9C2D4   *.PATCH AREA - ILBDCB1 COPYRIGHT IBM*  00C0A148
0002160  B102B104 B106B108 B10AF5F7 F4F660C3 C5F7F4F6 60D3D4F4 40C3D6D7 E8D9C9C7   *.........5746-CB1 COPYRIG*   00C0A168
0002180  40C3D6D9 D74B40F1 F9F7F36B F1F9F8F0 F5F7F4F6 60D3D4F4 F6F6F1F6 F3F0F238   * CORP. 1973,19805746-LM4 COPYRIG*  00C0A188
00021A0  C8E340C9 C2D440C3 D6D9D74B 40F1F9F7 F36BF1F9 F8F0F6C5 F6F6F1F6 3F0F238    *HT IBM CORP. 1973,1980FE661630.2*  00C0A1A8
00021C0  4FF0F016 C9D3C2C4 E3C3F2F0 F3F0F0F7 61F2F561 F8F190EC D00C05A0 5890A0A0   *.00.ILBDTC203007/25/81.........*   00C0A1C8
00021E0  12994780 A0549110 90004710 A05A9610 900050D0 9080188D 41D0907C 50D80008   *.r....j....o.........Q...*   00C0A1E8
0002200  12114780 A02E5811 000091C0 9004780  A04C58F0 A09805EF 941F9000 12114770   *....j......o......q..m...Q*  00C0A208
0002220  A04C58F0 A09405EF 58D09080 94EF9000 98ECD00C 07FE9180 9014710 A0869680    *..........0..m...q....j....fo.*  00C0A228
0002240  900158C0 A0540000 C0909210 C09450D0 0080188D 41D0907C 50D80008 05EF58D0   *..........0.m...q......j...*  00C0A248
0002260  90804780 A0540000 00000000 00000000 00000000 00000000 00000000 00000000   *...............0..k..m.....Q....*  00C0A268
0002280  00000000 00000000 00000000 00000000 9500706D 00010203 04050607 00000000   *.................0......n....*  00C0A288
00022A0  0C0D0E0F 10111213 14151617 18191A1B 1C1D1E1F 20212223 24252627            *................................*  00C0A2A8
00022C0  08090A0B 2C2D2E2F 30313233 34353637 38393A3B 3C3D3E3F 40414243 44454647   *................n...........*  00C0A2C8
00022E0  28292A2B 4C4D4E4F 50515253 54555657 58595A5B 5C5D5E5F 60616263 64656667   *..................................*  00C0A2E8
0002300  48494A4B 6C6D6E6F 70717273 74757677 7C7D7E7F 80818283 84858687            *..............(+......$*).;-/....*  00C0A308
0002320  68696A6B 0802F000 78797A7B 90919293 9C9D9E9F A0A1A2A3 A4A5A6A7            *..............'..=..abcdefg.*  00C0A328
0002340  8C8D8E8F 94959697 98999A9B B4B5B6B7 B8B9BABB BCBDBEBF C0C1C2C3 C4C5C6C7   *................jklmnopqr...stuvwx*  00C0A348
0002360  A8A9AAAB B0B1B2B3 ACADAEAF B4B5B6B7 B8B9BABB DCDDDEDF E0E1E2E3 E4E5E6E7   *.hi.............stuvwx*      00C0A368
0002380  C8C9CACB CCCDCECF D0D1D2D3 D8D9DADB DCDDDEDF E0E1E2E3 E4E5E6E7            *.yz............ABCDEFG*      00C0A388
00023A0  E8E9EAEB ECEDEEEF F0F1F2F3 F4F5F6F7 F8F9FAFB FCFDFEFF 01010101 01010101   *.YZ........JKLMNOPQR.*       00C0A3A8
00023C0  01010101 01010101 01010101 01010101 01010101 01010101 01010101 01010101   *.YZ........012345678 9.........*  00C0A3C8
00023E0  01010101 01010101 01010101 00000000 00000000 00000000 00000000 00000000   *..............................*  00C0A3E8
0002400  SAME AS ABOVE
LINES TO 0002480 SAME AS ABOVE
00024A0  01010101 00000000 00000000 00000101 01010101                              *.*                            00C0A4A8


PROGRAM STORAGE                          ADDRESS 00C0F808 TO 00C0F9DC      LENGTH 0001D5

00000000  E5C5D5C4 E2C5E340 00604040 00000000 D4C5D5E4 D4C1D740 01C500DC            *VENDSET  .  ........MENUMAP .E. *   00C0F808
00000020  00E50217 C04004E0 00185001 01100000 00000000 00701F0  00000000            *.V...  ..........0....*              00C0F828
00000040  00402F0  0042C4C1 E3C50000 00801F0  00470000 005D8C5C5 D5C4D6D9            *.V...DATE....0....0.)VENDOR*        00C0F848
00000060  404C1E2  E3C5D940 D4C5D5E4 40000000 0402F000 92E3C9D4 0802F001            * MASTER MENU...0.kTIME....0.*       00C0F868
00000080  97000000 0802F000 E2D6D7C5 D3000000 0301F001 EC000000 0802F001            *.p....0.SOPERATOR.......0.*         00C0F888
000000A0  32E3C5D9 D4C9D5C1 D3000000 1902F001 49F14040 4C4C9E2                      *.TERMINAL...0....0.DIS.*            00C0F8A8
000000C0  D7D3C1E8 40D4C1E2 E3C5D940 D9C5C3D6 D9C40000 00190290 01E9F240 4040D4C1   *PLAY MASTER RECORD....0.Z2  UP*     00C0F8C8
000000E0  C4C1E3C5 40D4C1E2 E3C5D940 D9C5C3D6 D9C40000 00001902 F0028F93 404040C1   *DATE MASTER RECORD....0.i3  A*      00C0F8E8
00000100  C4C440D4 C1E2E3C5 C3D6D9C4 40404040 40000019 02F00329 F4404040            *DD MASTER RECORD........0.4*        00C0F908
00000120  C4C5D3C5 E3C540D4 C1E2E3C5 D9C5C3D6 D9C40000 00001902 F903 C9F54040       *DELETE MASTER RECORD....0.I5*       00C0F928
00000140  40C5E7C9 E340D4C1 E2E3C5D9 40D4C5D5 E4400000 00190290 02F00E3E8            *EXIT MASTER MENU........0..TY*      00C0F948
00000160  D7C540C6 E4D5C3E3 C9D6D540 C3D6C4C5 404DF160 F55D4000 0000103  C104CBF1   *PE FUNCTION CODE (1-5)....A..1*     00C0F968
00000180  00000011 02F000CD C1D5C440 E5C5D5C4 D6D940D5 E4D4C2C5 D9000000 0603C104   *...0..AND VENDOR NUMBER....A.*      00C0F988
```

FIGURE 13.5. Continued

```
CUSTOMER INFORMATION CONTROL SYSTEM STORAGE DUMP    CODE=ASRA    TASK=VEND        DATE=11/04/86    TIME=20:04:11    PAGE    18

PROGRAM STORAGE                    ADDRESS 00C0F808 TO 00C0F9DC        LENGTH 0001D5

000001A0   DFD5D5D5 D5D5D500 00001002 F004E6E3   C8C5D540 D7D9C5E2 E240C5D5 E3C5D900   *.NNNNN.....0.WTHEN PRESS ENTER.*   00C0F9A8
000001C0   00004F01 F005A000 00004F01 F005F0FF   FFFFFFFF FF                          *....0........0.0.......*            00C0F9C8

END OF CICS/VS STORAGE DUMP
```

FIGURE 13.5.   Continued

Chapter Summary

The problem determination aids provided by CICS/VS can be extremely beneficial to an installation. Not only do they provide an alternative to using EDF during testing, they also provide a means to get debugging information after a system has been placed into production. An installation that develops good problem control procedures can use these aids to improve and maintain the reliability of their on-line systems. Your skills in using these aids can help your installation to reduce application down time. This is an important goal of every organization.

Discussion Questions

1. Through the use of EDF storage modification screens it is possible to use an update program to "patch up" a corrupted record in a file. How would this same capability cause potential security infringements?
2. The internal trace table is used to trace the activity of transactions running in the system. What is the primary limitation of this table?
3. What facility is provided to overcome the main limitation of the internal trace table?
4. When reading a transaction dump to determine the cause of a program check interruption, what information in the PSW is usually needed?
5. Describe the process of locating the EIB in a transaction dump.
6. Describe a quick way to locate the beginning of working-storage in a dump.
7. A very common reason for a program check interruption is the data exception (OC7 interrupt). What is the cause of this exception?
8. Discuss why an installation would make it standard operating procedure to have the Systems Support staff review all transaction dumps produced by the production CICS system.
9. How are EIP trace entries identified?
10. Each trace entry contains the address of register 14 at entry to each management program. How can this address be useful in tracing the flow of a command-level program?
11. A trace entry is made by EIP just prior to returning control back to the application program. Where in this trace entry is the return address in the COBOL program stored?
12. By what means can the application program make trace entries of its own? How could this be useful?
13. Which general register usually points to the COBOL INTI1 routine?

Review Exercises

1. Assume that the PSW information below is printed at the top of a transaction dump. Assume further that the program load address of the COBOL program is 60D050. What is the address of the instruction that caused the interrupt? What is the reason for the interrupt? What is the offset into the program where the interrupt occurred?

```
PSW   078D0000   0060E806   00060007 0000
```

2. Code a DUMP command to cause the contents of the field DATE-EMPLOYED below to be produced in a transaction dump. The dump code for this dump should be AX42.

```
01   RECORD-AREA.
     05   EMPLOYEE-NAME PIC X(30).
     05   EMPLOYEE-ADDRESS PIC X(24).
     05   DATE-EMPLOYED PIC S9(07) COMP-3.
     05   DATE-TERMINATED PIX S9(07) COMP-3.
```

3. Code a command to produce a trace entry. Display the first eight bytes of the commarea in the trace. Select any valid user trace identification. The resource name for the trace should be 'COMMAREA.'

Appendix A
CICS/VS Reference

CICS/VS Commands

GENERAL FORMAT

```
[EXECUTE | EXEC] CICS
    function [option[(argument)]]...
    END-EXEC
```

ARGUMENT VALUES

data-value Any COBOL data name of the correct type or a constant of the correct type.

data-area Any COBOL data name of the correct type.

name A COBOL data name of length equal to maximum allowed, or a literal constant.

hhmmss A COBOL data name defined as S9(7) COMP-3 or a constant.

EXCEPTIONAL CONDITIONS

```
HANDLE CONDITION
      condition [(label)]
      [condition [(label)]]
IGNORE CONDITION
      condition
      [condition]
NOHANDLE option
RESP option
POP HANDLE
PUSH HANDLE
```

ACCESS TO SYSTEM INFORMATION

```
ADDRESS    option (pointer-ref)   [option (pointer-ref)]
```

☐ **Options**

CSA	common system area
CWA	common work area
EIB	Execute Interface Block
TCTUA	Terminal Control Table user area
TWA	task work area

```
ASSIGN    option (data-area)    [option (data-area)]
```

□ **Options**

ABCODE 4-byte argument is set to the current abend code; blanks if an abend has not occurred.

APPLID 8-byte argument is set to the name of the application owning the transaction.

BTRANS 1-byte argument is set to high-values if the terminal supports background transparency; it is set to low-values if the terminal does not support background transparency.

COLOR 1-byte argument is set to high-values if the terminal supports extended color; it is set to low-values if the terminal does not support extended color.

CWALENG S9999 COMPUTATIONAL argument is set to the length of the CWA. If a CWA does not exist, the argument is set to zero.

DELIMITER 1-byte argument used for the IBM 3600 terminal.

DESTCOUNT S9999 COMPUTATIONAL argument used with advanced BMS commands.

DESTID 8-byte argument used with Batch Data Interface of CICS.

DESTIDLENG S9999 COMPUTATIONAL argument used with Batch Data Interface of CICS.

EXTDS 1-byte argument is set to high-values if the terminal supports extended attributes; it is set to low-values if the terminal does not support extended attributes.

FACILITY 4-byte character argument that contains the name of the facility that initiated the transaction.

FCI 1-byte character argument that contains the CICS facility control indicator for the task.

GCHARS S9999 COMPUTATIONAL argument used with graphic terminals.

GCODES S9999 COMPUTATIONAL argument used with graphic terminals.

HILIGHT 1 BYTE argument. If the terminal supports extended highlighting, it is set to high-values. It is set to low-values if the terminal does not support extended highlighting.

INPARTN 2-byte argument used for terminals with multiple partition support.

KATAKANA 1-byte argument used to determine if the terminal supports KATAKANA.

LDCMNEM 2-byte argument used with advanced BMS commands.

LDCNUM 1-byte argument used with advanced BMS commands.

MAPCOLUMN S9999 COMPUTATIONAL argument is set to the column number of the origin of the most recently positioned map.

MAPHEIGHT S9999 COMPUTATIONAL argument is set to the height of the most recently positioned map.

MAPLINE S9999 COMPUTATIONAL argument is set to the line number of the origin of the most recently positioned map.

MAPWIDTH S9999 COMPUTATIONAL argument is set to the width of the most recently positioned map.

MSRCONTROL 1-byte argument used to determine if the terminal supports the magnetic slot reader.

NETNAME 8-byte argument used to get the name of the logical unit with SNA networks.

NUMTAB 1-byte argument used with IBM 2980 terminals.

OPCLASS 3-byte character argument used to get the operator class codes. The three bytes contain 24 binary codes corresponding to each of the 24 available codes.

OPERKEYS 8-byte character argument used to get the operator security codes. The 8 bytes contain 64 binary codes corresponding to each of the 64 available security codes.

OPID   3-byte argument used to get the operator identification.

OPSECURITY   3-byte character argument used to get the standard transaction security codes. The 3 bytes contain 24 binary codes corresponding to each of the 24 available codes.

OUTLINE   1-byte argument is set to high-values if the terminal supports outlining; it is set to low-values if the terminal does not support outlining.

PAGENUM   S9999 COMPUTATIONAL argument used with advanced BMS commands.

PARTNPAGE   2-byte argument used with terminals that support multiple partitions.

PARTNS   1-byte argument used to determine if the terminal supports partitions.

PARTNSET   6-byte argument used with terminals that support partitions.

PRINSYSID   4-byte argument used with LU6 terminals.

PS   1-byte argument is set to high-values if the terminal supports programmed symbols; it is set to low-values if the terminal does not support programmed symbols.

QNAME   4-byte argument used to get the name of the transient data queue that started this transaction using ATI.

RESTART   1-byte argument set to high-values if the transaction has been restarted by the CICS; it is set to low-values for a normal transaction start.

SCRNHT   S9999 COMPUTATIONAL argument used to get the number of rows for the terminal.

SCRNWD   S9999 COMPUTATIONAL argument used to get the number of columns for the terminal.

SIGDATA   4-byte argument used to get signal data from the logical unit.

SOSI   1-byte argument used to determine if the terminal has the capability for mixed EBCDIC/DBCS fields.

STARTCODE   2-byte argument used to determine how the transaction was started. A value of TD will be stored in this field if the transaction was started due to terminal input. If started with the START command the argument will have a value of SD or S. A value of QD indicates that the transaction was started with the transient data trigger facility. A value of U indicates a user-attached task.

STATIONID   1-byte argument used with IBM 2980 terminals.

SYSID   4-byte argument used to get the name of the local CICS system.

TCTUALENG   S9999 COMPUTATIONAL argument used to get the length of the Terminal Control Table user area. The argument will contain zeros if no TCTUA is present.

TELLERID   1-byte character argument used with IBM 2980 terminals.

TERMCODE   2-byte value used to get the type and model of the terminal.

TWALENG   S9999 COMPUTATIONAL argument used to get the length of the task work area. The argument will contain zeros if no TWA is present.

UNATTEND   1-byte argument used to determine whether the terminal is operating in unattended mode.

VALIDATION   1-byte indicator used to determine whether the terminal has field validation capability. High-values indicates that the terminal has the feature. Low-values indicates that the terminal does not have the validation feature.

☐ **Conditions:** INVREQ

GENERAL SERVICE COMMANDS

```
ABEND               [ABCODE(name)]
                    [CANCEL]
                    [NOHANDLE]
                    [RESP (data-area)]
ALLOCATE            {SESSION(name) | SYSID (name)}
                    [PROFILE(name)]
                    [NOQUEUE | NOSUSPEND]
                    [NOHANDLE]
                    [RESP(data-area)]
```

□ **Conditions:** CBIDERR, EOC, INVREQ, SESSBUSY, SESSIONERR, SYSBUSY, SYSIDERR

```
ASKTIME             [ABSTIME(data-area)]
                    [NOHANDLE]
                    [RESP(data-area)]
BIF                 DEEDIT
                    FIELD(data-area)
                    LENGTH(data-value)
                    [NOHANDLE]
                    [RESP(data-area)]
CANCEL              [REQID(name)
                        [TRANSID(name)] [SYSID(name)]]
```

□ **Conditions:** INVREQ, ISCINVREQ, NOTAUTH, NOTFND, SYSIDERR

```
DELAY               [INTERVAL(hhmmss) | TIME (hhmmss)]
                    [REQID(name)]
                    [NOHANDLE]
                    [RESP(data-area)]
```

□ **Conditions:** EXPIRED, INVREQ

```
DELETE              DATASET(name)
                    [RIDFLD(data-area)]
                    [KEYLENGTH(data-value)]
                    [GENERIC [NUMREC(data-area)]]
                    [SYSID(name)]
                    [RBA | RRN]
                    [NOHANDLE]
                    [RESP(data-area)]
```

□ **Conditions:** DISABLED, DSIDERR, DUPKEY, ILLOGIC, INVREQ, IOERR, ISCINVREQ, NOTAUTH, NOTFND, NOTOPEN, SYSIDERR

```
DELETEQ TD          QUEUE(name)
                    [SYSID(name)]
                    [NOHANDLE]
                    [RESP(data-area)]
```

□ **Conditions:** ISCINVREQ, NOTAUTH, QIDERR, SYSIDERR

```
DELETEQ TS          QUEUE(name)
                    [SYSID(name)]
                    [NOHANDLE]
                    [RESP(data-area)]
```

□ **Conditions:** ISCINVREQ, NOTAUTH, QIDERR, SYSIDERR

```
DEQ                        RESOURCE(data-area)
                           [LENGTH(data-value)]
                           [NOHANDLE]
                           [RESP(data-area)]
DUMP                       DUMPCODE(name)
                           [FROM(data-area) {LENGTH(data-value)
                             FLENGTH(data-value)}]
                           [TASK]
                           [NOHANDLE]
                           [RESP(data-area)]
```

☐ **Conditions:** LENGERR

```
ENDBR                      DATASET(name)
                           [REQID(data-value)]
                           [SYSID(name)]
                           [NOHANDLE]
                           [RESP(data-area)]
```

☐ **Conditions:** DISABLED, DSIDERR, ILLOGIC, INVREQ, ISCINVREQ, NOTAUTH, NOTOPEN, SYSIDERR

```
ENTER                      TRACEID(data-value)
                           [FROM(data-area)]
                           [RESOURCE(name)]
                           [NOHANDLE]
                           [RESP(data-area)]
```

☐ **Condition:** INVREQ

```
ENQ                        RESOURCE(data-area)
                           [LENGTH(data-value)]
                           [NOSUSPEND]
                           [NOHANDLE]
                           [RESP(data-area)]
```

☐ **Conditions:** ENQBUSY

```
FORMATTIME                 ABSTIME(data-value)
                           [YYDDD(data-area)]
                           [YYMMDD(data-area)]
                           [YYDDMM(data-area)]
                           [DDMMYY(data-area)]
                           [MMDDYY(data-area)]
                           [DATE(data-area)]
                           [DATEFORM(data-area)]
                           [DATESEP(data-value)]
                           [DAYCOUNT(data-area)]
                           [DAYOFWEEK(data-area)]
                           [DAYOFMONTH(data-area)]
                           [MONTHOFYEAR(data-area)]
                           [YEAR(data-area)]
                           [YEAR(data-area)]
                           [TIME(data-area)
                             [TIMESEP(data-value)]]
                           [NOHANDLE]
                           [RESP(data-area)]
FREEMAIN                   DATA(data-area)
                           [NOHANDLE]
                           [RESP(data-area)]
```

```
GETMAIN              SET(pointer-ref)
                     {LENGTH(data-value) |
                      FLENGTH(data-value)}
                     [INTIMIG(data-value)]
                     [NOSUSPEND]
                     [NOHANDLE]
                     [RESP(data-area)]
```

☐ **Conditions:** LENGERR, NOSTG

```
HANDLE ABEND         {PROGRAM(name) | LABEL(name) |
                      CANCEL | RESET}
                     [NOHANDLE]
                     [RESP(data-area)]
```

☐ **Conditions:** NOTAUTH, PGMIDERR

```
JOURNAL              JFILEID(data-value)
                     JTYPEID(data-value)
                     FROM(data-area)
                     LENGTH(data-value)
                     [REQID(data-area)]
                     [PREFIX(data-value) PFLENG(data-value)]
                     [STARTIO]
                     [WAIT]
                     [NOHANDLE]
                     [RESP(data-area)]
```

☐ **Conditions:** JIDERR, INVREQ, LENGERR, NOJBUFSP, NOTOPEN

```
LINK                 PROGRAM(name)
                     [COMMAREA(data-area)
                      LENGTH(data-value)]
                     [NOHANDLE]
                     [RESP(data-area)]
```

☐ **Conditions:** NOTAUTH, PGMIDERR

```
LOAD                 PROGRAM(name)
                     [SET(pointer-ref)]
                     [LENGTH(data-area) |
                      FLENGTH(data-area)]
                     [ENTRY(pointer-ref)]
                     [HOLD]
                     [NOHANDLE]
                     [RESP(data-area)]
```

☐ **Conditions:** NOTAUTH, PGMIDERR

```
POST                 [INTERVAL(hhmmss) | TIME(hhmmss)]
                     [SET(pointer-ref)]
                     [REQID(name)]
                     [NOHANDLE]
                     [RESP(data-area)]
```

☐ **Conditions:** EXPIRED, INVREQ

```
PURGE MESSAGE
```

☐ **Condition:** TSIOERR

```
READ                     DATASET(name)
                         {INTO(data-area) | SET(pointer-ref)}
                         [LENGTH(data-area)]
                         RIDFLD(data-area)
                         [KEYLENGTH(data-value) [GENERIC]]
                         [SYSID(name)]
                         [RBA | RRN]
                         [GTEQ | EQUAL]
                         [UPDATE]
                         [NOHANDLE]
                         [RESP(data-area)]
```

☐ **Conditions:** DISABLED, DSIDERR, DUPKEY, ILLOGIC, INVREQ, IOERR, ISCINVREQ, LENGERR, NOTAUTH, NOTFND, NOTOPEN, SYSIDERR

```
READNEXT                 DATASET(name)
                         {INTO(data-area) | SET(pointer-ref)}
                         [LENGTH(data-area)]
                         RIDFLD(data-area)
                         [KEYLENGTH(data-value)]
                         [REQID(data-value)]
                         [SYSID(name)]
                         [RBA | RRN]
                         [NOHANDLE]
                         [RESP(data-area)]
```

☐ **Conditions:** DISABLED, DSIDERR, DUPKEY, ENDFILE, ILLOGIC, INVREQ, IOERR, ISCINVREQ, LENGERR, NOTAUTH, NOTFND, NOTOPEN, SYSIDERR

```
READPREV                 DATASET(name)
                         {INTO(data-area) | SET(pointer-ref)}
                         [LENGTH(data-area)]
                         RIDFLD(data-area)
                         [KEYLENGTH(data-value)]
                         [REQID(data-value)]
                         [SYSID(name)]
                         [RBA | RRN]
                         [NOHANDLE]
                         [RESP(data-area)]
```

☐ **Conditions:** DISABLED, DSIDERR, DUPKEY, ENDFILE, ILLOGIC, INVREQ, IOERR, ISCINVREQ, LENGERR, NOTAUTH, NOTFND, NOTOPEN, SYSIDERR

```
READQ TD                 QUEUE(name)
                         {INTO(data-area) | SET(pointer-ref)}
                         [LENGTH(data-area)]
                         [SYSID(name)]
                         [NOSUSPEND]
                         [NOHANDLE]
                         [RESP(data-area)]
```

☐ **Conditions:** IOERR, ISCINVREQ, LENGERR, NOTAUTH, NOTOPEN, QBUSY, QIDERR, QZERO, SYSIDERR

```
READQ TS              QUEUE(name)
                      {INTO(data-area) | SET(pointer-ref)}
                      [LENGTH(data-area)]
                      [ITEM(data-value) | NEXT]
                      [NUMITEMS(data-area)]
                      [SYSID(name)]
                      [NOHANDLE]
                      [RESP(data-area)]
```

☐ **Conditions:** INVREQ, IOERR, ISCINVREQ, ITEMERR, LENGERR, NOTAUTH, QIDERR, SYSIDERR

```
RECEIVE               {INTO(data-area) | SET(pointer-ref)}
                      [LENGTH(data-area)]
                      [MAXLENGTH[(data-value)]]
                      [NOTRUNCATE]
                      [ASIS]
                      [BUFFER]
                      [NOHANDLE]
                      [RESP(data-area)]
```

☐ **Conditions:** LENGERR

```
RECEIVE               MAP(name)
                      [MAPSET(name)]
                      [{INTO(data-area) | SET(pointer-ref)}]
                      [NOHANDLE]
                      [RESP(data-area)]
```

☐ **Conditions:** INVMPSZ, MAPFAIL, INVPARTN, PARTNFAIL

```
RELEASE               PROGRAM(name)
                      [NOHANDLE]
                      [RESP(data-area)]
```

☐ **Conditions:** NOTAUTH, PGMIDERR

```
RESETBR               DATASET(name)
                      RIDFLD(data-area)
                      [KEYLENGTH(data-value) [GENERIC]]
                      [REQID(data-value)]
                      [SYSID(name)]
                      [RBA | RRN]
                      [GTEQ | EQUAL]
                      [NOHANDLE]
                      [RESP(data-area)]
```

☐ **Conditions:** DISABLED, DSIDERR, ILLOGIC, INVREQ, IOERR, ISCINVREQ, NOTAUTH, NOTFND, NOTOPEN, SYSIDERR

```
RETRIEVE              [INTO(data-area) | SET(pointer-ref)]
                      [LENGTH(data-area)]
                      [RTRANSID(data-area)]
                      [RTERMID(data-area)]
                      [QUEUE]
                      [NOHANDLE]
                      [RESP(data-area)]
```

☐ **Conditions:** ENDDATA, ENVDEFERR, INVREQ, INVTSREQ, IOERR, LENGERR, NOTAUTH, NOTFND

```
RETURN                  [TRANSID(name)]
                        [COMMAREA(data-area)
                         LENGTH(data-value)]
                        [NOHANDLE]
                        [RESP(data-area)]
```

□ **Conditions:** INVREQ, NOTAUTH

```
REWRITE                 DATASET(name)
                        FROM(data-area)
                        [LENGTH(data-value)]
                        [SYSID(name)]
                        [NOHANDLE]
                        [RESP(data-area)]
```

□ **Conditions:** DISABLED, DSIDERR, DUPREC, ILLOGIC, INVREQ, IOERR, ISCINVREQ, LENGERR, NOSPACE, NOTAUTH, NOTOPEN, SYSIDERR

```
ROUTE                   [INTERVAL(hhmmss) | TIME(hhmmss)]
                        [ERRTERM(name)]
                        [TITLE(data-area)]
                        [LIST(data-area)]
                        [OPCLASS(data-area)]
                        [REQID(name)]
                        [LDC(name)]
                        [NLEOM]
                        [NOHANDLE]
                        [RESP(data-area)]
```

□ **Conditions:** INVERRTERM, INVLDC, INVREQ, RETFAIL, RTESOME

```
SEND                    FROM(data-area)
                        [LENGTH(data-value)]
                        [WAIT]
                        [ERASE]
                        [CTLCHAR(data-value)]
                        [NOHANDLE]
                        [RESP(data-area)]
SEND                    CONTROL
                        [ERASE | ERASEAUP]
                        [CURSOR[(data-value)]]
                        [FREEKB]
                        [ALARM]
                        [FRSET]
                        [ACCUM]
                        [PAGING | TERMINAL]
                        [NOHANDLE]
                        [RESP(data-area)]
```

□ **Conditions:** INVREQ, TSIOERR

```
SEND                    MAP(name)
                        [MAPSET(name)]
                        [DATAONLY | MAPONLY]
                        [ERASE | ERASEAUP]
                        [CURSOR[(data-value)]]
                        [FREEKB]
                        [ALARM]
                        [FRSET]
                        [ACCUM]
                        [PAGING | TERMINAL]
```

```
                          [NOHANDLE]
                          [RESP(data-area)]

☐ Conditions: INVMPSZ, INVREQ, OVERFLOW, TSIOERR

SEND                      PAGE
                          [RELEASE [TRANSID(name)] | RETAIN]
                          [TRAILER (data-area)]
                          [SET (pointer-ref)]
                          [AUTOPAGE | NOAUTOPAGE [CURRENT | ALL]]
                          [OPERPURGE]
                          [NOHANDLE]
                          [RESP(data-area)]


☐ Conditions: INVMPSZ, INVREQ, OVERFLOW, TSIOERR

SEND                      TEXT
                          FROM(data-area)
                          LENGTH(data-value)
                          [HEADER (data-area)]
                          [TRAILER (data-area)]
                          [ERASE]
                          [CURSOR (data-value)]
                          [FREEKB]
                          [ALARM]
                          [NOHANDLE]
                          [RESP(data-area)]


☐ Conditions: INVREQ, TSIOERR

START                     TRANSID(name)
                          [INTERVAL(hhmmss) | TIME(hhmmss)]
                          [REQID(name)]
                          [FROM(data-area)
                           LENGTH(data-value) [FMH]]
                          [TERMID(name)]
                          [SYSID(name)]
                          [RTRANSID(name)]
                          [RTERMID(name)]
                          [QUEUE(name)]
                          [NOCHECK]
                          [PROTECT]
                          [NOHANDLE]
                          [RESP(data-area)]


☐ Conditions: INVREQ, IOERR, ISCINVREQ, NOTAUTH, SYSIDERR, TERMIDERR, TRANSIDERR

STARTBR                   DATASET(name)
                          RIDFLD(data-area)
                          [KEYLENGTH(data-value) [GENERIC]]
                          [REQID(data-value)]
                          [SYSID (name)]
                          [RBA | RRN]
                          [GTEQ | EQUAL]
                          [NOHANDLE]
                          [RESP(data-area)]


☐ Conditions: DISABLED, DSIDERR, ILLOGIC, INVREQ, IOERR, ISCINVREQ, NOTAUTH, NOTFND,
              NOTOPEN, SYSIDERR
```

```
SUSPEND                     [NOHANDLE]
                            [RESP(data-area)]
SYNCPOINT                   [ROLLBACK]
                            [NOHANDLE]
                            [RESP(data-area)]
```

☐ **Conditions:** ROLLEDBACK

```
UNLOCK                      DATASET(name)
                            [SYSID(name)]
                            [NOHANDLE]
                            [RESP(data-area)]
```

☐ **Conditions:** DISABLED, DSIDERR, ILLOGIC, IOERR, ISCINVREQ, NOTAUTH, NOTOPEN, SYSIDERR

```
WAIT EVENT                  ECADDR(pointer-value)
                            [NOHANDLE]
                            [RESP(data-area)]
```

☐ **Condition:** INVREQ

```
WAIT JOURNAL                JFILEID(data-value)
                            [REQID(data-value)]
                            [STARTIO]
                            [NOHANDLE]
                            [RESP(data-area)]
```

☐ **Conditions:** JIDERR, INVREQ, IOERR, NOTOPEN

```
WRITE                       DATASET(name)
                            FROM(data-area)
                            [LENGTH(data-value)]
                            RIDFLD(data-area)
                            [KEYLENGTH(data-value)]
                            [SYSID(name)]
                            [RBA | RRN]
                            [MASSINSERT]
                            [NOHANDLE]
                            [RESP(data-area)]
```

☐ **Conditions:** DISABLED, DSIDERR, DUPREC, ILLOGIC, INVREQ, IOERR, ISCINVREQ, LENGERR, NOSPACE, NOTAUTH, NOTOPEN, SYSIDERR

```
WRITEQ TD                   QUEUE(name)
                            FROM(data-area)
                            LENGTH(data-area)
                            [SYSID(name)]
                            [NOHANDLE]
                            [RESP(data-area)]
```

☐ **Conditions:** IOERR, ISCINVREQ, LENGERR, NOSPACE, NOTAUTH, NOTOPEN, QIDERR, SYSIDERR

```
WRITEQ TS                   QUEUE(name)
                            FROM(data-area)
                            LENGTH(data-value)
                            [ITEM(data-area) [REWRITE]]
                            [SYSID(name)]
                            [MAIN | AUXILIARY]
```

```
                              [NOSUSPEND]
                              [NOHANDLE]
                              [RESP(data-area)]
```

☐ **Conditions:** INVREQ, IOERR, ISCINVREQ, ITEMERR, NOSPACE, NOSPACE, NOTAUTH, QIDERR, SYSIDERR

```
XCTL                          PROGRAM(name)
                              [COMMAREA(data-area)
                               LENGTH(data-value)]
                              [NOHANDLE]
                              [RESP(data-area)]
```

☐ **Conditions:** NOTAUTH, PGMIDERR

BMS Screen Definition Statements

```
mapset                        DFHMSD
                              [TYPE={DSECT | MAP}
                              [TIOAPFX=YES]
                              [STORAGE=AUTO]
                              [MODE={IN | OUT | INOUT}]
                              [LANG={ASM | COBOL | PLI | RPG}]
                              [CTRL=[PRINT][,FREEKB][,ALARM][,FRSET]]
                              [EXTATT={NO | MAPONLY | YES}]
                              [MAPATTS=(attr1,attr2,...)]
                              [DSATTS=(attr1,attr2,...)]
                              [COLOR={DEFAULT | color}]
                              [HILIGHT={OFF | BLINK | REVERSE | UNDERLINE}]
                              [SUFFIX=suffix | TERM=termtype]

map                           DFHMDI
                              [SIZE=(line,column)]
                              [LINE={number | NEXT | SAME}]
                              [COLUMN={number | NEXT | SAME}]
                              [JUSTIFY=([{LEFT | RIGHT}] [,{FIRST | LAST}])]
                              [HEADER=YES]
                              [TRAILER=YES]
                              [EXTATT={NO | MAPONLY | YES}]
                              [FIELDS=NO]
                              [CTRL=[PRINT][,FREEKB][,ALARM][,FRSET]]
                              [MAPATTS=(attr1,attr2,...)]
                              [DSATTS=(attr1,attr2,...)]
                              [COLOR={DEFAULT | color}]
                              [HILIGHT={OFF | BLINK | REVERSE | UNDERLINE}]

[fld]                         DFHMDF
                              [POS={number | (line,column)}]
                              [LENGTH=number]
                              [JUSTIFY=([{LEFT | RIGHT}][{BLANK | ZERO}])]
                              [INITIAL='char data'] | XINIT=hex data]
                              [ATTRB=([{ASKIP | PROT | UNPROT[,NUM}]
                              [{BRT | NORM | DRK}]
                              [DET][IC][FSET])]
```

```
[COLOR={DEFAULT | color}]
[PS={BASE | psid}]
[HILIGHT={OFF | BLINK | REVERSE | UNDERLINE}]
[VALIDN=([MUSTFILL][MUSTENTER][TRIGGER])]
[GRPNAME=group-name]
[OCCURS=number]
[PICIN='value']
[PICOUT='value']
```

Command Translator Options

CICS Assumed by default. Specifies that the translator is to process EXEC CICS commands.

COBOL2 specifies that the translator is to translate VS COBOL II programs.

DEBUG/NODEBUG specifies whether or not the translator is to pass the translator line number to the Execution Diagnostic Facility during program execution. The debug option may be useful in following the path of the program logic during program testing, and will cause only a small increase to the size of the load module.

DLI specifies that the translator is to process EXEC DLI commands.

FE specifies that the translator is to provide a hexadecimal listing of the first argument passed to EIP. This information is normally used only during internal problem determination.

FLAG [I | W | E | S] specifies the minimum severity of error that requires a message to be listed in the translator run.

LANGLVL(1) | LANGLVL(2) specifies the level of COBOL source code to be generated by the translator. LANGLVL(1) is the default.

LINECOUNT (n) specifies the number of lines to be listed on each page of the translator listing.

NOSPIE causes a dump to be produced when unrecoverable errors are encountered in the translator run.

NUM | NONUM If NUM is used, the translator generates its own line numbers for the translator listing. If NONUM is used, the programmer supplied line numbers are used.

OPT | NOOPT specifies whether the translator is to generate COBOL SERVICE RELOAD statements required by the optimizing COBOL compiler. If the COBOL compiler is not using the optimization feature, OPT is not needed.

OPTIONS | NOOPTIONS specifies whether the translator is to list the options used in this translator run.

QUOTE | APOST specifies whether the translator should recognize the character *quote* ('') or the character *apostrophe* (') to delineate literals.

SEQ/NOSEQ SEQ is the default and will cause the translator to flag source program statements that are out of sequence. Unless your text editor automatically generates line numbers, NOSEQ should be specified.

SOURCE/NOSOURCE SOURCE is the default. NOSOURCE allows the translator to suppress the listing of the COBOL input; this option may be desirable to save paper and print time during final stages of program debugging.

SPACE 1/SPACE 2/SPACE 3 indicates the required type of spacing in the translator listing. SPACE1 is the default and conserves on paper usage.

VBREF/NOVBREF indicates whether the translator is to provide a cross-reference list of all the commands used in the program.

COBOL Restrictions

The following compiler options cannot be used:

```
COUNT
FLOW
STATE
SYMDUMP
STXIT
ENDJOB
DYNAM
TEST
SYST
```

The following COBOL I/O statements cannot be used:

```
OPEN
CLOSE
READ
WRITE
ACCEPT
DISPLAY
DELETE
REWRITE
START
other I/O statements
```

The following statements requesting operating system services *should* not be used:

```
EXHIBIT
INSPECT
STOP RUN
SIGN IS SEPARATE
UNSTRING
CURRENT-DATE
DATE
DAY
TIME
```

For some versions of COBOL the following restrictions have been removed:

```
INSPECT
STRING
UNSTRING
```

The following special options cannot be used:

```
REPORT WRITER
SEGMENTATION
SORT
TRACE
```

EXEC Interface Block

EIBAID	X		attention identifier
EIBATT	X		RU attach header
EIBCALEN	S9999	COMP	commarea length
EIBCOMPL	X		terminal input complete indicator
EIBCONF	X		LU6.2 terminal confirm request indicator
EIBCPOSN	S9999	COMP	cursor position
EIBDATE	S9(7)	COMP-3	task start date
EIBDS	X(8)		last data-set name
EIBEOC	X		end of chain indicator
EIBERR	X		LU6.2 error indicator

```
EIBERRCD    XXXX            LU6.2 error code
EIBFMH      X               FMH received indicator
EIBFN       XX              hex function code of last command
EIBFREE     X               free facility indicator
EIBNODAT    X               LU6.2 no data indicator
EIBRCODE    X(6)            hex response from last command
EIBRECV     X               receive continue indicator
EIBREQID    X(8)            interval control request identifier
EIBRESP     S9(8) COMP      decimal response from last command
EIBRESP2    S9(8) COMP      decimal response from special commands
EIBRSRCE    X(8)            symbolic name of last-used resource
EIBSIG      X               signal received indicator
EIBSYNC     X               sync point needed indicator
EIBSYNRB    X               sync point rollback needed indicator
EIBTASKN    S9(7) COMP-3    CICS assigned task number
EIBTIME     S9(7) COMP-3    time task started or time of last ASKTIME
EIBTRMID    XXXX            terminal identification
EIBTRNID    XXXX            transaction identification of the task
```

EIBFN VALUES

EIP

```
0202   ADDRESS
0204   HANDLE CONDITION
0206   HANDLE AID
0208   ASSIGN
020A   IGNORE CONDITION
020C   PUSH
020E   POP
```

TERMINAL CONTROL

```
0402   RECEIVE
0404   SEND
0406   CONVERSE
0408   ISSUE EODS
040A   ISSUE COPY
040C   WAIT TERMINAL
040E   ISSUE LOAD
0410   WAIT SIGNAL
0412   ISSUE RESET
0414   ISSUE DISCONNECT
0416   ISSUE ENDOUTPUT
0418   ISSUE ERASEUP
041A   ISSUE ENDFILE
041C   ISSUE PRINT
041E   ISSUE SIGNAL
0420   ALLOCATE
0422   FREE
0424   POINT
0426   BUILD ATTACH
0428   EXTRACT ATTACH
042A   EXTRACT TCT
042C   WAID CONVID
042E   EXTRACT PROCESS
0430   ISSUE ABEND
0432   CONNECT PROCESS
0434   ISSUE CONFIRMATION
0436   ISSUE ERROR
```

```
0438   ISSUE PREPARE
043A   ISSUE PASS
043C   EXTRACT LOGONMSG
```

FILE CONTROL

```
0602   READ
0604   WRITE
0606   REWRITE
0608   DELETE
060A   UNLOCK
060C   STARTBR
060E   READNEXT
0610   READPREV
0612   ENDBR
0614   RESETBR
```

TRANSIENT DATA CONTROL

```
0802   WRITEQ TD
0804   READQ TD
0806   DELETEQ TD
```

TEMPORARY STORAGE CONTROL

```
0A02   WRITEQ TS
0A04   READQ TS
0A06   DELETEQ TS
```

STORAGE CONTROL

```
0C02   GETMAIN
0C04   FREEMAIN
```

PROGRAM CONTROL

```
0E02   LINK
0E04   XCTL
0E06   LOAD
0E08   RETURN
0E0A   RELEASE
0E0C   ABEND
0E0E   HANDLE ABEND
```

INTERVAL CONTROL

```
1002   ASKTIME
1004   DELAY
1006   POST
1008   START
100A   RETRIEVE
100C   CANCEL
4A02   ASKTIME ABSTIME
4A04   FORMATTIME
```

TASK CONTROL

```
1202   WAIT EVENT
1204   ENQ
1206   DEQ
1208   SUSPEND
```

JOURNAL CONTROL

```
1402   JOURNAL
1404   WAIT JOURNAL
```

SYNCPOINT CONTROL

```
1602   SYNCPOINT
```

BASIC MAPPING SUPPORT

```
1802   RECEIVE MAP
1804   SEND MAP
1806   SEND TEXT
1808   SEND PAGE
180A   PURGE MESSAGE
180C   ROUTE
180E   RECEIVE PARTITION
1810   SEND PARTNSET
1812   SEND CONTROL
```

TRACE CONTROL/DUMP CONTROL

```
1A02   TRACE ON/OFF
1A04   ENTER
1C02   DUMP
```

BATCH DATA INTERCHANGE

```
1E02   ISSUE ADD
1E04   ISSUE ERASE
1E06   ISSUE REPLACE
1E08   ISSUE ABORT
1E0A   ISSUE QUERY
1E0C   ISSUE END
1E0E   ISSUE RECEIVE
1E10   ISSUE NOTE
1E12   ISSUE WAIT
1E14   ISSUE SEND
```

BUILT-IN FUNCTIONS PROGRAM

```
2002   BIF DEEDIT
```

EIBRCODE VALUES

```
EIBFN EIBRCODE
```

EXECUTE INTERFACE PROGRAM

```
02XX   E0 XX XX XX XX XX   INVREQ
```

TERMINAL CONTROL

```
04XX   04 XX XX XX XX XX   EOF
       10 XX XX XX XX XX   EODS
       C1 XX XX XX XX XX   EOF
       C2 XX XX XX XX XX   ENDINPUT
       D0 YY XX XX XX XX   SYSIDERR
       XX 04 XX XX XX XX     NAME ERROR
       XX 08 XX XX XX XX     LINK OUT OF SERVICE
```

```
          XX OC XX XX XX XX          NAME UNKNOWN TO CICS
          D2 YY XX XX XX XX       SESSIONERR
          XX 04 XX XX XX XX          NAME ERROR
          XX 08 XX XX XX XX          LINK OUT OF SERVICE
          XX OC XX XX XX XX          NAME UNKNOWN TO CICS
          D3 XX XX XX XX XX       SYSBUSY
          D4 XX XX XX XX XX       SESSBUSY
          D5 XX XX XX XX XX       NOTALLOC
          E0 XX XX YY XX XX       INVREQ
          XX XX XX 04 XX XX          TCTTE ALREADY ALLOCATED
          XX XX XX 08 XX XX          TCTTE WRONG STATE FOR FREE
          XX XX XX OC XX XX          CONNECT SYNCLVL 2 NOT SUPPORTED
          XX XX XX 10 XX XX          INVALID DATA FOR EXTRACT ATTACH
          XX XX XX 14 XX XX          CONFIRM OPTION INVALID
          XX XX XX 18 XX XX          INVALID NETNAME FOR EXTRACT TCT
          XX XX XX 1C XX XX          INVALID COMMAND FOR TERMINAL
          XX XX XX 20 XX XX          INVALID COMMAND FOR LU6.2
          E1 YY XX XX XX XX       LENGERR
          XX 00 XX XX XX XX          INPUT DATA HAS BEEN TRUNCATED
          XX 04 XX XX XX XX          ON OUTPUT DATA > 32767 OR < 0
          XX 08 XX XX XX XX          ON INPUT TO LENGTH > 32767
          XX OC XX XX XX XX          COMMAND WAS ISSUE PASS
          E3 XX XX XX XX XX       WRBRK
          E4 XX XX XX XX XX       RDATT
          E5 XX XX XX XX XX       SIGNAL
          E6 XX XX XX XX XX       TERMIDERR
          E7 XX XX XX XX XX       NOPASSBKRD
          E8 XX XX XX XX XX       NOPASSKBWR
          EA XX XX XX XX XX       IGREQCD
          EB XX XX XX XX XX       CBIDERR
          F1 XX XX XX XX XX       TERMERR
          XX 20 XX XX XX XX          EOC
          XX 40 XX XX XX XX          INBFMH
          XX XX XX F6 XX XX          NOSTART
          XX XX XX F7 XX XX          NONVAL

      FILE CONTROL

06XX      01 XX XX XX XX XX XX    DSIDERR
          02 VR VE XX XX XX XX    ILLOGIC
                                  VR=VSAM RETURN CODE
                                  VE=VSAM ERROR CODE
          08 XX XX XX XX XX XX    INVREQ
          OC XX XX XX XX XX XX    NOTOPEN
          OD XX XX XX XX XX XX    DISABLED
          OF XX XX XX XX XX XX    ENDFILE
          80 E1 E2 E3 E4 XX XX    IOERR
                                  E1-E4 BDAM RESPONSE
          81 XX XX XX XX XX XX    NOTFND
          82 XX XX XX XX XX XX    DUPREC
          83 XX XX XX XX XX XX    NOSPACE
          84 XX XX XX XX XX XX    DUPKEY
          D0 YY XX XX XX XX XX    SYSIDERR
          XX 04 XX XX XX XX          NAME ERROR
          XX 08 XX XX XX XX          LINK OUT OF SERVICE
          XX OC XX XX XX XX          NAME UNKNOWN TO CICS
          D1 XX XX XX XX XX XX    ISCINVREQ
          D6 XX XX XX XX XX XX    NOTAUTH
          E1 XX XX XX XX XX XX    LENGERR
```

TRANSIENT DATA CONTROL

```
08XX    01 XX XX XX XX XX        QZERO
        02 XX XX XX XX XX        QIDERR
        04 XX XX XX XX XX        IOERR
        08 XX XX XX XX XX        NOTOPEN
        10 XX XX XX XX XX        NOSPACE
        C0 XX XX XX XX XX        QBUSY
        D0 XX XX XX XX XX        SYSIDERR
        XX 04 XX XX XX XX           NAME ERROR
        XX 08 XX XX XX XX           LINK OUT OF SERVICE
        XX 0C XX XX XX XX           NAME UNKNOWN TO CICS
        D1 XX XX XX XX XX        ISCINVREQ
        D6 XX XX XX XX XX        NOTAUTH
        E1 XX XX XX XX XX        LENGERR
```

TEMPORARY STORAGE CONTROL

```
0AXX    01 XX XX XX XX XX        ITEMERR
        02 XX XX XX XX XX        QIDERR
        04 XX XX XX XX XX        IOERR
        08 XX XX XX XX XX        NOSPACE
        20 XX XX XX XX XX        INVREQ
        D0 YY XX XX XX XX        SYSIDERR
        XX 04 XX XX XX XX           NAME ERROR
        XX 08 XX XX XX XX           LINK OUT OF SERVICE
        XX 0C XX XX XX XX           NAME UNKNOWN TO CICS
        D1 XX XX XX XX XX        ISCINVREQ
        D6 XX XX XX XX XX        NOTAUTH
        E1 XX XX XX XX XX        LENGERR
```

STORAGE CONTROL

```
0CXX    E1 XX XX XX XX XX        LENGERR
        E2 XX XX XX XX XX        NOSTG
```

PROGRAM CONTROL

```
0EXX    01 XX XX XX XX XX        PGMIDERR
        D6 XX XX XX XX XX        NOTAUTH
        E0 XX XX XX XX XX        INVREQ
```

INTERVAL CONTROL

```
10XX    01 XX XX XX XX XX        ENDDATA
        04 XX XX XX XX XX        IOERR
        11 XX XX XX XX XX        TRANSIDERR
        12 XX XX XX XX XX        TERMIDERR
        14 XX XX XX XX XX        INVTSREQ
        20 XX XX XX XX XX        EXPIRED
        81 XX XX XX XX XX        NOTFND
        D0 YY XX XX XX XX        SYSIDERR
        XX 04 XX XX XX XX           NAME ERROR
        XX 08 XX XX XX XX           LINK OUT OF SERVICE
        XX 0C XX XX XX XX           NAME UNKNOWN TO CICS
        D1 XX XX XX XX XX        ISCINVREQ
        D6 XX XX XX XX XX        NOTAUTH
        E1 XX XX XX XX XX        LENGERR
        E9 XX XX XX XX XX        ENVDEFERR
        FF XX XX XX XX XX        INVREQ
```

TASK CONTROL

```
12XX    32 XX XX XX XX XX       ENQBUSY
        E0 XX XX XX XX XX       INVREQ
```

JOURNAL CONTROL

```
14XX    01 XX XX XX XX XX       JIDERR
        02 XX XX XX XX XX       INVREQ
        05 XX XX XX XX XX       NOTOPEN
        06 XX XX XX XX XX       LENGERR
        07 XX XX XX XX XX       IOERR
        09 XX XX XX XX XX       NOJBUFSP
        D6 XX XX XX XX XX       NOTAUTH
```

SYNCPOINT CONTROL

```
16XX    01 XX XX XX XX XX       ROLLEDBACK
```

BASIC MAPPING SUPPORT

```
18XX    01 XX XX XX XX XX       INVREQ
        02 XX XX XX XX XX       RETPAGE
        04 XX XX XX XX XX       MAPFAIL
        08 XX XX TC XX XX       INVMPZ
                                TC=TYPE OF TERMINAL CODE
                                   I.E. L=3270 40 CHAR SCREEN
                                        M=3270 80 CHAR SCREEN
        20 XX XX XX XX XX       INVERRTERM
        40 XX XX XX XX XX       RTESOME
        80 XX XX XX XX XX       RTEFAIL
        E1 XX XX XX XX XX       LENGERR
        E3 XX XX XX XX XX       WRBRK
        E4 XX XX XX XX XX       RDATT
        XX 02 XX XX XX XX       PARTNFAIL
        XX 04 XX XX XX XX       INVPARTN
        XX 08 XX XX XX XX       INVPARTNSET
        XX 10 XX XX XX XX       INVLDC
        XX 20 XX XX XX XX       UNEXPIN
        XX 40 XX XX XX XX       IGREQCD
        XX 80 XX XX XX XX       TSIOERR
        XX XX 01 XX XX XX       OVERFLOW
        XX XX 04 XX XX XX       EODS
        XX XX 08 XX XX XX       EOC
        XX XX 10 XX XX XX       IGREQID
```

TRACE CONTROL

```
1AXX    E0 XX XX XX XX XX       INVREQ
```

BATCH DATA INTERCHANGE

```
1EXX    04 XX XX XX XX XX       DSSTAT
        08 XX XX XX XX XX       FUNCERR
        0C XX XX XX XX XX       SELNERR
        10 XX XX XX XX XX       UNEXPIN
        E1 XX XX XX XX XX       LENGERR
        XX 2B XX XX XX XX       IGREQCD
        XX XX 20 XX XX XX       EOC
```

FORMATTIME

```
4AXX    XX XX XX 01 XX XX    ERROR
```

EIBRESP VALUES

```
01      ERROR
02      RDATT
03      WRBRK
04      EOF
05      EODS
06      EOC
07      INBFMH
08      ENDINPT
09      NONVAL
10      NOSTART
11      TERMIDERR
12      DSIDERR
13      NOTFND
14      DUPREC
15      DUPKEY
16      INVREQ
17      IOERR
18      NOSPACE
19      NOTOPEN
20      ENDFILE
21      ILLOGIC
22      LENGERR
23      QZERO
24      SIGNAL
25      QBUSY
26      ITEMERR
27      PGMIDERR
28      TRANSIDERR
29      ENDDATA
30      INVTSREQ
31      EXPIRED
32      RETPAGE
33      RTEFAIL
34      RTESOME
35      TSIOERR
36      MAPFAIL
37      INVERRTERM
38      INVMPSZ
39      IGREQID
40      OVERFLOW
41      INVLDC
42      NOSTG
43      JIDERR
44      QIDERR
45      NOJBUFSP
46      DSSTAT
47      SELNERR
48      FUNCERR
49      UNEXPIN
50      NOPASSBKRD
51      NOPASSBKWR
52
53      SYSIDERR
54      ISCINVREQ
```

```
55      ENQBUSY
56      ENVDEFERR
57      IGREQCD
58      SESSIONERR
59      SYSBUSY
60      SESSBUSY
61      NOTALLOC
62      CBIDERR
63
64      INVPARTNSET
65      INVPARTN
66      PARTNFAIL
67
68
69
70      NOTAUTH
71
72
73
74
75
76
77
78
79
80      NOSPOOL
81      TERMERR
82      ROLLEDBACK
83      END
84      DISABLED
85      ALLOCERR
86      STRELERR
87      OPENERR
88      SPOLBUSY
89      SPOLERR
90      NODEIDER
```

Common Transaction Abend Codes

```
Abend Code              Description
AACA                    invalid error code
ABMA                    TIOA wrong length
ABMB                    cursor position exceeds screen size
ABMD                    bad return code from send
ABMG                    BMS service not present
ABMI                    not input map
ABML                    invalid output
ABMO                    not output map
ABMP                    undefined PF/PA key
ABMR                    BMS modules not generated
ABMO                    map not located
ABM1                    non-BMS-supported terminal
ABM2                    no user data
ABM3                    BMS used in non-terminal-oriented task
ABM4                    page error
ABM5                    invalid TS request
ABM7                    trailer too large
ABM8                    justify parm too large
ABM9                    trailer too large
```

```
ABNA                        no route list specified
ACSF                        invalid FREEMAIN address
AEC1                        CEMT, CECI, or CEDA used on unsupported terminal
AED1                        CEDF used on nonsupported terminal
AED2                        logic error in EDF
AED3                        EDF abnormally terminated
AFCA                        file disabled
AFCR                        illegal ISAM request
AFCS                        VSAM file control subtask error
AICA                        runaway (looping) task
AKCP                        stall condition
AKCS                        deadlock timeout
AKCT                        terminal read timeout
AMSA                        3270 SBA not followed by an address
APCC                        not proper support for COBOL
APCL                        shared library not present
APCS                        not proper support for COBOL
APC2                        Same
APC3                        Same
APC4                        Same
APLx                        PL/I abend code
ASPD                        error resetting dynamic log
ASPE                        rollback without dynamic transaction backout
ASRA                        program interrupt
ASRB                        operating system abnormal termination
```

Execute Interface Abend Codes

See figure 3.1, p. 37.

Appendix B
File Layouts for Lab Problems

Most chapters in this text contain a set of laboratory problems intended to apply your knowledge of the material presented in this book. Each lab is a complete program assignment that you should design, write, and then test on a CICS/VS system. Each lab assignment is similar in design to the sample programs contained within the chapters. Yet certain requirements have been changed enough to exercise your problem-solving abilities while applying the techniques illustrated in the chapter.

For some chapters, lab problems have one or more options that may be implemented. These options provide different levels of complexity for the same program. If you plan to try some of these options, I suggest that you begin by first completing the basic programming assignment. You can then expand the program by incorporating the optional features into the program. If the initial program is designed properly, adding the new features should be a simple matter.

Together, all of the lab problems represent a sample application. This sample application contains key elements of a "real-life" system. Some components of a real system have been omitted to allow assignments to be completed within the time frame of an academic term. Actually, if you look back now to the lab assignments, you will probably agree that there may be more programs than can be completed within a single course. You probably will not be able to complete all of these assignments. They are simply presented here to provide a variety of problems to test your CICS/VS programming abilities. Some may be assigned for extra credit. Others may not be assigned at all.

Our sample application contains several functions relating to a personnel master file. Most of these functions are common to all applications, so the experience you will get from developing these programs should be easily transferred to other programming systems. There are two files used by the programming assignments in this Appendix. These files are

personnel master file

system control file

Personnel Master File

The personnel master file is a VSAM key-sequenced data set (KSDS). The CICS/VS data-set name for the file is PERSFLE. It contains one record for each employee in our case organization. As with other enterprises, this organization has multiple employee categories, work locations, and departmental units. The record layout for our personnel master file is depicted below.

```
01  PERSONNEL-ROOT-RECORD.
*----PERSONAL INFORMATION----------------
    05   EMPLOYEE-NAME           PIC X(30).
    05   EMPLOYEE-SSN            PIC 9(09).
    05   EMPLOYEE-ADDRESS        PIC X(30).
    05   EMPLOYEE-CITY           PIC X(20).
    05   EMPLOYEE-STATE          PIC X(02).
    05   EMPLOYEE-ZIP            PIC X(09).
```

```
      05   EMPLOYEE-SSN2            PIC S9(09) COMP-3.
      05   EMPLOYEE-PHONE           PIC X(07).
      05   EMPLOYEE-ETHNIC          PIC X(01).
      05   EMPLOYEE-SEX             PIC X(01).
      05   EMPLOYEE-BDATE           PIC S9(07) COMP-3.
      05   PERSONAL-UPDATE-COUNTER  PIC S9 COMP-3.
*----COMPANY INFORMATION------------------
      05   EMPLOYEE-TYPE            PIC XX.
      05   EMPLOYEE-LOCATION        PIC XX.
      05   EMPLOYEE-DEPARTMENT      PIC XXXX.
      05   EMPLOYEE-JOB-TITLE       PIC XXXXX.
      05   EMPLOYEE-POSITION-NO     PIC XXXXX.
      05   EMPLOYEE-EDATE           PIC S9(07) COMP-3.
      05   EMPLOYEE-TDATE           PIC S9(07) COMP-3.
      05   EMPLOYEE-ANNUAL-SALARY   PIC S9(9)V99 COMP-3.
      05   COMPANY-UPDATE-COUNTER   PIC S9 COMP-3.
*----RECORD STATUS INFORMATION------------
      05   DATE-RECORD-ADDED        PIC S9(07) COMP-3.
      05   DATE-RECORD-UPDATED      PIC S9(07) COMP-3.
      05   LAST-UPDATE-OPERATOR     PIC XXX.
```

The master record contains three logical sections: personal information about the employee, company information for the employee, and record status information. Fields in the personal information section are

EMPLOYEE-NAME This field contains the name of the employee in the form, LAST NAME,FIRST NAME. A middle initial or middle name may follow the first name if space permits. A comma should be keyed between the surname and the first name. This surname indicator will allow batch programs to rearrange the name for personalized letters and mailing labels.

EMPLOYEE-SSN Contains the 9-digit Social Security number for this employee. This field is the primary key for the VSAM KSDS file. It is placed behind the employee name field to allow for a VSAM alternate index to be created using the name field. The alternate index could include both the name and SSN field to allow for a unique key to be defined even when more than one employee has the same name. For more information about VSAM alternate indexes see chapter 10

EMPLOYEE-ADDRESS Contains the street address or postal box for the employee. This field should not contain spaces.

EMPLOYEE-CITY Contains the city where the employee resides. Should not be spaces.

EMPLOYEE-STATE Contains the standard postal service abbreviation for the state of residence for the employee. Should not contain spaces.

EMPLOYEE-ZIP Contains the 9-digit postal zip code for the employee. Should be numeric.

EMPLOYEE-SSN2 This COMP-3 field contains a copy of the employee Social Security number. It is duplicated behind the zip code to allow for a VSAM alternate index to be created using the zip code. The alternate index could include both the zip code and second SSN field to allow for a unique VSAM key to be defined even though multiple records could contain the same zip code.

EMPLOYEE-PHONE Contains the 7-digit telephone number for the employee.

EMPLOYEE-ETHNIC This field contains a 1-digit code representing the ethnic (race) category for the employee.

EMPLOYEE-SEX Contains a 1-character code representing the sex of the employee. Valid codes are ''F'' for Females and ''M'' for Males.

EMPLOYEE-BDATE Contains the birth date of the employee in the form 0MMDDYY in Computational-3 format.

PERSONAL-UPDATE-COUNTER Update counter to provide protection against multiple updates with pseudoconversational update programs. See chapter 8 for more details of the use of an update counter.

Fields in the company information section are

EMPLOYEE-TYPE This field contains a value corresponding to the type of employee (i.e., faculty, staff, administrator). The system control file (described later) contains a table of valid employee type categories along with an employee type description corresponding to each valid code.

EMPLOYEE-LOCATION Contains a value corresponding to the work location for this employee. The system control file contains a table of valid location codes along with a location description corresponding to each valid code.

EMPLOYEE-DEPARTMENT Contains a value corresponding to the department for the employee. The system control file contains a table of valid department codes along with a department description corresponding to each valid code.

EMPLOYEE-JOB-TITLE Contains a code corresponding to the job title for this employee. All employees with the same job title have the same code.

EMPLOYEE-POSITION-NO Contains a position number value for the staffing table position for this employee.

EMPLOYEE-EDATE Contains the employment date (date hired) for the employee in the form 0MMDDYY in Computational-3 format.

EMPLOYEE-TDATE Contains the termination date for the employee in the form 0MMDDYY in Computational-3 format. Current employees have a value of zero stored in this field.

EMPLOYEE-ANNUAL-SALARY Contains the annual salary for the employee in Computational-3 format.

COMPANY-UPDATE-COUNTER Update counter to provide protection against multiple updates with pseudoconversational update programs. See chapter 8 for more details of the use of an update counter.

Fields in the record status section are

DATE-RECORD-ADDED Contains the date this record was added to the file in Computational-3 format.

DATE-RECORD-UPDATED Contains the date of the last on-line update operation for this record in Computational-3 format.

LAST-UPDATE-OPERATOR Contains the CICS/VS operator identification that added or last updated this record.

The System Control File

The system control file (data-set name is PERSCF) is an ancillary file used to store control and table records for the sample personnel system.

Control records contain information used by programs in the system. Table records contain the equivalent of table look-up values and associated table data. There are several tables stored in the system control file. Some of these tables were described earlier. For example, there is a department table that contains a code and description for each employee department. Another table contains a list of valid work location codes and descriptions.

The SCF is a VSAM KSDS file with variable length records. The general layout of the records in the system control file is depicted below.

Field Name	Format	Pos	Len	Description
PERSCF-RECORD-KEY	X(20)	1	20	group name
PERSCF-APPL-ID	XX	1	2	record group
PERSCF-TABLE-NAME	XXXX	3	4	table or control Record Name
PERSCF-TABLE-VALUE	X(14)	7	14	table look-up value
PERSCF-STATUS	X	21	1	active-inactive
PERSCF-VARIABLE-DATA	X(??)	22	Var	Variable Data

The **PERSCF-RECORD-KEY** is in the first 20 bytes of the record and is composed of the following subfields:

PERSCF-APPL-ID This 2-byte field contains an application group identifier for records in the file. Personnel control and table records contain a value of 'PE.' By using this application prefix, the system control file could support more than one application. For instance, records for the payroll application could contain a prefix value of 'PA.' By storing this code in the leftmost position of the key, all table and control records for an application would be grouped together.

PERSCF-TABLE-NAME This 4-byte subfield contains a value identifying the type of control record or, for table records, the name of the table. All records for a given table will have the same value stored in this field and will therefore be stored in consecutive records within the file.

PERSCF-TABLE-VALUE This 14-byte subfield contains the remainder of the key. For tables, this field represents the look-up or search code. The search code is justified in the leftmost positions of this field and is always padded on the right with spaces. Tables with short search strings will have more spaces to the right of the search string than tables with longer search values. Just in case you are now confused, here is an example of this phenomenon. Below are records from three tables (department, employee type, and location) and a help record. Only the record key is shown. Each of these tables has search arguments of different lengths, yet is stored with fixed-length keys required by the VSAM access method.

bbbb represents blanks (spaces)

```
PEDEPT2180bbbbbbbbbb.........
PEDEPT2190bbbbbbbbbb.........
PEDEPT2200bbbbbbbbbb.........
PEDEPT2300bbbbbbbbbb.........
PEEMPL01bbbbbbbbbbbb.........
PEEMPL02bbbbbbbbbbbb.........
PEHELPXY01bbbbbbbbbb.........
PEHELPXY02bbbbbbbbbb.........
PELOCN01bbbbbbbbbbbb.........
PELOCN02bbbbbbbbbbbb.........
PELOCN04bbbbbbbbbbbb.........
...
```

ACCESSING A TABLE OR CONTROL RECORD

A file control READ command would be used to access a control or table record. Prior to issuing the READ command, an appropriate record key would be constructed by the program. For example, let's assume that a program needs to access the location table (LOCN) using a search value stored in the field EMPLOYEE-LOCATION (PIC XX field). The statements below would be used. You should note that the desired padding of spaces in the field PERSCF-TABLE-VALUE will be done automatically by COBOL.

```
MOVE 'PE' TO PERSCF-APPL-ID.
MOVE 'LOCN' TO PERSCF-TABLE-NAME.
MOVE EMPLOYEE-LOCATION TO PERSCF-TABLE-VALUE.
EXEC CICS READ DATASET ('PERSCF')
         RIDFLD (PERSCF-RECORD-KEY)...
```

SCF DATA AREAS

The contents of each type of record in the system control file will vary. Some records may contain only a corresponding description code. Other records may contain multiple fields as needed by the application. This variable content approach adds to the versatility of the file. The general layout above depicted two fields in the data area. These are

PERSCF-STATUS This field is used to indicate the status of table records in our file. In some applications table search values must be maintained even though the value is no longer a valid code for the application. Some applications keep historical information. To support historical search codes, table records may be kept in the SCF and are marked with an "inactive" status code. When a code is marked as inactive, it would not be considered a valid code for update purposes.

PERSCF-VARIABLE-DATA This field would contain variable table and control record information needed by the application.

SCF PURPOSE

The purpose of storing these tables in the system control file is to eliminate program maintenance associated with table changes. The alternative to storing tables in the SCF is to "hard-code" each table within a program's working-storage. Then each time a table change is required, each program using that table would be modified and the program recataloged. With the SCF approach, however, table changes would be accomplished using an on-line file maintenance program. This file maintenance program would add, update, and delete table records in the system control file. Programs using these tables in the SCF would have access to updated table values immediately after the changes were made.

It is possible for both batch and CICS programs to use the system control file. Batch programs would normally define working-storage space to accommodate a large number of table entries for each table. These tables would initially be "empty." These empty tables would be "loaded" by table initialization routines written for the program. Loading the tables is a matter of positioning to the first record for the table (using a START verb), then reading each table record from the SCF into the empty table elements. Later, in the processing routines, the batch program would use standard table look-up methods to access the table values.

CICS/VS programs needing table information can be designed using a variety of techniques. The simplest technique is to use the table look-up value to construct the record key argument and then perform a random read to the SCF. If a file control not-found condition arises, the code is invalid. If the record is found, associated table information is retrieved from the record just read. Another technique is to "load" one or more tables from the SCF into working-storage in a similar way to batch programs. The image of the loaded table(s), however, can be saved as one or more items in Temporary-Storage. Later, if the table or tables are needed by a CICS program, they can be read from Temporary Storage.

SAMPLE RECORD LAYOUT FOR SCF

```
01  SYSTEM-CONTROL-RECORD.
*----RECORD-KEY----------------------------
    05  PERSCF-RECORD-KEY.
        07  PERSCF-APPL-ID          PIC XX VALUE 'PE'.
        07  PERSCF-TABLE-NAME       PIC XXXX.
        07  PERSCF-TABLE-VALUE      PIC X(14).
*----RECORD-DATA---------------------------
    05  PERSCF-ACTIVE-INACTIVE      PIC X.
    88  PERSCF-ACTIVE-RECORD VALUE 'A'.
        88  PERSCF-INACTIVE-RECORD    VALUE 'I'.
    05  PERSCF-VARIABLE-DATA        PIC X(2014).
01  PERSCF-EMPL-TABLE REDEFINES SYSTEM-CONTROL-RECORD.
    05  FILLER                      PIC X(21).
    05  PERSCF-EMPL-DESCR           PIC X(20).
01  PERSCF-LOCN-TABLE REDEFINES SYSTEM-CONTROL-RECORD.
    05  FILLER                      PIC X(21).
    05  PERSCF-LOCN-DESCR           PIC X(20).
01  PERSCF-DEPT-TABLE REDEFINES SYSTEM-CONTROL-RECORD.
    05  FILLER                      PIC X(21).
    05  PERSCF-DEPT-DESCR           PIC X(30).
01  PERSCF-HELP-RECORD REDEFINES SYSTEM-CONTROL-RECORD.
    05  FILLER                      PIC X(21).
    05  PERSCF-HELP-HEADER          PIC X(34).
    05  PERSCF-HELP-TRAILER         PIC X(34).
    05  PERSCF-HELP-TEXT            PIC X(1840).
```

DESCRIPTION OF SAMPLE RECORDS

PERSCF-EMPL-TABLE (table name "EMPL") These table records contain a list of employee type codes and corresponding descriptions used by several lab assignments.

PERSCF-LOCN-TABLE (table name "LOCN") These table records contain a list of location codes and corresponding descriptions used by several lab assignments.

PERSCF-DEPT-TABLE (table name "DEPT") These table records contain a list of department codes and corresponding descriptions used by several lab assignments.

PERSCF-HELP-RECORD These records contain help text records. The first 34 bytes contain a standard header block (including the 4-byte prefix). The second 34 bytes contain a trailer block. These header-trailer areas are followed by text characters. The BMS SEND TEXT command described in chapter 11 can be used to process these records.

Glossary

Abend   Abnormal End. A process whereby a program or task is canceled due to some error condition.

Access Method   A data management technique used to transfer data between main storage and an I/O device. Usually used within the context of IBM licensed programs and routines supplied with the operating system. For example, VSAM, ISAM, and VTAM.

Alternate Index   A file used by VSAM to access records using a field other than the primary key of the base data set.

Alternate Key   Used with VSAM files. A field containing one or more consecutive characters used to (1) access a data record from the base data set; (2) create an alternate index.

Application   A collection of related programs used by an enterprise in conducting its business or performing its mission. For example, payroll application.

Assembler Language   A language in which there is generally a one-to-one correspondence between a source statement and a machine language instruction.

Attention Identifier (AID)   A one-character code transmitted by an IBM 3270 terminal that identifies which key was used to transmit the message. For example, ENTER, CLEAR, PF1, PA1.

Attribute   A characteristic of a field transmitted to an IBM 3270 terminal. Fields generally contain multiple attributes such as dark, normal intensity, or high intensity; alphameric or numeric; protected or nonprotected; modified or not-modified.

Base Data Set   A VSAM file where data records are physically stored. Usually referred to in the context of building alternate indexes. May also be referred to as *base cluster.*

Base Locator (BL)   A COBOL internal pointer used to access an area of working-storage. Each base locator can allow access to 4096 bytes of working-storage.

Base Locator-Linkage (BLL)   A COBOL internal pointer used to access an area outside of the program. A BLL pointer is created for each 01 data structure in the Linkage Section. Each base locator can access up to 4096 bytes of working-storage. The EIB and commarea fields are addressed by BLL pointers.

Basic Mapping Support (BMS)   A collection CICS/VS application services program that simplifies the transmission of formatted data between the application program and the terminal.

Batch Processing   Processing performed by computer programs submitted to the computer using job control language (JCL) statements.

BDAM (Basic Direct Access Method)   An MVS access method used to provide update or retrieve records by block or physical key. Similar to DAM.

Browse   CICS term used to denote sequential processing of random access files.

BTAM (Basic Telecommunications Access Method)   An older access method used to communicate with on-line terminals.

CICS/VS   Customer Information Control System/Virtual Storage.

Command   A source statement used to request a CICS function. Commands have a format similar to high-level languages such as COBOL. With COBOL, each command begins with the keyword EXECUTE abbreviated EXEC and ends with the END-EXEC keyword.

Command-Level Interface   The collection of programs that allow application programs to be written using CICS commands. The interface consists of a batch mode command translator and a series of on-line programs. The command translator is used to prepare an application program for execution under CICS. The on-line programs provide an interface between the executing program and the various CICS control programs.

Command Translator   A batch program used to prepare programs containing CICS commands for execution. The translator modifies the source program to allow it to be compiled by the standard language compiler. The resulting program is suitable for execution under CICS.

Communications Area   An area used to pass data from one command-level program to another. The program may be in the same task or a different task. The communications area resides in CICS/VS dynamic storage.

Concurrent   The occurrence of two or more activities within the same time interval. For instance, concurrently active tasks indicates that more than one task has been initiated but not completed within a specified interval of time.

Control Block   An area of CICS/VS storage used to hold data needed by a CICS control program or application program. CICS/VS makes extensive use of control blocks to manage the various activities occurring within the system.

Control Interval   The physical unit of information transmitted to or from auxiliary storage by the VSAM access method. One or more logical records may be contained within a control interval.

Conversational Programming   A programming technique whereby a program maintains a dialog with an operator without terminating the task while awaiting an operator response.

Copy Library   A disk data set managed by MVS operating system and used for the purpose of storing source statements. These source statements are usually copied into a program during the compile process. Term synonymous with *source statement library* in VSE.

Core Image Library   A library maintained by the VSE operating system. Used to store core image (executable) modules. Similar to *load library* in MVS.

Core Image Module   A computer program in a format suitable for loading into main storage for execution. Term given to an executable program in VSE; called *load module* in MVS.

CSA (Common System Area)   This is the primary CICS control block, to which all other control blocks, tables, and control programs are anchored. This area is printed in a CICS dump but is not normally needed when using the Command-Level Interface.

Cursor   A visual symbol displayed on a terminal used to denote the location of the next character keyed by the operator.

DAM (Direct Access Method)   A VSE access method used to provide update or retrieve records by block or physical key. Similar to BDAM.

Data Base   A collection of data records used by an enterprise. Usually managed by a licensed product. For example, DL/I or IMS.

Data Communication   The process of transmitting and receiving data from one or more terminals.

Data Stream   The data transmitted to or from an input-output device. The data stream transmitted to or from a terminal can contain control codes and orders that are used by the hardware to perform special functions.

Device Independence The ability to transmit or receive data from a terminal without regard to the physical characteristics of the terminal.

Dispatch The process of selecting a CICS task to receive control of the CPU.

DOS (Disk Operating System) An older version of the VSE operating system. DOS, DOS/VS, and VSE are sometimes used interchangeably.

Dump A listing of control blocks, CICS tables, storage areas, and programs in character and hexadecimal format. Dumps are used during problem determination. A dump is normally produced when a task is abended but can also be requested by an application program using the DUMP command.

Dump Control A program used to write control blocks, CICS tables, and storage and program areas to a dump data set. Usually invoked automatically when a task has been abended.

Dynamic Storage A storage area maintained within the CICS partition or region. Storage areas are dynamically acquired and released during the execution of the various CICS tasks.

EDF (Execution Diagnostic Facility) An on-line testing and debugging facility provided by CICS.

EIB (Execute Interface Block) A control block containing system variables that can be used during a task. These variables can be used by an application program to obtain information such as terminal identification, transaction identification, date, time.

EIP (Execute Interface Program) One of the components of the Command-Level Interface. This program is used as an interface between an application program and the various CICS control programs.

Exceptional Condition An unusual condition that has caused the execution of a command to fail. The default action for most exceptional conditions is to cause the task to be abended. A program can override the default action in various ways.

Extended Attribute A characteristic of a field transmitted to an IBM 3270 terminal with extended field capabilities. For color terminals extended attributes define the color displayed for a field. Other extended attributes can cause a field to be displayed with underline, blinking, or reverse video.

FCT (File Control Table) A table used to describe the characteristics of all files to be managed by the File Control Program. A file cannot be used by a CICS program unless it has been defined in this table.

File Control The control program used to access random access files. The File Control Program uses the standard operating system access methods to provide both random and sequential access to records.

Format Independence The ability to transmit or receive data from a terminal without regard to its location or format on the terminal.

Generic Key The leftmost characters of the record key. Also known as *partial key*.

INIT1 Routine The first part of the COBOL load module used to initialize the program for execution. Address of INIT1 is used to compute the address of a failing instruction.

ISAM (Indexed Sequential Access Method) An older access method used to provide direct and sequential access to records in a file using a record key.

Linkage Editor A program used to link one or more object modules together to produce a load module, or core image module.

Load Library A library maintained by the MVS operating system. Used to store load (executable) modules. Similar to *core image library* in VSE.

Load Module A computer program in a format suitable for loading into main storage for execution. Term given to an executable program in MVS; called *core image module* in VSE.

Logical Level   Each program in a task is executed at some logical level. When a program at the highest level is terminated, the task is also terminated.

Macro   A CICS instruction similar in format to an Assembler language statement.

Map   A descriptive table that contains the format of a screen or part of a screen.

Mapping   The process of transferring data between a terminal and an application program using one or more BMS mapping commands.

Mapset   A physical entity where a set of related BMS maps are stored. When any related map is used by an application program, the entire mapset is loaded into storage. Each mapset requires an entry in the Program Processing Table (PPT).

Master Terminal Operator   Any operator having transaction security allowing use of the master terminal transaction.

Master Terminal Transaction   Either of the two transactions CSMT or CEMT which can be used to control system resources.

Modified Data Tag   A field attribute that can be set so the terminal will treat the field as if it had been modified by the operator. Usually all modified fields will be transmitted to CICS when the operator presses an attention key.

Multiprogramming   The capability to interleave the execution of two or more computer programs by a single computer system. Programs are usually running in different address spaces (regions or partitions).

Multitasking   The capability to have more than one program concurrently loaded and running within a single address space (region or partition).

Multithreading   The capability for the concurrent execution of the same program in two more separate tasks.

MVS (Multiple Virtual Storage)   An operating system normally used on larger processors. Provides many functions not available with the VSE operating system. A term used interchangeably with *OS/VS*.

Nucleus   The CICS management (control) programs and tables that are loaded during systems initialization.

Operating System   An organized collection of programs and routines licensed by IBM to control the resources of the computer. Current IBM operating systems are OS/VS2 (MVS) and VSE (DOS/VS).

OS (Operating System)   An older version of the OS/VS operating system. *OS, OS/VS2,* and *MVS* are sometimes used interchangeably.

Page Building   A BMS service that allows displays to be produced from multiple maps.

Partition   The term used in VSE to represent a user storage area of fixed size allocated to an application program.

PCT (Program Control Table)   A table created and maintained during CICS tailoring to identify the transactions that can be used by the installation. A program to be started for each transaction is identified in the table.

Physical Map   See *Map*.

PL/I   A programming language with features similar to COBOL, FORTRAN, and Assembler.

PPT   Program Processing Table. A table created and maintained during CICS tailoring to identify the programs to be used by the installation.

Priority   A ranking system used to determine the order in which a task receives control of the processor. With CICS, priorities are determined from the transaction code, terminal identification, and terminal operator.

Program Control   This is a CICS management function used to control all programs operating within CICS.

Protection Exception   An error condition where the operating system has determined that a program has attempted to modify storage in a different address space.

Pseudoconversational Program   A programming technique whereby a program interacts with an operator without remaining in storage while awaiting an operator reply.

Quasi Reentrant   A program that is "serially reusable" between CICS commands. A program is serially reusable if changes made to the data or instructions will not affect other tasks that may be concurrently using the program. CICS provides a copy of working-storage for each task using a COBOL program to enable the program to be quasi reenterant.

Queue   A group of records available for processing. Usually used within context of CICS Temporary Storage.

Random Access   The retrieval, or storage, of a single record by reference to its location. Access may be by record key, relative byte address, relative record number, or block reference, depending on the access method used. Contrast with *sequential access.*

Region   The term used in MVS to represent a user storage area of variable size allocated to an application program.

Resource   Some facility in the computing system available for use by one or more tasks. In CICS, resources can consist of storage, files, programs, transaction codes, and Temporary Storage queues.

Resource Security   A mechanism available to restrict access to certain CICS resources. Each resource can be assigned a security code. Operators can be assigned one or more resource codes to restrict access to certain resources.

Response Code   A value placed in the EIB after completion of a command. The program can interrogate the return code to determine whether a command was successful.

Response Time   The amount of elapsed time required to perform an action requested by an operator. Usually related to the time required to display information requested by an operator.

Sequential Access   Access to a record relative to the previously retrieved record.

Source Statement Library   A disk data set managed by VSE operating system, and used for the purpose of storing source statements. These source statements are usually copied into a program during the compile process. Term synonymous with *copy library* in MVS.

Storage Control   The program that acquires and releases dynamic storage for all tasks.

Storage Protection Key   A mechanism used to prevent a program from modifying storage in a different address space.

Storage Violation   The process whereby a program destroys storage accounting fields maintained by the Storage Control Program. Usually implies that some data area or control block is inadvertently corrupted.

Symbolic Cursor Positioning   A BMS service that allows a program to logically indicate the position of the cursor when data is displayed.

Symbolic Map   A data structure in the format of the application that is used by BMS to transfer variables between an application program and a terminal.

Table   In CICS, tables usually denote special CICS areas used by an installation. These tables reflect the transactions, programs, files, terminals, and other resources needed by the organization.

Tailoring   The process of generating a CICS system for use by an organization. Tailoring normally consists of creating and updating CICS tables. Tailoring can also involve regenerating certain CICS control programs. This tailoring process is usually performed by the Systems Support staff.

Task   The basic unit of work in CICS. One or more programs will be executed during a single task. A task usually begins as a result of some operator input. It ends when the last program in the task has completed execution.

Task Control   This is a CICS management function used to control all tasks operating within CICS.

Task Switching   The overlapping of input-output operations and processing unit (CPU) usage between one or more tasks.

TCA (Task Control Area)   A control block created during the initiation of a CICS task. The task control area contains register save areas, status indicators, and other operational data concerning the task. All transaction storage used by the task is addressed by pointers anchored in the TCA. Normally, it will only be needed when debugging a program using a storage dump.

TCAM (Telecommunications Access Method)   An older access method licensed by IBM; used to communicate with on-line terminals.

TCT (Terminal Control Table)   A CICS table containing information about every terminal used by the CICS system. Each table entry contains details concerning the status and features of a single terminal.

Temporary Storage Control   The CICS facility used to store and retrieve records in the Temporary Storage facility. Queues of records can be maintained in either main or auxiliary storage.

Terminal   A device equipped with a keyboard and display, capable of transferring or receiving data over a communication channel. As used in this text, a display device in the IBM 3270 family.

Terminal Control   The collection of programs and tables used to communicate with terminals connected to the CICS system.

Terminal Identification   A four-character code assigned to each terminal connected to the CICS system. This code is available to the program using a field in the EIB.

Terminal Operator   Anyone using a terminal to enter a transaction.

Terminal Paging   A BMS service that allows one or more screens to be stored in Temporary Storage. These screens can then be viewed by the operator using a series of page retrieval commands.

TGT (Task Global Table)   A part of the COBOL object module used during the execution of a COBOL program. This area contains special registers such as TALLY, work areas for COMPUTE statements, and base locator cells used to access working-storage fields. A copy of the TGT as well as working-storage is used for each task using a program.

TIOA (Terminal Input/Output Area)   A storage area where input and output messages are stored.

Trace Control   The CICS program that provides the ability to trace the activities of system and application programs.

Trace Table   1. An area of storage in which data is written to record the activities of system and application programs. 2. An area on a CICS dump listing that contains a printout of the most recent system and program activity.

Transaction   A processing activity that results in some action or result; usually from the operator viewpoint. For example, displaying a record. A transaction may require one or more CICS tasks.

Transaction Identification   A one-to-four-character code used to start a CICS task.

Transaction Security   A mechanism to prevent unauthorized use of CICS transaction identification codes by an operator.

Virtual Storage   Address space that appears to the program as main storage even though the storage address may not actually exist in the processor. This is accomplished through a combination of hardware and operating system routines. The different operating system features determine the amount of Virtual Storage that is available.

VSAM (Virtual Storage Access Method)   An access method licensed by IBM to allow random or sequential processing of records on direct access devices.

VSE (Virtual Storage Extended)   An operating system normally used on smaller processors. Provides fewer operating system functions than the full-featured MVS operating system.

VTAM (Virtual Telecommunications Access Method)   An access method used to communicate with on-line terminals directly. VTAM operates in a separate partition or region than the CICS system. CICS indirectly communicates with terminals using VTAM.

Working-Storage   An area defined in a COBOL program. Used to provide record areas, working variables, and constants needed by an application program. When using the Command-Level Interface, each new task using a program is provided a copy of the original working-storage areas.

Index